The Roots of Hinduism

The Roots of Hinduism

The Early Aryans and the Indus Civilization

Asko Parpola

OXFORD
UNIVERSITY PRESS

OXFORD
UNIVERSITY PRESS

Oxford University Press is a department of the University of Oxford. It furthers the University's objective of excellence in research, scholarship, and education by publishing worldwide.

Oxford New York
Auckland Cape Town Dar es Salaam Hong Kong Karachi
Kuala Lumpur Madrid Melbourne Mexico City Nairobi
New Delhi Shanghai Taipei Toronto

With offices in
Argentina Austria Brazil Chile Czech Republic France Greece
Guatemala Hungary Italy Japan Poland Portugal Singapore
South Korea Switzerland Thailand Turkey Ukraine Vietnam

Published in the United States of America by
Oxford University Press
198 Madison Avenue, New York, NY 10016

Cataloging-in-Publication data is on file at the Library of Congress
ISBN 978-0-19-022690-9 (hbk.); 978-0-19-022692-3 (pbk.)

3 5 7 9 8 6 4 2
Printed in the United States of America
on acid-free paper

Contents

Conclusion

Preface

India's earliest urban culture, which existed from 2600 until 1900 BCE, was discovered in the valley of the Indus River in the early 1920s. The Indus civilization had a population estimated at one million people, who lived in more than 1000 settlements, several of them cities of some 50,000 inhabitants, most notably Harappa and Mohenjo-daro, which display extraordinary town planning and water engineering, but not such splendid palaces and temples as ancient Egypt or Mesopotamia. With an area of nearly a million square kilometers, approximately a quarter the size of Europe, the Indus civilization was more extensive than the other key urban cultures of the time, in Mesopotamia and Egypt; it stretched eastwards from the Indus Valley as far as about Delhi and southwards almost as far as Mumbai (Fig. 4.2). It had long-distance contacts with West Asia, as proved by Indus objects and cuneiform records found in Mesopotamia. It also largely established a way of life that has continued in the villages of the subcontinent until the present day.

Yet, after almost a century of excavation and research, the Indus civilization remains comparatively little understood, especially in regard to its thought. What language did the Indus people speak? Is it related to the Sanskrit language of north India, to the Dravidian languages of south India, or to another surviving Indian language family? How might we decipher the exquisitely carved Indus inscriptions? What deities did the Indus civilization worship? Did these deities survive to become part of the religion described in the earliest surviving Indian literature, the Vedas, composed in Sanskrit, which are generally attributed to the centuries after 1500 BCE? Did the Aryan composers of the Vedas migrate to South Asia from outside the subcontinent? If so, where did they come from, and during what period did they migrate? Indeed, are the roots of contemporary Hinduism to be found in the religion of the Indus civilization as well as in the Vedic religion?

This book proposes answers to these fundamental questions about the beginning of Indian civilization. Some of the answers occurred to me soon after the start of my career in the study of Vedic literature and religion half a century ago, while others have struck me only in the last few years, following decades of research, both in Europe and in Asia. I have published most of them in the scholarly literature (where the interested reader will find more detail and full documentation). However, this literature is not well known outside a relatively small circle of experts. The time is ripe to introduce what I think are the most solid of my conclusions to a wider readership. My hope is that this book will stimulate further research and thus contribute to a solution that will be acceptable to many scholars.

Unfortunately, as I shall outline in the Introduction, at present there is little agreement on many of the issues I discuss. Since the 1980s, the above questions, especially the "Aryan problem," have been debated with increasing animosity, colored by the history of modern colonialism in India, and often by people without pertinent qualifications. Hence, it is vital to sort out the origins of the Vedic Aryans if we are to establish the true linguistic identity and religious affinity of the Indus civilization. Fortunately, the prospect for settling this vexed question has recently improved with the advance of archaeological excavations in Central Asia—where a major new Bronze Age civilization (Bactria and Margiana Archaeological Complex, BMAC, or the Oxus civilization), was discovered in the 1970s—and in Eurasia, including Russia.

Archaeological cultures have long been correlated with linguistic and ethnic groups. To take one relevant example, the proposal that people of the Andronovo cultures of Kazakhstan spoke an Indo-Iranian language was put forward by A. M. Tallgren in 1928. Various later scholars have had the same opinion, but while some speak of Proto-Aryan, others speak of Proto-Indo-Aryan, others of Proto-Iranian; others (e.g., Lamberg-Karlovsky 2002) deny the very possibility of such a correlation. I shall not discuss the methodology of archaeo-linguistic correlation here, but restrict myself only to some fundamental conclusions. Readers interested in the methodology should consult the publications of J. P. Mallory (1989 and later), who has developed this methodology remarkably.

The relatively uniform material "cultures" studied by archaeology reflect human communities, whose members must have communicated with each other by means of a language (in some cases more than one language). Shared material culture and shared language are both among the strongest sources of ethnic identity. They may change very little if people stay in the same place and receive no visitors from beyond their habitat, as has happened in Iceland since the early Viking Age. Contact with other communities has normally led to changes, the extent of which depends on the intensity of contact. Trade may introduce new artifacts and ideas, and loanwords denoting these artifacts and ideas. Conquest and immigration may lead to a community's abandoning its earlier culture and language in favor of a new culture and language. Language shifts involve a period of bilingualism, when part of the community speaks two (or more) languages.

Such continuities and change can be analyzed using a comparative method. Both archaeology and linguistics have developed techniques to do this. In principle, when correlating languages with archaeology, it is better not to assume long-distance migrations, except under exceptional circumstances, such as the combination of open steppe with wheeled vehicles or horses (cf. Nichols 1997:369). There must always be tangible archaeological evidence for assuming the existence of such movements.

The most important methodological principle is that isolated correlations are invalid, only a web of correlations similar to that of an entire language family can be convincing.

Every piece of evidence available from archaeology and linguistics should be used and should fit together. With this methodology in mind, I have been searching, since 1973, for an optimal solution to this puzzle: How can the Eurasian archaeological finds be correlated with the discoveries of Indo-European historical linguistics and the route of the Aryan migrations to India be established?

* * *

Given the above extremely contentious background, it is perhaps more than usually necessary for an author to present his credentials—linguistic, anthropological, archaeological, and otherwise—for writing on this subject in its many and varied aspects. I would therefore like to relate, fairly briefly, how and why I undertook the relevant research.

After seven years of Latin at school, I went to the University of Helsinki in 1959 to study classics, especially ancient Greek language and literature, but quickly switched to Sanskrit and comparative Indo-European linguistics. Unlike the study of Homer and Herodotus, which I loved, this major seemed to offer vast amounts of material virtually untouched by western scholarship. For my PhD dissertation my teacher, Pentti Aalto, suggested tackling the Drāhyāyaṇa-Śrautasūtra (DŚS), which had not been translated into any language. A critical edition of this text with the medieval commentary of Dhanvin had been started by a Finnish Sanskritist, J. N. Reuter, but only one-fifth had been published, back in 1904; the rest, in Reuter's unfinished manuscript, was kept in the university library.

The DŚS deals with the duties of the chanter priests in Vedic sacrificial rituals. I contacted Jan Gonda, a distinguished Dutch master of Vedic studies, who kindly got me started. Under his guidance I prepared an annotated English translation of the published portion of the DŚS and its commentary (1969), and for my dissertation I studied the relationship of this text to the closely parallel Lāṭyāyana-Śrautasūtra and other literature of the Sāmaveda (1968). This was interesting and exciting work, during which I chanced to discover a unique manuscript containing completely unknown portions of a second parallel text, the Jaiminīya-Śrautasūtra, at the library of the former maharaja of Tanjore (Thanjavur) in the south Indian state of Tamil Nadu (1967 [1968]; 2011d; 2012c; in press f). On my first visit to India in 1971, I photographed this manuscript, and started a search for all existing manuscripts of works belonging to the less-known Jaiminīya branch of the Sāmaveda (1973). Since then I have visited Kerala, Tamil Nadu, and Karnataka some twenty-five times, mainly pursuing and photographing Jaiminīya manuscripts. Ever since 1985, I have collaborated in this work and in the publication of the Jaiminīya texts with Masato Fujii, my former student (Fujii 2012). I am grateful to Fujii-san—and to Toshiki Osada—for making it possible for me to do research in Japan, as well as in India.

Vedic rituals and recitation by Brahmins have survived for some three millennia better in south India than in the north, which was long dominated by Muslim rulers. Frits Staal had documented them in Kerala in his book *Nambudiri Veda recitation* (1961), from which I learned that these particular Brahmins belong to the Jaiminīya school. Staal wanted to record this living oral tradition and invited me to join his project, which he inaugurated by tape-recording the songs of my future guru in studying the Sāmaveda, Śrī Iṭṭi Ravi Nambūdiri. In 1975, I had the opportunity to witness the entire performance of a Vedic *soma* sacrifice by sixteen officiating priests, who built the sacred enclosure with its huts and a fire altar of 1000 bricks. The resulting two-volume book edited by Staal, *Agni: The Vedic ritual of the Fire Altar* (1983), is a monumental study of Vedic religion. My three contributions include an attempt to penetrate the pre-Vedic Indian background of Vedic rituals. In 1983–1985, accompanied by my wife, Marjatta (who eventually wrote a book, *Kerala Brahmins in transition* [2000]) and two postgraduate students (Klaus Karttunen and Masato Fujii), I documented domestic rituals of Jaiminīya Sāmavedins by taking photographs and videos of actual and simulated performances, and reading with my guru unpublished manuals written in Malayalam, the Dravidian language of Kerala (2011e). Besides the Vedic heritage of the Brahmins, I also studied some other exciting Hindu traditions, such as the cult of Kuṭṭiccāttan, a little-known god of sorcery in Kerala (1999c).

My wish to understand better the formation of Hinduism was what encouraged my initial interest in the Indus civilization. But the impetus to study the Indus script came from Seppo Koskenniemi, a childhood friend who was a scientific advisor to IBM in Finland in the mid-1960s. He asked me, when I had just started working on my PhD, if I would like to use a computer—quite a new technique in those days!—for any research problem in my field. We could use IBM's facilities; Seppo would take care of programming.

Having recently read the Cambridge University classicist John Chadwick's fascinating book *The decipherment of Linear B* (1958), I suggested that we take up the decipherment of the Indus script as a hobby. Chadwick had explained in some detail the methods applied in this detective work by Michael Ventris and himself. Compilation of statistics and indexes to Linear B sign sequences played an important role. I thought a computer could ease this kind of analysis. My younger brother, Simo, who was studying Assyriology, joined our team and provided crucial expertise. In our spare time we collected the Indus texts from archaeological reports, drew up a provisional list of the different Indus signs, allotted a number to each sign, and punched the texts in numerical form onto cards. After the computer had processed all this information into lists, we transcribed the numbers back into pictograms, searched the lists for meaningful patterns, and tested automated methods of decipherment (Parpola, Parpola, & Koskenniemi 1966; Koskenniemi, Parpola, & Parpola 1970). Later the computer was programmed to draw in Indus signs the first concordance to all sign combinations, which was published in 1973. A three-volume revised version was produced in collaboration with Seppo's younger brother Kimmo Koskenniemi, a computer linguist, in 1979–1981 (see Fig. 5.1). Kimmo Koskenniemi (1981) developed automated syntactic methods for the study of the Indus script; these were implemented and tested in her M.Sc. thesis by my daughter Päivikki Parpola (1987; 1988).

Pentti Aalto, my Sanskrit teacher, was a code-breaker for military intelligence during the Second World War. He urged me to test whether some Indus signs could be read on the basis of our assumption that the underlying language was Dravidian (rather than Sanskrit). Since our trial substitutions seemed to yield sense, I quickly drafted a booklet, published in 1969, soon followed by two progress reports (Parpola et al. 1969a,b; 1970). These appeared under the joint names of our team, even though I could not easily consult my team-mates in Finland, because I was by now working in Copenhagen. My hurry was partly due to a rumor that a team of Soviet scholars was trying to decipher the Indus script. I made the mistake of including unripe ideas and presenting them with overconfidence and without proper checking. I was also quite unfamiliar with Dravidian languages in the 1960s, which led to some blunders. Understandably, these "first announcements" were received with severe and quite deserved criticism. The reviews, though painful reading, were a very useful and sobering lesson. But they did not shake my belief that our method and some of its fundamental hypotheses were correct. The decipherment work had to be continued.

Encouragement came from Gerard Clauson and John Chadwick (1969). Pentti Aalto and I were invited to give lectures in England in 1969, and in 1973 I was one of the speakers at the Royal Asiatic Society's sesquicentenary symposium on undeciphered scripts (1975a). Chadwick, whom I met several times in Cambridge, eventually recommended my book, *Deciphering the Indus script* (1994), for publication by Cambridge University Press. There I developed my early ideas, by proposing specific, carefully checked and tested, Proto-Dravidian readings for two dozen Indus signs.

Some critics continue to label this whole attempt at a partial decipherment abortive, because it allegedly has not made any progress. As if nothing has happened since the late 1960s, they still criticize the approach for those first announcements and for hypotheses abandoned long ago. Yet, a lot of advance was made between 1969 and 1994, and further steps forward have occurred since then.

To improve my grasp of Dravidian languages, in 1969 I started to learn Tamil in earnest with two Tamil scholars, R. Panneerselvam and P. R. Subramanian, who were attached for two years to the Scandinavian Institute of Asian Studies, my institute. They, together with my late friend Eric Grinstead, a specialist in East Asia, compiled for my personal use a reverse index to the seven-volume *Tamil lexicon*—a tool that turned out to be immensely useful in my study of the Indus script. Later, as Professor of Indology at the University of Helsinki, I arranged for Tamil and Malayalam to be taught there by native speakers on a regular basis.

During my first trip to South Asia in 1971, I was able to check the original inscriptions kept in various museums. I discovered hundreds of unpublished inscriptions in South Asian museums and initiated a major project to publish a comprehensive *Corpus of Indus Seals and Inscriptions* (CISI) as an international collaboration under the auspices of UNESCO. After many bureaucratic difficulties, three of the projected four volumes have appeared (1987, 1991, and 2010). This fundamental research tool is approaching completion.

Apart from Chadwick, my mentors in Cambridge included Bridget and Raymond Allchin, who specialized in South Asian archaeology. They published a fundamental survey of research, *The birth of Indian civilization: India and Pakistan before 500 B.C.* (1968), with later updated versions. This book, which I studied very closely, gave me basic knowledge of the current archaeological situation. In 1970, the Allchins established what is nowadays called the European Association of South Asian Archaeology and Art History, inviting me to be one of the founding members; and I had the privilege of serving on the board until 2002. Every second year, the association has arranged an international conference for scholars to present the results of their recent excavations and research. I attended most of these exciting meetings (and organized one of them, in 1993 [Parpola & Koskikallio 1994]), which provided a unique opportunity to follow the development of South Asian archaeology, including, of course, Indus archaeology.

Study of the iconographic motifs of inscriptions and painted pottery from the Indus Valley, as well as small statuettes and terracotta figurines, has suggested parallels in Iran and West Asia that have led to major insights into the history of Indian religions. Archaeological knowledge is required not only for comprehending the Indus civilization but also the evidence for Aryan migrations into India. Since the early 1970s (Parpola 1974), I have tried to gain a better understanding of how the emergence and dispersal of the Indo-European and Uralic (Finno-Ugric) language families are reflected in the archaeological record—for the prehistory of the Indo-Iranian languages involves both of these language families. I have learnt a lot from J. P. Mallory's important book, *In search of the Indo-Europeans* (1989), and from close collaboration with Christian Carpelan, a Finnish archaeologist specializing in northern and eastern Europe (Carpelan & Parpola 2001). I have also had the privilege of visiting some key archaeological sites, such as Gonur in Turkmenistan, the main location of the BMAC or Oxus civilization (two visits at the kind invitation of its excavator, Viktor I. Sarianidi); Botaj in Kazakhstan, important for the history of horse domestication (one visit thanks to David Anthony, a leading researcher; Parpola 1997c); and sites of the Abashevo culture in Russia. For this research I had to acquire a reading knowledge of Russian. My friend Sergej V. Kuz'minykh, an eminent Russian archaeologist, has kept me up-to-date with Russian publications.

In a work like this, one must constantly adjust to the advances made in international research and one's own better grasp of the problems. Just before the book went to press, I attended the twenty-second international conference of the European Association of South Asian Archaeology and Art held in Stockholm in mid-2014. One new piece of information slightly affecting this book may be mentioned. My dates for the Gandhāra Grave culture reported in chapter 8, established in the long-continued excavations of Giorgio Stacul, now require revision. Recent excavations with new radiocarbon dates, communicated by Vidale and colleagues (2014), suggest *c.* 1500–1100 BCE for period IV, *c.* 1200–800 BCE for period V, and *c.* 800–400/300 BCE for period VI.

I am immensely grateful to my friend Andrew Robinson, author of excellent books on the history of writing and decipherment (among many other things), for his willingness to make my text as accessible to the general reader as possible; and to the Building and Use of Linguistic Technology (BAULT) research community at the University of Helsinki and its director Kimmo Koskenniemi for funding Andrew's work and some of the illustrations. Andrew was a hard taskmaster, and without his constant prodding and encouragement I would not have been able to put this book together—or at least not so speedily. The work progressed chapter by chapter, as I sent my first draft to Andrew, who edited it, asking me to clarify everything that he could not follow. He also recommended including a short explanation of Indo-European linguistics and its methods for those readers coming to this subject for the first time (see chapter 3).

My cordial thanks go to Stephanie Jamison and Joel Brereton for generously allowing me to use their new translations of Rigvedic verses referring to the Dāsas and Dasyus in chapter 9. For very useful feedback I am indebted to the anonymous expert readers whom the publisher invited to read the book proposal, and especially the one who read the nearly final complete manuscript. Harry Falk and Xenia Zeiler also quickly read the text when it went to press and suggested some adjustments.

The illustrations are vital for understanding the ideas in the text. I am much obliged to the all the various copyright holders for granting permission to reproduce them. Many friends and colleagues helped in the task of collecting the permissions: Julian Reade, Dominique Collon, Mark Kenoyer, Ian Hodder, S. V. Kuz'minykh, N. B. Vinogradov, Yuri Rassamakin, Durre Ahmed, Gyula Wojtilla, Andrew Robinson, Dipankar Home, Dipak Bhattacharya, Sayan Bhattacharya, Joyoti Roy, and B. M. Pande. Anna Kurvinen graciously drew two nice maps according to my specifications.

My best thanks are due to Cynthia Read, my editor at Oxford University Press, USA, and her team, particularly Marcela Maxfield, Michael Durnin, and Sunoj Shankaran, for bringing this book out so nicely and in good cooperation.

I dedicate the book to my family: Marjatta, Päivikki and Pekka, and Mette.

Asko Parpola
Helsinki, October 2014

Abbreviations

ASI	Archaeological Survey of India
AV	Arto Vuohelainen
CISI	See CISI in References.
DAMGP	Department of Archaeology and Museums, Government of Pakistan
EL	Erja Lahdenperä
JL	Jyrki Lyytikkä
NMI	National Museum of India

VEDIC TEXTS WITH THEIR ABBREVIATIONS

For editions and translations see Gonda 1975; 1977; Jamison & Witzel 1992.

AĀ	Aitareya-Āraṇyaka
AB	Aitareya-Brāhmaṇa
ĀpŚS	Āpastamba-Śrautasūtra
ĀśvGS	Āśvalāyana-Gṛhyasūtra
AV(Ś)	Atharvaveda(-Saṁhitā) (Śaunaka-śākhā)
AVP	Atharvaveda-Saṁhitā, Paippalāda-śākhā
BĀU	Bṛhad-Āraṇyaka-Upaniṣad (Kāṇva-śākhā)
BŚS	Baudhāyana-Śrautasūtra
BŚu	Baudhāyana-Śulvasūtra
ChU	Chāndogya-Upaniṣad
DŚS	Drāhyāyaṇa-Śrautasūtra
GGS	Gobhila-Gṛhyasūtra
HGS	Hiraṇyakeśi-Gṛhyasūtra
JB	Jaiminīya-Brāhmaṇa
JGS	Jaiminīya-Gṛhyasūtra
JŚS	Jaiminīya-Śrautasūtra

JUB	Jaiminīya-Upaniṣad-Brāhmaṇa
KĀ	Kaṭha-Āraṇyaka
KauśS	Kauśika-Sūtra
KB	Kauṣītaki-Brāhmaṇa
KS	Kaṭha-Saṁhitā / Kāṭhaka-Saṁhitā
KŚS	Kātyāyana-Śrautasūtra
KŚu	Kātyāyana-Śulvasūtra
KU	Kaṭha-Upaniṣad
LŚS	Lāṭyāyana-Śrautasūtra
MS	Maitrāyaṇī Saṃhitā
PB	Pañcaviṁśa-Brāhmaṇa
PGS	Pāraskara-Gṛhyasūtra
RV	Rigveda (-Saṁhitā)
ŚĀ	Śāṅkhāyana-Āraṇyaka
ŚB(M)	Śatapatha-Brāhmaṇa (Mādhyandina-śākhā)
ŚBK	Śatapatha-Brāhmaṇa, Kāṇva-śākhā
ṢB	Ṣaḍviṁśa-Brāhmaṇa
ŚŚS	Śāṅkhāyana-Śrautasūtra
SV	Sāmaveda(-Saṁhitā) (Kauthuma-śākhā)
SVB	Sāmavidhāna-Brāhmaṇa
TĀ	Taittirīya-Āraṇyaka
TB	Taittirīya-Brāhmaṇa
TS	Taittirīya-Saṁhitā
VādhA	Vādhūla-Anvākhyāna
VādhŚS	Vādhūla-Śrautasūtra
VS(M)	Vājasaneyi-Saṁhitā (Mādhyandina-śākhā)

The Roots of Hinduism

Introduction

1

Defining "Hindu" and "Hinduism"

Before investigating the roots of Hinduism we must first define what is meant by the terms Hindu and Hinduism. The etymology of "Hindu" goes back to about 515 BCE, when the Persian king Darius the Great annexed the Indus Valley to his empire. *Sindhu*, the Sanskrit name of the Indus River and its southern province—the area now known as Sindh—became *Hindu* in the Persian language. The Ionian Greeks serving the Great King did not pronounce word-initial aspiration (like French-speakers today) and so in the Greek language Persian *Hindu* became *Indos* (whence, Latin *Indus*) and its surrounding country became *India*. But when the Persian-speaking Mughals conquered northern India in the sixteenth century, they called the country *Hindustan* and its people *Hindu*. During the Mughal empire, in the seventeenth century, the British, too, began to use "Hindu" (or "Hindoo") to describe the people living in the subcontinent. During the British period, in the nineteenth century, the term was adopted by those Indians who opposed colonialism, in order to distinguish themselves from Muslims. In the twentieth century, Hindu became the common label for all Indians who were not Muslims, Buddhists, Christians, Jains, Jews, Parsees, or Sikhs. V. D. Savarkar used the neologism *hindutva* (coined with the Sanskrit abstract noun suffix *-tva*) to mean "the quality of being a Hindu, Hindu identity" in his influential nationalist-political tract *Hindutva: Who is a Hindu?* (1938), first published under a pseudonym in 1923, and still in print.

An East India Company merchant and evangelical Christian, Charles Grant, is known to have used the term "Hindooism" for the earlier "Hindoo religion" or "Hindoo creed" as early as 1787. During the nineteenth century, Hinduism became the general name for the native religion(s) of India, excluding Buddhism, Jainism, and Sikhism (Pennington 2005). Some Indians object to having a foreign term for their religion, preferring the Sanskrit expression *sanātana dharma*, "eternal law or truth," despite the fact that this expression was not applied to any religious system in ancient texts.

Another objection is that "Hinduism" artificially bundles together different religions, such as the Vaiṣṇava, Śaiva, and Śākta traditions of worship, each with its own theology and cult. One may indeed say that:

> Hinduism *in toto*, with various contradicting systems and all the resulting inconsistencies, certainly does not meet the fundamental requirements for a historical religion of being a coherent system; but its distinct entities [the so called "sects"] do. They are indeed religions, while Hinduism is not. What we call "Hinduism" is a geographically defined group of distinct but related religions, that originated in the same region, developed under similar socio-economic and political conditions, incorporated largely the same traditions, influenced each other continuously, and jointly contributed to the Hindu culture. (von Stietencron 1989:20)

The classical Hindu gods Viṣṇu and Śiva go back, at least in part, to the polytheistic pantheon of the older Vedic religion. The Vedas are regarded as the ultimate scriptural authority by most Hindus, especially the "orthodox" Brahmins, but on the whole the Vedic religion plays a small role in classical Hinduism, many aspects of which differ fundamentally from the religion described in the Vedas. The more recent part of the Vedic religion, "Brahmanism," is sometimes counted as an older phase of Hinduism, since much of later Hindu philosophy is based on it. Usually, however, "classical" Hinduism is considered to be of post-Vedic date, beginning around 400–200 BCE, and epitomized in the epics the Mahābhārata and the Rāmāyaṇa, and the Purāṇas. In his masterly sketch, *Religions of ancient India*, the great French Indologist Louis Renou emphasizes the change that occurred between the Vedic religion and later Hinduism:

> The Vedic contribution to Hinduism, especially Hindu cult-practice and speculation, is not a large one; Vedic influence on mythology is rather stronger, though here also there has been a profound regeneration. Religious terminology is almost completely transformed between the Vedas and the Epics or the Purāṇas, a fact which has not been sufficiently emphasized; the old terms have disappeared or have so changed in meaning that they are hardly recognizable; a new terminology comes into being. Even in those cases where continuity has been suggested, as for Rudra-Śiva, the differences are really far more striking than the similarities. (Renou 1953:47–48)

But if this analysis is correct, as I believe it is, it prompts the question: where did the many, indeed dominant, elements of Hinduism that are non-Vedic come from? No doubt many local religious cults were absorbed into and assimilated by Hinduism in the course of its millennial development and expansion and a lot of ideological evolution took place, yet even so the Indus civilization seems a likely original source, in spite of its great antiquity.

Regarding the Aryans, Renou cautiously continues: "It would have been quicker to enumerate those elements [of Hinduism] that are demonstrably Aryan: they would consist of perhaps a few functional gods (as it is the fashion to describe them), the *soma* cult and the rudiments of a social system: little enough, in all conscience" (Renou 1953:47–48).

Regarding the Indus civilization, he suggests: "If the forms of religion revealed in the seals and figurines of the Indus have any remote connection with Indian forms, it is not so much with those of Vedism as with those of Hinduism, a Hinduism which, though known to us only by inference, must have already existed in Vedic times, and probably considerably earlier" (Renou 1953:3).

Part I of this book (The Early Aryans) examines the evidence for the Aryan migrations and the formation of the Vedic religion. Part II (The Indus Civilization) is devoted to the possible legacy of the Indus civilization to the Vedas and to later Hinduism. The treatment is basically in chronological order, but in some places it proved necessary to depart from this.

2

The Early Aryans

Both the Vedic literature and the fundamental texts of classical Hinduism are in Sanskrit, which is termed an Old Indo-Aryan language. The Prakrit languages, classed as Middle Indo-Aryan, were spoken in South Asia between about 300 BCE and 1000 CE. The Prakrits then changed into early forms of the New, or Modern, Indo-Aryan languages, which include Hindi, Punjabi, Bengali, Marathi, and many other South Asian languages spoken today. The name Indo-Aryan was given in order to distinguish all of these languages from the Aryan languages spoken outside South Asia. The latter consist mainly of the Iranian language family (the name Irano-Aryan would have been more logical), which has been spoken in modern times principally in Iran but also in the Caucasus area (the Ossetic language) and in Central Asia, Afghanistan, and Pakistan (the Tajik, Pashto, and other languages). In addition there is a small group of so-called Nuristani languages in northeastern Afghanistan (Nuristan), previously known as Kafiri ("pagan") languages; their speakers were forcibly converted to Islam by the Afghans in 1896. The Nuristani languages have both Iranian and Indo-Aryan features, and their classification is not yet settled.

Old Iranian languages include Old Persian, preserved in the inscriptions of Darius the Great and other kings of the Achaemenid empire (559–330 BCE), and Avestan, which is the language of the Avesta, the sacred literature of the Zoroastrians (who include the Parsees of India). The oldest parts of the Avesta are thought to date from around 1000 BCE, being of nearly the same age as the oldest Vedic text, the Rigveda. The Avesta and the Rigveda share a number of religious terms, for example, the words for "worship, sacrifice" (*yasna* in Avestan, *yajña* in Vedic) and "prayer, spell" (*manthra* in Avestan, *mantra* in Vedic), and the cultic phrase "with hands raised up in homage" (*ustānazastō . . . nəmaŋhā* in Avestan, *uttānahasto namasā* in Vedic).

Speakers of Old Indo-Aryan and speakers of Old Iranian called themselves by the same name, that is, *ārya* (Old Indo-Aryan) and *arya* (Old Iranian); the Old Iranian genitive plural *aryānām*, "(country) of the Aryas," in the course of time became shortened to the country name Iran. The meaning of this tribal self-appellation is debated, but many philologists think it originally stood for "hospitable, noble," or for "master of the household, lord." Together, Indo-Aryan and Iranian form the Aryan group of languages, though this collective is nowadays usually called Indo-Iranian (to avoid the connotation acquired by "Aryan" from its association with the racial prejudices and misconceptions culminating in the horrors of Nazi Germany). Indo-Aryan and Iranian are postulated to descend from a single original language, Proto-Indo-Iranian, with dialects that drifted apart and became separate languages, which in turn divided to give rise to the modern Indo-Iranian languages.

After Vasco da Gama reached India in 1498, he was followed by European missionaries, some of whom acquired remarkable mastery of Indian languages. They included an English Jesuit, Thomas Stephens (Tomáz Estêvão), who retold the story of the New Testament in Konkani under the title *Krista-purāṇa*, covering more than 10,000 verses, and also wrote the first Konkani grammar. Stephens noted the similarity of Sanskrit and European languages as early as 1583; so did the French Jesuit Gaston-Laurent Coeurdoux, author of *Moeurs et coutumes des Indiens* (pirated by Jean Antoine Dubois [{1825} 1906]), in a letter written in 1767 to A. H. Anquetil-Duperron, describing the relation of Sanskrit to Greek and Latin.

The idea that languages change, and that the ancestor of current related languages may have died out, was expressed with reference to Sanskrit and its cognates by Sir William Jones in his speech at the Asiatick Society in Calcutta on February 2, 1786. After studying Sanskrit with the help of a Bengali paṇḍit, Jones announced that:

> The *Sanscrit* language, whatever be its antiquity, is of a wonderful structure; more perfect than the *Greek*, more copious than the *Latin*, and more exquisitely refined than either, yet bearing to both of them a stronger affinity, both in the roots of verbs and in the forms of grammar, than could possibly have been produced by accident; so strong indeed, that no philologer could examine them all three, without believing them to have sprung from some common source, which, perhaps, no longer exists; there is a similar reason, though not quite so forcible, for supposing that both the *Gothick* and the *Celtick*, though blended with a very different idiom, had the same origin with the Sanscrit; and the old *Persian* might be added to the same family. (Jones 1788:422)

When published in the widely read journal *Asiatick Researches*, Jones's suggestion had a revolutionary impact. Some of the Romantics of the early nineteenth century imagined that Sanskrit was the mother tongue of the "Indo-European" language family (a term coined not by Jones but by another polymath, Thomas Young [1813:255]), and that India was the cradle of civilization.

But soon Sanskrit was relegated to the same status as the other Indo-European tongues, along with the area where it was spoken, India. Modern historical linguistics began with Franz Bopp's German publication, "On the conjugational system of the Sanskrit language compared with that of Greek, Latin, Persian and Germanic" (Bopp 1816). The unknown homeland of Proto-Indo-European was now thought to lie in an area of Eurasia yet to be precisely determined. Thus the Indo-Aryans were immigrants in South Asia. But when did they come?

Friedrich Max Müller, who taught Sanskrit, comparative philology, and comparative religion at Oxford University during the latter half of the nineteenth century, edited the earliest of the four principal Vedas, the Rigveda. In 1859, Max Müller estimated that the Rigveda was composed around 1200–1000 BCE. He arrived at this date by assigning the Sūtra texts of the Vedas to 600–200 BCE, then conjecturing that the earlier Brāhmaṇa texts were composed in 800–600 BCE, and the still earlier Mantra texts (the Atharvaveda and the Yajurveda Samhitās) in 1000–800 BCE. Although these estimated dates have been much discussed and criticized, they have turned out to be remarkably sagacious, and today many Vedic scholars (including myself) more or less agree with them. Moreover, philologists have long favored 1500–1200 BCE as the date for the migration of Indo-Aryan speakers into South Asia. One powerful piece of evidence comes from cuneiform documents in Anatolia, West Asia, and Egypt, according to which the rulers of the Mitanni kingdom of Syria in 1500–1300 BCE had Indo-Aryan names, swore oaths by Indo-Aryan gods, and trained chariot horses using Indo-Aryan technical terms (see chapter 8).

All the leading twentieth-century British archaeologists who have studied the Indus civilization—John Marshall (1931), Stuart Piggott (1950), Mortimer Wheeler (1968), and Bridget and Raymond Allchin (1982)—have placed the Aryan migrations in the second millennium BCE. It has proved difficult, however, to pin down specific archaeological evidence that could be connected with this event, for the Aryans were pastoralists and may therefore be assumed to have been mobile, with temporary settlements, at least for some time after their arrival. According to Renou, "In the very primitive architecture which we can infer from descriptions in the Vedic ritual texts there is nothing that can reasonably be compared with the buildings of Mohenjo-daro" (Renou 1953:4). Marshall (1931:I, 111) pointed out another important negative indicator: the horse seems to have been unknown in the Indus civilization, while prominent in the culture described in the Vedas.

The contrary "out of India" view, that the Indo-Aryan speakers originated in India, has recently been much propagated, as mentioned in the Preface. Thomas Trautmann writes in his edited collection *The Aryan debate* (2005):

> In the last several years a number of popular books and websites on the Aryan debate have appeared, many of them—but not all—by authors who are not scholars by their training in the skills of ancient history. Moreover, partisan politics and governments of the day have been making pronouncements about ancient history, and ordering changes in textbooks. The new writings have pressed various versions of the alternative view very strongly, arguing that the Aryans are indigenous to India and were the builders of the Indus civilization. (Trautmann 2005:xvii)

The Aryan debate undoubtedly has multiple causes, including the racial "theories" of the nineteenth and twentieth centuries endorsed by the Nazis. These have been thoroughly researched by Edwin Bryant in *The quest for the origins of Vedic culture: The Indo-Aryan migration debate* (2001). It is worrying, however, that Bryant does not want to take a stand on the issue after studying the arguments in depth. He concludes: "how the cognate languages got to be where they were in prehistory is as unresolved today, in my mind, as it was two hundred years ago when William Jones announced the Sanskrit language connection to a surprised Europe" (Bryant 2001:12). In my view, it is possible to go quite far toward establishing the truth about the Indo-Aryan migrations.

3

Indo-European Linguistics

Since some of this book requires a basic understanding of the concepts and methods of Indo-European (IE) linguistics, "iron rations" will be provided in this chapter. Those looking for a fuller account are advised to read a good introductory textbook, such as Lyle Campbell's *Historical linguistics* (2004) or, more particularly, Benjamin W. Fortson's *Indo-European language and culture* (2010).

Since languages are complex phenomena, linguistics has developed various subdisciplines, each with its own special terminology and methods. Here are some of the important subdisciplines. Phonetics studies how sounds are produced and classifies their different qualities. Phonology examines sounds as distinctive units (phonemes) and how phonemes combine into a sound system. Phonotactics investigates how phonemes behave when conjoined. Morphology is devoted to the grammatical markers and inflections of words. Lexicography concerns the vocabulary of a language. Syntactics involves the study of how words are combined to form phrases and sentences. Semantics grapples with how words convey meaning. Descriptive linguistics records all aspects of a language as it exists at a given point in its history.

All languages have a history: excepting the dead ones, they change constantly, in all their aspects. Especially important is phonological change, which often involves changes in morphology, too. Historical linguistics (unlike descriptive linguistics) documents how languages change over time, and tries to reconstruct prehistoric changes. It also aims to understand how and why linguistic change occurs, and to define how different languages are related to each other. That is, are the languages part of one family, in other words genetically related—in which case how closely related? If they are not genetically related, have they been in contact with each other at some point in their histories? Or are they totally distinct? The chief method of historical linguistics is therefore comparison of languages. IE linguistics is essentially historical linguistics.

The ancient Indian linguist Pāṇini's Sanskrit grammar (known as *Aṣṭādhyāyī*, "having eight chapters"), composed around 350 BCE, is a marvel of descriptive linguistics, the finest achievement in this field for more than two thousand years (Bloomfield 1933:11; Cardona 1976). Historical linguistics came into being only in the early nineteenth century CE. Before this, as early as the sixteenth century, the similarity of IE languages had been noted, but it was William Jones's observation (1788:422) of the similarity of Sanskrit, Greek, and Latin, among other European languages, that inaugurated modern historical linguistics (see chapter 2). Jones spelled out his new concept of a genetic relationship by suggesting that these languages had developed from a single original language, which no longer existed—now called Proto-Indo-European (PIE), from Greek _prôtos_, "foremost (in place, time, order), first."

The works of Franz Bopp (1816) and Rasmus Rask (1818) started to establish systematic phonological and grammatical correspondences between vocabulary words of similar meaning, in order to prove a genetic relationship between the IE languages; János (in Latin, Joannes) Sajnovics (1770) had initiated a similar study of the Uralic languages by comparing Hungarian and Saami.

People without linguistic training may draw radically incorrect conclusions from apparent similarities in sound and meaning between languages that in reality are unrelated and often quite distant from each other. For instance, in the Mayan language Kaqchikel, spoken in Central America, the word _mes_ denotes "mess, disorder, garbage," which happens to be similar in sound and meaning to the English word _mess_. But there is no regular sound correspondence between words beginning with _m-_ in English and their semantic counterparts in Kaqchikel for example, _man: ači, mouse: č'oy, moon: qatiʔt, mother: nan._

The English–Mayan situation contrasts with the IE languages, where there are regular sound correspondences. For instance, IE words denoting "father" include the following cognates (in the nominative singular):

Late PIE *_**p**ətḗr_ (< Early PIE *_**p**_H_2_tḗr_)
Indo-Iranian: Vedic Sanskrit _**p**itā́_, Old Avestan _**p**tā_, Younger Avestan _**p**ita_, Old Persian _**p**itā_
Greek _**p**atḗr_
Latin _**p**ater_
Celtic: Old Irish _athair/athir_
Germanic: Gothic _**f**adar_, Old Icelandic _**f**aðir/**f**aþer_, Old English _**f**æder_, Anglo-Saxon _**f**ader_
Tocharian A _**p**ācar_, B _**p**ācer_
Armenian _**h**ayr_

In the above cognates, the word-initial PIE *_p-_ (the asterisk denotes an unattested reconstruction) has been preserved as _p-_ in most languages, but in Celtic languages it has been lost, while in Germanic the change *_p-_ > _f-_ has taken place, and in Armenian so has the change *_p-_ > _h-_. (The symbol > means "changes into"; the symbol < means "has developed from.")

The important concept of regularity may be illustrated by taking a different word with a word-initial *_p-_ in PIE, the verb meaning "to ask" (in the first person present singular active). Here we again find exactly the same sound correspondences at the beginning of the cognates:

PIE *_**p**r̥ḱskṓ_
Indo-Iranian: Vedic Sanskrit _**p**r̥cchā́mi_, Old Avestan _**p**ərᵊsā_, Old Persian _**p**arsāmiy_
Latin: *_**p**orkskō_ > _**p**oscō_
Celtic: Old Irish _arco/arcu_

Germanic: Old High German _forscōm_
Baltic: Lithuanian **_peršù_**
Tocharian A **_praksam_**, B **_preksau_**
Armenian **_harc̕anem_**

Jakob Grimm (1822) noted that the change of PIE _*p_ into Proto-Germanic _*f_ was not an isolated phenomenon but part of a major change in the entire sound system, involving all labial, dental, and velar stops.

Stops are consonants articulated by first making a complete closure of the vocal tract, stopping the flow of air from the lungs, then abruptly opening the tract with an audible plosion. Stops can be voiced or voiceless, that is, articulated with or without an accompanying vibration of the vocal cords. Labial stops are articulated with the lips, dental stops with the teeth, and velar stops with the soft palate and the back of the tongue; palatals are pronounced with the blade of the tongue touching the hard palate. Aspirated stops are pronounced with an audible and forceful release of breath. Fricatives are continuant consonants produced by partial occlusion of the airstream, causing a friction-like sound.

The PIE voiceless stops changed into corresponding voiceless fricatives in Proto-Germanic: _*p_ > _*f_, _*t_ > _*θ_, _*k_ and _*ḱ_ > χ (written _h_). At the same time PIE voiced stops changed into corresponding voiceless stops in Proto-Germanic: _*b_ > _*p_, _*d_ > _*t_, _*g_ and _*ǵ_ > _*k_, _*g_^{w} > _*kw_. And PIE voiced aspirated stops changed into corresponding plain voiced stops in Proto-Germanic: _*bh_ > _*b_, _*dh_ > _*d_, _*gh_ and _*ǵh_ > _*g_, _*g_^{w}_h_ > _*gw/*w_. Before this, the PIE palatals _*ḱ_, _*ǵ_, _ǵh_ had merged with the PIE velar stops _*k_, _*g_, _*gh_. PIE _*k_^{w}, _*g_^{w} and _*g_^{w}_h_ were labiovelars, that is, velar stops pronounced with a simultaneous rounding of the lips.

Taken together, these Proto-Germanic sound changes are known as the "first Germanic sound shift," or Grimm's law. Such sound laws are expected to apply throughout a language, in all words and grammatical markers, unless the sound law is "conditioned," that is, applicable under restricted conditions. Grimm's law is conditioned, for it applies neither after fricatives (thus PIE _*sp_ > Proto-Germanic _*sp_, not _sf_) nor after stops (thus PIE _*kt_ > Proto-Germanic _*χt_, not _χθ_). Strict adherence to the rule that sound laws should have no exceptions is an immensely important methodological principle. Emphasized by the so-called neogrammarians during the last quarter of the nineteenth century, it led to great advances in linguistic science.

There are always isolated cases where a sound law does not apply in practice, but even then there is usually a valid explanation. A common reason for such exceptions is analogy. Analogical change is of many different kinds, seeking agreement or similarity with existing patterns or models. For example, the antiquated plural _brethren_ may be replaced with _brothers_ that is analogous to "normal" plurals. PIE _*penk_^{w}_e-_ yields English _five_ with Proto-Germanic _*f_ in accordance with Grimm's law, but the preceding numeral PIE _*kwetwor-_ becomes _four_ in English, with a possibly analogical _f_ that imitates the beginning of the following numeral _five_, instead of the expected _whour_. Latin _quinque_, "five" seems to involve a similar analogical change (but in the reverse direction), in imitation of _quattuor_, "four."

Besides analogy, there may be other reasons why there may be seeming exceptions to sound laws. One important reason can be that an IE language has not inherited a given IE word from its own earlier phase(s) of development, but borrowed the word from another IE language which has different sound laws.

Historical linguistics has progressed over the past two centuries, and the mechanics of language change are now fairly well understood, so that the same linguistic methodology can be applied to all languages. Certain sound changes tend to take place in many languages (even genetically unrelated ones). For example, dental, palatal, and velar stops often change into affricates when they are followed by front vowels, that is, vowels articulated in the front part of the mouth, *i* and *e*. Affricates are composite sounds consisting of a stop and a fricative articulated at the same point. Thus Latin *centum*, "hundred" (with *c* pronounced as *k*), has become *cento* in Italian (with *c* pronounced as an affricate, like *ch* in the English word *chess*).

The PIE palatal stops became affricated in early post-PIE times in Proto-Indo-Iranian, Proto-Balto-Slavic, Proto-Armenian and Proto-Albanian—apparently then contiguous languages spoken somewhere north of the Black Sea. These are called "*satem*-languages," as opposed to other IE "*centum*-languages." The word *satem* (a broad transcription for *satəm*) is Avestan for "hundred." The label derives from the fact that *satəm* and *centum* are prominent examples of this particular sound change.

The words for "hundred"—and for "ten," from which "hundred" is derived—have also been important in sorting out the development of PIE "syllabic nasals," *m*- and *n*-sounds that function like vowels when they occur alone between consonants; they have changed in different ways in the different branches of the IE languages. In Proto-Indo-Iranian the syllabic nasals changed into **a*, as in most dialects of Greek, whereas the Arcadian and Lesbian dialects of Greek have *o* instead of *a*. In the late phase of Proto-Indo-Aryan and Proto-Iranian, PIE **e* and **o* changed into **a*, but early Aryan loanwords in Uralic languages show that **e* and **o* were still preserved in their early phases. The two words also exemplify the important role that accent and shift of accent have played in the formation and inflection of IE words: the vowel *e* in the accented first syllable of **déḱm̥* is reduced and lost when the accent shifts away from the first syllable to the second syllable in **(d)ḱm̥tóm*.

Here is a selection of words meaning "hundred" and "ten" in various IE languages:

**(d)ḱm̥tóm*, "hundred" (possibly "tenth [ten]")
Old Irish *cét* [i.e., *kēt*]
Italic: Latin *centum*
Greek *hekatón* (*he-* < **sem*, "one")
Germanic: **χunda* > Gothic *hund*, English *hundred*
Indo-Iranian: **ćatám* [i.e., *tśatam*]
  > Proto-Indo-Aryan **ćatám/*śatám*
    > Old Indo-Aryan *śatám*
  > Proto-Iranian **catam* [i.e., *tsatam*]
    > Avestan *satəm*
    > Old Persian *θata*
Baltic: Lithuanian *šimtas*, Latvian *sìmts*
Old Church Slavonic *sŭto*, Russian *sto*
Tocharian **ḱm̥tóm* > ** käntæ* > A *känt*, B *kante*

PIE **déḱm̥(t)*, 'ten'
Old Irish: *deich*
Italic: Latin *decem*
Greek *déka*
Germanic: **teχun* > Gothic *taíhun*, English *ten*
Indo-Iranian: **deća* [i.e., *detśa*]
> Proto-Indo-Aryan **deća/*daśa* > Old Indo-Aryan *daśa*;
> Proto-Iranian **deca/*daca* [i.e., *datsa*]
> Proto-Nuristani *daca* [i.e., *datsa*] > Kati *duc*,
> Avestan *dasa*
Baltic: Old Prussian *dessempts/dessimpts*, Old Lithuanian *dešimtis*, Lithuanian *dẽšimt*
Old Church Slavonic *desętĭ*, Russian *désyat'*
Albanian *dhjetë*
Armenian *tasn*
Tocharian **tšäkä(n)* > **śäkä(n)* > A *śäk*, B *śak*

The hypothesis that all existing IE languages go back to a single PIE language once spoken in a relatively restricted area is now a generally accepted idea. Helpfully, there is an example in which this assumed process has been documented from the beginning. The Romance languages have developed out of the Vulgar Latin spoken in the Roman empire in the areas where nowadays Italian, French, Spanish, Portuguese, Romanian, and Rheto-Romanian are spoken. We know the Romance protolanguage from copious literary sources: it is Latin, which was originally spoken in a very restricted region of Latium in northern Italy but then spread widely along with the expansion of the Roman empire. Latin was just one member of an "Italic" branch of the IE language family, known from inscriptions since *c.* 600 BCE, which at one time included the dead languages Oscan, Umbrian, and Faliscan (known from scanty sources) but by the beginning of the Christian era consisted of only Latin.

Many other dead languages known from sources inadequate for proper linguistic analysis have been identified as members of the IE language family, more or less securely. Best known are Phrygian (*c.* 800 BCE – 400 CE) from Anatolia, Thracian and Illyrian from the Balkans, and Venetic and Messapic from Italy. If we ignore these additional members, ten main IE branches are generally acknowledged (Fig. 3.1). Listed by date of their first documentation (with the oldest language coming first), they are:

(1) The Anatolian branch in modern Turkey, which became extinct by about 300 BCE. Its principal members are Hittite (*c.* 1600–1200 BCE), Palaic (*c.* 1600–1500 BCE), and Luvian (*c.* 1300–750 BCE), all documented in Mesopotamian cuneiform, while Luvian is also written in its own hieroglyphic script. Luvian was probably the language spoken by the Trojans of Homer's *Iliad*. Lycian and Lydian are important later Anatolian languages, known from alphabetic inscriptions of the fifth and fourth centuries BCE. (For Anatolian, see chapter 6.)

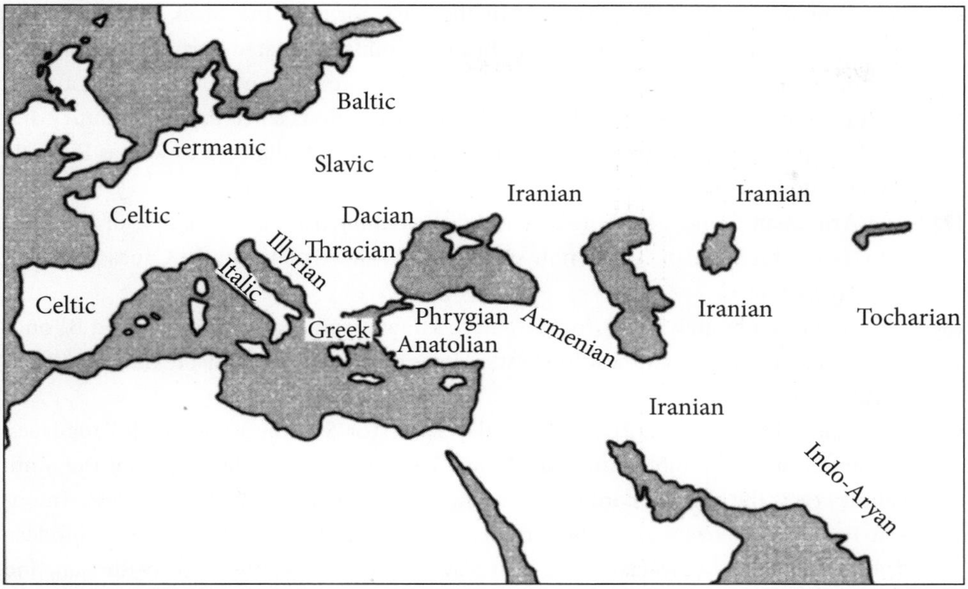

FIGURE 3.1 Generalized distribution of the principal Indo-European languages *c.* 500 BCE (after Mallory and Adams [1997:300]). Courtesy J. P. Mallory.

(2) The Indo-Iranian or Aryan branch, with many languages now spoken in India, Iran, and Central Asia, and in antiquity in the Eurasian steppes. Its scanty oldest testimonia are cuneiform documents from the ancient West Asia related to the Proto-Indo-Aryans of the Mitanni kingdom, dated *c.* 1500–1300 BCE (see chapter 8). The Old Indo-Aryan Rigveda containing 1028 hymns dates from *c.* 1300–1000 BCE, and the most ancient part of the Old Iranian Avesta from *c.* 1000 BCE (see chapter 9). However, loanwords borrowed from Proto-Indo-Aryan and Proto-Iranian into Proto-Uralic and its immediate successors between about 2300 and 1600 BCE represent the oldest known phase of Indo-Iranian (see chapter 7), although they were recorded only in modern times.

(3) The Greek branch with numerous dialects. Its earliest inscriptions in the Mycenaean Linear B script date from the thirteenth century BCE, Homeric literature from *c.* 800 BCE. The ancient Greeks had colonies in Italy, Africa, and Asia, as far as India (see chapter 6).

(4) The Italic branch, discussed above.

(5) The Celtic branch, divided into two groups. Insular Celtic of the British Isles and Brittany, attested in inscriptions since *c.* 400 CE, is the only one to survive today in Irish, Welsh, Cornish, and Breton. Continental Celtic, attested since *c.* 600 BCE, was the most widely spoken language in western and central Europe, ranging from Spain to France all the way east to the Black Sea; the Galatians even reached Anatolia. The spread of the Roman empire and Latin caused Continental Celtic to die out *c.* 300 CE.

(6) The Germanic branch, divided into three groups. North Germanic, currently represented by Icelandic, Norwegian, Danish, and Swedish, is known from runic inscriptions dating from *c.* 150 CE and extensive Old Norse literature from *c.* 900 CE. East Germanic

is synonymous with Gothic spoken in the area north of the Black Sea by Nordic immigrants. In the fourth century CE, Bishop Wulfila translated part of the Bible into Gothic, which died out in the sixteenth century. The most important current West Germanic languages are English (recorded in inscriptions since the fifth century and in literature since the eighth century CE), German with its dialects, as well as Flemish, Dutch, and Frisian.

(7) The Armenian branch, known since the fifth century from a translation of the Bible into classical Armenian. This is now spoken mainly in Armenia in the Caucasus and in eastern Turkey.

(8) The Tocharian branch, an extinct language known from two dialects (A and B) once spoken in Xinjiang or Chinese Turkestan. It is recorded in Buddhist texts dating from *c.* 600–800 CE.

(9) The Balto-Slavic branch, divided into the Slavic (or Slavonic) and Baltic languages. A translation of the Bible into Old Church Slavonic or Old Bulgarian from the ninth century CE is the oldest record of Slavic languages, which comprise South Slavic (modern Bulgarian, Slovenian, Serbo-Croatian, and Macedonian), West Slavic (modern Polish, Czech, and Slovacian), and East Slavic (modern Ukrainian, Belo-Russian, and Russian). The Baltic languages include the extinct Old Prussian (with some records from 1300–1600 CE), and modern Lithuanian and Latvian (with a literature since *c.* 1500 CE).

(10) The Albanian branch, spoken in Albania, Bosnia, and northern Italy. This is known in two dialects and has been recorded since the fifteenth century CE.

Scholars are unanimous that the Anatolian branch was the first to separate from the IE protolanguage. It is the only branch to preserve the so-called laryngeal phonemes that have been reconstructed for Early PIE. The other branches appear to have emerged from a Late PIE linguistic community, which disintegrated suddenly, dispersing in different directions. Many scholars think that Tocharian is the most archaic of the Late PIE languages.

4

The Indus Civilization

In 1924, Sir John Marshall, Director General of the Archaeological Survey of India, announced to the general public the discovery of a previously unknown Bronze Age culture. He named it the Indus civilization, because the finds came from two sites in the Upper and Lower Indus Valley, Harappa (near Lahore in the Punjab) and Mohenjo-daro (in Sindh), 600 km apart.

However, an archaeological culture is often named after the site of its first discovery. In this case, the site of Harappa had been described, by Alexander Cunningham, the first Director of the Archaeological Survey of India, as early as 1875. So "Harappan culture" has often been used, instead of "Indus civilization," to embrace both the earlier, developmental phase of the civilization and its mature phase, which is dated to *c.* 2600–1900 BCE. This followed the realization by the archaeologist M. Rafique Mughal in 1970 that urbanization and many concomitant technologies began before the Mature Harappan phase during the Early Harappan phase dated to *c.* 3200–2600 BCE; the term previously used for this earlier period, Pre-Harappan, did not convey the sense of close cultural continuity between the Early and Mature Harappan phases. It now appears that during a short transition period, *c.* 2600–2500 BCE, various Early Harappan cultures were largely transformed into the relatively unified Indus civilization.

Excavations at the sites of Mehrgarh, Nausharo, Sibri, and Pirak have provided an unbroken cultural sequence from about 7000 to 1000 BCE (Jarrige et al. 1995). These places were strategically located close to the Bolan Pass (connecting the Lower Indus Valley with the highlands of Baluchistan) on the ancient route to Afghanistan, the Iranian plateau, and Central Asia. The Mehrgarh cultural sequence has made it possible to understand the mutual relationship of the various small local Neolithic and Copper Age cultures of the Indo-Iranian borderlands, to follow their gradual evolution, and to sketch their migration to the Indus Valley and beyond so as to become Early Harappan cultures.

Variant Early Harappan cultures existed in the valley around Quetta (Damb Sadaat culture); in southern Afghanistan around Kandahar (Mundigak culture); in southern Baluchistan and southern Sindh (the Kulli, Nal, and Amri cultures), in the eastern plains of the Punjab, Haryana, and Uttar Pradesh (Ravi-Hakra and Sothi-Siswal cultures); and in nearly the whole Indus Valley (the Kot Diji culture) (Possehl 1999) (Fig. 4.1). Some of

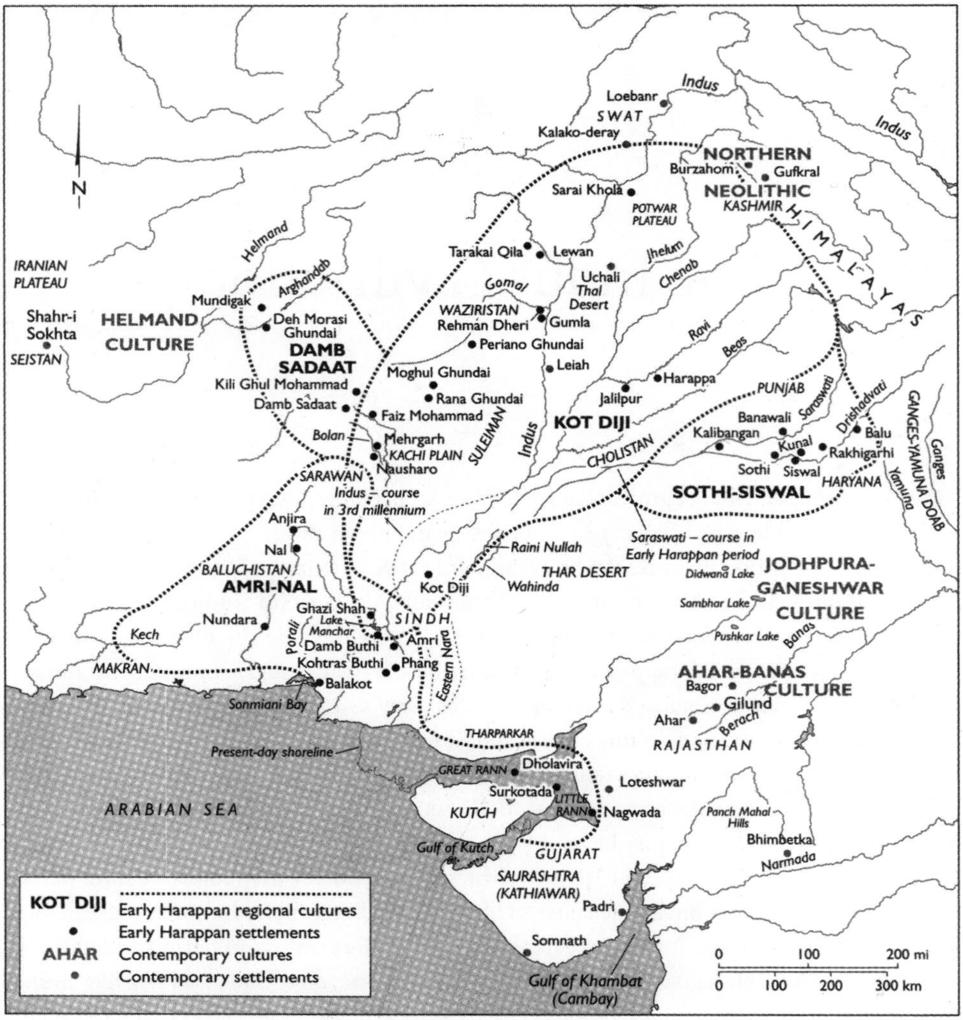

FIGURE 4.1 The Greater Indus Valley during the Early Harappan period, *c.* 3200–2600 BCE. After McIntosh 2008: map 1. © ABC-CLIO Inc.

these Early Harappan cultures continued to exist after the formation of the Indus civilization: the Kulli culture in southern Baluchistan, the Late Kot Diji culture in the northernmost Indus Valley and the Anarta tradition of Gujarat (derived from the Amri-Nal cultures). The post-Harappan Copper Age cultures of Rajasthan, the Deccan, and the Upper Gangetic Valley have a predominantly Harappan ancestry (Fig. 4.4).

The Indus Valley, with its wide plains watered and fertilized by annual floods, permitted cultivation on a larger scale than the mountain valleys of the borderlands. Yet the valley was not colonized immediately, for its environmental conditions also posed difficulties. Habitations had to survive the floods, which often required building on raised foundations. Villages started spreading, tentatively, from the piedmont to the plains as early as 3800 BCE.

With gradually increasing social skills and technological advances came walled towns on a grid pattern in the Early Harappan period. Where before, in the Neolithic and Copper Age villages, people had stored grain in communal granaries, now they stored it in large storage jars kept in separate houses. The novel concept of private ownership is also suggested by pot marks, and the adoption of stamp seals with geometrical motifs for administration. Cattle pulled plows in the fields: furrows excavated in the Early Harappan level at Kalibangan show the same pattern as today, running in two directions at right angles to each other (nowadays sown with two different seeds, horsegram and mustard). Transport was facilitated by ox-carts, still the most important vehicle in the South Asian countryside; its numerous representations in clay-model form were the Harappan counterpart of present-day model cars for children.

The Early Harappan cultures had overland trade contacts with southern Turkmenistan and with the Iranian plateau, where the Proto-Elamite culture (*c.* 3200–2600 BCE) had spread widely. Typically Proto-Elamite bevel-rimmed pottery comes even from Mir-i Qalat in Pakistani Baluchistan (Besenval 2011). Contact with Proto-Elamite people may have given Early Harappans the idea of creating a writing system, for the foundations of the Indus script were laid in late Kot Diji times, although the script itself bears scarcely any resemblance to the Proto-Elamite script.

The Early Harappans already possessed most of the basic cultural constituents of the Indus civilization. In the Mature Harappan period these became more refined and were applied on a grand scale. Early Harappan artifacts are clearly distinguishable from Mature Harappan ones on the basis of form and style. The most characteristic features of the Indus civilization include the following:

- the fully developed Indus script;
- finely carved stamp seals with writing and/or an animal or some other iconographic motif mostly, usually made of soft soapstone hardened by heating;
- standardized measures, including cubic weights made of chert carefully cut and polished, employing a combination of the binary and decimal systems, in the ratios $\frac{1}{16}$, $\frac{1}{8}$, $\frac{1}{6}$, $\frac{1}{4}$, $\frac{1}{2}$, 1, 2, 4, 8, 16, . . . 800;
- the large-scale use of burnt brick, standardized in size, with the ratio 1:2:4 the most effective for bonding;
- exquisite lapidary art, featuring highly developed microdrilling of very long beads made of hard carnelian, decorated with chemically stained motifs.

We do not know exactly where the Indus civilization came into being. But it is clear that it spread quickly over almost the entire Early Harappan area and even beyond (Fig. 4.2). The transitional period (2600–2500 BCE) may not have been altogether peaceful, for several Early Harappan towns were burned down and resettled in Mature Harappan fashion. Because rather few bronze weapons have been found, the Indus civilization has been imagined as being an exceptionally peaceful place, yet it seems unlikely that it could have dispensed with armed forces to maintain law and order, and as a defense against outside attack. Bows and arrows made of cane appear in Indus art but are hard to trace in the

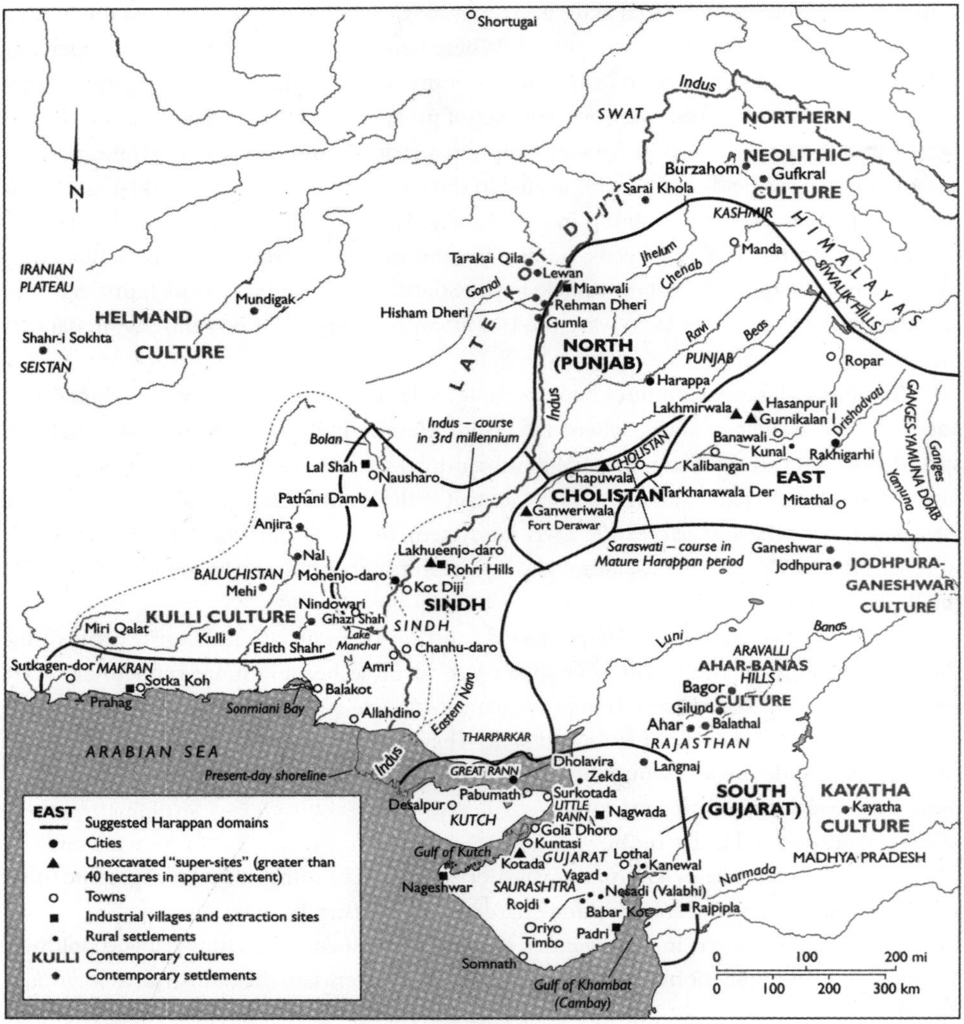

FIGURE 4.2 The Greater Indus Valley during the Indus civilization or Mature Harappan period, *c.* 2600–1900 BCE. After McIntosh 2008: map 2. © ABC-CLIO Inc.

archaeological record. They were the weapons of Indian soldiers in the fifth century BCE, according to Herodotus (7,65).

As during the Early Harappan period, the cities and their specialized craftsmen were fed by farmers and pastoralists. Humped cattle, sheep, and goats were kept and wheat and barley were cultivated from Neolithic times. In the Mature Harappan period the number of cultivars increased, and two growing seasons were introduced where feasible: barley, wheat, oats, lentils, beans, mustard, jujube, and linen were grown in winter; millets, cotton, sesamum, melons, jute, hemp, grapes, and dates in summer during the monsoon.

Mature Harappan metallurgists used copper (alloyed to make bronze mostly with tin), lead, silver, gold, and electrum. Lapidaries worked many kinds of stone. Analysis has shown that the Indus people procured their minerals from diverse sources, often far away (Law 2011). A Mature Harappan settlement was established beyond the Hindu Kush mountains in northeastern Afghanistan at Shortugai to control the mining of lapis lazuli, which was in great demand in West Asia (Francfort 1989). A major innovation was water transport. Rivers could be used for moving large and heavy loads long distances. Ships also transformed foreign trade.

While virtually no object of clearly West Asiatic origin has been discovered in the Greater Indus Valley, dozens of seals bearing the Indus script have been found in Mesopotamia and the Persian Gulf, along with Harappan weights and jewelry. Cuneiform texts also speak of sea trade with foreign countries, and there is nowadays wide agreement that the most distant of these countries, Meluhha, was the Greater Indus Valley. There are also references to Meluhhan people living in Mesopotamia, but unfortunately no record of their language, except that it required an interpreter (chapter 17).

Mohenjo-daro, built by 2400 BCE, is one of the largest Indus settlements, with an area of at least 100 hectares, possibly more, and a population of perhaps 50,000 people (Marshall 1931; Mackay 1938; Franke-Vogt 1991 [1992]). The acropolis, or "citadel," covering 20 hectares, stands to the west of the residential "lower city" on a 12 m high mud-brick platform. The purpose of its "public" buildings is largely guesswork: they include an "Assembly Hall"; a "Granary" or "Warehouse" (once ventilated); a "Great Bath," with a watertight pool measuring 7 m by 13 m surrounded by verandas, rooms, and a well; and a "College of Priests." The "lower city," too, was artificially raised above the flood plain and surrounded by a wall. Many houses had two stories and a central courtyard. The main street, 7.6 m wide, ran north–south. The real wonder of Mohenjo-daro is its water-engineering (Jansen 1993). It is estimated to have had 700 deep wells ingeniously built with tapering bricks to prevent them from collapsing. Many houses had waterproof bathing platforms and privies. Waste water was channeled away through pipes and chutes into covered drains that ran along level streets. The cesspits of these drains were regularly emptied.

Another major site, the 100-hectare town of Dholavira in Kutch, had three large water tanks to conserve drinking water (Fig. 4.3). Dholavira looks different from the brick-built Mohenjo-daro, because here stone was available as a building material. The town has grand walls and gates, one of which was found to carry a monumental inscription, the only example of its kind so far discovered: each of its ten signs is about 37 cm high, made of pieces of crystalline rock inlaid in a wooden plank three meters long.

Many Indus towns had an acropolis: Allahdino, Banawali, Chanhu-daro, Dholavira, Harappa, Kalibangan, Kot Diji, Lothal, Mohenjo-daro, Nausharo, Rakhigarhi, Surkotada, and Sutkagen-dor. The purpose of these varying monumental structures is thought to have been to impress people and thus reinforce political power. Some of them clearly had a protective function, too (Eltsov 2008). Kanmer in Kutch is a small site (115 m by 105 m), but its walls are 11 m high by 12–15 m wide (Kharakwal, Rawat, & Osada 2012).

FIGURE 4.3 The largest of several water reservoirs in the Indus town of Dholavira, Kutch, Gujarat. It is 73.4 m long, 29.3 m wide, and 10.6 m deep, with flights of thirty steps in three corners. Photo Asko Parpola 2008.

Around 2000–1900 BCE the Indus civilization came to an end. Multiple causes have been adduced for the gradual decline and eventual downfall of urban life in the Indus Valley, which resulted in the disappearance of the Indus script and seals. (The latest, definitely recognizable, samples of the Indus script are from the southernmost site of Daimabad, not too far from Mumbai, about 1800 BCE. Fig. 14.3) Stagnant water in the irrigation canals of the civilization may have dissolved ground salts and rendered the fields uncultivable. Thick layers of silt at Mohenjo-daro attest to catastrophic floods. Rivers, particularly the Indus and the Ghaggar-Hakra, also changed their courses. These events may have been connected with earthquakes. Recent palaeoclimatic research (Dixit, Hodell, & Petrie 2014) suggests an abrupt weakening of the summer monsoon in the northwestern plains of the Indian subcontinent about 2100 BCE, causing severe decline in summer overbank flooding that adversely affected monsoon-supported agriculture. (This aridification seems to have been widespread; it occurred in West Asia too.) All this coincided with the arrival of the first wave of Indo-Aryan speakers in South Asia (chapter 8), but there is no evidence of a massacre of Indus Valley populations by "Indra's hordes," as was once thought (Wheeler 1947; 1968); rather, the skeletons lying unburied in the streets of Mohenjo-daro are now known to have belonged to people who died from malaria and cholera, not armed assault.

The large Harappan population did not all of a sudden disappear. There is a clear continuity between the relatively unified Indus civilization and the varied regional cultures of the second millennium, that is, the Jhukar culture of Sindh and the Cemetery H culture of

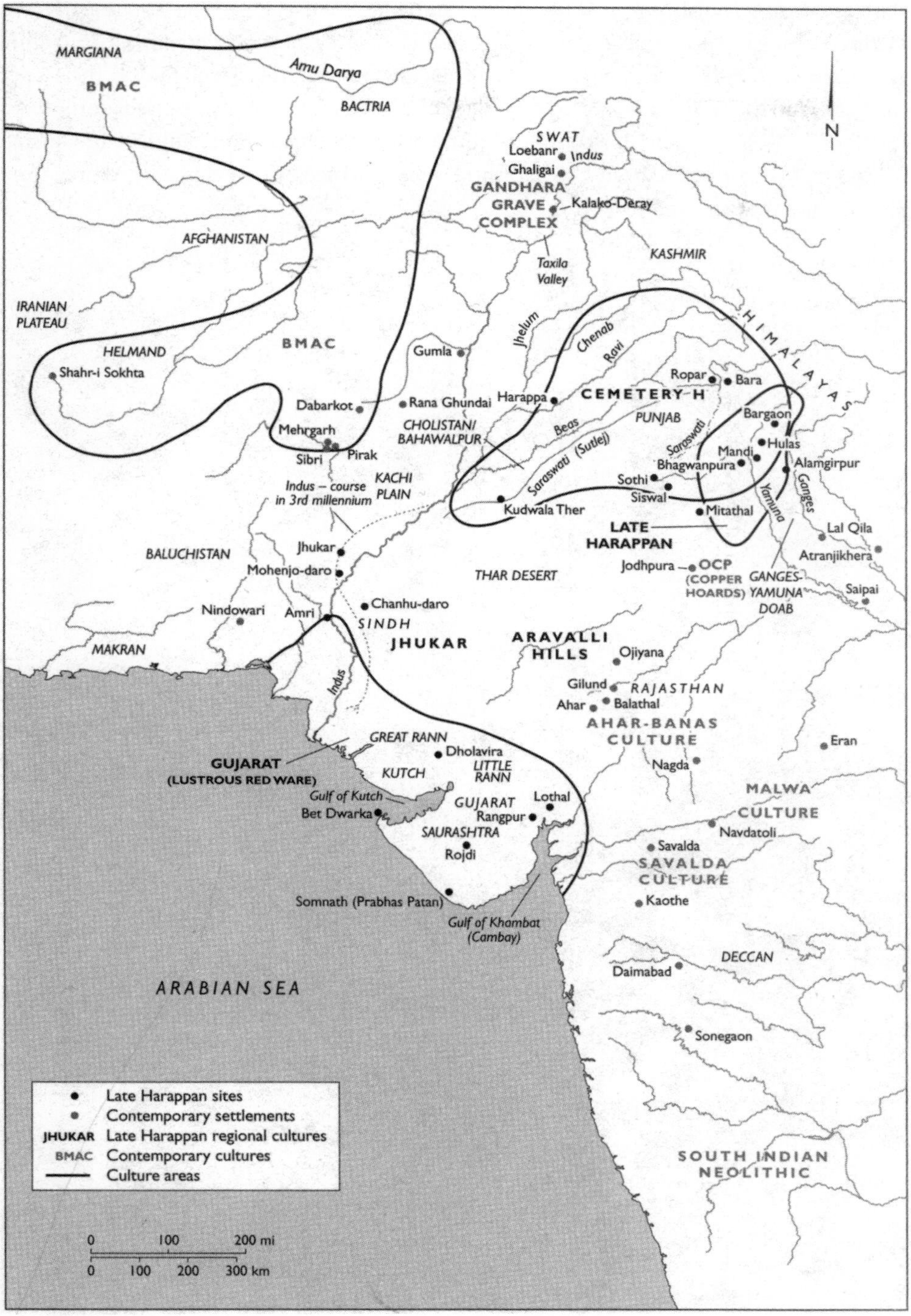

FIGURE 4.4 The Greater Indus Valley during the Late and Post-Harappan period, *c.* 1900–1300 BCE. After McIntosh 2008: map 4. © ABC-CLIO Inc.

Harappa, which is distributed in the Punjab and Cholistan. The heritage of the Early and Mature Harappan cultures likewise continues in the Ochre Coloured Pottery (OCP) culture associated with the copper hoards found in the Ganges–Yamuna Doab and in the Upper Gangetic Valley. In Gujarat and Maharashtra the Indus civilization lingered until about 1800 BCE. Harappan traditions continued in the various "Chalcolithic" cultures of Gujarat, Rajasthan, Madhya Pradesh, and Maharashtra, supplemented by new elements coming from the west and the east (Fig. 4.4).

5

The Indus Religion and the Indus Script

The Indus civilization was the fourth culture in the world to become literate. Around 3400 BCE, the Sumerians of the Late Uruk culture in Mesopotamia created the very first writing system, which inspired the Proto-Elamites of Iran and the Egyptians to devise their respective scripts by about 3200 BCE. But whereas abundant textual material sheds light on the Mesopotamian and Egyptian civilizations, only very short Harappan inscriptions survive, written in signs that are extremely difficult to decipher in the absence of bilingual texts. The archaic Sumerian script and the earliest Egyptian hieroglyphic are understood (on the basis of their later forms) to a considerable extent, Proto-Elamite very poorly.

The seal inscriptions, and the tiny clay, faience, and stone tablets labeled as Indus "amulets," are written in pictograms, often in conjunction with some iconographic motif, usually depicting an animal, but also sacred trees and anthropomorphic figures likely to be deities. In addition there are small statuettes and figurines of human beings and animals and what have been described as either gaming pieces or phalli. Furthermore, as has already been remarked, among the most noteworthy public structures at Mohenjo-daro are a remarkably advanced water drainage system and the so-called Great Bath, suggesting that the Indus people were preoccupied with ritual bathing.

These discoveries together persuaded Marshall, the leader of the first major excavations of the Indus civilization, to posit a connection with Hinduism. In a paper published in 1931, Marshall even identified as "Proto-Śiva" a human-like figure depicted on a seal as three-faced, seated on a throne in what appears to be a yogic posture, and surrounded by animals (fig. 16.6). Marshall's paper (Marshall 1931a), the most quoted study of the Indus religion, has been accepted by many scholars in its general conclusions, despite criticism of its details, including his identification of "Proto-Śiva." However, some scholars remain doubtful about any connection between the Indus civilization and later Indian religions. "We should not impose the meaning of the later icons upon the earlier images," writes a skeptical Wendy Doniger in one of the best current assessments of the Indus religion. Yet even Doniger admits:

> once we have explored the meaning of the Indus representations within the context of their own limited context, we can go on to speculate how they may have contributed to the evolution of a later iconography that they sometimes superficially resemble. For the resemblances between some aspects of the IVC [Indus Valley Civilization] and later Hinduism are simply too stunning to ignore. (Doniger 2009:82–83)

I of course agree with this, while accepting the need for caution in my speculations. In the second half of this book, I attempt to elucidate the roots of Hinduism in the Indus civilization with novel interpretations of Indus iconography—in the seals, tablets, painted pottery, and other objects, such as the well-known statuette of the "priest-king"—based not only on later Indian parallels but also on the contemporaneous evidence from Mesopotamia and elsewhere in West Asia. The examination of the Indus iconography occupies most of part II of the book, where I suggest that the Western Asian parallels yield unprecedented insights into the Harappan religion. This evidence is largely independent of the results achieved in the study of the Indus script, summarized in chapter 21 before the conclusion.

But first we must ask whether the Indus script was actually *writing*, in the sense of a system for visually recording spoken language, that wonderful means of communication capable of expressing the full range of thought. The earliest writing systems started as fairly primitive "proto-writing," which normally did not record the grammatical forms of words, and mostly operated with "logographic" pictograms (symbols that in principle could be read as words in any language); yet all of the systems used punning to express words or syllables phonetically. They were thus at least partially language-based, although they required centuries to evolve a writing system sufficiently sophisticated to express all parts of a spoken language. There are also nonlinguistic sign systems, such as mathematical or musical notation, which can be understood without reference to language, but they can express only a limited range of thought.

This issue of whether the Indus script is writing has been hotly debated after a team consisting of a historian, Steve Farmer, a computer linguist, Richard Sproat, and an Indologist, Michael Witzel, claimed that the Indus signs do not constitute a language-based writing system, but are merely nonlinguistic symbols of political and religious significance (Farmer, Sproat, & Witzel 2004; see also Lawler 2004). The authors admit that the Indus people were in contact with Mesopotamia and were thus acquainted with its cuneiform script; but they suggest that the Indus people made a deliberate decision not to adopt a writing system, probably in order to keep their esoteric knowledge secret. However, the existence of esoteric or religious knowledge—which was transmitted orally—was no obstacle to the adoption of writing by Indian people from Persia for administrative and economic purposes during the latter half of the first millennium BCE.

As to their other arguments, plain statistical tests, such as the distribution of sign frequencies, can prove neither that the signs represent writing nor that they do not represent writing, as Sproat admits. The claim that there is no sign repetition within any one Indus "inscription" (beyond reduplications, which they exclude) is simply false—there are many cases of sign repetition. What about the authors' principal claim, that all real writing systems have produced longer texts than found in the Indus script? The average length of an Indus inscription is five signs. The shortest texts have just one sign; the longest has twenty-six signs divided on three sides of a tablet; the longest single-side text has fourteen signs divided into three lines (Fig. 21.3a); and the longest single-line texts have fourteen signs. (The trio promise to pay a large sum of money to anyone who finds a genuine Indus text with more than fifty signs.) This thesis stumbles on the fact that in the earliest phase of Egyptian hieroglyphic writing, texts consisting of one or two signs can be read phonetically and meaningfully on the basis of later Egyptian hieroglyphic writing.

It appears that a phoneticized writing system was in use in Egypt in Pre-Dynastic times as early as 3200 BC, but it was not until the beginning of the Third Dynasty of the Old Kingdom, some 500 years later, that the Egyptians started to write complete sentences and longer documents. "Many inscribed artifacts are preserved from the first two Dynasties, the most numerous categories being cylinder seals and sealings, cursive annotations on pottery, and tags originally attached to tomb equipment, especially of the First Dynasty kings. Continuous language was still not recorded," writes the Egyptologist John Baines (1999:883). Fuller administrative documents are assumed to have existed in this early period but have not survived. It is perfectly possible that the same could have happened in the Indus civilization. This also takes care of the argument of Farmer and his colleagues that any Indus texts assumed to be lost never actually existed.

During the early half of the third millennium BCE, systems of "potter's marks" existed at several locations in the Indus Valley and the Iranian Plateau (Quivron 1980; Vidale 2007). Each used between about thirty and seventy different incised or painted symbols, which were probably nonlinguistic, as they never form longer sequences. Some of the Early Harappan "potter's marks" excavated at Harappa resemble some of the approximately 400 standardized signs of the Indus script. Farmer and colleagues do not take into account the fact that many groups of three Indus signs recur in the same sequence having the very same order at several different sites (Fig. 5.1), which is hard to explain unless they represent language rather than decorative designs. By contrast, the graffiti on pots excavated at the Megalithic site of Sanur in southern India are nonlinguistic symbols, for three different signs can be seen occurring in the following sequences: 123 three times, 132 twice, 231 four times, 312 four times, 213 once (Parpola 2008c). In addition, there are Indus inscriptions where the signs are squeezed together to fit into the end of a line, implying that the signs were written sequentially in one direction. "If the sequence matters, it's a language," writes Doniger (2009:69).

The Indus inscriptions are more than 1500 years older than the earliest presently readable texts of the subcontinent, the stone inscriptions of the Emperor Asoka, written in the third century BCE in the Kharoṣṭhī and Brāhmī scripts. The potential of the Indus inscriptions to shed new light on the dark prehistory of South Asia has attracted more than 100 published claims of decipherment since the 1920s, none of which has been widely accepted.

The most formidable obstacle to decipherment is the absence of any bilingual inscription written in Indus signs and translated into a known script. Such translations have usually provided the key to unknown scripts, most famously in the case of the Rosetta Stone, where

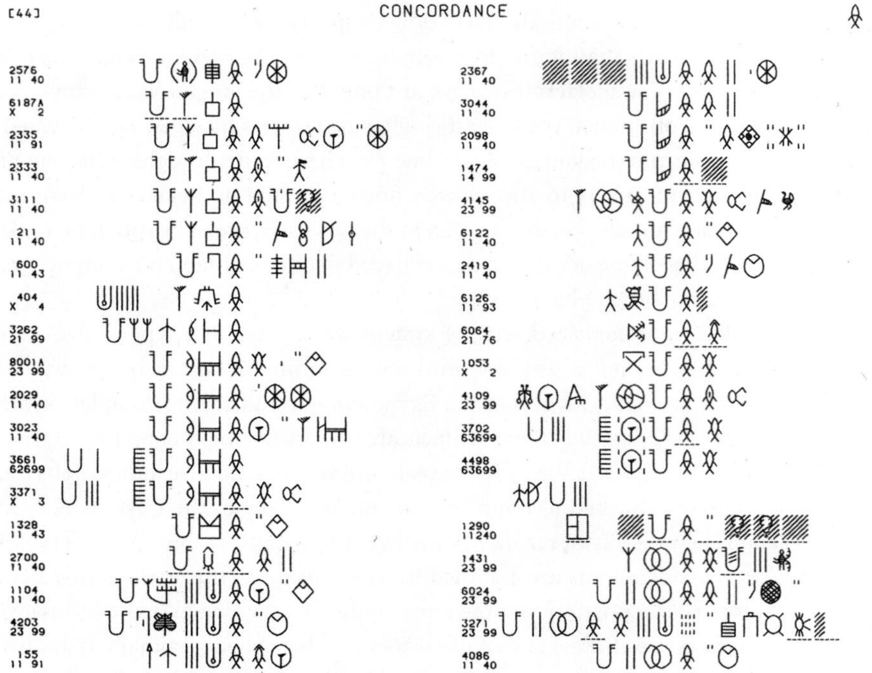

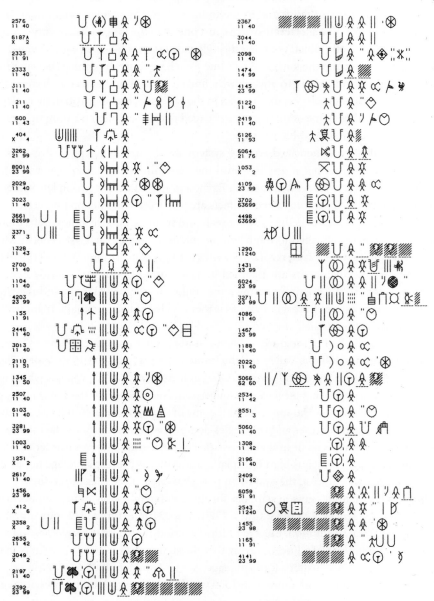

FIGURE 5.1 A sample page from the concordance to Indus inscriptions by K. Koskenniemi & A. Parpola 1982.

its Greek alphabetic inscription provided the key to its Egyptian hieroglyphic equivalent. Although no bilingual came to the aid of the decipherers of the many varieties of the cuneiform script, the names and genealogies of Persian kings, known from Herodotus and the Bible, provided a clue to Old Persian cuneiform. But this kind of information, too, is lacking for the Indus civilization, which collapsed before historically documented times.

Attempts to decipher the script started even before the ruins of Harappa and Mohenjo-daro were investigated and the Indus civilization was recognized in 1924. As early as 1875, Sir Alexander Cunningham reported the first known Indus seal, which was collected from the site of Harappa. He assumed that the seal was a foreign import because the bull depicted on the seal did not have the hump of the Indian zebu. A few years later, he suggested that the unique seal might bear signs of the Brāhmī script in a hitherto unknown early form.

After Cunningham, many other scholars connected the Indus script with the Brāhmī script, which is the ancestor of no fewer than about 200 South Asian and Southeast Asian scripts. To take one example, G. R. Hunter studied the Indus inscriptions at first hand in the 1920s and analyzed them structurally in a valuable doctoral dissertation (published as Hunter 1934), where he compared the script with other early writing systems. However, it has long been quite clear that the Kharoṣṭhī script is based on the Aramaic variant of the Semitic consonantal alphabet, which was brought to the Indus Valley by the bureaucracy of the Persian empire around 500 BCE, while the Brāhmī script may have been influenced in addition by the Greek script, which came to India with Alexander the Great in 326 BCE (Salomon 1996; Falk 1993). These two scripts, Kharoṣṭhī and Brāhmī, thus have nothing to do with the Indus script, the last traces of which date from around 1800 BCE.

Nonetheless, to take a second example of a published decipherment, the archaeologist S. R. Rao tried to assert that the Indus script is the basis of not only of the Brāhmī characters but also of the Semitic alphabet. In *The decipherment of the Indus script* (1982) and elsewhere (Rao 1991), Rao proposes that the Indus script developed thirty-four basic cursive signs, reduced to twenty-four in the Late Harappan period. He then finds somewhat similar Semitic parallels to seventeen of these basic cursive signs and so reads these seventeen Indus signs with their "equivalent" Semitic phonetic values. Other, pictographic, Indus signs, however, Rao reads phonetically on the basis of the Sanskrit names for the pictograms, but rather arbitrarily: the "man" pictogram is read as *ṛ* from Sanskrit *nṛ-* "man," whereas some other signs are read acrophonically. It requires a lot of trust to believe that Rao's proposed readings make sense in an Aryan language close to Vedic Sanskrit, as he claims. The consensus view is that the Semitic alphabet was created in the mid-second millennium BCE on the basis of the uniconsonantal signs of the neighboring Egyptian hieroglyphic script.

Others have looked to the Mesopotamian scripts for clues to the Indus script. Immediately after the discovery of the Indus civilization was announced, the British Assyriologists A. H. Sayce (1924) and C. J. Gadd and Sidney Smith (1924) pointed to its resemblance to the Elamite and Mesopotamian civilizations. They compared the Indus signs with the pictograms of the Proto-Elamite and archaic Sumerian scripts. The resemblance proved to be superficial, yet in 1925, the amateur Tibetologist L. A. Waddell published *The Indo-Sumerian seals deciphered*, with a subtitle summarizing a radical revision of the early history of mankind: *Discovering Sumerians of the Indus Valley as Phoenicians, Barats, Goths and famous Vedic Aryans, 3100–2300 B.C.* Waddell simply read the Indus signs with the phonetic values of somewhat similar-looking Sumerian signs and identified the inscriptions as "revised forms" of the names of Sumerian and Aryan kings.

Waddell's is an example of the most common approach used in would-be decipherments. But such sign comparison works only when the scripts involved are closely related, and even then there are pitfalls. For example, the Roman script is closely related to the Greek script but the Greek P has the phonetic value of the Roman R. The Indus script has no obvious genetic affinity with any other known script. It is true that some Indus signs have close formal parallels in many other ancient scripts, for example, the sign looking like a mountain resembles signs in the Sumerian, Egyptian, Hittite, and Chinese scripts. But each of these signs has a different phonetic value, even if their meaning may be the same or similar.

Perhaps the strangest Indus "decipherment" was that of a Hungarian engineer, Vilmos Hevesy (Hévesy 1933). In 1932, he suggested a connection between the Indus inscriptions and the *rongorongo* tablets of Easter Island in the Pacific Ocean. The two scripts are separated by more than 20,000 kilometers and some 3500 years, yet Hevesy's comparative lists of similar-looking Indus and *rongorongo* signs have been taken seriously by some scholars. It is, however, a particularly useless speculation, given that the *rongorongo* tablets are to a large extent undeciphered.

In my view, the most productive line of enquiry has proved to focus on identifying the underlying language of the Indus script. As far back as 1924, Marshall suggested that the Indus people may have spoken a Dravidian language, because the Indus civilization is pre-Aryan and a Dravidian language, Brahui, is even today represented in the Indus Valley and Baluchistan by a substantial number of Brahui speakers. Piero Meriggi, later an acknowledged authority on the Hittite and Proto-Elamite scripts, agreed with Marshall about the likelihood of this Dravidian linguistic affinity (Meriggi 1934), but refrained from a phonetic decipherment because he thought that reconstruction of the ancient Indus language was impossible. The Dravidian hypothesis was the basis of Father Henry Heras's ambitious attempt to decipher the Indus script, culminating in a large book in 1953. Heras was, I think, right in his readings of a couple of signs, but these were fatally undermined by a mass of nonsensical interpretations.

My own approach, launched in 1964 with Seppo Koskenniemi and Simo Parpola, was also based on the Dravidian hypothesis (see the preface and Parpola et al. 1969ab; 1970). The "rival" Soviet team agreed that the underlying language was probably Dravidian. The team was led by Yuri Knorozov, who had initiated the successful decipherment of the Mayan script in 1952, and it included a Dravidian specialist, Nikita Gurov (Knorozov et al 1968). (I appreciate Gurov's work—see chapters 14 and 24—but doubt the Soviet team's claims published in their final report [Knorozov, Albedil, & Volchok 1981], which confidently reads all of the Indus signs in Dravidian.) In India, Iravatham Mahadevan, who has done remarkable work in the field of Old Tamil epigraphy (Mahadevan 2003), has also published several papers offering Dravidian readings for Indus signs. Mahadevan started working on Indus material in 1971, and brought out his useful Indus computer corpus and concordance in 1977.

John Marshall underlined that success in study of the Indus script would require a many-sided professional approach. Effective interpretation "can be accomplished, now or in the future, by specialists conversant with the subject in all its bearings. I cannot refrain from stressing this point here, because the antiquities from Mohenjo-daro and Harappa . . . have been made the subject of much nonsensical writing, which can be nothing but a hindrance in the way of useful research" (Marshall 1931:I,ix). I believe Marshall would have extended the same advice to all those involved in the Aryan debate, if this had raged in his time as it does today.

PART I

The Early Aryans

6

Proto-Indo-European Homelands

In searching for the origins of the Indo-Iranian languages we naturally want to identify the homeland of the Proto-Indo-European speakers. The vocabulary common to the different Indo-European languages permits some conclusions about the natural and cultural environment of the PIE language. More than a century ago, Theodor Benfey, one of the leading Indo-Europeanists of his time, proposed that the PIE homeland was likely to have been in southern Russia (Benfey 1869:597–600). Otto Schrader, author of the still valuable encyclopedia of IE antiquity (2nd ed. in two volumes, revised by A. Nehring, 1917–1929) and who wrote a major work on comparative linguistics and prehistory (3rd ed. 1907), came to the conclusion that the Pontic steppes north of the Black Sea provided the most likely solution to the PIE homeland problem. Schrader noted that this location could explain the differences in the agricultural and environmental vocabulary of the IE languages spoken in Europe and Asia. Placing the homeland between the areas where the Uralic and Semitic languages are spoken also fits the assumed prehistoric contact of these language families with PIE. One of the most esteemed archaeologists of the first half of the twentieth century, V. Gordon Childe, opted for the same solution in his book *The Aryans: A study of Indo-European origins* (1926).

Marija Gimbutas correlated the PIE language with what she called the "Kurgan culture" of the south Russian steppes, and traced its impact on the archaeological cultures of Europe on a broad scale (Gimbutas 1997). Gimbutas's work was insightful, but her extensive and often pioneering syntheses were bound to be somewhat controversial. Her studies have been conservatively revised and carried further by her student J. P. Mallory. In his classic book *In search of the Indo-Europeans* (1989) and numerous other studies, Mallory has in many ways established—in my opinion convincingly—the thesis that the Early PIE homeland indeed was in the Pontic-Caspian steppes in southern Ukraine and southern Russia. In recent decades, Valentin Dergachev (1998; 2007) and David Anthony (1995; 2007) have contributed important support to this view, which is most widely accepted by both archaeologists and linguists.

The Pontic-Caspian steppes account for more than 40 percent of the wild-horse remains in Europe from the period *c.* 5000 BCE. The people of the Late Neolithic and Copper Age cultures of the Pontic-Caspian steppes not only hunted and ate the horse (at one site in the Mid-Volga River region 66 percent of the 3,602 identified bones were from horses), but also sacrificed it (cultic deposits of horse heads and hooves have been found) and made bone-plaque horse figurines. Not surprisingly, Early PIE had a word for horse, **h́éḱwos*. Moreover, the horse is the only animal to figure prominently in the personal names of several peoples speaking early IE languages, such as Old Indo-Aryan, Old Iranian, ancient Greek, Gaulish Celtic, and Old English, who in addition worshipped deities associated with the horse and offered horse sacrifices.

The horse was probably at first kept for meat and milk and only later used for traction. Many archaeozoologists consider the evidence for horse domestication uncertain before about 2500 BCE. I also doubt that the steppe pastoralists of the Copper Age rode domesticated horses in order to control their herds and make raids as early as 4100 BCE, as claimed by some scholars, notably Anthony (2007). If they had done so, then surely we would see pictures of horse-riders from this time? In fact, the first picture of a horse with a human rider dates from *c.* 2040 BCE and comes from Ur III dynasty Mesopotamia (Oates 2003), while those from the steppes date from later still, *c.* 1500 BCE (Figs. 9.4, 9.5), after which horse-rider images become increasingly prominent, especially in the cultures of mounted pastoralists, such as the Scythians. The handles of the Sejma-Turbino knives of the Asiatic steppes and European forest-steppe in the early second millennium still depict a single plain horse or a pair of horses (Fig. 7.8), except in one case. In the Eurasian steppes, a man is for the first time represented with a horse in the handle of a knife from the Rostovka cemetery. But this man is neither riding the horse, nor, as Anthony (2007:446) prefers, "roping" it; he is actually leaning backwards while standing on skis, using the horse for traction on snow (Fig. 7.10). Could horse-riding really have existed to any significant extent for two thousand years without being depicted? By contrast, the first wagons were depicted almost immediately after the invention of wheeled vehicles. They were so heavy—a wagon with four solid wheels could weigh 800 kg—that they could be pulled only by oxen, which are often depicted. Horses were harnessed to pull light, two-wheeled, chariots, but this did not happen before *c.* 2100 BCE (see chapter 7). It also seems significant that words for "riding" and "rider" cannot be reconstructed for PIE, nor even for Proto-Indo-Iranian.

When people of the Late Neolithic culture called Khvalynsk (*c.* 5000–3800 BCE) of the Volga steppes moved westwards and took control of the Dnieper-Donets culture, they fused with this earlier local population to form the Copper Age culture called Srednij Stog II (*c.* 4700–3400 BCE) in the steppes between the Don and Dnieper rivers north of the Black Sea. The Khvalynsk and Srednij Stog II peoples were pastoralists, who traded with the thriving Carpatho-Balkan cultures of agriculturalists. Together all these cultures formed the world's first great "metallurgical domain," where production (mining and working) was in the hands of agriculturalists (Chernykh 1992; 2007). The pastoralists were the receiving partners. Their closest neighbors, just beyond the steppes, were the farmers of the Cucuteni–Tripolye culture (known as the Cucuteni culture in Romania and Moldavia, the Tripolye culture in Ukraine), hereafter simply termed the Tripolye culture from which the eastern pastoralists received their metal and other prestige goods (Fig. 6.1). The Tripolye culture is divided into three major phases, A, B, and C, spanning *c.* 5700–2900 BCE, but the last sub-phase C2 (*c.* 3400–2900 BCE) is nowadays considered Post-Tripolye.

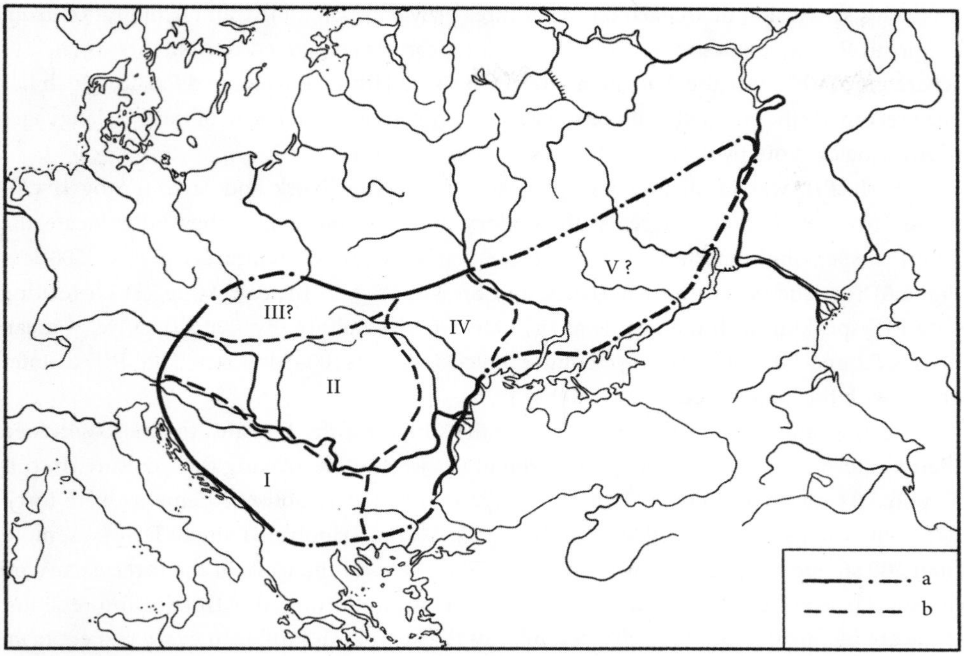

FIGURE 6.1 The "Carpatho-Balkan Metallurgical Province" of the fifth millennium BCE, according to E. N. Chernykh (1992:49, fig. 15). Courtesy E. N. Chernykh and Cambridge University Press. The steppe area (zone V)—here supposed to be the Early PIE homeland—was just importing metal from the west, mainly from the Cucuteni–Tripolye culture (the northern half of zone IV), which is here supposed to have been the Late PIE homeland *c.* 4200–3400 BCE.

An early phase of the Srednij Stog II culture (represented by the sites of Stril'cha Skelya, Chapli, Mariupol', Novodanilovka, and Suvorovo) was named the Skelya culture (*c.* 4300–4000 BCE) by Yuri Rassamakin (1999; 2004). During the last quarter of the fifth millennium, Skelya pastoralists invaded the Balkans. Widely distributed Skelya-type burials with characteristic Skelya grave goods are newly introduced cultural items in this area. Some 600 sites of the Carpatho-Balkan cultures were abandoned, many after burning down, and their voluminous metal production stopped almost completely.

The surviving local cultures of the eastern Balkans were transformed into the Cernavoda culture (*c.* 4000–3200 BCE) with notable new cultural components brought from the steppe in its economy, religion and social hierarchy. It is likely to have spoken the Early PIE of the Skelya invaders. About a millennium later, the Cernavoda culture fused with steppe invaders from the Yamnaya culture to form the Ezero culture (*c.* 3300–2700 BCE). This latter culture has ceramics supposed to be ancestral to the pottery of the Troy I culture (*c.* 3000–2600 BCE) of Anatolia. The most widely accepted date for the intrusion of IE speakers from Europe into Anatolia is *c.* 2700 BCE. Then, in western and southern Anatolia, more than 100 Early Bronze Age II (*c.* 2600–2250 BCE) sites were abandoned and all major sites destroyed, while Troy V-type ceramics (*c.* 2000–1800 BCE) spread eastwards along with the *megaron*-type architecture that characterizes early Greece.

This succession of archaeological cultures provides a credible trail for migration from the north Pontic steppes to Anatolia. Indo-Europeanists are agreed that the first branch to separate from PIE was the Anatolian one, comprising Hittite, Luvian, and Palaic, which has been recorded since the sixteenth century BCE (as noted in chapter 3, all of these IE languages of Anatolia died out by the end of the first millennium BCE).

Early PIE was in all probability spoken in the Khvalynsk and Srednij Stog II cultures. However, I do not agree with Mallory and Anthony when they both locate the Late-PIE-speaking homeland in the same place, that is, the Yamnaya cultures (*c.* 3300–2500 BCE, Fig. 6.6) that succeeded the Khvalynsk and Srednij Stog II. Instead, I suggest correlating Late-PIE-speaking with the people of the Late Tripolye culture. By "Late Tripolye," I mean phases B2 and C1 of the Tripolye culture, dated from *c.* 4100–3400 BCE. Late PIE disintegrated with the Tripolye culture *c.* 3400 BCE.

At the same time as the Skelya pastoralists invaded the Balkans, they also subdued their western neighbors, the Tripolye people, but without destroying their culture. In this Tripolye B1 phase (*c.* 4300–4000 BCE), a large number of Tripolye settlements were fortified, which suggests that they were under attack. At the Tripolye B1 site of Drutsy 1, more than 100 steppe-type flint arrowheads were found around the walls of the three excavated houses. Drutsy 1 also had "Cucuteni C-type" ceramics decorated with cord impressions; these are identical with the Skelya ceramics of the steppe, and differ in every respect from the traditional beautiful Tripolye painted pottery. This intrusive ware appeared at first sporadically in a number of settlements, then with increasing frequency until it became the predominant ceramic in the final phase of the Tripolye culture.

Some of the earliest Tripolye sites to yield this steppe-type pottery also produced knobbed maces (a few of them in the shape of a horse's head), which spread from the steppes to the Balkans and the Tripolye area in 4300–4000 BCE (Fig. 6.2). These weapons were symbols of power, very probably reflecting the spread of a new type of social organization—strongly hierarchical chieftainship—instrumental in the spread of Early IE. Effective new leadership

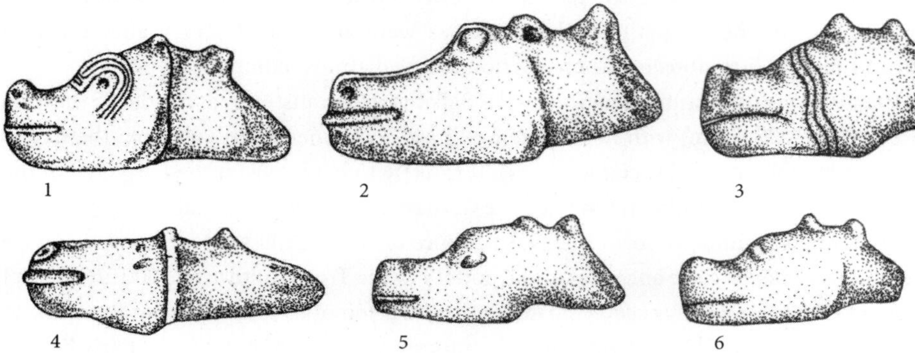

FIGURE 6.2 Skelya-type scepters with stone mace-heads sometimes shaped like a horse-head, *c.* 4300–4000 BCE. These come from the following sites: (1) Casimcea; (2) Terekli-Mekteb; (3) Salcuta; (4) Suvorovo (this one is 17 cm long); (5) Fedeleseni; (6) Rzhevo. After Mallory 1989:234, fig. 129. Courtesy J. P. Mallory.

seems to have invigorated the Tripolye culture, which expanded northwards and eastwards, creating ever-larger towns, some covering hundreds of hectares. There was now internal strife between the rival eastern and western parts of the Tripolye culture. Perhaps this was the age of warring heroes described in IE epic poetry with poetic formulae, such as Greek _kléos áphthiton_ (Iliad 9,413) and Sanskrit _śrávo . . . ákṣitam_ (RV 1,9,7), both of which mean "imperishable fame" and derive from PIE _*ḱlewes *n̥dhg^{w}hitom_ (Schmitt 1967; Watkins 1995; West 2007).

The most important means of relating archaeological cultures with the speaking of Late PIE is the PIE vocabulary associated with wheeled vehicles. On the one hand, these technical terms imply that Late PIE-speakers used wheeled vehicles, on the other, they date the disintegration of Late PIE to a period after the invention of wheeled vehicles—a date that can in principle be deduced from the archaeological record. That Late PIE had at least five terms associated with wheeled vehicles has been very widely agreed for more than a century, although in my view as many as twelve terms are plausible. The five more-or-less certain terms are now discussed to show the extent and solidity of the evidence for Late PIE-speaking use of wheeled vehicles and the origin of these words.

(1) PIE _*k^{w}é-k^{w}l-o-/*k$^{w}_{e}$k^{w}l-á_, "wheel" is the origin of Greek _kúklos_, Tocharian A _kukäl_ / B _kokale_, "wagon," Sanskrit _cakrá-_, Old Norse _hvél, hjól_, Old English _hwēol_. There is even a PIE poetic phrase that speaks of "the wheel of the sun": Vedic _sūryasya cakrá-_, Old Norse _sunnu . . . hvél_, Greek _hēlíou kúklos_. This word is derived by intensifying reduplication from the PIE root _*k^{w}el-_, "to turn (around), move in a circle." PIE _*k^{w}ol-o-/*k^{w}el-es-_ derived from the unreduplicated root is represented by Old Irish _cul_, "wagon"; Latin _colus_, "distaff, the rod on which wool is wound before spinning"; Old Norse _hvel_ (with a short _e_), "wheel"; Old Church Slavonic _kolo_, "wheel" (pl. _kola_, "wagon"); Greek _pólos_, "axle."

(2) The PIE verbal root _*weǵ^{h}-_ is the basis of PIE nominal derivatives denoting "vehicle, wagon" (the number of which attests to the importance of wagon building and wagon traffic in Late PIE and early post-PIE-speaking times):
   (a) PIE _*wóǵ^{h}-o-_, "wagon": Greek _ókhos_, Old Church Slavonic _voz_; Sanskrit _vāhá_, "vehicle, draught animal";
   (b) PIE _*wóǵ^{h}-a-_: Mycenaean Greek _wo-ka-_ (i.e., _wokha-_), "two-wheeled wagon";
   (c) PIE _*wéǵ^{h}-os_ (n.), "wagon": Greek (Homer, Pindar) _ókhos_ (n., pl. _ókhea_); Sanskrit _váhas-_ (n.), "shoulder of a draught animal";
   (d) PIE _*weǵ^{h}-no-_, "wagon": Old Irish _fēn_, Welsh _gwain_;
   (e) PIE _*woǵ^{h}-no-_, "wagon": Proto-Germanic _*wagnaz_ > Old Norse _vagn_, etc.; cf. Sanskrit _vāhana-_, "vehicle, draught animal";
   (f) PIE _*weǵ^{h}-e-tlom_, "device for transport": Latin _vehiculum_, Sanskrit _vahitram_, "ship, vehicle"; cf. Greek (Hesychius) _ókhetla_, "carriages."

The verbal root _*weǵ^{h}-_ is securely reconstructed to mean "convey in a vehicle, drive": Luwian Hieroglyphic _wa-za-_, "drive"; Sanskrit _váhati_, "conveys"; Avestan _vazaiti_, "conveys"; Greek _ékhō_, "I bring" (Pamphylian Greek _wekhétō_), _ókheomai_, "I convey"; Latin _vehō_, "I convey, bring"; Old Norse _vega_, "to move"; Lithuanian _vežù_, "I convey"; Russian _vezu_, "I convey."

Before the invention of wheeled vehicles, this native PIE root is likely to have meant mainly "moving a heavy load" by means of a lever, litter, travois, sledge, or draught animal. For this older meaning (which agrees with the generally accepted hypothesis of how the wheeled vehicles were invented) we have the following attestations: Proto-Germanic **wegan*, "move"; Old Norse *vǫg*, "lever," pl. *vagar*, "sledge," *vǫgur, vāgir*, "litter, travois," *vagn*, "wagon, sledge, litter," *vāg*, "lever, weighing machine, weight"; Old Prussian *wessis*, Lithuanian *vãžis, važỹs*, Latvian *važus, važas*, "sledge"; Greek *okhleús*, "lever," *okhlízō*, "to move by a lever, heave up."

(3) PIE **aḱs-*, "axle" survives with various extensions in different branches:
  (a) PIE **aḱs-o-* in Vedic Sanskrit *ákṣa-*;
  (b) PIE **aḱs-i-* in Latin *axis*, Lithuanian *ašìs*, Old Church Slavonic *osь*;
  (c) PIE **aḱs-on-* in Greek *áksōn* (gen. *áksonos*), Mycenaean Greek *a-ko-so-ne*;
  (d) PIE **aḱs-a* in West Germanic **ahsō*, Old High German *ahsa*, German *Achse*, Old English *eax*; English *axle* from Old Norse *ǫxull* from **ahsula*; also Greek *hámaksa*, "cart with a single axle," from PIE **sm-aḱs-a*.

PIE **aḱs-*, "axle," is probably an **-es*-derivative from PIE **aǵ-*, "to drive, move, lead" (Sanskrit *aj-, ájati*, Latin *agō*, Greek *ágō*, Armenian *acem*, Tokharian *āk-*; intransitive in Old Norse *aka*, "to drive," Welsh *af*, "to go"). Lithuanian *ašìs* denotes, besides "axle," also "fathom" = "outstretched arms," while Avestan *aša-* (which formally corresponds to Sanskrit *ákṣa-*, "axle") means "shoulder," like the Old Norse *ǫxl*, German *Achsel*. The axle enables the movement of wheels as the shoulders enable movement of the arms and wings. Thus the axle is what makes the wagon "move" (**aǵ-*). The term could also denote the axle as the "moving part," for in its most primitive form, the axle was fixed to the wheels, which did not rotate independent of it.

(4) PIE **nebʰ-/*nobʰ-/*n̥bʰ-*, "navel, nave": the older meaning is the more widely distributed "navel," but the word is attested in the meaning "nave of the wheel" in Sanskrit *nábhya-*, *nābhi-*; Old Prussian *nabis*; Latvian *naba*; Old High German *naba*, German *Nabe*, Old Norse *nof*, Old English *nafu* and of course English *nave*.

(5) PIE **yug-ó-*, "yoke": Hittite *iukan*, Sanskrit *yugám*, Greek *zugón*, Latin *iugum*, Gothic *juk*, Old Norse *ok*, Old High German *juch, joch*, Lithuanian *jùngas*, Russian *igo*, Welsh *iau*, Armenian *luc*. This word is derived from the PIE verbal root **yeug-*, "yoke, join, unite, harness": Sanskrit *yuj-, yunákti*, Greek *zeúgnumi*, Latin *iungō*, Lithuanian *jùngti*. The yoke was needed not only for wheeled vehicles but also for the plow, which is likely to have been a slightly earlier invention. In both cases PIE-speakers used a native term.

Anthony, who locates the Late PIE homeland in the Pontic-Caspian steppes in his graphic map of the distribution of PIE vehicle terms (Fig. 6.3), has difficulties with the origin of this terminology. He explicitly denies proposing "that wheeled vehicle technology originated in the PIE homeland," admitting "only that most of the IE *vocabulary* for wheeled vehicles originated in PIE" (Anthony 1995:558).

> If they learned about the invention of the wheel from others they did not adopt the foreign name for it, so the social setting in which the transfer took place probably was brief, between people who remained socially distant. The alternative, that wheels were invented within the Proto-Indo-European language community, seems unlikely for archaeological and historical reasons, though it remains possible. (Anthony 2007:34)

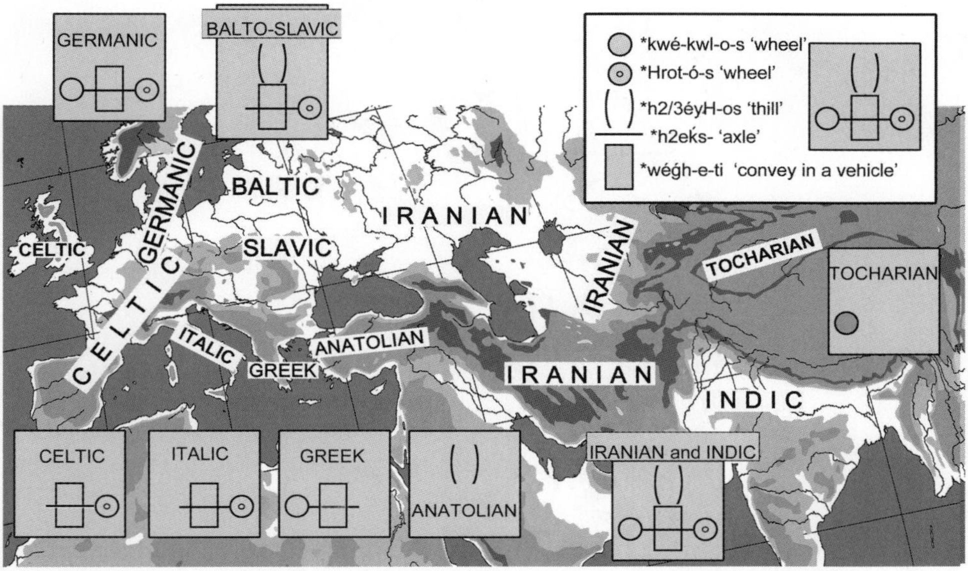

FIGURE 6.3 Distribution of select Proto-Indo-European terms referring to wheeled vehicles, according to David W. Anthony. Modified from Anthony 1995:557, fig. 1. Courtesy David W. Anthony. In the 1995 map, Anthony placed the "Proto-Indo-European homeland" in the Pontic-Caspian steppes, as he did in the map of Anthony 2007:84 (where he dates this homeland to "about 3500–3000 BCE").

All of the earlier discussed five terms are native PIE words: they have been formed by deriving them from PIE verbal roots. This is important because, with any new technology, the inventor of the technology is the one who names it, and thereafter the inventor's name usually spreads with the spread of the technology.

For example, in the Uralic (Finno-Ugric) languages, the traditional vehicle terminology is predominantly borrowed from IE languages. All the five common words for "wagon" or "cart" in Finnish are IE loanwords:

- *vaunut* (pl.) from North Germanic: Old Norse *vagn*, etc.;
- *rattaat* (pl.)/*ratas* (sg.), "wheel," from Baltic: Lithuanian *rãtai* (pl.)/*rãtas* (sg.), "wheel";
- *kärryt* (pl.) from Old Swedish *kärra* (Latin *carrus*);
- *kiesit, keesit, kääsit* (pl.) from Swedish *schäs* (French *chaise*);
- *vankkurit* (pl.), perhaps from Swedish *vagn* or German *Wagen*.

Likewise, the Finnish terms for the parts of the cart or wagon are IE loanwords: *akseli*, "axle," *aisa*, "thill," *napa*, "nave," and *ies* (gen. *ikeen*), "yoke"; an exception is the native word *pyörä*,

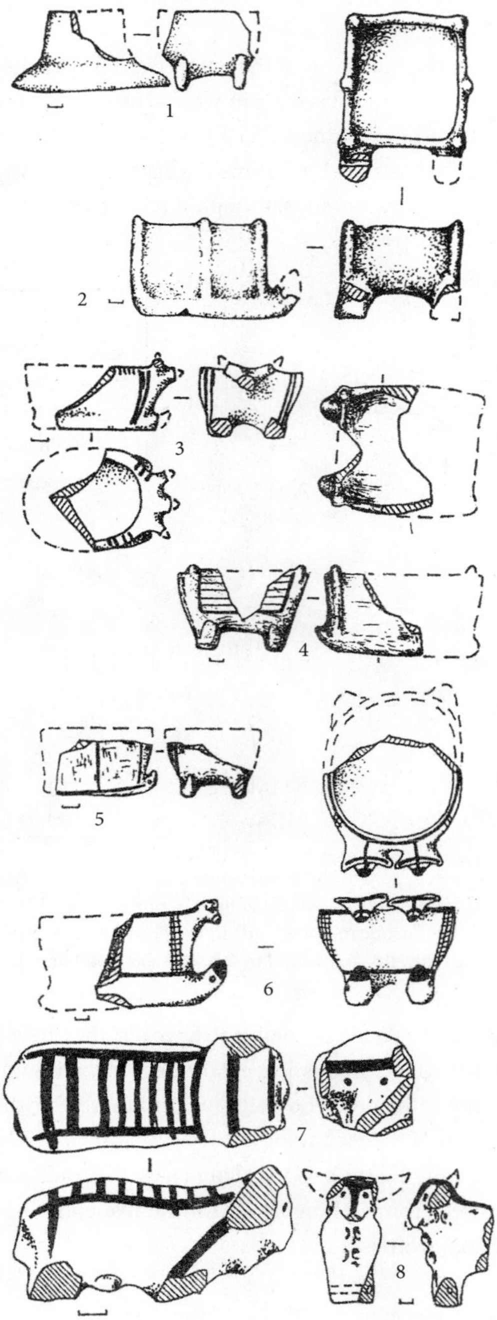

FIGURE 6.4 (a) Pottery cups in the shape of a sledge with bent runners, some with the head(s) of one or two oxen, and figurines of oxen wearing painted straps, from five different Tripolye culture sites of phase C1 (*c.*3800–3400 BCE): Nezvis'ko [1], Majdanets'ke [2], Tal'yanky [3–6], Chychyrkozivka [7] and Volodymyrivka [8]. After Ryzhov 2003:56–57, figs. 1, 2. Courtesy Sergej M. Ryzhov. Many Tripolye C1 sites have also produced round or rectangular pottery cups with or without ox protomes, and pairs of front and hind legs often perforated for an axle and two wheels (see Gusev 1998; Parpola 2008:15–17, fig. 4e–k), as well as separate perforated model wheels of clay (Gusev 1998:18 figs. 3:3–3:10; Parpola 2008:14, fig. 4a). (b) A pottery cup in the shape of a wheeled wagon from the Baden/Pécel culture site, Budakalász, Hungary (late fourth millennium BCE). After Piggott 1983:46, fig. 15. Courtesy Ferenczy Múzeum, Szentendre, Hungary.

(b)

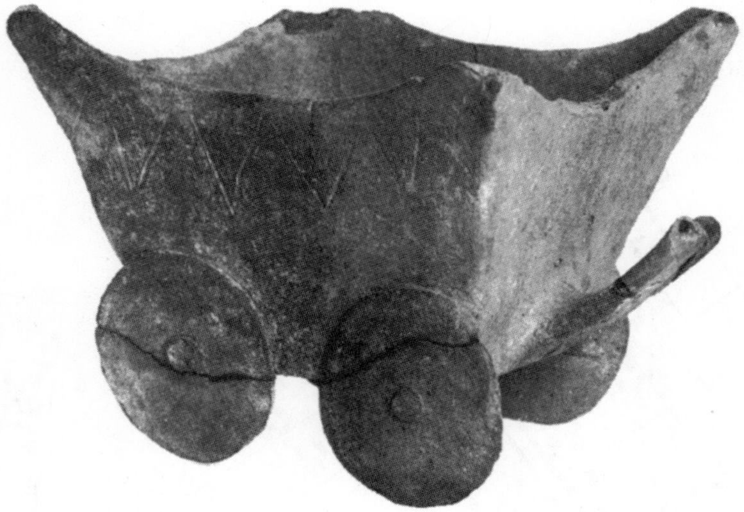

FIGURE 6.4 (Continued)

"wheel" (also "bicycle"), "whorl, whirl," with such derivatives as *pyöreä*, "round," and *pyöriä*, "roll, turn."

Following this logic, the answer to the important question—who did the PIE speakers get their wheeled vehicles from?—can be answered with fair certainty: from themselves. In my view, it was PIE-speakers who invented the wheeled vehicle.

Until recently, it has been assumed that the wheeled vehicle was invented in the Late Uruk culture of Mesopotamia *c.* 3500–3300 BCE. However, wheeled vehicle finds of comparable date have been made not only in West Asia but also in many places in Europe. Furthermore, Johannes Renger (2004) and Josef Maran (2004b) observe that the marshlands of Sumer were not favorable terrain for wheeled vehicles; sledges would have worked in ordinary life much better than wheeled vehicles in marshy Mesopotamia, and indeed stayed in use there long after the Late Uruk period. It is true that the Uruk pictograms show sledges with four wheels; however, these "wheels" may depict rolling logs over which the sledges ran. Logs rolling beneath sledges were probably the initial stage in the invention of the wheel for carts and wagons (Littauer & Crouwel 1979).

Maran (2004a,b) suggests the Late Tripolye culture as the most likely place of origin for wheeled vehicles. Late Tripolye is the only culture to show evidence of wagons predating 3500 BCE (Burmeister 2004), in the form of drinking cups provided with rotating model wheels and with ox foreparts protruding from the front of the cup. In addition to these wagon-shaped drinking cups, there are numerous Late Tripolye drinking cups in the shape of an ox-pulled sledge, which is thought to be the immediate predecessor of the ox-pulled wagon (Fig. 6.4).

Between 4000 and 3400 BCE, the Late Tripolye culture was the most thriving and populous agricultural community in the entire Copper Age world, cultivating extremely fertile black soil, in villages covering hundreds of hectares and housing up to 15,000 people (Fig. 6.5). These agriculturalist people needed transport, whether by sledge or wheeled

(a)

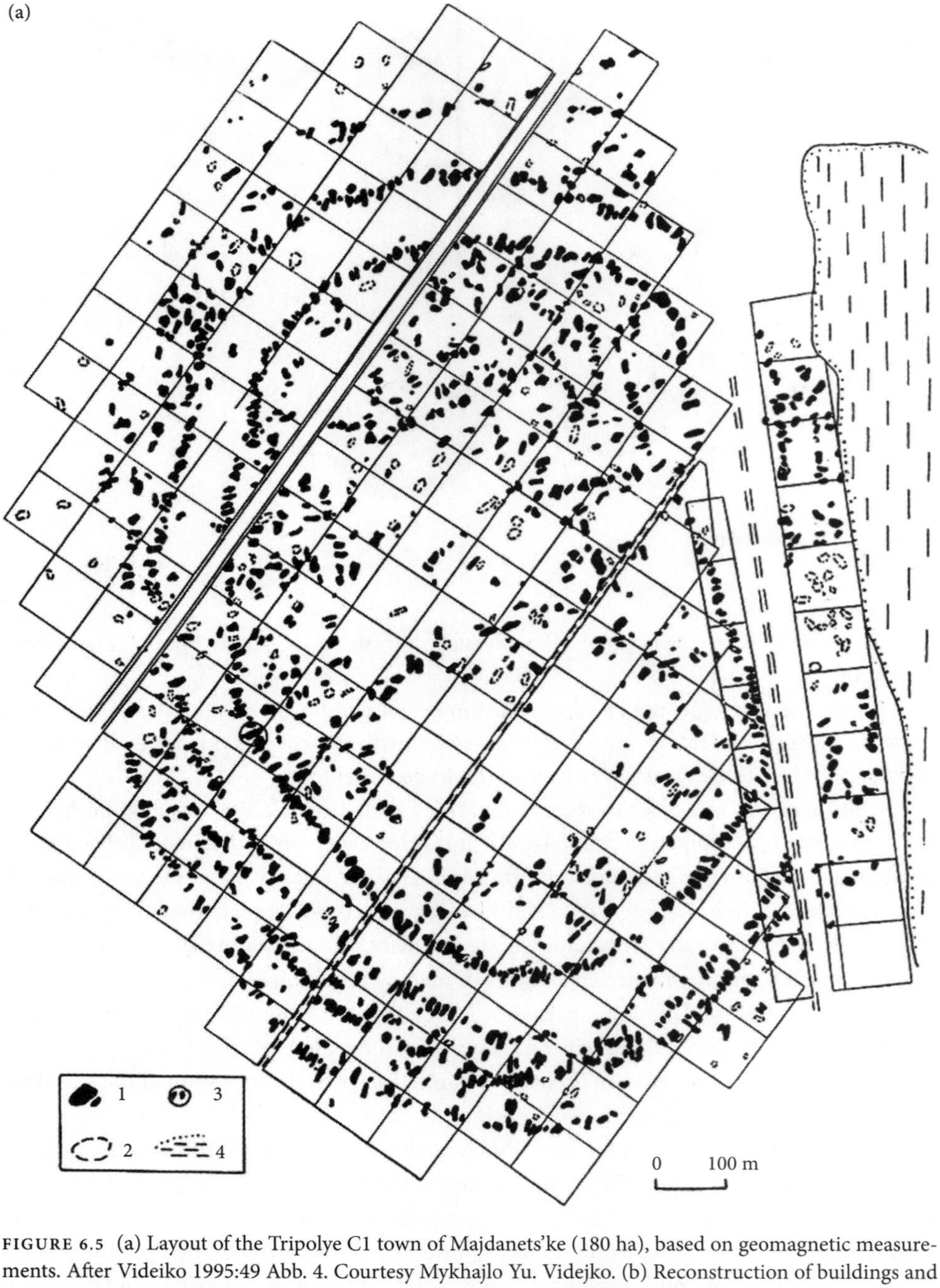

FIGURE 6.5 (a) Layout of the Tripolye C1 town of Majdanets'ke (180 ha), based on geomagnetic measurements. After Videiko 1995:49 Abb. 4. Courtesy Mykhajlo Yu. Videjko. (b) Reconstruction of buildings and fortifications at Majdanets'ke: 1–2 part of the town excavated in 1987–1991. After Videiko 1994:23, fig. 13. Courtesy Mykhajlo Yu. Videjko.

(b)

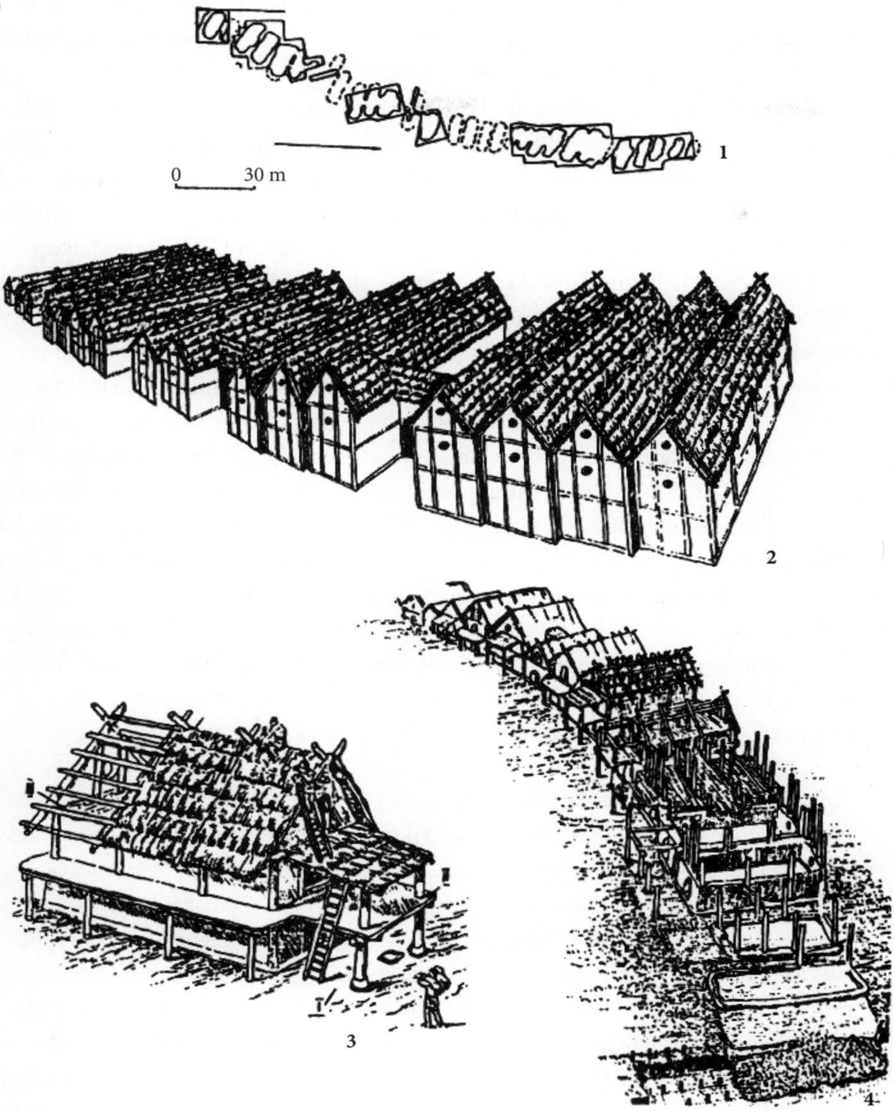

FIGURE 6.5 (Continued)

wagon. The local forest-steppe provided enough trees for the construction of primitive solid wheels but also sufficient open and level fields for the movement of wheeled traffic, unlike the forested and hilly landscape that covered most of Europe.

I am connecting Maran's hypothesis that wheeled vehicles were invented in the Late Tripolye culture with the hypothesis that the Tripolye culture was taken over by PIE speakers by *c.* 4000 BCE. The PIE speakers would have largely assimilated the earlier Tripolye population linguistically by the time wheeled vehicles were invented, probably *c.* 3600 BCE. The location of Late Tripolye culture makes sense as the geographical center for the spread of the wheeled vehicles; it is also very near the middle of the IE-speaking area and is a good candidate for being the Late PIE homeland from this point of view.

Vehicle technology was probably transmitted to West Asia from the Tripolye culture via the Caucasus, where the Pontic-Caspian and West Asian cultural spheres interacted with each other during the fourth millennium BCE. From both the south and the north there was great interest in possessing the copper resources of the Caucasus. This led to the formation of the south Caucasian Kura-Araxes culture and the north Caucasian Majkop culture (*c.* 3950–3300 BCE). While the Kura-Araxes culture continued the local traditions with heavy influence of the Uruk expansion from Mesopotamia, the Majkop culture has long been considered a splendid mixture of the steppe and West Asian traditions. The pastoralists of the east European steppes had received their copper mainly from the Balkans during the Copper Age, but after the collapse of the Balkano-Carpathian "metallurgical domain," around 4000 BCE, the Caucasus became their main source of metal during the Early and Middle Bronze Age (Chernykh 1992; 2007). Out of the approximately 300 graves belonging to the last phase (*c.* 3500–3300 BCE) of the Majkop culture, two elite burials under a barrow contain a wagon, one at Starokorsunskaya in the Kuban steppe, the other at Koldyri on the Lower River Don. From the immediately succeeding Novotitarovskaya culture (*c.* 3300–2800 BCE) of the Kuban steppe, 116 wagon graves are known. The wagons apparently reached the Caucasus from the west, from the forest-steppe region between the Prut and the Bug rivers. Several clay models of wheels are known from the associated post-Tripolye phase C2 sites.

Mallory leaves the origin of wheeled vehicles an open question but comments:

> Tomas Gamkrelidze and Vyacheslav Ivanov [1995:I,622] . . . have noted that . . . Proto-Indo-European **kʷekʷlo-* bears striking similarity to the words for vehicles in Sumerian *gigir*, Semitic **galgal-*, and Kartvelian **grgar*. With the putative origin of wheeled vehicles set variously to the Pontic-Caspian, Transcaucasia or to Sumer, we may be witnessing the original word for a wheeled vehicle in four different language families. Furthermore, as the Proto-Indo-European form is built on an Indo-European verbal root **kʷel-*, "to turn, to twist", it is unlikely that the Indo-Europeans borrowed their word from one of the other languages. This need not, of course, indicate that the Indo-Europeans invented wheeled vehicles, but it might suggest that they were in some form of contact relation with these Near Eastern languages in the fourth millennium BC. (Mallory 1989:163)

Sumerian *gigir*, inscribed in the cuneiform tablets of the third millennium BCE, may indeed provide the earliest written testimony for an originally PIE word.

While there is fair agreement concerning the Anatolian branch as the first language group to separate from the PIE unity, the same cannot be said of the construction of a family tree for the other branches of the IE language family. The reason seems to be that Late PIE disintegrated suddenly in all directions. When the Late Tripolye culture dissolved, around 3400 BCE, it gave way not only to local Post-Tripolye cultures (phase C2, *c.* 3400–2900 BCE), but also created new cultures all around, cultures that shared components of Tripolye and steppe origin. And these new cultures spread to the very regions where the various IE languages first made their appearance, or a fair distance along the route leading to their final destinations (Iran and India in the case of Indo-Iranian). It is assumed that climatic change influenced the transformation of the Late Tripolye culture of thriving settled farmers (with significant animal husbandry) into several cultures of more mobile pastoralists. Tens of thousands of people started moving with their cattle and ox-drawn wagons in all directions (Kohl 2007), mixing with the various earlier local populations and eventually bringing about a language shift.

Starting about 3200 BCE, probably from the Post-Tripolye Middle Dnieper and Sub-Carpathian cultures, the Corded Ware (or Battle Axe) cultures (*c.* 3100–2300/2000 BCE) spread within a couple of centuries over a vast area, spanning from the Netherlands to the coasts of Finland and to the region of the Upper Volga River. In Finland, their beginning is dated 3200 or 3000 BCE. In the Upper Volga region, the local Corded Ware variant, the Fatyanovo culture (*c.* 2800–1900 BCE), belongs visibly to the Bronze Age from about 2300 BCE, when it developed a metal-working Balanovo extension as far east as the area between the mouths of the Oka and Kama rivers (Fig. 6.6). The language of the Corded Ware people, who were mobile pastoralists, can be assumed to be "Northwest IE," still quite close to Late PIE, the common ancestor of the later Celtic, Germanic, and Balto-Slavic branches of the IE language family, which all emerge into history within the area occupied by the Corded Ware cultures.

On the basis of their rapid spread to the areas where various branches of IE were spoken in historical times, the Corded Ware cultures have long been connected with the early expansion of IE. But it has been difficult to reconcile this with the assumption that Late PIE was spoken in the Yamnaya cultures, as these two cultures cannot easily be derived directly from one another. There is no such difficulty if Late PIE is correlated with the Late Tripolye culture.

In its final C phase, the Tripolye culture expanded to the Pontic steppes and eventually (in C2 phase) differentiated into a number of regional cultures (Horodistea-Foltesti, Kasperovtsy, Usatovo, Gorodsk, and Sofievka) (*c.* 3400–2900 BCE). In the steppes these Post-Tripolye cultures fused with the various Late Srednij Stog II pastoralist cultures (Stogovska, Kvitanska, Dereivka, and Nizhne-Mikhailovka) that had flourished in the Pontic-Caspian steppes during the preceding period, *c.* 4000–3400 BCE. This resulted in the formation of the Yamnaya cultural complex (*c.* 3300–2500 BCE), which eventually extended from the Danube River to the Urals (Fig. 6.6). A large number of wagon graves belonging to the Yamnaya archaeological horizon have been found, attesting to a pastoral economy based on mobility (Fig. 7.1). The Yamnaya cultures can be assumed to have spoken variants of "Southeast IE," which was still close to Late PIE, but undoubtedly soon split into a number of local dialects. Its eastern extension and successors connected with the Indo-Iranian branch of IE language family will be discussed in chapter 7.

A spearhead of the earliest Yamnaya-related eastward movement reached as far as southern Siberia (the Minussinsk basin) and Mongolia, founding there the Afanasyevo culture, dated *c.* 3100–2500 BCE. This culture is very similar to the early Yamnaya cultures in many respects, including the burial of the body in supine position with legs flexed and

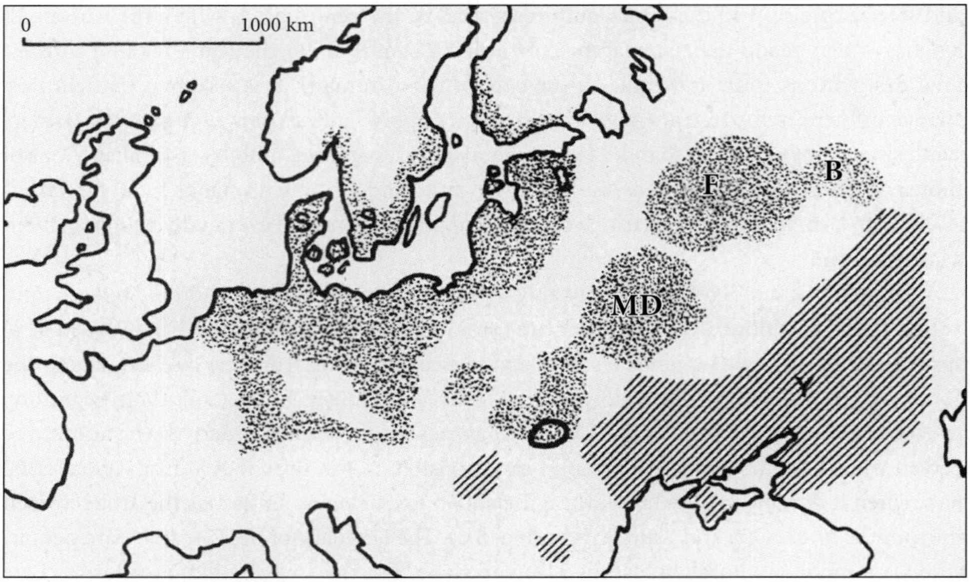

FIGURE 6.6 The Yamnaya (Y and diagonal lines) and Corded Ware cultures (stippled) (*c.* 3300–2000 BCE). Within the Corded Ware: circle = Sub-Carpathian culture; MD = Middle Dnieper culture; S = Scandinavian Corded Ware (from *c.* 2800 BCE); F = Fatyanovo culture (*c.* 2800–1900 BCE); B = Balanovo culture (*c.* 2300–1900 BCE). After Carpelan & Parpola 2001:65, fig. 6, modified.

sprinkled with ochre, pointed-base vessels, "censer" bowls, copper knives, and awls. The roof over an Afanasyevo grave at the recently excavated site of Khurgak-Govi in Mongolia, radiocarbon dated to *c.* 2900–2500 BCE, is interpreted as a wagon chassis. The sites of the Afanasyevo culture are some 1500 km distant from the easternmost Yamnaya sites in the Urals, but a few related sites (such at Karagash near Karaganda) have been found in the intervening area. Afanasyevo-like new cultural components coming from the northern steppes have also been found at Sarazm in the Zeravshan Valley of Tajikistan (in the fourth cultural phase dated to *c.* 2500–2000 BCE).

The Afanasyevo culture has been correlated with the Tocharian languages spoken in the first millennium CE in Chinese Turkestan (Sinkiang/Xinjiang) (Mallory & Mair 2000). Tocharian has retained many archaic features of PIE, and is widely considered to be the next oldest PIE branch after Anatolian. Particularly noteworthy is that Tocharian has not participated in the satemization that affected among others the Indo-Iranian languages before they spread widely to the Asiatic steppes around 2000 BCE (as will be argued in chapter 7), so Tocharian must have come to its distant speaking area before the satemization happened. There are some difficulties with this Afanasyevo–Tocharian correlation, nevertheless the archaeological record bears witness to an early offshoot of the Late Tripolye/Yamnaya cultures of southeastern Europe far off in the Asiatic steppes not too far from the Tocharian-speaking areas.

Penetrating deep into the Danube Valley and the Balkans, the western extensions of the Yamnaya cultural community formed an interaction sphere, which can be correlated with the later emergence in these regions of various branches of the IE language family. The Greek speakers are supposed to have migrated to Greece in two or three waves. The most widely suggested slot for the first wave is the archaeological shift from Early Helladic II to Early Helladic III, *c.* 2300 BCE, during which EH II sites in Corinthia and the Argolid were destroyed and abandoned, and new types of architecture (apsidal houses), burials (tumuli), weapons (perforated stone hammer-axes), and pottery (Minyan Ware) were introduced.

As discussed in chapter 7, the horse-drawn chariot was developed in the Sintashta culture of the south Ural steppes at the end of the third millennium BCE, from where it spread quickly east and west. Steppe-style cheek-pieces for driving chariot horses are known from Mycenae, too (Usachuk 2004; 2013). The horse-chariot, swords, and status burials under a barrow mound were probably introduced via Albania by a small body of intruding warriors, who gave rise to the sudden emergence of Mycenaean chiefdoms, which flourished during the Late Helladic period, *c.* 1700–1100 BCE. They might have originated from the late phase of the Catacomb Grave cultures of the Pontic steppes, where it was the custom to bury a chief with a face-mask made of clay: an artifact considered to be a possible model for the famous golden face-masks in the shaft graves of Mycenae (see chapter 7).

The last major wave of migration to Greece is associated with the collapse of the Mycenaean civilization around 1300 BCE. The general unrest of these times pushed speakers of Dorian dialects into Greece and Proto-Armenian speakers into Anatolia. (In Anatolia many sites were destroyed around 1200 BCE; a connection has been suggested between the Proto-Armenians and the people called Muski, who were said to have had an army of 20,000 men on the Upper Euphrates, according to Assyrian sources in 1165 BCE.) One factor undoubtedly connected with the unrest was the large-scale adoption of riding, which seems to have started among the probably Proto-Iranian speaking roller-pottery cultures of the Pontic-Caspian steppes around 1500 BCE (see chapters 7 and 9). The Dorians introduced riding into Greece along with their cult of the divine horsemen, Kastor and Poludeukes (chapter 10).

My goal in this chapter has been to demonstrate that the PIE terminology for wheeled vehicles is the most secure criterion for locating the Late PIE-speaking homeland. The terminology is of native PIE origin and suggests that PIE speakers were the inventors of wheeled vehicles. On this basis, Late PIE was spoken in the Late Tripolye culture of agriculturalists, where the wheeled vehicles were most likely invented. This hypothesis is in agreement with the assumption that Early PIE was spoken by the Skelya pastoralists of the Pontic Caspian steppes, who invaded and took control of the Tripolye culture *c.* 4300–4000 BCE. At the same time another group of Skelya pastoralists invaded the Balkans, with the result that their Early PIE eventually came to Anatolia. Both the Corded Ware cultures of northeastern Europe and the Yamnaya cultures of southeastern Europe came into being when the tens of thousands of Late Tripolye people became mobile pastoralists and spread in all directions with wheeled vehicles around 3400 BCE. From these two extensive cultural communities of the Early Bronze Age (*c.* 3300–2500 BCE and later) it is possible, through successive cultures with one ultimate origin, to trace the trail of the major branches of the IE language family to the areas where they are first historically attested.

7

Early Indo-Iranians on the Eurasian Steppes

The Yamnaya cultural community is the umbrella name for the different regional cultures that prevailed from about 3300 to 2500 BCE in the Pontic-Caspian steppes north of the Black Sea, spanning some 3000 kilometers from the Danube to the Urals (Fig. 6.6). The name derives from Russian, in which *yama* means "pit, grave"; indeed, the Yamnaya cultural community was formerly known as the "Pit Grave culture." Its constituent cultures are identifiable almost exclusively from their graves, which were fairly simple pits. The dead were normally placed on their backs, but sometimes on their sides, in each case with their legs flexed and their head facing east or northeast, lying either directly on the ground or on wooden planks or reeds. The body was often sprinkled with red ocher, to represent life-giving blood. Early burials are poor in grave goods, but later graves include pots, flint or copper knives, flint spear-heads, stone axes, bone harpoons, sickles with flint blades, and ornaments such as hammer-headed bone-pins and boar's-tusk pendants. Any animal bones probably come from food provisions for the dead, partly from cultic sacrifices; the skulls and forelegs of sheep or more rarely horse occur, as do sheep knucklebones, which may have served as gaming dice. The burial site might be covered with planks or stone slabs or surrounded by a stone circle, but as a rule, above it was a barrow or kurgan, an earthen mound, which could be used for further burials. Sometimes, anthropomorphic stone stelae top the mound.

The Yamnaya cultures came into being when people of the Late Tripolye culture, who very probably spoke Late Proto-Indo-European, rapidly spread with their wheeled vehicles to the Pontic-Caspian steppes, which had until this time been occupied predominantly by the Skelya/Srednij Stog II and (in the eastern parts) Late Khvalynsk people, whose language was probably based on Early PIE. These Early PIE substrata may have had an archaizing effect, leaving traces of laryngeal phonemes which were probably lost in the assumed Late PIE of the Tripolye area.

It seems that the ancestors of the Greeks and Armenians occupied the westernmost part of the Yamnaya continuum, and that the future Armenian speakers, whose language is close to Greek but shares the *satem* innovation (see chapter 3) with Indo-Iranian, stayed longer in the steppes than the future Greek speakers. The steppes east of the Dnieper River were probably the ancestral homeland of the Indo-Iranian speakers. Greek and Indo-Iranian have some common post-PIE linguistic innovations (such as several derivational suffixes and the augment, i.e., a prefixed past tense marker of the verb).

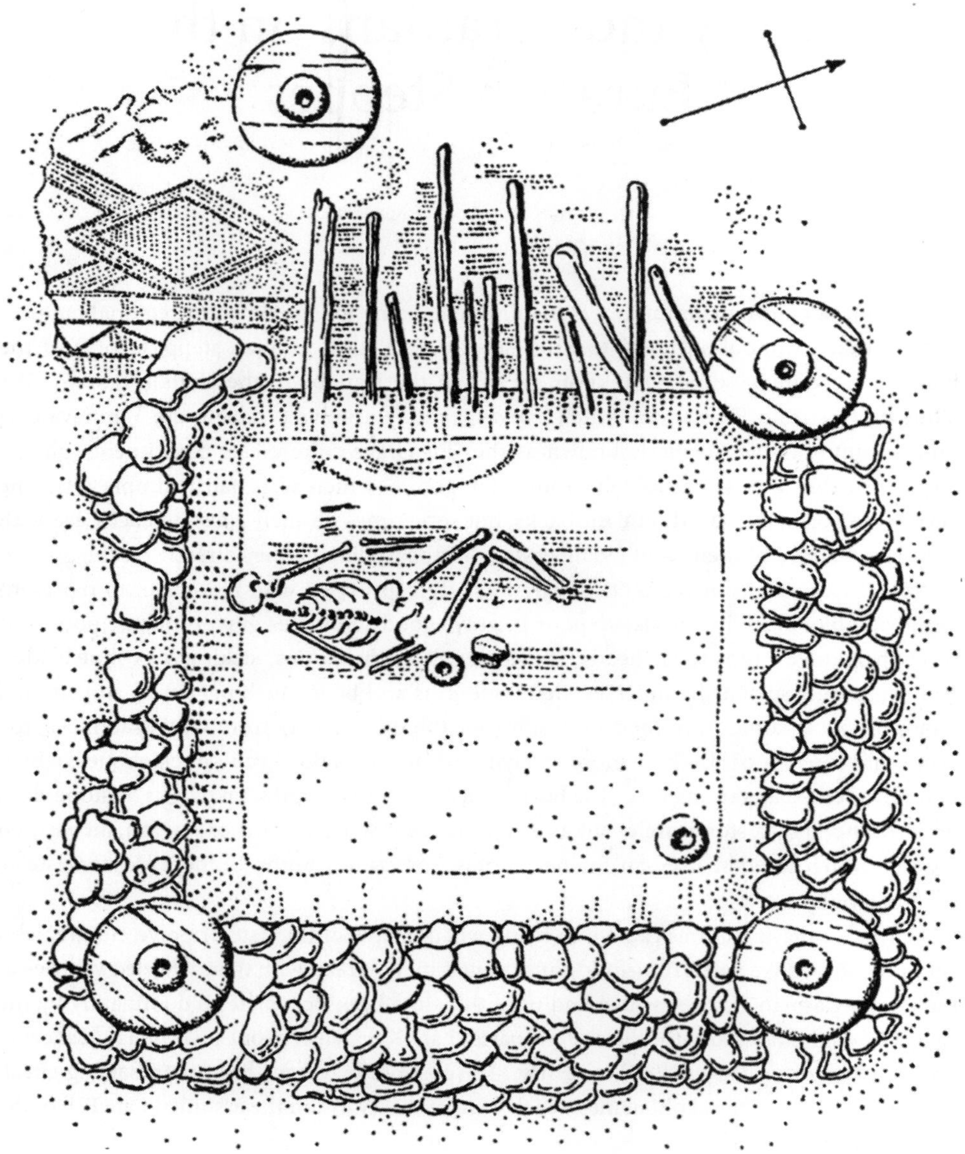

FIGURE 7.1 A wagon grave of the Yamnaya culture at Tri Brata. After Piggott 1983:55, fig. 23. Courtesy Alison and Stewart Sanderson.

Numerous Yamnaya graves contain the remains of entire wagons or carts, with two or four solid wheels, pulled by oxen (Fig. 7.1). They were essential for the exploitation of the open steppe, not only for transport purposes but also as mobile homes for a family. This mobility explains why occupational sites of the Yamnaya culture are rare, although a number of temporary camps typical of mobile pastoralists have been found. A few settlements are known, however, notably at Mikhajlovka in the Lower Dnieper River region. This settlement overlies a layer representing the earlier Skelya culture. It eventually covered 1.5 hectares. The first houses were oval in shape and half dug into the soil; later they were larger and rectangular, with three rooms, built of wood on stone foundations. Mikhajlovka was surrounded by a moat and 2.5-meter stone fortification. Warfare is suggested by the discovery of weapons: arrowheads and knives of flint, mace-heads, and battle-axes of stone.

The animal bones excavated at Mikhajlovka attest to animal husbandry and hunting. Besides domestic animals—chiefly sheep, goats, and cattle, with a fair number of horses and some pigs—there are the bones of wild asses, wild bulls, wild boar, red deer, saiga antelopes, and, in small numbers, those of hares, foxes, wolves, otters, beavers, and other wild animals. Agriculture on the open steppe is limited by salty and sandy soils and the absence of water, but its practice in the river valleys is implied by the discovery of sickles with flint blades and querns for grinding grain. Metallurgy was practiced locally, though the metal itself and the forms of the tools (knives, awls, chisels, and adzes) came from the Caucasus, apart from in the Volga and Ural regions, which had their own copper. Flint, stone, bone, and antler remained important materials for tools and weapons. Handmade pottery continued earlier local traditions, and was decorated with cord and comb impressions. An important diagnostic item is the "censer," a ceramic bowl with ceramic feet probably used for burning hemp, in the manner of the much later Scythians mentioned by Herodotus (4,73-75).

Between the Dnieper and Volga rivers, the Yamnaya cultural community was succeeded around 2500 BCE by the Catacomb Grave cultural community, which continued until about 1950 BCE. Its economy was very similar to the Yamnaya culture, though it included specialized crafts, particularly bronze working, weapons manufacture, and weaving. Most of the sparse Catacomb Grave settlements are seasonal camps; but a fortress with stone walls surrounded by a moat is known. The name derives from a catacomb-like side-niche at the bottom of the grave pit, into which the dead person was placed in the flexed position on his or her right side. The catacomb is ascribed to cultural influence from the Caucasus, as is the style of the metal objects. Some graves contain animal offerings, such as the head and hooves of sheep, goats, and cattle. Such diagnostic cultural items as a hammer-headed bone-pin and the "censer" continue to be used. Presumably elite graves under barrows contained wagons, scepters, stone and metal axes, stone mace-heads with knobs, daggers, arrows, and, remarkably, face-masks made of clay (about a hundred examples are known), supposed to be prototypes for the golden face-masks of the Mycenaean shaft-grave burials. There is also evidence of the practice of skull deformation of young people.

The Catacomb Grave cultures are likely to have formed the ancestral speech community of the "Iranian" branch of Indo-Iranian. Of course "Iranian" (or "Irano-Aryan") and "Indo-Aryan" are anachronistic terms for groups of languages spoken in the Eurasian steppes and the forest steppes. These terms simply reflect the fact that these languages were ancestral to the two chief branches of the Aryan languages nowadays spoken mainly in Iran and India, respectively. Millennial cultural and linguistic continuity in the Pontic-Caspian steppes is suggested by the fact that after the Catacomb Grave cultures the same large area was occupied by very similar and genetically related pastoralist cultures.

West of the Don River, the Catacomb Grave cultures were transformed into a culture with multiroller ceramics (in Russian, *kul'tura mnogovalikovoj keramiki* = KMK), also called the Babino III culture (*c.* 2100–1850 BCE). ("Roller" here denotes a rope-like band of clay attached to the outer surface of a pot before firing.) The Srubnaya culture (*c.* 1850–1450 BCE) is also known as Timber Grave culture, from Russian *srub*, "timber work," which is sometimes found with the burials. The Srubnaya culture succeeded not only the KMK culture but also the Abashevo culture (discussed below) over the latter's entire area, and expanded to the southern Urals where it coexisted with the contemporary Andronovo culture (also discussed below). The Pozdnyakovo culture (*c.* 1850–1450 BCE) of the Volga-Oka interfluve represents a Srubnaya expansion into the forest zone of central Russia.

In the Late Bronze Age (*c.* 1500–800 BCE), the Srubnaya culture was followed by cultures distinguished by roller pottery (Russian *valikovaya keramika*) (Fig. 9.7). With their adoption of riding about 1500 BCE, the peoples of the roller-pottery cultures were powerful warriors who enlarged the earlier Srubnaya area westwards, northwards (to the Kama River basin), and eastwards. In the east, roller-pottery cultures came to cover the whole of Kazakhstan and Turkmenistan (previously occupied by the Andronovo cultures); in chapter 9 it is argued that their language was Proto-East-Iranian. In the steppe and forest steppe of northern Kazakhstan between the Tobol and Ishim Rivers, the roller-pottery tradition is represented by the Alekseevka, alias Sargary, culture (*c.* 1500–900 BCE) (Fig. 9.7, no. 8). All of these roller-pottery cultures were the immediate ancestors of the Iranian-speaking mounted horsemen known as Scythians, Sarmatians, and Sakas, who ruled the Eurasian steppes from the Danube to Mongolia in the first millennium BCE and the early first millennium CE. Many of the river names in the European steppe have an Iranian etymology; for example, Don (and its diminutive, Donets) comes from Old Iranian (Avestan) *dānu*, "river," which is also behind the initial part of the river names Dnieper and Dniester.

It has been debated which way the speakers of West Iranian languages came from their homeland in the northern Pontic steppes to the Iranian Plateau and West Asia—via the Caspian Gates in the eastern Caucasus, which according to Herodotus was the route taken by the Scythians who in 652–625 BCE ruled the Median empire, or via the eastern route around the Caspian Sea and through Khorasan. The cultural change associated with the shift from Yaz I to Yaz II in southern Central Asia around 1000 BCE is likely to be connected with the arrival of the West Iranian speakers. The Medes and Persians are first mentioned in Neo-Assyrian royal inscriptions dating from 881–835; they contain Median names and announce that twenty-seven kings of Parsuva situated in the area around Lake Urmia paid tribute to the Assyrian king Shalmaneser III in 835 BCE. Cuyler Young (1985) connects the early Medes and Persians with the Late West Iranian Buff Ware (*c.* 900–700 BCE) and traces this ceramic back to southern Central Asia where it first appears around 1100 BCE.

In any case, the West Iranian languages have been spoken in most parts of Iran since the early first millennium BCE. The Median empire flourished in northern Iran (with its capital Ecbatana at modern Hamadan) *c.* 678–549 BCE. Conquered by Cyrus the Great in 549 BCE, it was succeeded by the Old Persian-speaking Achaemenid empire (559–330 BCE), which stretched from Egypt and Anatolia to the Indus Valley. After the conquest of Alexander the Great, the empire was divided by his generals, of whom Seleucus received the eastern part from Syria to the Indus Valley. The Hellenistic Seleucid empire that thus came into being lasted from 312 to 63 BCE. In 247 BCE Arsaces of the Parna tribe (see chapter 9) conquered Parthia in northern Iran from the Seleucids, founding the Arsacid or Parthian empire (247 BCE–224 CE); it was greatly expanded by Mithridates I (ruled *c.* 171–138 BCE), who took Media and Mesopotamia from the Seleucids. The Parthians were succeeded by the Sasanids, who ruled Iran *c.* 224–651 CE, until the Muslim conquest of the country.

The West Iranian language called Baluchi is closely related with Kurdish spoken in eastern Turkey, northwestern Iran, and northern Iraq. According to the Baluchi tradition—for which there is some confirmation in historical sources—the Baluchi speakers in the seventh or eighth century CE migrated from the west to their present habitat that extends from Iranian Makran to Pakistani Baluchistan.

Having sketched the early history of the Iranian branch, which probably derives from the Catacomb Grave culture of the Pontic-Caspian steppes, we return to the split of Proto-Indo-Iranian. A dialectal differentiation that eventually resulted in the formation of the two branches seems to have started about 2500 BCE. The "Indo-Aryan" branch probably originated in the Late Yamnaya culture of the Upper Don and the Poltavka culture of the Volga-Urals, which are contemporary with Early Catacomb graves, *c.* 2500–2100 BCE.

The Abashevo culture (*c.* 2300–1850 BCE), named after a site in the Chuvash Republic on the Mid-Volga, extended along the border of the forest steppe and the forest zone from the Upper Don to the Upper Tobol River in western Siberia (Fig. 7.3). That it had its origin in the eastern Late Yamnaya cultures is indicated by its burial customs (the dead placed on their backs with their legs flexed, beneath a barrow) and its pottery, which contains crushed shell mixed with clay to strengthen it, as do all the steppe ceramics from Neolithic times onward. Metal sickles and stone querns testify to the existence of agriculture. The main means of subsistence was animal husbandry; almost all the bone finds belong to domesticated animals: cattle, sheep, goats, and small numbers of horses and pigs.

The eastward expansion of the Abashevo culture was motivated by the deposits in sandstone of rich, pure copper on the Mid-Volga and the Lower Kama and Belaya rivers (Fig. 7.2). The Abashevo people fought for copper with the Balanovo people. An Abashevo burial at Pepkino contained twenty-eight men, some of whom had been hit on the head with an ax. The Balanovo culture (*c.* 2300–1900 BCE) forms the easternmost branch of the Fatyanovo culture (*c.* 2800–1900 BCE), which constituted the eastern variant of the Corded Ware/Battle Axe cultures (Fig. 6.6). The Fatyanovo-Balanovo people almost certainly spoke Proto-Balto-Slavic, an early branch of Indo-European that is known to have been in early contact with Indo-Iranian. Balto-Slavic and Indo-Iranian share some early linguistic changes, in particular satemization, and (partially) the so-called *ruki* rule (change of **s* into **š* after *r, u, k*, and *i*). While Abashevo burials are similar to Yamnaya burials but differ from the flat burials of the Fatyanovo people (which are in shafts, with men on their right side, heads facing the southwest, women on their left side, heads facing northeast), the early Abashevo ceramics and metal objects, especially the ax forms, are very similar to those of

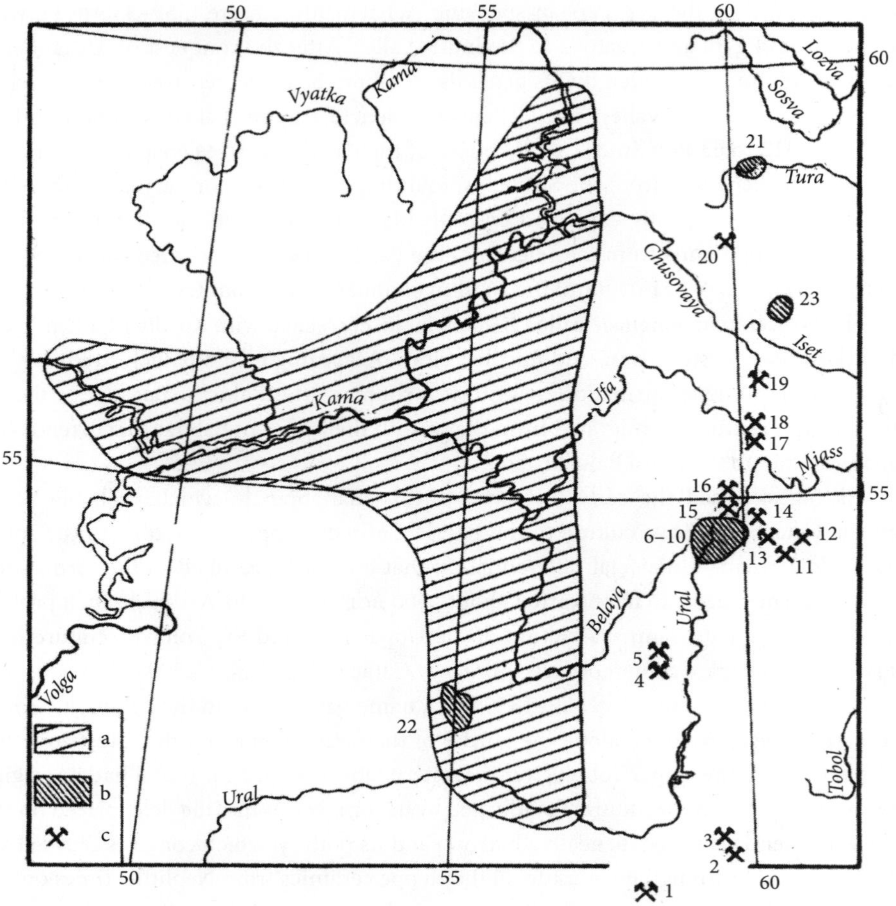

FIGURE 7.2 Copper deposits in the Urals: (a) area of copper sandstone ores, (b) groups of mines, (c) copper deposit. After Koryakova & Epimakhov 2007:29, fig. 1.1.B (based on Chernykh 1970). Copyright © Ludmila Koryakova and Andrej Epimakhov. Reprinted with the permission of Cambridge University Press.

the Fatyanovo-Balanovo Corded Ware culture. This indicates a fair amount of interaction between the two cultures, including presumably linguistic interaction.

The Abashevo culture was an important early center of metallurgy. Its metal production was initially based on the pure copper ores of the Volga-Kama-Belaya area, but afterwards moved just east of the Urals, where the arsenical copper was more suitable for producing harder weapons and tools. Around the twenty-second century BCE, part of the Abashevo people moved southwards to take possession of the rich metal ores and pastures until then occupied by the Poltavka culture. This resulted in the emergence of the Potapovka culture in the Mid-Volga (*c.* 2100–1700 BCE) and the powerful Sintashta culture (*c.* 2100–1800 BCE) in the southeast Urals, where huge copper mines have been located (Fig. 7.3).

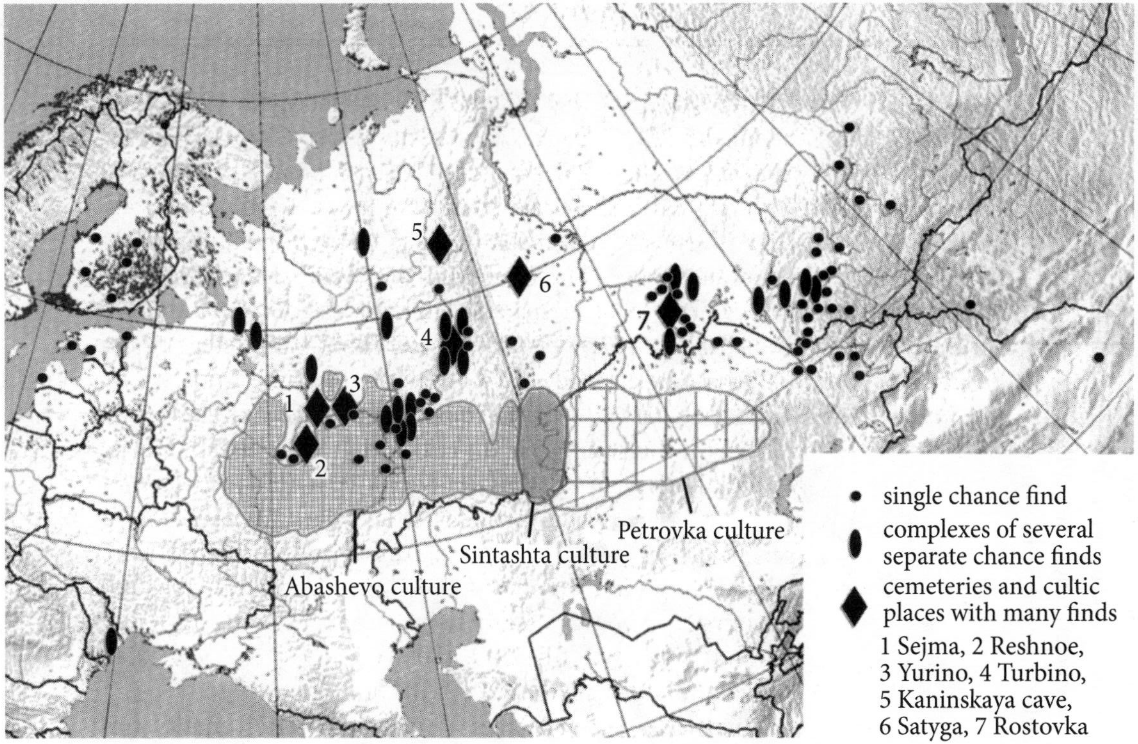

FIGURE 7.3 Find spots of artifacts distributed by the Sejma-Turbino intercultural trader network, and the areas of the most important participating cultures: Abashevo, Sintashta, Petrovka. After Parpola 2012 (2013):157, fig. 8 (based on Chernykh 2007:77).

The Sintashta culture had fortified settlements surrounded by an earth wall and a moat, the best known being Sintashta and Arkaim. The walls are usually formed in a circle about 150 meters in diameter, defending houses that taper inwards so as to create the impression of a spoked wheel (Fig. 7.4). At Sintashta there are two concentric defense lines and between them rectangular houses half sunken into the ground, many of them with metallurgical furnaces. There are several cemeteries near the settlements; at Sintashta one cemetery contained forty graves. The burials under the barrows have wooden rooms, where chiefs were placed

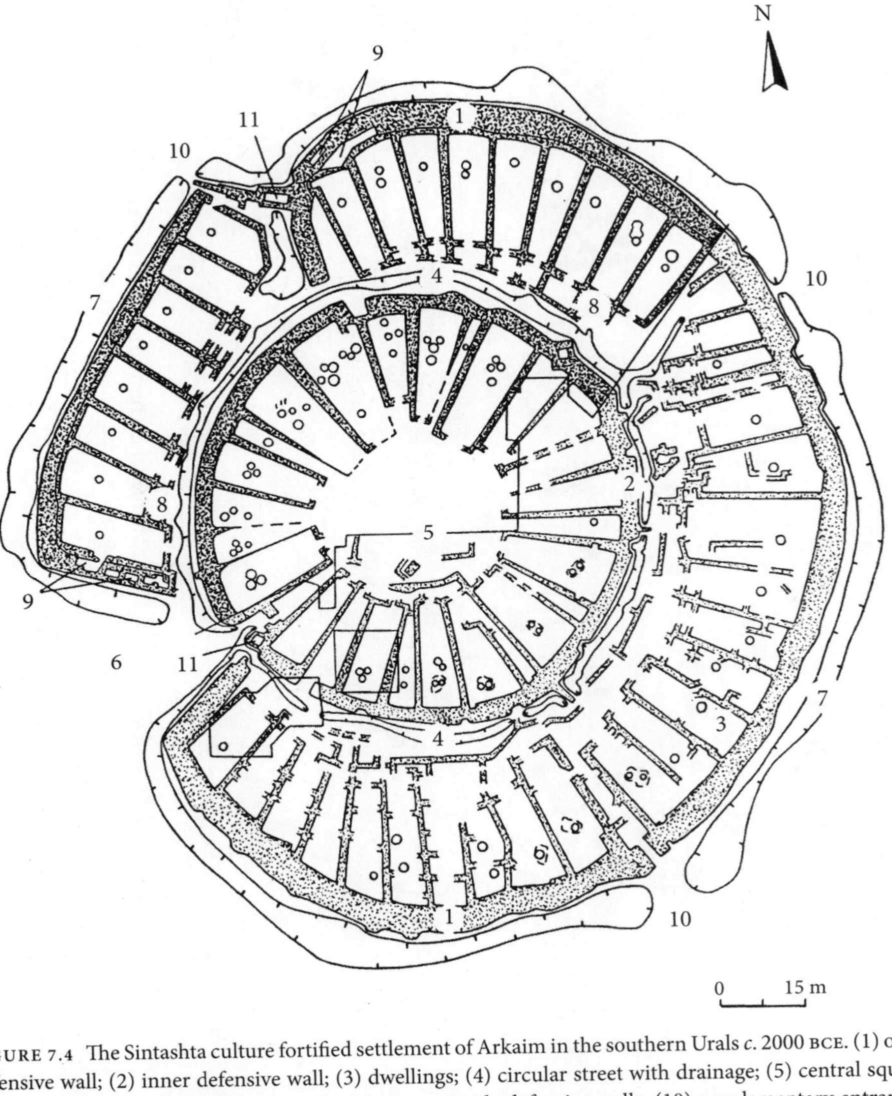

FIGURE 7.4 The Sintashta culture fortified settlement of Arkaim in the southern Urals *c.* 2000 BCE. (1) outer defensive wall; (2) inner defensive wall; (3) dwellings; (4) circular street with drainage; (5) central square; (6) main entrance; (7) a moat; (8) yards; (9) rooms inside defensive walls; (10) supplementary entrances; (11) basement of gate tower. The circles within the rooms are hearths and well-pits. After Zdanovich & Zdanovich 2002:256, fig. 16.3. Courtesy Gennady B. Zdanovich.

with their weapons, horse-drawn chariots, and often animal offerings, pottery, and other grave goods, as well as fireplaces (Fig. 7.5). While it seems that the Catacomb Grave culture already used ox-drawn chariots, the Sintashta culture seems to be the first to have used horse-drawn chariots, with both solid and spoked wheels.

The "daughter branch" of the Sintashta culture, the Petrovka culture (*c.* 2000–1800 BCE), expanded eastwards into the Tobol-Ishim interfluve of northern Kazakhstan. Evidently its goal was the Altai Mountains, rich in not only copper but also tin, needed for alloying copper into bronze. Together the three cultures—Abashevo, Sintashta, and Petrovka—formed the backbone of the "Sejma-Turbino transcultural network" (*c.* 2100–1600 BCE). Within this network armed traders transmitted high-quality weapons from Siberia to the Urals and even as far west as Finland (Fig. 7.3). This network probably played a major role in the early dispersal of the Uralic languages.

The Sintashta and Petrovka cultures also gave rise to the extensive Andronovo cultural community, which also possessed horse-drawn chariots and was likewise engaged in metallurgy and stockbreeding. Dispersed all over the Asiatic steppes between the Ural and Altai mountains, the Andronovo community was divided into two main branches: the Alakul' Andronovo culture (*c.* 2000–1700 BCE), distributed mainly in the steppe and forest steppe of the Trans-Urals and northern, western, and central Kazakhstan, and the Fëdorovo Andronovo culture (*c.* 1850–1450 BCE), which covered practically the whole of Turkmenistan and Kazakhstan; in the north it is connected especially with the forest steppe, from the Trans-Urals in the west to eastern Kazakhstan and the Upper Yenissei River. The symbiosis of the Fëdorovo Andronovans with the probably Proto-East-Uralic speaking people of the Cherkaskul' culture will be discussed shortly (Fig. 7.6).

On the basis of linguistic criteria, the Uralic, alias Finno-Ugric, languages form three major groups. Western Uralic comprises Saami, Finnic (Finnish, Estonian, Livonian, Karelian, etc.), and Mordvin; Central Uralic consists of Mari (formerly called Cheremiss) and the Permic languages (Udmurt, formerly called Votyak, and Komi, formerly called Zyryan or Zyryene); and East Uralic (with shared innovations established by Jaakko Häkkinen 2009) consists of the Samoyed languages distributed very widely in Siberia and the Ugric languages (Hanti or Khanty, previously called Ostyak; Mansi, previously called Vogul; and Hungarian, which arrived in Hungary from the southern Urals by the tenth century CE).

The region around the Kama River valley has long been suspected to be the original homeland of the Uralic (Finno-Ugric) language family. The Proto-Uralic vocabulary suggests a Mesolithic/sub-Neolithic hunter-gatherer economy, with no indication of agriculture or animal husbandry. The present distribution of the Uralic languages, and what is known of the history of the peoples speaking Uralic languages, suggests their origin lies in the forested northeastern part of European Russia. The homeland should be in the neighborhood of the Ural Mountains, because Proto-Uralic has words for the Cembra pine, **sïksi*, and the Siberian fir, **ńulka*, and these trees do not grow west of the Kama and Pechora rivers. In addition, Proto-Uralic has native terms for metals, the most important being **wäśka*, "copper or bronze," which suggests primitive native metallurgy, such as that of the Chalcolithic Garino-Bor culture of the Kama Valley before the arrival of the Abashevo people (Fig. 7.2).

(a)

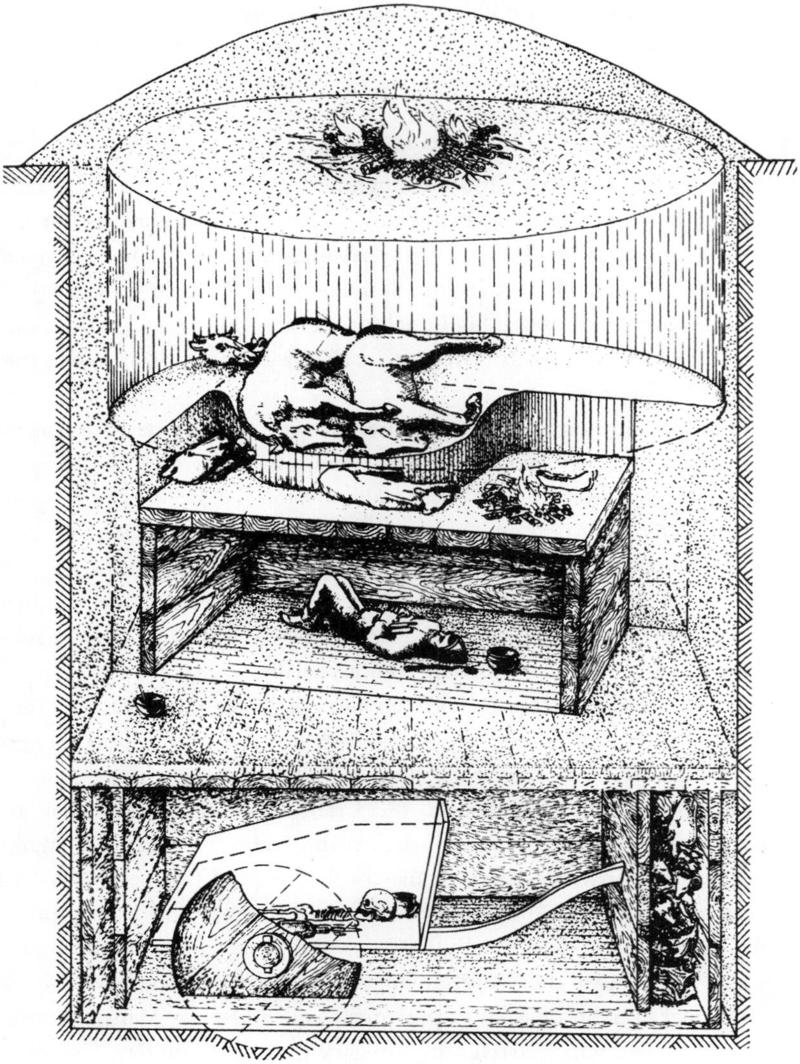

FIGURE 7.5 Horse-chariots in the graves of the Sintashta culture of the southern Trans-Urals, Russia, *c.* 2100–1800 BCE. (a) Reconstruction of the burials 10 and 16 in the area SM south of the Great Kurgan at Sintashta. A warrior with his weapons lies in a chariot and a charioteer or groom with two horses. After Gening, Zdanovich, & Gening 1992:154, fig. 72. Courtesy Gennady B. Zdanovich.

(b)

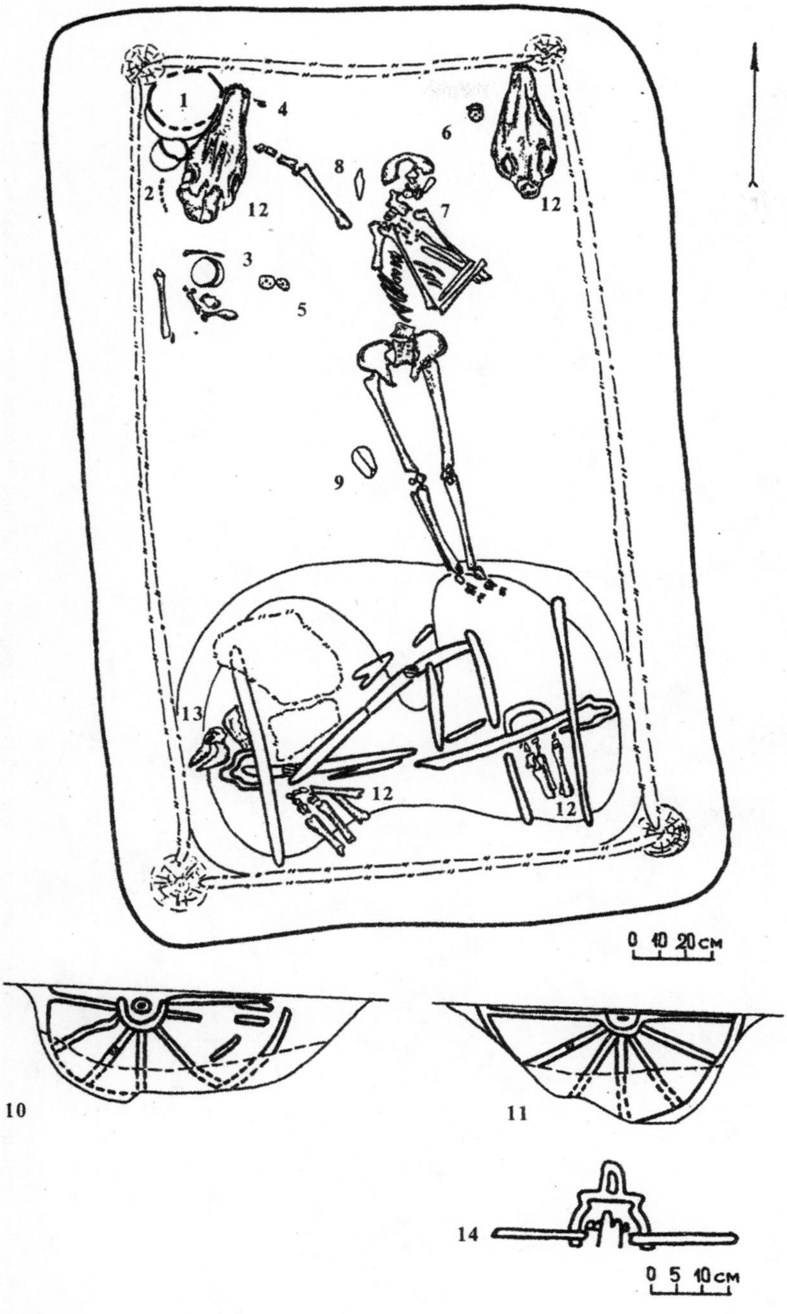

FIGURE 7.5 (b) Grave 1 of kurgan 9 in the cemetery of Krivoe Ozero had the following finds on the bottom: (1–3) ceramics; (4) arrow-heads made of stone and bone; (5–6) pairs of cheek-pieces made of horn; (7) bronze ax-head; (8) bronze dagger; (9) whetstone; (10–11) chariot wheels (in section view; (14) view of the wheel navel); (12) skulls and leg bones of two horses; (13) bones of sheep or goat. After Vinogradov 2003:85, fig. 34. Courtesy Nikolaj B. Vinogradov.

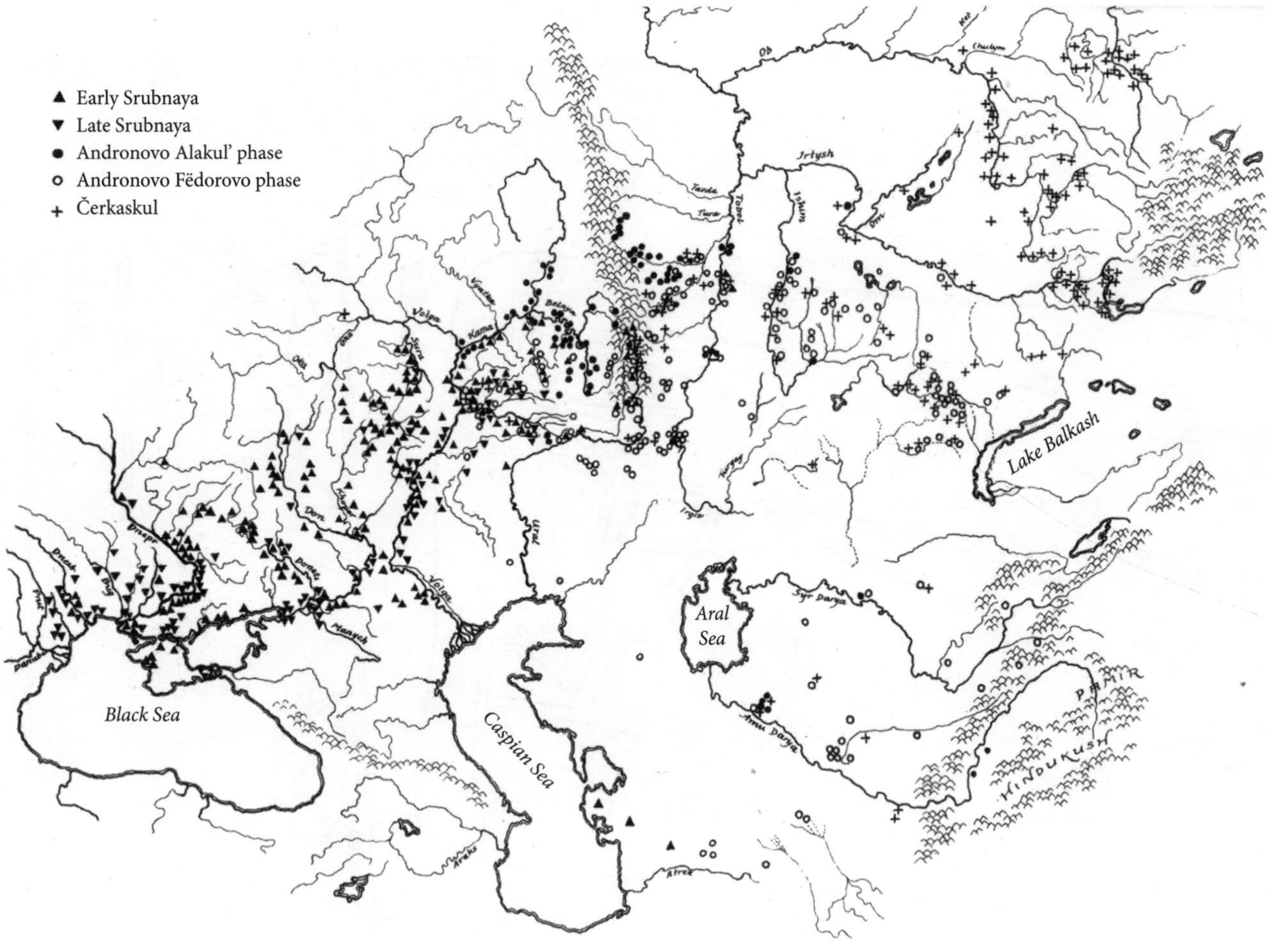

FIGURE 7.6 The distribution of Srubnaya (Timber Grave, early and late), Andronovo (Alakul' and Fëdorovo variants), and Cherkaskul' monuments. Map drawn by Virpi Hämeen-Anttila for Parpola 1994a:146, fig. 8.15, based on Chlenova 1984: map facing p. 100; reproduced here after the slightly revised version of Parpola 2012 (2013):165, fig. 10. © The Finno-Ugrian Society, Asko Parpola, and Virpi Hämeen-Anttila.

But Proto-Uralic also had terms for "tin" and "lead," **äsa* and **olna* / **olni*, respectively; the former occurs in the compound **äsa-wäśka*, which can only denote the tin-bronze produced in, and imported from, the eastern wing of the Sejma-Turbino network. In addition, Proto-Uralic has a loanword **ora*, "awl," from Proto-Indo-Aryan **ārā*, "awl," a word not attested in any Iranian language. Another loanword for a metal object is Proto-West-Uralic **vaśara*, "hammer, ax," from Proto-Indo-Aryan **vaj'ra-*, "weapon of the war-god"; it probably originally denoted the ax or mace of the Sejma-Turbino warriors, but later acquired the meaning "hammer" from the Nordic war-god Thor. The Proto-Indo-Aryan compound **madhu-śišta-*, preserved in Sanskrit *madhu-śiṣṭa-*, "beeswax," literally "what is left over of honey," survives in Komi *ma-śis*, "beeswax," while the latter part of the compound is found also in several other Uralic languages (Mordvin, Mari, and Udmurt) with the meaning "beeswax." Beeswax is very important for metal-casting, and the word (or even the verb **śiš-*, "to leave," from which it is derived) has no Iranian cognate.

Some Aryan loanwords in Proto-Uralic attest to an early stage of language development, between Proto-Indo-European and the Proto-Indo-Iranian reconstructed on the basis of the attested Indo-Aryan and Iranian languages, that is, predating sound changes typical of Proto-Aryan; compare Proto-West-Uralic **kekrä*, "circular thing, cycle," with Sanskrit *cakra-*, "wheel, cycle" (see chapter 6). The PIE word **medhu-*, "honey," also still

FIGURE 7.7 A horse skull and cheek-plates from grave 11 of the monument SM in Sintashta, southern Trans-Urals. After the excavation of the grave had been documented, the cheek-plates were placed next to the skull in order to show students how they had been used. The excavation report, however, failed to note that the photograph does not represent the finds as they were excavated. After Gening, Zdanovich, & Gening 1992:157, fig. 74,1. Courtesy Nikolaj B. Vinogradov.

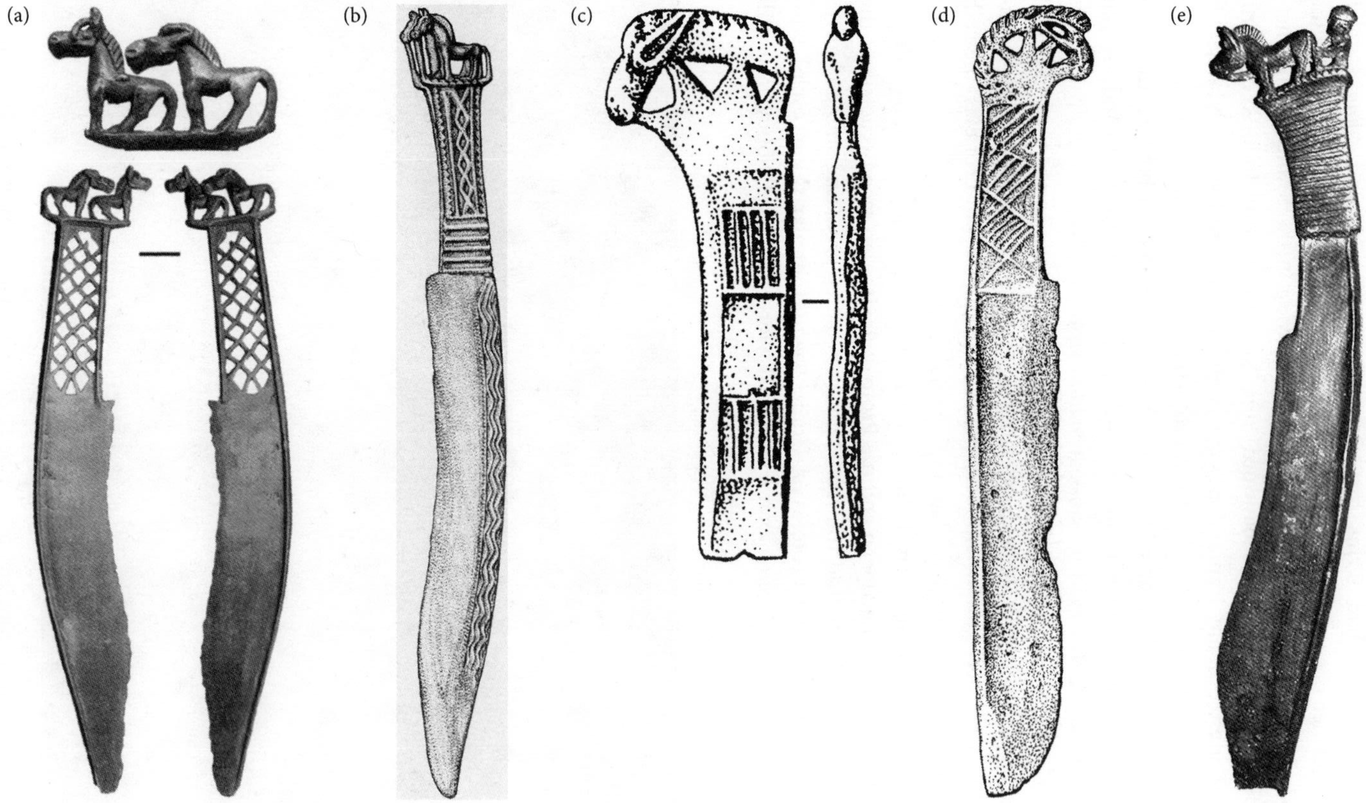

FIGURE 7.8 Sejma-Turbino type metal knives with horse-tops. (a) Sejma. (b) Omsk. (c) Ust'-Muta, Altai. (d) Elunino 1. (e) Rostovka. After Kovtun 2013: t. 2.2; 2.4; 1.2; 1.1; 2.3. Courtesy Igor V. Kovtun.

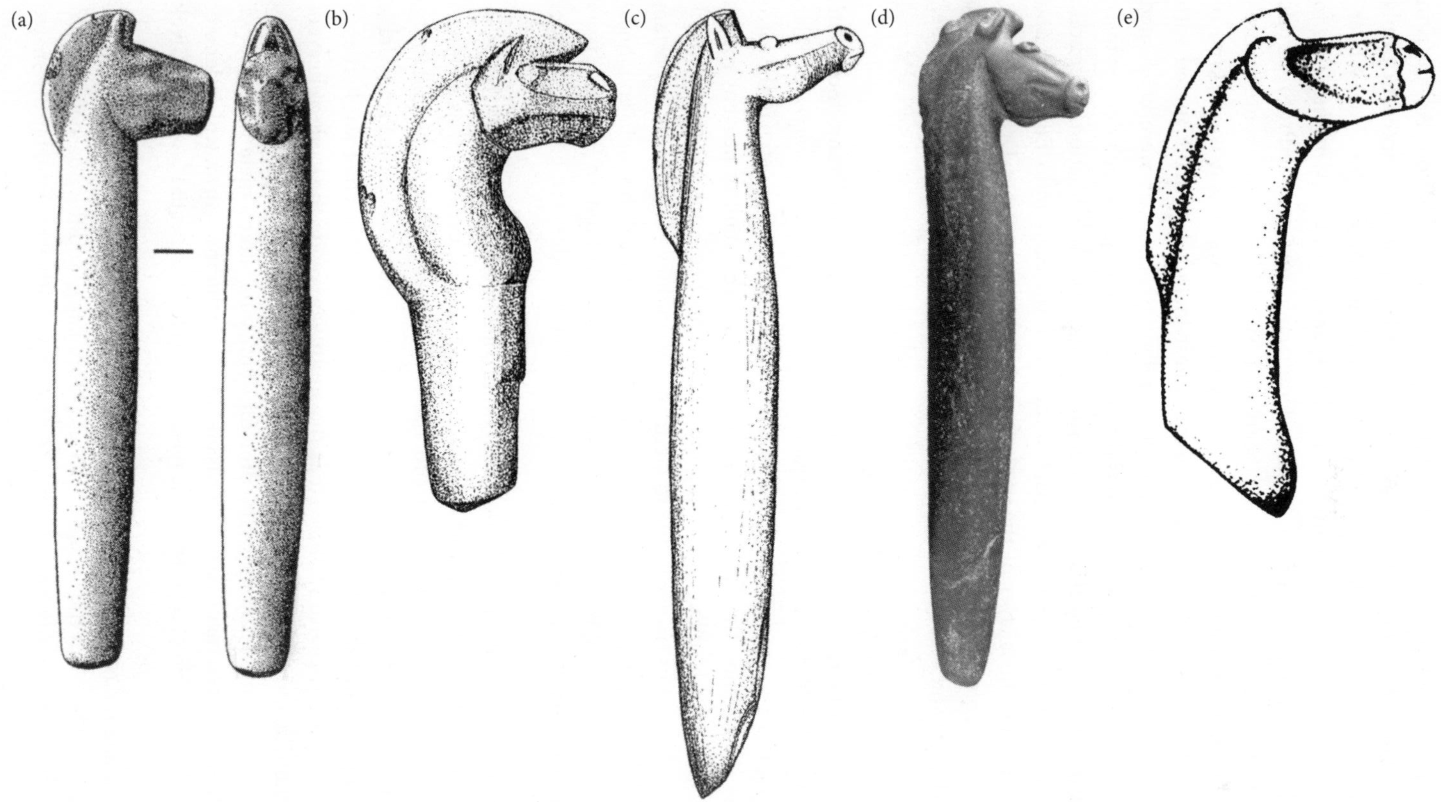

FIGURE 7.9 Sejma-Turbino-related horse-head stone scepters from the steppes. (a) Shipunovo 5, Chelyabinsk. (b) Omsk. (c) Semipalatinsk. (d) Bukhtarma, Irtysh. (e) Kizil', Chelyabinsk. After Kovtun 2013: t. 14.1, 14.3, 14.2, 14.4, 14.5. Courtesy Igor V. Kovtun.

retained its original **e* (not yet changed into **a*) in that early form of Proto-Aryan from which it was borrowed into Proto-Uralic as **mete-*. In PIE **medhu-* denoted not only "honey," but also an alcoholic drink made from honey known as "mead" or "honey-beer" in the historic cultures of Celtic, Germanic, and Baltic speakers; in Greek *méthu* came to mean "wine." The loanwords from Proto-Aryan in Uralic languages include Proto-Permic **sur*, "beer," corresponding to Sanskrit *surā*, "beer" and Avestan *hurā*, "fermented mare's milk, kumiss"; the Komi compound *ma-sur*, "honey-beer," shows that it was a kind of mead. In Vedic India, the reception of a respected guest included a "drink mixed with honey" (*madhu-parka, madhu-mantha*). Important religious occasions were celebrated with feasts that involved drinking, called *peijas* [i.e., *peiyas*] in Finnish, which derives from Proto-Indo-Aryan **paiya-s* > Old Indo-Aryan *peya-*, "drink, drinking; libation." Alcoholic drinks are assumed to have played a vital part in the life of the early Indo-European and Aryan elites. This uppermost layer of the society is represented in Proto-Uralic **asera / *asira*, "prince, lord," from Proto-(Indo-)Aryan **asura-*, "lord." Proto-Uralic contains also Aryan loanwords that indicated dealings with valued objects: PU **arva-*, "price, value," from Proto-Aryan **argha-*, "price, value," and the numerals for 100 (PU **śata* < PIA **śata-*) and 1000 (PU **śosra* < Proto-Aryan **źhasra-*).

Several Proto-Aryan religious terms have become part of Proto-Uralic, too. From Proto-Indo-Aryan **stambha-s*, "pillar, world-pillar," comes Proto-Finnic **sampas*, "pillar, world pillar"; it figures as a much coveted treasure in ancient Finnic epic poetry in the form of a magic mill called Sampo that has a star-speckled cover. (The vault of heavens rotates around the axis of the world-pillar supporting the heavens; its being conceived as a magic mill that grinds riches for its owner is due to Germanic mythology.) Even more important is **juma-* (in this spelling *j* is the semivowel corresponding to *y* in English *yoke*), "god, highest god, heaven" (*Jumala* is the word for "God" with a capital G in modern Finnish), from Proto-Indo-Aryan **dyuma(n)t-*, "heavenly, shining; epithet of Indra, the god of thunder and war."

In view of this religious intercourse and interethnic collaboration of peoples who probably spoke Proto-Indo-Aryan and Proto-East-Uralic in the steppes, even as far as southern Turkmenistan (see below), I have ventured to propose that the name of the Aryan god Indra, which has defied earlier etymological explanations, might come from that of the Proto-Uralic god of weather, thunder and sky, **Ilmar / *Inmar*. Ilmarinen, one of the chief war heroes in ancient Finnic epic poetry, is also mentioned as the smith who made the vault of heavens and Sampo; in Finnish, *ilma* is the usual word for "air, atmosphere, weather." The change of the Udmurt form *Inmar* into *Indra* is not too difficult to imagine: after a metathesis *ar* > *ra*, occasioned by the fact that so many Aryan words end in *-ra* (including **vaj'ra*, which denotes Indra's weapon), the insertion of *d* between the nasal and *r* is to be expected (compare Greek *anēr*, "man," genitive *an-d-ros*).

The best explanation of the many early Aryan loanwords in Uralic languages seems to be a lengthy symbiosis between the local Kama Valley population and the Abashevo people. Some loanwords come specifically from the Indo-Aryan branch. They presumably originated with the Abashevo people, ancestors of the many above-mentioned cultures that dominated the Asiatic steppes until about 1500 BCE, when they were overrun by horsemen (who in all likelihood spoke Iranian) from the Pontic-Caspian steppes. Even the Abashevo culture was succeeded by people who probably spoke Proto-Iranian when its area was taken over by the early Srubnaya culture about 1850 BCE.

I have suggested that those Proto-Indo-Aryan-speakers who remained in the Volga-Kama area of pure copper sandstone (Fig. 7.2) eventually started speaking Proto-Uralic, yet retained an ability to communicate in Proto-Indo-Aryan with the Siberian side of the Sejma-Turbino international network of metal production and marketing. In this way Proto-Uralic would have become the language of the European side of Sejma-Turbino metal production and its network of warrior traders (Fig. 7.3). The westward spread of the Uralic protolanguage with the Sejma-Turbino network is suggested by its temporal closeness to the disintegration of Proto-Uralic, which must postdate its adoption of many Proto-Indo-Aryan loanwords.

It is currently thought that the PIE language probably to a large extent spread through language shifts initiated by local leaders who came to the side of small but powerful groups of PIE-speaking immigrants. The latter would have an effective, strongly hierarchical social system, good weapons, and a military backing, plus coveted luxury goods as external markers of

FIGURE 7.10 A ski-jorer pulled by a horse. The top of a Sejma-Turbino knife (see Fig. 7.8e) from Rostovka. After Kovtun 2013: photo 49.3. Courtesy Igor V. Kovtun.

their power. Joining such a network of foreign chiefs would guarantee local leaders both their existing positions and additional advantages. The loyalty of new network members could be guaranteed by matrimonial alliances (Mallory 2002a). That the Uralic languages very probably spread by similar means, with language shifts initiated by Sejma-Turbino warrior-traders, can be substantiated: a detailed demonstration of how this assumed dispersal of the Uralic languages to their present areas of speech matches the archaeological record is available (Parpola 2012 [2013]), but cannot be included here.

While on this topic, I would however like to mention that the collaboration between Uralic and Aryan speakers continued even into later times, especially between the probably Proto-East Uralic speaking people of the Cherkaskul' culture (*c.* 1850–1500 BCE) of Bashkiria and the Mid- and South Trans-Urals, and the Proto-Indo-Aryan speaking Fëdorovo Andronovans (Chlenova 1984). Part of the Cherkaskul' people adopted pastoralism and accompanied the Andronovans in long migrations in the steppe, even as far east as the Altai Mountains and as far south as southern Central Asia (Fig. 7.6). In these migrations the Cherkaskul' people, like the later Hungarians who adopted mobile pastoralism, could retain their original language: some of them apparently remained near the Altai Mountains and became the ancestors of the speakers of Samoyed languages.

In the light of the evidence presented in this chapter, the early Proto-Indo-Aryan speakers were not only metalsmiths and arms merchants but also pastoralists and inventors of the horse-drawn chariot. Remains of chariots and chariot horses with their cheek-plates (Fig. 7.7) have been found in the elite graves of the Sintashta and Petrovka cultures (2100–1800 BCE) and those of the succeeding Andronovo cultures (2000–1450 BCE), spreading widely over the steppes of southern Siberia, Kazakhstan, and Turkmenistan. Hundreds of petroglyphs in Central and Inner Asia depict the horse-drawn chariot. The horse is the favorite animal depicted in the knives and scepters of the Sejma-Turbino intercultural network of warrior-traders (Figs. 7.8, 7.9,). It is remarkable, however, that these objects never represent a horse-rider, although the image of a ski-jorer pulled by a horse decorates the top of one Sejma-Turbino knife (Fig. 7.10). The horse-drawn chariot, first attested in the Sintashta culture, also diffused to the European steppes in the early second millennium BCE (Usachuk 2004; 2013), and it went on to revolutionize warfare in the ancient West Asia, where the first horse-drawn chariots appeared in the twentieth century BCE.

8

The BMAC of Central Asia and the Mitanni of Syria

Afghanistan and the surrounding areas of southern Central Asia, through which the Rigvedic Aryans must have passed on their way to South Asia, were until quite recently a blank on the Bronze Age archaeological map. In the 1970s, a previously unknown civilization was discovered in this area, mainly by Viktor I. Sarianidi, a Russian archaeologist of Greek descent, who excavated it unceasingly until his death "on the spot" at Gonur in 2013. As a token of respect for a good friend, this book uses Sarianidi's name for the new civilization, the Bactria and Margiana Archaeological Complex (BMAC). Bactria and Margiana are derived from the ancient Greek names for, respectively, northern Afghanistan around modern Balkh and southeastern Turkmenistan, the satrapy of Marguš in the Persian empire of the Achaemenids, around the modern city of Merv. It should be noted, however, that an alternative and perhaps more elegant name, the Oxus civilization (from the ancient Greek name of the Amu Darya River whose upper reaches flow through the BMAC), has been suggested by Henri-Paul Francfort.

Francfort (2005) distinguishes three principal periods of the BMAC:

- 3000–2500/2400 BCE is the formative phase, containing handmade ceramics painted with many colors, mainly with cross and rhombus motifs; stone objects made of alabaster and steatite; and the first compartmented metal seals. The wide formative area comprised the piedmont sites of the Kopet Dagh range of southwestern Turkmenistan (Namazga Depe, Altyn Depe, Ulug Depe, Khapuz Depe), the delta of the Tedzen River (Geoksyur), western Tajikistan (Sarazm in the Zeravshan Valley), central and northern Afghanistan (Mundigak and Taliqan), and Iranian Seistan (Shahr-i Sokhta). A particularly important influence was that of the Proto-Elamite civilization (attested by an inscribed tablet at Shahr-i Sokhta and cylinder seals in Bactria and Sarazm), manifested in monumental architecture (Mundigak and Sarazm) and seal motifs. There was influence, too, from the Early Harappan cultures of the Greater Indus Valley and from the northern steppes, manifested in the Afanasyevo-like burial at Sarazm, where ceramics of the Kelteminar culture have also been found.

- 2500/2400–1700 BCE is the mature "urban" phase, largely contemporaneous with the mature Indus civilization, with its most dynamic period, *c.* 2200–1750 BCE. Its area, the core area of the BMAC, consists of the oases of southern Turkmenistan (Taip, Gonur, Togolok, and Kelleli in Margiana; and Namazga, Ulug, Khapuz, Altyn in Kopet Dagh), northern Afghanistan (Daulatabad, Dashly, and Farukabad), and southern Uzbekistan (Sapalli and Dzharkutan). Some 300 sites are known altogether, representing a considerable population. The economy was based on irrigation agriculture using wheat and barley, and commanded considerable mineral resources, including copper, tin, lead, gold, silver, lapis lazuli, and turquoise. Numerous settlements were strongly fortified with walls up to 10 meters wide, employing towers and gates, sometimes with two further inner walls. Inside were residential houses, workshops, and "palaces" or "temples" (Fig. 8.1).

The "palace" at Gonur, the capital of Margiana, measures 150 × 140 meters, along with a slightly smaller "temple." A necropolis of 10 hectares situated 200 m to the west of Gonur contains more than 1500 excavated graves; a smaller graveyard with royal burials was discovered south of the "temple." The latter contained, among other things, a wagon with bronze-rimmed wheels exactly paralleling those found in Susa. There are many remarkable finds at Gonur, but I mention here only a few datable to the late third millennium. These include ivory objects (combs and pins) of the Indus civilization, a large square Harappan stamp seal with an image of an elephant and an inscription in the Indus script. A cylinder seal that according to its cuneiform inscription belonged to the cup-bearer of a Mesopotamian king (whose name is unfortunately illegible) is concrete evidence of relations with Mesopotamia, where the BMAC was probably known as the far-off country Šimaški (Potts 2008 [2009]).

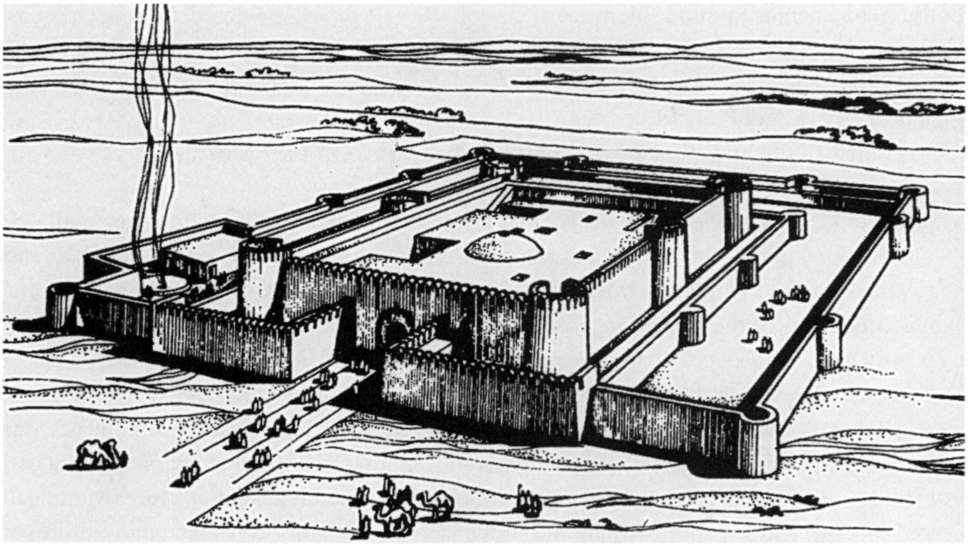

FIGURE 8.1 The BMAC fortress of Togolok-21 in southern Turkmenistan (ancient Margiana). After Sarianidi 1987:52. Courtesy Margiana Archaeological Expedition.

The material culture comprises a wide variety of beautiful artifacts, including fine wheel-made ceramics, bronze tools and weapons such as swords and hatchets, and impressive symbols of power in the form of decorated ritual axes, mace heads, and long stone scepters. The numerous uninscribed metal and stone seals (Fig. 20.2) form an important category of objects (Baghestani 1997; Sarianidi 1998; Winkelmann 2004; Franke 2010). The eagle (sometimes with two heads), snake, scorpion, mountain goat, camel, wild boar, and lion are among the animals represented on the seals, toilet pins, axes, and maces. Wine cups of gold and silver give a rare insight into the life of the BMAC people. They depict men plowing fields with teams of oxen, driving ox-pulled wagons and chariots, feasting on meat and drink, listening to harp music, hunting game, fighting battles, becoming wounded, and being buried (Fig. 8.2). These men wear the Sumerian flounced *kaunakes* garment, as do the statuettes of seated females, who are likely to be goddesses, made of soft stone (steatite and alabaster), which is the material of many other objects too. Semiprecious stones (lapis lazuli, turquoise, and carnelian) are used for jewelry. Pierre Amiet (1986) calls the iconography "Trans-Elamite"; it has a lot in common with the art of Kerman (Jiroft), ultimately going back to the Proto-Elamite art of western Iran and Uruk-period Mesopotamia.

- 1700–1500 BCE is the late or post-"urban" phase of the BMAC, which is represented by the Takhirbaj period in Margiana, the Kuzali, Mollali, and Bustan periods in northern Bactria, and the Namazga VI period in the Kopet Dagh region. In this impoverished phase, the small finds distinctive of the mature phase of the BMAC such as seals and ax-heads disappear, and architecture continues only to a limited extent. At Gonur, the building complexes appear to have been abandoned suddenly at the end of the "urban" phase: valuable grinding stones were left behind, along with unbaked ceramics near pottery kilns. The situation appears similar at Togolok 1 and Togolok 21. The desiccation that occurred around 1750 BCE is thought to be a major cause of the collapse of the BMAC at the beginning of its post-"urban" phase; it is probably associated with another likely contributing cause, namely the arrival of steppe nomads representing the Fëdorovo variant of the Andronovo cultures.

Neither Andronovo pottery nor barrows typical of the steppe culture are found south of the line defined by the Kopet Dagh, Hindukush, and Pamir mountains. Yet, Aryan languages originally spoken in the northern steppes (see chapter 7) had reached Syria and South Asia by the middle of the second millennium. In Parpola (1988a), I proposed that the BMAC must have expanded in these two directions as the archaeological counterpart of this later linguistic spread. This proposal implied that an elite of Aryan-speaking pastoralist warriors from the steppes took over the leadership in the BMAC. I compared this with a takeover of power by an immigrant Proto-Indo-Aryan-speaking elite in the Mitanni kingdom a few centuries later. The takeover of the BMAC could have occurred relatively peacefully, as there is little evidence of violence; it could have given the BMAC a more effective hierarchical leadership, which in turn would provide a plausible explanation for the BMAC's increased dynamism and aggressiveness in the later part of its "urban" phase.

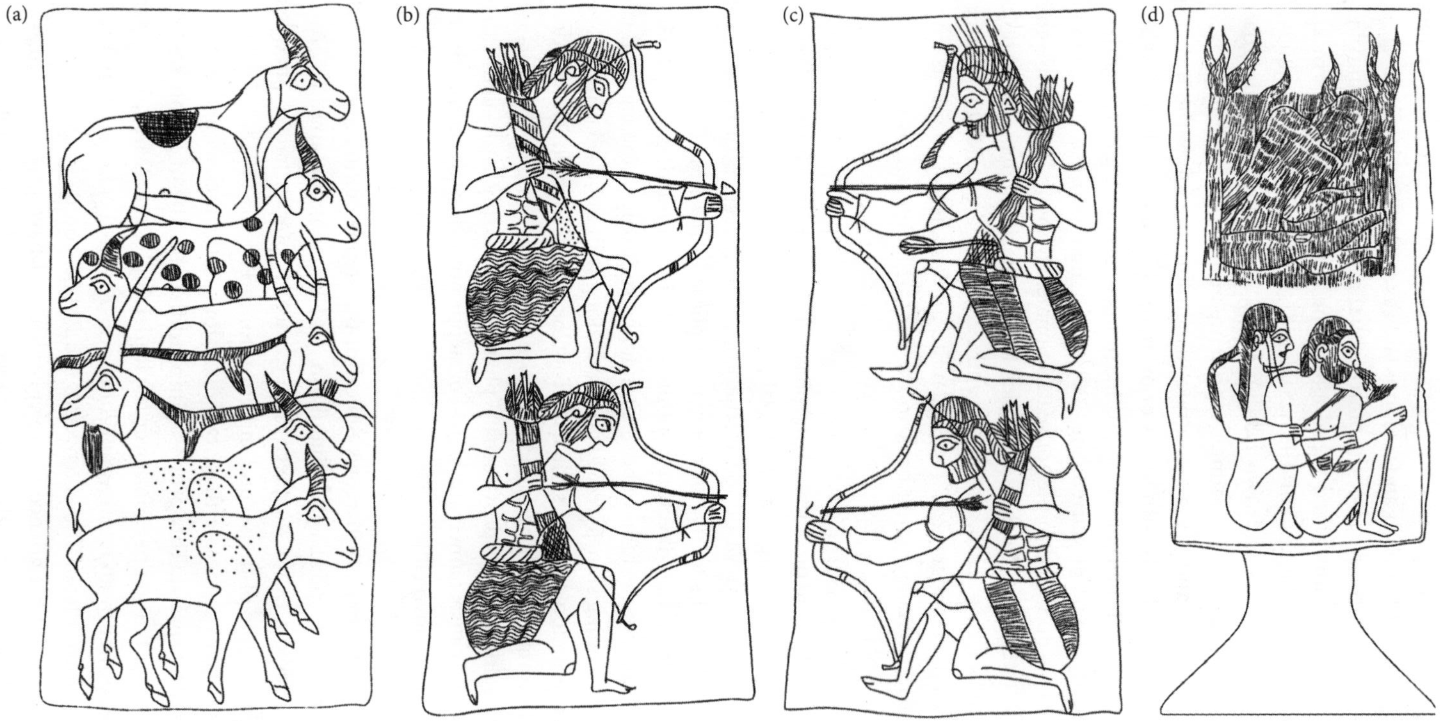

FIGURE 8.2 Four BMAC silver cups illustrating the life of the elite. (a–d) A group of goats, archers fighting each other, and the burial of a hero hit with an arrow. Private collection. After Francfort 2005: fig. 28 a–d. Drawing J. Svire, courtesy H.-P. Francfort.

(e)

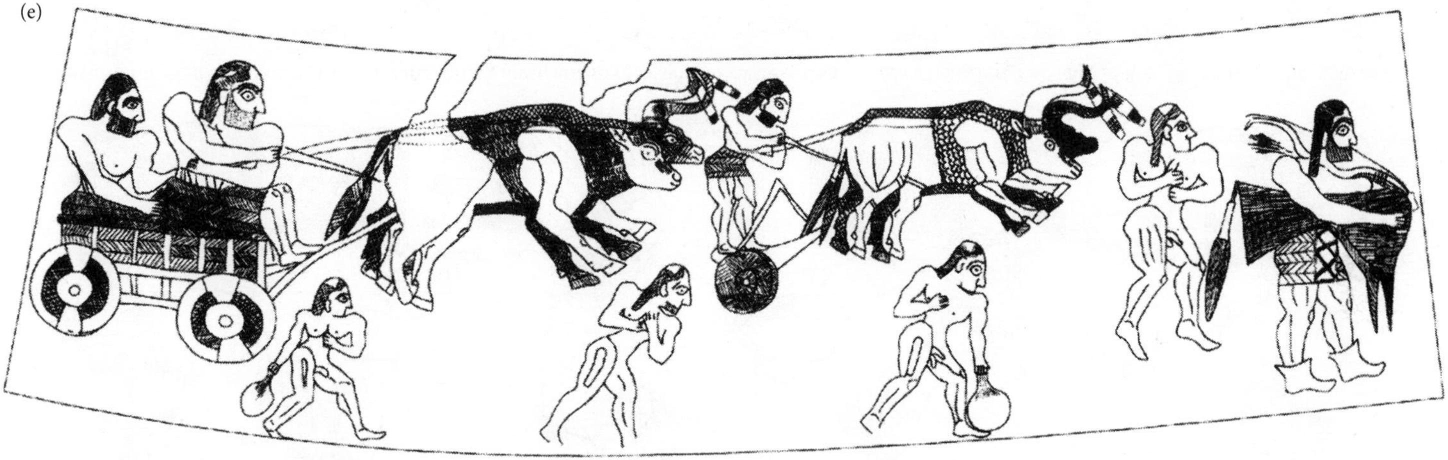

FIGURE 8.2 (e) A procession in which an archer wearing boots carries an unrecognized object, nude men carry heavy round objects, and a one-man chariot and a four-wheeled wagon with two seated men are pulled by pairs of galloping oxen. Musée du Louvre (AO 28518). After Francfort 2005: fig. 6. Drawing H. David, courtesy H.-P. Francfort and Musée du Louvre/Béatrice André-Salvini.

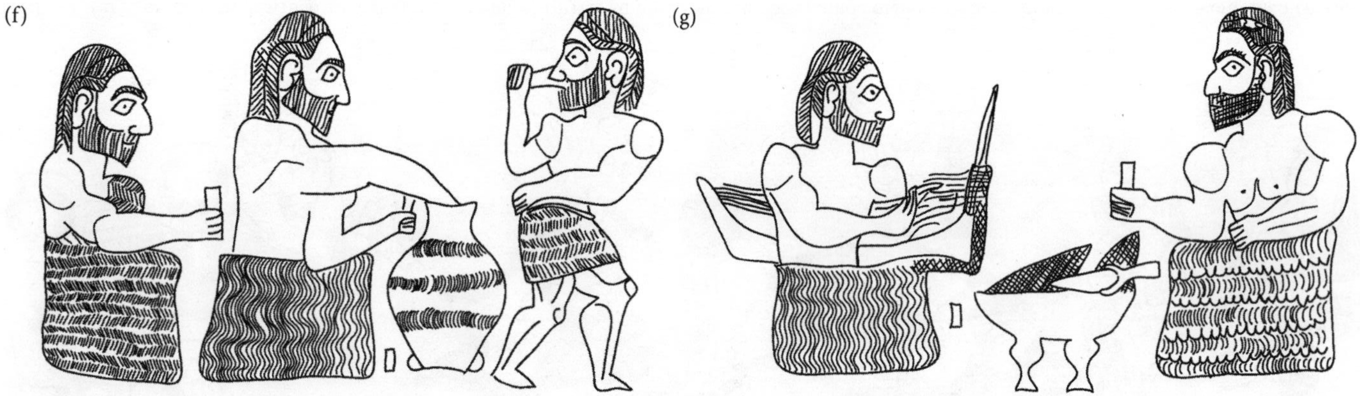

FIGURE 8.2 (f–g)A banquet with drinking, eating meat, and harp-playing. Private collection. After Francfort 2005: fig. 26 a–b. Drawing J. Svire, courtesy H.-P. Francfort.

(h)

FIGURE 8.2 (h) Cylindrical cup with an agricultural and ceremonial scene in the Miho Museum, Shiga, Japan (SF03.055), showing banqueting and plowing with oxen. After Jansen, Mulloy, & Urban 1991:169, pl. 148(h). Courtesy © Miho Museum.

Fred Hiebert agrees that the expansion of the BMAC people to the Iranian plateau and the Indus Valley borderlands at the beginning of the second millennium BCE is "the best candidate for an archaeological correlate of the introduction of Indo-Iranian speakers to Iran and South Asia" (Hiebert 1995:192). J. P. Mallory embraces this hypothesis, too, and has developed his well-known *Kultur-Kugel* model to support it up theoretically (Mallory 1998; 2002a). Francfort (2005:298), however, excludes the presence of Aryan-speakers from the "urban" period between 2500 and 1700 BCE, when the BMAC was ruled by a Trans-Elamite elite, according to him; the Indo-Aryan speakers were in charge during the post-"urban" period 1700–1500 BCE, while the Iranian speakers came to southern Central Asia around 1500 BCE.

At present, given the BMAC's links with South Asia and especially with northern Iran and Mitanni, and the necessity of having the Rigvedic Aryans as the second (later) wave of Indo-Aryan immigrants in South Asia (chapter 12), I remain convinced that an early wave of Proto-Indo-Aryan speakers took charge of the BMAC around 2000 BCE. Some may have come to the BMAC even earlier, when they had not yet yoked the horses to the chariot but were racing with chariots pulled by bulls (cf. Fig. 8.2e), though certainly the culture remained thoroughly "Trans-Elamite." The mature "urban" phase, however, saw the introduction of the horse and camel. Horse, camel, and donkey bones have been identified. The necropolis of Gonur was found to contain two horse burials, which in both cases lacked the head, and which can plausibly be linked with the prehistory of the Vedic horse sacrifice (chapter 11). Along with the camel, the domesticated horse is represented in BMAC weapon-scepters (Fig. 8.3) and some stamp and cylinder seals. By its late phase the BMAC people appear to have gained great mobility and spread widely both westwards and eastwards. They were in contact with the Indus civilization, with eastern and western Iran, with the Gulf, with Syria and Anatolia, and with the steppes, where typical BMAC metal seals have been found as far east as the Ordos Plateau in the Inner Mongolia autonomous region of China (Baghestani 1997).

A rich grave accidentally found at Zardcha Khalifa in the Zeravshan Valley in Tajikistan (Bobomulloev 1997) contained, besides ceramics and other grave goods typical of the BMAC (Sarianidi 2001:434), the remains of a chariot and two horses, which once had cheek-plates (*psalia*) of precisely the same type as at Sintashta culture, and mouth bits (Fig. 8.4; cf. Fig. 7.7). In addition, there was a bronze pin, whose horse-top is paralleled by the horse-tops of the Sejma-Turbino knives and scepters (Figs. 7.8, 7.9). This find suggests that Indo-Aryan speakers had come from the southern Urals and entered the ruling elite of the BMAC probably as early as the twentieth century BCE. Sintashta-type cheek-plates have recently been excavated also in grave 2 at Sazagan in the Zeravshan Valley, here too with BMAC ceramics of the Sapalli phase (*c.* 2000–1800 BCE) (Avanesova 2010). Teufer (2012) points out that the metal bits of Zardcha Khalifa do not come from the Sintashta culture but from West Asia; he suggests that the spoke-wheeled war chariot was elaborated in southern Central Asia, which formed a contact zone between the northern (steppe) and southern traditions about 2000 BCE.

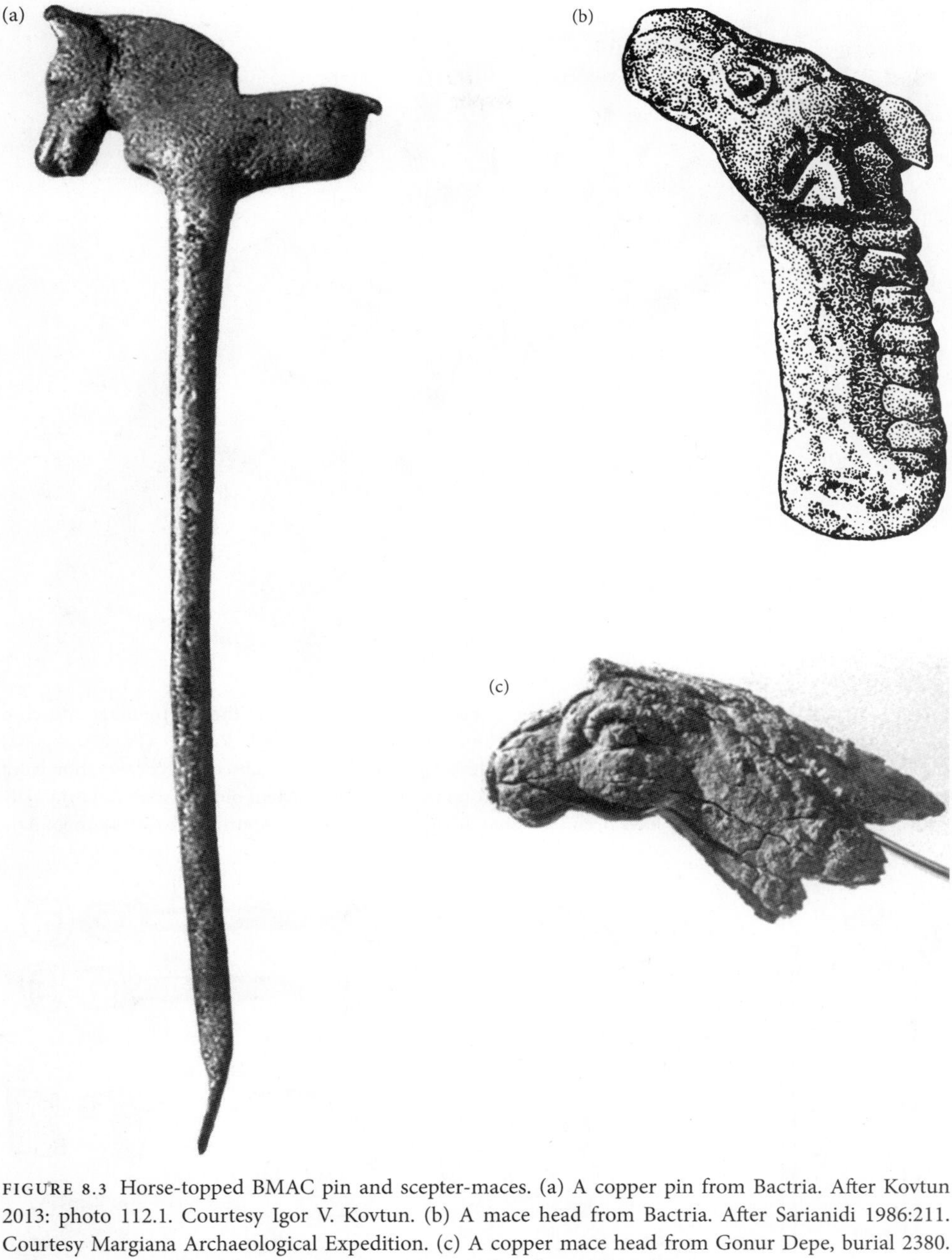

FIGURE 8.3 Horse-topped BMAC pin and scepter-maces. (a) A copper pin from Bactria. After Kovtun 2013: photo 112.1. Courtesy Igor V. Kovtun. (b) A mace head from Bactria. After Sarianidi 1986:211. Courtesy Margiana Archaeological Expedition. (c) A copper mace head from Gonur Depe, burial 2380. After Sarianidi 2007:127, fig. 3. Courtesy Margiana Archaeological Expedition.

FIGURE 8.3 (d) An unprovenanced copper scepter head from Afghanistan in the Metropolitan Museum of Art, New York (1989.281.39, gift of Norbert Schimmel Trust). When Holly Pittman (1984:70, fig. 32) published this object thirty years ago, it was united with a bronze mace head. Subsequent conservation work has determined that the mace head and the horse protome, while both ancient objects, were not originally part of the same piece, and they have been separated. Image courtesy © The Metropolitan Museum of Art.

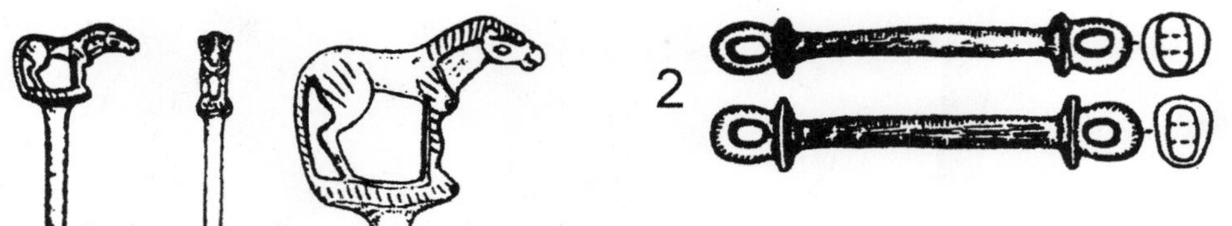

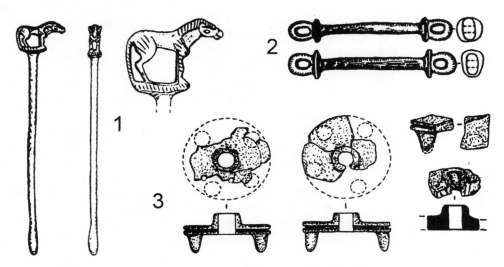

FIGURE 8.4 Finds from a BMAC elite grave at Zardcha Khalifa in Tajikistan. (1) A horse-topped bronze pin. (2) Bronze horse-bits. (3) Sintashta-type cheek-pieces for chariot-horses made of bone. After Carpelan & Parpola 2001:138, fig. 37, based on Bobomulloev 1997:126, Abb. 3.14 (1), 3.12–13 (2) and 128, Abb. 4.1–4 (3).

On the other hand, surface surveys in Margiana (Gubaev, Koshelenko, & Tosi 1998) revealed that in the late phase of the BMAC, up to the fifteenth century BCE, practically all BMAC settlements in south Turkmenistan were surrounded by pastoralist campsites with late Andronovo ceramics, attesting to an ever-increasing presence of steppe pastoralists who very probably spoke Proto-Indo-Aryan.

During 2000–1900 BCE, the BMAC spread to Pakistani Baluchistan. A rich BMAC graveyard was accidentally discovered at Quetta, while other BMAC graves were found at Mehrgarh VIII and Sibri near the Bolan Pass. That BMAC people (not just traders) moved to Pakistani Baluchistan is evident from the fact that the entire cultural complex was imported, including burials (Jarrige 1991). BMAC-type seals and seal impressions have been found in small numbers in the late phase of the Indus civilization at Mohenjo-daro and Harappa (Parpola 2005d; Franke 2010), and in post-Harappan times in the southern Indus Valley (the so-called Jhukar seals in Chanhu-daro) (Mackay 1943), Gujarat (Somnath, alias Prabhas Patan), and even Rajasthan, where about a hundred seal impressions were collected in a pot at Gilund (Shinde, Possehl, & Ameri 2005) (Fig. 8.5). The

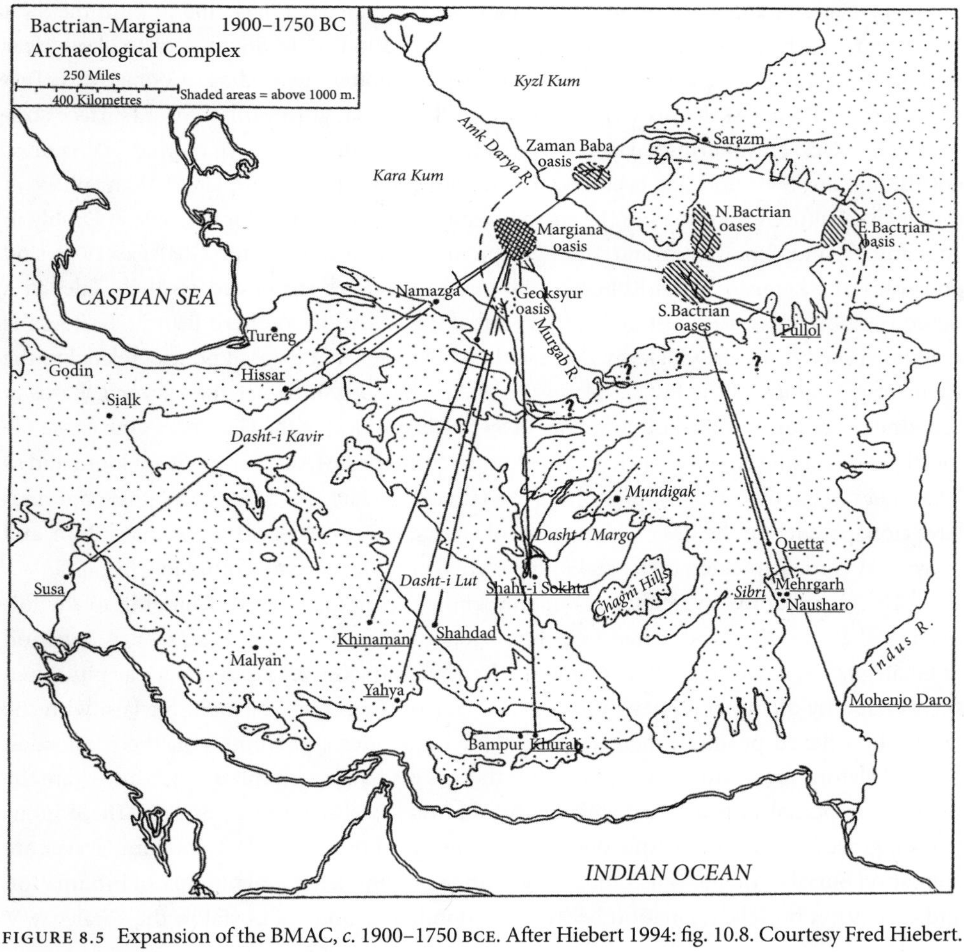

FIGURE 8.5 Expansion of the BMAC, *c.* 1900–1750 BCE. After Hiebert 1994: fig. 10.8. Courtesy Fred Hiebert.

(a)

(b)

FIGURE 8.6 Antennae-hilted swords: (a) from Bactria, northern Afghanistan, length 52 cm, and (b) from Fatehgarh, Uttar Pradesh, India, length 63.5 cm. After Parpola 1988a: 285, fig. 10, based on (a) Sarianidi 1986: 198, fig. 75 and (b) Gordon 1960: pl. XXVII b.

Gangetic copper hoards have antennae-hilted swords similar to those coming from plundered BMAC sites of Afghanistan, which dates the hoards to about the twentieth century BCE or later (Fig. 8.6; Fig. 4.4).

The Gandhara Grave culture of the Ghālegay IV phase (*c.* 1700–1400 BCE) in the Swat Valley starts with the arrival of a new culture, one of the first in South Asia to show clear evidence for domesticated horse, in motifs of painted pottery as well as in bone finds. Two well-preserved horse skeletons were excavated in the Kātelai graveyard of Swat (surface stratum). The black-gray, burnished pottery introduced from the beginning of phase IV is present throughout Swat and has been connected with the pottery of the late "urban" phase of the BMAC culture widespread in the surrounding areas at this time, for example at Dashly in Afghanistan and Tepe Hissar and Tureng Tepe in northern Iran. In the Ghālegay IV Period graveyard at Kherai in Indus Kohistan, the inhumed bodies are placed on their sides in a flexed position, this burial custom being typical of the BMAC in southern Bactria. Besides the gray-burnished ware, the Ghālegay IV Period had black-on-red painted pottery related to the Cemetery H culture of the Punjab plains (Fig. 4.4). The horse is depicted on several shards of this kind of ceramics at Bīr-kōṭ-ghwaṇḍai in Swāt. Very typical of the Gandhāra Graves are the metal pins for fixing clothing; such pins are known from the BMAC necropolis at Gonur and as imported foreign objects from graves in Syria (Chagar Bazar). The terracotta female figurines have close parallels in the BMAC necropolis of Gonur, at Tepe Hissar III in northern Iran, and in Syria. A compartmented metal seal of the BMAC type was recently found in Chitral.

The Gandhāra Grave culture is mainly known from graveyards belonging to the following Ghālegay V Period, dated to *c.* 1400–1000 BCE, and the following Iron Age Period of Ghālegay VI, dated to *c.* 1000–600 BCE. The Gandhāra Graves are rectangular pits, often surrounded by a ring of stones. About two-thirds of them are interment burials, with the bodies in a flexed position, men lying on their right sides and women on their left sides. Some skeletons are anatomically intact, but there is also a large number of graves where the bones were placed in heaps, yet with the head always in the upmost position. These inhumation graves are covered with stones. About one-third of these later Gandhāra Graves are cremation burials. After a transition period with approximately equal number of inhumation and cremation burials, cremation became the dominant mode of burial in the Ghālegay V

Period (the characteristic "face urns" are discussed in chapter 11), while during the Ghālegay VI Period cremation gradually disappeared. Both inhumation and cremation burials contain both single persons and (quite often) two persons, usually couples that mostly seem to have been buried at different times.

The Gandhāra Graves of the Ghālegay V period have been compared with the cemeteries of the Vakhsh and Beshkent Valleys of southern Tajikistan. These represent a fusion of the local north Bactrian variant of the BMAC in its late Molali-Bustān Phase (*c.* 1700–1400 bce) and of steppe nomads of the Fëdorovo Andronovo culture, which is attested at several sites in southern Tajikistan. In both Vakhsh and Beshkent interment in a flexed position is the predominant mode of burial, but at Beshkent secondary and cremation burials are also found. At the necropolis of Bustān 6 in southern Uzbekistan it is quite clear that the cremation tradition was introduced by the Fëdorovo Andronovo culture (recognized from ceramics and terracotta human and horse figurines). This late variant of the Andronovo culture practiced cremation widely in the steppes of Kazakhstan.

When the BMAC people moved to South Asia, they probably spoke both the original BMAC language and Proto-Indo-Aryan, which may have been influenced by the original BMAC language. This situation should be reflected in the available linguistic evidence. But how could one know anything about the BMAC language which had no written documents, and how could one judge its influence on Proto-Indo-Aryan? Alexander Lubotsky (2001) has collected "all Sanskrit etyma which have Iranian correspondences, but lack clear cognates outside Indo-Iranian," numbering about 120. He concludes that some of these words may have been borrowed from Uralic languages, but that the major portion is likely to have come from the language of the BMAC, which he considers non-Indo-European. One criterion is the non-Proto-Indo-European structure of many of these loanwords. He refers to trisyllabic words in which the first and third syllable have a short vowel and the medial syllable a long vowel (∪–∪). According to Lubotsky, "the Indo-Aryans were presumably the first who came in contact with foreign tribes" in Central Asia "and sometimes 'passed on' loanwords to the Iranians." He also points out that these Indo-Iranian loanwords, likely to have been borrowed mainly from the language of the BMAC, are phonologically and morphologically similar to many loanwords found in Sanskrit alone. Indeed, a large part of the 383 "foreign words" from the Rigveda listed by F. B. J. Kuiper (1991) probably comes from the BMAC language.

I would like to note some characteristics of this hypothetical BMAC language not specified by Lubotsky. The vocalic *ṛ* occurs in the first syllable in several of Lubotsky's loanwords, such as *ṛbīsa-*, "oven," and *śṛgāla-*, "jackal" (both having the trisyllabic structure with long middle syllable), *gṛda-*, "penis" (here Lubotsky notes the two unaspirated voiced stops in the same word, a root structure impossible for an IE word); moreover, the vocalic *ṛ* in the initial syllable is anomalously accented in **ṛ́ši-*, "seer," and this is the case too in several proper names recorded in the Rigveda as names of the Dāsas, Dasyus, and Paṇis (see chapter 9), namely Dṛbhīka, Sṛbinda, Bṛsaya (with the anomalous dental *s* after *ṛ*, also found in later Vedic *bṛsī-*, "roll of twisted grass, cushion"); an unaccented *ṛ* in the first syllable is found in the Dāsa proper names Bṛbu (but accented in *bṛbūka-*, "thick") and Pipru Mṛgaya (from *mṛga-*, which is listed as a likely loanword). Bṛsaya is particularly important, because it can be located in the regions west of the Indus Valley with the help of Greek sources (see chapter 9).

Another peculiarity in the above BMAC/Dāsa words is the phoneme *b* (cf. *ṛbīsa-*, Sṛbinda, Bṛbu), which in Indo-Aryan only rarely goes back to PIE **b*, but occurs in many words of probably foreign origin. Among these words are further Dāsa names, Balbūtha, and Ilībiśa. These again have the phoneme *l* not found in the main dialect of the Rigveda (chapter 12). Both *b* and *l* occur in *kilbiṣa-*, "injury, transgression, injustice, sin, guilt."

Some probable BMAC loanwords occur outside the Indo-Iranian material discussed by Lubotsky. For example, the following Sanskrit words have the trisyllabic structure with a long middle syllable as well as the phoneme *l*:

- *kulāla-/kaulāla-*, "potter," "potter's ware"; this word is not attested in the Rigveda but does appear in the Yajurveda (Vājasaneyi-Saṃhitā), with cognates in modern Dardic languages of the northwest (Pashai and Kashmiri), as well as in the modern Iranian language Parachi. Both the BMAC and the Indo-Aryan speakers coming from the northern steppes to the BMAC produced pottery. But whereas the BMAC potters threw their pots on a wheel, the people of the northern steppes made their new pots using inverted cloth-covered old pots as molds upon which the wet clay for the new pot was patted. All clay vessels needed in the Vedic ritual had to be made by hand only by an Āryan. In the Vedic texts, a potter who uses the wheel is described as being a Śūdra, of low social standing; wheel-turned pottery is said to belong to the worshippers of demons (*asura*).
- *kīlāla-*, "some kind of milk product" (RV 10,91,14, *kīlāla-pa-*, "drinking *kīlāla*"; *kīlāla-* appears seven times in the Atharvaveda), Classical Sanskrit (Suśruta) *kilāṭa-*; of modern languages, the etymon is found almost exclusively in Nuristani and Dardic languages, where it means mostly "fresh cheese"; in addition comes only Sindhi *kiroṭu, kirūṭu*, "cheese made from skimmed milk." Although the word is found also in Burushaski as *kīlāy* and in Dravidian (Tamil *kiḻāan̲*, "curds," etc.), a BMAC origin seems likely to me.
- *palālī-* (Atharvaveda) / *palāla-*, "stalk, straw."

The BMAC people expanded not only eastwards to South Asia and south to Afghanistan and eastern Iran, but also west, to northern Iran, Syria, and Anatolia. We shall now examine this western extension of the BMAC. Locally manufactured seals from Anatolia and Syria testify that the horse-chariot reached these areas in the twentieth century BCE. According to the cuneiform archives found at the Assyrian trading colony Kanesh, present Kültepe in Cappadocia, the Assyrian merchants settled there imported textiles and enormous amounts of tin from Assur, bartering these goods for silver and gold in Anatolia. This trade, which flourished for seventy years in 1920–1850 BC, affected all areas involved (Brisch & Bartl 1995). The source of the tin was in the east, probably in southern Central Asia (Cierny, Stöllner, & Weisgerber 2005).

The trade contacts are reflected in the seals of the various regions. From about 1850 BC Syria was in close contact with Egypt, and many Egyptian motifs started appearing in the Syrian glyptics (Eder 1996). Among them is the "twist," which appears on locally made but clearly Syrian-inspired stamp-cylinders and their impressions excavated at BMAC sites in Margiana, such as at Taip-depe (Collon 1987:142–143). Conversely the two-humped Bactrian camel of Central Asia, which figures on BMAC seals and ax-scepters, is attested also on Syrian seals.

The BMAC expanded to the Gorgan region near the southeastern shore of the Caspian Sea in northern Iran, where it is represented by the Tepe Hissar IIIC culture (*c.* 1900–1750 BCE). The large number of its bronze weapons suggests that this rich culture was ruled by a warring aristocracy (Schmidt 1937). An alabaster cylinder seal excavated from the IIIB phase at Tepe Hissar depicts a two-wheeled horse-drawn chariot (Fig. 8.7). Roman Ghirshman (1977) suggested that the trumpets made of gold, silver, and copper, now also found in Bactria and Margiana—altogether some fifty trumpets are known (Lawergren 2003)—were used for giving signals in both training chariot horses (as depicted in an Egyptian wall painting) and for directing chariots in battles (Fig. 8.8). Ghirshman also proposed that the Indo-Aryan-speaking nobles of the Mitanni kingdom of Syria came from the Tepe Hissar IIIC culture.

The beginning of Indo-Aryan rule in Mitanni can be narrowed down to the sixteenth century BCE. Cuyler Young (1985) has plausibly linked the arrival of these Indo-Aryans in Syria with the sudden appearance of the Early West Iranian Gray Ware in great quantities all along the Elburz Mountains, in Azerbaijan, and around Lake Urmia around 1500 BCE. Young sees this ceramic, which is new to western Iran, as an evolved form of the Gorgan Gray Ware of the Tepe Hissar IIIC phase, which continued in an impoverished form at Tureng Tepe until about 1600 BCE. Young's reconstruction provides a chronologically and typologically acceptable link between the Mitanni Aryans, the Tepe Hissar III culture of Gorgan, and the BMAC.

In the sixteenth century, the Syrian kingdom of the Mitanni or Mittani dramatically overpowered Assyria and became one of the greatest powers in West Asia, rivalling the Hittites of Anatolia and the Egyptians (Fig. 8.9). While the population of Mitanni consisted of local Hurrian people (whose language seems to be a member of the Caucasian family), its ruling dynasty had Indo-Aryan names. Exactly how this Proto-Indo-Aryan-speaking aristocracy took control is unclear. A cuneiform letter (L.87–887) recently recovered from the archives of Tall Leilan in the Khabur Valley, as early as about 1760 BCE, speaks of *mary-anni* soldiers that served Hurrian rulers as an elite troop. This may have been a vanguard of Proto-Indo-Aryan-speaking mercenaries. More might soon become known from the ongoing excavations at Tall Fakhariya and Tall Hamidiya, since there are good reasons to suspect that these mounds contain the ancient Mitanni capitals Vaššukanni and Taidu, which are expected to have royal archives of cuneiform tablets (Eidem 2014). In any case,

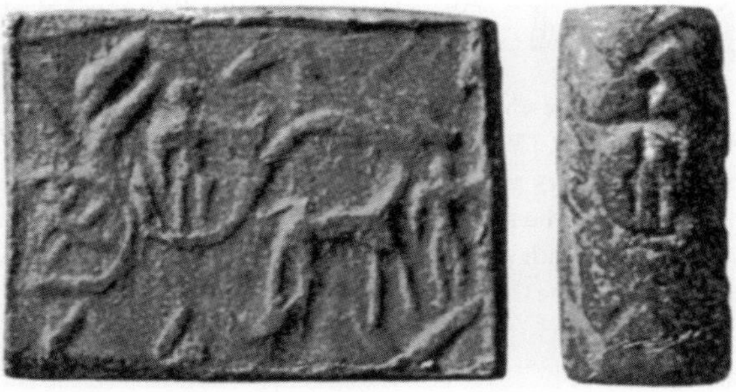

FIGURE 8.7 An alabaster cylinder seal depicting a horse-drawn chariot with cross-bar wheels. Excavated at Tepe Hissar, Gorgan, northeastern Iran, phase III B. After Schmidt 1937:198, fig. 118. Courtesy University of Pennsylvania Museum of Archaeology and Anthropology.

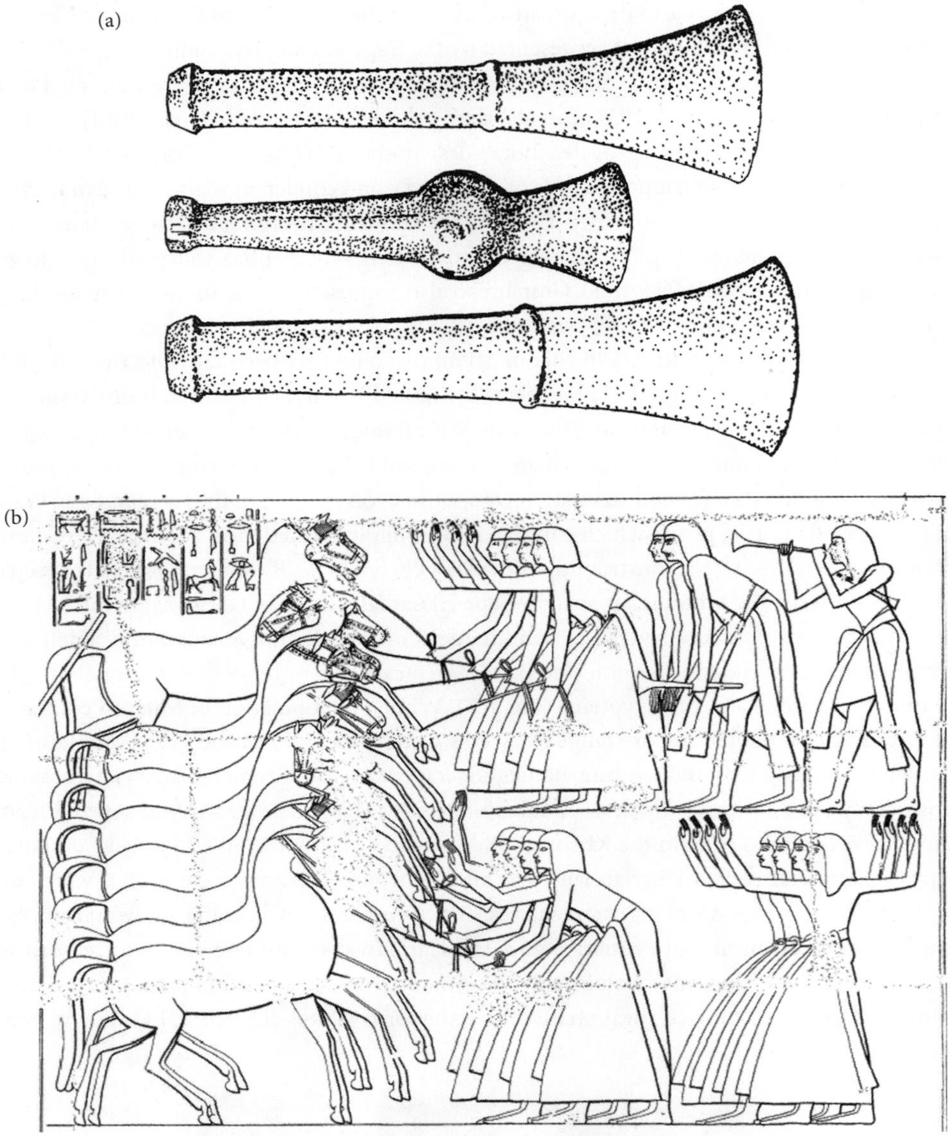

FIGURE 8.8 Trumpets and the horse-chariot. (a) Golden and silver signal trumpets from Tepe Hissar III C. After Mallowan 1965:124, fig. 139, based on Schmidt 1937:209, fig. 121. Courtesy University of Pennsylvania Museum of Archaeology and Anthropology. (b) An order being given to the horses with a trumpet when the pharaoh inspects the royal stables. Relief in the temple of Ramses III (ruled 1194–1163 BCE) at Medinet Habu, First court, south wall, west end. After Nelson et al. 1932: fig. 109, upper right corner. Courtesy of the Oriental Institute of the University of Chicago. On the trumpet in Egypt see Hickmann 1946.

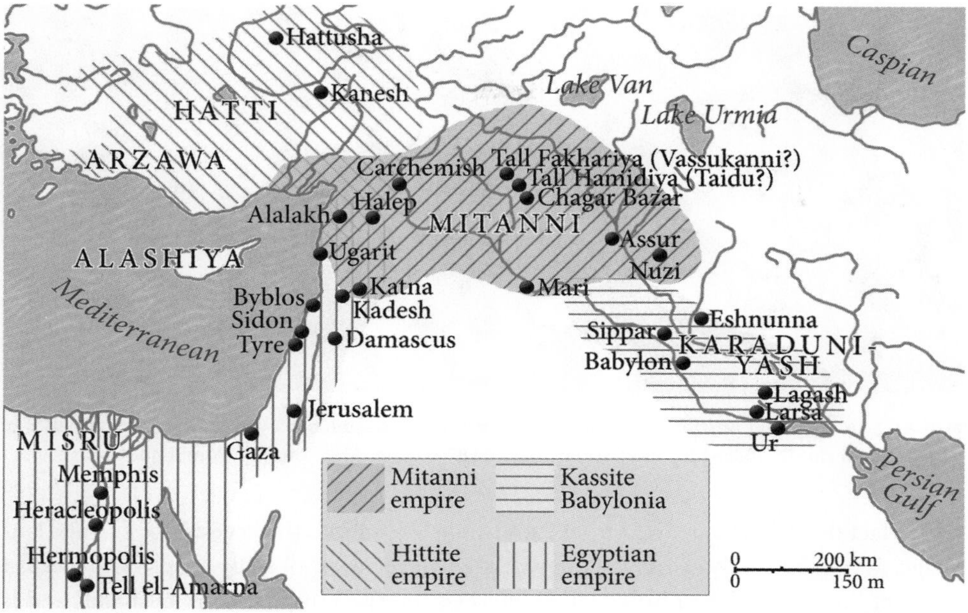

FIGURE 8.9 The Mitanni empire and its neighbors. Map © Anna Kurvinen and Asko Parpola.

the Proto-Indo-Aryan takeover resulted (as in the PIE takeover of the Tripolye culture; see chapter 6) in the vitalization of the Hurrian power, though we of course reject earlier racist interpretations. It is clear that the new Indo-Aryan-speaking rulers totally adjusted to the local culture, for instance, they communicated with other rulers in the Akkadian language, written in cuneiform by the local scribes.

The Mitanni dynasty introduced a mastery of warfare with horse-drawn chariots, although both the horse and the chariot had come to West Asia (including Anatolia) centuries earlier (Fig. 8.10). At Alalaḫ there is even evidence for the use of horse-drawn chariots in warfare in the seventeenth century BCE, but chariotry did not become a regular component of the West Asian and Egyptian armies before the fifteenth century BCE. That the impetus came from Mitanni is suggested by the associated terminology that spread all over West Asia and Egypt. Thus, the Indo-Aryan elite was denoted after the fifteenth century BCE by the term *maryanni*, which consists of the Indo-Aryan word *márya-* plus the Hurrian derivational suffix *-nni* (the Hurrian plural is *maryannina*). The word also occurs in the Semitized form *maryannu*, plural *maryannūma* (in West Semitic), or *mariyannū*, plural *maryannūtu* (in Akkadian)—the actual spelling in cuneiform varies (for example, *ma-ri-ya-an-nu*). In the Egyptian language the word is *maryana*, spelled in various hieroglyphic texts as *ma-ra-ya-na, m-ra-ya-na,* ma_3*-ra-ya-n*, etc. Everywhere this term denotes a "nobleman" of a high status, close to the local ruler, and in the possession of a war chariot (von Dassow 2008). In the Rigveda, *marya-* means "young man, young warrior, suitor, lover, husband," corresponding to Avestan *mairiia-*, "rascal" (this pejorative sense refers to those who opposed the Zoroastrian religion). The early history of this word is illustrated

FIGURE 8.10 A chariot warrior and a charioteer in battle. Impression of a cylinder seal from Alalaḫ V of early Mitanni rule (*c.* 1525–1460 BCE). After Collon 1987:160, no. 731. Courtesy Dominique Collon.

by the fact that it was borrowed from Proto-Indo-Aryan into the ancestor of a Uralic language, Mari (previously called Cheremiss), a language now spoken by people who live just north of the Mid-Volga in Russia; there *mari* (< **marya-*) means "man, husband" and is now the ethnic name of this people.

The royal archives at El Amarna in Egypt preserved 382 letters of the fourteenth century BCE where the rulers of Egypt, Babylonia, Assyria, Mitanni, Arzawa (to the west of Cilicia), Alašia (Cyprus), and Hatti (the Hittite country) correspond with each other more or less on the basis of equality, addressing each other as "brothers." The great importance attached to the chariot by the kings is evident from the fact that it is, along with horses, regularly included in the stereotyped salutation formula. For example, in a letter from Tušratta, the king of Mitanni, to Nimmureya (i.e., Amenophis III), the king of Egypt (ruled *c.* 1390–1352), the formula is as follows: "For me all goes well. For you may all go well. For your household, for my daughter [the wife of Nimmureya], for the rest of your wives, for your sons, for your chariots, for your horses, for your warriors, for your country, and for whatever else belongs to you, may all go very, very well" (El Amarna 19 = BM 29791, translated Moran 1992:43).

Tušratta also details many *maninnu* necklaces (meant to decorate chariot horses) that he has sent to his son-in-law Nimmureya, the king of Egypt, among many other gifts on the occasion of his wedding to Tušratta's daughter. For instance: "1 *maninnu*-necklace, cut: 37 genuine lapis lazuli stones, 39 (pieces of) gold leaf; the centerpiece a genuine *ḫulalu*-stone mounted on gold" (El Amarna 25, translated Moran 1992:73).

The Akkadian word *maninnu* (with its Akkadian suffix *-nnu*) contained in this text is one of the few Mitanni Indo-Aryan words that have been etymologically identified: it corresponds to Vedic *maṇí-*, "necklace" (Rigveda 1,122,14, *maṇi-grīvá-*, "wearing a *maṇi*-necklace on one's neck"). Some other identified Mitanni Indo-Aryan words are *maganni* = Vedic *maghá-*, "present, gift" (with the Hurrian suffix *-nni*); *martianni* = Vedic *mártiya-*, "man, warrior"; and (with the Akkadian suffix *-nnu*) *mištannu*, "bounty" = Proto-Indo-Aryan **miždha-* > Vedic *mīḍhá-*, "booty." A marriage document from Alalaḫ IV contains Proto-Indo-Aryan *vadūranni*, "bride-price" = Sanskrit **vadhū-rā-*.

The royal archive of the Hittite kings was excavated at Boğazköy (ancient Hattuša) in Turkey in 1906–1907. It included a manual for training chariot horses. (Raulwing 2005 [2006].) The text consists of four cuneiform tablets written in the Hittite language, which are a thirteenth-century copy of a lost original written in the fifteenth century. It contains a training program for the chariot horses stretching over at least 184 days, with some differences in the autumn, winter, and spring: it specifies how many days a given training unit lasts; at what time of the day the exercise is performed (the time frame extending from early morning to midnight); how many rounds in the stadium the horses are made to run; how exactly defined rations of fodder and water are to be given and sometimes withheld; how the horses are kept in the stables, massaged, greased, covered with a blanket, and if necessary fitted with a muzzle; and how they are let out to graze on pasture. The manual opens with the words: "Thus (speaks) Kikkuli (Ki-ik-ku-li), a horse trainer from the country of Mittanni (Mi-it-ta-an-ni)." The term used for "horse trainer" is *aššuššanni* = Indo-Aryan *aśva-śā-ḥ*, "one who tires or exhausts [*śam-*] the horse (during training to use up all its strength)." The text contains some other technical terms in Proto-Indo-Aryan:

va-ša-an-na and Indo-Aryan genitive case *va-ša-an-na-ša-ya*, "racecourse, stadium" = Proto-Indo-Aryan **vaźhana-*, gen. **vaźhanasya* > Sanskrit *vahana-*, gen. *vahanasya*, "the act of driving"

va-ar-ta-an-zi, "to turn" = Indo-Aryan *vart-*, "to turn"

va-ar-ta-an-na, "turn" or "round" (in the following compounds) = Indo-Aryan *vartana-*, "the act of turning; wheel-track, path"; this word is compounded with five numerals:

a-i-ka-va-ar-ta-an-na = Proto-Indo-Aryan **aika-*, "one" > Sanskrit *eka-* (in contrast, "one" was in Proto-Iranian **aiva-*)

ti-e-ra-va-ar-ta-an-na = Indo-Aryan *tri-*, "three"

pa-an-za-va-ar-ta-an-na = Indo-Aryan *pañca-*, "five"

ša-at-ta-va-ar-ta-an-na = Old Indo-Aryan *sapta-* (whence Middle-Indo-Aryan *satta-*), "seven"

na-a-va-ar-ta-an-na and Hittite dative-locative case *na-va-ar-ta-an-ni* (with haplology, i.e., omission of one of two identical *va* syllables in **navavartana-*) = Indo-Aryan *nava-*, "nine"

Cuneiform texts from Mitanni-ruled Nuzi in Syria contain Indo-Aryan color terms connected with horses (with the Akkadian suffix *-nnu*, and, importantly, with the rhotacism **l* > *r* characteristic of the original dialect of the Rigveda, see chapter 12):

paprunnu / *babrunnu* = Vedic Sanskrit *babhrú-*, "brown"

pinkarannu = Vedic Sanskrit *piṅgalá-*, "reddish brown"

parittannu = Vedic Sanskrit *palitá-*, "gray"

"A man of Uniga, son of Kukki," is mentioned as "a maker of an *a-šu-wa-ni-in-ni* chariot" in a tablet from Alalaḫ; the word written as *a-šu-wa-ni* and *aš-wa-ni* (plus the Hurrian suffix *-nni*) almost certainly contains the Indo-Aryan word *aśva-*, "horse."

The Alalaḫ tablet mentions a chariot with six-spoked wheels, where the term for "chariot" is the Hurrian word *aradiyanni*, probably based on Indo-Aryan *rathya-*, "chariot."

The kings of Mitanni bear Indo-Aryan names, although it has not been possible to provide all with an etymology.

Kirta (*Ki-ir-ta*) (father of:)
Šuttarna (*Šu-ut-tar-na*) I (son of Kirta)
Parsatatar (*Par-sa-ta-tar*) (father of Sauštatar)
Saušsatat(t)ar, Sauštatar (*Sa-uš-sa-ta-(at-)tar* in Alalaḫ, *Sa-uš-ta-at-tar* in Nuzi) (son of Parsatatar) ruled *c.* 1450–1425
Artatama (*Ar-ta-ta-a-ma*) (son or descendant of Sauštatar) = Vedic *ṛtá-dhāman-*, "having Law as his abode" (for Arta-, cf. also the Old Persian names in Greek sources, such as Artabazos, Artaphernes)
Šuttarna (*Šu-ut-tar-na*) II
Artaššumara (*Ar-ta-aš-šu-ma-ra*) (son of Šuttarna) = *Ṛta-smara-
Tušratta (*Tu-uš-rat-ta, Tu-iš-e-rat-ta, Tu-uš-e-rat-ta*) (younger son of Šuttarna) = Proto-Indo-Aryan *Tvaišaratha > Vedic *tveṣá-ratha-*, "having a rushing chariot"
Parattarna (*Par-ra-at-tar-na*) I
Šattivaza (*KUR-ti-ú-a(z)-za*) = *Sāti-vāja-, "obtaining booty" (cf. Vedic *vāja-sāti-*, *vājasya sāti-*)

Two previously unexplained royal Mitanni names, Sauštattar and Parsatattar, can be explained, I believe, from the Indo-Aryan terms *savyasthātar* and *prasthātar*, which both denote "chariot-warrior" (Fig. 8.11). Mayrhofer (1974) has mentioned **Su-sthātar-*, "provided with good horse drivers," as the most likely earlier proposal, noting that such a compound would be semantically suitable as the name of a nobleman; the problem is that this compound is not attested in Vedic or Avestan. Mayrhofer has suggested reading Parsatattar as *Puraḥ-sthātar-*, "one who stands in front, leader," attested in Rigveda 8,46,13. As Sauštattar's descendants' names are all connected with Vedic chariotry, I propose **Savya-šthātar-*, "one who stands on the left (in the chariot), chariot-warrior" (as opposed to the charioteer, who stands on the right in the chariot, cf. TB 1,7,9,1 *dvau savyeṣṭha-sārathī*; other parallels in Vedic texts are *savya-ṣṭhā-* in AV 8,8,23, and *savya-ṣṭha-* in ŚB 5,2,4,9; 5,3,1,8; 5,4,3,17–18). Parsatattar could be **Pra-sthātar-*, "chariot-fighter who stands in front." In the Veda, the "adhvaryu-pair" of priests, that is, the Adhvaryu and the Pratiprasthātar, are equated with the two Aśvins, the divine charioteers (Taittirīya-Āraṇyaka 3,3 *aśvinādhvaryū*). These two priests are actually in charge of the *gharma* ritual, in which hot milk is offered to the Aśvins (chapter 11). The word *adhvaryu-* literally means "one connected with the road(s)" and may originally have meant "charioteer," who keeps the chariot on the road. Thus the word *prati-prasthātar-* may originally have denoted the "chariot-warrior who stands in front opposite (to the charioteer)." The unexplained name of Kirta, Sauštattar's father, might

FIGURE 8.11 Impression of the seal of "Sauštattar, son of Parsatattar, King of Mitanni" (*sa-uš-ta-at-tar DUMU par-sata-tar LUGAL ma-i-ta-ni*), from *c.* 1420 BCE, preserved on clay tablets found at Nuzi and at Tell Brak. After Stein 1994:297, fig. 2. Courtesy Diana L. Stein.

stand for **kṛta-*, "praised, famed," from the Indo-Iranian root *kar- carkarti*, "to praise," for Sanskrit grammarians mention *kṛta-* besides *kīrṇa-* as the past participle of the homonymous root *kar-*, "to kill."

The royal archive of the Hittite kings at Boğazköy also contained a peace treaty between the Hittite king Suppiluliuma I and the Mitanni king Šattivaza. This contract, made around 1350 BCE, reduced the Mitanni empire to a vassal kingdom. Four Indo-Aryan deities are asked to be divine witness of the treaty: Mitra (*Mi-it-ra-*), Varuṇa (*A-ru-na-*), Indra (*In-da-ra-*), and the Nāsatya twins (*Na-aš-ša-at-ti-ya-*). After the text has mentioned about a hundred divine witnesses on the Hittite side follow two dozen divine witnesses of the Mitanni king, the Indo-Aryan gods being in the middle. These same deities are mentioned, in the same order, in Rigveda 10,125,1: *aham mitrāvaruṇobhā bibharmy aham indrāgnī aham aśvinobhā*; the only difference is that instead of Indra in the treaty, Indra-and-Agni are mentioned here, and the divine charioteer twins are mentioned by a different name; yet the name Nāsatya, "rescuer, savior" is very commonly used in the Rigveda for the Aśvins (Thieme 1960).

In addition to the Indo-Aryan gods mentioned in this treaty come two further Indo-Aryan deities, the fire-god Agni (*A-ak-ni-iš*), mentioned in Hittite ritual texts, and the sun-god Sūrya (*Šu-ri-ya-áš*), equated with the Akkadian sun-god Šamaš in a glossarial cuneiform tablet from Babylonia during the Kassite rule (*c.* 1570–1155 BCE). The Kassite rulers were a minority elite (like the Indo-Aryans of Mitanni) whose homeland since the eighteenth century BCE seems to have been Luristan in the Zagros Mountains east of Babylonia; their language is without known relatives.

Besides the names of the Mitanni kings, a number of other Proto-Indo-Aryan personal names are known, many of them being *maryanni*. Several names are compounds ending in *atti*, that is, **atthi*, which corresponds to Vedic *atithi*-, "guest." Five names formed with *atithi* as the last part, "having X as his guest," usually with a god's name as the first part, occur in the hymns of the Kāṇva poets of the Rigveda: Medhyātithi, Medhātithi, Nīpātithi, Mitrātithi, and Devātithi.

Aššuratti, Ašuratti = *Asurātthi
Biriyatti, Biryatti = *Priyātthi
Intaratti = Indrātthi
Maryatti = *Maryātthi
Mitaratti = Vedic Mitrātithi, as a proper name in the Rigveda
Šauššatti
Šuwatti, Šuwatiti = *Suvatthi
Šuryatti = Sūryātthi
Paratti = *Prātthi

Other Proto-Indo-Aryan proper names are

Ar-ta-am-na = *Ṛta-mna-, "having the mind of Law" (cf. Vedic *ṛtásya . . . mánas* and the Persian name Artamenēs in Greek sources)
Aššuzzana = *Aśva-canas- (cf. Aspa-canah- as a personal name in Old Persian)
Bi-ri-ya-aš-šu-va = Indo-Aryan *Priyāśva-
Biridašva = *Prītāśva-
Bi-ir-ya-ma-aš-da = Proto-Indo-Aryan *Priya-mazdha- > Vedic Priyá-medha-, as a personal name in the Rigveda
Indaruta (*In-tar-ú-da, En-dar-ú-ta*) = Vedic Indrotá- (= Indra-ūtá-)
Šattavaza = *Sāta-vāja- (cf. Sāti-vāja as the name of a Mitanni king)
Šu-ba-an-du = Vedic Sanskrit Subandhu-, as a personal name in the Rigveda
Zantarmiyašta = Proto-Indo-Aryan *-*miyazdha*- > Vedic -*miyédha*-, "sacrificial meal"
Zitra = Vedic *Citrá*-, 'brilliant, radiant', occurring as a personal name in the Rigveda.

To conclude, the culture and proper names of the Mitanni Indo-Aryans were dominated by the horse and the chariot. Indeed, the Mitanni Indo-Aryans seem to have been the prime motors in the introduction of chariotry into the West Asian warfare around 1500 BCE. This raises the question whether or not Proto-Indo-Aryan speakers were involved in the Hyksos conquest of Lower Egypt and the introduction of chariotry there. The Mitanni rule came to an end in the thirteenth century BCE, by which time there is reason to assume the Proto-Indo-Aryan language had ceased to be spoken in West Asia. Aryan speakers are not mentioned in cuneiform documents until the middle of the ninth century BCE, when the West Iranian-speaking Medians and Persians emerge (see chapter 7). The BMAC settlements in southern Central Asia were for many centuries surrounded by steppe pastoralists, and so Proto-Indo-Aryan, being constantly replenished, could prevail there; but in Syria it was assimilated to local languages, undoubtedly because the Mitanni Indo-Aryans, after their takeover of power, eventually became isolated from their linguistic relatives further east.

Linguistically, Mitanni Indo-Aryan (1500-1300 BCE) represents an older stage of development than Rigvedic Indo-Aryan. Though the available Mitanni vocabulary is very limited, four cases can be cited where the Mitanni word equals the Proto-Indo-Aryan reconstruction, while a subsequent sound change has taken place in the Rigvedic counterpart (Mayrhofer 1966:18–20):

Table 8.1

Sound change	**Mitanni**	**Rigveda**	**Avesta**
ai > e	*aika-*	*eka-*	*aēva- < *aiva*
az > e	*-mazdha-*	*-medha-*	*mazdā-*
źh > h	*vaźhana-*	*vahana-*	*vaz-*
ižd(h) > īḍ(h)	*miždha-*	**miẓḍha- > mīḍha-*	*mižda-*

9

The Rigvedic Indo-Aryans and the Dāsas

When did the Indo-Aryan speakers associated with the Rigvedic hymns move from Central Asia to South Asia? This has been, and continues to be, one of the chief problems of Vedic research and Indian history as a whole. If we ignore the impossible hypothesis that the Vedic Aryans were indigenous to South Asia, and some implausibly ancient dates for their existence, we find that current scholarly estimates for the date of their migration vary between about 2000 and 1000 BCE. Often, comparison is made with the fragments of Mitanni Indo-Aryan discussed in chapter 8 and the immigration is dated at around 1400–1200 BCE. My own approach relies on studying the ethnic and linguistic identity of the people known as Dāsa, Dasyu, and Paṇi, against whom the Rigvedic Aryans were fighting.

First, some basic data about the Rigveda are required. The Rigvedic hymns were collected from the priestly clans, who had composed them, and systematized at the time of the Kuru kingdom around 1000 BCE (see chapter 13). The Rigveda is divided into ten books (1–10) called "circles" (*maṇḍala*). The so-called "family books" (2–7) are each ascribed by later tradition (confirmed by internal indications) to a particular family of poets (*kavi*) or sages (*ṛṣi*). Each family descends from a sage: Gṛtsamada (Book 2), Viśvāmitra (3), Vāmadeva (4), Atri (5), Bharadvāja (6), and Vasiṣṭha (7). Within each book, the hymns are arranged according to three hierarchical criteria: by deity (first Agni, then Indra, then other gods, in the order of the frequency of hymns addressed to them), by meter and by the number of verses in the hymn (in decreasing order).

The family books represent the oldest stratum of the Rigveda. Almost equally old is the next layer of hymns, the second half (hymns 51–191) of Book 1, where the hymns are arranged according to the same principles: first according to their authors (nine poets or families), then gods, meters, and the number of verses. The next addition is Book 8, composed by poets of the Kaṇva (hymns 1–66) and Aṅgiras (hymns 67–103) families. The first half of Book 1 (hymns 1–50), the subsequent addition, is closely connected with Book 8, most of its hymns being ascribed to the Kaṇva and Aṅgiras families; it shares with Book 8 a predilection for tristichs, song units consisting of three verses, and some other characteristics. Book 9 was created by extracting all the hymns addressed to Soma (the deified sacrificial drink) from Books 1–8, for liturgical purposes. Book 10 is by far the most recent addition to the Rigveda, the first half (hymns 1–84) being older than the second (hymns 85–191): the total number of hymns is similar to that of Book 1. Finally, in addition to the Rigveda proper, there are a few "supplementary verses" (*khila*).

The Rigveda mentions names of countries, mountains, and rivers. The river names are especially important as their referents can often be identified with certainty. Particularly prominent is the Indus River, along with its main tributaries, which are intended in the phrase *sapta sindhavaḥ*, "the seven streams," much repeated in the Rigveda. Hymn 75 of Book 10, "In praise of streams," lists all the major rivers of the northwest Indian plains, particularly of the Indus system. In verses 1–4, *Sindhu* (= Indus); in verse 5, *Gaṅgā* (= Ganges), *Yamunā* (= Jumna), *Sarasvatī* (= Sarsuti and Ghaggar-Hakra), *Śutudrī* (= Sutlej), *Paruṣṇī* (= Irāvatī > Ravi), *Marudvṛdhā* with *Asiknī* (= Chenab), *Vitastā* (= Jhelum), and *Ārjīkīyā* with *Suṣomā* (=?Sohan); and in verse 6, the western tributaries of the Indus are listed as *Tṛṣṭāmā, Susartu, Rasā, Śvetyā, Kubhā* (= Kabul), *Gomatī* (= Gomal), *Krumu* (= Kurum, Kurram), and *Mehatnū*. *Suvāstu* (= Swat) is missing from this list, but is mentioned in RV 8,19,37; it may be one of the listed but unidentified western tributaries of the Indus. The geographical names connect the Rigveda mostly with the northwest and the Punjab, whereas eastern references occur rarely in the Rigveda (Gaṅgā only here, in 10,75,5; Yamunā also in 5,52,17 and 7,18,19). This is in contrast with later Vedic literature, where the geographical horizon widens eastwards and southwards.

It seems that several other names of rivers (or river systems) have, or had, referents in Central Asia, Afghanistan, and Baluchistan; and that some of these names were transferred to the Indian subcontinent by early Rigvedic immigrants. They include:

- *Rasā* (= Avestan *Raŋhā* =?Oxus / Amu Darya; *Rasā* becoming **Rahā* in Iranian is the most likely source for *Rhā*, which Ammianus Marcellinus has recorded as the ancient name of the Volga, one of the main rivers of the assumed Indo-Iranian homeland) (see chapter 7);
- *Sarayū* (=?Avestan *Haroiva*, "name of a country" = Old Persian *Haraiva*, "province of the Persian empire," *Aria*, "Ariana" = the Herat province of Afghanistan);
- *Sarasvatī* (= Avestan *Harax*^{v}*aiti*, "name of a country" = Old Persian *Hara*^{h}*uvati*, "province of the Persian empire, Arachosia" = the Kandahar province of Afghanistan, named after its principal river, present-day Arghandab + Helmand; later Sarsuti and Ghaggar-Hakra in India);
- *Yavyavatī* (=?Zhob in northern Baluchistan);
- *Bhalāna*, "name of a tribe" (= ?Bolan River in Baluchistan).

The Rigveda mentions by name some thirty Aryan tribes and clans. A term meaning "five peoples" is used throughout the Rigveda to refer to the major tribes, of which four are regularly paired: Yadu with Turvaśa, Anu with Druhyu. These four tribes seem to have been among the first wave of Indo-Aryan-speaking immigrants to the northwest of the subcontinent from Afghanistan. A fifth tribe, Pūru, together with its ally or subtribe Bharata, appears to have arrived later, again from Afghanistan, overpowering the earlier tribes. The principal agents in the Rigvedic hymns are Bharata and Pūru dynasties of three to five generations (Bharata: Atithigva > Divodāsa > Sudās; Pūru: Girikṣit > Purukutsa > Trasadasyu > Tṛkṣi), so the family books seem to reflect their times. The latest Bharata or Pūru king mentioned in Books 2–7 is Trasadasyu's son, Tṛkṣi, so probably the family books were collected fairly soon after his reign (Witzel 1995a,b).

The Pūru king Purukutsa and the Bharata king Divodāsa seem to have led this immigration over the Hindukush mountains to the Indus Valley. In the celebrated "battle of ten kings" (Book 7, hymns 18, 33, and 83) on the river Paruṣṇī (modern Ravi), the Bharata king Sudās, son or grandson of Divodāsa, defeated the Pūru king (probably Trasadasyu, the son of Purukutsa) and his many allies, becoming the ruler of the Punjab. The first Kuru king mentioned in the Rigveda is Kuruśravaṇa, a descendant of Trasadasyu, suggesting that the Pūrus moved to the area later called Kurukṣetra (the Kuru kings are discussed in chapter 13). Alexander the Great defeated King Pōros, whose Middle Indo-Aryan name Pora comes from Sanskrit Paurava, "descendant of Pūru"; his realm lay between the Jhelum and Ravi rivers.

Indra and his protégés, particularly kings Divodāsa and Purukutsa, are said to have vanquished "black-skinned" enemies called Dāsa, Dasyu, and Paṇi, who neither worshipped Indra nor sacrificed *soma* but had their own observances (*vrata*) and were rich in cattle. Indra and Agni helped the Aryans to destroy the numerous enemy strongholds, in particular those of Dāsa Śambara situated among mountains. Though human foes are undoubtedly meant, many of these enemies are presented as demons. The following anthology of verses about the Dāsas and Dasyus, taken from a new translation of the entire Rigveda by Stephanie Jamison and Joel Brereton (2014), will give the reader some idea of the evidence for the hostile nature of these peoples.

1,51,5 With your wiles you blew away the wily ones, who, according to their own customs, poured (their offering) "on the shoulder."
You broke through the strongholds of Pipru, O you of manly mind; you helped Ṛjiśvan through in the smashing of Dasyus.
6 You helped Kutsa in the smashing of Śuṣṇa, and you made Śambara subject to Atithigva.
With your foot you trampled down Arbuda, though he was great. Indeed, from long ago you were born to smash Dasyus.
8 Distinguish between the Āryas and those who are Dasyus. Chastising those who follow no commandment, make them subject to the man who provides ritual grass.
Become the potent inciter of the sacrificer. I take pleasure in all these (deeds) of yours at our joint revelries.

1,103,3 He who by nature provides support, being trusted for his power, roved widely, splitting apart the Dāsa strongholds.
As knowing one, O possessor of the mace, cast your missile at the Dasyu; strengthen Ārya might and brilliance, O Indra.

2,12,4 By whom all these exploits have been done: who has put the Dāsa tribe below and hidden away,
who has taken the riches of the stranger, as a winning gambling champion does the wager—he, O peoples, is Indra.
10 Who has struck with his arrow those constantly creating for themselves great guilt, the unthinking ones;
who does not concede arrogance to the arrogant man; who is the smasher of the Dasyu—he, O peoples, is Indra.
11 Who in the fortieth autumn discovered Śambara dwelling in the mountains;
who smashed the serpent displaying its strength, the son of Dānu, (thereby) lying (dead)—he, O peoples, is Indra.

2,20, 6 The god famed as Indra by name, he the most wondrous, rose upright for Manu.
The able, independent one carried away the Dāsa Arśasāna's very own head.
7 Smasher of Vṛtra, splitter of fortresses, Indra razed the Dāsa (fortresses) with their dark wombs.
He gave birth to the earth and the waters for Manu. In every way, he makes the sacrificer's laud powerful.

4,16,10 Drive here to the home (of Uśanā Kāvya) with your Dasyu-smashing mind. In companionship with you, Kutsa will become eager.
Do you two, having the same form, sit down each in his own womb. She is trying to distinguish between you two—she is a woman who distinguishes the truth.
12 For Kutsa you laid low insatiable Śuṣṇa, who brings bad harvest, with his thousands, before the day's first meal.
Immediately crush out the Dasyus with (the weapon) that is Kutsa, and then tear off the wheel of the Sun at the moment of encounter.
13 You subjugated Pipru Mṛgaya, swollen with power, to Ṛjiśvan, the son of Vidathin.
You scattered down the dark fifty thousand. You shredded their fortresses, like worn-out age a cloak—

5,34,6 Very energetic in the clash, affixing the wheel (to the chariot?), he is antagonistic to the non-presser, but strengthener of the presser.
Indra is the dominator of all, spreading fear; the Ārya leads the Dāsa as he wishes.

6,20,10 Might we win anew through your help, Indra. The Pūrus start up the praise with this (hymn) along with sacrifices.
When he split the seven autumnal strongholds, their shelter, he smote the Dāsa (clans), doing his best for Purukutsa.

6,26,5 You made that hymn (endowed) with might, Indra, so that you could tear out hundreds and thousands (of goods), o champion.
You struck the Dāsa Śambara down from the mountain and furthered Divodāsa with glittering help.

6,47,21 Day after day he drove off from their seat the other half, the black kindred all of the same appearance.
The bull smashed the two Dāsas, mercenaries, Varcin and Śambara, at the moated place.

7,6,3 Down with those of no intelligence, those tying in knots, those of disdainful words: the Paṇis, not giving hospitality, not giving strength, not giving sacrifices.
Onward and onward Agni has pursued those Dasyus. The first has made the last to be without sacrifices.

7,19,2 Just you, O Indra, helped Kutsa, while seeking fame for yourself with your own body in the clash,
when for him you weakened the Dāsa Śuṣṇa bringing bad harvest, doing your best for Arjuna's offspring.
4 You—whose mind is inclined towards men in their pursuit of the gods—along with men you smash many obstacles, you of the fallow bays;
you put to sleep the Dasyu Cumuri and Dhuni, easy to smash, for Dabhīti.
5 Yours are these exploits, you with the mace in hand—that nine and ninety fortifications at once
along with the hundredth you worked to the end, in bringing them to rest [= collapse]. You smashed Vṛtra, and moreover Namuci you smashed.

8,70,10 You are the one who seeks the truth for us, Indra. You find no satisfaction in him who reviles you.
Gird yourself in between your thighs, O you of mighty manliness. Jab down the Dāsa with your blows.
11 The man who follows other commandments, who is no son of Manu, no sacrificer, no devotee of the gods—
him should your own comrade, the mountain, send tumbling down; the mountain (should send down) the Dasyu for easy smiting.

10,22,8 The Dasyu of non-deeds, of non-thought, the non-man whose commandments are other, is against us.
You smasher of non-allies, humble the weapon of this Dāsa.

10,138,3 The sun unhitched his chariot in the middle of heaven. The Ārya found a match for the Dāsa.
The firm fortifications of the crafty lord Pipru did Indra throw open, having acted together with Ṛjiśvan.
4 Defiant, he threw open the undefiable (fortifications); the unbridled one pulverized the ungodly treasure-houses.
Like the sun with the moon, he took for his own the goods found in the fortress. Being sung, he shattered his rivals with his flashing (weapon).

When Mortimer Wheeler exposed the mighty walls of Harappa in 1946, he identified the fortified Indus cities with the forts of the Dāsas broken up by Indra and the Aryan kings, according to the Rigveda (Wheeler 1947). However, as Wilhelm Rau (1976) pointed out in his examination of the Rigvedic descriptions, the Dāsa forts are described as having many concentric and circular walls—which do not match the layout of the Indus cities. In 1988, I spotted an archaeological counterpart to this description of the Dāsa forts in the so-called "temple-fort" of the BMAC in Dashly-3, excavated in the 1970s in northern Afghanistan (Sarianidi 1977): it has three concentric circular walls (Fig. 20.3a). This suggested to me that the major fights between the Aryans and the Dāsas probably took place not in the Indus Valley but in the Indo-Iranian borderlands, en route to the Indus Valley. Dashly-3 is dated to about 1900 BCE and therefore belongs to the Proto-Indo-Aryan phase of the BMAC. However, the tradition of building such fortresses with three concentric walls continued in Afghanistan until historical times, as is shown by the Achaemenid fort of Kutlug Tepe in Bactria (Fig. 20.3b).

There are in the Rigveda as many as twenty-four references to a Dāsa called Śambara. The Aryan king Divodāsa Atithigva, Indra's protégé, is said to have vanquished Śambara in the fortieth autumn, breaking his ninety-nine fortifications. The descriptions of the fights between Śambara and Divodāsa are the most realistic, and apparently the oldest, in Book 6; it has been suggested that the enmity between the Dāsas and Aryans was at its greatest in the period represented by Book 6, which contains several indications that its poems refer to places near to or west of the Hindukush. The repeated references to (great) mountains as Śambara's habitat are a significant pointer to the geographical location of the Dāsa forts, ruling out the Indus Valley.

A second important pointer appears in RV 6,61,1–3. Here the mighty River Sarasvatī is said to have given the powerful Divodāsa as a son to Vadhryaśva, who worshipped Sarasvatī with offerings. It is most likely that Divodāsa, the son of Vadhryaśva, is the same person as Divodāsa Atithigva, and that it was his son, or more likely his grandson, Sudās, who fought the famous battle of ten kings in the Punjab, in which both Aryans and Dāsas participated. The description of Sarasvatī in RV 6,61,2 does not at all fit the sacred stream Sarasvatī in India (both the Sarsuti and the Ghaggar, with which it is identified, descend from the low Siwalik Mountains): "By means of her gushing and powerful waves, this (Sarasvatī) has crushed the ridge of the mountains, (breaking river banks) like a man who digs for lotus roots; with praises and prayers, we solicit Sarasvatī for her help, (Sarasvatī) who slays the foreigners." It is widely accepted that the Sarasvatī mentioned here is the river that gave the name Harax^{v}aitī- (in Avestan) or Hara^{h}uvati- (in Old Persian) or Arachosia (in Greek) to the province of the Persian empire in southeastern Afghanistan that is chiefly watered by this river. It is generally identified with the Arghandab that descends from a height of nearly four kilometers down to about 700 meters, when it joins the Helmand River, which eventually forms shallow lakes; and the name Sarasvatī means "(river) having ponds or lakes." The Helmand's present Pashto name comes from Avestan Haētumant-, "having dams." In the dry season the Arghandab, too, may become a series of lakes.

In RV 6,61,3, the Sarasvatī is asked to throw down the *deva* revilers, the descendants of "every Bṛsaya." In Alexander the Great's time, the satrap of Arachosia and Drangiana (Seistan) was a man called Barsaéntēs (Arrian, *Anabasis* 3,8,3; 3,21,1), a name that resembles Bṛsaya. The latter appears to have been a hereditary royal title, as suggested by the expression "every Bṛsaya." By way of comparison, every king of Taxila was called Taxiles, according to Q. Curtius Rufus (8,12,14), and Pōros, the name of the king whom Alexander the Great defeated in the Punjab, is clearly a dynastic title, meaning "descendant of Pūru." Bṛsaya has features (*b-* and *-ṛs-*) suggesting that it may come from the original language of the BMAC (see chapter 8).

Now I return to the Rigveda's repeated references to Śambara's mountainous domicile. If Divodāsa was born in Arachosia and his son or grandson Sudās fought in the Punjab, Divodāsa is likely to have crossed the Afghan highlands roughly from Kandahar to Kabul and from there entered Swat. The highest mountains are in the northern part of this itinerary, in Waziristan, now well known as one of the principal bases of today's Taliban insurgents.

This very region where Divodāsa may have fought against the Dāsa is the only area of modern-day Afghanistan where the habitations consist of large traditional farm compounds surrounded by massive walls of kneaded mud and provided with defense towers. These fortified manors are presently inhabited by Pashto-speaking farmers and called *qala*, "fortress" (Figs. 9.1, 9.2).

There is an evident similarity between these present-day *qalas* and their possible Bronze Age predecessors, the fortified manors of the BMAC (Fig. 8.1). The BMAC-type "*qala*" architecture started in Margiana around 2300 BCE, spread to Bactria about 1900 BCE and was continued in the "post-urban" Takhirbaj period (*c.* 1750–1500). It is important to note that the BMAC-type citadels and manors survived until the Yaz I–related cultures of the Early Iron Age, for instance at Tillya Tepe in northern Afghanistan (Fig. 9.3), and indeed until medieval and modern times. "Massive exterior walls made of mud brick are typical of the later (Parthian, Sasanian, and medieval) architecture of the Margiana oasis . . . and can be used as an analogy for the deflated remains of the massive exterior walls in Bronze Age Margiana to suggest that these walls functioned both for defence and for insulation against summer heat and winter sandstorms" (Hiebert 1994:115).

According to the Zoroastrian text Vīdēvdād (2,21–43), Ahura Mazda ordered the first Aryan/Iranian king Yima to build a fortress (*vara-*), "long as a riding ground on every side of the square" in the "Aryan expanse" (*airyānəm vaējō*), which contained plenty of grass for cattle but offered no shelter during the long winter. The text describes the method of construction, which also matches that of the current Afghan *qala* with its thick *pakhsa* walls: Yima had to crush earth and knead it with his fingers, as the potter kneads clay, to build the *vara*, establishing there "dwelling places, consisting of a house with a balcony, a courtyard, and a gallery," and then stock it with an inexhaustible supply of seeds.

Michael Witzel (2000) has discussed the old problem of locating this "home of the Aryans" [i.e., early East Iranians], where Yima built his fort, on the basis of the climatic conditions and geographical distribution of the various Iranian tribes mentioned in the first chapter of the Vīdēvdād. The highlands of Afghanistan lie in the center of the places mentioned, even though the precise identification of many geographical references remains hypothetical. Witzel's proposal of locating the homeland in Afghanistan is supported by the transhumance that for thousands of years has brought together nomadic tribes in the highlands of Afghanistan from all directions to utilize fresh pastures during the summer months. In addition to grazing their animals, the tribes use this time for celebrating marriages.

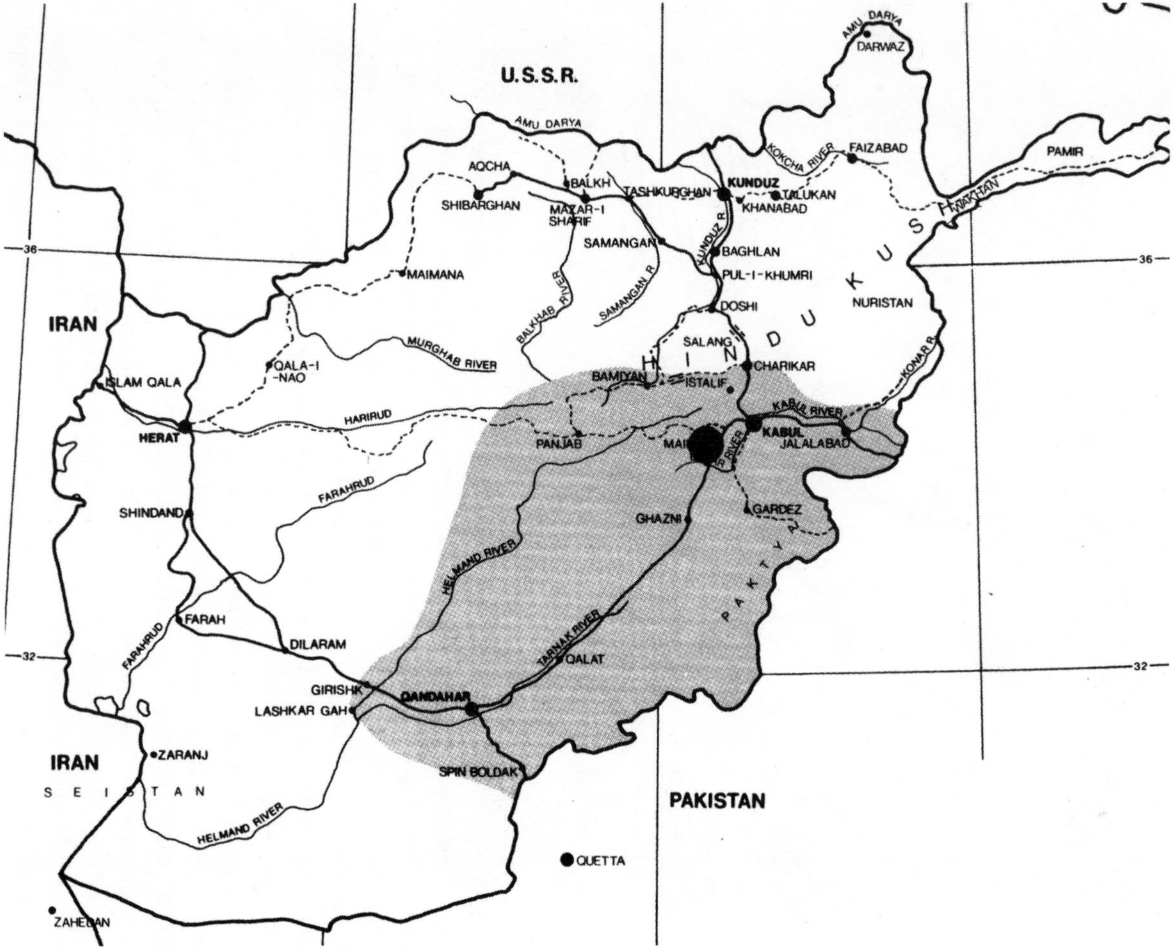

FIGURE 9.1 Distribution of the fortified manors with massive *pakhsa* walls in eastern Afghanistan. After Szabo & Barfield 1991:140. Courtesy Thomas J. Barfield.

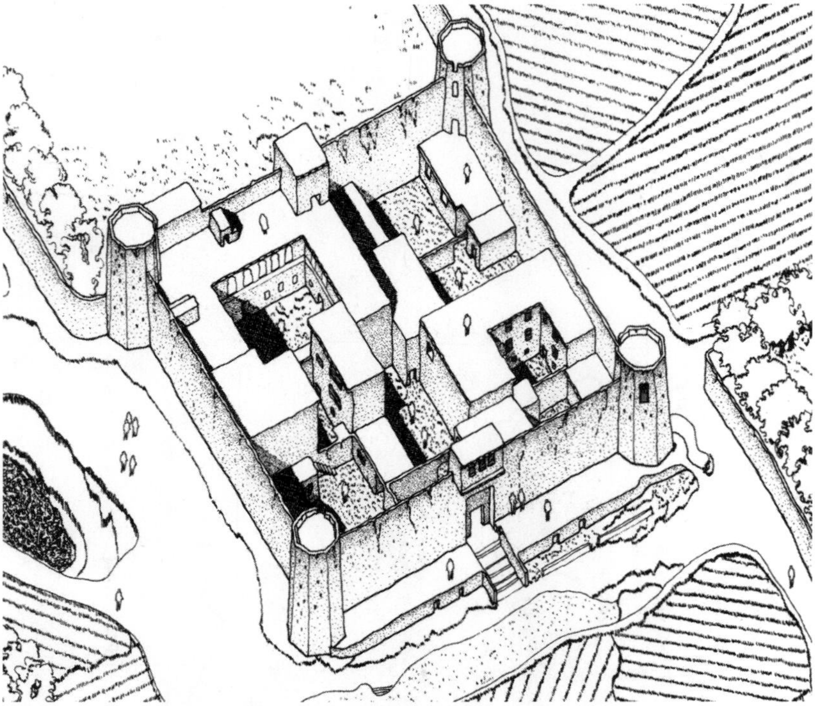

FIGURE 9.2 A fortified manor (*qala*) of eastern Afghanistan. After Szabo & Barfield 1991:188. Courtesy Thomas J. Barfield.

In the Rigveda, *dāsá-* normally appears to mean "member of an enemy tribe" or "enemy demon." These meanings are implicated in the corresponding adjective or derived noun *dā́sa-*, which in classical Sanskrit (as *dāsa-*) means "slave"; this meaning occurs four times in the Rigveda. We may note many historical parallels in which the name of a people captured in war comes to mean "slave," for instance, Finnish *orja*, "slave," derived from *ārya-*, "Aryan," and also English *slave*, which derives via French *esclave* and late Latin *sclavus* from Byzantine Greek *esklabēnós*, "Slav taken as war-captive, slave."

In Iranian languages, Proto-Iranian **s* became *h* before a following vowel at a relatively late period, perhaps around 850–600 BCE. Old Persian *Ūǰa-* < **Hūža-* "(the country of) Elam" (which corresponds to Parthian *Xūzestān*, "Elam") is supposed to have come from the Elamite name of the city of Susa, **Sūša(n)*, and since the Persians could not have been in contact with the Elamites before the ninth century BCE, the sound law **s* > *h* is supposed to have been operating at the time when the Persians came to Elam. Another piece of evidence for a relatively late date is a Neo-Assyrian cuneiform tablet from the library of Assurbanipal (*c.* 668–630 BCE) that records a god's name, *ᵈAs-sa-ra ᵈMa-za-áš*; this may render Median **Asura-Mazdās*, where the change *Asura-* > *Ahura-* had not yet taken place. (It has been argued, though, that this Neo-Assyrian tablet might be a copy of a Middle Assyrian text from the second millennium BCE; Hintze 1998; Schmitt 2000.)

Sanskrit *Dāsa-* as an ethnic name thus has an exact counterpart in Avestan *Dåŋha-*, which stands for **Dāha-*. The corresponding Old Persian ethnic name is *Daha-*. The plural

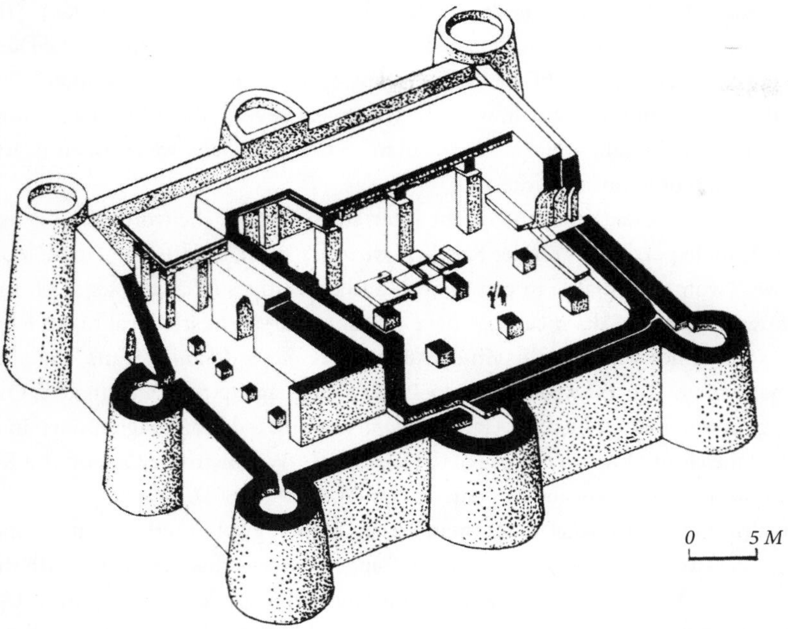

FIGURE 9.3 The fort of Tillya Tepe in eastern Afghanistan, *c.* 1500–1000 BCE. After Sarianidi 1989:19, fig. 5:1. Courtesy Margiana Archaeological Expedition.

form *Dahā* is included among the subjects of the Great King in the "empire list" of Xerxes, immediately before the two kinds of *Sakā*. Herodotus (1,125) includes the *Dáai* / *Dáoi* (intervocalic *h* is omitted in Greek) among the nomadic tribes of the Persians. According to Q. Curtius Rufus (8,3), the *Dahae* lived on the lower course of the river Margus (modern Murghab) in Margiana, where they are also located in Ptolemy's *Geography* (6,10,2). Eratosthenes, quoted by Pomponius Mela (3,42), notes that the great bend of the Oxus towards the northwest begins near the *Dahae*. Tacitus (*Annales* 11,10) places the *Dahae* on the border river (Sindes, modern Tejend) between Areia and Margiana.

The same Rigvedic verse which mentions Divodāsa's birth as a gift of the Sarasvatī (of Arachosia), RV 6,61,1, also says that the river took away from the (enemy) Paṇi his nourishment (pasture or cattle). The Paṇis are often mentioned as enemies of Rigvedic kings, sometimes along with the Dāsas and Dasyus, and in very similar terms. *Paṇí* is supposed to be a Prakritic development of **Pṛṇi*, a reduced-grade variant of an ethnic name that has a full grade in *Parṇáya*, the name of an enemy of King (Divodāsa) Atithigva in RV 1,53,8 and 10,48,8. Strabo (11,9,2) describes the foundation of the Parthian empire of the Arsacids around 240 BCE as follows: "Arsakēs, a Scythian man, who had (in his command) some men of the *Dāai*, namely nomads called *Párnoi*, who were living along the River Okhos (modern Tejend), invaded Parthia and conquered it."

A Roman author characterized the Parthian language as being between Median and Scythian (i.e., Saka) and as a mixture of both tongues (Iustinus 41,2,3: "sermo his inter Scythicum Medicumque medius et utrimque mixtus"). A number of words in Parthian have been identified as phonetically and lexically East Iranian and ascribed to the language of these Parna people belonging to the Dahae, who therefore apparently spoke Saka.

According to RV 6,21,11, gods "made Mánu superior/successor to Dása." This is the only occurrence of the word *dása-* in Sanskrit; it may denote the ancestor of the Dāsas, while Mánu is the mythical ancestor of the Vedic Aryans. Sanskrit *mánu-* means "man." *Dasa-* is the original Proto-Iranian form which, with the (relatively late, cf. above) Iranian sound change **s > h*, became in Khotanese Saka *daha-*, "man." Khotanese Saka was spoken in Khotan, in western Sinkiang or Chinese Turkestan.

In Khotanese Saka there is no doubt about the meaning. The word *daha-* is used in the sense "man, male person" to render Sanskrit *puruṣa-*, "man," and *nara-*, "man," contrasting with *strīyā-*, "woman, female"; in compounds and derivatives it has the sense of "manliness, virility, bravery." These Saka meanings have a counterpart in nearby Wakhi, an East Iranian language spoken nowadays in the Hindukush, where *δay* < **daha-* means "man, male person, human being." The only further Indo-Iranian language to have a cognate is Ossetic, for Ossetic *läg*, "man," may go back to Alanian **dahaka-*. This Saka language spoken in northern Caucasus is the closest known relative of the Khotanese-Wakhi group: Ossetic and Khotanese Saka share some seventy vocabulary entries (Bailey 1959 [1960]).

It is clear that Proto-Saka **dasa*, "man," is the etymology of the ethnic name which in Old Persian appears as *Daha-*, for many ethnic self-appellations go back to words with this meaning; for instance the native ethnic name of the *Mari*, who speak a Uralic (Finno-Ugric) language, goes back to Proto-Indo-Aryan **marya-*, "man" (literally "one who has to die, mortal").

It is true that **dasa- / *dāsa-* and **dasyu-* have a limited distribution in Indo-Iranian. "There are several suggestions for an Indo-European etymology, but they are all doubtful," observed Alexander Lubotsky (2001:313). I shall not go into these earlier etymologies here, but repeat only my own observation (Parpola 2002b). These words could go back to the PIE root **dens-*, "to be(come) clever or wise," if the accent was originally on the derivative suffix (**-á-* and **-yú-*), as in Vedic *das-rá-* (< **dn̥s-ró-*), "clever, skillful," which occurs especially as an epithet of the wonder-working Aśvins. In the Rigveda, the Aśvins are called *dasrā́* nine times, *dásrā* nine times, and *dásrau* four times, with the variation in accent attested in a single standing formula (*dasrā́ híraṇyavartanī* in RV 1,92,18b, *dásrā híraṇyavartanī* in RV 5,75,2c, RV 8,5,11b, RV 8,8,1c, and RV 8,87,5c). Therefore, the accent in the unique RV VI,21,11 *dása-*, instead of the expected **dasá-*, is no obstacle to this etymology. For *dásyu-* instead of the expected **dasyú-*, one may compare RV 7,18,5c *śimyú-* against RV 1,100,18a *śímyu-*, this being likewise a name of an enemy people.

Semantically it makes good sense to derive a word meaning "man" from a root expressing cleverness and skillfulness. One can compare the possible derivation of Sanskrit *mánu-*, "man," from the root *man-* < PIE **men-*, "to think." An even closer parallel is the ethnic name Śaka-, which is most likely derived from the root *śak-*, "to be able, powerful, skillful" (the Rigveda has *su-śáka-*, "well able," as an epithet of "men"; one may also compare the use of *śak-rá-*, "strong, mighty," as an attribute and later as a proper name of god Indra; the synonymous *ugrá-*, "strong, mighty," is used as an ethnic name). In Iranian the root *sak-* means "to understand, to know," which makes Śaka < *śak-* an even closer parallel to Dasa- < PIE **dens-*.

The royal inscriptions of Darius contain five versions of the "empire list" enumerating the countries known to be subjects of the Great King; in addition there is one version by Xerxes. The two shortest lists of Darius (from the Behistun and Susa foundation charters) contain twenty-three names, in which the eleven last ones relate to the eastern part of the empire: Parthia, Drangiana, Aria, Chorasmia, Bactria, Sogdiana, Gandhara, Saka, Sattagydia, Arachosia, and Makran or Quadia. The list of twenty-four names from Persepolis adds Indus (after Arachosia and before Gandhara and Saka). In the lists of twenty-seven and twenty-nine countries, after Gandhara and Indus follow the Sakas now divided into two varieties, *Sakā haumavargā*, "Sakas with hauma cult," and *Sakā tigraxaudā*, "Sakas wearing pointed caps." In the list of Xerxes, the thirty-one (or thirty) names are in a rather haphazard order in the following sequence (Cappadocia being out of place): Gandhara, Indus, Cappadocia, Dahae, Sakā Haumavargā, and Sakā Tigraxaudā. Here the Dahae figure for the first time in Old Persian.

Herodotus (7,64), describing the army of Xerxes, lumps the two kinds of Saka together: "The Sacae, or Skyths, were clad in trousers, and had on their heads tall stiff caps rising to a point. They bore the bow of their country and the dagger: besides which they carried the battle-axe, or *sagaris*. They were in truth Amyrgian Scythians, but the Persians called them Sacae, since that is the name they give to all Scythians" (translated Rawlinson [1860] 1942:524). The Amyrgian Scythians are considered to correspond to *Sakā haumavargā*. *Hauma* is Avestan *haoma*, the Iranian counterpart of Sanskrit *soma*, Indra's sacred drink.

The Khotanese and the Wakhis are considered descendants of the Scythian tribes of eastern central Asia, probably the Scythians with pointed caps. It seems to me that the Khotanese Saka and the Wakhis originally called themselves Dasa/Dāsa, and that this ethnic name, although Dahae were added as a separate people by Xerxes, may in fact be coterminous with *Sakā tigraxaudā*. The following evidence suggests that the immigrants to southern Central Asia associated with the Yaz I and related cultures (*c.* 1500–1000 BC) were horsemen and that they wore pointed caps.

There are only two places in the Rigveda (1,162,17 and 5,61,2–3) that clearly refer to riding; in four other verses the reference is dubious (Falk 1994). Compared to the prominence of the horse chariot (a creation of the Proto-Indo-Aryans of the Sintashta culture), horse-riding played a very marginal role among the Rigvedic Aryans. But they knew of it, which suggests the presence of mounted horsemen in their neighborhood. Among animal remains, there is a very significant increase in the numbers of horse (7–18 percent) in the Early Iron Age of southern Central Asia compared to the immediately preceding Late BMAC (Takhirbaj) period (only 2.6 percent). There is one Late BMAC cylinder seal depicting a horse-rider (Fig. 9.4). From the first two periods (*c.* 1750–1300 and 1300–1100 BCE) of Pirak in Baluchistan near the Bolan Pass come terracotta figurines of horse-riders, with bowed legs to fit them on the back of the horse, armless torsos and heads with faces ending in a bird-like beak (Fig. 9.5). I detect a striking resemblance to the rider's bird-head in the pointed felt caps topped by beaked bird heads that have survived in frozen tombs of mounted Saka nomads in the Altai Mountains, dated to *c.* 500–200 BCE (Fig. 9.6).

That the Early Iron Age cultures of southern Central Asia related to Yaz I (Fig. 9.7) are linked to Iranian-speakers is suggested by the fact that so far no graves have been found in this vast area from about 1500 BCE to Hellenistic times (Teufer 2013). This absence of graves points to the practice of exposure burial, which is associated with the Zoroastrian religion. Burials are not permitted for the Zoroastrians, because they would defile earth, which is one of Ahura Mazdā's creations.

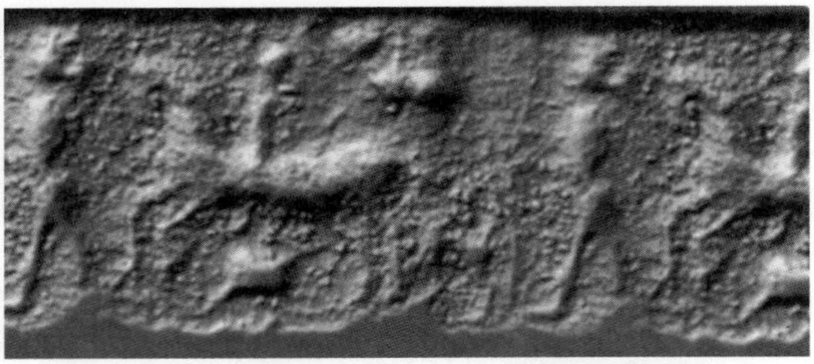

FIGURE 9.4 A BMAC cylinder seal from tombs looted in Afghanistan around 1985, showing a horse-rider. Probably sixteenth century BCE. After Sarianidi 1998b:169, no. 1482. Courtesy Margiana Archaeological Expedition.

FIGURE 9.5 A clay figurine of a bird-headed horse-rider from Pirak, Pakistani Baluchistan, *c.* 1500 BCE. After Jarrige 1985:245. Courtesy Mission Archéologique de l'Indus, CNRS/Musée Guimet, Paris.

FIGURE 9.6 Pointed felt caps topped by a bird head, belonging to Saka mounted nomads, from frozen tombs in the Altai Mountains. After Polos'mak 2001:124, fig. 21. Courtesy Nataliya V. Polos'mak.

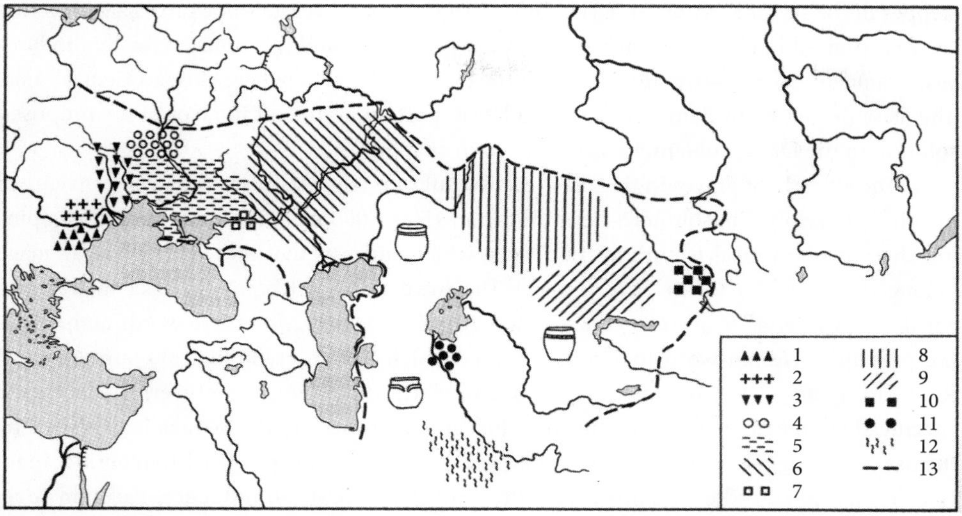

FIGURE 9.7 The distribution of the "Roller Pottery" cultures, among them the late Srubnaya cultures (6), the Sargary culture (8), and the Yaz I culture (12). After Chernykh 1992: 236, fig. 79. Courtesy E. N. Chernykh and Cambridge University Press.

Important linguistic evidence supporting the identification of the Dāsas as Proto-Sakas is provided by the Nuristani languages spoken in northeastern Afghanistan. The Nuristani languages are unique in their preservation, in etymologically correct words, of the sounds called dental affricates (*ts, dz, dz*) that have been reconstructed for Proto-Iranian, but which have developed further and differently in Avestan (*s, z, z*) and Old Persian (*th, d, d*); these Proto-Iranian sounds are the expected developments of Proto-Indo-Iranian palatal affricates (*ć, j, jh*) from PIE palatal stops (*ḱ, ǵ, ǵh*), the Iranian development being different from Proto-Indo-Aryan (*ś, j, h*). If the ancestors of the Nuristani speakers belonged to the very first Iranians in Central Asia, and became isolated from other Aryan speakers early on, they could well have preserved this very archaic stage of phonological development. The exact affiliation of the Nuristani languages is an old problem, but Almuth Degener (2002) has suggested a plausible solution: the Nuristani languages are likely to be a mixture of the Proto-Indo-Aryan spoken in the BMAC and the Proto-Iranian that came to southern Central Asia with the Yaz I-related cultures.

Some of the Dāsa proper names, in particular Balbūtha Tarukṣa (RV 8,46,32), Bṛsaya (RV 1,93,4; 6,61,3), Bṛbu (RV 6,45,31 and 33), and Sṛbinda (RV 8,32,2), seem to come from the original, pre-Aryan language of the BMAC (chapter 8), suggesting that its speakers had survived the Proto-Indo-Aryan rule (*c.* 2000–1500 BCE) and were now part of the Saka community of the Dāsas, Dasyus, and Paṇis. While there are several Aryan-looking Dāsa names, it is important to note that there is an elite proper name that is undoubtedly of Saka affinity. In RV 8,46,21 and 24 a chief called Pṛthuśravas, "widely famed," is praised as having presented to the poet 60,000 horses, 2,000 camels, 1000 dark brown mares, 10,000 cows, and a golden chariot. This liberal sponsor has the patronym *Kānītá*, which has been compared, no doubt correctly, to the Scythian personal names *Kanī́tēs* and *Kánitos* recorded in the Pontic steppes in the second century BCE (Hoffmann 1940:142). Dāsa Balbūtha Tarukṣa mentioned above is praised in the same hymn for a similar generosity, and it is noteworthy that in both cases camels are given—an indication that the location lies somewhere close to Central Asia. The Dāsa proper name Śambara is yet another important argument in favor of my proposed solution to the Dāsa problem, to be discussed in chapter 20.

The absence of graves in the Yaz I–related cultures suggests that Proto-Zoroastrianism may have developed in southern Central Asia in 1500–1000 BCE (Teufer 2013). In my opinion there is one lexical feature in the Avesta which suggests that its Old Iranian language belonged specifically to the Saka branch. The word used in Khotanese Saka to translate Sanskrit *deva*, "god," is *gyasta-*, *jasta-*, and in Tumshuq Saka *jezda-*; these words come from the principal Avestan word for "god," *yazata-*, which has an etymological counterpart in Rigvedic *yajata-*, "worthy of worship or sacrifice" (in the Rigveda, however, it is not used specifically to mean "god"). That this word for "god" goes back to Proto-Saka is suggested by the use of the cognate word *zäd* or *izäg* for "god" in Ossetic in the pre-Christian period: there is no reason to consider that this usage is due to any Zoroastrian influence. Parthian *yazd*, "god," besides *bg-*, "god," may also go back to the Saka language of the Dahae. By contrast, in Sogdian Buddhist texts *deva-* is translated with βγ- from *baga-*, which denotes "god" in Old Persian, with cognates in most Iranian languages, but is rare in the Avesta. That *baga*, "god," comes from a dialect of Proto-Iranian which originally had a more western location than Proto-Saka is suggested by its semantic borrowing into Old Slavic *bogŭ*, "god."

The religion of the early Iranians of the Saka branch coming to Central Asia around 1500 BCE must surely have been much influenced by the Proto-Indo-Aryan religion prevailing there during their arrival. This question, among others, will be considered in the next chapter. What this chapter has endeavored to show is that my ethnic and linguistic identification of the Dāsas, Dasyus, and Paṇis of the Rigveda with the Yaz I–related cultures has provided a new and forceful argument that the migration of the Rigvedic tribes of Pūru and Bharata into northwestern South Asia in all likelihood took place *c.* 1400–1200 BCE. This agrees with the estimated date most often proposed by others.

10

The Aśvins and Mitra-Varuṇa

The Rigvedic hymns are addressed to gods, whom they praise, whom they invite to a sacrificial meal and to whom they pray for long life, sons, cattle, victory in battle, or fame. The central myths are repeated over and over, but the Rigveda abounds in references to myths, legends, and happenings supposedly well known to the audience but obscure to us. Only later Vedic literature provides more coherent accounts of the gods' doings.

Indra, the god of war and thunder, is described as a robust and bearded warrior, who wields the lightning bolt as his mace (*vajra*), is victorious in battle, and has an insatiable thirst for his *soma* drink. Indra is the chief divinity of the Rigvedic people, to whom more than one-quarter of the collection of 1028 hymns is addressed. Indra's most important feat is the release of the waters by killing the dragon Vṛtra, whose name means "enclosure, obstruction." Maruts, the storm winds, assist Indra. Indra also helps in finding the cattle captured by the enemy, especially the demon Vala, who keeps the cows in a cave; in this Indra is helped by Bṛhaspati with magic spells. Indra helps Aryan kings to destroy the fortifications of the Dāsas. He is also a demiurge who creates the sun, the heaven, and the dawns.

Second in popularity is Agni, the god of fire (*agni-*, related to Latin *ignis*, "fire," and Russian *ogon'*, "fire"). As the ritual fire into which libations of ghee and *soma* are poured and other offerings placed, Agni is the mouth of the gods, and the divine priest and messenger. He assists Indra in burning the enemy forts. Third most popular (as measured by the number of hymns devoted to him) is Soma, the god praised in Book 9. Soma is the invigorating divine juice that enhances a warrior's performance and keeps a poet inspired and vigilant. It is pressed, using stones, from the stalks of the *soma* plant, after they have been soaked in hot water. *Soma* is both sacrificed to gods, especially Indra, and imbibed by the priests and poets.

Vedic *soma* corresponds to Avestan *haoma*, both from older **sauma*, derived from the verb **sau-*, "to press out." The botanical identity of the plant has been much debated. Rhubarb, hops, fly-agaric mushroom, and harmel or wild rue are some of the alternative candidates proposed, but nowadays the identification of the *soma* plant as belonging to the genus *Ephedra* is widely accepted. *Ephedra* is the source of ephedrine, a banned drug among modern sportsmen, thus fit to enhance Indra's martial feats. Moreover, *Ephedra* has been used for many centuries for *haoma* by Zoroastrians in both central Iran and India. In Nepal *Ephedra* is called *soma-latā*, "soma creeper," which suggests its use for *soma* in North India. In South India, where *Ephedra* does not grow, *Sarcostemma brevistigma*, a leafless climber similar to *Ephedra*, has been used as a substitute (Flattery & Schwartz 1989; Falk 1989; Nyberg 1995).

Important deities, to whom relatively few hymns are addressed in the Rigveda, are Mitra ("contract"), the divine guardian of pacts, and Varuṇa (perhaps "true speech"), the upholder of the cosmic and social order, who punishes sinners; these two usually appear as a dual divinity, Mitra-Varuṇa; they are the foremost in the group of divinities called Ādityas, to be discussed below. Also important are the horse-owning twins, Aśvins or Nāsatyas, whose sister and bride is the most important goddess of the Rigveda, the beautiful goddess of Dawn, Uṣas (whose name is related to Greek Ēōs and Latin Aurora). Other nature gods are the sun god, Sūrya; the wind god, Vāyu or Vāta; the rain god, Parjanya; Dyaus, "Heaven, Sky"; and Pṛthivī, "Earth." The latter two are the father and mother of the gods and the world; they were inherited from the Proto-Indo-European pantheon, although Dyaus is less important than Greek Zeus and Roman Jupiter. Minor divinities are many, including Pūṣan, a pastoral deity who helps in finding paths, the creator god Tvaṣṭar ("carpenter, fashioner") and Savitar ("impeller, commander"). Viṣṇu and Śiva, who dominate the later Hindu pantheon, are to some extent already present in the Rigveda, the latter under the name Rudra (see chapter 12), but as rather marginal divinities. Viṣṇu is a friend and helper of Indra. His Rigvedic feat of measuring the universe in three steps is often referred to in later Vedic literature and forms the basis of his dwarf (Vāmana) incarnation in classical Hinduism.

Vedic scholars have long noted a marked contrast between the somewhat barbaric main hero god, Indra, and Varuṇa, the majestic guardian of the universe, who through his spies watches out that people speak truth. Varuṇa has been considered a remarkably "ethical" and "civilized" deity; yet, in spite of his high rank, he is the deity of relatively few Rigvedic hymns. A certain antagonism and rivalry between Indra and Varuṇa is seen in the Rigvedic hymn 4,42, where these two deities in turn laud themselves as kings, emphasizing their achievements and prerogatives. Particular importance has been given to RV 10,124,5, a verse in which Indra addresses Varuṇa as follows: "Those Asuras have just now become devoid of their magic power; If you desire me, come to my overlordship of dominion, distinguishing Falsity from Truth, O king!" (translated Proferes 2007:108). According to Karl Geldner and many others, Indra here declares that the older generation of gods called *asuras* have now lost their struggle with the new generation of gods called *devas*, and Indra offers Varuṇa, the leading Asura, a chance to join the ranks of the *devas* if he accepts becoming a vassal of Indra. In my opinion, the verse could indeed reflect such a compromise between Varuṇa and Indra worshippers at the time when the first and second waves of Proto-Indo-Aryan immigrants to the BMAC mingled in Central Asia, and then again in the Indus Valley, when the Rigvedic Aryans mingled with the earlier Indo-Aryan immigrants.

In the Rigveda, Indra is the king (Varuṇa anoints Indra in hymn 10,124); but in the Brāhmaṇas, Varuṇa is generally the divine king. In the Rigveda, Indra is addressed as *deva*, "god," but Varuṇa as *asura* (a title borrowed from Proto-Indo-Aryan into Uralic languages in the meaning "prince, lord"); in the Brāhmaṇas, *asura* means "demon," which often is an appellation of enemy gods; some contexts indeed show that there were non-Vedic peoples in eastern India who worshipped asuras. Indra's drink is *soma*, Varuṇa's beer (*surā*); the barley from which *surā* is made belongs to Varuṇa. Vedic texts usually condemn *surā* as a manifestation of untruth. In the Vedic *vājapeya* ritual, which includes a chariot race, *soma* is offered to Indra and other deities and consumed by the priests, but *surā* is prepared and given to the charioteers, while the winner receives a bowl of honey (*madhu*). Honey is associated with the Aśvins; honey-beer was the ritual drink of the PIE speakers, and figures also among the early Aryan loanwords of the Uralic languages (chapter 7).

This chapter discusses the Aśvins, alias Nāsatyas, and the dual divinity Mitra-and-Varuṇa, whom I see as a double of the Aśvins. I explain the above-mentioned cultic conflicts within Indra worship—which appear to have been partially resolved by various compromises—by postulating a fundamental religious difference between the two waves of Proto-Indo-Aryan speakers who successively took over power in the BMAC. Archaeological evidence suggests that the first wave came from the south Uralic Sintashta culture, where the horse-drawn chariot first appeared (see chapter 8, and Figs. 7.7 and 8.4). I see the Aśvins as the divinized chariot-team, who were probably the highest gods representing their mundane counterparts, dual kings, although in the Vedas they are divinities of a low rank. The second wave of Proto-Indo-Aryan speakers was that of the Fëdorovo Andronovans, steppe pastoralists whose arrival more or less coincided with the beginning of the impoverished "post-urban" phase of the BMAC. Their main god was Indra, whose name may come from **Inmar*, the name of the sky and thunder god of their Uralic-speaking companions (see chapter 7). *Soma*, Indra's cultic drink, does not have an ancient Indo-European background like the *madhu* of the Aśvins, and was probably adopted by the Fëdorovo Andronovans in Central Asia.

Thus I see the cult of the Nāsatyas as being not of Proto-Indo-European origin (as is often so maintained) but as going back to the times when the horse-drawn chariot evolved, that is, the end of the third millennium BCE. The chariot was a prestigious and effective new instrument of war and sport, which was quickly adopted by the elites of neighboring peoples. Together with the chariot, the mythology and cult of the deified chariot team also spread. Placing its origin in the steppes of the south Urals best explains the distribution of the early chariot lore among the Aryans, Greeks, and Balts.

In the Rigveda, the Aśvins are several times called "sons of the sky," *divó nápātā* or *dívo napātā*. It relates them historically to the horse-riding divine twins of early Greece who are called *Dioskouroi*, "youths of Zeus" (i.e., sons of the sky god), and to the horse-riding "sons of the God" (Latvian *Dieva dēli*, Lithuanian *Dievo sūneliai*) in the pre-Christian religion of the Balts. Moreover, all three sets of equestrian twins have a sister or wife or bride either associated with the dawn or called the daughter of the sun (Uṣas or Sūryā in India, Helénē < **svelénā*, "sunshine," in Greece, and in the Baltics, Latvian *saules meita*, "maiden or daughter of the sun," and Lithuanian *saules dukryte*, "daughter of the sun").

The Aśvins of the Ṛgveda move in a chariot, but the Greek Dioskouroi and the Baltic "sons of the God" are horse-riders. The difference is understandable. In much of the ancient world, throughout the second millennium BCE, the chariot drawn by a pair of horses was "the vehicle of prestige—the only approved conveyance for the chieftain and his noble entourage in ceremony and ritual, hunting and its counterpart, warfare" (Piggott 1992:48). But the situation changed in the early first millennium BCE, when the Dioskouroi first make their appearance (eighth or seventh century BCE):

> The beginnings of regal horse-riding were tentative. In the ancient Near Eastern tradition the king, if he did not appear in a chariot, might on occasion ride on a mule or a donkey. . . . In the early second millennium a well-known letter to Zimri-Lin, King of Mari, gives him advice on this matter—"Let my lord not ride horses. Let him mount only chariots or mules and honour his kingly head." . . . But . . . cavalry was taking over chariotry in Assyria by the ninth century BC and the king Shalmaneser III (858–823 BC) is depicted as riding on horseback. Thenceforward the monarch as a warrior on horseback became the accepted convention in the ancient Orient. (Piggott 1992:69–70)

Significantly, the Assyrian mounted warriors of the ninth century "always go in pairs, translated directly from the chariot: the bowman and the driver, who still holds the reins of both horses, both riders with cramped and unhorsemanlike seats. These Assyrians use the weapon they used in the chariot and, no matter how awkwardly at first, they persist in fighting mounted, thus continuing their chariot-fighting tradition" (Littauer in Littauer & Crouwel 2002:63–64).

The existence of a two-man team associated with the chariot in the Sintashta-Arkaim culture of the southern Urals (*c.* 2200–1800 BCE) is suggested by a burial at Sintashta (Fig. 7.5a). Here the warrior was buried together with his weapons and his car at the bottom of the grave, while another man was buried together with a pair of horses and a burning fireplace in an upper chamber. In the Vedic religion, the charioteer and the chariot-fighter are expressly equated with the Aśvins. When, in the royal consecration, the king goes to the house of his charioteer (*samgrahītár-*), he "prepares a cake on two potsherds for the Aśvins; for the two Aśvins are of the same womb; and so are the chariot fighter [*savyaṣṭhá-*] and the driver [*sā́rathi-*] of the same womb (standing-place), since they stand on one and the same chariot: hence it is for the Aśvins" (ŚB 5,3,1,8, translated Eggeling 1894:III,62).

Of the Greek Dioskouroi, too, one was a fighter and the other took care of horses: according to their standing Homeric attributes (e.g., *Iliad* 3,237), Poludeukes was good at fistfighting (*pùks agathós*), while Kastor was good at taming horses (*hippódamos*). The Rigveda, too, differentiates between the two Aśvins: "one of you is respected as the victorious lord of Sumakha, and the other as the fortunate son of heaven" (RV 1,181,4, translated Insler 1996:183). This passage suggests that *divó nápātā* is an elliptic dual, that is, based on the name of just one member of the pair, "the son of heaven/sky," just like *nā́satyā*, derived as it seems to be from the charioteer member of the team. A similar case is the elliptic plural *Castores*, "Castor and Pollux" of Latin (which lacks the dual) for the Greek dual *tô Kástore*.

Nā́satya- is a derivative of **nasatí-*, "safe return home," and belongs to the same PIE root **nes-* as the Greek agent noun *Néstōr*—known from Homer (*Iliad* 23,301–350 and 638–642) as a *hippóta*, "horseman," and a masterly charioteer; it refers to the charioteer's task of bringing the hero safely back from the battle (Frame 1978; 2010). In the Indian epics, "the rule of protecting the knight is formal. 'In battle the knight, if confused, must be guarded by the charioteer'; or, 'ever must the man of the war-car be guarded'; and when the charioteer risks his life in saving his master, he does so because he 'bears in mind the rule'" (Hopkins 1889:196). In the Rigvedic verse just quoted the "victorious lord of Sumakha" appears to be the chariot-warrior. The meaning of the words *sú-makha-* and *makhá-*, *-makhas-* is debated, but this context suits the old etymology that connects them with Greek *mákhē*, "battle, combat," and *makhésasthai*, "to fight."

All over the ancient West Asia at the times of the Mitanni empire, the chariot was the prerogative of the king and the noblemen close to the ruler, and the same was the case in Vedic India. When the horse-drawn chariot had just been invented, it must have symbolized royal power in the highest degree, and is indeed found only in elite graves. The chariot crew normally consisted of two men, the warrior and the charioteer, and the two were normally of equal aristocratic status: in the Mahābhārata, it is usual for kings to serve as charioteers of kings in the battle, as in the case of Kṛṣṇa driving Arjuna's car, or Śalya driving Karṇa's. Putting all these things together, I argue that among the inherited features that the Aśvins share with their Greek counterparts we should include dual kingship. Among the Dorian Greeks, the Dioskouroi were the greatest gods, and they were widely worshipped in Greece as "the two kings" (*ánake*). According to Herodotus (5,75), their images accompanied the two kings of Sparta on war expeditions. In the Buddhist tradition of India, the universal emperor wielding supreme political power (*rājā cakkavattin*) is paralleled by the *buddha-*, who wields supreme spiritual power (Aṅguttara-Nikāya I,76 and III,150). The idea of such a dual kingship manifests itself above all in the integral connection of *kṣatrá-*, "political power" and *bráhman-*, "sacred power," these two being represented by the king and the royal chief priest, the *puróhita-*.

This dual kingship is associated with the chariot (and therewith the Aśvins), for, according to the Jaiminīya-Brāhmaṇa (3,94), "formerly the kings' chief priests used to be their charioteers so that they could oversee that the king did not commit any sin." The Āśvalāyana-Gṛhyasūtra (3,12) details the royal *purohita*'s duties in battle. Standing behind the chariot, he makes the king put on the coat of mail, hands the bow and the quiver to the king, blesses the weapons and the chariot with its horses. Then the *purohita* mounts the chariot and makes the king repeat the Rigvedic hymn 10,174, in which the king asks Bṛhaspati to help him overpower his rivals. In the battle hymn called *ápratiratha-*, which the *purohita* recites next, Bṛhaspati, the charioteer and *purohita* of Indra, the king of gods, is asked to "fly around" in his chariot, warding off enemies and helping the chariots of the *purohita*'s side.

In RV 2,24, Bṛhaspati is mentioned as an excellent charioteer and winner of races. In the chariot race of the *vājapeya*, the sacrificer announces he will win the race with the help of Bṛhaspati. Indeed, the Śatapatha-Brāhmaṇa (5,1,1,11) states that "this [*vājapeya*] is a sacrifice of the Brāhmaṇa, inasmuch as Bṛhaspati sacrificed with it; for Bṛhaspati is *brahman*, the priesthood, and the Brāhmaṇa is *brahman*, the priesthood." The *vājapeya* was prescribed for the royal *purohita* (LŚS 8,11,1); both before and after the *vājapeya*, the sacrificer was supposed to perform the *sava* rite of Bṛhaspati (LŚS 8,11,12), and it was by performing the *bṛhaspatisava* sacrifice that Bṛhaspati became the *purohita* of the gods (PB 17,11,5–6).

The charioteer and the royal priest were expected to be wise and crafty. *Dasrá-*, "having marvelous skill," is one of the most distinctive epithets of the Aśvins, often referring especially to their skill in chariot driving. By the time of the epics, Dasra became the proper name of one of the Aśvins. The Aśvins are also called *purudáṁsa(s)-*, "having many skills," which is etymologically related to the Greek epithet *polúdḗnēs*, "having many counsels, plans or arts; very wise." One is reminded of the crafty designs and plots of Kṛṣṇa, the charioteer of Arjuna, in the Mahābhārata (see chapter 13).

There is a problem with the dual kingship of the Aśvins proposed here. In his book on kingship in the Rigveda and the Atharvaveda (1960), Bernfried Schlerath finds no evidence for the Aśvins being themselves kings, although they are mentioned as bestowers of royal power—especially because they make the king's chariot victorious. However, on one occasion (in RV 3,38,5) "the two sons of the sky" are addressed as two kings (*rājānā*). According to Rigveda 8,35,13, the two Aśvins are "possessed of Mitra and Varuṇa as well as of Dharma" (*mitrā́váruṇavantā utá dhármavantā*). The primary meaning of *mitrá-* is "contractual alliance, pact of friendship," and of *váruṇa-* probably "true speech." Thus these personified notions of social nature—important in illiterate tribal societies—were associated with the Aśvins. The Nāsatyas are, together with Mitra and Varuṇa, and Indra, Proto-Indo-Aryan oath deities sworn by in the Hittite-Mitanni treaty of about 1350 BCE (chapter 8). In RV 8,35,12 and 1,120,8, the Aśvins are invoked to guard against the breach of a treaty. An etymology of the name Nāsatya quoted by Yāska on Nirukta 6,13 shows that they were regarded as protectors of the truth: they are "true and not false (*na-asatya*)," says Aurṇavābha; "they are promoters of the truth," says Āgrāyaṇa (*satyāv eva nāsatyāv ity aurṇavābhaḥ / satyasya praṇetārāv ity āgrāyaṇaḥ*). The Dioskouroi, too, were oath deities.

The winged solar disk in Achae, menid art, representing the highest god of Zoroastrianism, Ahura Mazdā, has been taken over from Assyrian art, where it is one of the principal symbols of the Assyrian high god, Aššur. The conception of Ahura Mazdā as a monotheistic god with the Ameša Spəṇtas, "Holy Immortals," representing his qualities or powers, is also strikingly similar to that of Aššur. The cuneiform texts present also the "great gods" of the Babylonian pantheon as functions, powers, and attributes of the Babylonian national god Marduk: as his "kingship, might, wisdom, victory, strength, counsel, judgment," and so on. It is widely agreed that this conception was not a creation of Zarathuštra. The Iranian god Mithra, too, was surrounded by friendship, obedience, justice, courage, and divine grace.

The Zoroastrian Ameša Spəṇtas have long been compared to the Ādityas of the Veda: these "personalized powers . . . represented the principles on which human action depended" (Brereton 1981:ix). Two of the Ādityas, Mitra ("Alliance") and Varuṇa ("Commandment" or "True Speech"), are invoked in the Mitanni treaty. In addition, the Ādityas comprised such abstract deities as Aryaman ("Civility") and Bhaga ("Fortune"), Aṁśa ("Share"), and Dakṣa ("Ability") (Brereton 1981). I have proposed that the creation of the Ādityas was inspired by the Assyrian religion, where deified social virtues are aspects of Aššur, the highest god, comparable to the advisors who surround the great king. The Assyrian religion is likely to have influenced Proto-Indo-Aryan religion during the late twentieth and early nineteenth centuries BCE, when Assyrian traders operating from Syria and Cappadocia imported tin from Central Asia. Ideological influence is evidenced by the Syrian and Egyptian motifs adopted in seals of the BMAC (see chapter 8).

Mitra-and-Varuṇa early on seem to have overtaken the Aśvins' royal function. The Śatapatha-Brāhmaṇa (4,1,4) actually describes the relationship between Mitra and Varuṇa as that prevailing between the king and his high priest. Yet the Aśvins, as the deified chariot-team corresponding to the Dioskouroi, seem to be the original deities of dual kingship.

According to RV 3,58,8, the chariot of the Aśvins goes around the heaven and earth in one day. In the *āśvinaśastra*, a text praising the Aśvins, the same is said of the sun's horses. In another verse (RV 1,115,5), the sun is said to show the colors of Mitra and Varuṇa in the lap of heaven: the one appearance is infinitely white, the other one is black. Here the sun is conceived of as one divinity having two forms, the white day-sun and the black night-sun, and these two forms are connected with Mitra and Varuṇa. Some verses of the Rigveda suggest that the sun is the chariot of the Aśvins. According to RV 6,9,1, "the white day and the black day—(the pair of) light and darkness—manifestly turn around."

If the white day and the black night are the two Aśvins, their association with the red dawn as their sister-wife is most natural: the three are mentioned together for example in RV 7,80,1, where the Vasiṣṭhas praise Uṣas as one who turns around the darkness and the light, the two contiguous ones. In RV 10,39,12, the Aśvins are asked to come with their chariot manufactured by the Ṛbhus, which is quicker than the mind and at the yoking of which is born the daughter of the sky (i.e., the dawn) and Vivasvant's two beautiful days (i.e., the white day and the black day = night). Vivasvant is the sun god, who according to RV 10,17,2 is the father of the Aśvins. In the Atharvaveda (13,3,13), Mitra and Varuṇa are connected with the two forms that the fire god Agni has during the day and night: "This Agni becomes Varuṇa in the evening; in the morning, rising, he becomes Mitra." Thus Mitra and Varuṇa are the sun and the fire, the deities of the *agnihotra* sacrifice—which, in my opinion, is an early variant of the *gharma* offering to the Aśvins. The *agnihotra* is performed at sunset and sunrise, to Agni (Fire) and Sūrya (Sun). In RV 10,88,6, "Agni is the head of the earth in the night, of him is the rising sun born in the morning." Both Mitra and Varuṇa and the two Aśvins are equated with day and night in the Brāhmaṇa texts.

The sun and the fire—the day-sun and the night-sun—thus seem to be the cosmic and atmospheric phenomena that the two Aśvins were originally conceived of as representing. Instead of the fire, the moon could conceivably represent the nocturnal counterpart of the day-sun; in addition, the rising sun and the moon are not infrequently seen together in the sky in the morning. The Atharvaveda (7,81,1) offers a characterization of the sun and moon (to whom the hymn is addressed) that fits well with the youthful Aśvins: "these two playing young ones by their magic power move eastwards and westwards around the ocean." In comparison to the sun and moon, the morning and evening star are much less significant phenomena to qualify as royal symbols; though they are connected with the Dioskouroi in the classical (but not the earliest) Greek tradition as well as with the "sons of God" in Baltic folk songs, this can be seen as a natural later development with these deities of the dawn and dusk, a development that could have taken place independently in Greece and the Baltics. In India, a different astral identification took place: the Aśvins were associated with one of the calendrical asterisms consisting of two stars, called *aśvayújau*. They have also been equated with the zodiacal stars of Gemini.

Mithra and Ahura are the Avestan counterpart of Vedic Mitra-and-Varuṇa. The original meaning of Asura, the principal epithet of Varuṇa, can be seen from **asera-*, "lord, prince," attested in Uralic languages as an early loanword from Proto-Indo-Aryan (in Proto-Uralic, labial vowels could occur only in the first syllable, so **u* was replaced with **e*). In Zarathuštra's pantheon, Asura Varuṇa became Ahura Mazdā, "Lord Wisdom," whose supreme symbol is fire. The Vedic word *medhā́-*, "wisdom," which is the etymological counterpart of Avestan *mazdā-* (both go back to Proto-Aryan **mn̥z-dhā́-*), is connected especially with the fire god Agni. As we have seen, Varuṇa is the night/fire partner of the pair Mitra-and-Varuṇa, alias Day-Sun-and-Night-Sun, alias Sun-and-Fire.

This agrees with the fact that Apąm Napāt, "son of the waters," is called Ahura and is coupled with Mithra in the Avesta, while in the Veda, Apāṃ Napāt is another name of the fire god Agni and is conceived of as a horse-shaped sun-fire in the waters. Varuṇa, too, is connected with the waters as their lord, *Apāṃ pati*. According to the Kauṣītaki-Brāhmaṇa (18,9), the sun becomes Varuṇa after it has entered the waters. The horse (*áśva-*) is often said to belong to Varuṇa.

In Iran, Mithra's name eventually came to mean the sun. In the Avesta, Mithra is a warrior god wielding the *vazra* as his weapon, and in front of him runs the god of victory, *Vərəθrayna*, in the shape of a wild boar. In the Veda, the *vajra*-wielding Indra, slayer of Vṛtra (*vṛtrahan-*), is the counterpart of Mithra, the chariot-warrior, the solar god of the day. In the Veda, Indra's charioteer is Bṛhaspati, the *purohita* of the gods. Bṛhaspati or Brahmaṇaspati, "Lord of the Magic Song," was originally an epithet of Indra himself, whose kingship thus also comprised the priestly function. Bṛhaspati's becoming a separate *purohita*-figure, and the creation of the dual divinities Indra-Bṛhaspatī and Indra-Agnī, was undoubtedly in imitation of the old pair Mitra-and-Varuṇa (Gonda 1974:52–53, 276, 281, 291–292, 325–330). Bṛhaspáti- is also an epithet of Agni, the *purohita* of the gods.

Indra's charioteer in the Mahābhārata is called Mā́talī. In the form Mā́talī, this name is attested for the first time in the funeral hymn RV 10,14. One of the three occurrences in the Atharvaveda mentions the chariot-brought immortal medicine known to Mā́talī that is in the waters; it resembles the Rigvedic verse (by Medhātithi Kāṇva) 1,23,1, which mentions "the nectar in the waters, the medicine in the waters"—this is recited at the *vājapeya* rite before the chariot race, when the horses are bathed in water. *Bheṣajá-*, "medicine," and the chariot associate Mā́talī with the Aśvins, the divine charioteers and divine physicians. *Mā́talī* is a pet name abbreviation of *Mātaríśvan-*, who is mentioned twenty-seven times in the Rigveda (mostly in Books 1 and 10) and twenty-one times in the Atharvaveda. In several passages Mātaríśvan is the name of Agni, and once (RV 1,190,2) he is a form of Bṛhaspati (the *purohita* and charioteer of Indra). Otherwise Mātaríśvan is mostly spoken of as an Indian counterpart of the Greek Prometheus, who brought the hidden fire (Agni) to men from heaven or who produced it by friction.

Stanley Insler has convincingly proposed that *Mātaríśvan-* comes from earlier **Ātaríśvan-*, "master of fire" (see Parpola 2005a:26–27). The latter part of the compound, *íśvan-*, has preserved the original unreduplicated root *iś-*, "to master"; it has a direct equivalent in Avestan *isvan-*, "master." In about one-third of the occurrences of the name Mātariśvan, it is preceded by a word ending in *-m*, and the sequence . . . *m *ātaríśvā* was reinterpreted as . . . *mātaríśvā*, folk-etymologically associating the name with *mātar-*, "mother." The reason for this reworking was that the word **ātar-*, "fire," had become obsolete in the Vedic language, where *agní-*, "fire," has completely supplanted **ātar-*, just as *ātar-* has replaced *agní-* in Avestan. There is no myth among the Iranians about the theft of fire from the gods, because fire is the creation and protected offspring of Ahura Mazdā. I suspect that *Ātar-iśvan originally was a Proto-Iranian deity and came to South Asia with the Dāsas.

Mātariśvan has a close Greek parallel in Prometheus (Promātheús in the Dorian dialects), whose name is likely to have originally meant "robber," etymologically related to the root *math-*, "to steal, rob," which is often used in connection with Mātaríśvan (cf. also Sanskrit *pramātha-*, "robbery"). I have no doubt that the myth is also connected with the homophonous root *math- / manth-*, "to whirl round, to rotate" (so as to produce cream by rotating a churning-stick in milk, or fire by rapidly rotating a dry wooden stick in a hole of a dry wooden plank, that is, a "fire-drill"). Mātariśvan also kindled the hidden fire for the Bhṛgus, who are spoken of as ancient sacrificers along with the Atharvans and Āṅgirasas. The Bhṛgus are not only a priestly clan who discovered fire for mankind, they are also mentioned as chariot builders in the Rigveda. In the Brāhmaṇa texts, Bhṛgu is the son of Varuṇa. The word *bhṛgu-* is considered etymologically related to *bhárgas-*, "effulgence," which characterizes Agni when the fire is born out of "power" (i.e., the strong friction of the kindling stick); these words seem to have a cognate in Greek *phlóks* (gen. *phlogós*) and Latin *flamma*. Mātaríśvan's double association with the origin of the fire and with the chariot (as Indra's charioteer) is paralleled by the chariot-driving Aśvins' association with the two pieces of wood used for producing fire by friction in the Rigveda (10,184,3). Generation of fire with a fire-drill is compared to generation of offspring, and also in this sense connected with the Aśvins (see the end of chapter 11).

Agni is the divine priest, the *purohita* of the gods. As Agni conveys the offerings to the gods, he is "the charioteer of the rites" (TS 2,5,9,2–3 *rathī́r adhvarā́ṇām*). "Fire" is therefore called *váhni-*, "driver, charioteer," from the root *vah-*, "to drive in a chariot, convey by carriage." Varuṇa's connection with the charioteer is apparent from an episode in the royal consecration: when the king goes to the house of the *sūtá-*, "herald, bard," he makes an offering to Varuṇa and gives a horse as a sacrificial gift (ŚB 5,3,1,5). In the Indian epics, the charioteer gives the hero advice and encourages him in battle by singing of the feats of his ancestors; hence *sūtá-* means both "charioteer" and "bard."

Varuṇa has the title *samrā́j-*, generally understood to denote "universal ruler," but in my opinion literally "co-ruling" (a title which in itself suggests dual kingship) in the sense of "priest-king." According to the Śatapatha-Brāhmaṇa (5,1,1,12–13), "the royal consecration (*rājasūya*) is only for the king. For he who performs the royal consecration becomes the king; and unsuited for kingship is the Brāhmaṇa. . . . By performing the *vājapeya* [which is a sacrifice of the Brāhmaṇa and of Bṛhaspati, the *purohita* of the gods, see ŚB 5,1,1,11], one becomes the *samrā́j*; and the office of the king is the lower, and that of the *samrā́j* the higher. . . ." The performer of the *vājapeya*, who becomes *samrā́j*, is not supposed to stand up in front of anybody—the symbol of the *samrā́j* is the throne (*āsandī*, ŚB 12,8,3,4). Here we can see how the Brahmins are making the priest-king higher than the mundane king. Varuṇa was originally the *samrā́j* in the sense of the priest-king, but came to be considered as the ruling king: in Śatapatha-Brāhmaṇa 4,1,4,1–6, Varuṇa represents *kṣatrá-*, the ruling power, and Mitra is the *purohita* and *bráhman-*, representing priesthood. This led to Mitra's being practically eclipsed from the dual kingship by Varuṇa; and in Zoroastrianism, too, Ahura Mazdā ousted Mithra.

However, in Śatapatha-Brāhmaṇa 11,4,3,10–11, while Varuṇa is called *samrā́j*, it is Mitra who is connected with the ruling power (*váruṇaḥ samrā́ṭ samrā́ṭpatiḥ . . . mitráḥ kṣatrám̥ kṣatrápatiḥ*). Moreover, in RV 6,68,3, Varuṇa is called a *vípra*, "[sacred] poet," in contrast to the warrior Indra, who slays Vṛtra with his mace. "There can be no doubt whatever that Mitra's characteristic role is that of a king and not that of a priest: the evidence of the RV is overwhelming and confirmed as genuine by the Avesta" (Thieme 1957:8). Thus originally Mitra represented mundane kingship, Varuṇa priesthood. In the Atharvaveda, Varuṇa is a master of the magic, which was the domain of the royal *purohita*.

11

The Aśvins as Funerary Gods

The Aśvins and Mitra-Varuṇa stood for the two sides of kingship and of the solar god, the sun and the fire, day and night. In the Vedas, the night, darkness and Varuṇa are all associated with death. That the Aśvins were linked not only with day and night but also with life and death as early as Proto-Aryan times is suggested by Greek evidence. According to Homer, the Dioskouroi "have this honour from Zeus, albeit in the nether world, they pass from death to life and life to death on alternate days, and enjoy equal honors with the Gods" (*Odyssey* 11,298–304, translated Farnell 1921:181). Sometimes one of the Dioskouroi is depicted on a white horse and the other on a black horse—corresponding with the idea that one is immortal, belonging to the celestials, the other mortal and belonging to the deceased.

The Dioskouroi were "saviors" (*sōtêres*) assisting in all kinds of trouble, notably at sea, on the battlefield and during illness; they also figure in funerary inscriptions and frequently appear on Roman sarcophagi. In *The myth of return in early Greek epic* (1978), Douglas Frame argues that *nóstos*, "homecoming, return," in early Greek religion, primarily meant "return from (darkness and) death," "coming back to (light and) life," and that the miracles performed by the Dioskouroi as saviors largely denote revivals from death. "In the Iliad . . . the role of the chariot seems to be chiefly as a means of transport to and from the battlefield. Generally the warrior leaps down to fight—his charioteer standing by to carry him out of danger if things go badly" (Wace and Stubbings 1962:521). The rescue function thus belonged to the charioteer, and the term *nāsatya-*, "effecting safe homecoming, rescuer, savior," therefore denotes this member of the chariot team, although it is used in the Rigveda in an elliptic dual (which omits the other member) of both Aśvin twins. Sanskrit *nāsatya-* is related to Greek *néstōr*, which in Homer is the name of the old king of Pylos, famed as a horseman (*hippóta*) and an experienced charioteer (Frame 2010). Both words go back to a Proto-Indo-European root **nes-*, "to come home safely," from which also derive Greek *nóstos*, Sanskrit *astam-aya-*, "homecoming, sunset," Gothic *ganisan*, "to be saved," and Modern German *genesen*, "to be healed."

In India, the equestrian twins were conceived of as saviors, too. That this is due to an Indo-Iranian heritage is suggested by the fact that the twins were also invoked by people in peril at sea, despite the Vedic people no longer having any direct contact with the sea.

A funerary function for the Aśvins is suggested by the stories of Atri, Kakṣīvant, Cyavāna, Vandana, and several other persons whom the Aśvins rescued from distress or rejuvenated, even though they were lying buried, as if dead. The rejuvenation accomplished by the Aśvins is several times compared to the renovation of an old chariot. That the Aśvins were often funerary divinities who resurrected the dead is clear from their assistance to Vandana. Vandana had become decrepit with age; his regeneration out of the ground (also: womb) is compared to the skillful repair of an old chariot that threatens to fall into pieces (RV 1,119,7). Vandana had been buried and was like one sleeping in the lap of the goddess of destruction (i.e., a dead person); he rested like the sun in darkness; the Aśvins dug him up like a buried ornament of gold, beautiful to look at (RV 1,117,5). In another hymn, the dug-up Vandana is compared to a dug-up hidden treasure (RV 1,116,11). The Aśvins lifted him up so he could see the sun (RV 1,112,5), that is, live. The Aśvins dug Vandana up from a pit (RV 10,39,8), that is, a grave.

In the Sintashta culture of the southern Urals, deceased chieftains were buried with their horses and chariots. The chariot was intimately involved with burial rites, and was probably assumed to take the dead to the next world. In the twenty-third song of the *Iliad*, Homer, describing the funeral of Patroclus, reports (verses 171–172) that four horses were cast upon his pyre. The chariot was involved, too, but in a different way. In athletic contests to honor the dead hero, his belongings were divided up as victory prizes. The most important of these contests was the chariot race. Describing it, King Nestor refers to another funeral chariot race, in which he was beaten by the sons of Aktor, "Siamese twins," one of whom held the reins while the other brandished the whip. A comparable horse race, performed by riders on the day of the burial, occurred in the pre-Christian traditions of the Baltic people (Caland 1914). There the prize consisted either of money placed on top of the goal post, or of property of the deceased, placed at certain intervals along the route. The day ended in a drinking bout.

One would expect a funeral chariot race to have survived in ancient India, but despite considerable research, no such connection has been found (Sparreboom 1985). I believe that a reference has survived in a hymn to the Aśvins, RV 1,116,2: "O you two, who had triumphed with (your) strong-winged (horses), urged to a fast course, or through the incitements of the gods, (your) ass won a thousand (cows) in Yama's prize-contest, O Nāsatyas." Many scholars have commented upon this verse, but none has interpreted the phrase "Yama's prize-contest" (*ājā́ yamásya pradháne*) as referring to a funeral chariot race, although Yama is the god of death and the Yama hymns of Book 10 of the Rigveda were used in funeral rites. Éric Pirart (1995), however, significantly observes that the verb *śad-*, "to triumph," used here of the Aśvins with regard to the chariot race, is derived from the same Indo-European root as the Greek name *Kástōr*, born by one of the Dioskouroi twins, the "tamer of horses."

The Rigveda specifies that the Aśvins won a thousand cows or verses with their ass in Yama's prize-contest. Such a race won by the Aśvins with asses is described in Aitareya-Brāhmaṇa 4,7–9. The context is the 1000-versed *āśvina-śastra-* ("praise to the Aśvins"). The *āśvina-śastra-* is recited at dawn, when ending an "overnight" (*atirātrá-*) *soma* sacrifice, which has lasted a whole day (representing a full life) and continued throughout the following night. Night represents death, and dawn rebirth. The text stresses the generative power of the ass, and this seems to be an important reason why the Aśvins drive a chariot pulled by asses in the funeral race of Yama; another reason is undoubtedly that the wild ass, which is stronger than the horse, is associated with death (Parpola & Janhunen 2011).

The symbolism of the *āśvina-śastra-* suits the funeral context well, for "the *āśvina* is . . . the chariot of the gods. With this chariot of the gods he attains in safety the world of heaven. (The *śastra*) should include the *suparṇa* [the 'good-feathered' bird]; the *suparṇa* is a bird; becoming, like it, a winged one, a bird, he attains in safety the world of heaven." (KB 18,4) The *suparṇa*, which flies to heaven, is Varuṇa's messenger at the seat of Yama (RV 10,123,6), and thus associated with death. In funerary pots of the Late Harappan Cemetery H culture of the Punjab (*c.* 1900–1300 BCE), the peacock is depicted as carrying the dead (who lie horizontal inside the peacock) to the stars in heaven (Fig. 15.9). Birds are connected with the Aśvins, too, for the horses pulling their airborne chariot are compared to birds (RV 6,63,7).

The *āśvina-śastra-* contains a thousand verses. The Aitareya-Brāhmaṇa (2,17) explains their meaning: "A thousand [verses] should be recited for one desiring heaven; the world of heaven is at a distance of a thousand journeys of a horse hence; (they serve) for the attainment of the world of heaven, the securing, the going to (the world of heaven)." The number is also connected with the sun, which is said to have a thousand rays—and the sun's rays are often understood as cattle; one thousand cows or verses was the prize in Yama's chariot race won by the Aśvins.

The funeral context of the *āśvina-śastra* has gone unnoticed, because the Rigveda Brāhmaṇas introduce its exposition by associating it with the marriage of Soma (the Moon) and the Solar Maiden: "Now when Savitṛ gave Sūryā to Soma, the king, he made over to his daughter whether she was Prajāpati's (or his own) on marriage this thousand (of verses) that was in the possession of these deities; they said, 'Let us run a race for this thousand'; they ran the race, then the Aśvins were victorious by means of the ass" (Kauṣītaki-Brāhmaṇa 18,1, translated Keith 1920:444–445).

Actually, the marriage context is also very relevant, for the conclusion of funeral rituals aiming at rejuvenation and the attainment of heaven coincides with the beginning of new life in the impregnation that occurs at a wedding. The mythical explanation of the cup of *soma* offered to the Aśvins (*āśvinagraha-*) at the morning pressing of the *soma* plant also links marriage and rejuvenation. Cyavana, a sage decrepit with old age, lay ghost-like on the ground, and was offended by the people of Śaryāta Mānava—they threw clods of earth at him (*loṣṭa*, the word used here for "clod," is also used of the earthen "bricks" of the funeral monument, *loṣṭa-citi-*). The angered sage caused problems for Śaryāta, who gave his beautiful daughter Sukanyā to the sage in atonement. Through Sukanyā, Cyavana made the Aśvins rejuvenate him: Cyavana was thrown into water (or: pool of youth in the River Sarasvatī), and emerged young again. Finally, he sacrificed with a thousand cows (the prize won by the Aśvins in the race).

Regeneration implies reentering the womb: "A son is a light in the highest heaven. The husband enters the wife; having become a germ (he enters) the mother; having becoming renewed in her, he is born in the tenth month" (*Ślokas* of the Śunaḥśepa legend recited at the royal consecration, according to Aitareya-Brāhmaṇa 7,13). The Aśvins are deities of both death and (re)birth, saving people by helping them make the dangerous, liminal passage. They appear in the morning and evening, at the junctures between night and day, or death and life: Janus-like, their white-and-black appearance unites these opposites. In this, they resemble the Dioskouroi.

Among the singer families of the Rigveda, the Kāṇvas and Atris are prominent worshippers of the Nāsatyas. Of the fifty-four complete hymns addressed to the Aśvins, as many as thirty-three are in "Kāṇva" books: sixteen in Book 1, twelve in Book 8, and five in Book 10. Six hymns are in the Atri book, Book 5. There are eight Aśvin hymns in Book 7, which belongs to the Varuṇa-worshipping Vasiṣṭhas. The contrast with the remaining "family books" is great: Book 2 has just one hymn, Book 3 just one hymn, Book 4 has three hymns, and Book 6 only two. The references to the *gharma* rite, which is special to the Aśvins, are of similar distribution: they occur most frequently in Books 1, 5, 7, 8, and 10.

Kāṇva poets of the Rigveda resided in Gandhāra, the area of the Gandhāra Grave culture (*c.* 1700–900 BCE), the first culture in northern Indus Valley to possess the domesticated horse (Fig. 11.1; Fig. 4.4). Suvāstu, the ancient name of the Swāt River, is mentioned in the Rigveda only in the Kāṇva hymn 8,19 (verse 37). Women from Gandhāra are mentioned once in book I. Besides toponyms, cultural criteria back up the location of the Kāṇva poets. Thus, in contrast to the family books, the Kāṇva hymns repeatedly refer to shepherding and to plowing, which were both practised in Gandhāra. Out of the five Rigvedic occurrences of the word *uṣṭra*, "camel," four are in Book 8 and one in Book 1. The Kāṇva hymns are the only

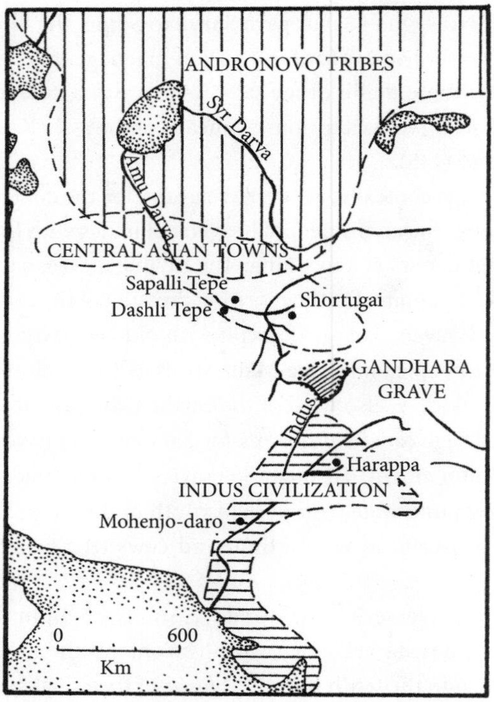

FIGURE 11.1 The location of the Gandhāra Grave culture in relation to the Andronovo cultures, the BMAC ("Central Asian towns"), and the Late Indus civilization. After Mallory 1989:230, ill. 127. Courtesy J.P. Mallory.

ones in the Rigveda to have proper names of the type "having god NN as his guest," such as Medhātithi. This name type connects them with the Proto-Indo-Aryans of Mitanni, who took northern Syria in their control by 1500 BCE and fairly certainly came from the north Iranian branch of the BMAC (chapter 8). This migration took place around the same time as the Ghālegay IV Period immigration of the Gandhāra Grave culture from the BMAC into the Swāt Valley and surrounding regions, probably bringing the Kāṇvas to Gandhāra.

The great majority of the Rigvedic Aryans connected with the family books are likely to have crossed the Gandhāra and pushed on to the plains. The Atri clan associated with Book 5, however, remained in Gandhāra. Atri hymn 5,53 mentions the Kābul and Kurum rivers, along with other rivers of Afghanistan and northwest Pakistan. The Atris were in close and friendly contact with the Kāṇvas, which suggests that they resided in each other's neighborhood. The *gharma* rite appears to have originally been an independent rite connected with the worship of the Aśvins that was developed by the Atri clan. Even the Atris predominantly worship Indra. We may assume that they introduced the *gharma* rite into the Indra cult, as a result of coming under the influence of the Aśvin-worshipping Kāṇvas in Gandhāra. The post-Rigvedic legends telling how the Aśvins obtained a share in the *soma* sacrifice are likely to refer to this stage of development. The incorporation of the Aśvins' *gharma* offering as a minor component in the *soma* sacrifice, one of its many heterogeneous elements, and the Aśvins' obtaining a share of *soma* signal the Aśvins' submission to Indra. The Aśvins were now second-rank deities of the Vedic pantheon, mainly associated with healing. They are expressly called physicians, and were looked down by other gods on account of their too close relationship with human beings.

According to the Maitrāyaṇī Saṁhitā (4,6,2), the Aśvins were not originally *soma*-drinkers, and asked for the *āśvina* cup of *soma* (offered in the morning outside the actual place of sacrifice) as a reward for healing the originally "headless" *soma* sacrifice. The Aśvins healed the sacrifice by providing it with a "head" in the form of the introductory *pravargya* rite, which originally belonged to them. Consequently, a Vedic sacrificer was not supposed to perform the *pravargya* rite in his first *soma* sacrifice (which was at first "headless"), only in his second sacrifice and thereafter.

The account of the origin of the *pravargya* rite in the Śatapatha-Brāhmaṇa (14,1,1) may be summarized as follows. (1–5) The gods, excluding the Aśvins, performed a sacrificial session in order to attain glory. They agreed that whoever among them would first reach the end of the sacrifice would be the most excellent among them, and the glory would then be common to them all. Makha-Viṣṇu did so, and became the most excellent. (6) Viṣṇu, who personified the sacrifice (*makha*) and the sun, was unable to contain his love of glory. (7–10) Taking his bow and three arrows, he stepped forth and rested his head on the bow. The other gods did not dare attack, but instead asked the ants to gnaw Viṣṇu's bowstring. When the ends of the bow sprang asunder, they cut off Viṣṇu's head, which fell and became the sun. His headless trunk lay stretched out with its top part pointing toward the east. (11) The gods said: Our great hero (*mahān vīraḥ*) has fallen. That is why the *pravargya* vessel is called Mahāvīra. With their hands the gods wiped up (*sam-mṛj-*) the vital sap that flowed out of him, and that is why the Mahāvīra is Emperor (*samrāj*). (12) The gods rushed forward to him, eager to gain his glory. Indra reached him first, applied himself to him, limb by limb, and became possessed of his glory. (13) Indra became *makhavat-*, "possessed of Makha," this being (mystically) the same as *maghavat-*, "possessed of booty" (Indra's usual epithet). (14–17) The gods rewarded the ants, divided among themselves Viṣṇu's body into three parts (i.e., the three services of the *soma* sacrifice), and continued their worship with a headless sacrifice. (It failed, however, because the sacrifice was headless.)

(18) Dadhyañc Ātharvaṇa knew this *śukra*, "essence, seed," the secret of how the head of the sacrifice is put on again, how the sacrifice becomes complete again. (19) Indra (who had obtained only the glory of the headless body) threatened to cut off Dadhyañc's head if he told the secret to anybody. (20–22) The Aśvins heard that Dadhyañc possessed this secret knowledge and asked to become his disciples, but Dadhyañc refused to teach them, mentioning Indra's threat. (23) The Aśvins suggested the following scheme: after they became his pupils, they would cut off Dadhyañc's head and replace it with a horse's head. Dadhyañc would then teach them with this horse's head, and when Indra cut the head off, the Aśvins would put Dadhyañc's own head back again. (24–25) This scheme was then realized, as told in Rigveda 1,116,12 (where it is said that horse-headed Dadhyañc Ātharvaṇa taught *madhu*, "honey," to the Aśvins; in ŚB 4,1,5,18, which deals with the *āśvina* cup of *soma* to the honey-loving Aśvins, Dadhyañc is said to have told them "the secret knowledge called Honey," *madhu nāma brāhmaṇam*).

Also the *pravargya* chapter of the Taittirīya-Āraṇyaka (5,1) calls the decapitated hero Makha Vaiṣṇava, but in the Kaṭha-Āraṇyaka (chapter 3) it is Rudra whose head is cut off. This suggests that Makha is the original name, and indeed the hero is called just Makha in the oldest version in the Maitrāyaṇī Saṁhitā (4,5,9) as well as in the Pañcaviṁśa-Brāhmaṇa (7,5,6). Makha reminds one of the name Sumakha associated with one of the Aśvins and its probable etymological connection with Greek *mákhē*, "fight." Sumakha would have personified the chariot-warrior; this Aśvin would have become the god Mitra, whose name later in Iran denoted the sun. The body of the hero fell with its top to the east, and its cut-off head became the sun. In the Bṛhad-Āraṇyaka-Upaniṣad (1,1), the sacrificial horse is equated with the cosmos, and its head with the dawn. The fact that the secret of the *pravargya* is told by a decapitated sage wearing the head of a decapitated horse seems most significant.

From the oldest source available on the Vedic horse sacrifice, the Rigvedic hymns 1,162–163, we know that the horse was slaughtered by cutting off its head with an ax or a butcher's knife (*svadhiti-*, RV 1,163,9), not by strangling, as in the "classical" Vedic ritual. Hence, it would appear, the existence of two burials of a headless body of a horse in the BMAC capital Gonur (chapter 8). The Dadhyañc legend also speaks of providing a human sage with a horse's head. Such an operation may have been an integral part of the secret rite of reviving a dead hero. It is tempting to see this Aśvin-related revival rite revealed in a human skeleton with the skull of a horse, which was excavated in a unique grave near Samara in the Mid-Volga region of Russia; it belongs to the Potapovka culture, dated to *c.* 2100–1700 BCE, and was very probably the skeleton of a Proto-Indo-Aryan speaker (chapter 7) (Fig. 11.2). The secret knowledge of revival is, moreover, connected with honey, which the Vedas connect above all with the Aśvins, the divine healers. In Finnic epic poems of Kalevala, which contain survivals of Proto-Aryan religious concepts (chapter 7), the mother of a dead hero

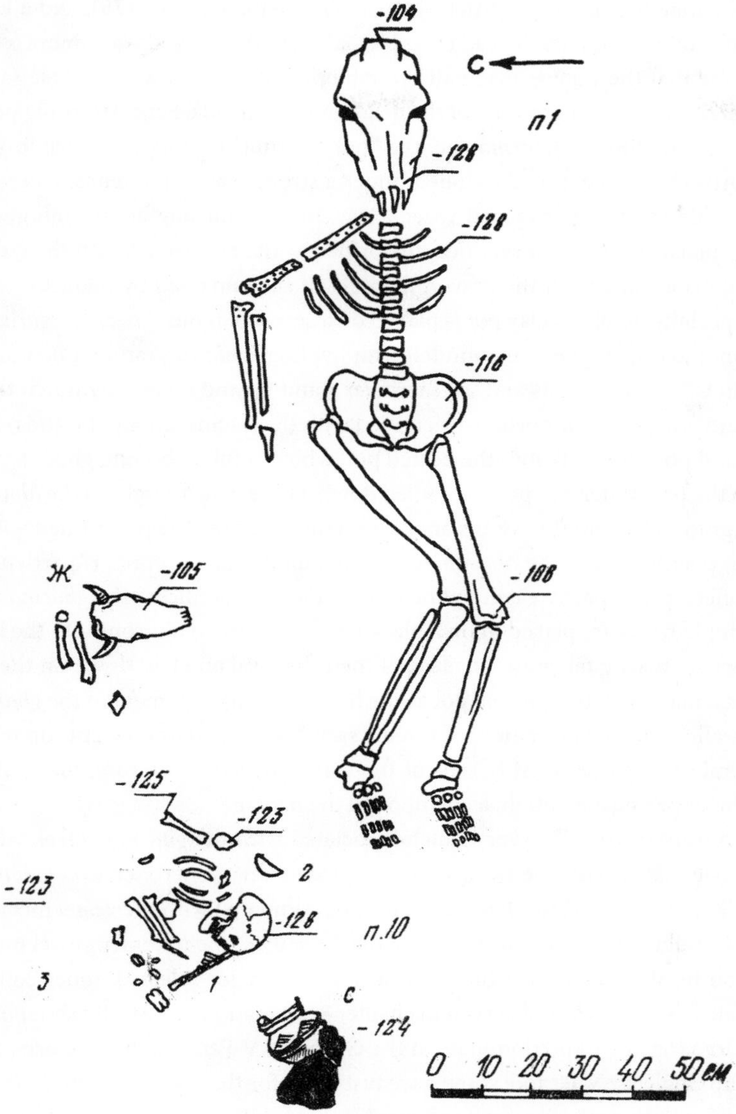

FIGURE 11.2 A human skeleton with a horse's skull. Potapovka kurgan burial, grave 1, near Samara on the mid-Volga in Russia, *c.* 2100–1700 BCE. The arrow points to the north (C). After Vasil'ev et al. 1994:115, fig. 11. Courtesy Pavel V. Kuznetsov.

collects his dismembered corpse and revives it by means of honey (Uralic **mete* from early Proto-Aryan **medhu*) fetched from the highest heaven by a bee.

It must be noted, however, that the evidence of the Potapovka grave has been questioned, because of a suspected mixing of the archaeological layers. Moreover, some molded tablets from Harappa show anthropomorphic deities with animal heads: a dancer resembling later Śiva Naṭarāja has the head of the water buffalo (CISI 1:207 H-175), and a long-armed deity within a fig tree has a ram's head (Fig. 21.16a) like the later god Naigameṣa (chapter 21).

I assume that the Kāṇvas originally worshipped the Aśvins with a horse sacrifice and with funeral rituals implying revival of the dead. In the Rigveda, Sage Atri is the person most closely connected with the *gharma* rite, the "hot offering" of milk and ghee to the Aśvins, which the Atri clan apparently developed under a strong Kāṇva influence. Later called *pravargya*, this offering was performed twice a day, in the morning and evening, during the preparatory phase of the *soma* sacrifice, the principal rite connected with the cult of Indra. Some of the principal acts in the *pravargya* rite—all accompanied by mantras—are the following. A specially prepared clay pot is placed on a separate mound near the *gārhapatya* fire, filled and anointed with ghee, surrounded with live coals and fuel, and fanned until the pot glows red-hot. Then all priests and the sacrificer stand up and reverently watch the pot. The *adhvaryu* and *pratiprasthātar* priests (identified with the Aśvins among the gods) milk a cow and a goat and pour the milk into the heated pot, which is full of boiling ghee. A pillar of fire issues from the pot. When the pot has cooled down a little, it is brought to the *āhavanīya* fire, and offerings to Indra and the Aśvins are poured into the fire. The pot is filled with curds or milk, which overflows into the *āhavanīya*. The remainder of the curds is partly used for an *agnihotra* offering and partly eaten by the priests and the sacrificer. The *gharma* pot and all accessory implements are placed upon a black antelope skin on a throne. On the last day the *gharma* implements are taken to the place of their disposal and laid down on the ground in the shape of a man, with the *gharma* pot as the head. This displacement of the *gharma* implements is paralleled by the placement of a Vedic sacrificer's ritual implements upon his corpse in the funeral. In the fractional burials of the Gandhāra Grave culture, the skull is always placed in the uppermost position, as mentioned in chapter 8.

The concept of "head" is very much associated with the *gharma* vessel, which, as we have seen, is equated with the head of a decapitated divine hero, called *mahāvīra*, "great hero," and "Makha's head." The *gharma* pot may be compared with the vessel most characteristic of the Gandhāra Grave culture, namely the "face urn," the funerary vessel made to look like a human head. Such an urn functions as an ossuary for selected bones collected after cremation burials. As already observed in chapter 8, cremations constitute about one-third of the Gandhāra Graves and predominate in the Ghālegay V Period. The face urns are characteristic of the Ghālegay V Period; some have just holes for the "eyes" and the "mouth," others have both these holes and a protruding "nose" (Fig. 11.3a).

Attempts have been made to trace parallels with this distinctive artifact in other archaeological cultures of Eurasia. Giorgio Stacul (1971) suggested a connection with the anthropomorphically inspired face urns with cremation remains found in the final phase of the Middle Danubian culture of Baden-Pécel (*c.* 2000 BCE). In the Balkans and the Middle Danube, anthropomorphic containers go back to the Late Neolithic period, where they were not as yet related to burial rites. In spite of the several other parallels noted by Stacul between the Gandhāra Graves and the cultures of the Great Hungarian Plain, it has not been possible to confirm any historical connection. The distance in space, and to some extent in time, is considerable. The Gandhāran face urns seem to be an independent local development.

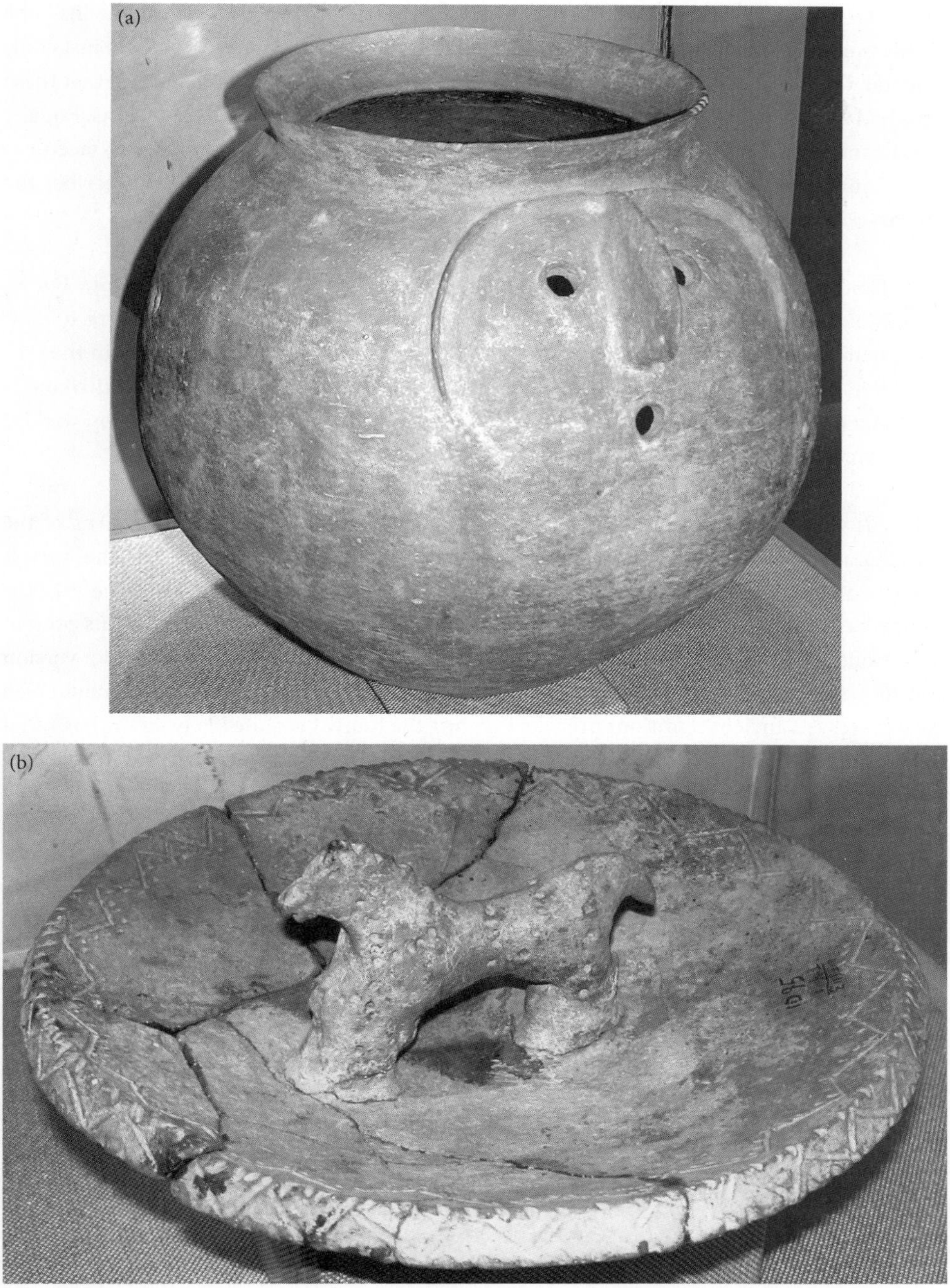

FIGURE 11.3 Funerary "face urns" of the Gandhāra Grave culture. (a) An urn from Zarif Karuna, near Peshawar, with a human-like face including a big nose. Photo Asko Parpola. (b) A lid with a horse-shaped handle from Loebanr, Swat. Photo Asko Parpola.

The symbolic parallels between the *gharma* vessel in the cult of the Aśvins—the "possessors of horses"—and the face urn of the Gandhāra Graves appear not to be just coincidental, for the horse-shaped handle of the lid of a face urn (Fig. 11.3b) suggests that these urns had a cultic relationship with the horse and therefore probably with the Aśvins. Equally significant is the fact that the conspicuous three-dimensional "nose" of the later face urns has a counterpart in the *gharma* vessel. The Śatapatha-Brāhmaṇa (14,1,2,17) describes the preparation of the *gharma* vessel thus:

> He then takes a lump of clay and makes the Mahāvīra (pot) with [the mantra], "For Makha thee! for Makha's head thee!" . . . a span high, for the head is, as it were, a span high;—contracted in the middle, for the head is, as it were, contracted in the middle. At the top he then draws it out [*unnayati*] (so as to form) a spout [*mukham* "mouth"] of three thumb's breadths (high): he thereby makes a nose [*nāsikām*] to this (Mahāvīra, or Pravargya).

It is true that this description does not exactly match the making of the face urns of the Gandhāra Graves, but it is remarkable that the *gharma* pot, alone of all the vessels described in the Vedic literature, is expressly told to have a "nose." It is also true that the Śatapatha-Brāhmaṇa is the only Vedic text to mention this "nose," and although its present redactions are younger than the texts of the Black Yajurveda, it goes back to an earlier version and its contents in some respects differ entirely from all the other texts. That it could well have preserved ancient traditions prevalent among the Kāṇvas is quite likely on the basis that one of the two redactions belongs to the Kāṇvas. The "nose" of the face urn and the *gharma* pot should have some specific function, and indeed it is meaningful when considered in the context of the Aśvin cult.

Comparing the *gharma* vessel with the cinerary urn of the Gandhāra Grave culture implies that there should be a close relationship between the *gharma* rite and the funeral. I think such a relationship does exist. According to the Rigveda, the *gharma* rite was instituted by Atri and offered by his descendants out of gratitude to the Aśvins, because the Aśvins had saved Atri from the distress of the *ṛbīsa* pit. It was the Aśvins who had first given the hot *gharma* drink to Atri while saving him, so the *gharma* rite imitates the service rendered by the Aśvins. I hereby argue that the Atri legend reflects the Atri clan's cremation burial and its association with the adopted cult of the Aśvins as funeral deities, who revive the dead by means of their drink. This funeral cult the Atris took over from the Kāṇvas, with whom they had established friendly relations while settling in Gandhāra. In RV 6,50,10, the Aśvins "delivered Atri from great darkness," in RV 7,71,5 "from a narrow place and darkness." These expressions usually refer to death and to the state of an embryo. Atri's case is similar to that of Vandana and many persons saved by the Aśvins when they seem to be already dead or in a death-like state. As "healers" and "saviors" the Aśvins were thus essentially revivers of the dead, in other words, funeral gods, though this function has not been generally recognized.

What, then, is the meaning of the "nose" of the *gharma* pot and the face urn of the Gandhāra Graves? In PIE, the verbal root **nes-* meant "to come home safely," and, as noted above, from this are derived Gothic *ganisan*, "to be saved," and Modern German *genesen*, "to be healed." As a result of the sound change that turned PIE **e* into Indo-Iranian **a*, that root became homonymous with the word *nas-*, "nose." In the Vedas, the Nāsatyas were associated with the nose. The word *nas-*, "nose," occurs only twice in the Rigveda. In RV 2,39,6 the two Aśvins are compared to the nose with its two nostrils (*nāsā* in the dual)—the nose of one Gandhāran face urn has the detail of two nostrils. Secondly, in RV 5,61,2c, in a hymn addressed to the Maruts, the gods of storm and battle, who in verses 12–13 are represented as driving a chariot, but in verse 2 apparently are riders: "(where is) the saddle (literally, seat) on the back (of the horse), (where) the rein (literally, the restrainer) of the two nostrils (of the horse)?" (*pṛṣṭhé sádo nasór yámaḥ*). This verse shows that the Sanskrit words *yama-* (meaning "twin" as well as "rein") and *nas-* (meaning "nose" as well as "to save")—both associated with the Aśvins in the Rigvedic language—had connotations definitely linked with a key equestrian skill, the control of a horse through its nostrils. (This is one of the two certain references to riding in the Rigveda.)

The Aśvins are invoked as deities of generation, and in Vedic rites of human fertility, the nose plays a central role. In RV 10, 184, 2–3, a prayer for the birth of a son, the two Aśvins, the lotus-garlanded gods, are asked to place an embryo in the wife. The embryo is equated with the fire, the embryo of the waters, who is hidden in the *aśvattha* wood used as the fire-drill: "The embryo, whom the Aśvins rub out of the two golden kindling woods, him we call hither for you, so that you may bear him in the tenth month." Fire is generated by rotating a vertical male kindling-stick of *aśvattha* wood in a hole of a horizontal female plank of *śamī* wood. In the Atharvaveda (AVŚ 6,1), this act is conceived of as sexual intercourse, and Fire as the son of these two pieces of wood. According to the Kauśika-Sūtra (35, 6–10) of the Atharvaveda, the life-cycle rite of *puṁsavana* aiming at the birth of a son is performed as follows. After fire has been produced with the fire-drill, it is ground into powder, which is mixed with butter coming from a cow that has born a male calf. The mixture is put with the thumb of the right hand into the right nostril of the wife.

The myth about the "nose-birth" of the Aśvins is told briefly in a Rigvedic Yama hymn (10,17,1–2) and more extensively in the Nirukta (12,10), in the Bṛhaddevatā (6,127–7,6 ed. Tokunaga 1997) and elsewhere. Saraṇyū, the mother of the divine twins, had assumed the shape of a mare. She became pregnant with the Aśvins when sniffing the seed of her husband, the bright sun god, Vivasvant, who had assumed the shape of a stallion but in haste had emitted his seed on the ground.

This "nose-birth" of the Nāsatyas is ritually included also in the *pravargya* rite. When collecting the clay out of which the *gharma* pot is to be fashioned, at the moment when a goat is milked so that its milk flows over the clay, a horse is made to sniff at the clay while the *adhvaryu* priest recites: "Grant life, grant *prāṇa, apāna*, and *vyāna*, sight, hearing, mind, voice, body, strength, mass—grant me all this!" (ĀpŚS 15,2,2–3). The milk symbolizes the generating seed, as does the reviving *gharma* drink that the Aśvins gave to Atri. According to the Aitareya-Brāhmaṇa (1,22), the *gharma* vessel is the male member, and the milk is the seed. The seed is poured into the fire, the womb of the gods, as generation, so one who sacrifices with the *pravargya* rite is reborn as an immortal god.

Thus there are many reasons to connect the funeral face-urn of Gandhāra, with its prominent "nose," to the *gharma* pot of the Aśvin cult, which also has a "nose," representing the head of a great hero called Makha. Here at last we have a very concrete link between archaeological evidence and Vedic culture, a link that many people have been missing.

The *gharma/pravargya* ritual is the only context in the Rigveda in which *sāmans* (ritual songs) are mentioned by name. The name of the most important *sāman, rathantara*, refers to the chariot (*ratha-*), the vehicle of the Aśvins. The name occurs in the Rigveda just twice: in RV 1,164,25, immediately before the verses 26–29, which speak of the *gharma/pravargya* rite of the Aśvins; and in RV 1,180,1 (along with the also important *bṛhat sāman* mentioned in verse 2), immediately before the *gharma* ritual (mentioned in verse 3). The *gharma* rite of the Aśvins is the only ritual, besides the *soma* sacrifice, that is mentioned a number of times in the Rigveda. The hymns addressed to *soma* were collected from all the "family" books of the Rigveda in order to make Book 9—the basis for the Sāmavedic ritual. In view of the almost complete absence of *sāman* names, and the omission of chanter priests from the Rigvedic enumerations of priests, it would seem that the Sāmavedic liturgy for the *soma* sacrifice was created out of the tradition of *sāman* singing in Aśvin rituals.

The *sāmans* in the *gharma* rite are much simpler than those sung in praise of *soma*; they are solo songs chanted by just one person, although all participants sing the finale. In the *soma* sacrifice, the *sāmans* are chanted by a trio of priests, consisting of the *prastotar* (literally, "pre-lauder"), who sings the first portion, the *pratihartar* ("the receiver"), who sings the second portion, the *udgātar* ("high-chanter"), who sings the most important portion, the *udgītha* ("high chant"), while all three priests sing the finale, joined by other participants in the ritual on certain occasions. This scheme seems to me to be an elaboration of the solo *sāmans*, devised when the Sāmavedic ritual was created for the *soma* sacrifice.

The relatively simple preparation of the *haoma* juice in the Zoroastrian *yasna* ritual includes filtering, but without the praise songs that in the Vedic *soma* sacrifice are addressed to Soma Pavamāna, "Soma that is being purified," by being strained through sheep's wool. I suspect that Soma's praise songs may have been inspired by an earlier liturgy that praised the *surā*, the beer made of barley that is sacred to Varuṇa. We know from the *sautrāmaṇī* ritual that *surā* was also purified, using a horse-hair (*vāla- / vāra-*) filter. In this ritual, the king, after first becoming a brāhmaṇa and a *soma* drinker for the royal consecration (*rājasūya*), is transformed back into a warrior (*kṣatriya*) and therewith a *surā* drinker in this "reconsecration" (*punar-abhiṣeka*). Perhaps the original drink of *pavamāna* hymns was *surā*, but the laud-singing was transferred to *soma* when the Rigvedic community expanded to include Kāṇva and Āṅgirasa poets, who were initially worshippers of the Aśvins and Mitra-Varuṇa but later converted to the Indra cult after the Aśvins became accepted as *soma* drinkers.

It is the Kāṇva and Āṅgirasa clans who must have created the Sāmaveda, for in addition to Book 9, the Sāmaveda-Saṁhitā mainly consists of their hymns in Books 8 and 1. The Aṅgirases are mentioned as composers of *sāmans* in the latest books of the Rigveda, in RV 1,107,2 (*áṅgirasāṃ sā́mabhiḥ stūyámānāḥ*) and RV 10,78,5 (*áṅgiraso ná sā́mabhiḥ*). The Sāmaveda favors the meters (*gāyatrī* and *pragātha*) and the strophic structure (tristichs) characteristic of the poetry of the Kāṇva and Āṅgirasa clans, which in this respect differs from the poetry of the "family" books (Oldenberg 1884). The same applies to some extent to the language: thus the root *gā(y)-*, "to sing, chant," which is fundamental to Sāmavedic terminology, is seldom attested in the "family" books, mostly in *gāyatrī* or *pragātha* stanzas in hymns with tristich structure (Hopkins 1896). The words *gāyatrá-* and *gāyatrí-* are found in Books 2–7 only in the admittedly late hymn RV 2,43, which is the last of Book 2.

The Sāmavedic priest *udgātár-* is mentioned in the Rigveda just once, in this late three-versed hymn 2,43, which also speaks of singing a *sāman* in verse 2a (*udgātéva . . . sā́ma gāyasi*) and of "a *sāman* singer who speaks in two ways, mastering the songs in *gāyatrī* and *triṣṭubh* meters." Though the Sāmaveda appears to have been created in South Asia, Aṅgiras, the ancestor of the Āṅgirasa clan, already figures in the "family" books', so the Rigvedic Indo-Aryans must have met Aṅgirases already in southern Central Asia. The Old Iranian Avesta has two different poetic traditions: Zarathuštra's *gāthās* resemble the "family" books of the Rigveda, while the later Yašt hymns are comparable to the Kāṇva and Āṅgirasa poetry. Probably, the Yašt hymns were collected and recorded later than the *gāthās* for reasons similar to the reasons why the Atharvavedic hymns were collected later than the hymns of the Rigveda.

12

The Atharvaveda and the Vrātyas

The hymns of the Atharvaveda form the second-oldest text collection of the Vedic literature after the Rigveda. The Atharvaveda of the Śaunaka school (AVŚ)—the most commonly used recension—contains 730 hymns divided into twenty books. By contrast, the recension of the Paippalāda school (AVP) has 923 hymns also divided into twenty books, but arranged in an order different from that of the Śaunaka school. The AVP first became known from a single corrupt manuscript discovered in Kashmir in 1873, but remained largely incomprehensible until a living Paippalāda tradition with many manuscripts was discovered in Orissa about 1950 by Durgamohan Bhattacharyya. Its publication and exegesis are one of the most exciting current projects of Vedic philology.

The hymn collections of the Rigveda, Sāmaveda, and Yajurveda mainly relate to the *soma* sacrifice or other *śrauta* rituals and have therefore been considered to represent the "hieratic religion" of the Vedas, in contrast to the "popular religion" of the Atharvaveda, with its "white and black magic" and domestic (*gṛhya*) rituals such as initiation into learning (*upanayana*), marriage, and funerals. These labels represent an attempt to understand the "Triple Veda" and the Atharvaveda as two sides of a single integral religion, rather than a single phase in the acculturation of two different religions: "Rigvedic" and "Atharvavedic." Actually, "popular" is not a good fit as a label, given that royal rituals and the duties of the king's court priest (for whom "magic" was important) are among the central topics of the Atharvaveda and its ritual manual, Kauśika-Sūtra.

The "Atharvavedic" religion had already started to be accepted into the fold of the Rigvedic religion in Books 1 and 10 of the Rigveda, which contain many hymns of clearly Atharvavedic character, including the marriage and funeral rituals and the (not so "popular") cosmogonical, speculative, and riddle hymns. "Most western scholars are . . . agreed that the Rigveda contains a number of hymns which by their special characteristics in subject, metre and language differ from the main body of the poems and associate themselves instead with the Atharvaveda. They are generally described as 'popular' and regarded as later additions . . ." (Gonda 1975:28).

By the time the Atharvavedic hymns were collected, their poets had accepted the Rigvedic tradition, and vice versa. Many Atharvavedic hymns copy and imitate Rigvedic hymns, yet without handling the poetical meters nearly as skillfully as in the Rigveda. This partial adoption of Rigvedic traditions cannot, however, hide the fact that the Atharvaveda goes back to a separate, and in many respects more archaic, Indo-Aryan tradition. The language of the Atharvaveda, continued in the Brāhmaṇas and other later Vedic texts, as well as in epic and classical Sanskrit, cannot be directly derived from the Rigvedic language. This is clear above all from the fact that the "Atharvavedic" language has preserved the Proto-Indo-European distinction between the sounds *l* and *r* in many words. The original Rigvedic language, on the other hand, had completely lost the PIE **l* as a result of so-called rhotacism, which merged every **l* with **r*; and this change must have happened in southern Central Asia, before the migrants entered South Asia, because the **l/*r* distinction was also lost in Mitanni Indo-Aryan (chapter 8) as well as in Avestan and Old Persian (Mayrhofer 2002 [2004]). Words with PIE **l* start to infiltrate the Rigveda in Books 1 and 10, in which *l* occurs eight times more frequently than in the "family" books, while in the AV *l* occurs seven times more frequently than in the RV. In the "family" books, *l* occurs mainly in foreign loanwords and proper names (see chapter 9), but no verbs preserve PIE **l* ("to hear" is *śru-* against Greek *klúō*, Latin *cluēre*, Russian *slušat'*) and only a few nouns (*uloka-/loka-*, *śloka-*, *-miśla-*), which have crept in when the text of the Rigveda was finally fixed around 700 BCE (Pinault 1989:36–37).

The dialectal difference between the Rigvedic language on the one hand and the Atharvavedic language and classical Sanskrit on the other was proposed by Maurice Bloomfield (1899:46–47) and seconded by M. B. Emeneau (1966) and a number of other scholars. The loss or preservation of the **r/*l* distinction is paralleled in other linguistic traits. In the declination of the nouns with *a*-stems, the Rigvedic dialect has innovated in the masculine plural nominative by adding a second plural nominative marker *-as* (used in consonantal stems) to the ending *-ās*, which continues the original PIE ending; the resulting double ending *-āsas* is parallelled in Avestan (*-āŋhō*), Old Persian (*-āha*), and Pāli (*-āse*). Besides this innovated double ending, the original *-ās* is also found in the Rigvedic language (though *-ās* is often to be read as *-āsas* to mend defective meter) as it is found in Avestan (*-ā*) and Old Persian (*-ā*). While *-ās* is about twice as frequent as *-āsas* in the Rigveda, in the Atharvaveda it is twenty-four times as frequent, and classical Sanskrit knows only *-ās*. Similarly, in the instrumental plural of the *a*-stems, the Rigvedic language has the innovative ending *-ebhis* (paralleled by Old Persian *-aibiš*) besides the slightly more common inherited ending *-ais* (Avestan *-āiš*); while Rigvedic *-ebhis* is continued in Pāli *-ehi* and Prakrit *-ehiṃ*, in the Atharvaveda *-ais* is five times as common as *-ebhis*, and classical Sanskrit knows only *-ais*. In the verbal conjugation, the innovative ending *-masi* of the first-person plural present active (paralleled by Old Iranian *-mahi*) is about five times as common as the inherited ending *-mas*, while in the Atharvaveda *-mas* is commoner than *-masi*, which is no longer used in classical Sanskrit. There are many further differences, not least in the lexicon.

In chapter 11 we saw that some poets of the Kāṇva and Āṅgirasa families early on joined the Rigvedic culture, composing hymns in Books 1, 8, and 9, which form the basis of the Sāmaveda that they apparently created. Evidently other Kāṇvas and Āṅgirasas remained more faithful to their own traditions and composed the Atharvaveda, the oldest name of which is *atharvāṅgirasaḥ*. This name divides the contents of this fourth Veda into two parts and relates them to these two clans: the Atharvans are associated with the peaceful (*śānta*) and auspicious (*pauṣṭika*) rituals of medication (*bheṣajāni*), while the Āṅgirasas are connected with the terrible (*ghora*) rituals of sorcery (*ābhicārika*).

Comparing the Śaunaka and Paippalāda versions of the Atharvaveda, Stanley Insler has studied the methods by which their composers have pieced their hymns together. "This is made possible because both known recensions of the Atharvan Saṃhitā often present versions of the same hymn that differ not only in the choice of forms, words, phrases or whole lines (*pāda*), but that also differ in the sequence and number of stanzas constituting a recognized *sūkta* ['hymn'] in the respective collections." Insler concludes that the Kāṇva and Āṅgirasa poets of the Rigveda belong to the same tradition as the poets of the Atharvaveda:

> This proposal can be supported linguistically, which I shall undertake on another occasion. If the Kaṇva and Āṅgirasa bards were in fact the poets of the Atharvan compositions, an interesting question arises: Do the Dharma texts state that one should stop studying the Veda if the singing of *sāmans* is overheard because the Kaṇvas and Āṅgirases, the *sāman*-singers par excellence, were also *yātudhānas* [i.e., sorcerers]? How else is their bad reputation to be explained, a matter so clearly unpleasant that the singing of *sāmans* is mentioned along with the noise of dogs, jackals, asses and owls? Support for this idea stems from the fact that the black spells among Atharvan hyms (*ghora, yātu, ābhicārika*) are called *āṅgirasa*. (Insler 1998:17)

Káṇva- (whence the patronym *Kāṇvá-*) is among those words of the Rigveda that exhibit a sound change characteristic of the later development of the Old Indo-Aryan language (Sanskrit) into Middle Indo-Aryan (Prakrit), in this case *ṛ* >*a*. (Such Prakritisms one would expect to find in the "Atharvavedic" language, which had supposedly been subject to Dravidian substratum influence for centuries in the Indus Valley [chapter 14]. In this connection one can also point to the unusually high number of non-IE retroflex phonemes in Book 8 of the Rigveda, belonging to the Kāṇvas and Āṅgirasas.) Karl Hoffmann (1940) convincingly derived *káṇva-* from **kṛṇva-*, "acting (magically)." The name appears to mean "bewitcher, sorcerer." The root *kṛ-*, "to do," is itself used in the meaning "to bewitch" in the Atharvaveda (AVŚ 5,14,9 *yáś cakā́ra tám íj jahi*) and has such derivatives as *kártra-* and *kṛtyā-*, "sorcery." Moreover, in the hymn AVŚ 2,25, *káṇva-* denotes demoniac beings who eat embryos (verse 3) and obstruct life (verses 4 and 5), while AVP 13,10,4 speaks of "a *káṇva-* associated with a sorcerer (*yātumāvān*)."

As we shall now see, key sorcery terms are more or less totally absent from the "family" books of the Rigveda and occur mainly in Books 1 and 10, whereas they occur frequently in the Atharvaveda (here AVŚ). The word *abhicārá-*, "sorcery, witchcraft," is not found anywhere in the Rigveda, but it is implied in the only Rigvedic verse (10,34,14b) where the verb *abhi + car-* is attested: *mā́ no ghoréṇa* (scil. *abhicāréṇa*) *caratābhí dhṛṣṇú*, "do ye not mightily bewitch us with terrible (sorcery)!" In the AVŚ, on the other hand, *abhicārá-* occurs four times; *abhicārín-*, "one commanding sorcery," once; *pratyabhicáraṇa-*, "counter-incantation" once; while the verb *abhi + car-*, "to bewitch," is used three times. Another key sorcery term, *kṛtyā-*, "witchcraft," occurs only twice in the Rigveda, in 10,85,28–29, that is, in the marriage hymn of Book 10. In the AVŚ, on the other hand, it is attested as many as fifty-eight times, plus twenty-six times in the compound *kṛtyā-kṛt-*, "practicing witchcraft."

The sorcery rites are usually directed against a rival, and favor the words *bhrā́tṛvya-* and *sapátna-*. The first of these originally meant "brother's son" or "cousin," a relative who for a king or prince is a dangerous rival as a potential seizer of royal power. In the Rigveda *bhrā́tṛvya-* is attested just once (with a privative prefix) in RV 8,21,13, used by a Kāṇva poet, while in the Atharvaveda, it occurs fifteen times, sometimes in prose passages, including three instances of compound words that denote "destroying," "killing," or "driving away" the rival. The second term, *sapátna-*, "rival," is derived from the corresponding feminine gender term *sa-pátnī-*, "co-wife, wife having the same husband," which is attested twice in the old "family" books of the Rigveda, but without originally implying rivalry, since both hymns (RV 3,1,10 and 3,6,4) speak of the two world halves (*ródasī*), heaven and earth, as co-wives of the fire god Agni. Female rivals are involved, however, in two hymns belonging to the late books of the Rigveda: RV 1,105,8 (the hymn is ascribed to Kutsa Āṅgirasa) and 10,145,1–5. The masculine *sapátna-*, "rival," is attested four times in the Rigveda, all in Book 10, along with the compound *sapatna-hán-*, "killing the rival." In the Atharvaveda, on the other hand, *sapátna-* occurs sixty-seven times, along with various compounds meaning "killing the rival" or the like: *sapatna-hán-* (twenty-two times), *sapatna-kṣáyaṇa-* (five times), and *sapatna-kárśana-*, *sapatna-cā́tana-*, and *sapatna-dámbhana-* (once each).

I return to Insler's question about the Sāmavedins as sorcerers. The Sāmavedic texts are the first to prescribe some *soma* sacrifices specifically for witchcraft purposes. But the Sāmavedic singers can also fulfil wishes by other, less drastic means. The following list of options is not exhaustive. One may choose between several different *stomas*, that is, how many verses are to be chanted in a laud; between several different *viṣṭutis*, that is, ways of counting the verses repeated to fulfil the *stoma*; between several alternative verses on which the *sāmans* are chanted; between several alternative *sāmans* and within individual *sāmans*, between alternative syllable numbers in the parts of the *sāmans*; and between several different finales (*nidhana*). We may exemplify the use of the song's finale by quoting Pañcaviṁśa-Brāhmaṇa 7,1,11, which gives the following options for replacement of the regular finale *ā* of the *gāyatra sāman*: "As the finale he should take (the word) *iḍā* (literally 'refreshment,' but often equated with cattle) for one who desires cattle; *svaḥ* ('heaven') for one who wishes (to attain) heaven; *yaśaḥ* ('fame') for one who desires spiritual luster; *āyuḥ* ('long life') for one who suffers from disease; *haṁsi* ('you kill') for one who practices sorcery." Similar options exist for all the means enumerated above; they usually include witchcraft.

Before continuing with the Sāmaveda, the mention of the options to fulfil specific wishes leads me to comment briefly on the beginnings of the Yajurveda. The principal Yajurvedic priests are the Adhvaryu and the Pratiprasthātar, human representatives of the Aśvins, whom they worship as the main priests of the *pravargya* ritual (see chapter 11). The earliest Yajurvedic texts, the Maitrāyaṇī and Kāṭhaka Saṁhitās, introduce to the Vedic *śrauta* ritual many *kāmya-iṣṭi* rites, devised to fulfil all kinds of wishes, including the desire to harm rivals and enemies (Caland 1908). The principal ritual manual of the Atharvavedins, the Kauśika-Sūtra, consists of two parts; while the latter part describes domestic (*gṛhya*) rites, the first fifty-two chapters are devoted to *kāmya-iṣṭis* of the same kind (Caland 1900). This suggests an ultimately "Atharvavedic" background for the *iṣṭi* rites, where the sacrificial oblations usually consist of cakes baked of rice or barley (grains sacred to Varuṇa). These sacrifices differ from the original Rigvedic *soma* sacrifice (*yajña*), which probably resembled the *yasna* of the Zoroastrians. In chapter 11, I compared the milk offerings to the Aśvins of the *pravargya* to the daily *agnihotra* offerings of milk to sun and fire (equated with Mitra and Varuṇa, respectively), which, with the slightly more complicated *iṣṭi*s of the new- and full-moon days, constitute the very core of the "classical" Vedic *śrauta* ritual; the *iṣṭi*s function also as models for the simpler domestic sacrifices (which first emerge in the late hymns of the Rigveda and the Atharvaveda). The origins of the Yajurveda thus also seem to lie in the "Atharvavedic" worship of the Aśvins and their doubles Mitra-Varuṇa.

The earliest sources on *soma* sacrifices connected with sorcery belong to the Sāmaveda, which is the source for most texts dealing with these rites in the other Vedas. The original Tāṇḍya-Brāhmaṇa seems to have been purged of most "barbaric" material, including the rites of sorcery, which are missing in the twenty-five chapters of the Pañcaviṁśa-Brāhmaṇa (in contrast to the Jaiminīya-Brāhmaṇa) but appear in its supplementary twenty-sixth chapter, the Ṣaḍviṁśa-Brāhmaṇa (Caland 1931:xx–xxi). ṢB 3,8–11 contains the sorcery rites called *śyena* ("falcon"), *iṣu* ("arrow"), *saṃdaṁśa* ("tongs"), and *vajra* ("mace, thunderbolt"). The *śyena* rite is described as follows in the Sāmavedic Lāṭyāyana-Śrautasūtra (8,5):

> As officiating priests of the "falcon" rite one should choose learned sons of warriors (*yaudha-*) who form (raiding) gangs (*vrātīna-*); (learned sons) of worthy persons (*arhat-*), according to Śāṇḍilya. One should churn butter for sacrificial ghee from the milk of cows which are among sick cows but are not yet sick. After cutting down all the many plant stems and trees that have grown in a given place they should make the sacrificial area there; or on a burning hot ground. The words *śavanabhye adhiṣavaṇe* (in the Ṣaḍviṁśa-Brāhmaṇa) mean: they should make the two planks on which the *soma* is pressed from the nave(-plank)s of a cart with which the corpse (*śava*), i.e., dead person, is carried away (to the place of funeral). The sacrificial stake should not have the (usual) *caṣāla*-ring (at top) but instead a wooden sword as its tip. The officiating priests should perform their duties wearing red turbans, dressed in red clothes, having their sacred thread hung from the neck (as is done when one defecates), carrying quivers and bows with strings strung. . . . [instructions for *sāmans* as deadly weapons omitted] . . . (The prescription about the sacrificial fees given in the Ṣaḍviṁśa-Brāhmaṇa means that) in groups of nine (animals), one should give as many as possible cows that are blind in one eye, lame, without horns, and without tails. Moreover, these (defective animals) they should make bleed at the time the animals are given as priestly fees.

The term *vrātīna-* connects these performers of the "falcon" and other sorcery rites with people termed *vrātya-* in Vedic texts. The Vrātyas are known especially from rites called *vrātyastoma*, the oldest sources on which belong to the Sāmaveda: Jaiminīya-Brāhmaṇa 2,221–227, and Pañcaviṁśa-Brāhmaṇa 17,1–4; the Lāṭyāyana-Śrautasūtra (8,6) gives divergent explanations of ritual authorities for the obsolete terms used in PB 17,1. The *vrātyastomas* and related rites are centrally important for understanding the prehistory of the Vedic ritual, for they have many features and components not normally found in the *śrauta* rites. Actually it is nowadays widely agreed that they are a kind of fossil remains of an earlier, more archaic stage of ritual development. Discussing them without giving the reader a chance to form an idea of them from the source texts seems futile. I therefore start by quoting the Pañcaviṁśa-Brāhmaṇa's exposition of the first, basic *vrātyastoma*, omitting much irrelevant data, but adding some clarifications in brackets:

> The Gods, forsooth, went to the world of heaven; of them the adherents of "the God" [i.e., Rudra] were left behind (on earth), leading a Vrātya-life. . . . Those who lead the life of a joined group [*vrāta-*] are destitute, left behind. For they neither practise the study of the Veda nor do they plough or trade. . . . The joined group is unequal [among its members], as it were. . . . Swallowing poison are those, who eat foreign food as Brahman's food, who call good words bad, who use a stick to strike the guiltless [JB 2,225 is more explicit by stating that the Vrātyas violate a Brahmin who should not be violated], who, though being not initiated, speak the speech of the initiated [according to JB 2,222 the Vrātyas speak with their voice what is impure and unsuited for sacrifice; in front of elder people they speak obscene things, *āhanasyaṃ vadanti*]. The guilt of these may be removed by the sixteen-versed *stoma* . . .
>
> A turban, a goad, a bow without arrow, a board-covered rough vehicle [*vipathaḥ phalakāstīrṇaḥ*; according to LŚS 8,6,9–11, *vipatha-* is an uncovered chariot of the people living in the east (i.e., Magadha), *prācyaratho nāstīrṇaḥ*; it is yoked with an agile pair of a horse and a mule, according to Śāṇḍilya, or with any pair of horses or mules, according to Dhānaṃjayya], a garment with black fringes, two goat-skins: one white, one black, a silver ornament (worn around the neck), (all) that is (the equipment) of the Gṛhapati [i.e., the leader]. The other (Vrātyas) have (upper garments) with red borders and corded fringes, with strings at each side; each of them has a pair of shoes and doubly-joined goat's hides. This is the possession of the Vrātyas; on him, to whom they bestow (this possession), they transfer (their) guilt (or unworthiness, so that henceforth they are qualified to take part in the sacrifice of the Āryas). [LŚS 8,6,28–29 specifies that those who give up roaming around as Vrātyas should give their equipment to Vrātyas (who practice this way of life), or to a religious student from the country of Magadha, *brahmabandhu- māgadhadeśīya-*; after having performed the *vrātyastoma* rites they should live following the three Vedas.] Each of them brings to their Gṛhapati thirty-three (cows). For thirty-three adherents of "the God" had come (through this *vrātyastoma*) to prospering. (So this rite serves) for prospering. (PB 17,1, translated Caland 1931:454–458)

Besides Sāmavedic texts, the earliest source on the Vrātyas is the Atharvaveda, which devotes a whole book with eighteen chapters in Brāhmaṇa prose to this topic (AVŚ 15, AVP 18,27–43); the description of the *vrātyastoma* in the old Yajurvedic Baudhāyana-Śrautasūtra (BŚS) 18,24–26 clearly follows the Atharvavedic tradition and provides important specifications.

AVŚ 15,1: The Vrātya-Book of the Atharvaveda begins with a cosmogony. In the beginning this universe was the Vrātya, going around making requests (*īyamāna-*); he stirred up the creator god Prajāpati who started to create. This resulted in the birth of the Great God (*mahādeva*), the Lord (*īśāna*), who became the "solitary" Eka-Vrātya (this expression may refer to the sun as the protypal solitary wanderer). He took to himself a bow, which became the rainbow: its belly is dark blue (*nīla*), its back red (*lohita*); with the dark blue he envelops a hostile cousin or rival (*bhrātṛvya-*), with the red he pierces one hating him. The quarters of space are connected with the Vrātya's archers (*iṣvāsa-*), called Bhava, Śarva, Paśupati, Ugro devaḥ, Rudra, Mahādeva, and Īśāna (these same plus Vajra as the eighth are the eight names of Rudra in Kauṣītaki-Brāhmaṇa 6,1–9).

AVŚ 15,2: The Vrātya is described as moving through all the directions of space, starting from the east. He (BŚS: the agreed leader, *sthapati*, of the Vrātyas, who performs the vows, *vrata-*, on behalf on the whole group: he sleeps on the ground, does not eat meat, and does not have sex) is dressed in a garment (*vāsas*, BŚS: it is black with black fringes, this being the garment of one who has been initiated), wears a turban (*uṣṇīṣa*, BŚS: it is black, as he is initiated), two round ornaments (*pravarta-*, BŚS: radiant disks, *rukma-*, of gold and silver: the BŚS expressly connects them with the golden and silvery disk placed on both sides of the heated *gharma* vessel which symbolizes the head of the Great Hero in the *pravargya* rite of the Aśvins; cf. also the golden disk, *rukma-*, hung from his neck by the sacrificer when he is about to carry the fire-pot *ukhā* in the *agnicayana*), a jewel-necklace (*maṇi*). (BŚS: A bow with three arrows in a quiver made of leather serves as his stick of the initiated; he speaks the speech of the Vrātyas, which serves as the speech of the initiated. He wears hoofed sandals, *khuryāv upānahau*, because as an initiated one, he should not tread on anything impure.)

He drives around in a "rough vehicle" (*vipatha-*, "able to move in roadless terrain") pulled by two draught-animals (*vipatha-vāha-*) and driven by a charioteer (*sārathi-*) with a whip (*pratoda-*). (BŚS 18,24 here speaks of the leader as having a war chariot, *ratha-*, and correlates the chariot's parts with the components of the sacrificial area of the Vedic *śrauta* ritual: the whip's handle and lash, the chariot front, the two shafts of the forked pole, the two yokes, the two bow-stands, the two sides of the chariot, the railing, the stands of the servants, the seat of the charioteer, the chariot-lap, i.e., its floor, the standing-place of the chariot. BŚS 18,25 however mentions an inauspicious old chariot yoked with old draught-animals.) Running on each side of the Vrātya's carriage are two footmen (*pariṣkanda*), while in front of it run two other men (*puraḥ-sara*). A prostitute (*puṁścalī*) and a bard (*māgadha*) accompany the Vrātya. (BŚS 18,25 enigmatically states that among the Vrātyas is "a celibate man who is not a *māgadha* but is called a *māgadha*," *brahmabandhur amāgadho māgadhavākyaḥ*, and "a celibate nonprostitute who is called a prostitute," *brahmabandhur apuṁścalū puṁścalūvākyā*.)

AVŚ 15,10: When the Vrātya comes to royal houses as a guest (*atithi-*), the king should esteem him higher than himself; "thus he will not offend against the royal rule (*rāṣṭra-*)." From this arose spiritual power (*brahman-*) and mundane power (*kṣatra-*), which entered Bṛhaspati (the divine *purohita*) and Indra (the divine king) respectively.

AVŚ 15,3: After standing for a year erect, the Vrātya asked for a throne-seat (*āsandī-*) to be brought. The four seasons (spring, summer, rains, autumn) are represented in its four feet, the *sāman* songs *rathantara, bṛhad, vāmadevya*, and *yajñāyajñīya* in its two lengthwise and two crosswise frames, the Rigvedic verses in its forward cords and the Yajurvedic formulae in its cross-cords, the Vedas in its cushion, and the Brahman in its pillow, the *sāman* in its seat and the *udgītha* in its rest. On this seat the Vrātya ascended. (The principal chanter priest Udgātar ascends a throne seat with almost identical ritual at the *mahāvrata*, see LŚS 3,12 below.)

AVŚ 15,2: The *sāmans* move with the Vrātya, starting with *rathantara* and *bṛhad* in the east, *vāmadevya* and *yajñāyajñīya* in the south, *vairāja* and *vairūpa* in the west, and *naudhasa* and *śyaita* in the north.

The Rigveda mentions by name very few *sāmans*, all in connection with the *gharma/pravargya* rite of the Aśvins, where they are sung as solo songs (chapter 11).

In the Atharvaveda, *sāmans* mentioned by name occur mostly in this *vrātya*-book (other references, almost all of them just to *rathantara* and *bṛhat*—probably connected with the *gharma* rite, as in AVŚ 9,10,3, which repeats RV 1,64,25—occur in 8,9,4, 8,10,13–17, 11,3,16, and 13,3,11–12). All those mentioned in the *vrātya*-book are important *sāmans*, mostly used at the *pṛṣṭha* lauds sung at the midday service of a *soma* sacrifice in the Sāmavedic liturgy. This particular combination of *sāmans* in AVŚ 15,2, however, suggests that the ritual context probably is the *mahāvrata* laud chanted at the midday service of the *mahāvrata* day, at the end of a ritual year, when solo *sāmans* are sung around the completed fire altar as a part of the *mahāvrata* laud (PB 5,1–4; LŚS 1,5,11–22, 3,9–4,4). Other reasons, too, require a closer examination of the *mahāvrata* day, as we shall now conduct using the Lāṭyāyana-Śrautasūtra.

LŚS 3,9: The Sāmavedic Lāṭyāyana-Śrautasūtra begins its description of the *mahāvrata* day with the solo *sāmans* around the fire altar: when, by whom and where exactly they should be chanted; the finale parts are sung in chorus.

LŚS 3,10: Next, the king and the warriors who follow him in a minimum of two chariots are made to put on armor and hand protection, then to string the bow, equip themselves with three arrows, and board the chariot. Two pieces of antelope skin are tied up for targets on the north side of the fire-kindler's hearth, one to the east, the other to the west. The king is instructed to drive sunwise around the sacrificial ground three times, on each round piercing the eastern target skin, so that each arrow pierces the skin higher than the previous arrow, and without the arrow falling to the ground. The other charioteers should in the same way pierce the western skin with three arrows. After shooting the third arrow the king should drive northwards and shoot a fourth arrow in any direction he likes, stopping his drive after he has seen cows. There his armor will be taken off.

LŚS 3,11: A hole has been dug in the ground west of the fire-kindler's hearth, so that it is half inside and half outside the sacrificial area. A bull's hide with its hair side upwards is fixed over the hole so that it is fully covered. They hit (*ā-han-*) this earth-drum (*bhūmi-dundubhi*) with the tail (of the bull hide), uttering the mantra: "You are (Goddess) Vāc! Announce, O drum, success . . . for us! Contradict (i.e., ward off by sound) him who hates (us), contradict (him by emitting) a terrible sound (*ghorāṃ vācam*)! Then announce noble fame for us, O drum, (by emitting) a sound that is kind and friendly (for us)! . . ."—The verb *ā-han-*, here used for the "beating" of the drum, has two connotations: the "slaying" of the bull and the bull's "pushing his penis" (symbolized by the bull's tail with which the drum is beaten) into the vagina of the Goddess. From this verb is derived *āhanasya-*, "obscenity," which JB 2,222 says the Vrātyas impudently speak in front of elders, and which denotes the obscene dialogue taking place during the sexual union of the horse sacrifice.

LŚS 3,12: Then a throne seat (*āsandī-*) made of the wood of the *udumbara* fig tree and cords of woven *muñja* grass is brought to the north side of the pillar made of *udumbara* wood in the sitting hall (*sadas*). The Udgātar touches the four feet of the throne, which he calls the *rathantara* and *bṛhat, naudhasa* and *śyaita* (*sāmans*), and the four horizontal beams, which he calls *vairāja* and *vairūpa*, and *raivata* and *śākvara* (*sāmans*). Then he touches the crosswise and lengthwise woven strings, which he verbally equates with Rigvedic verses and Yajurvedic formulae, he touches the seat, which he equates with Sāmavedic *sāmans*, and so on. The Udgātar then ascends the seat, according to the mantra he thereby utters, for becoming Samrāj, "the Universal King" (on this term, see chapter 10). (The Vrātya ascends a throne with an almost identical ritual according to AVŚ 15,3, see above.)

LŚS 4,1: A harp (*vāṇa-*) has been made of *udumbara* wood, with its soundbox covered with the hide of a red bull, hair side out. Ten holes are made in the rear part of the harp, in each of which ten strings of *muñja* grass are fixed (alternatively, there are three holes, with thirty-three, thirty-four, and thirty-three strings each). The Udgātar priest now plays this hundred-stringed harp by stroking it with a reed plectrum, pronouncing a mantra, linking its sound with goddess Vāc, who overpowers the enemies and grants life for a hundred years.

LŚS 4,2: Now different stringed instruments (*alābuvīṇā, vakrā, kapiśīrṣṇī, mahāvīṇā,* and *apiśīlavīṇā*) are played by professional musicians at the eastern and western doors of the sitting hall. Choristers accompany them with mantras. To the west of them, the wives of the participants play the *kāṇḍavīṇā* (with a plectrum) and the *picchorā* (upon the mouth) alternately in pairs.

LŚS 4,3: A Brahmanical praiser (*abhigara-*) sits at the eastern door of the hall facing westwards and praises the accomplishment of the participants in the sacrificial session. A commoner reviler (*apagara-*) sits at the western door facing eastwards and blames the participants for their failure.

A man belonging to an Aryan social class stands south of the *mārjālīya* hearth (the fireplace for washing utensils) inside the sacrificial area facing southwards. Opposite him, outside the sacrificial area, a man of the Śūdra class faces northwards. These two men fight for a round white skin by pulling it alternately toward themselves, starting with the Śūdra; eventually the Aryan man wins, the Śūdra drops the skin and runs away, while the Aryan man follows him, beating him with the skin.

East of the fire-kindler's hearth a celibate student (*brahmacārin-*) stands inside the sacrificial area facing north, while a prostitute (*puṁścalī-*) stands outside the sacrificial area, facing southwards. They scold each other, she blaming him for bad conduct and emitting semen, while he blames her for being a wretched prostitute, the cleanser of the host, and the washer of every man's penis. West of the fire-kindler's hearth outside the sacrificial area in an enclosed space couples (of men and women) should copulate, without caring about their social class. At least five, maximally 500, but ideally twenty-five slave girls (*dāsī-*) of the Gṛhapati should go sunwise around the *mārjālīya* hearth, carrying new vessels full of water, shouting "*Haimahā*, this is honey!" in an increasingly higher voice. Drums tied in all corners (of the sitting hall or the sacrificial area) are beaten. All sounds should become increasingly louder and continue as long as the *mahāvrata* laud is chanted by the Sāmavedic priests.

The *vrātya*-book was the first sample of the Atharvaveda to appear in a Western language; it was translated into German by Theodor Aufrecht in 1849. At the same time, Albrecht Weber (1849) published a pioneering survey of the Sāmaveda literature, in which he drew attention to passages in the Pañcaviṁśa-Brāhmana (PB 17,1–4) and the Lāṭyāyana-Śrautasūtra (LŚS 8,6) that deal with the *vrātyastomas*. Weber saw them as rituals by means of which Aryan people living in a non-brahmanical manner could enter the Vedic community. He also connected the *vrātya*s with the sorcery rites of the *vrātīnas*, noting that the terms used for the warrior (*yaudha*) and the priestly class (*arhat*) differ from those normally used in Vedic literature but have a parallel in the Buddhist title *arhat*. Weber also noted another pointer to eastern India in the phrase *brahmabandhu māgadhadeśīya*, which refers to the country of Magadha. Jarl Charpentier (1911), on the basis of AVŚ 15, saw the Vrātyas as early worshippers of Rudra-Śiva. J. W. Hauer (1927) on the basis of the Vrātyas' association with a prostitute and a *brahmabandhu māgadha* recognized the "popular" celebrations on the *mahāvrata* day as a Vrātya rite. Hauer also pointed to the similarity between the dialogue of the *mahāvrata* couple with the highly erotic *kuntāpa* verses of AVŚ 20,136 applied during the "sacred marriage" of the stallion and the chief queen at the culmination of the royal horse sacrifice.

In two papers, "Vrātya and sacrifice" (1962) and "The case of the severed head" (1967), Jan Heesterman laid the foundations for the hypothesis that he and others (especially Harry Falk 1986) have developed, that the *vrātyastoma*s were rites for purifying military sodalities after raiding expeditions, and that they, as well as the *mahāvrata* and some other rites, in particular the horse sacrifice (*aśvamedha*), the royal consecration (*rājasūya*), the *vājapeya*, and the building of the fire altar (*agnicayana*), are "fossils" preserving earlier, sexually more explicit "preclassical" forms of Vedic ritual that also included more violence and competition between two antagonistic parties.

The *vrātyastoma* texts speak of "beating with a stick people who should not be beaten," or "violating a Brahmin who should not be harmed." What is meant is clarified by Śatapatha-Brāhmaṇa 13,4,2,17, where the following advice is given to the guardians of the sacrificial horse when they start their year-long expedition: "Whenever ye meet with any kind of Brāhmaṇas, ask ye them, 'O Brāhmaṇas, how much know ye of the Aśvamedha?' and those who know naught of the Aśvamedha, know naught of anything, he is not a Brāhmaṇa, and as such liable to be despoiled." It is for the sake of such ritualistic and theological disputations that the *vrātīnas* should select the most learned among them as their leaders. Ignorance was used as a pretext for robbing and killing, and such ancient practice seems to be reflected in the learned disputations of the Upaniṣads, where we sometimes come across threats like the following: "He went off to that sacrifice which had already been begun. There . . . he said to the Prastotar priest: 'Prastotar, if you shall sing the *prastāva* (the initial part of the laud) without knowing the divinity which is connected with the *prastāva*, your head will fall off' " (ChU 1,10,7–9).

The military escort of the sacrificial horse had to prevent the horse from mounting any mare during its year-long expedition and to guard it from all sorts of dangers, including enemies of the sacrificing king who might wish to obstruct the sacrifice. This army consisted of four socially different groups close to the royal household, associated with the numbers four to one, expressed by the respective number of chariot horses. The most detailed description of them is given in the Vādhūla-Śrautasūtra (11,10): four lots of 300 chariot teams and four lots of 300 footmen; each group of 300 is divided into four batches, seventy-five on either side of the horse and seventy-five behind and in front of it. The four different kinds of chariot teams are the following: (1) 300 royal princes armed for battle, clad in bronze mail on both sides, with charioteers armed for battle, driving chariots covered with shields and yoked with four horses; (2) 300 nonroyal warriors armed for battle, with charioteers not armed for battle, driving chariots covered with shields and yoked with three horses; (3) 300 heralds and headmen not armed for battle, driving chariots not covered with shields and yoked with two horses; (4) 300 meat carvers and charioteers, who drive on off-track carts (yoked with one horse).

The reading *viprthu-* in Śāṅkhāyana-Śrautasūtra 14,72,3 for the last-mentioned type of vehicle may throw some further light on the *vipathá-*, "off-track cart," which according to the *vrātyastoma* texts and the *vrātya*-Book of the Atharvaveda is the vehicle of the Vrātya leader. *Viprthu-* might be just a corruption of *vipatha-*, but it might also represent the original, non-Prakritized form of the word, meaning "not broad" = "narrow" = one-man chariot.

The chief queen of the sacrificing king, who is to lie with the main victim, the horse (or the male chief victim of the otherwise identical human sacrifice, *puruṣamedha*, to be discussed in more detail shortly, and also in chapters 16 and 19), and the three other queens, are escorted by the corresponding number of young maidens from the same four social classes as the male guardians of the horse. All these women, including the junior queens, go around the couple of the "sacred marriage," smiting their thighs and fanning the couple with their clothing. The sexually loaded mantras uttered on this occasion mention three "mothers" (*ambā, ambikā, ambālikā*) that seem to connect the chief victim with Rudra, one of whose epithets is Tryambaka, "having three mothers." Actually the victim of the horse/human sacrifice is at this culmination of the rite addressed as "the host-leader of the hosts" in the mantra *gaṇānāṃ tvā gaṇapatim* . . . (ŚB 13,2,8,4; ĀpŚS 20,18,1). He would indeed have led for one year the armed host accompanying him, thus resembling the Vrātya leader, who is armed with a bow and directly identified with Rudra in no uncertain terms: in AVŚ 15,1,4–5 he is the Great God (*mahādeva*) and the Lord (*īśāna*); in AVŚ 15,5 he is escorted by the archers Bhava, Śarva, Paśupati, Ugra Deva, Rudra, Mahādeva, and Īśāna, which are all names of Rudra. From the mantras of the *śatarudriya* section of the Vājasaneyi-Saṁhitā (Book 16), which accompany the 425 oblations to Rudra at the completion of the fire altar (supposed to coincide with the completion of a ritual year, just like the horse/human sacrifice), it is plain that Rudra was feared as "leader of hosts," "lord of robbers," a hero mailed and armored, whose bow, arrows, and wrath were much feared. Rudra's Hindu successor, Skanda, is the divine army leader (*senāpati*), who is escorted by a host of "mothers." In this respect he is like the Hindu god Gaṇapati, alias Ganeśa, who is also escorted by "mothers" and whose title *gaṇapati*, "host-leader," can be understood also as a military title. Gaṇapati therefore appears to be a duplication of Skanda and the leader of Śiva's *gaṇas* in later mythology.

Gaṇa- is a synonym of *vrāta-*, "group, troop," and is also used of a *vrātya-gaṇa-* in Kātyāyana-Śrautasūtra 22,4,3. But Śiva's *gaṇas* in classical Hinduism consist also of singers and dancers like the *kinnaras* and *gandharvas*. Actually, *gaṇānāṃ tvā gaṇapatiṃ* in Rigveda 2,23,1—words addressed to the sacrificial horse—were originally addressed to Bṛhaspati/Brahmaṇaspati, singer of magic songs. In the Atharvavedic Kauśika-Sūtra (135,9) Bṛhaspati is an Āṅgirasa, and in the Mahābhārata Bṛhaspati is frequently called "the best of Aṅgirases" (*aṅgirasāṃ śreṣṭhaḥ*). As the divine *purohita* and charioteer, Bṛhaspati was a *sūta-*, "charioteer" and "bard," whose task it was to advise the chariot's warrior and to encourage him by singing of the brave deeds of his ancestors. During the year-long expedition of the sacrificial horse, there are "revolving" (*pāriplava*) oral performances of all sorts of literary genres for the entertainment of the sacrificing king and the general public. On this occasion, also, "master musicians accompanied by hosts (*gaṇa*) of harp players" (*vīṇāgaṇakinaḥ*) are present and the Adhvaryu asks them to sing about the sacrificing king and about the righteous kings of former times. A Brahmin harp-player-singer (*vīṇāgāthī*) sings three strophes composed by himself on such topics as "Such a sacrifice he performed, Such gifts he gave" (ŚB 13,4,2,8). Likewise, a *rājanya* harp-player and singer sings three strophes about "Such war he waged, Such battle he won" (ŚB 13,4,3,5; TB 3,9,14,1–3). These tristichs agree with the tradition of the Kāṇvas and Āṅgirasas, poets of the Rigvedic Proto-Sāmaveda and the Atharvaveda, who favored tristich composition. The Brāhmaṇas and Upaniṣads have preserved a number of *gāthā*s and *śloka*s, including those of the Śunaḥśepa legend recited at the royal consecration, which on the one hand are connected with the *vrātya* tradition, and on the other feed into the epic tradition (Horsch 1966).

The Sāmavedins of the "classical" Vedic ritual do not play harp, but at the culmination of the *mahāvrata* the Udgātar ascends a throne (*āsandī*) and plays a hundred-stringed harp with a plectrum. And just before the horse is killed in the *aśvamedha*, the horse is chosen to be the Udgātar priest and made to "sing" the *udgītha* of the out-of-doors laud by neighing, which is deliberately provoked by the proximity of a mare (cf. ĀpŚS 20,13,5–8; LŚS 9,9,18–23); in other words, the horse personifies the principal chanter priest Udgātar. According to the Vādhūla-Śrautasūtra (11,12,2–3), "after having decorated him, they bring to the place the son of the noblest bard (*sūtaśreṣṭhasya putraṃ*), a virginal youth (*kumāram asiktaretasam*) to be the cutter of the horse, lamenting him as if he was to die (*rudanto yathā mariṣyantam evam*). For they say that formerly the head of him would fall off severed who was the first to make a cut." The next sūtras (4–12) tell how this custom came to be changed and the youth to survive. I have suggested that this youth (*kumāra*) personified god Rudra, whose name the Brāhmaṇa texts derive from the root *rud-*, "to cry," and who is also called Kumāra. Rudra was thus represented by a bard—in the Rigveda (1,43,4) Rudra is called *gāthapati-*, "lord of the song"—and his *gaṇas* were also groups of singers, comparable not only to the *kinnaras* of classical Hinduism but also, for example, to the Bāul singers of today's Bengal. In later Hinduism, Rudra's successor, Śiva, is said to be fond of the Sāmaveda; in south Indian iconography one of Śiva's manifestations is "lute-holder," Vīṇādharamūrti, and the classical Indian musical instruments include the *Rudra-vīṇā*.

The fourth *vrātyastoma* in Pañcaviṁśa-Brāhmaṇa 17,4 is "for those Vrātyas whose penis is quiet and hangs down (*śama-nīca-meḍhrāḥ*)," which the Lātyāyana-Śrautasūtra

(8,6,4) explains to be "those who by old age are precluded from sexual intercourse." From this it is clear that by early Vedic times Rudra's wandering troops included old people or perhaps even men like today's naked ascetics who assemble at the Kumbha Melā and have literally destroyed their virility by self-castration. Both *gaṇa-* and *saṅgha-* are used as synonyms of *vrāta-* in the case of the *vrātyas*. They are also the terms used by the early ascetic communities of Jains and Buddhists.

The Jaiminīya-Brāhmaṇa (2,69–70) describes a sacrificial contest between the creator god Prajāpati (predecessor of the Hindu god Brahmā and the divine representative of the Brahmins in the Brāhmaṇa texts) and Mṛtyu, the god of death. This contest continued for a long time, many years, as neither could triumph. Eventually Prajāpati "saw" the ritualistic technique of establishing equations or identifications between the components of the microcosm of the ritual and the macrocosm of the universe, so that cosmic events could be controlled by means of ritualistic symbols, especially numerical matches between entities (manipulating for instance the number of syllables in a poetic meter). Thereby he conquered Mṛtyu, whose sacrifice gradually vanished, leaving Prajāpati's sacrifice as the only existing one. Prajāpati's army is said to have consisted of the Sāmavedic lauds, Rigvedic *śastras*, and Yajurvedic operations of the *soma* sacrifice, while Mṛtyu's army consisted of singing to the accompaniment of the harp, dancing, and frivolous activities. Particular attention is paid to Mṛtyu's harp (*vīṇā*), which clearly played a vital role in Mṛtyu's ritual, as its various parts—such as the stick (*daṇḍa*) of the harp, its body (*sūnā*) and its seven strings—are enumerated and compared with elements of the classical sacrifice. There is no doubt that rites such as the *mahāvrata* are hereby meant (at the *mahāvrata*, the Udgātar seated on a throne plays a harp, slave girls perform a dance around the *mārjālīya* hearth, slapping their thighs, and sexual intercourse is performed). These archaic practices are described in the Vedic texts, some of which however declare them as obsolete (*utsanna*) and not to be done. Thus Prajāpati's victorious sacrifice represents the reformed "classical" Vedic ritual and Mṛtyu's the "pre-classical" ritual of the *vrātya* rites.

From the description of Mṛtyu's sacrifice it is clear that Mṛtyu stands for Rudra, the chief god of the Vrātyas as raiding gangs, also known as *bhūtapati-*, "lord of ghosts or evil spirits of the dead." The name Mṛtyu of course means "Death." The building of the funeral monument (for a someone who during his lifetime built a fire altar) and the burial of the vessel with the ashes or bones of the deceased is accompanied with ritual acts that are clearly connected with the Vrātya type of sacrifice, such as music (with harps, conches, pipes, flutes, and a metal vessel beaten with an old shoe), songs and dances by male and female relatives, as well as professional dancing women, and feasting. Sexual intercourse also takes place, at least symbolically. A *brahmabandhu* or a Śūdra asks the seniormost widow for sexual intercourse on behalf of her deceased husband; she denies him twice but then agrees for one night. The vessel with the ashes or bones is placed under a tripod holding a pot with a hundred holes, and sour milk with curds is poured into it. This symbolic seed-laying is accompanied by a "fanning" (*dhuvanam*) similar to that around the senior wife lying in "sacred marriage" with the chief victim in the horse sacrifice (ŚB 13,2,8,4). These archaic practices were soon regarded as obsolete, since they were declared optional in the Pitṛmedhasūtras (Caland 1896).

Only a man who had built a fire altar (*agni-citi*) was entitled to a funeral monument. The close connection between these two kinds of monuments is underlined by the fact that it is Yama, the god of death, who recommends the building of a fire altar as a means to overcome death in the Kaṭha-Upaniṣad. Significantly, Yama tempts Naciketas not to ask for the ultimate secret by offering him "these lovely maidens, with chariots and harps" (*imā rāmāḥ sarathāḥ satūryāḥ*), which Naciketas rejects as follows: "thine be the vehicles, thine the songs and dances!" (*tavaiva vāhās tava nṛtyagīte*) (KU 1,25–26).

In the Kāfir pantheon of northeastern Afghanistan, the high god is Imra, from *Yama-rāja, "King Yama." He is also called Māra, "Killer, Death." Māra had seven daughters, worshipped as goddesses of fertility who protect agriculture. In the Buddhist legend, Māra, ruler of the phenomenal world, in vain tries to prevent Buddha Śākyamuni from attaining enlightenment by sending his terrible armies to threaten him, followed by his three appealing daughters to seduce him. Mṛtyu corresponds to Maccu in Pāli texts, and some early Buddhist texts speak of this deity as a king, Maccu-rājā and Mṛtyu-rāj, providing thus a counterpart to the Kāfir name Imra and to Yama-rājan- in RV 10,16,9, as well as to King Yima in the Avesta. The "evil Death" (*māro pāpimā*) of the Buddhist texts corresponds to the synonymous deity called *pāpmā mṛtyuḥ* in the Atharvaveda and Middle Vedic texts, where he is equated with Yama and Śarva (= Rudra). There are many correspondences between the Vrātya rituals and the Kāfir religion, in which raiding expeditions, circular dances, and heroic songs sung to the accompaniment of the "Kāfir harp" (similar to the classical—not modern—Indian *vīṇā*) play a very central role, so the concordance between Kāfir Māra and Atharvavedic/Vrātya Mṛtyu is significant.

Yama, the son of Vivasvat, as the king of the dead appears in the Rigveda mainly in Books 1 and 10. Yama as the first mortal or first man duplicates Manu ("man"), the son of Vivasvat, the first sacrificer and the ancestor of the Rigvedic Indo-Aryans. Avestan Yima, the son of Vīvaŋhvat, as the first sacrificer of *haoma* and the first king of the Aryans/Iranians, plays an important role in Old Iranian religion, while in the Vedic religion Yama seems to duplicate also Varuṇa, who has an ancient Indo-Aryan background; according to RV 10,14,7–8, the pious dead arriving in the highest heaven see there the two kings, Yama and Varuṇa. Yama seems to me to have come to the Vedic pantheon from the religion of the Dāsas who were Iranians (see chapter 9) and whose religion seems to have survived in the Kāfir religion of Nuristan (see chapter 20). In Rigveda 10,10,13, Yama's twin sister Yamī exclaims "*bato batāsi*," when Yama declines her advances. Hereafter the word *bata* is attested in Indo-Aryan only as an interjection of reproach or frustration. It is found only in this Rigvedic verse as a noun, in the nominative and vocative cases, probably denoting "weakling." Is it a mere coincidence that Khotanese Saka has an adjective *bata* meaning "small, weak, bad," with cognates in Zoroastrian Persian and other Iranian languages?

Yama's vehicle in Hinduism is the water buffalo, but there is no record of this in the Vedas. In the single context of a buffalo sacrifice in the Brāhmaṇa and Sūtra texts, the water buffalo is sacred to Varuṇa. The water buffalo is an animal native to South Asia, not originally connected with Aryan deities. On the other hand, it is connected with Harappan "Proto-Śiva," who wears the horns of a water buffalo. So the buffalo's connection with Yama, the god of death, suggests something about Proto-Śiva, too: Proto-Śiva may have been a god of death, but most probably he was also a divine king, like Varuṇa, who guarded the cosmic order (*ṛta-*), as well as Yama, known as the king of righteousness, *dharma-rāja*. Yama of the Hindu period and Vedic Varuṇa also share the attribute of a "noose" (*pāśa-*), with which to catch and bind the sinners who are to die. "Indeed, Varuṇa is Death" (*mṛtyur vai varuṇaḥ*, KS 13,2).

13

The Megalithic Culture and the Great Epics

In the preceding chapters, I have tried to throw new light on the religion of the early Aryan-speaking peoples chiefly by reference to archaeological evidence. In this chapter, archaeology continues to make a key contribution. I shall consider three major archaeological complexes of the first millennium BCE: those of the Painted Grey Ware (PGW), the Northern Black Polished Ware (NBPW) (Fig. 13.1), and the Black-and-Red Ware (BRW). The last of these is largely associated with Megalithic graves, which seem to represent a further Aryan immigration to South Asia. Their archaeological data provide reasons to suggest a wholly new interpretation of the Mahābhārata war. In addition to archaeology, there are textual sources: Vedic literature for the period before about 400 BCE, and thereafter Pāṇini and the beginnings of the Mahābhārata and Rāmāyaṇa, although we know them only from later versions. This chapter focuses on the central narratives of these great epics, which involve the transition from Vedic to Hindu religion in the field of Viṣṇuism.

This is contested scholarly territory, with an unavoidably imprecise chronology until we reach the inscriptions of Asoka in the third century BCE. To make it easier for the reader to follow my arguments, I shall sum up at the outset the main theses of this chapter, while noting that they are not likely to be accepted by all scholars working on these texts. In my view, the first phase of the PGW reflects the stabilization of the Vedic/Brahmanical culture in the powerful Kuru kingdom, while its second phase temporally and geographically coincides with the Mahābhārata war. The Pāṇḍava heroes of the Mahābhārata appear to have been originally "pale" (*pāṇḍu*) Iranian horsemen; they entered western India from about 800 BCE and during the following centuries spread widely to peninsular India and Sri Lanka. The Pāṇḍava takeover of the Kuru kingdom is the main theme of the Mahābhārata, while the Pāṇḍava takeover of Sri Lanka appears to be reflected in the Rāmāyaṇa. The latter event is associated with the introduction of Aryan rulers from north India (the Mathurā region and Gujarat) into Tamil Nadu. In Hinduism these events are connected with the formation and spread of the Vaiṣṇava or Bhāgavata religion, in the form of worship of Bala-Rāma and Kṛṣṇa. To my mind, these divine brothers are continuations partly of the divine Aśvin twins in Vedic worship—this again is a new idea—and partly of the earlier religion of the Harappan age founded in agriculture and pastoralism.

The Rigvedic and Atharvavedic traditions had fused by the time the earliest texts of the Yajurveda were created. These codified the complex Vedic *śrauta* ritual in more or less its final form. Around this time—perhaps 1000 BCE—the existing hymns of the Rigveda and the Atharvaveda were assembled and arranged systematically into text collections that from now on were memorized and handed down as faithfully as possible. This unification of the Vedic community took place in the Kuru or Kaurava kingdom. The first hint of its emergence is the name of King Kuruśravaṇa, mentioned as a descendant of King Trasadasyu in two hymns of the late tenth book of the Rigveda. Instead of about thirty tribes referred to in the Rigveda, the Brāhmaṇa texts mostly speak of just the Kurus, or of the Kurus and the Pañcālas, who clearly were closely allied. The geographical distribution of the Vedic culture is defined by the place-names occurring in the texts, and seems to offer a close match with the iron-, horse-, and rice-using culture of the PGW culture (*c.* 1100–350 BCE) discovered by archaeologists in the northwestern plains (Fig. 13.1). The early phase of this culture (*c.* 1100–700 BC), with few and small towns, appears to represent the Middle Vedic culture and its Kuru kingdom.

Archaic Vedic rituals such as the horse sacrifice and the royal consecration included "proto-epic" bardic performances. They included both praise songs by priestly singers, praising the ritual achievements and liberality of their sponsors, as well as praise songs by warrior bards who lauded the king's military feats. In addition, there were narratives for the entertainment of the crowds in the audience. According to the Śatapatha-Brāhmaṇa (13,4,3,2–14), the *pāriplava* narratives of the horse sacrifice included also *purāṇas* and *itihāsas*, ancient myths and legends, anticipating those of the epic and Purāṇa texts. The "proto-epic" Vedic verse preserved in the Brāhmaṇas (AB 8,21,3, and ŚB 13,5,4,2) glorifies the horse sacrifice of King Janamejaya, a descendant of the Kuru king Parikṣit known from the Atharvaveda. A mythical snake sacrifice is described in Vedic texts (PB 25,15 and BŚS 17,18), in which royal snakes take human form and officiate as priests; they include Kings Janamejaya and Dhṛtarāṣṭra. The second of these names is also the name of the blind Kaurava king against whom the Pāṇḍava brothers fight in the Mahābhārata. Indeed, the epic states in its first book that it was first recited at Janamejaya's snake sacrifice.

The war between the Kauravas and the Pāṇḍavas takes place in Kurukṣetra, the "Kuru plain," located in the Ganges-Yamuna Doab. The PGW is found in the lowest strata of all major sites associated with the main story of the Mahābhārata. The late phase of the PGW culture (*c.* 700–350 BCE) may represent the period of the Mahābhārata war, which has been difficult to date; the oldest parts of the epic were in existence in 400–350 BCE, when the grammarian Pāṇini mentions the Mahābhārata by name (6,2,38), along with some of its places (Hāstinapura in 6,2,101) and personalities (Vāsudeva and Arjuna 4,3,98; Yudhiṣṭhira 8,3,95; the Vṛṣṇi and Andhaka tribes 6,2,34). On the other hand, King Pāṇḍu and the five Pāṇḍava brothers are not mentioned even once in any older Vedic text; the Mahābhārata and its reciter at Janamejaya's snake sacrifice, Vaiśampāyana, are mentioned only in the Āśvalāyana- and Kauṣītaki-Gṛhyasūtras, which belong to the latest phase of Vedic literature. The Pāṇḍavas, therefore, arrived on the scene only after the completion of most of the Vedic literature. They

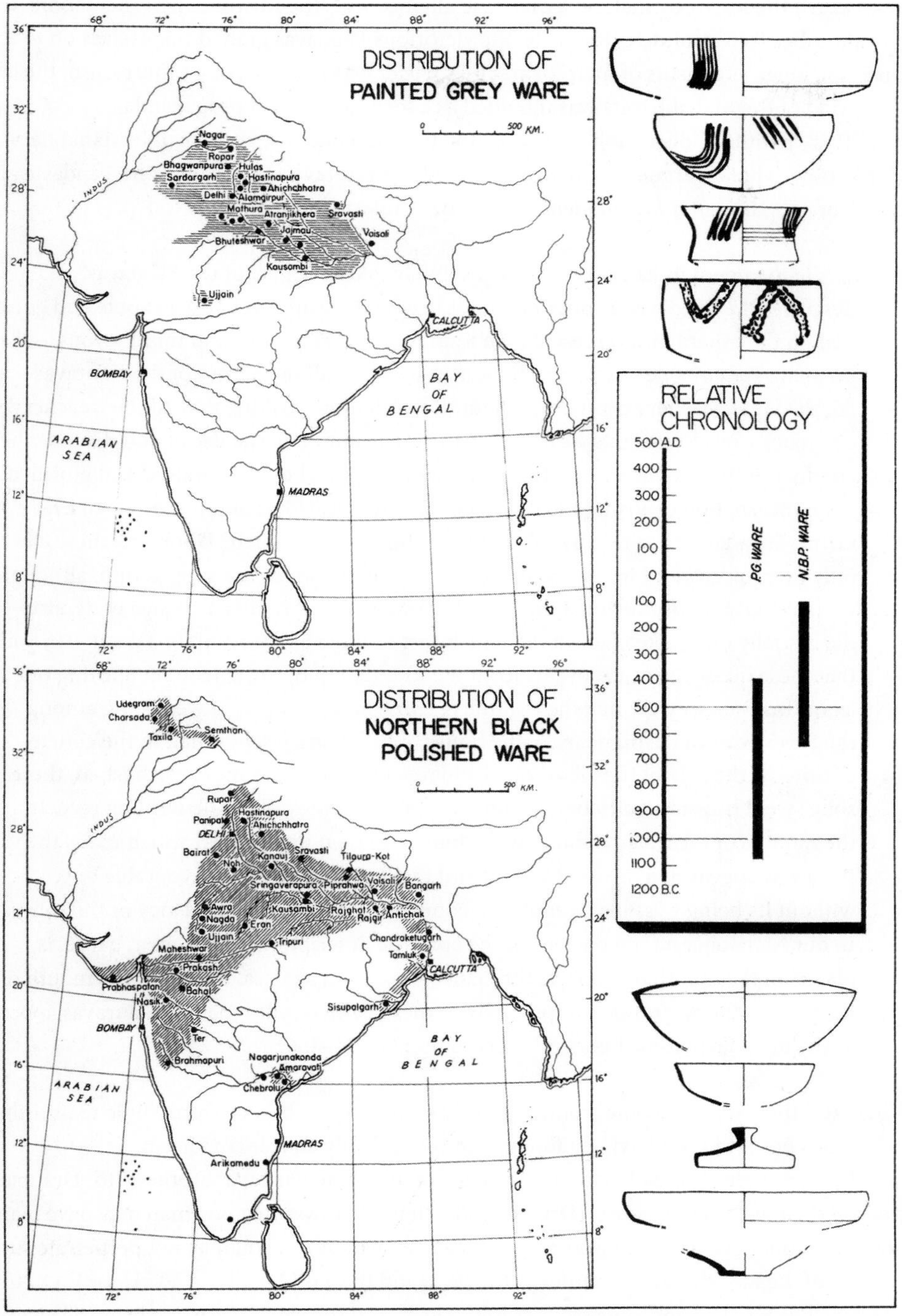

FIGURE 13.1 Distribution of the Painted Grey Ware and the Northern Black Polished Ware. After Thapar 1985:122. Courtesy ASI.

could crush the Kurus by making a marriage alliance with the Kurus' eastern neighbors, the Pañcāla tribe. To consolidate their rule, the victorious Pāṇḍavas grafted themselves on to the Kuru genealogy as cousins of their former foes, the defeated Kauravas. In this regard, the latest version of the Mahābhārata was intended as a form of political propaganda.

This "political" distortion may account for the contradictions in the Mahābhārata, which some scholars argue originally celebrated the Kauravas rather than the Pāṇḍavas. In his celebrated *History of Indian literature*, Moriz Winternitz comments:

> While the poem in its present form absolutely takes the part of the Pāṇḍavas, and describes the Pāṇḍavas as not only brave beyond measure, but also as noble and good, and on the other hand represents the Kauravas as treacherous and mischievous,—the poem, in remarkable self-contradiction, relates that all the heroes of the Kauravas fall through treachery or in unfair fight. It is still more striking that all the treachery emanates from Kṛṣṇa, that *he* is always the instigator of all the deceit and defends the conduct of the Pāṇḍavas. And this is the same Kṛṣṇa who . . . is praised and glorified as an incarnation of Viṣṇu, the highest god, and as the ideal and prototype of every virtue. How can these remarkable contradictions be explained? Upon this there can only be conjectures. First, there is probably justification for the supposition, although we have only the authority of the Mahābhārata itself for it, that a change of dynasty did actually once take place in the Northwest of India as the result of a great war, and that these quasi-historical events form the foundation of the epic itself. Starting out from this, we can well imagine that the original heroic songs . . . were sung among the bards who were still near . . . the house of the Kauravas, but that, in the course of time, as the rule of the victorious Pāṇḍavas was more and more established, these songs were transmitted to bards who were in the employ of the new ruling race. In the mouths of these bards those alterations were then undertaken which made the Pāṇḍavas appear in a favourable light and the Kauravas in an unfavourable one, without its being possible to eradicate completely the original tendency of the songs. In our Mahābhārata the nucleus of the epic, the descriptions of the great battle, is placed in the mouth of Sañjaya, the charioteer of Dhṛtarāṣṭra, that is, in the mouth of the bard of the Kauravas. It is precisely in these battle-scenes that the Kauravas appear in the most favourable light. (Winternitz 1927:I,454–456)

Where did the Pāṇḍavas come from? Apart from their total absence from Vedic texts, other indications point to their having a foreign, and specifically an Iranian, origin.

For example, the polyandric marriage of the five Pāṇḍava brothers to Draupadī shocked their audience at court: "Drupada said: 'It is laid down that one man may have many queens, . . . but *never* that one woman may have many men! . . . you may not perpetrate such a breach of the Law that runs counter to the Veda and the world . . . !' . . . Vyāsa said: 'On this Law, which is mocked and runs counter to the Veda and the world, I wish to hear the view of each of you . . . .'" (Mahābhārata 1,187–188, translated van Buitenen 1973:I,367–368, modified). This Pāṇḍava custom may be compared to that of the Iranian tribe of the Massagetae who were formidable warriors, according to Herodotus: "The following are some of their customs: Each man has but one wife, yet all the wives are held in common. . . . When a man desires a woman he hangs his quiver in front of her wagon and has intercourse with her unhindered" (Herodotus 1,216, translated Rawlinson [1860] 1942:114). The name of the Massagetae is thought to contain Proto-Iranian **masya-* from Proto-Aryan **matsya-*, "fish," and the tribe has been compared to that of the Matsyas, among whom the Pāṇḍavas were hiding in Virāṭanagara.

A foreign, northerly origin is suggested by the Pāṇḍavas' pale skin. The Mahābhārata (1,100,17–18) notes that their father, King Pāṇḍu, was destined to be born pale because his mother was pale with fright at the sight of his horrid-looking father during the conception of Pāṇḍu. In Sanskrit, *pāṇḍu-, pāṇḍura-, pāṇḍara-*, "white, whitish, yellowish, pale," attested since about 800 BCE, are loanwords from a Proto-Dravidian root **paḻ- / *paṇḍ-*. This implies that the appellation of the foreign immigrants as "pale" may have originated among the local population in an area with a Dravidian linguistic substratum. The Pāṇḍavas' hiding in Virāṭanagara (Bairāṭ near Jaipur), their alliance with Kṛṣṇa Vāsudeva of Mathurā, and the location of their first kingdom in the wooded southern half of Kurukṣetra, all suggest that these foreigners of probably West Iranian descent entered the subcontinent from the west, via Sindh, Gujarat, and Rajasthan. The Mahābhārata (2,23–29) and early northern Buddhist texts speak of the Pāṇḍavas as marauders over wide areas.

Is there any counterpart in the archaeological record for the Pāṇḍavas as foreigners of Iranian affinity coming to India *c.* 800–400 BCE? In my view, a good match is the "Megalithic" culture, first attested around 800 BCE at sites such as Mahurjhari and Khapa in Vidarbha in northeastern Maharashtra. These graves are simple stone circles, in which people were buried with weapons and horses; the horse equipment resembles that found in Central Asia, the Caucasus, and western Iran. The circular huts with wooden posts and a fireplace are similar to the yurts used by the nomads of the Central and Inner Asian steppes. The Megalithic immigrants could have belonged to the West Iranian speakers, who were assumed (see chapter 7) to have initiated the Yaz II culture (*c.*1000–500 BCE) of southern Central Asia and to have continued also westward along the southern shore of the Caspian Sea to emerge in history as the Medians and Persians. About 518 BCE, the Achaemenid king Darius I annexed the Indus Valley to the Persian empire. The Persians might be mentioned in Baudhāyana-Śrautasūtra 18,44, which lists the Gāndhāris, Parśus (emended from Sparśus), and Araṭṭas as western peoples, while according to 18,13 the countries of Āraṭṭa (see chapter 17) and Gāndhāra were non-Brahmanical.

After their arrival in western India, the carriers of the Megalithic culture adopted the Black-and-Red Ware pottery (of local Chalcolithic origin) and during the following several centuries spread over wide areas, mainly southwards to the Deccan, south India, and Sri Lanka. In many regions, folklore associates the megaliths with the Pāṇḍavas; this is very understandable, especially in Tamil Nadu, where the megaliths are called *paṇḍu-kal*, "old stones" (Leshnik 1974). (Tamil *paḻa / paṇḍu*, "old," goes back to the Proto-Dravidian root **paḻ- / *paṇḍ-*, "to be old." With the sense "to become old" it can be linked, I suggest, with the homonymous root meaning, "[fruit] to become ripe, be[come] yellowish, be pale," which is attested in Rigvedic Sanskrit *phalam*, "fruit," from Proto-Dravidian **paḻam*, "ripe fruit.") Numerous iron tridents suggest a Śaiva religion. Martial traditions of Megalithic origin still continue in the Deccan, where horsemen accompanied by dogs worship Śaiva deities such as Bhairava, Khaṇḍobā, and Birobā with tridents in yurt-like shrines (Sontheimer 1989:26–27). In Tamil Nadu the Megalithic culture continued till the second century CE and is reflected in the Old Tamil heroic poetry.

While the focus of the Mahābhārata is the Upper Ganges Valley, the Rāmāyaṇa situates itself in the middle Ganges Valley. Its oldest portions are estimated to date from *c.* 750–300 BCE, and correlate with the early Northern Black Polished Ware culture (*c.* 550–400 BCE), found at sites identified with various places mentioned in the Rāmāyaṇa, including Ayodhyā (Fig. 13.1). Thus the two epics reflect a gradual eastwards movement of the Brahmanical culture. The distribution of the NBPW appears to coincide with the formation of the kingdom of Magadha and the expansion of its power. Magadhas and Aṅgas are mentioned in a medicinal spell of the Atharvaveda as a far-off and undesirable people of the east, to whom the disease of fever is banished.

The possible BMAC origin of the Gangetic copper hoards (mentioned in chapter 8) suggests that Indo-Aryan speakers moved to the middle Ganges Valley so early that they did not become part of the Vedic culture. Such early Indo-Aryan speakers of the "Atharvavedic" wave of immigration seem to be meant when Vedic texts refer to "easterners" as *asura* worshippers and speakers of a language resembling eastern Middle Indo-Aryan, the Māgadhī Prakrit. According to the Śatapatha Brāhmaṇa (13,8,1,5), Vedic people who worship *devas*, make their funeral monument four-cornered; but their enemies, who worship *asuras*, the "easterners" and others, make their funeral monument round. The Buddhist stūpa must surely have developed from these round funeral monuments of eastern India, which preserve the round layout of most of the *kurgans* (tumuli) of the Eurasian steppes. It is significant that the Atharvavedins of the Śaunaka school prescribe either a round or a rectangular shape for the funeral monument, giving preference to the circular form (Kauśika-Sūtra 85,8). In the Brāhmaṇa period, however, the Vedic culture expanded to the middle Ganges Valley, which led to an upsurge of ideas and practices in the Upaniṣads that were novel from the Vedic point of view but that had been developing for a longer time in eastern India, as is evident from their heterodox religions.

Christian Lassen (1847:I,535) early on proposed that Vālmīki's Rāmāyaṇa "contains the legend of the first attempt of the Āryans to extend their power southwards by warring expeditions." Albrecht Weber (1870 [1871]) was inclined to accept this view, although he believed that the epic was composed in north India and that its author did not have any exact knowledge of the southern parts of the subcontinent. Yet it is clear that "the poet knew of an island kingdom, whether real or mythical, said to lie some distance off the coast of the Indian mainland" (Goldman 1984:I,28). Indeed, as early as the second or third century CE, an Old Tamil poem (Akanāṉūṟu 70) refers to Kōṭi (= Dhanuṣkōṭi, the tip of the mainland, opposite to Adam's Bridge in Sri Lanka) as the place from which the victorious Rāma crossed over to Laṅkā.

The archaeology of early historical Sri Lanka, so far largely ignored in this connection, has only recently become clearer (Coningham & Allchin 1995). The oldest, "Mesolithic," period is evidenced by locally manufactured stone tools. In the second, "Iron Age," period (*c.* 600–450 BCE) the habitation area of Anurādhapura was about 18 hectares with circular huts indicated by postholes. People had "typical Black-and-Red burnished ware," iron, and cattle. In the "Early Historic 1" period (*c.* 450–350 BCE), the site and the circular huts are larger, and there are strong similarities with south Indian Megalithic burials. The pottery is still dominated by Black-and-Red burnished ware. Horse bones are found, and indications of a major expansion of trade in conch shells, iron ore, amethyst and quartz. In the "Early Historic 2" period (*c.* 350–275 BCE), the site was more than 66 hectares and surrounded by a defensive wall. Finds include mother of pearl, cowrie and conch shells, lapis lazuli from Afghanistan, and carnelian from Gujarat, five Brahmi inscriptions on potsherds, and, toward the end, coins stamped with a single arched hill or *caitya*. The "Early Historic 3 and 4" periods (*c.* 275–225 and 225–150 BCE) have yielded also typically Hellenistic objects. It must be noted that the dates given here, though said to be radiocarbon-based, have been very seriously questioned, together with the claim of a pre-Aśokan date for Brahmi script in Sri Lanka.

Widespread evidence covering the entire island suggests that Sri Lanka was inhabited only by tribes of Mesolithic hunter-gatherers until *c.* 800–600 BCE, when agriculture and cattle-raising were introduced by an Iron Age culture characterized by "Megalithic" burials and Black-and-Red Ware. It is so similar to the Iron Age Megalithic culture of the Indian mainland that its spread must be ascribed to actual movements of people. But where exactly did these settlers come from? It is sensible to seek an answer from the legends in the chronicles of Sri Lanka.

The legend of the colonization of Sri Lanka is related in the Dīpavaṁsa (chapters 9–11) and with slight variation in the Mahāvaṁsa (chapters 6–10), written in about 400 and 500 CE, respectively, but based on older records. This legend derives the Simhalas from Gujarat, which is most reasonable on the basis of linguistic evidence, which generally classifies Sinhalese with Gujarati and Marathi. Pāli, the Middle Indo-Aryan language of the Theravāda Buddhism of Sri Lanka, is closest to Aśoka's inscriptions at Gīrnār in Gujarat, and is generally considered nowadays to have originated in western India. Gujarat and Maharashtra are also precisely the areas where the Megalithic culture seems to have spread first.

According to legend, at first 700 Simhalas led by Prince Vijaya came to Sri Lanka from Sīhapura (Siṁhapura) in Lāḷa (Lāṭa in southern Gujarat). "Prince Vijaya was daring and uneducated; he committed most wicked and fearful things, plundering the people."He was therefore expelled from Sīhapura by his father, King Sīhabāhu. Vijaya and his men sailed down the west coast of the subcontinent, stopping at the cities of Bhārukaccha (Broach in Gujarat) and Suppāra (Śūrpāraka = Sopāra near Mumbai). In both places they were offered hospitality and honors, but they exasperated the inhabitants with their "cruel, savage, terrible, and most dreadful deeds," which included "drinking, theft, adultery, falsehood, and slander." Finally they arrived at the island of Laṅkā—by coincidence at the time when the Buddha reached the complete extinction (*parinirvāṇa*). In nine months Vijaya and his men exterminated the island's indigenous population of *yakkhas* (Sanskrit *yakṣas*), who may denote the Mesolithic hunter-gatherer population of Sri Lanka, ancestors of the Veḍḍa aboriginals. Vijaya founded Tambapaṇṇi, the first town in the island of Laṅkā. After ruling for thirty-eight years, Vijaya sent a message to his brother Sumitta in Sīhapura, asking that a relative succeed him in Laṅkā after his death.

Vijaya is usually dated to 1–38 after the Buddha's *parinirvāṇa*, that is (according to the traditional chronology) *c.* 486–448 BCE; his successor, Paṇḍu-Vāsudeva, to 38–39 (448–447 BCE), and so on. However, Laṅkā is said to have been kingless for one year, and Paṇḍu-Vāsudeva to have come from Siṁhapura on a separate mission. The Vijaya story may be just an attempt to fill the earlier history with a vague memory of the first immigration: it seems to me that regular dynastic record was started only with the arrival of Paṇḍu-Vāsudeva, whereafter it was continuous. Indeed, Lassen (1852:II,96) suggested that "Vijaya" did not refer to any specific person but rather to an event: the "conquest" of Sri Lanka. The "cruel and savage" Vijaya, like the demon king Rāvaṇa of the Rāmāyaṇa, may simply symbolize the early rulers of the island.

The Purāṇas associate Rāvaṇa and his brother Kubera (the god of riches) with the Himalayas. When people migrate, they often transfer the name of their old domicile to their new habitat. Siṁhapura, Vijaya's home town in Gujarat, has a namesake, Siṁhapura, in the Indus Valley, conquered by the Pāṇḍavas (Mahābhārata 2,24,19); according to the Chinese pilgrim Xuan-Zang/Hsüan Tsang, this Siṁhapura was some 200 km southeast of Taxila. In the next verse (2,24,20), the Mahābhārata mentions the Cola as a people crushed by the Pāṇḍavas. Moreover, Vijaya's brother Sumitta, King of Siṁhapura, married a princess of the Madra country, which is situated in the Upper Indus Valley. Cola is otherwise known only as the name of another dynasty of ancient Tamil kings; like the Pāṇḍyas, this royal house is also likely to have come to Tamil Nadu from north India.

The second Siṁhala king was called Paṇḍu-Vāsudeva. The word Paṇḍu(ka) figures in the names of other ancient Sinhalese kings as well, and associates them with the Pāṇḍavas of the Mahābhārata, whose father Pāṇḍu is called Paṇḍu or Paṇḍu-rājā in Buddhist texts written in Pāli. Paṇḍu-Vāsudeva's father-in-law, who ruled in a kingdom on the Ganges River, was likewise called Paṇḍu. He belonged to the Śākya clan, being a relative of the Buddha. Śākya is derived from Śaka, one of the principal names of Iranian steppe nomads. Its association with the name Paṇḍu is an additional hint of the Iranian origin of the Pāṇḍavas.

The beginning of the second phase (*c.* 450–350 BCE) of the Megalithic culture of Sri Lanka coincides almost exactly with the traditional dates for Paṇḍu-Vāsudeva's rule. The phase is said to resemble much the Megalithic culture of South India. These archaeological parallels are mirrored in the chronicles. According to the Mahāvaṁsa (chapter 7), a fierce demoness (*yakkhinī*) called Kuveṇī or Kuvaṇṇā had fallen in love with Prince Vijaya and helped the invader to kill the *yakkhas*, who lived in their cities of Laṅkāpura and Sirīsavatthu. She bore him children. But when his companions proposed to perform the Vedic sacrifice necessary to consecrate King Vijaya, he accepted only if they procured him a queen of high rank. So they sent a delegation with jewels and other presents to southern Madhurā (*dakkhiṇa-madhurā*). Its ruler, called Paṇḍu/Paṇḍava, decided to send his daughter Vijayā in marriage to Prince Vijaya along with 700 daughters of his nobility for Vijaya's retinue of 700 men. After marrying Paṇḍava's daughter, Vijaya rejected Kuveṇī, sending her away from his house but promising to maintain her as a goddess with a thousand bloody *bali* offerings.

Southern Madhurā is modern Madurai in Tamil Nadu, the capital of the Pāṇḍya kings. The dynastic name Pāṇḍya is derived from Pāṇḍu, according to Patañjali's commentary on Pāṇini's grammar (4,1,168). Sri Lankan kings kept contact with the city of southern Madhurā later on, as well. The Greek ambassador to the Mauryan kingdom, Megasthenes, writing about 300 BCE, refers to the Pāṇḍya country when speaking of an Indian "Heracles":

> this Heracles . . . had only one daughter. Her name was Pandaea [Pandaíē], and the country in which she was born, the government of which Heracles entrusted to her, was called Pandaea after the girl. . . . Some other Indians tell of Heracles that, after he had traversed every land and sea, and purged them of all evil monsters, he found in the sea a new form of womanly ornament . . . the sea *margarita* [pearl] as it is called in the Indian tongue. Heracles was in fact so taken with the beauty of the ornament that he collected this pearl from every sea and brought it to India to adorn his daughter . . . among the Indians too the pearl is worth three times its weight in refined gold. (Arrian, *Indica* 8,6–13, translated Brunt 1983:II,329–331)

The Arthaśāstra (2,11), ascribed to Megasthenes's contemporary, the Maurya minister Kauṭilya (although it actually dates from a somewhat later time), mentions as sources of pearls several places on the coasts of southernmost India and northern Sri Lanka, among them Pāṇḍya-kavāṭa and Tāmraparṇī. Tāmraparṇī is the name of the chief river of the southernmost (Tirunelveli) district of Tamil Nadu, at the mouth of which was the Pāṇḍya port town of Koṟkai, famed in Old Tamil literature for its pearl fishery. Tāmraparṇī is also the name of the first Sinhalese capital on the north coast of Sri Lanka, called Tambapaṇṇi in Mahāvaṁsa 7,38–42 and Taprobane by Onesicritus, the admiral of Alexander the Great, who learned it as the name of the whole island in 325 BCE in the Indus Valley. Vijaya's contacts would have been with Koṟkai, before the Pāṇḍya capital was moved to Madhurā inland.

The Pāṇḍya capital is called Southern Madhurā to distinguish it from the northern Madhurā, that is, Mathurā, the famed domicile of Kṛṣṇa Vāsudeva, after which the Pāṇḍya Madhurā obviously was named. This is suggested also by the name of the second Siṁhala king coming from Gujarat, Paṇḍu-Vāsudeva. It seems to me that it was this second wave of Paṇḍu princes coming by sea to Sri Lanka and Tamil Nadu that brought the Vaiṣṇava religion to the south. This is suggested further by the legend of the God Uppalavaṇṇa (Sanskrit Utpalavarṇa, "having the color of blue lotus") being appointed by the Buddha as the guardian deity of the island and taking the immigrants under his protection, even if the Mahāvaṁsa (chapter 7) associates this with Vijaya. The earliest form of Vaiṣṇava religion in south India is supposed to be the Pañcavīra cult, that is, the worship of the five Vṛṣṇi or Yādava heroes, in particular Kṛṣṇa Vāsudeva and his elder brother Bala-Rāma, worshipped both independently and together in Tamil Nadu in the early centuries CE. Such a migration of the Yādavas seems to be hinted at in the northern Sanskrit sources too: Kṛṣṇa Vāsudeva moved from Mathurā to Gujarat, where he founded the coastal city of Dvārakā or Dvāravatī. Sanskrit *dvāra*, "door," corresponds to Tamil *kavāṭam/kapāṭam*, "fold of a door," found in the names Pāṇḍya-kavāṭa (one of the pearl sources in Arthaśāstra 2,11,2) and Kapāṭapuram (the legendary seat of one of the ancient Tamil literary academies). According Old Tamil tradition, Sage Agastya brought the eighteen Vēḷir chiefs and the rulers of the Aruvāḷa country from Dvārakā. The Āy rulers of the eighth- to ninth-century south Travancore likewise traced their descent from the Yādavas.

Who was the Indian Heracles? "This Heracles is chiefly honoured by the Surasenians, an Indian tribe, with two great cities, Methora and Clisobora [Kleisóbora]; the navigable river Iomanes flows through their territory. Megasthenes says that the garb this Heracles wore was like that of the Theban Heracles by the account of the Indians themselves; he also had a great many sons in this country, for this Heracles too wedded many wives, but he had only one daughter. Her name was Pandaea" (Arrian, *Indica* 8,5–7, translated Brunt 1983:II,327–329). Practically all scholars have identified the Indian Heracles with Kṛṣṇa worshipped by Śūrasenas in Mathurā on the Yamunā river. An exception was James Tod, who in 1835 identified Heracles with Bala-Deva, the god of strength (*bala*). Strength is of course a characteristic of the Greek Heracles; and there is other evidence suggesting that Tod was right. Cicero, while discussing the six appearances of Heracles, states that in India he was called Belus (Cicero, *De natura deorum* 3,42). Bala-Rāma's strength is mentioned in the Old Tamil poems of the first centuries CE: "In Pur̲[an̲ānūr̲u] 56, Krishna is invoked for his fame, Balarāma for his strength. Krishna is described as having a body like blue sapphire, having a bird (presumably the *garuḍa*) on his flag, and being accompanied by Balarāma, who has a body the colour of a conch, a plow for his weapon, and a palmyra for his banner" (Hart 1975:57)

Textual and iconographic evidence from about 400 BCE onwards shows that Bala-Rāma was in early Viṣṇuism a very important deity, especially in the Mathurā area. Mathurā is called Madhurā not only in Pāli sources but also by Patañjali in his Mahābhāṣya, around 150 BCE. The form Madhurā figures in the Mahābhārata, too, which derives the name from the demon Madhu, who lived in the Madhu-vana forest on the Yamunā river but was slain by Kṛṣṇa, who is therefore called Madhusūdana, "the killer of Madhu." The "demoniac" god earlier worshipped at Madhurā seems to have been a snake deity connected with plowing and identified with Śiva (Śiva's names listed in the Mahābhārata include Madhu) and who was addicted to drinking wine (*madhu*). Madhu's cult was then absorbed into that of Kṛṣṇa Vāsudeva by transferring all the attributes of this earlier local god to Kṛṣṇa's "elder brother" Bala-Rāma, who, among other things, is a great wine drinker. Demon Madhu (with the demon Kaiṭabha, whose name may be compared with Pāli *keṭubha*, "Brahmin ritualist") is said to have stolen the Vedas from the god Brahmā, which were then regained by Viṣṇu; this myth seems to imply that a Vedic tradition prevailed at Mathurā before Viṣṇuism.

In the Vedas, *madhu* is specifically associated with the Aśvins. As discussed in chapter 10, these divine charioteers, twin sons of the Sky (*divo napātā*), probably represent, among other things, the (white) day and the (black) night. In Rigveda 3,55,11, day and night are spoken of as twin sisters (*yamyā*) who have assumed different colors, one shining bright (*tayor anyad rocate*), the other black (*kṛṣṇam anyat*); the Aśvins, too, are twins and are identified with day and night (MS 3,4,4: *ahorātre vā aśvinā*). Some verses of the Rigveda suggest that the sun is the chariot of the Aśvins. According to RV 6,9,1, "the white day and the black day—(the pair of) light and darkness—manifestly turn around." The color terms here used of day and night, *árjuna-*, "white," and *kṛṣṇá-*, "black," are connected with the two members of the chariot team in the Mahābhārata. The mightiest warrior of the Pāṇḍavas is Arjuna, whose name means "white." Arjuna's charioteer is the wise and crafty Kṛṣṇa, whose name means "black." Originally Kṛṣṇa's teammate was undoubtedly his elder brother, the strong Balarāma, who is white in color. When the Vedic king at the royal consecration as a warrior (*kṣatriya*) ascends his chariot, he calls himself Arjuna in the mantra that he thereby utters (ŚB 5,4,3,7, where Arjuna is said to be Indra's secret name).

The Aśvins drive around the world in a triple chariot accompanied by the fair goddess of Dawn (Uṣas), daughter of the Sky or Sun (Sūre/Sūro duhitā, Sūryā), their sister and wife. This trio has a counterpart in the divine horsemen of the Greeks, Kastor and Poludeukes (originally *Poluleúkēs*, "much shining")—who are sons of the sky god Zeus and brothers of Helen—as well as in the Lithuanian twin gods expressly identified with the morning and evening star wooing the daughter of the Sun. Many of the Aśvin hymns of the Rigveda belong to the Kāṇva family of poets that was associated with the early Vedic tribe of Yadu, from which Kṛṣṇa's Yādava tribe is descended. It therefore appears likely to me that the trio of Aśvins and their sister/wife is the model of the early Vaiṣṇava trio consisting of two brothers connected with the colors white and black and their sister/wife. Chariotry is one further characteristic in common. The Aśvins are chariot gods, and in the Mahābhārata, the "black" Vāsudeva is the charioteer of the "white" chariot-warrior Arjuna. The two brothers Kṛṣṇa-Vāsudeva and Bala-Rāma and their sister were a popular trio in early Vaiṣṇava iconography and are still worshipped as such at Puri in Orissa.

Megasthenes, in the above-quoted passage, gave Pandaíē as the name of Heracles's daughter and of the country called after her, the source of pearls (i.e., the Pāṇḍya country of south India). This name may correspond to Sanskrit Pāṇḍeyā, "daughter of Pāṇḍu." In Megasthenes's account, Heracles is both the father and husband of Pandaíē:

> In this country where Heracles' daughter was queen, the girls are marriageable at seven years, and the men do not live longer than forty years. There is a story about this among the Indians, that Heracles, whose daughter was born to him late in life, realizing that his own end was near, and having no man of his own worth to whom he might give his daughter, copulated with her himself when she was seven, so that their progeny might be left behind as Indian kings. Thus Heracles made her marriageable, and thenceforward the whole of this line which began with Pandaea inherited this very same privilege from Heracles. (Arrian, *Indica* 9,1–3, translated Brunt 1983:II,331)

I quote this account, because it parallels a well-known Sāvitrī legend, one of the many side-episodes included in the Mahābhārata, and one of importance for the topic of chapter 19. Princess Sāvitrī's father, King Aśvapati of Madra (in the northern Indus Valley), fails to marry off his daughter in time, and therefore sends her to search for and choose a husband on her own. The texts do not directly indicate that the king had an incestuous relationship with Princess Sāvitrī, but they do quote in this context a law text stating that if a girl experiences her first menses in her father's house, the father incurs a great sin. According to the Mahābhārata 3,277,32, Aśvapati asks Sāvitrī to find a husband "equal to *herself*" (*sadṛśam ātmanaḥ*) as no wooer is forthcoming, but according to the Skanda-Purāṇa (7,166,16), Aśvapati says that however much he looks, he cannot find for his daughter a bridegroom who in worth is equal to *himself* (*vicārayan na paśyāmi varaṃ tulyam ihātmanaḥ*).

In the Sāvitrī legend, the human couple (Princess Sāvitrī and Prince Satyavat) corresponds to the divine couple (Goddess Sāvitrī and God Brahmā). It was through the grace of Goddess Sāvitrī and her husband that the princess was born, and both the human and the divine Sāvitrī along with their husbands are to be worshipped in the vow and ritual of *vaṭa-sāvitrī-vrata* that is associated with the legend. Even the fate of the human couple has its counterpart at the divine level. In accordance with the prophesy of Sage Nārada, the husband (Satyavat, alias Citrāśva, the young "alter ego" of Sāvitrī's father Aśvapati) dies after one year has passed from his wedding, with his head on the lap of Princess Sāvitrī. Sāvitrī, as a faithful wife, Satī, follows her husband to death when Yama comes to fetch him, and with her loyalty gains his life back. The *vaṭa-sāvitrī-vrata* is still today centrally important for married Hindu women whose husband is alive.

Parallel to the Sāvitrī legend, the Skanda-Purāṇa (3,1,40) tells how the creator god Brahmā, alias Prajāpati, has sex with his own daughter Vāc and is therefore killed by Śiva, but Brahmā's wives Sarasvatī and Gāyatrī pacify Śiva and make him join Brahmā's severed head with the body. This myth is directly based on a Vedic myth most explicitly told in Aitareya-Brāhmaṇa 3,33: Prajāpati is guilty of incest with his daughter Vāc and is killed by Rudra in punishment. Vāc ("speech, voice, sound") is another name of Goddess Sāvitrī, known best as the holiest stanza of the Veda composed in the *gāyatrī* meter: its recitation at sunrise and sunset, and (later) at noon are considered to manifest the goddesses Gāyatrī, Sāvitrī, and Sarasvatī.

Prajāpati thus had an incestuous relationship with his daughter Vāc, who is explicitly identified with the goddess of Dawn (Uṣas or Sūryā or Sāvitrī), and had to die, in punishment for this sin. Pandaíē's incestuous father Heracles also died soon after the copulation. Pāṇḍu, the father of the Pāṇḍava heroes (and of Pandaíē = Pāṇḍeyā), after he had killed a mating deer, was cursed to die if he ever copulated again, which came to pass when he had intercourse with his wife Mādrī. Mādrī was a princess of the Madra country, and ascended the funeral pyre of Pāṇḍu, resolute as the goddess Dhṛti. In both respects Mādrī resembles another princess of the Madra country, namely Sāvitrī, who is the prototype of a Satī, and the human counterpart of goddess Sāvitrī, the wife-daughter of Brahmā/Prajāpati. We have seen that the female member of the early Vaiṣṇava trio (Kṛṣṇa's sister Subhadrā, Rāma's wife Sītā) seems to continue the goddess of dawn (Sūryā/Sāvitrī) in the trio that she forms with the two Aśvins. Not only Sāvitrī but this entire earlier trio appears to have been worshipped in the Madra country, because Nakula (clever like Kṛṣṇa) and Saha-Deva (whose name is a synonym of Bala-Deva as "the god of strength"), the two Pāṇḍavas sired by the Aśvins, had Mādrī as their mother. Mādrī's brother Śalya, King of Madra, had Goddess Sītā in his banner, and the Vedic Taittirīya-Brāhmaṇa 2,3,10 mentions Sītā Sāvitrī as the daughter of Prajāpati. All this suggests that Pandaíē, Uṣas/Sūryā/Sāvitrī, and Sītā are each other's aliases.

I agree with Weber (1850), who considered Rāma's spouse Sītā to be at least partly mythical. An agricultural goddess, Sītā, the personified furrow, is known from the Rigveda (4,57,6–7), and her worship is described in detail in Pāraskara-Gṛhyasūtra 2,17; according to the Gobhila-Gṛhyasūtra (4,4,27–29), she was to be worshipped at plowing. It makes sense that the husband of "Furrow" is the god of plowing. Weber therefore thought that the hero of the Rāmāyaṇa had developed from Rāma Halabhṛt ("carrier of the plow," i.e., Bala-Rāma), and that he too personified an agricultural divinity, like Sītā. Bala-Rāma's distinctive iconographic emblems, the plow (*lāṅgala, hala*, and *phāla*) and pestle for pounding grain (*muṣala*) definitely mark him as primarily an agrarian deity. The agricultural connection is also plain from his alternative name, Saṃkarṣaṇa, which is derived from the activity of plowing (*kṛṣi*). Weber's hypothesis that the Rāma of the Rāmāyaṇa is actually Bala-Rāma is supported by the fact that the name Bala-Rāma is not found in the Mahābhārata, where Bala-Rāma is called simply Rāma (143 times).

The plow is instrumental in placing the seed in the womb of the earth, and plowing thus symbolizes sexual intercourse. But the plow also creates the furrow, thus representing its generator. In Rāmāyaṇa 1,66,14–15, Sītā emerges out of the furrow when Janaka, the king of Mithilā, is plowing a field, and is given the name Sītā and raised as his daughter by Janaka. In Rāmāyaṇa 7,88,9–14, Sītā finally returns to her mother Earth: the goddess comes to fetch her and the two disappear underground. Janaka's name denotes "progenitor, father." It is one of the names used in the Purāṇas of the Hindu creator god Brahmā, and Brahmā directly continues Vedic Prajāpati, whom Taittirīya-Brāhmaṇa 2,3,10 mentions as the father of Sītā Sāvitrī. On the other hand, as noted above, the plow and the field plowed (or the furrow) form a couple, so that Prajāpati is also Sītā Sāvitrī's husband through incest. In the Rāmāyaṇa, a plow-god seems to be both Sītā's father (Janaka) and husband (Rāma = Bala-Rāma).

Queen Pandaíē of Megasthenes has been compared with the guardian Goddess of the Pāṇḍya capital Madurai, Mīnākṣī. In the local Tamil Tiruviḷaiyāṭaṟ-Purāṇam (twelfth to sixteenth centuries CE), Mīnākṣī is the daughter of a Pāṇḍya king of Madurai and his queen, who was the daughter of a Cōḻa king called Śūrasena. Childless, they performed a Vedic sacrifice to obtain a son, but received from the sacrificial fire a girl. (The birth of Princess Sāvitrī to King Aśvapati in the Indus Valley was similar.) The girl had three breasts, and a voice from heaven told that she should be educated in the military arts like a prince, and that she would conquer the whole world. The third breast would disappear when she met her future husband. All this happened, and finally when fighting at Mount Kailasa, she met God Śiva and the third breast disappeared. After their marriage, Śiva ruled Madurai as King Sundara-Pāṇḍyan.

Here the spouse of Mīnākṣī is called Sundareśvara, "Beautiful Lord," and considered to be Śiva. However, there is in Madurai a local form of Viṣṇu whose Tamil name is Aḻakar, "Beautiful Lord." Aḻakar is the brother of Mīnākṣī who gives the bride away to the groom. The Aḻakar-Malai temple near Madurai, with a standing form of Viṣṇu, dates to pre-Pallavan times, and is one of the oldest in Tamil Nadu. Especially in a city called Madhurā, Aḻakar could have been both the brother and the husband of the goddess in ancient times, as was the case with Rāma and Sītā according to the Dasaratha-Jātaka. Both Sundara and Aḻakar might render Sanskrit Rāma, which in classical Sanskrit means "pleasing, charming, handsome, lovely, beautiful." Some iconographic manuals prescribe that Rāma is to be depicted as beautiful (*sundara*), others that Rāma and Lakṣmaṇa are to be exceedingly handsome. According to Bhāgavata-Purāṇa 10,2,13, Bala-Rāma was called Rāma because he charmed people (*rāmeti lokaramaṇād*) with his beauty.

Vijaya's Sri Lankan *yakkhinī* wife Kuveṇī or Kuvaṇṇā likewise had three breasts, and she had also been told that one of them would vanish when she would see her future husband, which happened when she saw Vijaya. As David Shulman (1980) has pointed out, the Tamil word *kaṇ* in Mīnākṣī's Tamil name, Aṅ-kayaṟ-kaṇṇ-ammaiyār, "lady of the beautiful carp-eyes," means both "eye" and "breast-nipple." In the Śrīvidyārṇava-Tantra, Sītā is three-eyed and wears the crescent of the moon on her head; she has four arms holding a noose, a goad, a bow, and an arrow. Sītā Sāvitrī is an aspect of the warrior goddess Durgā, as is sometimes made explicit in texts. In the case of Mīnākṣī, this relationship with Durgā is clear from her local legend. This legend must be old, for in the Mahāvaṁsa (*c.* 500 CE), the daughter of King Paṇḍu of the southern Madhurā is called Vijayā, which designates her as the goddess of victory.

The legend of a three-breasted princess recurs even at Nāgapaṭṭinam in Tamil Nadu: here this "lady of the long dark eyes" (Karun-taṭaṅ-kaṇṇi) is the daughter of Ādi-Śeṣa, king of the snakes, an ardent worshipper of Śiva. Of her, too, it was prophesied that the third breast would disappear as soon as she saw the king who would wed her, in some variants a Nāgarāja. Shulman (1980) has discussed her relationship with Mīnākṣī and with Kaṇṇaki, the heroine of the Tamil epic Cilappatikāram, who destroys the city of Madurai with one of her breasts: all multiforms of the three-eyed warrior goddess Durgā-Kālī. At Madurai, too, the bridegroom appears to have been the local Śiva-related snake god, called in Tamil Āla-vāy (Sanskrit *hālāsya*, "having poison in its mouth").

Bala-Rāma incarnates a snake deity connected with fertility and the subterranean regions, called Śeṣa, "remainder" (the name seems to refer to the seed grain left over for next sowing), or Ananta, "endless." Serpent Śeṣa drinks palm-wine, and has the palmyra palm and the wine cup as his iconographic attributes. In this regard he is like Bala-Rāma, who in turn has the triple-bended (*tri-bhaṅga*) pose associated with snake deities. Buddhist Sanskrit texts know Pāṇḍuka, Pāṇḍuraka, Paṇḍulaka, and Paṇḍaraka as names of a *nāga* king, one of the guardians of the great treasures.

The Mathurā region is considered to be the stronghold of Saṃkarṣaṇa-Baladeva worship. The identity of Bala-Rāma is likely to have been pasted on the earlier local divinity there. The myth of Kṛṣṇa's subduing the snake Kāliya living in the Yamunā River and driving him away from his home has been explained to symbolize the replacement of a snake cult earlier prevalent at Mathurā with the cult of Kṛṣṇa. Excavations at Sonkh near Mathurā have confirmed that snake worship prevailed to a remarkable degree at Mathurā still around the beginning of the Christian era. The only major shrine discovered is a *nāga* temple. The associated finds comprise images and panels representing serpent deities and inscriptions referring to their cult. Nāga, Nāga Bhūmo, and Nāgarāja Dadhikarṇṇa are mentioned by name.

> Although Saṅkarṣaṇa appears as a Vaiṣṇavite divinity in the Mahābhārata and the Purāṇas, there are traces of his close connection with the cult of Rudra-Śiva also. The Pañcarātra Saṃhitās often identify Saṅkarṣaṇa with Rudra-Śiva. The Brahmāṇḍa Purāṇa states that Rudra was known as Halāyudha ["having the plow as his weapon"]. The Viṣṇu Purāṇa speaks of Saṅkarṣaṇa-Rudra, who comes out of the mouth of the serpent Śeṣa at the end of every aeon. . . . Śiva also is intimately associated with the *nāgas*. (Jaiswal 1981:54)

In Bengal, Śiva is worshipped as Lāṅgaleśvara, "lord of the plow," and the most important phallic god of Hinduism could really be expected to be the god of plowing and generation. Megasthenes's account (*c.* 300 BCE) of the so-called Indian "Dionysus" almost certainly describes the cult of Śiva, underlining his connection with agriculture and the plow: "The Indians, he [Megasthenes] says, were originally nomads . . . until Dionysus reached India. But when he arrived and became master of India, he founded cities, gave them laws, bestowed wine on the Indians as on the Greeks, and taught them to sow their land, giving them seed. . . . Dionysus first yoked oxen to the plough and made most of the Indians agriculturalists instead of nomads, and equipped them also with the arms of warfare" (Arrian, *Indica* 7,2–7, translated Brunt 1983:II,325–327.)

All these sources preserve important information about the earlier, pre-Aśvin background of the Vaiṣṇava/Bhāgavata religion, connecting it with the Vedic and Hindu myths of the incestuous father-and-daughter couple and the young prince-husband (an alter ego of the father) resurrected from death, to be discussed in chapter 19. The agricultural divinities involved here are very likely to have their origin in the indigenous, Harappan religion.

PART II

The Indus Civilization

14

The Language of the Indus Civilization

The identity of the Indus language is perhaps the most important puzzle about the Indus civilization. At the present time, a number of languages are spoken in the Indus Valley. Indo-Aryan languages include Sindhi in Sindh and Punjabi in the Punjab (with its dialects Siraiki and Lahnda) and a number of languages of the Dardic subgroup (Shina, Khowar, Kohistani, and others) with relatively few speakers in the northernmost part of the valley. Other Indo-Aryan languages border the Indus Valley in the east, chiefly Hindi, with its dialect Marwari in Rajasthan, and in the south, Gujarati, in Gujarat. Iranian languages are spoken immediately west of the Indus Valley: Baluchi in Baluchistan, Dari and Pashto in Afghanistan (Pashto extending also to the northern Indus Valley), plus Wakhi and some others with relatively few speakers in the Hindu Kush. The Nuristani languages, spoken in northeastern Afghanistan, have both ancient Iranian and ancient Indo-Aryan features. Outside the group of Indo-Iranian languages is the Dravidian language Brahui, spoken in Baluchistan and Sindh, and the isolated Burushaski, spoken in the northernmost part of Pakistan, close to the Chinese border.

In the third millennium BCE, it is quite likely that many dialects, and perhaps even languages, were spoken in the Indus Valley. But we may be sure that just one language was used in writing the Indus script, because the sign sequences of its inscriptions are repeated throughout the Indus realm. Only in the West Asian Indus seals do we find clearly different sign sequences testifying to the use of another language (probably Sumerian or Akkadian in Mesopotamia, an early West Semitic language in the Arabian or Persian Gulf).

Some of the West Asian Indus seals are of the typically square-stamp Harappan type, and their inscriptions, too, agree with South Asian Indus texts. Others, however, have common Indus signs in sequences dissimilar to seals from the Indus Valley (Fig. 14.1). It appears that the owners of these latter West Asian seals had adopted local, Mesopotamian names along with the local language(s) they needed to know for their business, just as some of these Harappan trade agents in Mesopotamia adopted the local cylinder type of seal. That the language of Meluhha (the probable Sumerian name for the Greater Indus Valley, see chapter 17)

FIGURE 14.1 A round Gulf-type stamp seal (see chapter 17) of glazed white steatite in the British Museum (Reg. No. 1883,116.1, BM 120228). A Harappan-type bison bull feeds from a manger beneath an inscription engraved with five frequently occurring Indus script signs, which, however, are arranged in a unique order. Image 272276001 © The Trustees of the British Museum.

was not understood in Mesopotamia is clear from an inscription found on an Akkadian cylinder seal, which reads: "Šu-ilišu, interpreter of the Meluhhan language" (Fig. 17.4). This, plus the fact that hardly a single object of clearly West Asian origin has been excavated in the Indus realm, makes it very unlikely that the language spoken by the Harappans was any of the West Asian languages.

What about the Indo-Aryan languages? As demonstrated in Part I, there is an unbroken chain of archaeologically connected cultures via which the Indo-Iranian languages passed from their Proto-Indo-European homeland in the Ukraine to their earliest recorded areas of speech. (Even today, the distribution of the Indo-Iranian languages covers almost the entire distance from the Ukraine to India; the steppes north of the Black Sea, in Ukraine and southern Russia, are now void of Indo-Iranian, but the Scythian tribes, who lived there as nomads, spoke an Old Iranian language in the fifth century BCE, as we know from Herodotus.) Since the Indo-Iranian languages started arriving in the South Asia only in the Late Harappan period, around the twentieth century BCE, they cannot account for the Harappan language. Archaeology supports this conclusion. The domesticated horse is totally absent from the art and faunal finds of the Indus civilization. (The published claims to the contrary are based on ambiguous bones, which may have belonged to the wild ass; Meadow 1991; Meadow & Patel 1997; Parpola & Janhunen 2011.) This fact is in drastic contrast with the important role played by the horse in the culture and religion of the early Indo-Iranian speakers. No less striking is the difference between the primitive wooden huts of the Vedic people and the Harappan brick-built and preplanned cities and towns with their elaborate water engineering.

Speakers of the language of the Bactria and Margiana Archaeological Complex (BMAC), too, are likely to have arrived in greater numbers to the Indus Valley only around the twentieth century BCE, accompanying the first wave of Indo-Aryan speakers. As discussed in chapter 8, the original non-Indo-European BMAC language appears to have given a large number of loanwords to Old Indo-Aryan. Indeed, the majority of the many (more than 300) foreign words of unknown origin in the Rigveda seem to have come from this source.

Burushaski, a language isolate in northernmost Pakistan, must have come from the north and never spread further, as there are no linguistic traces of Burushaski south of its present area of speech. The Tibeto-Burman languages (which belong to the great Sinitic family of China, Tibet, and the Southeast Asian mainland) are spoken on the fringes of the Himalaya. They probably came from the north prior to Burushaski; they may have been spoken in the Northern Neolithic culture (2800–1500 BCE) of Kashmir and the Swat Valley. Characteristic features of this culture, such as semisubterranean dwellings and dog burials, are paralleled in China. The Northern Neolithic was in some contact with the Early Harappan Kot Diji culture (Figs. 4.1 and 15.2b), but not demonstrably with the Mature Harappan culture, which did not spread to the northernmost Indus Valley.

The Munda languages spoken in eastern India and belonging to the Austro-Asiatic family have linguistic relatives in Southeast Asia; their westernmost language, Korku in central India, is evidently an offshoot from eastern India. Toshiki Osada (2006), following a remark made by Norman Zide (1969:420), another leading authority on the Munda languages, has shown the untenable nature of many of the most frequently quoted Proto-Munda or Austro-Asiatic etymologies proposed for Sanskrit words (including *lāṅgala-*, "plow," *kadala- / kadalī-*, "banana," *marīca-*, "pepper," and *karpāsa-*, "cotton"). Osada argues that the role of the Munda/Austro-Asiatic languages in the linguistic history of South Asia has been overestimated (cf. also Anderson 2008). Yet Michael Witzel (2005:176–180), followed by Franklin Southworth (2005:64–69,325), considers "Para-Munda" as the most likely language of the Indus civilization. All the linguistic evidence adduced in support, however, is questionable: among the "clearest cases" of a Munda prefix cited from the Rigveda is the word *vi-bhindu-* (Witzel 2005:177), which however is a *-ú-* derivative from the present stem of the Indo-Aryan root *bhi(n)d-*, preceded by the Indo-Aryan prefix *vi-* (thus Wackernagel & Debrunner 1954:II.2:473). Among the words allegedly formed with the Austro-Asiatic prefixes *ka-* and *ki-* (no Austro-Asiatic cognates are given) are *kaparda-* and *kiyāmbu-*, which can be explained as loanwords from Dravidian (see below and chapter 18).

Burushaski, the Tibeto-Burman languages, and the Austro-Asiatic languages are all spoken by very small linguistic minorities in South Asia and have been restricted to the marginal geographical areas, so far as is known. The Austro-Asiatic-speakers, who form the largest group, amount to just 1.13 percent of India's population (as of the 1991 census). None of these minority languages has contributed generally recognized loanwords to the Rigvedic vocabulary. They cannot be considered to be serious candidates for the Harappan language, spoken by about one million people, a remarkably large population in the Bronze Age.

Only one group of South Asian languages remains as a candidate for the Indus language: the Dravidian language family, by far the second largest after the Indo-Iranian family, spoken by 22.53 percent of India's population in 1991. As early as 1816, Francis Whyte Ellis noted that Tamil, Malayalam, Kannada, Kodagu, Telugu, and Malto "form a distinct family of languages" with which "the Sanscrit has, in later times, especially, intermixed, but with which it has no radical connection." In 1856, Robert Caldwell published the first edition of his pioneering *Comparative grammar of the Dravidian or South-Indian family of languages*, in which he named the language family "Dravidian," taking it from the Sanskrit word *draviḍa-*, used of the Tamil language and its speakers and more vaguely of other south Indian peoples.

Caldwell described just twelve Dravidian languages, adding Brahui in his second edition published in 1875. Today, some twenty-six Dravidian languages are recognized, which early on branched into three or four subgroups: North, Central, and South Dravidian, the last of which split into two (Fig. 14.2). Four are major languages, Tamil, Malayalam, Kannada, and Telugu, with roughly fifty-three, thirty, thirty-three, and sixty-six million speakers, respectively (in the 1991 census), and long literary traditions. Linguistically and culturally Tamil is the most important, as it has remained highly conservative in structure and has a rich literature going back some 2000 years, and even earlier in the case of some short inscriptions. Most of the other Dravidian languages have relatively few speakers, many being tribal languages with only an oral literature.

Most Dravidian speakers inhabit south and central India. The exceptions are the speakers of Brahui, Kurukh, and Malto. Brahui-speakers live close to the Indus Valley in Baluchistan, now mainly in Pakistan, but previously also in Iranian Baluchistan. Though Dravidian, Brahui is very heavily influenced by Baluchi, the West Iranian language that arrived in Baluchistan from the northwest in several waves between 700 and 1200 CE (chapter 7). Brahui was probably spoken in Baluchistan before this time, for its speakers had higher social prestige than Baluchi-speakers until 1750, when the situation was reversed. Until quite recently, all speakers of Brahui knew Baluchi, and vice versa, and families were often bilingual in Brahui and Baluchi. The two other members of the North Dravidian subbranch, Kurukh and Malto, which are closely related, are mainly spoken in mountainous regions of Bihar. It is possible that the two languages branched off from Brahui in the first millennium CE, perhaps because Gurjara or Muslim invasions prevented some Brahuis from returning to Baluchistan from Sindh, where many of them had spent the winter season in an age-old transhumance from the mountains to the plains and back.

The Dravidian languages appear to have spread to central and southern India from the area of the Indus Valley. Copper Age cultures of the Deccan, which derive from the Early and Mature Harappan cultures of the Greater Indus Valley, spread farming and animal husbandry to central and southern India, in place of hunter-gathering—an archaeological configuration that matches the current distribution of the Dravidian languages in central and southern India (Fig. 4.4; Fig. 14.2). The Indus civilization itself covered Gujarat and the northern part of Maharashtra (Fig. 4.2), where a Late Harappan seal with Indus script was excavated at Daimabad (Fig. 14.3). Gujarati and especially Marathi, despite being Indo-Aryan languages, are acknowledged to contain a considerable number of loanwords of Dravidian origin, while the evidence of place names also suggests a Dravidian substratum. Particularly common are the suffixes *-ul, -uli, -ol, -oli, -vli, -vali, -valli, -vāli, -vāl, -palli, -pāli*, and *-pāl*, all of which are supposed to go back (via North and Central Dravidian **palli*) to Proto-Dravidian **paḷḷi*, "small village, hamlet" (Southworth 2005).

Not only loanwords reveal a Dravidian substratum; so do kinship relations. In theory, Dravidian and Indo-Aryan-speakers adhere to two fundamentally different kinship systems. Dravidian kinship terminology is based on the cross-cousin marriage, where a man may marry his mother's brother's daughter or his father's sister's daughter (both of whom are cross cousins), but not his mother's sister's daughter or his father's brother's daughter (who are both parallel cousins, because they are the children of same-sex siblings). By contrast,

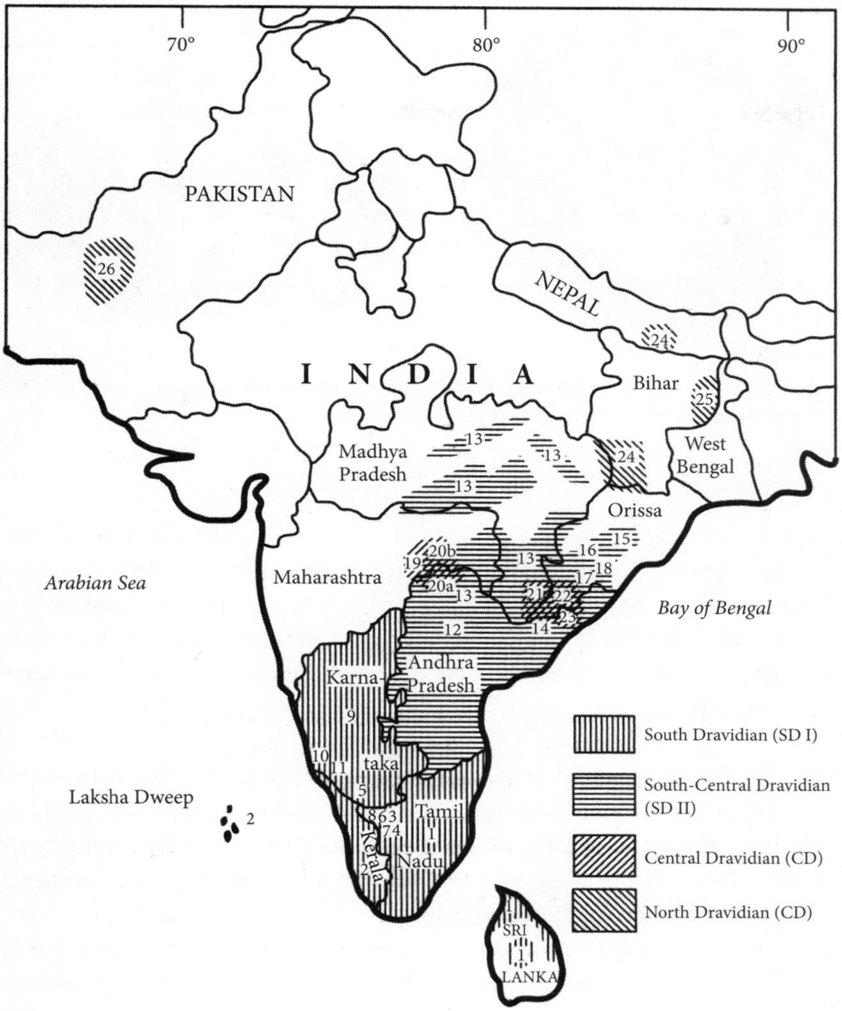

FIGURE 14.2 The geographical distribution of the Dravidian languages in South Asia: (1) Tamil (Tamil̲); (2) Malayalam (Malayāḷam); (3) Irula (Ir̲uḷa); (4) Kurumba (Kur̲umba); (5) Kodagu (Koḍagu, Kuḍagu, Coorg); (6) Toda (Tuda); (7) Kota (Kōta); (8) Badaga (Baḍaga); (9) Kannada (Kannaḍa, Kanarese, Canarese); (10) Koraga; (11) Tulu (Tuḷu); (12 Telugu (Teluṅgu, Teliṅga, Tenugu, Tenuṅgu); (13) Gondi (Gōṇḍī); (14) Konda (Koṇḍa, Kūbi); (15) Kui (Kūi); (16) Kuvi (Kuwi, Kūvi); (17) Pengo; (18) Manda (Manḍa); (19) Kolami (Kōlāmī); (20a) Naikri (Naikṛi); (20b) Naiki of Chanda; (21) Parji; (22) Ollari; (23) (Koṇḍēkōr) Gadaba (Gaḍba); (24) Kurukh (Kuṛukh̲, Kuṛux, Orāōn, Urāōn, Kisan); (25) Malto (Maltō); (26) Brahui (Brāhūī). After Krishnamurti 2003:18, with the caption enlarged to include alternative spellings of the language names and their synonyms. Copyright © 2003 Bhadriraju Krishnamurti. Reprinted with the permission of Cambridge University Press.

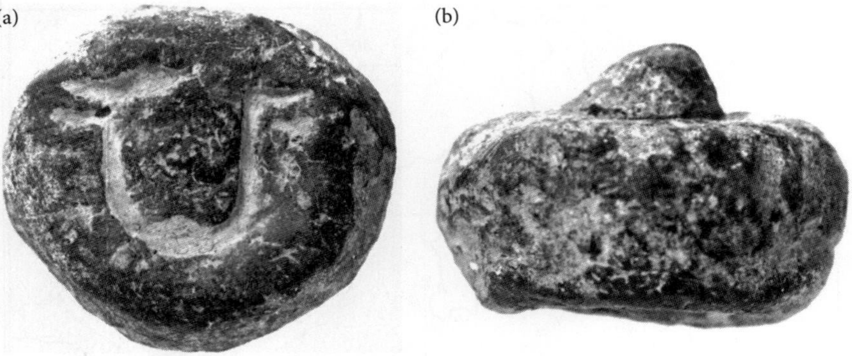

FIGURE 14.3 A Late Harappan stamp seal (Dmb-1) from Daimabad, Maharashtra, period II, *c.* 1800 BCE. (a) The obverse; (b) a side view. After CISI 1:352. Photo EL, courtesy ASI.

in the Indo-Aryan marriage system exogamy of consanguines prevails, although the exact rules vary. For instance, among the Rajputs one may not marry any member of the *gotras* (extended patrilineages) of one's four grandparents, and according to the even more restrictive *sapiṇḍa* rules of the Sanskrit law texts, marriage is prohibited with all near-relatives by birth, not just patrilineal relatives. In practice, however, some Indo-Aryan speakers follow Dravidian kinship practices.

> Although for the most part Dravidian speakers are also Dravidian in kinship and Indo-Aryan speakers are Indo-Aryan in kinship, that is by no means wholly the case. In particular, the kinship map serves to establish a Dravidian presence right up the western coast of India, well to the north of the limit of Dravidian speech, through Maharashtra and into Saurashtra in Gujarat. This is a matter of great historical significance . . . there are a number of communities that, although they speak Indo-Aryan languages, nevertheless have a Dravidian system of kinship. (Trautmann 1981:112)

If the Harappan population numbered about one million in the last quarter of the third millennium BCE, its language is bound to have left some trace in the Vedic language that was spoken in the Indus Valley a thousand years later. Indeed, even structural features in the Vedic language not found in the closely related Old Iranian have been ascribed to Dravidian substratum influence. These involve both phonology and syntax, including the retroflex consonants as phonemes; an increasing use of the gerund; the quotative construction with the particle *iti* following direct speech; and onomatopoeic expressions with echo-duplication (e.g., Rigvedic *budbuda-*, "bubbling" ~ Telugu *buḍa-buḍa*, "with a bubbling noise"; Atharvavedic *kurkura-*, "dog" ~ Kannada *kure kure* and Malto *kur kur*, "call to a dog"; Rāmāyaṇa *kaṭakaṭāpayati*, "gnashes the teeth" ~ Kannada *kaṭakaṭa kaḍi*, "to grind one's teeth"). From later Indo-Aryan one may mention the simplification of the syllable structure and the use of dative-subject constructions as evidence of Dravidian influence. Moreover, it is widely recognized that the following seven Rigvedic words, at least, are derived from Proto-Dravidian words:

phalam, "fruit" < **paḻam*, "ripe fruit"
mukham, "mouth, face, beginning" < **mukam*, "mouth, face, beginning"
khala-, "threshing floor" < **kaḷam*, "threshing floor"
lāṅgalam, "plow" < **ñāṅgal*, "plow" (in my opinion, *ñāṅgal* is originally a compound of Proto-Dravidian **ñāl*, "earth, ground" + **kal*, "to dig, excavate")
ukham, "hip" < **ukkam*, "hip"
kāṇa-, "blind in one eye" < **kāṉ-*, "to see" + negative marker **-aH-*, "to see not"
kaṭuka-, "pungent, bitter" < **kaṭu* "pungent, bitter"

Although the Rigveda is the earliest recorded text collection in Indo-Aryan, it was composed by the later wave of immigrants, who may be assumed to have met fewer Dravidian speakers in the Indus Valley than the Indo-Aryan speakers who came earlier to the Indus Valley. The number of Dravidian loanwords in the later Vedic texts and the epics that continue the Atharvavedic tradition is well over 150; and there are many more if still later Indo-Aryan is taken into consideration. For instance, the following two words central in cultic Hinduism, discussed in the next chapter, are very likely to have Dravidian origins: *pūjā* and *ghāṭ*. I now consider six further early Vedic words that in my personal view offer fairly convincing examples of Dravidian loanwords. The first two concern the flora and fauna of the Indus Valley; the remaining four are my own etymologies.

1. *kiyāmbu*, a kind of aquatic plant

This word is known only from variants of a single Vedic verse. The Rigvedic phrase (10,16,13c) *kiyāmbu atra rohatu*, "may *kiyāmbu* grow here," appears as *kyāmbūr atra rohatu* in the Atharvaveda (18,3,6c). There is general agreement that *kiyāmbu* denotes a kind of aquatic plant, because the context of the verse concerns cooling the place of corpse cremation with plenty of water. No cognates have been recorded from later forms of Indo-Aryan, and the etymology has been considered unclear. However, Nikita Gurov (2000) has proposed an excellent etymology from Proto-Dravidian **kiyampu*, which through regular sound changes became Tamil *cēmpu*, a flowering plant known variously as taro, aroid, and *Colacasia*. The lengthened *-ā-* in the Rigveda and Atharvaveda may result from the idea that *kiyāmbu* is a compound with Sanskrit *ambu-*, "water," as the last member (although *ambu-* is not attested before the Upaniṣads). Incidentally, this etymology is important for the botanical history of South Asia, as it suggests that taro was present in the Indus Valley in 1000 BCE; in a recent survey by a leading researcher, taro is supposed to have come to south India from Orissa or eastern India (D. Q. Fuller 2006:41,46–47).

2. *gardabha*, "donkey" (sometimes also "wild ass")

The wild ass is the only native equid of South Asia, its habitat being restricted mainly to the extensive saline soils and salt marshes of Sindh and Gujarat. Its bones have been found at many Harappan sites and the animal itself is depicted on one Indus seal from Kanmer in

Kutch, as well as in a sign of the Indus script, and in several terracotta figurines. After the similar-looking donkey was introduced (besides the domesticated horse and the camel) from Central Asia to the Indus Valley by Indo-Aryan speakers, the native Dravidian word for "wild ass" was also used for "donkey." Proto-Dravidian **kaẓutay*, which is preserved in Tamil *kaḻutai*, "donkey," seems originally to have meant "the kicking animal of the salt marsh" (from **kaẓ-*, "saline soil, salt marsh" + **utay*, "to kick"). How Proto-Dravidian **kaẓ(u)ta(y)* became *garda-* in Sanskrit may be easier to understand if we note that it has become *kaḻte* in Kannada and *gāṛde* in Kuvi. Adding the ancient Indo-Aryan suffix *-bha-* to animal names has parallels even in later Indo-Aryan (Parpola & Janhunen 2011).

3. *oṁ*

The sacred syllable is not attested in the form *oṁ* in the Rigveda, but is thought to be implied by the expression *akṣara* "syllable" in three verses of the riddle hymn RV 1,164. It is, however, much used in the later Vedic liturgy. When the Rigvedic, Sāmavedic, and Yajurvedic priests ask the Brahman priest for permission to carry out an action (e.g., *brahman apaḥ praṇeṣyāmi*, "O Brahman, I am about to carry forwards the water"), *oṁ* introduces the permission (*anujñā*), followed by an imperative of the appropriate verb (e.g., *oṁ, praṇaya*, "yes, do carry it forward!"). The meaning of *oṁ* is explicitly stated in the Chāndogya-Upaniṣad (1,1,8): "This syllable is one of permission; for when one permits anything, he says *oṁ*." When the Śunaḥśepa legend is related during the royal consecration, "*oṁ* is the response to a Rigvedic verse (*ṛc*), *tathā* ('be it so') to a profane verse (*gāthā*); *oṁ* is divine, *tathā* is human" (AB 7,18). Distinction is made here between the hieratic speech of the sacrifice, where *oṁ* is used to express agreement, and ordinary mundane conversation, where *tathā* or *tathāstu* is used. But occasionally *oṁ* and *na* are used for "yes" and "no" in ordinary prose dialogue as replies to questions (e.g., in BĀU 6,2,1). I therefore propose that *oṁ* (with a long *ō*, as always in Sanskrit) derives from Proto-Dravidian **ām*, "yes," a contracted variant of **ākum*, the non-past (habitual present-future without personal endings) regularly formed with the suffix **-um* of the very basic auxiliary verb **ā* / **āku*, meaning "it is, it is so, yes." This usage of *ām* to mean "yes" is still very common in Dravidian languages, for instance Tamil, and in the Jaffna dialect of Tamil in Sri Lanka, where *ām* has become *ōm*, "yes," clearly repeating the same phonetic process (vocalic anticipation of *m*) that resulted in Vedic *ōm*. Hindi *hāṁ*, "yes," owes its initial *h-* to North Dravidian, where all initial vowels are introduced with a glottal stop (Parpola 1981).

4. *śakaṭī-, śakaṭam*, "ox-cart"

This word is attested once in the latest book of the Rigveda (10,156,3), where it has the feminine gender (*śakaṭī-*), apparently because it is connected with the goddess of the forest. Thereafter it mostly appears in the neuter gender as *śakaṭam*, which in later Vedic texts replaces the inherited Indo-Aryan word *anas-*, "ox-cart" (cognate with Latin *onus*, "load"). This suggests that the local, Indus Valley, name of the much-used ox-cart broke through to Vedic usage, given that the population of the Indus Valley had an ox-cart from the Early Harappan period, around 3000 BCE. The cognates of *śakaṭam* in the various modern Indo-Aryan languages presuppose variant forms **śakkaṭam* and **śaggaṭam* (Turner

1966:709; Mayrhofer 1996:II,601). I therefore suggest derivation, with metathetical sound transposition, from Proto-Dravidian **caṭṭakam*, "wooden frame or platform of a cart" (also used of the "frame of a door, bedstead, bier"). The Harappan terracotta models of carts consist of a platform-like frame with holes for vertical pins, and separate wheels; ox-carts of the same type are still used in Sindh (Parpola, in press d).

5. *bhekuri/bekuri*, "calendrical asterism, mistress of the moon"

The oldest Yajurvedic texts in one context refer to the *nakṣatras*—that is, the calendrical asterisms (lunar mansions of Hindu astrology)—by the name *bhekuri* or *bekuri*. They treat the *nakṣatras* as heavenly mistresses of the moon. Śatapatha-Brāhmaṇa (9,4,1,9) compares the moon joining the *nakṣatras* to a heavenly playboy (*gandharva*) having sexual intercourse with dancing girls (*apsaras*); and gives a folk-etymological explanation of *bhekuri* by stating that the *nakṣatras* "make light" (in Sanskrit, *bhāṃ kurvanti*). A more plausible etymology, in my view, is to trace *b(h)ekuri* back to what seems to be the original Dravidian appellation of the *nakṣatras*, preserved in several Dravidian languages in words denoting "morning star," particularly Old Tamil *vaikuṟu mīṉ*, derived from the Proto-Dravidian roots **vayku*, "to stay overnight, to outlast the night, to begin to grow light, to dawn," and **uṟu*, "to be joined, to be close together, touch, have sexual intercourse." The alternations *v-/b-* and *ai/e* are very common in Dravidian languages, for example in the representation of the Proto-Dravidian root **vayku* in Tulu, *baiku*, Telugu, *vēgu*, Kuvi, *vēy-* and Malto, *bije* (Parpola 1994a:206–207).

6. *kiṃpuruṣa* and *kinnara*, mythical musicians

In epic and classical Sanskrit literature, *kiṃpuruṣa* and *kinnara* are imagined to be half-human, half-animal (usually a horse). According to Māgha's Śiśupālavadha (4,38), the *kiṃpuruṣa* has a horse's head and a human body, while the *kinnara* has a human head and an equine body. Both words can be analyzed as compounds consisting of Sanskrit words meaning "what?" (*kim*) and "man" (*puruṣa* and *nara*), yielding the overall sense, "what kind of man?"

Of the two words, only *kiṃpuruṣa* occurs in the Vedic literature, in Brāhmaṇa texts. These specify that when a fire altar is built of bricks, five victims are sacrificed and their heads deposited in the *ukhā* pot in the center of the lowest layer of the altar. These five victims (including a man) are spoken of as "animals of the village": man (*puruṣa*), horse (*aśva*), cow, sheep, and goat. They are correlated with five "animals of the forest," which have been kept imprisoned but are then released in order to remove any evil created by the distress and pain suffered by the victims of the sacrifice. The five "wild" animals are: *kiṃpuruṣa*, wild ass (*gaura*), bison, urial or camel, and markhor or ibex. "Mock-man," "depraved man," "deformed man," "dwarf," "savage," and "ape" have been suggested as possible meanings for *kiṃpuruṣa*.

Because *kiṃpuruṣa* occurs in the Vedic literature but *kinnara* does not, *kinnara* has generally been considered to be a later transformation of *kiṃpuruṣa*. In my view, however, *kinnara* predates *kiṃpuruṣa*: it is a Dravidian word, which was misunderstood to be Sanskrit, so that *nara-*, which in Sanskrit means "man," was rendered by Sanskrit *puruṣa-*, "man."

Indeed, *kinnara(m)* is probably the very earliest Dravidian word on record. The Harappans may have brought the word to Mesopotamia, because it seems to be written in cuneiform sources. It appears first with the cuneiform logogram for "harp." Then, from the eighteenth century BCE onwards, it is written phonetically in Old Babylonian cuneiform as ^{GIŠ}*ki-in-na-ratim* and in the Ugaritic cuneiform and alphabet as ^{GIŠ}*ki-na-rum, knr*. These words definitely denote a "stringed musical instrument," and in this meaning cognates are known from a wide range of languages used at various times in the region: New Kingdom Egyptian *k[]-nù-rú* and *k.nn.r*, Syriac *kennārā*, Arabic *kinnāra, kinnīra*, and *kinārum*, Hebrew *kinnōr*, Greek *kinúrā* and *kinnúrā*. In Hittite, *kinirtalla* denotes "a musician (zither player?)." Assyriologists have suspected that the stringed musical instrument denoted by these words is an import from India to West Asia; the words are considered decidedly non-Semitic in structure.

I regard *kinnaram* as a compound word, where the first part is the Proto-Dravidian root **kil*, "to sound, resound," used in Old Tamil to express the sound of a harp; its final **-l* has been assimilated to the initial **n-* of the second member of the compound. This second member is Proto-Dravidian **naram* < **ñaram*, "nerve, tendon, sinew, vein," in Old Tamil "string of the harp" (made of tendon). The original meaning of *kinnaram* is therefore "a resounding stringed musical instrument," and in this meaning the compound word is attested in nine Dravidian languages: Tamil and Malayalam *kinnaram, kinnari*, Kannada and Tulu *kinnari*, Telugu *kinnara, kinnera*, Parji *kindri*, Kuvi *kinēri*, Kurukh *kendrā*, and Malto *kendre*. Moreover, three Indo-Aryan languages have words with the same meaning: Sanskrit *kiṃnarā* (attested only in a native Sanskrit lexicon), *kiṃnarī* (in Hemacandra's lexicon and the Kathāsaritsāgara), Sindhi *kīniro, kīnaro*, and Old Marathi *kinarī*. According to Hemacandra, *kiṃnarī* is "a lute of the tribals, *caṇḍālas*" (Parpola 1983).

Based on textual evidence (partly discussed in chapters 12 and 19), I propose that the human victim in Vedic sacrifices was a harp-playing bard, who was called (like any member of a modern orchestra) after his musical instrument. The sacrifice included a "revival" ritual that involved swapping the severed heads of the human victim and the animal (horse) victim, resulting in two "mythical" creatures of the kind described above by Māgha (see chapter 11).

Thus *kiṃpuruṣa*, an old problem relating to human sacrifice in the early layer of Vedic rituals, turns out to be a folk-etymological translation loan from Dravidian *kinnara*, which may be the earliest recorded word from any South Asian language.

Sanskrit *śakaṭam*, derived from Proto-Dravidian **caṭṭakam*, denotes the ox-cart, the most important transport vehicle of South Asia from Early Harappan to modern times. The sacred syllable *oṁ*, nowadays one of the primary symbols for Hinduism, also has a Dravidian etymology. These new etymologies increase the probability that Proto-Dravidian was the language of the Indus civilization—a conclusion reinforced by the evidence of the Indus script, as we shall see in chapter 21.

15

Fertility Cults in Folk Religion

Excavation in the Neolithic villages of Baluchistan, such as Mehrgarh, has brought to light not only evidence for the cultivation of crops and the rearing of animals for food but also what appear to be religious images: terracotta figurines of human females and bulls as the principal cultic artifacts. They suggest that the earliest village religion involved prayers for the fertility of plants, animals, and people. The female figurines are thought to represent the goddess Earth, the progenitor of plants from seeds sown into her womb and the nurturer of worshippers, like a mother who gives birth to children and takes care of them. The bull figurines relate to animal husbandry. They represent the thundering and pouring Sky, which is conceived in many archaic religions as a roaring bull, a powerful male god whose semen fertilizes his spouse, the Earth. This interpretation is endorsed by West Asian parallels, to be discussed in chapter 19.

Numerous terracotta figurines of human females and a variety of male animals show that this fertility cult continued into the Early and Mature Harappan periods dated several thousand years later, and indeed even up to our times in South Asian villages. Male human figurines make their appearance in the Early Harappan period, first at Mehrgarh, where they usually are turbaned and sometimes have a child in their arms. Of the human figurines excavated at Harappa, 1,143 have been identified as female (some also holding infants) and 407 as male. Most of the 500 or so human and animal figurines excavated at Mohenjo-daro were found in rooms with just one door, that is, in a private part of the house. Thus the cult images were granted a special place comparable to the *pūjā* room or alcove in Hindu homes.

The Indo-Iranians—and the Vedic priests who followed them—did not worship their deities in image form. They invited the invisible gods to come and sit on the grass next to the sacrificial fire, into which they poured food and drink for the gods, while praising them with newly composed hymns. The Hindus, by contrast, perform their ritual of worship directly and concretely upon the divinity, be it a statue, statuette, an icon, or a living being, either human (such as bride and groom during the wedding, when they personify Śiva and Pārvatī, or a guru) or animal (such as cattle during the yearly festival, snakes on the *nāgapañcamī* day), the banyan tree (while performing the *vaṭasāvitrīvrata*) or a lifeless object (such as a book or a weapon during the *navarātri* festival, or wooden sandals of saintly persons).

The Hindu image worship, called in Sanskrit *pūjā*, according to the learned manuals (written by Brahmins) normally consists of sixteen "services," but this number can vary from 1 to 108. Some of the earliest (post-Vedic) texts list these as follows: (1) invocation, (2) seat, (3) water for washing the feet, (4) *arghya* water offered to an honored guest, (5) water for sipping, (6) bath, (7) garments, (8) sacred thread, (9) anointing with unguents or sandalwood paste, (10) flowers, (11) incense, (12) lamp, (13) food, (14) mouth perfume, (15) (praise hymn and) prostration, and (16) circumambulation and gift or dismissal. One can immediately see that items (2) to (5) come from the Vedic ritual for receiving an honored guest, and (8) the sacred thread likewise belongs to the Brahmanical tradition.

The original non-Aryan mode of treating an honored guest, human or divine, seems to be first recorded in our sources in some rituals described in late Vedic texts. One is the *sarpa-bali*, offerings made without sacrificial fire to the snakes, another the ancestor rituals. The main thing seems to be bathing the object of worship, anointing the person's, animal's, or image's body with unguents, and giving garments and various adornments and items of toiletry (eye-liner, comb, mirror) and flower garlands. In temple worship, the image may be bathed with many different kinds of liquid (milk, curds, ghee, honey, sugar-cane juice . . .). It is also important for the worshipper to drink part of the bathing water and eat the remnants of the god's meal, which are charged with holy power from the divine touch.

If one turns from textual sources and temple ritual, which have been in the care of Brahmins, to the actual worship of simple villagers, Jarl Charpentier (1926) has collected several pages of references from all over India from the nineteenth century, where the worship consists of anointing the icon—which may be nothing but a peculiar stone under a sacred tree—with oil and vermilion paste. The red ointment, the red kunkuma powder, and the yellow turmeric powder, which all are so often used in smearing Hindu objects of worship, are supposed to stand for blood, which is poured on the icon of the goddess in animal sacrifices in south India and Bengal. In the Vedic ritual this has one singular parallel, which is undoubtedly of non-Aryan origin. In the horse sacrifice the blood of this chief victim is poured on the head of a bald old man with projecting teeth, who, up to his head in water, personifies the god Varuṇa. The description of the man and his being in water reminds one of the crocodile as Varuṇa's mount, discussed in the sequel. Chapter 19 will argue that the Vedic horse sacrifice has replaced a buffalo sacrifice of Harappan origin.

The Sanskrit root *pūj-*, "to worship, honor," with its derivates, is not used in Vedic texts before the Gṛhyasūtras, where the object of worship can, in Hindu fashion, be an animal such as the bull (GGS 3,6,11). Its etymology from the Proto-Dravidian root **pūcu*, "to smear, anoint," suggested by Hermann Gundert (1869), agrees well with the central act of the simplest form of Hindu *pūjā*. Dravidian *pūcu* corresponds in its meaning to the Sanskrit verbs *lip-* and *añj-*, "to smear, anoint," both of which occur in the descriptions of the *sarpa-bali* ritual.

The emphasis on bathing in Hindu rituals may possibly be traced back to the Indus civilization, as first suggested by Marshall. Mortimer Wheeler agreed, noting as follows:

> the importance . . . of water in the life of the Harappans is stressed by the Great Bath on the citadel of Mohenjo-daro and by the almost extravagant provision for bathing

> and drainage throughout the city, and may provide yet another link with the later Hinduism. The universal use of 'tanks' in modern Indian ritual, and the practice of bathing at the beginning of the day and before principal meals, may well derive ultimately from a usage of the pre-Āryan era as represented in the Indus civilization. (Wheeler 1968:110)

In my view Hindu bathing places, such as the ghats at Varanasi, may have existed from the time of the Indus civilization. It is supposed that a canal or a branch of the Indus flowed next to the lower city of Mohenjo-daro, which appears to have been surrounded by revetments functioning as flood defences. Next to what Ernest Mackay took to be "a small fort on the city wall," he found a "ghat-like staircase" that "led down at least as far as the present water-level" (Wheeler 1968:47). In any case the derivation of Sanskrit *ghaṭṭa-* from Dravidian **kaṭṭa*, "river bank, embankment, dam," is fairly generally accepted for the Hindi word *ghāṭ*, "bathing place," and its cognates in many modern Indo-Aryan languages; and it is surprising that the corresponding Sanskrit word *ghaṭṭa-* is not attested in Vedic, Epic, or Purāṇic literature, but only in the works of lexicographers. All the nuances of the equivalent Indo-Aryan term *tīrtha*, "ford, sacred bathing place," are supplemented by a near homophone of Dravidian **kaṭṭa*, namely **kaṭa*, "to cross over, ford, transgress" (Parpola 2003).

Early Harappans used the plow and the ox-cart; indeed all their basic crafts were well developed. In practical respects, South Asian villages have changed little until very recently. We can probably expect the same to be true of religion, since folk religion in all cultures is notably conservative. Speaking of Gujarat, a nineteenth-century scholar noted: "Every village has its own special guardian mother, called Mātā or Ambā"—some 140 different "mothers" in all. "Generally there is also a male deity, who protects like the female from all adverse and demoniacal influences. But the mother is the favourite object of adoration" (Monier-Williams 1885:222). The same held true in India at large, not least in the Dravidian-speaking south India. In every village the mother goddess personified the place and its soil, out of which her cult images were made by the local potter. She was prayed to for blessings such as children, good health, and animals, but also feared, for she could bring about terrible calamities such as a pestilence, if she were neglected or angered.

Early Harappan cultures started moving toward the east and south in about 3000 BCE, and later waves of influence in these same directions came from the Indus civilization (Figs.4.1–2). That the Harappan water-buffalo cult (Figs. 15.2, 16.6) had reached peninsular India by the Late Harappan or Chalcolithic times is suggested by the large bronze sculpture of water buffalo (Fig. 15.1) discovered in 1974 in a hoard at Daimabad, the southernmost Indus site in Maharashtra (Figs. 4.4, 14.3). Throughout south India, until relatively recently, village goddesses have been worshipped through water-buffalo sacrifices. The goddesses have been associated with a male deity called the "buffalo king," represented by a wooden post or a pillar made of stone, or by the pipal tree (Biardeau 2004).

In the form of worship at Kannapuram, a south Indian village in Tamil Nadu studied by Brenda Beck (1981), the tree-trunk (known as *kampam* in Tamil, from Sanskrit *skambha*, "pillar") in front of which the sacrificial buffaloes are decapitated, is said to be the husband of the goddess. At the end of the annual marriage rite, after the last victim has been slaughtered,

FIGURE 15.1 A water buffalo, 31 cm high and 25 cm long, standing on a platform attached to four solid wheels. One of four bronze sculptures weighing together over 60 kg, found in a hoard at Daimabad, Maharashtra, the southernmost Indus site, and ascribed to the Late Harappan or Chalcolithic period. Photo Asko Parpola.

this trunk is uprooted and the goddess divested of her ornaments like a widow. The pillar and its uprooting correspond to Śiva's phallus and its castration. The sacrificial post used to be burned after the divine marriage festival.

In a story about the origin of the tree-trunk, the goddess is said to have implanted herself in the womb of a Brahmin woman and been born as a Brahmin girl. An untouchable Paṟaiya boy fell in love with her and obtained her parents' consent to marry her. His untouchable status was discovered only later, to the anger of the goddess. With a scorching look she burned her husband to ashes and from them caused a margosa tree to grow, to stand forever outside her house. This is a typical version of the myths explaining the origin of the trees and posts symbolizing the male divinity who is the low-caste guardian or servant of the goddess.

The myth of Śiva and Kāma, known all over India, is quite parallel. With an angry look from his third eye, Śiva incinerated Kāma, the god of love and sexual lust, in revenge for Kāma's having shot Śiva with arrows of desire that made him fall for goddess Pārvatī. The ashes covering Śiva's ascetic body are said to be those of Kāma. According to some variants of this myth, Kāma became a tree. In contemporary Sri Lanka, a Tamil festival enacts Śiva's burning of Kāma, in which Kāma is impersonated by a post, which is also burnt. In central and south India, the spring festival of Holi (at the vernal equinox) commemorates the death and resurrection of Kāma with a big bonfire. Human figures representing Kāma and his wife

Rati ("sexual pleasure") are made and the male figure thrown into the fire. In Maharashtra, people walk around the fire shouting words for female genitals, and dances imitating copulation are performed. In Kumaon, Holi is celebrated by planting a pole in ground, dancing around it, singing erotic songs, and burning the pole on the last day of the festival.

In the Vedic ritual, the animal victim was tied to a wooden sacrificial stake (*yūpa*). This symbolized the primeval cosmic tree growing from the navel of the earth, upholding the sky and thus leading to heaven. "It is through the sacrificial stake that the offerings go to the heavenly world," says the Maitrāyaṇī Saṃhitā (4,8,8). After a Vedic sacrifice the post was either left standing or thrown into the sacred fire. The burning of the stake is explained by saying that the fireplace is the womb of the gods, and the sacrificer will be born in heaven with a body of gold (AB 2,3).

That the sacrificial post also had a phallic connotation, even in the Vedas, is evident from the Vedic rite of *puṁsavana*, "causing the birth of a male child." Here various symbols of the male generative organ are used, for example, two beans (for testicles) together with a barley corn (for the phallus), a shoot of the banyan tree with a fruit on either side and an aerial root of the banyan. The banyan shoots and air roots are pounded with millstones (an activity symbolizing sexual intercourse) and the husband inserts the resulting paste—expressly equated with sperm—into the right nostril of his wife. Among the other things that may be mixed with this potent paste is "a splinter of a sacrificial post . . . exposed to the fire" (HGS 2,1,2,6).

The deity prayed to in the *puṁsavana* ritual is Prajāpati, "the lord of offspring"; but the means used in it, barley and beans (KS 36,6; MS 1,10,12), as well as the banyan-tree (GGS 4,7,24), are all said to belong to Varuṇa. According to the Śunaḥśepa legend (discussed in the next chapter), Varuṇa is the deity to approach in order to conceive a son. This fact underlines Varuṇa's phallic nature and his relationship with Prajāpati, Śiva, and *liṅga* worship, which has become such a vital part of Hinduism.

In descriptions of the south Indian folk religion the guardian goddess of the village and the bloody sacrifices to her indeed occupy a central position:

> On the night before the day appointed for the offering of animal sacrifices by the villagers, a male buffalo, called Devara Potu, i.e. devoted to the deity, is sacrificed on behalf of the whole village. First, the buffalo is washed with water, smeared with yellow turmeric and red kunkuma, and then garlanded with flowers and the leaves of the sacred margosa tree. It is brought before the image; and a Mādigā cuts off its head, if possible at one blow, over a heap of boiled rice, which becomes soaked with the blood. The right foreleg is then cut off and placed crosswise in its mouth, according to the widespread custom prevailing in South India, the fat of the entrails is smeared over the eyes and the forehead, and the head is placed in front of the image. A lighted lamp is placed, not as in other villages on the head itself, but on the heap of rice soaked with blood. This rice is then put into a basket; and a Mādigā, the village *vetty* or sweeper, carries it round the site of the village, sprinkling it on the ground as he goes. The whole village goes with him, but there is no music or tom-toms. The people shout out as they go "Poli! Poli!" i.e. "Food! Food!" and clap their hands and wave their sticks above their

> heads to keep off the evil spirits. The rice offered to the goddess, but not soaked with blood, is then distributed to the people. . . . On the next day . . . various householders, even Brāhmans and Bunniahs, bring animals for sacrifice. All are killed by a Mādigā, and then the heads are all presented and placed in a heap before the goddess. Sometimes an extraordinary number of animals is sacrificed on occasions of this kind, as many as a thousand sheep on a single day. (Whitehead 1921:56–57)

If the buffalo sacrifice is common in south Indian village religion, it is absent from north Indian village religion. The reason is probably the conscious efforts of Vedic Brahmins to eradicate it. Extravagant buffalo sacrifices were at first adopted by the Rigvedic Aryans in the Indus Valley (cf. RV 5,29,7–8, etc.), but thereafter this mode of worship is not heard of. In the later Vedic literature a buffalo sacrifice (to Varuṇa) is mentioned in only a single context, in a list of hundreds of different animals offered as subsidiary victims in the horse sacrifice. It appears that generally speaking, the Brahmins have been fighting against bloody sacrifices from Rigvedic times onwards. In the Rigveda, the cow is called *aghnyā*, "not to be slain," and while the Gṛhyasūtra rules (apparently reflecting the behavioral code of the Atharvavedic Indo-Aryans) include the slaughter of a cow when a guest of honor is received, a later rule leaves it to the guest to decide whether this is done or the cow is set free. The Brāhmaṇa and Śrautasūtra texts record, even mentioning the names of the Brahmins concerned, how in the Vedic sacrifices human, horse, and other animal victims were successively discontinued, and a final rule says that the prescribed victims should be made out of rice and barley paste.

In the Indus civilization the water buffalo was connected with an important divinity, for the famous "Proto-Śiva" on a seal from Mohenjo-daro wears the horns of a water buffalo and this animal itself is also depicted on the seal (Hiltebeitel 1978) (Fig. 16.6). The water buffalo is prominent among the motifs on painted pottery in the Early Harappan Kot Diji culture; it is attested in different corners of the Indus Valley: at Kot Diji in Sindh, Gumla in the northwest and even in a vessel imported to the Northern Neolithic site of Burzahom in Kashmir (Fig. 15.2).

Even without the buffalo sacrifice, the religion of North Indian villages, too, largely goes back to traditions established in Early Harappan times. Buddhist and Jain texts describe in detail early folk cults, in which male and female deities, called in Sanskrit *yakṣa* and *yakṣī* or *yakṣiṇī*, occupy a central position. These deities are connected with sacred trees. For example:

> Near Campā there was a sanctuary (*cēïya*) named Puṇṇabhadde. It was of ancient origin . . . and well known. It had umbrellas, banners, and bells; it had flags . . . to adorn it. . . . It had daises (*veyaḍḍi*) built in it, and was reverentially adorned with a coating of dry cow-dung, and bore figures of the five-fingered hand painted in . . . sandal. There was a great store of ritual pitchers. . . . It smelt pleasantly . . . with sweet-smelling fine scents. . . . It was haunted by actors, dancers, rope-walkers, wrestlers, boxers, jesters, jumpers, reciters, ballad-singers, story-tellers, pole-dancers, picture-showmen, pipers, lute-players, and minstrels. . . . This sanctuary was

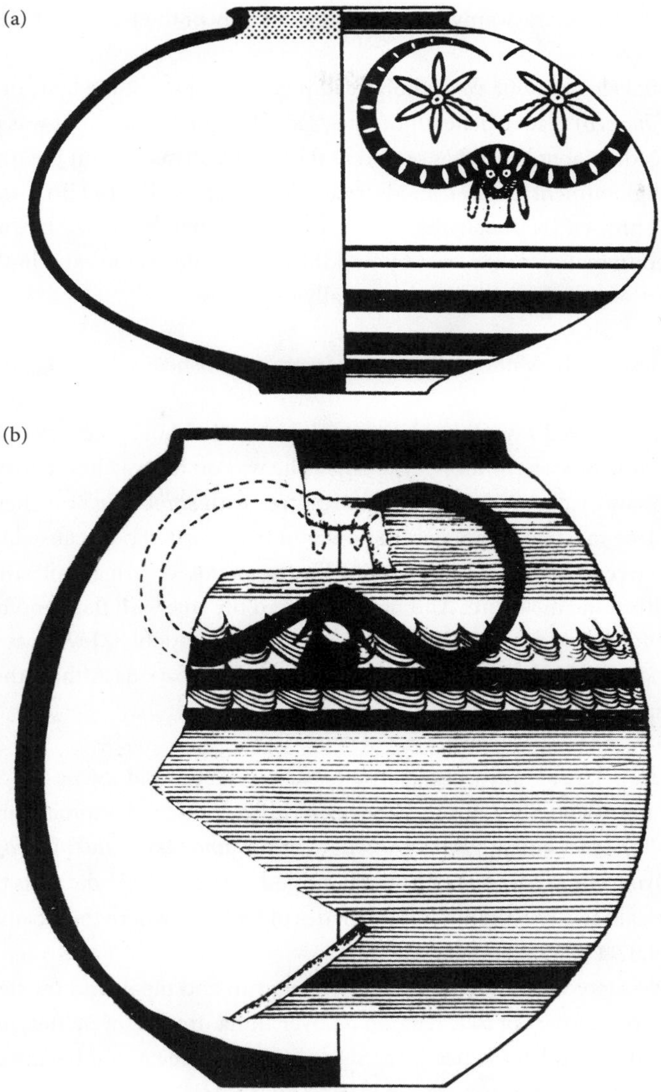

FIGURE 15.2 Water buffalo on painted pots of the Early Harappan Kot Diji culture. (a) A pot excavated at Kot Diji. After Khan 1965:58, fig. 16. Courtesy DAMGP. (b) A pot imported to the Northern Neolithic site of Burzahom in Kashmir, period II. After Kaw 1989:88, fig. 7. Courtesy ASI.

encompassed round about by a great wood . . . . In this wood was a broad mid-space. Therein . . . was a great and fine Aśoka tree. It had its roots pure with *kuśa* and *vikuśa* grass. . . . Underneath this fine Aśoka tree, somewhat close to its trunk was . . . a large dais of earthen blocks. . . . It was shaped like a throne. (Aupapātika-sūtra, translated Barnett 1907; quoted in Coomaraswamy 1928:I,19–21)

As noted by A. K. Coomaraswamy in his important study of the *yakṣa* cult (1928:I,17):

> the essential element of a *yakṣa* holystead [i.e., shrine] is a stone table or altar (*veyaḍḍi, mañco*) placed beneath the tree sacred to the Yakṣa. . . . It was just such an altar beneath a sacred tree that served as the Bodhisattva's seat on the night of the Great Enlightenment; Sujātā's maidservant, indeed, mistakes the Bodhisattva for the tree-spirit himself (Nidānakathā). It is very evident that the sacred tree and altar represent a combination taken over by Buddhism from older cults, and in the case of the Bodhi-tree we see the transference actually in process.

The texts also describe how new *yakṣa* shrines were established:

> At Sāvatthī . . . lived a householder named Great-Wealth. . . . He was rich . . ., but at the same time he was childless. One day, as he was on his way home from bathing at a ghāṭ, he saw by the roadside a large forest tree with spreading branches. Thought he, "This tree must be tenanted by a powerful tree-spirit." So he caused the ground under the tree to be cleared, the tree itself to be enclosed with a wall, and sand to be spread within the inclosure. And having decked the tree with flags and banners, he made the following vow: "Should I obtain a son or a daughter, I will pay you great honour." Having so done, he went on his way. (Dhammapada Atthakathā, translated Burlingame 1921:146)

The Mahābhārata refers to holy trees (*caitya-vṛkṣa*) in villages and towns (6,3,37); these trees should not be injured as they are the abodes of gods, *yakṣas*, demonic spirits, and so on (12,69,39–40). The epics and other texts often mention *gandharvas* and *apsaras* together with the *yakṣas* and *yakṣiṇīs* as subjects of Kubera, the god of riches. In Vedic texts the *gandharvas* and *apsaras* are said to reside in different varieties of fig trees, where their cymbals and harps resound (AVŚ 4,37,4; TS 3,4,8,4).

Worship of sacred trees, especially the figs banyan and pipal, and the neem, continues to be a very important part of folk religion all over India. Images of deities, including snake deities (*nāgas*), are often kept beneath the sacred trees. There cannot be any doubt that this tree worship, using the mightiest trees native to South Asia, has its origin in the Early and Mature Harappan culture, where fig trees are important art motifs. Several Indus seals and tablets depict an anthropomorphic deity standing inside a fig tree, sometimes with a worshipper kneeling in front of the tree, hands raised up, as if in prayer. Trees with railings around them are depicted in Indus tablets. A possible tree temple has been identified at Mohenjo-daro: it has a higher floor, to which lead two flights of steps on opposite sides of the room, which contains the remains of what may have been a railing for a sacred tree. In the fig deity seal from Mohenjo-daro we see in front of the sacred tree with its deity a throne-shaped altar table (Fig. 21.9). One tablet shows a cobra on such a throne beneath a sacred tree. Many anthropomorphic deities are shown to wear a branch of a fig or some other sacred tree in their horned headdress (Figs. 18.12, 19.5, 21.6b).

Besides the water buffalo and the fig tree, the fish is among the much repeated motifs of Early Harappan painted pottery that continue as conspicuous symbols in the Indus civilization. Fish constituted a significant part of the Harappan diet, but there were certainly other reasons, too, that made the fish an important symbol. Fish breed rapidly, have a phallic shape, and are the principal creatures inhabiting water, which is of course vital for life and vegetation. For all these reasons, the fish has remained an auspicious symbol of fertility in South Asia.

In Tamil, the Hindu water god Varuṇa is called *mīṉ-ūrti,* "having the fish for his mount"; usually in Hindu iconography, the mythical water monster, the *makara*, is Varuṇa's mount. Kāma, the god of sexual love, likewise rides on a *makara* and has the emblem of fish in his flag. As the most important aquatic animal, fish symbolizes water, and fish are offered waters in the Vedic horse sacrifice (MS 3,14,2 *abdhyo matsyān*).

On a tablet from Mohenjo-daro, a seated anthropomorphic god with a horned crown is flanked on either side by a fish and a long-snouted crocodile, as well as a wavy line that might represent water or a snake (Fig. 15.3). A cylinder seal probably made in Mesopotamia by a Harappan craftsman seems to represent the same divinity, because here, too, there is on either side a fish and a horned snake; in addition, a pair of water buffaloes is depicted under the throne on which this god is seated; this god wears a crown of buffalo horns topped by a branch of a fig tree (Fig. 18.12). The water buffalo, the fish, and the crocodile are all animals connected with water, and their presence strongly suggests that this anthropomorphic deity is the Harappan predecessor of the Hindu water god Varuṇa. (In Vedic texts, Varuṇa is, among other things, the god of waters, including the heavenly waters, and the master of all kinds of aquatic animals.) The fish symbol of this Harappan water-god reminds one of Sumerian Enki, the god of waters, who is depicted with rivers issuing from both sides of his body, with fish swimming either in those rivers or around the god (Fig. 15.4). Enki is praised as a phallic god, who fertilizes the soil with flood or rain water considered to be his semen.

FIGURE 15.3 An anthropomorphic deity with a crown of water buffalo horns, seated on a throne with bovine legs, flanked on either side by a fish, a crocodile, and a wavy line that may represent a snake or water. One side of a triangular prism from Mohenjo-daro (M-2033 B), in the Department of Eastern Art (Md 013), Ashmolean Museum, Oxford. After CISI 3.1:404 no. 101. Photo courtesy Ashmolean Museum, Oxford.

(a) (b)

FIGURE 15.4 The Sumerian water god Enki with rivers containing fish flowing from his shoulders or loins. (a) An Akkadian greenstone cylinder seal from Sippar, Mesopotamia, in the British Museum (Reg. No. 1891,0509.2553, BM 89115), inscribed "Adda, scribe" (cf. Collon 1987: no. 761). Image 135126001 © The Trustees of the British Museum. (b) Portion of an Akkadian cylinder seal from Tell Asmar (As. 32:593). After Frankfort 1955: no. 619. Courtesy of the Oriental Institute of the University of Chicago.

The Indus seals and tablets often depict the long-snouted fish-eating crocodile of north Indian rivers (Fig. 15.5). Known as the gharial, this crocodile is in danger of becoming extinct, because it has been hunted for the swelling protuberance on the tip of the male gharial's long snout, which is thought to represent a phallus and is believed to be an aphrodisiac (Fig. 15.6a). An Indus tablet from Harappa appears to represent the gharial in the act of fertilizing a woman by pushing its snout into her vagina (Fig. 15.6b). According to Marshall (1931:52) in this tablet "a nude female figure is depicted upside down with legs apart and with a plant issuing from her womb," this being a "striking representation of the Earth Goddess with a plant growing from her womb." Marshall's interpretation has been often quoted ever since, although already Mortimer Wheeler (1968:106) thought that "what has been interpreted as a plant . . . may equally well be . . . even a crocodile."

Childless young married women are reported to have fed crocodiles "in the hope of being blessed with offspring" (Crooke 1906:112). Before the British stopped this cruel practice in the early nineteenth century, "women in performance of a vow used to throw a first-born son to the crocodiles at the mouth of the Hooghly [river] in the hope that such an offering would secure them additional offspring" (Crooke 1926: 377, based on Ward 1811). Symbolic feeding of a baby to a crocodile continues in Bengali Hinduism. During the *gājan* festival of Śiva, in some temples a crocodile is made of clay, its mouth colored red with vermilion, and a baby made of clay is placed near its mouth (cf. Mahapatra 1972:132–133). A tablet from Dholavira in Kutch, Gujarat, suggests that the Harappans offered human children in sacrifice to a crocodile god.

In his essay on the Indus religion, Marshall discussed the present-day Hindu worship of the various animals depicted on their seals and tablets by the Harappans. Stating that these parallels "afford, of course, no proof that they were similarly worshipped five thousand years ago," yet considering the conservatism of India's religious cults, he thought that "we are justified in inferring that much of the zoolatry which characterizes Hinduism and which is demonstrably non-Aryan, is also derived from the prehistoric age" (Marshall 1931:I,73). Yet

FIGURE 15.5 The gharial with fish in its mouth. (a) The Indus seal M-410 (DK 8037, ASI 63.10.191) from Mohenjo-daro. After CISI 1:98. Photo EL, courtesy ASI. (b) The reverse side of the molded tablet M-482 (E 2500, NMI 69) from Mohenjo-daro in the collection of the National Museum of India, New Delhi. After CISI 3.1:387. Photo JL, courtesy NMI. (c) One side (C) of the molded terracotta prism M-1429 (UPM/MD-602, Exc. Branch) from Mohenjo-daro. After CISI 3.1:386. Photo courtesy © J. M. Kenoyer and DAMGP. (d) The reverse side of the molded tablet H-172 (XXXII,22, ASI 63.11.144) from Harappa. After CISI 1:207. Photo EL, courtesy ASI.

(a)

(b)

FIGURE 15.6 The fish-eating river crocodile (gharial) and fertility. (a). The snout of the male gharial. Photo Bo Link 2006, Wikipedia Commons. (b) A gharial depicted as fertilizing a human female on a moulded tablet H-180 (649, NMI 32) from Harappa in the collection of the National Museum of India, New Delhi. After CISI 3.1:398. Photo EL, courtesy NMI.

FIGURE 15.7 Two crocodiles set on poles. A Mature Harappan painted pot from Amri, southern Indus Valley. After Casal 1964: II, fig. 75 no. 323. Courtesy Mission Archéologique de l'Indus, CNRS/Musée Guimet, Paris.

FIGURE 15.8 The Devlimadi sanctuary of crocodile gods in southern Gujarat. After Fischer and Shah 1971: pl. 2. Photo courtesy © Eberhard Fischer 1970.

FIGURE 15.9 Peacocks carrying dead people to the stars. Painting on a funerary urn of the Late Harappan Cemetery H at Harappa. After Piggott 1950:234, fig. 29.

serious doubts have often been expressed with regard to the assumed religious continuity from the Indus civilization to historical times. It seems possible to demonstrate, however, that cults of Harappan origin have survived with little change even to the present day.

One such case concerns the crocodile, often depicted on Harappan "sacrificial tablets" and some seals. A Mature Harappan potsherd from Amri in Sindh shows two crocodiles who, instead of hind legs, have a 90° sideways projecting extension (Fig. 15.7). An explanation of this image comes from the unique way in which the crocodile is worshipped in some fifty villages of three tribes in southern Gujarat, documented by Fischer and Shah (1971). Images of crocodiles, normally a couple, are made of wood and installed on wooden posts, which goes through the middle or back part of the body (Fig. 15. 8). The installation ceremony celebrates their wedding, and the images are worshipped by smearing them with red vermilion paste and with offerings of chicken and goats, milk or alcohol afterwards consumed by the adorants. The male crocodile can be substituted with a *liṅga*-like post, or the couple by a single crocodile with a head at either end. This now rapidly declining crocodile cult is both communal and individual: people ask the crocodile gods for cows to give milk and calves, for good crops, for offspring, and for help against illness and sorcery, making a vow to install and worship the god if the boon is granted (Parpola 2011a).

The peacock is yet one important motif of Early, Mature, and Late Harappan painted pottery. One clue to its meaning for the Indus people is given by the funeral urns of the Late Harappan Cemetery H at Harappa, where the bird is seen carrying dead people to the stars (Fig. 15.9). At the funerals of the Dravidian-speaking Maria Gonds of Bastar in central India, wooden posts with rude representations of peacocks are set up next to the grave. In classical Hinduism, the peacock is the vehicle of Skanda, the successor of Vedic Rudra and the "son" of Śiva, who in south India is connected with a snake cult. Śiva is called Nīlakaṇṭha, "blue-necked," because he drank the deadly poison created at the churning of the milk ocean, which threatened to destroy the world. The Sanskrit word *nīlakaṇṭha* also denotes the peacock, which is a blue-necked bird. Possibly the color of the peacock's neck was imagined to result from the peacock's habit of eating poisonous snakes.

This chapter has dealt with some important religious conceptions and practices in present-day folk Hinduism that with great likelihood can be traced back to Harappan times and even earlier. Most of them are connected with outstanding aspects of South Asian nature, notably its fauna and flora. They all attest to a remarkable religious continuity over millennia. But there is no doubt that the Harappan religion also included the priestly elaborations of the elite.

16

Astronomy, Time-Reckoning, and Cosmology

The calendrical asterisms of the Vedas were not brought to South Asia by the Rigvedic Indo-Aryans, for they are not mentioned in the family books and have no counterpart in Iranian or other Indo-European traditions. Some *nakṣatras* are mentioned in the late Rigvedic "marriage" hymn 10,85, but not until the Atharvaveda and Yajurveda are all twenty-seven or twenty-eight *nakṣatras* listed for the first time. The Yajurvedic texts connect the *nakṣatras* and the full and new moon with specific "bricks" laid down in brick-built fire altars (*agni-citi*), which are unknown to the Rigveda and belong to the archaic layer of Vedic rituals connected with the Atharvavedic tradition (chapter 12). The relatively late Vedic Śulvasūtras describe the elaborate geometry and rules of orientation used in the construction of these altars. This Śulvasūtra tradition probably goes back to the Indus people, who lived for a millennium in brick-built cities and needed solar time-reckoning, as did other agriculturally based riverine and urban early cultures, for example, in Mesopotamia and Egypt, in which astronomy and astrology invariably form an important part of religion.

The planets cannot have failed to draw the attention of early astronomers, in whatever civilization, because they differ from other heavenly bodies through their independent movement and sometimes belong to the brightest phenomena of the night sky. Venus was the symbol of the Great Goddess as early as the fourth millennium BCE in Mesopotamia; in China astronomers were observing planetary movements by 1576 BCE; and in Old Tamil texts, there are native Dravidian names for the planets, some of which can be read in the Indus texts (see chapter 21). So it is surprising to come across no reference at all to the planets in the Rigveda. This might be taken as further proof that the Rigvedic Aryans did not create the Vedic star calendar, although it is at least conceivable that the Vedic Brahmins who descended from the Rigvedic Aryans actually knew about the planets but chose to avoid referring to them because they had a significant role in the pre-Rigvedic religion of South Asia.

Indeed, certain proper names in the Vedic literature reveal that the planets were not unknown to Vedic Aryans. The clearest example connects the planets with the Atharvavedic tradition of the Vrātyas. According to Pañcaviṁśa-Brāhmaṇa (24,18), the *daiva vrātyas* (who were adherents of "the God," i.e., Rudra), had Budha, the son of Soma, as their leader. Budha means "wise" and is the later Sanskrit name of the planet Mercury, while Soma denotes not only the sacred drink of Vedic Aryans but also the moon. One of the best-known astral myths of classical India, told in many Purāṇas and the Mahābhārata, concerns the birth of the planet Mercury. Soma the moon abducts Tārā ("the star"), lawful wife of Bṛhaspati, the planet Jupiter, and produces a splendid son, Budha. Willibald Kirfel (1952) speculates that this myth may have come from Mesopotamia, and that Tārā might be the bright star Spica in Virgo. (I propose a different explanation later in this chapter.)

Among the ritualistic fossils of the Veda, also connected with the Vrātyas, is the *mahāvrata* day, discussed in chapter 12 (and again in chapter 19). The *mahāvrata* concludes year-long rites and celebrates one of the turning-points of the year. A fire altar piled with bricks, some of which represent the *nakṣatras*, is a necessary part of the rite; when completed, it is praised with special songs on the *mahāvrata* day. The god Rudra, who is otherwise ignored in Vedic *soma* sacrifices, is identified with the fire-god Agni and receives on the completed altar an elaborate burnt offering of hundreds of libations of liquid butter (*śatarudriya*). The fire altar is an image of the creator god Prajāpati, whose body is said to consist of both the cosmos (space) and the year (time). There are various types of fire altar, but one common type has five layers and 10,800 bricks. The year is reckoned to comprise 360 days-and-nights, each having thirty *muhūrtas* ("hours" of forty-eight minutes), so that one year has 10,800 *muhūrtas*.

The thirty *muhūrtas* are based on the parallelism of three principal time cycles, each split into luminous and dark halves in the Veda: (1) a (twenty-four-hour) nychthemeron of thirty *muhūrtas* comprising a day of fifteen *muhūrtas* and a night of fifteen *muhūrtas*; (2) a month of thirty days comprising the "white half" of the waxing moon (fifteen days) and the "black half" of the waning moon (fifteen days); and (3) a year of twelve months (twenty-four half-months), comprising the auspicious "northern course" of the sun (six months or twelve half-months), and its ominous "southern course" (again six months or twelve half-months). In Yajurvedic ritual, it was of the greatest importance to make a sacrifice to accompany every transition from one half to the other in these three time cycles.

The idea of a year of 360 days, attested in the late riddle hymn of the Rigveda (1,164,11) arises naturally from twelve solar months of approximately thirty days. Of course, this round number 360 falls short of the actual length of a solar year, so the difference had to be regulated with an intercalary thirteenth month (implied in the late Rigvedic hymn 1,25,8 ascribed to Śunaḥśepa, who figures later in this chapter); this extra month was added once during every five-year cycle. Five times 360 plus 30 equals 1830 days, and 1830 divided by five yields 366 days, which is less than a day longer than the actual solar year.

Ancient astronomers determined the seasons by observing the position of the sun among the stars on its heavenly path known as the ecliptic. In Egypt, and in West Asia until about 1100 BCE, heliacal risings of stars were observed just before sunrise, in order to discover which asterism was closest to the rising sun. However, this method leaves little time for observation and the star is difficult to spot, on account of the brightness of the sun and atmospheric disturbances on the horizon. Chinese and Indian astronomers avoided this difficulty by adopting a different method, based on the fact that the full moon is exactly opposite to the sun. Asterisms were chosen in pairs with the two members exactly opposite each other (Fig. 16.1). From the conjunction of the full moon with a given asterism the astronomer knew that the sun was in conjunction with the opposite asterism. Even relatively small stars were selected in preference to more luminous ones. The Chinese and Indian calendars are therefore luni-solar; a purely lunar calendar based on just the observation of the moon's phases is out of step with the seasons, as exemplified by the movement of the Muslim month of Ramadan around the solar year.

The relationship between the Indian, Chinese, and Mesopotamian calendars has been much debated. Recent archaeological discoveries in China strongly suggest that the Chinese and Indian calendars developed independently of each other, despite their similarity. It just so happened that they evolved in much the same way. A Mesopotamian origin for the Chinese and Indian calendars, suspected by Joseph Needham (1959), is unlikely, because the opposition of the sun and the full moon was utilized only at a late phase of Mesopotamian astronomy, around 1000 BCE, and was not the basis of the regular calendar.

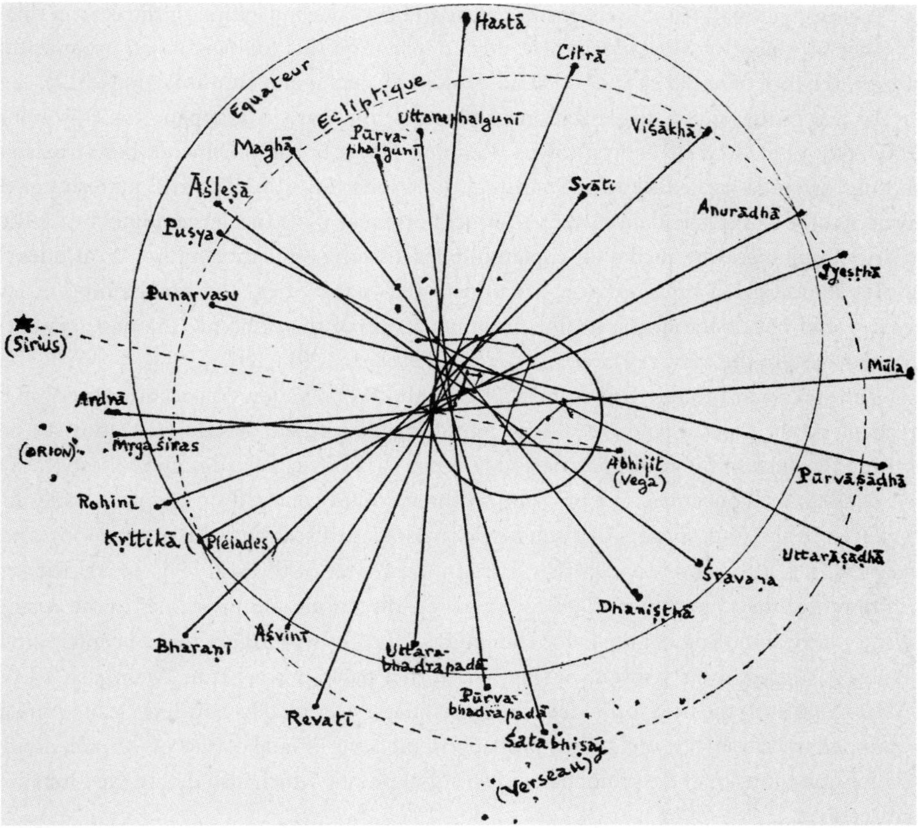

FIGURE 16.1 The *nakṣatras* as pairs of opposing asterisms. A sketch by Jean Filliozat. After Filliozat 1962:350, fig. 3. Courtesy Pierre-Sylvain Filliozat.

The opposite asterisms of the luni-solar calendar are never simultaneously visible; however, the position of the invisible asterism below the horizon could be figured out from the position of the pole star and the circumpolar stars, especially the seven bright stars in the Big Dipper of Ursa Major, which never rise or set. Chinese astronomers are known to have observed the circumpolar stars systematically. The rotation of Ursa Major functioned as a celestial clock marking the hours of the night as well as the seasons. The circumpolar stars play a dominant role in Chinese astronomy and cosmology. In addition to the four "palaces" defined by the equinoctial and solstitial points, the Chinese distinguished a fifth, central "palace," which was the celestial archetype cosmically empowering the Chinese emperor. Around 500 BCE, Confucius equated the emperor with the pole star, as follows: "The Master said: To conduct the government by virtue may be compared to the Northern Asterism: it occupies its place, while all other stars revolve around it." (*Lunyu* 2,1, translated Pankenier 2004:288). The Chinese concept of this particular astral-terrestrial correspondence goes back to the Bronze Age or even the Neolithic. The heavenly prototype (of the center ruling the four quarters) was used for political legitimation. Ever since the earliest dynastic state Xia (from 2000 BCE), palatial structures and royal tombs are quadrilateral and cardinally oriented.

The usual presumption is that a calendar was created to fulfil the needs of agriculturalists. "Farmers generally find the signs of nature to be a safer indication of the season than a civil [official] calendar. The latter is probably an invention that followed upon urbanization, not least as a tool of social control" (David Pankenier, personal communication 2012).

In the Indus Valley, urbanization began with the Early Harappan Kot Diji culture (3200–2600 BCE). One of its first towns, Rahman Dheri in the northwest, has streets and buildings oriented according to the cardinal directions (Fig. 16.2). A grid pattern enables easy access for ox-carts and an instant allotment of house plots to a large number of settlers arriving simultaneously. Such a town plan implies a strong regulating authority, as does the use of a standardized brick for construction in the Indus cities. The preplanning of level streets would have been necessary for the functioning of the elaborate drainage system of Mohenjo-daro in the Mature Harappan period (Ratnagar 1991).

The spread of the Kot Diji culture all over the Indus Valley was accompanied by the spread of a new type of stamp seal—an important instrument of administration—which continued to exist in the Harappan period (Uesugi 2011). The basic design of these Kot Diji seals consists of "concentric circles" (one to three circles centered on a dot): usually four sets placed in the four corners of a square or cross-shaped seal but with a common variant consisting of a fifth set of concentric circles in the center of the seal (Fig. 16.3). The seals seem to reflect the importance of the four cardinal directions and the center in the cosmology and political ideology of the Early Harappans. "Rays" surrounding the concentric circles in one seal suggest solar symbolism (Fig. 16.4). In a painted bowl from Mehrgarh VI–VII (*c.* 3200–2600 BCE) the field is divided into four squares occupied by sun-like circular images surrounded by "rays" (Fig. 16.5). This probably depicts the annual course of the sun, divided into four quadrants by the equinoctial and solstitial points, which also define the four cardinal directions.

The Rigvedic and Atharvavedic hymns often refer to four directions of space, which are undoubtedly the four main directions, for example, RV 7,72,5. The occasionally mentioned

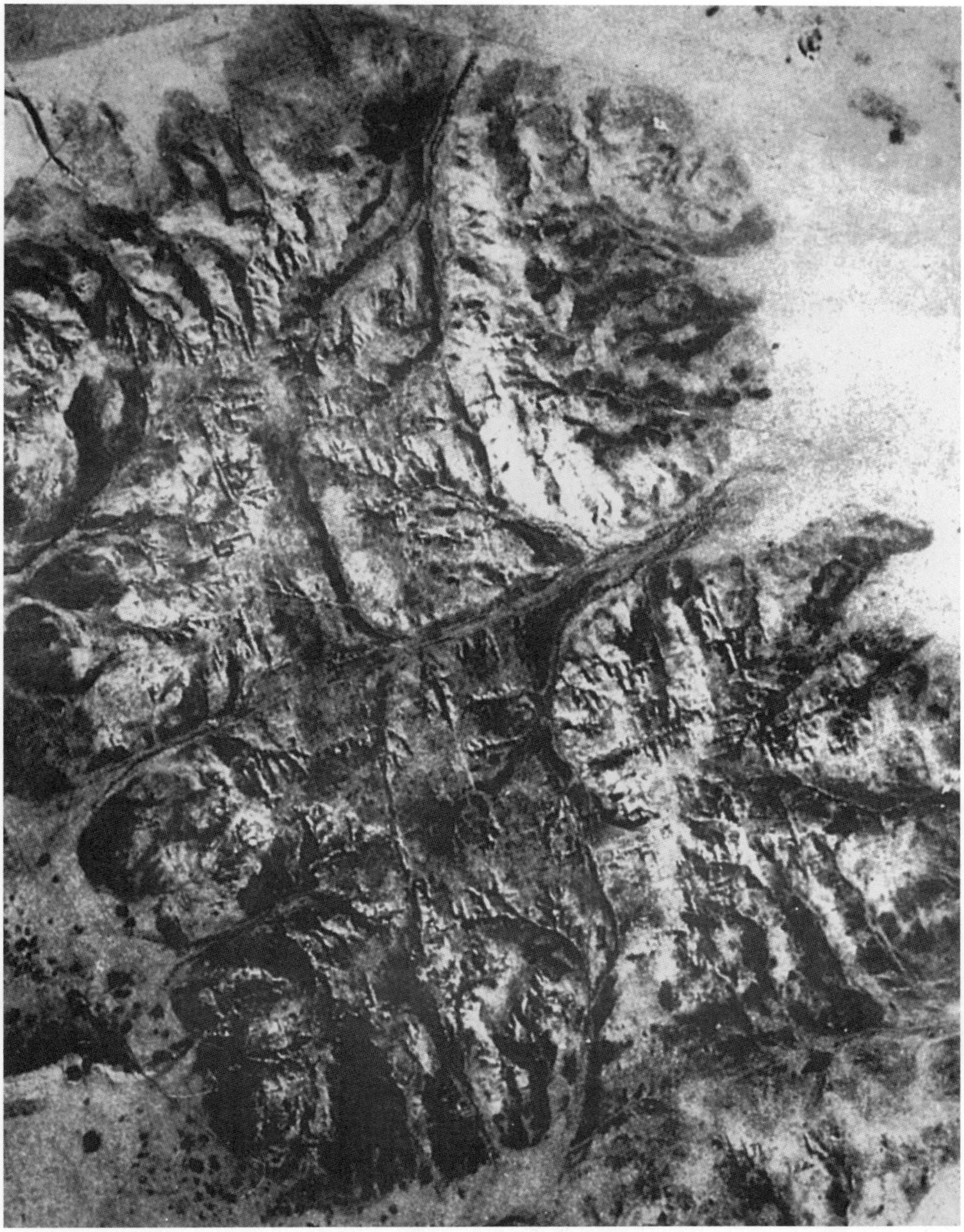

FIGURE 16.2 The Early Harappan town of Rahman Dheri from the air. After Durrani 1988:210, pl. 6. Courtesy Directorate of Archaeology and Museums, Government of Khyber Pakhtunkhwa, Peshawar, Pakistan.

FIGURE 16.3 Kot Diji type seals. (a) Trq -2, and (b) Trq-3 from Taraqai Qila. After CISI 2:414. Photo (a) JL and (b) J. R. Knox, courtesy Directorate of Archaeology and Museums, Government of Khyber Pakhtunkhwa, Peshawar, Pakistan. (c) H-638 (725, HM 13377) from Harappa. After CISI 2:304. Photo S. M. Ilyas. Courtesy DAMGP. (d) H-1535 (H00-4495, 9597-0001) from Harappa. After CISI 3.1:211. Photo Richard Meadow, courtesy Harappa Archaeological Research Project.

FIGURE 16.4 A seal from Rahman Dheri with the motif of "rays around concentric circles." After Durrani, Ali, & Erdosy 1994–1995:207. Courtesy Directorate of Archaeology and Museums, Government of Khyber Pakhtunkhwa, Peshawar, Pakistan.

FIGURE 16.5 "The sun in the four quadrants" painted on a Faiz Mohammad style gray ware bowl from Mehrgarh, period VI (*c.* 3200–2900 BCE). After C. Jarrige et al. 1995:160. Courtesy Mission Archéologique de l'Indus, CNRS/Musée Guimet, Paris.

fifth direction is the center. In the Yajurvedic Saṁhitās and Brāhmaṇas, the fifth point is the zenith; it is consistently associated with Bṛhaspati, the Vedic predecessor of the Hindu god Brahmā, who in classical Sanskrit texts occupies the center (Wessels-Mevissen 2001). One Vedic ritual connected with the directions of space is crucially important for understanding their ideological significance. This is the "mounting of the regions" during the royal consecration. The king first dons the *tārpya* garment, the royal robe of the divine king Varuṇa (which is likely to derive from the trefoil-ornamented "sky garment" of the Harappan "priest-king," modeled on Mesopotamian prototypes, as discussed in chapter 18). Then the king makes five steps, one after the other, in each of the five directions, thereby ascending to the zenith: "from the quarters he goes to the heaven," for "the heaven is the quarters of space" (MS 4,4,4). As the Śatapatha-Brāhmaṇa (5,4,1,8) explains: "It is the seasons, the year, that he [the *adhvaryu* priest] thereby makes him [the king] ascend; and having ascended the seasons, the year, he is high, high above everything here." In a parallel consecration ritual, in the *vājapeya* sacrifice, also known as the Bṛhaspati-sava, the ascent to the zenith is more concrete: the king dons the *tārpya* garment and with the help of a ladder ascends the sacrificial post; reaching the top he declares: "We have reached the sun/heaven, we have become immortal." He then descends and seats himself on the throne placed at the foot of the pillar.

In the Mahābhārata, Yudhiṣṭhira, the eldest of the five Pāṇḍava brothers, aspires to perform the royal consecration (*rājasūya*). Since only a king of the whole world is entitled to perform this, Yudhiṣṭhira sends his four younger brothers to conquer the four cardinal directions. In such a *digvijaya*, a "conquest of the directions," the victorious king has the sun as his role model: it rises in the east, creating light and expelling darkness, and goes through all the regions (cf. MS 4,14,14; ŚB 10,3,5,3). The sun is accordingly known as "four-cornered": the directions are his corners (ŚB 14,3,1,17). The sun defines these four directions through its daily as well as its annual course through the equinoxes and solstices (cf. JB 2,26). It is the sun that the gods anoint on the royal throne, and the person who knows this, when he sits on the royal throne, becomes the sun (cf. JB 2,25–26).

On the basis of the Kot Diji seals, I suggest that the connection of the ruler with the sun and the center of the four directions defined by the sun's daily and annual course, important in Vedic and epic royal ideology, may have originated in the Early Harappan culture. Further evidence that it prevailed in the Indus civilization comes from the so-called Proto-Śiva seal of Mohenjo-daro, in which an anthropomorphic figure wearing the horns of a water buffalo is seated on a throne (Fig. 16.6). The throne is a major symbol of royal authority in Vedic culture (cf. ŚB 12,8,3,4; TB 1,3,9,2). John Marshall (1931a:52–55), who coined the name "Proto-Śiva," suggested that the figure is three-faced, like many later Hindu images of Śiva. I prefer the alternative idea that the figure has four faces, like Śiva in the shape of *caturmukha-liṅga*, symbolizing the *axis mundi* or the Hindu god Brahmā, whom Indian architectural texts connect with the center. The fourth face is hidden, because it faces away from the viewer.

I further suggest that the four faces looking in four directions are in all likelihood related to the four male animals depicted on either side of "Proto-Śiva," arranged so as to form a rectangle: elephant above tiger on one side, rhinoceros above water buffalo on the other. (The fact that there are definitely four animals, rather than three, supports the hypothesis

FIGURE 16.6 The four-faced "Proto-Śiva" seated on a throne and surrounded by four animals on the seal M-304 (DK 5175, NMI 143) from Mohenjo-daro in the collection of the National Museum of India, New Delhi. After CISI 1:382. Photo EL, courtesy NMI.

of a four-faced, rather than a three-faced, figure.) Marshall himself suggested their connection with the four directions. Four animals are associated with the four heavenly palaces in China: blue dragon with east, red bird with south, white tiger with west, and black tortoise with north.

Among the principal ways to find due east is to observe the points where the sun rises during the year. The same method may be applied with other visible stars. Holger Wanzke (1987) studied the axes of the buildings and streets in Mohenjo-daro and found that they diverge one to two degrees clockwise from the cardinal directions, which would match the setting of the star Aldebaran in the west against the horizon of the Kirthar Mountains. Although no likely astronomical observatory has been identified in Mohenjo-daro, Mayank Vahia and Srikumar Menon (2011), two Indian astronomers, have suggested that a peculiar circular stone structure near the acropolis of Dholavira in Kutch, Gujarat, may have been an astronomical observatory.

Another way to find out the directions of space is by means of a sundial or gnomon, the oldest astronomical instrument, comprising a straight peg orthogonal to a level base. By recording the length and the direction of the peg's shadow every day of the year one can define the hours of the day, and from measurements made at noon discover the solstices and equinoxes. The Kātyāyana-Śulvasūtra (1,2–3) gives the rules for finding the cardinal directions as follows:

> Having fixed a peg on level ground and having drawn a circle around it by means of a rope that has the same length as the peg (and is attached to it), he fixes two pegs at the two points where the shadow of the tip of the peg falls on the line (of the circle in the fore- and afternoon); that (line joining these two new pegs) (is) the east(-west line). After adding to the rope its length and making two loops (at its either end), he fixes the loops at the two pegs marking the east-west line. Stretching the rope (draw a circle around each of the pegs) and fix a peg south and north in the middle (area where these two large circles meet). That (line joining these new pegs) is the north(-south) line.

In this case, I propose that ten stone pedestals excavated at Mohenjo-daro may have been made for wooden gnomons, rather than being the bases of *liṅgas* (cult images of Śiva's phallus), as suggested by Ernest Mackay (1938). One stand made of dark red stone is decorated with the trefoil motif that almost certainly had an astral significance in both the Indus Valley and Mesopotamia (Fig. 16.7). Great care was taken to make the bottom of the base flat and to secure the stability and uprightness of the shaft fixed in the round depression in the middle with two dowels (the dowel holes survive). For a gnomon the ground and the base must be as level as possible, and the peg as straight, stable, and orthogonal as possible. The Kātyāyana-Śulvasūtra (7,4) states that nothing is more level than the surface of still water, and that the peg should be made of the particularly stable core part of old, hard-wooded acacia tree.

The Baudhāyana-Śulvasūtra (1,22–28) describes a method to construct an oriented square and thus to define the cardinal and intermediate directions by using a gnomon and

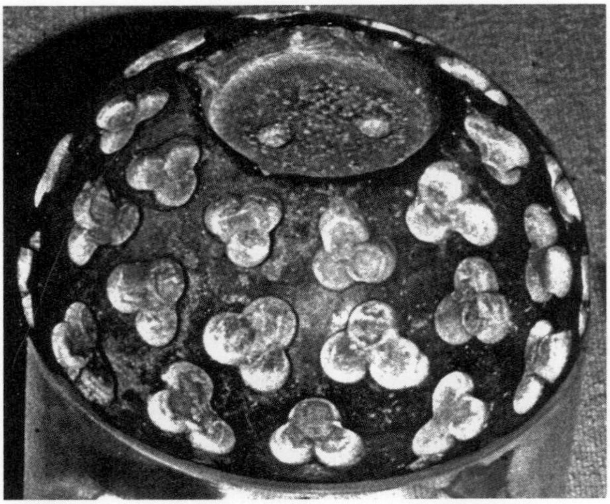

FIGURE 16.7 A finely polished pedestal made of dark red stone and decorated with trefoil figures, probably meant for a gnomon (sun-stick). Excavated in Mohenjo-daro (DK 4480, cf. Mackay 1938:I,412 and II, pl. 107.35), in the National Museum of Pakistan, Karachi. After Parpola 1985: fig. 9a. Photo Asko Parpola 1971, courtesy DAMGP.

a cord with marked midpoint. This produces a pattern of "intersecting circles," which is an important motif on Early and Mature Harappan painted pottery, and also a favorite motif on Harappan bathroom floors and "bath tubs." I suspect this motif relates to the necessity of leveling the ground for the gnomon by means of water. In later Indian astronomical texts water is recommended for making ground perfectly level.

It is of the greatest importance to note that the first calendrical asterism in the Vedic *nakṣatra* lists is the Pleiades. We can fully appreciate this fact only by noting carefully how the Vedic texts comment on the position of the Pleiades. As is well known, the priestly Brahmins established themselves as the highest social class of Vedic society; the Kṣatriyas or Rājanyas, warriors and nobility, were the second social class; and the Vaiśyas, the common people, were the third class. The oldest Yajurvedic texts prescribe that a Brahmin should establish his sacred fires in the spring, the first of the seasons, a Rājanya in the summer, and a Vaiśya in the autumn. A Brahmin should establish his fires under the Pleiades (*kṛttikāḥ*), the first among the calendrical asterisms, for the Pleiades belong to the fire-god Agni, the "foremost" of the gods (since he is always mentioned first, being the *purohita*, literally "set in front"), and the Brahmin, a member of the priestly class, belongs to Agni, who is the priest of the gods. The Pleiades are said to be seven, and since there are seven "breaths" in the head, the Pleiades are regarded as the head of the creator god Prajāpati, while Agni, who eats the offerings, is his mouth (*mukham*, "mouth, beginning"). The Śatapatha-Brāhmaṇa (2,1,2,1–5) adds that originally the Pleiades were the wives of the Seven Sages, but are now precluded from intercourse with their husbands, as the Seven Sages rise in the north, the Pleiades in the east. So now the Pleiades have Agni as their mate. In the early Vedic texts, Agni is the god of the east, the direction of the rising sun.

In this context, the Śatapatha-Brāhmaṇa (2,1,2,3) states that the Pleiades "do not move away from the eastern quarter, whilst the other asterisms do move from the eastern quarter." Jean Filliozat (1962) interpreted this to mean that while the east is defined by the sun's rising above the horizon, the east par excellence is defined by the sun's rising in the east at the vernal equinox, since at this point of time the sun rises into the northern hemisphere, too, beginning its so-called "northern course."

In the same context, the Śatapatha-Brāhmaṇa (2,1,2,4) also states: "the Seven Sages (*ṛṣayaḥ*) were in former times called Bears (*ṛkṣāḥ*)." Sanskrit *ṛkṣa-* means both "bear" and "star"; it occurs in Rigveda 1,24,10, which asks: "In the daytime, where have those bears/stars gone that are seen in the night sky as fixed high up?" Since this verse belongs to the Śunaḥśepa hymn (to be discussed below), it is fairly certain that the stars of Ursa Major are intended. In Greek antiquity the stars of Ursa Major were conceived as a mother bear (Greek *árktos*) followed by three bear cubs.

From the time of the Atharvaveda, however, Ursa Major was almost exclusively called *sapta ṛṣayaḥ*, "Seven Sages." The choice of the word *ṛṣi-*, "sage, seer, holy man, rishi" (a word the Indo-Aryans probably adopted from the original language of the BMAC, see chapter 8) was influenced by the inherited Graeco-Aryan term *ṛkṣa-*, "bear." But the semantic content of the new name undoubtedly goes back to conceptions that prevailed in pre-Vedic India. Harappan parentage, ultimately going back to Mesopotamia, may be involved here, for the Sumerians also spoke of "Seven Sages" (Sumerian *abgal*). They were supposed to be kings who ruled before the Flood, and servants of Enki, the god of water and wisdom, represented in Sumerian art as half-man half-fish. The Indian "Seven Sages" are also connected with a Flood, for according to the Mahābhārata (3,185,1–54), they were on an ark with Manu, the first man and ancestor of the human race. This conception may be due to the fact that the seven stars of Ursa Major being near the pole of heaven, never go beneath the horizon. Homer says that Ursa Major "circles ever in her place, and alone has no part in the baths of Ocean" (*Iliad* 18,489).

Late Harappan people were much more numerous than the first Indo-Aryan-speaking immigrants. The fusion of these two population groups probably started right away with mixed marriages and growing bilingualism. The newcomers needed middlemen to deal with the local population, and this gave the local leaders and priests a chance to obtain important positions in the emerging new social order.

The Seven Sages are considered to be the ancestors of the Brahmanical clans since the Rigveda; they are probably the same as the "seven sacrificers" of yore (*sapta hotrāḥ*), with whom Manu performed the first sacrifice to the gods (cf. RV 10,63,7). The Mahābhārata (3,43) says the ancient saints shine with a light of their own, acquired by their merits, standing ablaze on their own hearths (*dhiṣṇya*): these lights are seen as the stars looking from the earth below, like tiny oil-lamp flames because of the distance. This conception can be traced to early Vedic texts. While dealing with the building of the fire altar, the Taittirīya-Saṁhitā (5,4,1,3–4) states: "He puts down the constellation bricks; these are the lights of the sky; verily he wins them, the Nakṣatras are the lights of the doers of good deeds." The Maitrāyaṇī Saṃhitā (1,8,6) is most explicit in connecting the stars with ancient sacrificers. In the Vedic ritual, the word *dhiṣṇ(i)ya* in the strict sense denotes the fireplaces of seven priests officiating in a *soma* sacrifice; six of them are built in a row in the sitting hall, one is outside the hall on the border of the sacrificial area. A very similar row of seven Indus Valley fireplaces has been excavated on a ceremonial brick platform in the acropolis of Kalibangan.

The Śatapatha-Brāhmaṇa's account of the divorce of the Seven Sages and the Pleiades is the earliest version of the famous Hindu myth of the birth of the war-god Skanda, whose metronym *Kārttikeya* connects him with the Pleiades (*kṛttikāḥ*). According to the fuller epic and Purāṇic versions, Agni or Śiva seduced the Pleiades in the absence of their husbands, the Seven Sages. In one variant, the Seven Sages cursed Śiva to lose his fiery phallus, which dropped down and started burning the world, and did not stop until it was placed in the female member—the *yoni* base upon which Śiva's cult image (symbolizing an erect phallus) is installed. Thus the origins of *liṅga* worship come from this myth. Śiva's four-faced *liṅga* represents the *axis mundi*, and in the earliest Vedic texts, the rising sun (representing the mate of the Pleiades, Agni or Śiva) is described as a pillar which separates heaven and earth and props up the sky. (On the burning pillar or tree symbolizing the phallus, Kāma, or the husband of the goddess, and its connection with the spring festival, see chapter 15.)

The Vedic *nakṣatra* lists start with the asterism *kṛttikāḥ* because the heliacal rising of the Pleiades at the vernal equinox started the new year. The Pleiades were closest to the equinoctial point in about 2240 BCE. Through the equinoctial precession, the position of the asterism marking the vernal equinox with its heliacal rising slowly changed. Therefore, by 80 CE Indian astronomers had revised the *nakṣatra* list to make it start with Aśvinī, the constellation closest to the equinoctial point between 655 BCE and 300 CE. A similar calendrical adjustment was apparently made by Indus astronomers at the peak of the Mature Harappan period, for there are good reasons to suspect, with Albrecht Weber (1861 [1862]:275–277), that it was originally Rohiṇī, the second *nakṣatra* in the old list, that launched the calendar. Rohiṇī, "the red (female)," is Aldebaran, the large red star Alpha Tauri, which was closest to the equinoctial point in 3054 BCE.

According to the Brāhmaṇas, the creator god Prajāpati gave his daughters, the *nakṣatras*, in marriage to the moon. However, the moon neglected all his other astral wives and cohabited only with Rohiṇī, his favorite. The other wives in anger returned to their father, who severely reprimanded his son-in-law. The moon promised to treat all his wives equally but still continued to cohabit only with Rohiṇī; so he was inflicted with an illness that makes him wane. Both the Mahābhārata (3,219,10) and the Rāmāyaṇa (5,31,5) speak of the time when "Rohiṇī was the first of the stars." In the Atharvaveda (AVŚ 13,1,22), Rohiṇī is actually said to be the devoted wife of Rohita, the "Red," that is, the rising sun. The Jaiminīya-Upaniṣad-Brāhmaṇa (4,27) mentions Savitṛ, the "instigator" god, that is, the rising sun, and his mate, the "solar maiden" Sāvitrī, as the archetypal couple. But in the marriage hymn of the Rigveda (10,85), Soma, the moon, is the bride of Sāvitrī. These references suggest to me that it was the *heliacal* rising of Rohiṇī, together with the sun, that originally marked the beginning of the new year in India. The old astral myth, known already from Rigveda 10,109, in which Soma abducts (and eventually returns) the wife of Bṛhaspati, therefore originally seems to refer to the changeover from the solar to the luni-solar calendar. Bṛhaspati, who is later the planet Jupiter, is here the rising sun, and Tārā, the "star" par excellence, was originally Rohiṇī. The Vedic texts have preserved an obsolete word for "calendrical asterism," *b(h)ekuri*; its Dravidian original, discussed in chapter 14, suggests that it was an asterism observed at dawn, that is, when it rose heliacally with the sun.

To begin with, there were only twenty-four *nakṣatras*, corresponding to the twenty-four half-months of the solar year, with twenty-four separate names. Three more were later added by doubling three *nakṣatras* and adding the qualifications "former" and "latter" to the original three names. This was to provide the moon with twenty-seven mansions, one for each night of its sidereal revolution (the period it takes the moon to return to a given point in its orbit: twenty-seven days, seven hours, forty-three minutes). Thus it became possible to refer to each day of the month: according to Pāṇini (4,2,4), the statement "today is Puṣya" meant that the moon was in the Puṣya asterism.

In one version of the earliest *nakṣatra* list (Taittirīya-Saṃhitā 4,4,10) there is another star with same name, Rohiṇī, exactly opposite to Aldebaran. This is the large red star Alpha Scorpii. Weber (1861 [1862]) proposed that the two stars were both called Rohiṇī because originally each of them marked the beginning of a half-year period at the two equinoxes. Maybe at that time these were the only calendrical stars in use. In most versions of the old *nakṣatra* list, the second Rohiṇī (Alpha Scorpii) is called Jyeṣṭhā. This word means "the eldest (lady)," and the asterism is connected with the goddess of misfortune, the elder sister of Lakṣmī, the goddess of fortune. However, Jyeṣṭhā is likely to abbreviate *jyeṣṭhaghnī*, "killer of the eldest (son)," a word mentioned in the Atharvaveda as the name of an ominous constellation. This name recalls the sacrifice of a first-born child mentioned in the Śunaḥśepa legend, the recitation of which was an integral part of the royal consecration, the rite mentioned above as involving such components of probable Harappan origin as the donning of the *tārpya* garment and ascending the regions of space.

The Śunaḥśepa legend tells of King Hariścandra, who had a thousand wives but no son. He was advised to resort to Varuṇa. The god granted him a son, but only on condition that Hariścandra would sacrifice the child to Varuṇa. The boy, named Rohita, was demanded by Varuṇa several times, but each time Hariścandra postponed the sacrifice on various pretexts. When Rohita turned sixteen—the coming of age of a warrior youth—the father told the son that he would redeem his promise to Varuṇa. Rohita, however, took his bow and arrows and disappeared into the forest. His father was punished by Varuṇa with dropsy (an illness supposed to make the moon swell). Eventually Rohita purchased a surrogate victim, a Brahmin boy called Śunaḥśepa, whose father was prepared to slaughter his son for money. Bound to the sacrificial stake, Śunaḥśepa prayed to Varuṇa and other gods, who set him free. At the same time, Hariścandra was healed of his illness.

In chapter 15 we saw that Varuṇa was the successor to the Harappan god of water and fertility, which had the crocodile (Varuṇa's mount in Hinduism) among his symbols. The crocodile's long snout with a swelling protuberance at its tip represents a phallus. Crocodiles are believed to grant babies, and Hindus are known to have sacrificed their first-born child to crocodiles in the hope of further offspring. Now the Taittirīya-Āraṇyaka (2,19) speaks of a *divyaḥ śākvaraḥ śiśumāraḥ*, "a mighty divine crocodile" with a tail (*puccha*) of four sections. Because fore and hind legs are also mentioned among this creature's body parts represented by various stars, *śiśumāra-* cannot here have the alternative meaning "dolphin," but must denote "crocodile." Literally, *śiśumāra-* means "baby-killer."

The context of this heavenly crocodile is the worship of Brahma, which a Vedic householder is supposed to perform by uttering a prayer at dusk while facing the region of the pole star, Dhruva. This prayer begins with "*dhruvas tvam asi, dhruvasya kṣitam*" ("You are firm, foundation of the firm"), and ends with "obeisance to Śiśukumāra" (perhaps a corrupt reading for Śiśumāra). The oldest parts of the cosmographic descriptions of the Purāṇas tell that the god Viṣṇu appears in the sky in the shape of a crocodile consisting of stars, and that the pole star is in the tail of the crocodile. Thus the pole star occupies in the sky a position comparable to that of the pole in the back part of the body of the cultic crocodile images in Gujarati tribal villages and in the Harappan painted pot from Amri discussed in chapter 15 (Figs. 15.7, 15.8). In the sky the heavenly crocodile turns around with the pole star as its pivot, in the same way as tribal crocodile images. Moreover, on the Indus tablets depicting a procession of animals, the crocodile appears not in the lower register with the other animals but in the upper register corresponding to the sky.

In the Śunaḥśepa legend, Hariścandra's name means "Yellow Moon," and his thousand wives apparently stand for stars. His son Rohita has a name used of the rising sun in the Atharvaveda. Weber (1853:237) suggested that the name Śunaḥśepa has an astral denotation. It means literally "dog's tail," and corresponds exactly to Greek *kunósoura* and its Latin translation *canis cauda*, "dog's tail," which describes the asterism Ursa Minor (actually *kunosourìs árktos*, "female bear with a dog's tail") in the Greek and Roman tradition. Śunaḥśepa is thus an astral term of Indo-European origin for a circumpolar constellation, which moreover has the concept of "tail" in it. Śunaḥśepa is therefore the most natural inherited term that the Indo-Aryans had for what seems to have been the Harappan conception of Ursa Minor—the tail of a celestial crocodile, with the pole star in that tail. The heavenly crocodile itself might be compared to the Draco constellation (Fig. 16.8).

The Gṛhyasūtras prescribe that the groom should show the bride the pole star as a paragon of faithfulness. In the old *khila* verse interpolated as the last stanza of the marriage hymn Rigveda 10,85, the groom says: "be faithful!" (*dhruvaidhi*). In 4000–1900 BCE the pole star was Thuban (Alpha Draconis). In 2780 BC, Thuban was only 0.6° distant from the heavenly pole. Thuban is the only star that could really be called the "fixed" (*dhruva*) center of the rotating heavens before our own Polaris (Fig. 16.8). Therefore, the conception of the pole star as "fixed" must date from a much earlier time than the Gṛhyasūtras, that is, from the time of the Indus civilization.

The Hiraṇyakeśi-Gṛhyasūtra (1,22–23) prescribes that the groom should actually address the pole star. The contents of the groom's mantra suggest that it was originally the king who spoke this mantra, probably in the royal consecration, known as "Varuṇa's sacrifice":

I know thee as the nave [hub] of the universe. May I become the nave of this country.
I know thee as the center of the universe. May I become the center of this country.
I know thee as the string that holds the universe. May I become the string that holds this country.
I know thee as the pillar of the universe. May I become the pillar of this country.
I know thee as the navel of the universe. May I become the navel of this country . . .

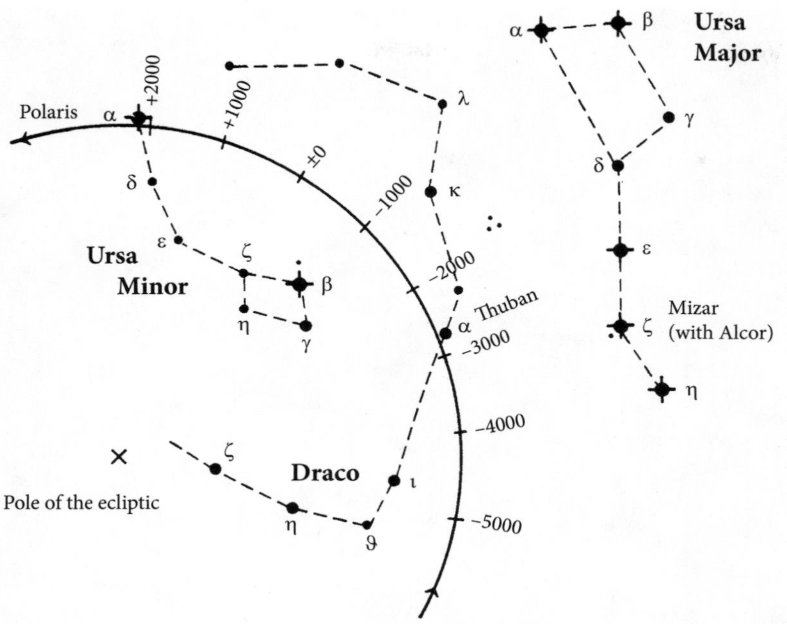

FIGURE 16.8 The circumpolar stars. After Parpola 1994a:243, fig. 14.4, based on Liebert 1968 (1969):168.

Varuṇa is the divine king, and in the mantra the pole star is a symbol of royalty, just as in imperial China.

In the Old Tamil epic Cilappatikāram, the groom points out the pole star, known as *vaṭa-mīṉ*, to the bride in the wedding ceremony, and this is still the custom in south India and Sri Lanka. The phrase actually means "north star" and can be read in the Indus inscriptions, as shown in chapter 21. A homonym of Dravidian *vaṭa*, "north," is *vaṭam*, "banyan fig," the mighty tree with rope-like air-roots from which it takes its name (Dravidian *vaṭam* means "rope") (Fig. 16.9). This original Dravidian appellation of the pole star with its homonyms opens up a new way to comprehend some fundamental conceptions of ancient Indian cosmology and kingship.

Immediately after speaking of the starry crocodile with the pole star in its tail, the Purāṇas describe the crucial function of the pole star as the hub and upholder of the entire stellar system: "As the pole star revolves, it causes the moon, sun and other planets to turn also, and the lunar asterisms follow that revolving (pole star) in the manner of a wheel (turning around the nave). The sun and the moon, the stars, the lunar asterisms along with the planets are all in fact bound to the pole star by cords consisting of an array of winds." (Viṣṇu-Purāṇa 2,9,2–3)

A Rigvedic hymn, in which reference is made to Śunaḥśepa, speaks of a banyan tree in the sky: "King Varuṇa holds up the crown of the (heavenly banyan) tree in infinite space; high up is the base of its (aerial roots) which hang down: may these beams of light be fixed on us!" (RV 1,24,7). The Vedic and Hindu texts repeatedly refer to a heavenly fig tree. This conception seems to be pictured on an Indus tablet (H-179), which depicts an

FIGURE 16.9 The banyan tree with its hanging air roots. After Parpola 1994a:242, fig. 14.2. Photo Asko Parpola.

anthropomorphic deity inside a fig tree: at bottom, the fig tree is flanked on either side by a star, which suggests a heavenly connection for the tree (Fig. 16.10). All principal varieties of fig trees are associated with kingship in the Aitareya-Brāhmaṇa (7,27–34); the mightiest of them, the banyan tree, belongs to Varuṇa (GGS 4,7,24). It is Varuṇa who holds the heavenly banyan tree in the sky. The "ropes of wind," which, according to the Purāṇas, bind the stars and planets to the pole star and prevent them from falling out of the sky, are undoubtedly the imagined air roots of this cosmic banyan tree. These conceptions follow naturally from the original Dravidian name of the pole star: *vaṭa-mīn*, "north star" = "banyan star" = "rope star."

The most fundamental change in the passage from Vedic to later Indian cosmology, shared by the Hindu, Buddhist, and Jaina traditions, is the addition of a golden mountain which rises from the center of the earth to the zenith. On the top of the mountain is the city of Brahmā or Indra, and directly above it is the pole star. The slopes of the mountain in the different directions have different colors. Willibald Kirfel (1920:2*–3*, 14*–19*) connects this central mountain with the astronomical conceptions associated with the pole star. Since the pole-star-related cosmological ideas seem to be much more ancient than has been thought, the central mountain and its name, Meru, attested in all three traditions, could also go back to the Indus civilization. The etymology of *Mēru* has remained unclear; I propose deriving it from Proto-Dravidian **mēl / *mēlu*, basically "what is over or above," hence also "the upper part of anything, high place, top." While Old Tamil has *mēl-ulakam*, "the celestial world," a modern Tamil lexicon uses the word *mēl* in its explanation of *ucci*, "zenith": *talaikku nēr mēlāka irukkum vāṉattiṉ pakuti*, "the part of the sky that is directly

FIGURE 16.10 The heavenly fig tree with its deity, flanked by a star on either side, on the molded tablet H-179 (2410, NMI 30) from Harappa. After Parpola 1994a:244, fig. 14.5; cf. CISI 1:209. Photo EL, courtesy NMI. The stars are surrounded by extensions of the tree's arch curving like the horns of a buffalo; compare the Indus deity with stars in the loops of the horned headdress in fig 21.6 b.

above the head" (Kriyā 2008:177). Semantically *mēl(u)* resembles *ucci*, "crown of the head, top, summit, zenith," which is supposed to be of Dravidian origin (DEDR 579), but actually can hardly be separated from the Sanskrit adverbs *uccā, uccais*, "high, above," derived from the Sanskrit verbal and nominal prefix *ud*, "up."

From Rigveda 1,24,7, it appears that the air roots of the heavenly banyan tree were conceived as beams of light that supply human beings with life energy. A parallel idea connected with the sun and its rays is found in the Purāṇic cosmology (Brahmāṇḍa-Purāṇa 24,64–72; Liṅga-Purāṇa 60,18–26; Vāyu-Purāṇa 53,44–50): the sun is said to feed the other planets and stars with its thousands of rays (*raśmi*). The seven principal rays nourish the moon, the calendrical stars (*nakṣatra/ṛkṣa*), and the planets Mercury (*budha*), Venus (*śukra*), Mars (*lohita*), Jupiter (*bṛhaspati*), and Saturn (*śanaiścara*). The solar ray that brings nourishment to the moon is called *suṣumṇa-*, "very benevolent."

The Buddhist tradition ascribes different colors to the rays of the sun. Thus according to the Avadānaśataka (ed. Speyer 1906:I,4–6), when the Buddha smiles, "a myriad band of light with a thousand colours comes out of his mouth and illuminates the ten directions like a rising sun"; the text specifies that "whenever the Blessed Buddhas produce a smile, rays of blue, yellow, red and white light issue from their mouths." David Fiordalis (2013) has compared this with the Pravargya-Brāhmaṇa of the Taittirīya-Āraṇyaka (5,1,2), where brilliant energy (*tejas*) escaped from Makha when he smiled. In chapter 11 we saw that Makha's severed head became the sun.

The solar ray *suṣumṇa* (*suṣumṇaḥ sūrya-raśmiḥ*) is mentioned in a mantra occurring in the Yajurvedic Saṃhitās (MS 2,12,2; KS 18,14; VS 18,40; and as *suṣumnaḥ* in TS 3,4,7,1) and the Śatapatha-Brāhmaṇa (9,4,1,9). In this mantra, which is used in the fire-altar ritual, the stars are said to have the name *bekuri* / *bhekuri-*, which probably comes from Dravidian (see chapter 14), and they are connected with the *gandharvas* and *apsarases*, whose abode is the banyan and other fig trees (TS 3,4,8,4).

In *haṭha-yoga* or *kuṇḍalinī-yoga*, which is supposed to have emerged around 1000 CE and best known from such texts as the Gorakṣaśataka (*c.* 1400 CE) and Haṭhayogapradīpikā (*c.* 1450 CE), *suṣumṇā* is the name of the central and most important one of the 72,000 veins or arteries (*nāḍī-*) of the human body, connecting the nerve center of the *mūlādhāra* at the bottom of the spinal cord with the *brahma-randhra* and its *cakra* of 1000-petaled lotus (which represents the 1000-rayed sun). This tradition is very late, but its elements can be traced back to the Upaniṣads. The Bṛhad-Āraṇyaka-Upaniṣad (2,1,19) mentions 72,000 arteries, and the Maitrī-Upaniṣad (6,21) names one of these as *suṣumṇā*. *Suṣumṇā* is meant also in one of the early *ślokas* (associated with the *vrātya* tradition, cf. Horsch 1966) quoted in the Chāndogya-Upaniṣad (8,6,6) and the Kaṭha-Upaniṣad (6,16):

> One hundred and one, the veins of the heart,
> Of them one runs up to the crown of the head.
> Going up by it, he reaches the immortal.
> The rest, in their ascent, spread out in all directions. (Translated Olivelle 1998:279)

The foregoing passage of the Chāndogya-Upaniṣad (8,6,1–5) explains this verse:

> 1. Now, these veins [*nāḍī*-] of the heart consist of the finest essence of orange [*piṅgala*-], white [*śukla*-], blue [*nīla*-], yellow [*pīta*-], and red [*lohita*-]. The sun up there, likewise, is orange, white, blue, yellow, and red. 2. Just as a long highway traverses both the villages, the one near by and the one far away, so also these rays of the sun traverse both the worlds, the one down here and the one up above. Extending out from the sun there, they slip into these veins here, and extending out from these veins here, they slip into the sun up there. 3. So, when someone is sound asleep here, totally collected and serene, and sees no dreams, he has then slipped into these veins. No evil thing can touch him, for he is then linked with radiance. 4. Now, when someone here has become extremely infirm, people sit around him and ask: "Do you recognize me?" "Do you recognize me?" As long as he has not departed from the body, he would recognize them. But when he is departing from his body, he rises up along those same rays. He goes up with the sound "Oṃ." No sooner does he think of it than he reaches the sun. It is the door to the farther world, open to those who have the knowledge but closed to those who do not. (Translated Olivelle 1998:279)

Here only five rays of different colors are mentioned, apparently those that feed the five planets, for according to the earliest detailed descriptions of the planets, in texts such as Yājñavalkya-Smṛti 1,290–303 and Jaiminīya-Gṛhyasūtra 2,9, Jupiter is golden, Venus white, Saturn dark-blue or black, Mercury greenish-yellow, and Mars red. The passage makes clear that the many veins bringing nourishment (blood) to all parts of the human body are thought to be connected with the rays of the sun, understood to be similar channels bringing nourishment from the sun to all beings of the universe. The human body with its center in the heart and the universe with its center in the sun are two networks that correspond to, and are connected with, each other.

The parallelism between the microcosm of the human body and the macrocosm of the universe is indeed one of the very basic conceptions of the *haṭha*- or *kuṇḍalinī-yoga*. The spinal column is called in Sanskrit *meru-daṇḍa*, a word that equates the column with the central mountain of the universe, Mount Meru. At the top of the human body is the head, and at the top of the head the *brahma-randhra*, "Brahma's crevice," the suture or aperture in the crown that is still open in a new-born child, and through which the soul is said to escape at death. In the macrocosm, the *brahma-randhra* would correspond to the sun in the zenith, which the Upaniṣads present as the gate to the Brahma-*loka* beyond the universe.

The conception that the universe has the shape of a human body—also prevalent in later Jaina cosmology—emerges in one of the latest hymns of the Rigveda (which are of Atharvavedic affinity). According to RV 10,90, the primeval cosmic "man" (*puruṣa*), who had a thousand heads, a thousand eyes, and a thousand feet (these descriptions refer to the sun, which is often said to be thousand-rayed), rose up and expanded to fill the entire universe. Verse 4 uses the verb *vi+kram*-, "to stride through," which older hymns of the Rigveda use to describe the three steps with which the solar god Viṣṇu traversed the universe. This primeval man was the victim of the first-ever sacrifice performed by the gods, the model of the Vedic human sacrifice (*puruṣa-medha*) and other sacrificial rituals. The manifested cosmos arose from the dismembered body parts of this primeval cosmic man: the moon from his mind, the sun from his eyes, the wind from his breath, the atmosphere from his navel, the sky from his head, the earth from his feet, and the directions of space from his ears.

Herman Tull (1989) has pointed out that this idea of an originally anthropomorphic cosmos that becomes dismembered differs fundamentally from the earlier Rigvedic cosmogonies. While the idea that the universe resulted from the union and separation of Father Heaven and Mother Earth goes back to Proto-Indo-European conceptions, "the chief cosmogonic myth of the early Ṛgveda is the slaying of Vṛtra by Indra and Indra's subsequent separation of the heavens and the earth through propping up the sky with the cosmic tree or pillar" (Tull 1989:54). Tull concentrates on showing in the ideology of Brāhmaṇa texts, on the other hand, that the concept of cosmic Puruṣa and his dismemberment remains central, particularly in the fire-altar ritual (which is unknown to the Rigveda).

In the Brāhmaṇa texts, Puruṣa becomes the creator god Prajāpati, as is explicitly stated in the Śatapatha-Brāhmaṇa (6,1,1,5). In the sequel (ŚB 6,1,2,12–26) this text notes that creating the universe out of himself, Prajāpati exhausted himself and came to fall apart, that is, to die. He asked his son Agni, "Fire," to restore his body by building up the fire altar (*agni-citi*). Prajāpati is here equated with the year and the cosmos, and his disjointed body parts are equated with the seasons and the directions, as well as the layers of brick in the fire altar. The fire laid on the completed altar is identified with the sun, and Prajāpati, the father of Agni, is also said to be his own son Agni, while Agni as the restorer of Prajāpati is said to be Prajāpati's father. (This somewhat paradoxical notion may be explained thus: when the sun has completed its yearly round and "brought out" all the seasons, it "dies" as the old or past year, but is restored in the new year when the sun is "reborn" as the successor and is thus the "son" of his own self.)

In miniature the same solar process takes place in the sun's diurnal cycle. During the day, the sun in the zenith represents the ruler of the universe. In the night this central position is held by the pole star, to which all planets, stars, and beings are bound with invisible "ropes of wind" (*vāta-raśmi*)—a conception I have endeavored to show goes back to the Indus civilization: Dravidian *vaṭa-mīn*, "north star," also means "rope star" and "banyan star." The pole star is thus the nightly counterpart of the sun, and indeed RV 1,24,7 refers to the (invisible) air ropes of Varuṇa's heavenly banyan tree as "beams of light" (*ketávaḥ*). According to an astronomical conception current in Vedic times, which is probably of Harappan origin, the sun actually never rises or sets but is in the sky all the time. The sun has a bright and a dark side. In the evening it simply turns its dark side toward the earth and its bright side toward the sky, returns invisible from west to east, and turns around again in the morning. (This idea is most explicitly stated in AB 3,44, less clearly in MS 4,6,3; KS 27,8; and TS 6,4,10,2–3.)

The pole star is the pivot on which the whole sky turns. In this respect it is like the tortoise (Sanskrit *kūrma*), which in the epic and Purāṇic myth of the churning of the milk ocean serves as the pivot and firm foundation of the floating earth and its cosmic mountain Meru (alias Mandara), used as a churning stick by gods and demons (cf. Mahābhārata 1,15–17; Matsya-Purāṇa 249–251). The etymology of Sanskrit *kūrma* has not been settled, but as the word is not attested in the Rigveda and lacks clear Indo-European cognates, it is likely to be a loanword from a South Asian language. Moreover, it is a local South Asian animal, and one that is represented in the molded tablets from Harappa and among the terracotta figurines from Mohenjo-daro; further, one sign of the Indus script (no. 350 in Parpola 1994a:77) may depict the tortoise. A possible Dravidian etymology for *kūrma* is suggested by Tamil *kuruḷai*, "tortoise," with cognates in other Dravidian languages denoting "shell," such as Kannada *guruḷe*; these words are probably derived from the root *kur-uḷ*, "to curl," which at least in Tulu has the further meaning "to contract, shrink" (cf. further the root *kur-aṅku*, "to bend, curve, crouch, contract, shrink"). A potential Proto-Dravidian homonym of *kūrma* is provided by the root **kūr*, "to be sharp, pointed or tapering," from which Tamil derives *kūr*, "pivot on which door swings," and *kūrmai*, "sharpness, pointedness." In Vedic texts, the lower shell of the tortoise is said to be the earth "which is firmly fixed (*pratiṣṭhitam*)," and the upper shell is the sky, "which has its ends bent down" (ŚB 7,5,1,2).

The tortoise is the shape assumed by the creator god Prajāpati when he created the living beings (ŚB 7,5,1,3). The tortoise is the life-sap and the life-breath (*prāṇa*), and a living tortoise is placed at the bottom of the brick-built fire altar, a Vedic cosmogram and restructured image of Prajāpati, in order to provide it with life-sap and breath (ŚB 7,5,1,1.3.7). "Now this tortoise is the same as yonder sun. . . . (It is placed beneath the altar, wrapped in water plants, with the mantras VS 13,30–32 beginning) 'Seat thee in the depth of waters . . .', for that indeed is the deepest (place) of the (heavenly) waters where yonder (sun) burns; 'the lord of waters, the bull of bricks' " (ŚB 7,5,1,6–9). As observed by John Brockington (1998:279), the tortoise as the lord of waters is here "a representative of Varuṇa." The heavenly banyan tree (i.e., the pole star) also belongs to Varuṇa.

The tortoise as a representative of the sun can be connected particularly with the setting sun or night sun. The most common tortoise of South Asia, from Sindh to Kerala, is the starred tortoise (Fig. 16.11). As we have seen, the Vedic texts equate the tortoise with the sun, and state that during the night the black side of the sun is turned towards the earth. The black shell of the starred tortoise is ornamented by several star-like figures, so that it looks like the black night sky studded with stars.

When setting, the sun draws in its rays, as the tortoise draws in its limbs. Three different Dravidian words for "tortoise" are derived from this characteristic: besides the above-mentioned Tamil *kuruḷai*, North Dravidian *ekkā, eke*, "tortoise," from Proto-Dravidian **ekku*, "to contract the abdominal muscles, to draw in the stomach," and Tamil *oṭunki*, "tortoise (as that which contracts)." The Proto-Dravidian verb **oṭuṅku*, "to contract, shrink, become reduced, become hidden" is also used in Tamil in the sense of "to be restrained, as the senses or desires, to become tranquil," and the transitive form (used when the verb requires a direct object) *oṭukku* in the meaning "to restrain the senses." Patañjali, in his Yogasūtra (2,54), advises the yogi to withdraw the senses from their objects to attain complete mastery of the sense organs. The Mahābhārata often compares this yogic sense-retraction (*pratyāhāra*) to the tortoise's drawing in its limbs (thus Bhagavadgītā 2,58). This comparison is also made in Tirukkuṟaḷ 126, where the Proto-Dravidian verb **aṭaṅku* / **aṭakku* is used. Besides meanings similar to those of **oṭuṅku* / **oṭukku*, this verb is also attested in Tamil in the sense of "to disappear, set as a heavenly body."

FIGURE 16.11 The starred tortoise (*Geochelone elegans*). After Daniel 1983: opposite p. 30. Photo courtesy © Isaac D. Kehimkar.

In post-Vedic worship of planetary gods, Saturn may be represented as riding a tortoise, and the Indus script suggests that Saturn was understood to have the tortoise as his vehicle already in Harappan times (chapter 21). According to the epics and Purāṇas, Saturn is the son of the sun; and as his color is, moreover, black or dark blue and the main deity presiding over Saturn is Yama (the Righteous King judging the dead and ruling over them), Saturn seems to represent the nightly aspect of the sun. In Babylonian astrology, too, Saturn is the "black star," representing the sun, and functions as the judge of the dead (Jeremias 1929:176).

We have seen that the tortoise placed at the bottom of the fire altar in water plants is said to be the sun in the deepest place of heavenly waters (ŚB 7,5,1,6–9). This suggests its connection with the night sun in the region of the pole star, which seems to correspond to the skull suture (*brahma-randhra*) of the macrocosmic man. The Śatapatha-Brāhmaṇa (7,5,1,35) indeed says that "the tortoise (is) the head (of the fire altar), and the vital airs in the tortoise are the vital airs in the head." The heads of the five principal victims are placed in the middle of the lowest brick layer of the fire altar, the human head in the center, surrounded by those of the horse, the cow, the ram, and the sheep, and the sacrificer is required to put into each head seven chips of gold, one into each of the "seven vital airs of the head": the two eyes, the two ears, the two nostrils, and the mouth (ŚB 7,5,2,8–12). One reason why the tortoise is connected with the head is likely to be its shell, for words denoting "shell" often stand also for the "shell of the head": English *skull*, for instance, has such a derivation, and Dravidian *ōṭu*, "shell," has the meanings "tortoise shell" and "skull" in several languages.

According to one of best-known late Rigvedic cosmogonic speculations, there was neither *asat*, "nonexistent," nor *sat*, "existent," in the beginning (RV 10,129,1). Śatapatha-Brāhmaṇa (6,1,1,1–7) modifies this by saying that in the beginning there was *asat*, and this *asat* was the Seven Sages, who were the seven vital airs. The creation could start only after these seven *puruṣas* were made into one Puruṣa, who became Prajāpati; the life-sap of those seven *puruṣas* is concentrated in Prajāpati's head. The seven circumpolar stars of Ursa Major are thus in Vedic texts evidently connected with the head of the cosmic man (*puruṣa*) as its seven openings (see Ehlers 2007). Being close to the pole star, to which other stars are bound with "ropes of wind" (*vāta-raśmi*), the "Seven Sages" of Ursa Major may be meant when the Rigveda (10,136) speaks of the long-haired, orange-clothed, and wind-girdled (*vāta-raśmi*) ascetics (*muni*) who, having drunk poison from Rudra's cup, fly through the air carrying fire.

The above passage, speaking of the seven openings of the head and their connection with the Seven Sages, mentions seven vital airs. Normally only five kinds of air in the body are spoken of, are enumerated and identified with the five directions. Just two are important, however, namely the inhalation (*prāṇa*) and exhalation (*apāna*), which the Seven Sages are said to observe in a *śloka* verse and its commentary contained in Jaiminīya-Brāhmaṇa 2,27. This looks like a reference to the regulation of breathing (*prāṇāyāma*), which is yet another important component of Patañjali's yoga. The words *prāṇa* and *apāna* do not occur in the Rigveda at all, while both words occur many times in the Atharvaveda; in the Vrātya book, the breaths of the Vrātya are identified with different elements of the universe (AVŚ 15,15–17), as are his body parts (AVŚ 15,18), rather like the body parts of the primeval Puruṣa in RV 10,90.

Ever since its discovery, the Indus civilization has been regarded as a possible source for the traditions of yoga. So far, the principal evidence for this hypothesis has consisted of the postures of seated Indus divinities on the seals, especially the "Proto-Śiva" (Fig. 16.6), whom John Marshall (1931a) compared with Śiva as Yogeśvara, "master of yoga." However, this posture seems to be an artistic convention taken from Proto-Elamite art (see Fig. 17.2). While this does not prevent it from also being a prototype of a particular yogic *āsana*, it somewhat weakens its power as evidence for the Harappan beginnings of the yoga. On the other hand, the human body plays an important role in the Tantric ritual, and the meditative practices of yoga undoubtedly do feel rather un-Aryan and native to South Asia, given the latter's strong ascetic traditions evident from the dawn of the historical period. This chapter has linked some central concepts and practices of the yogic tradition with a cosmology that can with good reason be linked to the Indus civilization, and thus it provides new evidence for the view that yoga, too, is a part of the Harappan cultural heritage.

17

Dilmun, Magan, and Meluhha

There were overland and then maritime contacts between West Asia and the Indus Valley during the third millennium BCE (Fig. 17.1). The eastward expansion of the Proto-Elamite civilization started around 3200 BCE and reached Seistan, Kerman, and Makran in eastern Iran by about 2900 BCE (Lamberg-Karlovsky 1986). Typically Proto-Elamite bevel-rimmed vessels (along with compartmented copper seals known widely from the Iranian plateau) have been discovered at Mir-i Qalat in Pakistani Baluchistan (end of period IIIa, *c.* 2900–2800 BCE). The layer above this one (IIIb, *c.* 2800–2600 BCE) has various kinds of pottery with motifs such as zebu bulls, leopards, and fish that are very similar to pottery motifs in the Early Harappan cultures of the Indo-Iranian borderlands. Still younger layers demonstrate the transition period (IIIc, 2600–2500 BCE) and the mature period (IV, *c.* 2500–2000 BCE) of the Indus civilization, respectively (Besenval 2011; Didier 2013).

More debatable evidence for overland contact is the so-called yoga posture of the Harappan deity dubbed "Proto-Śiva" (Fig. 16.6), which seems to derive from the way in which seated bulls are represented in Proto-Elamite art (Fig. 17.2) (Parpola 1984a). On the other hand, the motif may have been borrowed *c.* 2500–2400 BCE from the so-called "Trans-Elamite" art, which flourished in the Jiroft region of Kerman and in the BMAC of southern Central Asia; it may even have come from Mesopotamia itself in Early Dynastic IIIAB times (2600–2334 BCE) via maritime contacts between Indus Valley merchants and Sumerian rulers.

In the second half of the third millennium BCE, the Indus people began to travel in the opposite direction, westwards to Mesopotamia. During the transition from the Early to Mature Harappan phase (2600–2500 BCE), the Indus people built boats and ships that enabled them to navigate the Indus River and other waterways with large and heavy loads. Harappan seals and tablets depict ships with a hut-like cabin and a steersman at the helm with an oar. These ships resemble quite closely the present-day houseboats of the Mohanas, fishermen of the Lower Indus and the Manchar Lake. In the early Mature Harappan period (2500–2200 BCE), there was a dynamic cultural expansion. Enterprising seafaring merchants from the Indus Valley founded outposts on the Makran coast (Sotka-koh, Sutkagen-dor), in Oman

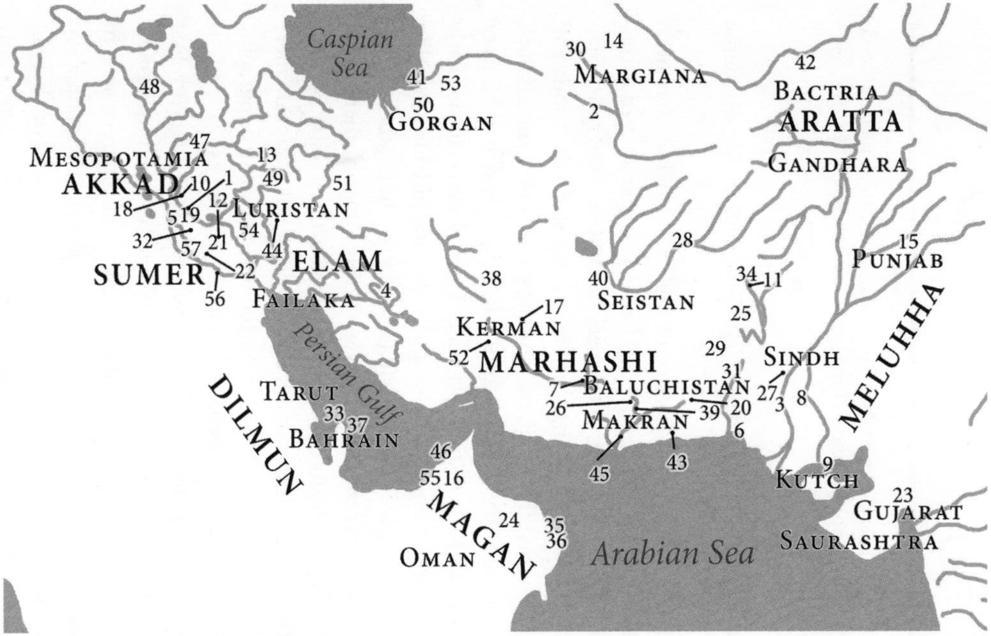

FIGURE 17.1 Map illustrating interaction between West, Central, and South Asia, *c.* 2600–1900 BCE. © Anna Kurvinen and Asko Parpola. Country names in bold versals are those of cuneiform sources. The approximate location of archaeological sites is indicated with numbers: (1) Akkad; Al Hiba, see Lagash; (2) Altyn Depe; (3) Amri; (4) Anshan (Tall-i Malyan); (5) Babylon; (6) Bala-kot; (7) Bampur; (8) Chanhu-daro; (9) Dholavira; Djokha, see Umma; (10) Eshnunna (Tell Asmar); (11) Faiz Mohammad; (12) Girsu (Tello); (13) Godin Tepe; (14) Gonur; (15) Harappa; (16) Hili; (17) Jiroft; (18) Khafajeh; (19) Kish; (20) Kulli; (21) Lagash (Al Hiba); (22) Larsa; (23) Lothal; (24) Maysar; (25) Mehrgarh; (26) Mir-i Qalat; (27) Mohenjo-Daro; (28) Mundigak; (29) Nal; (30) Namazga; (31) Nindowari; (32) Nippur; (33) Qala'at al-Bahrain; (34) Quetta; (35) Ra's al-Hadd; (36) Ra's al-Jinz/al-Junayz; (37) Sar; (38) Shahdad; (39) Shah-i Tump; (40) Shahr-i Sokhta; (41) Shah Tepe; (42) Shortughai; (43) Sotka-koh; (44) Susa; (45) Sutkagen-dor; Tall-i Malyan, see Anshan; (46) Tell Abraq; Tell Asmar, see Eshnunna; (47) Tell es-Sulema; Tello, see Girsu; (48) Tepe Gawra; (49) Tepe Giyan; (50) Tepe Hissar; (51) Tepe Sialk; (52) Tepe Yahya; (53) Tureng Tepe; (54) Umma (Djokha); (55) Umm an-Nar; (56) Ur; (57) Uruk.

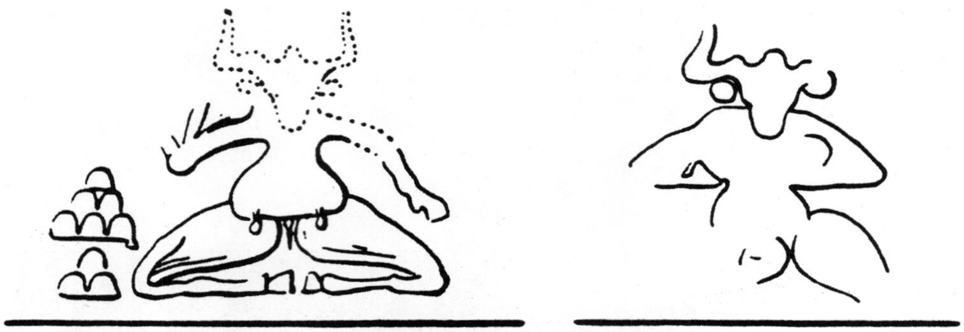

FIGURE 17.2 Sitting bulls on two Proto-Elamite seal impressions from Susa. After Amiet 1980: nos. 581, 582. Courtesy Pierre Amiet. Compare the sitting posture of the "Proto-Śiva" (Fig. 16.6).

(Ra's al-Junayz, Ra's al-Hadd, Maysar, Hili), along the Persian Gulf, and in Mesopotamia itself.

Among the items they traded was Harappan jewelry of high value, which has been found in Mesopotamia. Exceptionally long (more than 5 cm) barrel-cylinder-shaped carnelian beads involved the difficult drilling of long holes in this very hard stone. Other carnelian beads were stained with white designs by first drawing a pattern on the stone with soda and then heating it until the carnelian absorbed the alkali, making the pattern permanent. Such "etched" carnelian has survived as an industry in Sindh until our times. These two kinds of distinctive bead—excavated at Kish and in the Royal Graves at Ur, and dated to the Early Dynastic (ED) IIIA period—are the earliest objects of Harappan manufacture discovered in Mesopotamia. According to the conventional chronology followed in this book, their date is 2600–2500 BCE, but according to a more recent chronology gathering support, their actual date may be as late as 2400–2300 BCE (Reade 2008). It is possible that the jewelry reached Mesopotamia via middle men, either overland (through Iran) or by sea. But it appears more likely that the Harappans were already present in Sumer, on the basis of the iconographic motifs of ED III date borrowed into Harappan art, to be discussed in chapter 18.

Some Indus seals excavated in Mesopotamia in 1923–1925 provided the very first intimation of the high age of the Indus civilization. About twenty seals or seal impressions connected in one way or another with the Indus civilization come from different sites in Mesopotamia (Ur, Telloh/Girsu near ancient Lagash, Djokha/Umma, Babylon, Nippur, Kish, Tell Asmar/Eshnunna, and Tell es-Sulema) and Elam (Susa); in addition, about a further ten seals are unprovenanced but probably come from Mesopotamia or Elam. Unfortunately, only a few of these seals can be dated with fair certainty.

The earliest of the seals are attributed to the Akkadian period (2334–2154 BCE). They have the typically Mesopotamian cylindrical shape but, given their Harappan style and motifs (including a frieze of an elephant, a rhinoceros, and a crocodile), they were almost certainly carved by Harappan craftsmen residing in Mesopotamia. Two come from stratified contexts in the northerly sites Tell es-Sulema and Tell Asmar, and lack an inscription. An iconographically important cylinder seal without provenance is very probably contemporary with these first two (Fig. 18.12). A clumsily carved cylinder seal with an inscription excavated at Susa but in an unknown context may also be contemporary with them.

A corroded square copper seal and an Akkadian-style cylinder seal of lapis lazuli (without an inscription) attached to a metal cloak pin were excavated next to the arm of a skeleton buried in Private Grave no. 489 at the cemetery of Ur (Reade 1995). In an X-ray image of this copper seal shown to me in 1992, an Indus inscription with sign sequences common in the Indus Valley was clearly visible. A closely similar square copper seal was excavated at Ra's al Jinz (Ra's al-Junayz) in Oman, an important source of copper for the Indus people and the Mesopotamians (see Parpola 1994b: nos. 21 and 2). Only a single copper seal is known from the Greater Indus Valley, discovered in Lothal, a port town in Gujarat that served as an international entrepôt. Steatite square seals with native Harappan sign sequences have been excavated at Nippur and Kish, but cannot be dated with certainty; they were probably imported from the Indus Valley, like the single rectangular stamp seal with an inscription found at Telloh, dating from the time of Gudea (*c.* 2141–2122 BCE).

The round stone seals found in West Asia fall into two categories (Laursen 2010). The first category is known as "Gulf type." It depicts a Harappan-type bison (with or without a "manger"), with or without signs of the Indus script, and has a Harappan-type knob (with a single groove) on the reverse. A total of twenty-eight Gulf-type seals with an inscription are known. Twelve are from Mesopotamia (half being from Ur), three are from Iran (one from Susa, another of unknown source with an inscription in Linear Elamite), nine are from the Gulf (seven from Bahrain, two from Failaka), and five are from the Lower Indus Valley (four from Mohenjo-daro, one from Chanhu-daro). On one of these last, Harappan-style animal front parts are united into a whorl, a motif common in West Asia after 2000 BCE. There are also ninety-five Gulf-type seals without an inscription, almost all of them (eighty-seven) from Bahrain, the rest from elsewhere in the Gulf, except for one from Iran (Tepe Yahya in Kerman).

The oldest of the Gulf-type seals, dated *c.* 2100–2050, come from Mesopotamia and Iran. After this period, it appears that a community of Harappan merchants moved from Mesopotamia/Iran to Bahrain and settled there, for the majority of Gulf-type seals, dated *c.* 2050–2000 BCE, come from Bahrain, and there is evidence of local seal manufacture. Cubic weights of polished stone typical of the Indus civilization have been found in Bahrain, with numerous seals in the rooms of an ancient customs house next to the city gate of Qala'at al-Bahrain (Fig. 17.3). The majority of the seals come from burial mounds typical of the local culture, which suggests that the Indus people married into the local society. This supposition is reinforced by the fact that a great number of the Gulf-type seal inscriptions show sequences not known in the Indus Valley seals (Fig. 14.1). They probably write local proper names, given by bilingual Harappan merchants to their children now running the business. One seal from Bahrain was found with a small cuneiform tablet containing three Amorite proper names, datable on the grounds of the forms and combinations of its signs to *c.* 2050–1900 BCE. This suggests that the local language in Bahrain may have belonged to the West Semitic group.

The Gulf-type seal was a model for the second category of round seals, the "Dilmun type," hundreds of which replaced the Gulf type in Bahrain and Failaka around 2000 BCE and

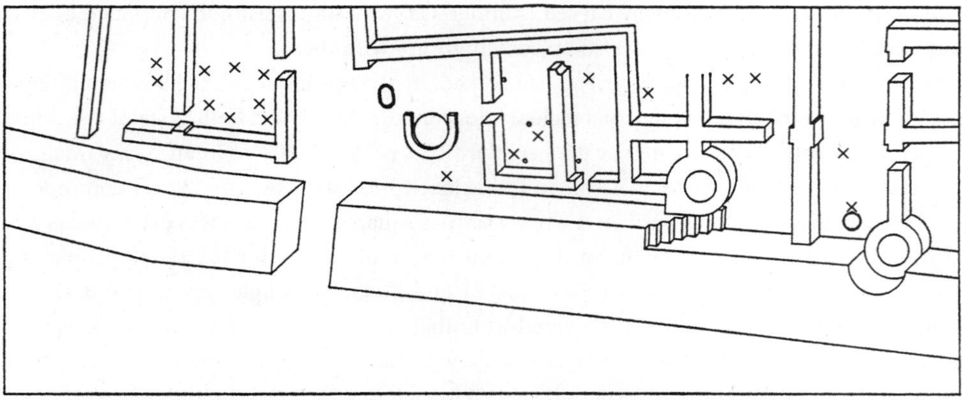

FIGURE 17.3 An ancient customs house in the City II area within the north wall at Qala'at al-Bahrain in the Gulf. To the right is the cul-de-sac, to the left the city gate, and between them the guard room with its well and staircase to the ramparts. Find spots of the seals (×) and weights (•) are marked. After Bibby 1972:368. Courtesy Moesgaard Museum, Højbjerg, Denmark.

continued in use for about a century. These later seals have Mesopotamian-influenced motifs, no inscriptions, and three grooves on a convex reverse, flanked by two dots-in-a-circle on either side. One Dilmun-type seal was excavated at Lothal in 1963. This is practically the only object in the Greater Indus Valley that clearly comes from West Asia, apart from some Mesopotamian-type "barrel weights" from Mohenjo-daro and Harappa that were used in the Gulf in the early second millennium BCE. The Lothal seal suggests that the maritime trade between Mesopotamia and the Indus Valley was wholly in the hands of sailors from the valley and Gulf merchants of Indus descent, and that Mesopotamian people did not come to South Asia.

Dilmun is a mythical paradise in a Sumerian creation myth, but cuneiform texts mention it as a real place, too, where Mesopotamian sailors could replenish their stocks of drinking water. It was an important center of trade to which goods came from a number of places. Dilmun figured in Mesopotamian maritime trade from the late fourth millennium but especially in the late ED III and Akkadian periods (*c.* 2500–2200 BCE). It is scarcely mentioned between 2200 and 2000 BCE, but becomes prominent again thereafter. Both archaeological and textual evidence suggests that Dilmun stretched from the island of Failaka in the north of the Persian Gulf to the island of Bahrain in the south, which acted as the center of Dilmun. Bahrain, with its thousands of tombs and its flourishing date palms, fits the image of paradise described in the Sumerian myth.

Another key location in cuneiform texts, Magan, was an important source of copper for the Sumerians. Archaeological excavations and surveys have identified Magan with Oman (especially Umm an-Nar) during the third millennium. Magan may, however, have included the Makran coast of Iran on the opposite side of the Gulf from Oman. For one thing, the name Magan may be related to that of Makran, which goes back to Maka, one of the satrapies of the Persian empire. Besides, "the *meš* wood of Magan," mentioned in the trilingual inscriptions of Darius the Great, was imported from northwest India (Gandhāra) and southeastern

FIGURE 17.4 Impression of an Akkadian cylinder seal that, according to its inscription, belonged to "Šu-ilišu, interpreter of the Meluhhan language" (for Dominique Collon's comments on this seal, see the caption of fig. 8.4 in Parpola 1994:132). Collection De Clercq, Département des Antiquités Orientales (AO 22310), Musée du Louvre. Photo courtesy Musée du Louvre/Béatrice André-Salvini.

Iran (Kerman). The wood is called *yakā-* in Old Persian; its modern Iranian cognate, *ǰag*, denotes sissoo wood from a large tree growing in the mountains of Oman, the Makran coast of southern Iran, and Pakistan.

While Dilmun and Magan are mentioned in early cuneiform texts, the third foreign country involved in the Mesopotamian sea trade, Meluḫḫa, appears for the first time in an Akkadian inscription of Sargon the Great (ruled 2334–2279 BCE). Sargon boasts that ships from Meluhha, Magan, and Dilmun docked in his new capital Akkad. To impress his readers, Sargon has reversed the order in which these countries were usually listed, putting the most distant place first. Several administrative texts mention food rations for "men of Meluhha" boarding "ships of Meluhha." The identification of Meluhha with the Greater Indus Valley is now almost universally accepted.

How did the Mesopotamians communicate with the Meluhhans? An Akkadian cylinder seal is inscribed "Šu-ilišu, interpreter of the Meluhhan language" (Fig. 17.4). This indicates that the Meluhhan language was not widely understood in Mesopotamia and that some Meluhhan speakers took local names, in this case a typical Semitic name.

The Akkadian kings endeavored to expand their power to the east, but never reached Meluhha. Apparently the easternmost country they conquered, first under Sargon himself, was called Marḫaši (in Sumerian) or Paraḫšum (in Akkadian). A historical text relates how other Iranian countries and Meluhha allied themselves with Marhaši against Sargon's son and successor Rimuš (ruled 2278–2270 BCE), who reconquered Parahšum: "[Rimuš, king of the world, in battle] was victorious over Abalgamaš, King of Parahšum. Zahar, Elam, Gupin and Meluhha assembled in Parahšum for battle, but [. . .]."

An Old Babylonian text, "Gula-AN and the seventeen kings against Narām-Sīn," recounts how almost the whole world rebelled against Narām-Sīn (ruled 2254–2218 BCE), the grandson of Sargon. This text, unfortunately mutilated, lists eighteen countries or peoples with their mutinous kings, most of whom lack the first part of their names. In eleventh place comes: "[. . .]-ib-ra, man of Meluhha." This tantalizing reference is the single historical name we have for a person from Meluhha, that is, from the Indus civilization. The eighteen countries or peoples are, in order: Gutium, Kakmum, Lullubum, Hahhum, Turukkum, Kaniš, Amurru, Dēr, Arrites, Kassites, Meluhha, Aratta, Marhaši, the confederacy of Elam, Land of Apum/the Canebrake, Land of Fifty, Land of Armanum, Land of Hana.

Aratta, the country listed between Meluhha and Marhaši, is chiefly known in Mesopotamian sources from the late Sumerian epic, "Enmerkar and the Lord of Aratta," in which King Enmerkar of Uruk negotiates the importation of lapis lazuli with the king of Aratta, a legendary country situated far away to the east. This is presumably the same country as that mentioned under the non-Aryan name Araṭṭa/Āraṭṭa/Arāṭṭa/Ārāṭṭa in Indian sources, such as the Vedic Baudhāyana-Śrautasūtra (18,13 and 18,44) and the Mahābhārata, where Āraṭṭa comprises the "immoral" regions of the northwest: Sindh, Gandhāra, and the western Punjab. The Mahābhārata includes within Āraṭṭa a region called Vāhīka or Bāhīka, which frequently occurs as a variant spelling of Bāhlīka/Bālhīka/Bahlika/Balhika/Balhīka. Vāhīka or Bāhīka was apparently created by ancient grammarians (who derived it from Sanskrit *bahiṣ*, "outside") in an attempt to understand these Sanskrit counterparts (Bāhlīka, etc.) of the Avestan name Bākhdī and Bākhtrī, that is, Bactria, modern Bālkh in northern Afghanistan—which is of course "outside" the Indian plains. A Harappan colony in Bactria, at Shortugai, controlled the nearby lapis lazuli mines of Badakhshan.

Narām-Sīn's son and successor, Šarkališarri (ruled 2217–2193 BCE), married a princess from Marhaši. He seems to have visited the country and received a delegation from it at Nippur. During the Third Dynasty of Ur, Marhaši had good diplomatic relations with Sumer and close economic relations with Magan. As tribute, Marhaši presented to Ibbi-Sīn, the last king of Ur III (whose rule ended in 2004 BCE), a "speckled dog of Meluhha"—possibly a leopard (cheetah), although this is a cat rather than dog, or the fierce Indian wild dog known as the *dhole* (*Cuon alpinus*), although this animal is red rather than speckled. (A hyena would perhaps suit the description best, were it not for the fact that hyenas were already known in West Asia.) It even appears that Marhaši could export Indian animals to Mesopotamia, for in the Old Babylonian text "Curse over Akkad," holy Inanna arranges that: "foreigners would cruise about [in Akkad] like unusual birds in the sky; that even Marhaši would be reentered in the tribute rolls; that monkeys, mighty elephants, water buffaloes, exotic animals, as well as thoroughbred dogs, lions, mountain ibexes, and *alum* sheep with long wool would jostle each other in the public squares."

Marhaši/Parahšum has been identified with great probability as the above-mentioned Jiroft region of Kerman, where dramatic archaeological finds were recently made, around 2000. Hundreds, if not thousands, of vases, cups, boxes, plaques, and handled "weights" with beautiful iconography carved in soft stone (chlorite, serpentine, steatite) were illegally excavated from five vast graveyards. Part of this trove was confiscated by police and published by Iranian archaeologists, who have since excavated the related habitation site Konar Sandal B near Jiroft. Important evidence supporting Marhaši's identification with Kerman comes from the cuneiform inscription "Rimuš, King of Kiš, the slayer of Elam and Parahšum," carved on two Jiroft-like chlorite bowls, one from Ur and another of unknown provenance. They probably belonged to the booty consisting of various kinds of stones that Rimuš states he brought from Parahšum to Mesopotamia (Steinkeller 1982).

Sumerian literary texts composed in the Old Babylonian period (*c.* 1800–1600 BCE) reflect Mesopotamian conceptions of foreign countries in the third millennium BCE. A composition entitled "Enki and the World Order" contains interesting information about Meluhha. It describes how the wise water god Enki moves around organizing the world and decreeing the fate of different countries. Lines 124–130 speak of foreign partners in maritime trade: "Let the lands of Meluhha, Magan and Dilmun look upon me, upon Enki. Let the Dilmun boats be loaded with timber. Let the Magan boats be loaded with treasure. Let the *magilum* boats of Meluhha transport gold and silver and bring them to Nibru for Enlil, the king of all lands" (translated Maekawa & Mori 2011:262).

Sumerian *magilum* (^{giš}ma$_2$-gi$_4$-lum) is a word exclusively used of the boats of Meluhha. In my opinion, it might well render Proto-Dravidian **maṅki* (**maṅgi*), a form that can be reconstructed as the ancestor of South Dravidian **mañci* (**mañji*), as an affrication of **k/g* due to the following *i* may be assumed. The meaning of this latter word, attested in Tamil, Malayalam, Kannada, and Tulu, is as follows: "single-masted large cargo boat with a raised platform used in coasting trade, holding 10–40 tons"—which matches remarkably well the contextual meaning of *magilum* in the above Sumerian passage. The above Proto-Dravidian reconstruction is supported by the following Sanskrit words recorded only by the twelfth-century Gujarati lexicographer Hemacandra and some other lexica (including one for Hindi): *maṅginī-*, "ship, boat," and *maṅga-*, "forepart of a ship, mast."

Lines 219–234 of "Enki and the World Order" deal with Meluhha itself:

> Then he proceeded to the land (*kur*) of Meluhha. Enki, Lord of Abzu (the Sweet-Water Ocean), decreed its fate: "Black land/mountain (*kur*), may your trees be great trees, may your forests be forests of highland (*kur*) *meš* trees! Chairs made from them will grace royal palaces! May your reeds be great reeds [. . .]! Heroes shall [. . .] them as weapons in the battlefields! May your bulls be great bulls, may they be bulls of the mountains/highland (*kur*)! May their roar be the roar of wild bulls of the mountains/highland (*kur*)! The great powers (*me*) of the gods shall be made perfect for you! May the francolins (*dar*) of the mountains/highland (*kur*) wear carnelian beards! May your birds all be peacocks (*haia*)! May their cries grace royal palaces! May all your silver be gold! May your copper be tin-bronze! Land (*kur*), may everything you possess be plentiful! May your people be [. . .]!" (Translated Maekawa & Mori 2011:262, modified)

The reference to "reeds" and "battlefields" relates to the fact that arrows have traditionally been made of reeds in India: Sanskrit *śara*, a principal word for "arrow," has as its primary meaning "reed" (*Saccharum sara*). Cuneiform texts inform us that reeds from Magan were used to make spears or arrow shafts. The reference to peacocks calls for a comparison with the much later Buddhist Bāveru-Jātaka. A story that may date from the Achaemenid times (sixth to fourth centuries BCE) speaks of Indian merchants who "came to the kingdom of Bāveru (i.e., Babylon, called in Babylonian *Bābilu* and in Old Persian *Bābiru*) [and] brought a royal peacock which they had trained to scream at the snapping of the fingers and to dance at the clapping of the hands"; the Babylonians bought it for a thousand gold coins, and paid the royal peacock high honor. Evidently the beautiful Indian bird has always been a desired luxury item of export.

Sumerian *kur*, "mountains, highland," which occurs many times in the above passage, usually refers to the Iranian plateau and to the foreign countries east of Mesopotamia. "Black land" could mean either "country of dark-skinned people" or "country of dark soil." I opt for the second alternative. The south Indian state Karnataka derives its name from Dravidian *karu-nāṭu* "black land," on account of its black loamy soil. In the Indus Valley, "very characteristic of Sind is the '*kalar*,' soil which contains an excessive proportion of salts. Its composition has been known to include nearly forty per cent of sodium sulphate. In such ground, almost black in colour, and glutinous, no vegetation can subsist, but in the darkish brown medium *kalar* several species of salvadora . . . flourish, particularly in lower Sind." (Lambrick 1964:16). The Sindhi word *kalar* goes back to Proto-Dravidian **kaḻu / *kaḻar / *kaḷar* "saline soil."

"Black land" recurs as an attribute of Meluhha in the "Curse over Akkad," which describes events in the times of Narām-Sīn. In lines 43–50, people from many foreign countries bring goods to the city of Akkad:

> At the city gate, like the Tigris flowing toward the sea, holy Inanna opened the portal of its gate. Sumer brings its own possessions upstream by boat. The highland Martu, people ignorant of agriculture, brought befitting cattle and kids for her. The Meluhhans, people of the black country, brought exotic wares to her. Elam and Subir loaded pack-asses with goods for her. (Translated Maekawa & Mori 2011:260, modified)

"Black country," denoting Meluhha, also occurs in an interesting inscription (B, lines 218–220) of King Šulgi of Ur from the Neo-Sumerian period (ruled 2094–2047 BCE). The king boasts that he can answer in five languages, being those of Elam, Sumer, the "black country" (Meluhha), Martu, and Subir. From precisely this reign, there are six Gulf-type Indus seals found at Ur.

During a period of at least thirty-five years (2105–2071 BCE), a village called Meluhha existed near the city of Lagash during the Third Dynasty of Ur. Meluhha is also the proper name of some of those who resided there, while its other residents have purely Sumerian names (S. Parpola, A. Parpola, & Brunswig 1977). One Ur III cuneiform tablet connects the "Meluhha village" with Guabba. This does not mean that the village was identical with the well-known large town called Guabba, as Vermaak (2008) has understood, but simply its location in the Guabba ("Sea-shore") province south of Lagash (Simo Parpola, personal communication). The dates of this Meluhha village agree closely with those of the early Gulf-type seals of Mesopotamia, such as the one from Telloh/Girsu, near Lagash. A little bit earlier, Gudea, the Sumerian king of Lagash (ruled 2141–2122 BCE), states in his inscriptions that "the Meluhhans came from their country" and supplied *ušū* wood, gold dust, carnelian, and other luxury items for the construction of the main temple in Gudea's capital.

The Old Babylonian text "Enki and Ninhursag" tells of the countries from which various goods came to Mesopotamia:

> May Dilmun become a storehouse on the quay for the land. May the land of Tukriš hand over to you gold of Harali, lapis lazuli and [. . .]. May the land of Meluhha load precious desirable carnelian, *meš* wood of Magan and the best *abba* wood into large ships for you. May the land of Marhaši yield you precious stones, *dušia* stone. May the land of Magan offer you strong, powerful copper, diorite, *ú* stone, and *šumin* stone. May the Sea-land offer you its own ebony wood, [. . .] of a king. May the "tent"-lands [i.e., the country of shepherds?] offer you fine multicoloured wools. May the land of Elam hand over to you selected wools, its tribute. (Translated Maekawa & Mori 2011:261)

The *abba* ("sea") wood imported from Meluhha for making chairs and dagger sheaths during the Third Dynasty of Ur was in all likelihood the very hard wood of the mangrove tree growing on the coast of east Baluchistan and Sindh. The *ú* stone was used to drill carnelian; the Harappans employed for this purpose "a type of indurated tonstein flint clay that has been deliberately heated to produce or enhance properties that made it a highly effective material for drilling hard stone beads" (Law 2011:83).

Ivory, though unmentioned in "Enki and Ninhursag," was another product of Meluhha that was imported into Mesopotamia via the Gulf (the texts mention it as coming from Magan and Dilmun). But after the end of the Isin-Larsa dynasty about 1800 BC, it ceases to be mentioned in cuneiform texts. Indeed, the very name Meluhha disappears altogether until the fifteenth century BCE, when it reappears referring to a new source of ivory: Nubia or Ethiopia, places that had been unknown to Mesopotamians in the third millennium BCE. Now the texts clearly speak of "black men of Meluhha," instead of the earlier "black land of Meluhha."

18

Royal Symbols from West Asia

The Harappan people, although technologically advanced in some respects—in water engineering, textile weaving, and bead making—were undoubtedly greatly impressed by the achievements of the Mesopotamian civilization. The elements they borrowed from Mesopotamia were, however, adapted to their own art traditions and environment by Harappan craftsmen; there is no evidence for Mesopotamian craftsmen working in the Indus Valley. Of these borrowed elements the most important were several royal symbols that embrace the so-called contest motif, which constitutes the principal iconography of the Sumerian and Akkadian royal seals, coupled with its associated details: the hairstyle of the royal hero and the "victory pose" of his foot. A further stylistic borrowing is the royal robe known as a "sky garment." This chapter explores the origin and significance of the "contest" motif and the above-noted details in Mesopotamia.

Five Indus seals from Mohenjo-daro and six molded tablets from Harappa depict a standing male hero who holds back two rearing tigers with his bare hands. Ernest Mackay (1938:I,337) noted that although the seals were manufactured in the Indus Valley they copied a Mesopotamian motif. This shows a male figure with two rearing lions, reminiscent of the epic of Gilgamesh: an example of a "contest scene" in West Asian iconography, which could involve combat with a range of animals. The replacement of the Sumerian lions with tigers, in the scene's Harappan equivalent, seems to be a natural adaptation of the "contest" motif to the ecology of the Indus Valley. (The lion is not represented anywhere in Indus iconography, but it is depicted in the seals of the BMAC, see Fig. 20.2, and also occurs in the Rigveda as *siṁha-*, "lion," a foreign loanword in Sanskrit.) However, as Heinz Mode (1944) pointed out, the Harappan representation has a closer parallel in the Nile Valley than on the royal seals of Mesopotamia, notably on an ancient Egyptian flint knife from Gebel el-Arak, which will be examined below (Fig. 18.1). Moreover, the man fighting with lions in Sumerian art (and also in later Assyrian and Persian glyptics) is often the king—a figure for whom the evidence from the Indus Valley is dubious.

The "contest" motif has an interesting history, which provides clues to understanding its symbolism. Its background is the "master of animals" or "divine hunter" of the upland tribes of southwestern Iran, who lived in symbiosis with the people of Susa in the adjacent lowlands of Elam. He was originally an anthropomorphic figure surrounded on either side by a snake, or sometimes also by a game animal, an eagle, or a panther. But around 4500–4000 BCE, in the stamp seals of Archaic Luristan and the style-A seals of Susa, the "master of animals" is depicted with the head of a wild goat. Later, in a style-B stamp seal from Susa (4000–3500 BCE), while retaining the horns of a wild goat, the figure holds back two rearing lions, one on either side. When the Mesopotamians of the Uruk culture expanded their power to Elam shortly before 3500 BCE, this "contest" motif became part of their iconography. Seal impressions from Uruk and Susa II depict an apparently naked hero holding back two lions. The next manifestations of the "contest" motif are from the subsequent Late Uruk period; but they come, somewhat surprisingly, from Upper Egypt.

The Late Uruk period, 3500–3100 BCE, was one of the most dynamic periods in Mesopotamian history, which witnessed the birth of the world's oldest writing system around 3400 BCE in Uruk. Before this, in the fifth millennium, southern Mesopotamia had already exerted influence, but now, during the so-called Uruk expansion, large-scale Late Uruk colonies—Habuba Kabira, Jebel Aruda, and Sheikh Hassan—were established on the Upper Euphrates (3500–3000 BCE) (Rothman 2001). They are nowadays reckoned to have played a significant role in the relations of the Uruk culture with Egypt, by linking Upper Egypt with West Asia via Lower Egypt and the Levant, rather than via the Persian Gulf and the Red Sea, as was previously thought. Egypt undoubtedly had trading contacts with West Asia from the Middle Uruk period onwards. Lapis lazuli, originally from Badakshan in Afghanistan, has been found in the Naqada region of Upper Egypt, dating from as early as 3800–3600 BCE, and at several Upper Egyptian sites in great quantities, dating from 3500–3300 BCE. Cylinder seals are another item providing clear proof of early Western Asiatic influence in Egypt. The cylinder seal was invented in Mesopotamia around 3750–3550 BCE as an administrative tool that would be more efficient than the existing stamp seal, because much larger areas of wet clay could be quickly and continuously marked by rolling the cylinder. The five earliest cylinder seals in Egypt come from the richest graves in the Naqada region and date from 3500–3300 BCE; and on the basis of their material (limestone), iconography, and style, they were all imported from Mesopotamia (Boehmer 1974; Honoré 2007).

In this period, the Egyptians were still behind the Uruk people in cultural development, for instance in their knowledge of metallurgy, and not nearly so well organized. It should have been possible for a well-armed group of well-traveled Uruk traders—already familiar with the local conditions, people, and language (at least via interpreters)—to take over Upper Egypt. I would like to resurrect the suggestion that the first pharaohs were Sumerian or Elamite invaders, proposed by the eminent Egyptologist Flinders Petrie (1853–1942) and strongly supported by many of his colleagues until about 1960. It was then generally rejected, because of the undoubted untenability of its associated ideas: a "Dynastic race" and a sudden invasion of Egypt via a sea route from Mesopotamia through the Persian Gulf around the Arabian peninsula and into the Red Sea.

The creation of the Egyptian state in Upper Egypt demanded above all strong leadership, and Uruk trader-invaders could have introduced Uruk's effective methods of administration: cylinder seals and record-keeping with logosyllabic protowriting. It is true that the Egyptian hieroglyphic script used its own, non-Mesopotamian, signs and language from its beginning at the end of the fourth millennium; but this may be explained by postulating that the Uruk rulers left such matters to preexisting local officials, as did the Indo-Aryan kings of Mitanni. The palaces and royal tombs of Pre-Dynastic Egypt resemble the so-called recess-buttress architecture typical of Late Uruk culture, which spread widely in West Asia with the Uruk expansion (Sievertsen 1999). The king's name was written within the façade of such a buttressed palace, as depicted in a so-called *serekh* frame; this frame may have been the origin of the later cartouche of the classical hieroglyphic script.

We might envision a parallel between prehistoric Uruk traders sailing up the Nile and taking over power in administratively weak Upper Egypt and the birth of the Russian state in historic time. By 750 CE, if not before, armed Viking traders were sailing from Scandinavia to the Black Sea and the Caspian Sea along the rivers of Russia, Belorussia, and the Ukraine. The Old Russian *Nestor's Chronicle* (the work of a monk called Nestor) records that sometime after 862 the Russians, who lacked laws and a firm government, invited the Vikings to be their rulers. From this same source we know that these chiefs of Viking origin had Scandinavian names in the first two generations, but thereafter Russian names. Likewise, adventurers of Uruk origin in Upper Egypt might have become Egyptianized within a couple of generations.

At least this is what happened to Uruk art objects in Egypt. The superb flint knife from Gebel el-Arak is without clear provenance but can be dated to 3300–3200 BCE on the basis of other similar luxury knives with ivory handles found in context in Upper Egypt, all locally made but decorated with Late Uruk motifs (Sievertsen 1992). The blade made of yellowish Egyptian chert is of extremely high quality, being considered the most accomplished example of the silex tool-making technique. The Gebel el-Arak knife is clearly a royal object, made in Upper Egypt for the king of Upper Egypt. The handle is exquisitely carved in pure Late Uruk style, by a native Uruk craftsman working in Egypt. It contains both Egyptian and Sumerian motifs, depicting two kinds of boats, and a combat between almost nude men wearing penis sheaths. Uppermost on one side of the handle is a bearded man holding back two lions, which stand up on their hind legs on either side (Fig. 18.1). He wears the long frock and head-band of the priest-king of the Late Uruk culture, matching exactly the royal dress on a number of Late Uruk artifacts from Mesopotamia, such as a stone stela from Uruk, where the king is shown hunting lions (Fig. 18.3). The craftsmanship of the Gebel el-Arak knife handle attests to the real presence of Sumerians in Upper Egypt, working for the king of Upper Egypt; it is logical to conclude that the Late Uruk priest-king depicted here is a Pre-Dynastic pharaoh. Thus this particular "contest" scene—royal motif par excellence—is of extraordinary importance for understanding the Egyptian state formation and the extent of the Uruk expansion.

The Egyptian slate palettes of Late Naqada III times (3200–3100 BCE) are already Egyptianized in style, but still have Late Uruk motifs. In the famous stone palette of Narmer, the monsters with intertwined snake-like necks closely parallel a Late Uruk seal. At the bottom of one side of Narmer's palette the king is depicted as a wild bull, goring his enemy, the chief of Lower Egypt; the other side depicts conflict with an enemy, but here the king is shown in human shape. In another palette, from Abydos, the king is represented as a bull, and in yet another, the "battle" palette in the British Museum, the king is shown in the shape of a lion. So the two most feared beasts, the wild bull and the lion, both manifest the royal power.

FIGURE 18.1 A Late Uruk style priest-king with two lions on the ivory handle of a royal flint knife from Gebel el-Arak, Egypt, *c.* 3300–3200 BCE. Musée du Louvre (AE 11517). Photo courtesy Musée du Louvre/ Béatrice André-Salvini.

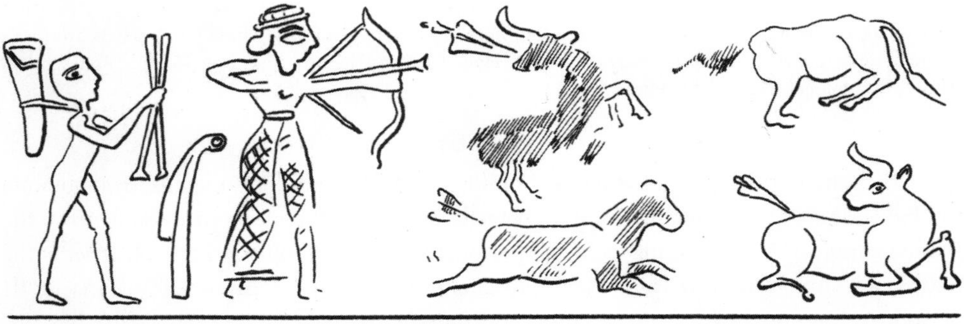

FIGURE 18.2 The Sumerian priest-king hunting wild bulls on a Late Uruk–style cylinder seal. After Amiet 1980: no. 1614. Courtesy Pierre Amiet.

While the already mentioned (Fig. 18.3) stone stela from Uruk shows the king shooting lions, a Mesopotamian Late Uruk cylinder seal depicts the king hunting wild bulls (Fig. 18.2). These depictions convey the message that the king is more powerful than the lion and the bull, or that he is a match for these kings of the beasts. But the Late Uruk king was not only a warrior; he was also the high priest, who is shown performing priestly duties.

FIGURE 18.3 The Sumerian priest-king hunting lions on a Late Uruk–style basalt stone stela from the Eanna temple in Uruk, Mesopotamia, *c.* 3200 BCE. Height 78 cm. The Iraq Museum (IM 23477), Baghdad. After Strommenger 1962: pl. 18. Photo Max Hirmer, © Hirmer Fotoarchiv, Munich.

The Late Uruk depiction of a king holding back two lions continued in Mesopotamia until at least about 2600 BCE (the Early Dynastic II period). It appears in a plaque from the Inanna temple of Nippur dating from this period; the two bulls confronting each other at the bottom are similar to some Harappan representations (Fig. 18.4a). In the Early Dynastic III period the Mesopotamian "contest" scene continues in the old fashion (Fig. 18.4b), but also changes (Fig. 18.4c), as a result of the influence of Proto-Elamite seals.

In Proto-Elamite art, 3200–2600 BCE, human activities are, as a rule, expressed through animal actors. The lion and the bull dominate, often shown in the "pose of power." In a variant of the man-plus-two-lions "contest" motif, the lion and the bull are shown as adversaries. Particularly interesting and important are seals in which these two animals are alternately represented as victorious or defeated, the killer or the killed. On one seal, a standing lion shoots a seated bull with a bow and arrow, and a standing bull clubs a seated lion (Fig. 19.8). On two others, an enormous bull masters two small lions and, conversely, an equally

(a)

(b)

(c)

FIGURE 18.4 "Contest" with two lions in the Near East of the Early Dynastic II–III periods, *c.* 2750–2334 BCE. (a) An ED II (*c.* 2750–2600 BCE) plaque from Nippur. After Parpola 1994:248, fig. 14.10. Drawn after Pritchard 1969:356 no. 646. (b) An ED III cylinder seal from Susa, southwestern Iran. After Legrain 1921:252. Courtesy Musée du Louvre/Béatrice André-Salvini. (c) An ED II–III cylinder seal from Fara. After Amiet 1980: no. 893. Courtesy Pierre Amiet.

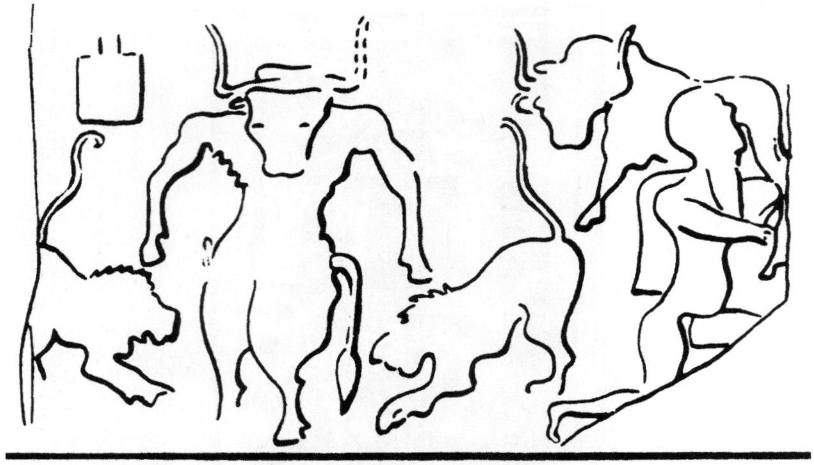

FIGURE 18.5 A Proto-Elamite "contest" seal with a man lifting a bull. After Amiet 1980: no. 586. Courtesy Pierre Amiet.

disproportionately big lion dominates two small bulls (Fig.19.2). Edith Porada (1950) and Pierre Amiet (1956) have plausibly suggested that the lion and bull are personifications of cosmic forces, whose alternation between strength and weakness preserves equilibrium in nature, as manifested in the cycle of day, night, and the seasons. Indeed, the golden-colored lion may stand for the sun, day, light, heat, and fire; the darker bull with crescent-shaped horns for the moon, night, darkness, cold, and water. Other dualities, too, seem to have been ascribed to these two forces: male versus female, heaven versus earth, life versus death; these will be discussed in the next chapter.

In one Proto-Elamite seal impression, a large bull dominating two small lions is balanced by a second scene where a man lifts a bull (Fig. 18.5). Amiet (1980:109) has suggested that in this composition, the bull is the prototype of the "bull-man" Enkidu, who in later Mesopotamian seals fights lions alongside the naked human-shaped hero Gilgamesh, who in turn kills the sky-god An's "Bull of Heaven." To Amiet's observation I add the fact that the human figure (rarely seen in Proto-Elamite seals) has here been substituted for the expected lion. In Sumerian seals, the human hero has six locks of hair, arranged in three hair curls on either side of his head, reminding one of the way the lion's mane is represented on some seals. Thus, this particular Proto-Elamite seal impression links the Proto-Elamite "contest" between animal adversaries with the most important motif of the Mesopotamian royal seals of the Early Dynastic III and Old Akkadian periods.

The Harappan seals with the "contest" motif suggest that the Late Uruk–style "contest" motif continued in Mesopotamia until Early Dynastic III times (2600–2334 BCE) (Fig. 18.4). In the same period, there are six dots over the head of the hero who holds back two tigers in a seal from Mohenjo-daro (Fig. 18.6). The dots correspond to the six curling locks of hair in the "contest" scenes in Early Dynastic III seals, including those of the Fara style (Fig. 18.4c), and in the Old Akkadian seals of Sargonic times. In the

FIGURE 18.6 "Contest" of a six-locked hero with two tigers on the seal stamp M-308 (DK 11794, ASI 63.10.388) from Mohenjo-daro. After CISI 1:384. Photo EL, courtesy ASI.

Old Akkadian period (2334–2200 BCE), this hairstyle was replaced by a conical cap, but toward Neo-Sumerian times (2200–2000 BCE) the six locks come back.

The plaited double-bun or chignon of the Mesopotamian hero is an important indicator of the period and place of origin of West Asian influence on Mature Harappan glyptics. Mesopotamian kings wore their hair in this fashion in the Late Early Dynastic period. The golden helmet of the Sumerian king Meskalamdug from the Royal Cemetery of Ur comes from the Early Dynastic IIIA period (2600–2500 BCE). The helmet shows "a large encircling braid holding the hair in place. Perhaps in the Early Dynastic period this braid replaced the fillet . . . that binds the hair of earlier rulers in Uruk and Jamdat Nasr representations" (Hansen 2003a:34–35). The same plaited chignon is worn by Eannatum, the Sumerian king of Lagash (but not by ordinary soldiers) in the battle scene carved on the ED IIIA "Stele of Vultures" (Fig. 18.7a), and in other depictions of rulers, for example that of Ishqi-Mari, who ruled Mari in Syria during the ED IIIB period (2500–2334 BC). Sargon the Great (*c.* 2334–2279 BCE) wears his hair in this fashion in a stela found at Susa, but by the time of Sargon's Old Akkadian successors, the plaited chignon had already changed into something more elaborate.

Indus people visiting Mesopotamia from their native Meluhha must have been deeply impressed by this royal symbol, given its prominence in their own art and iconography. This

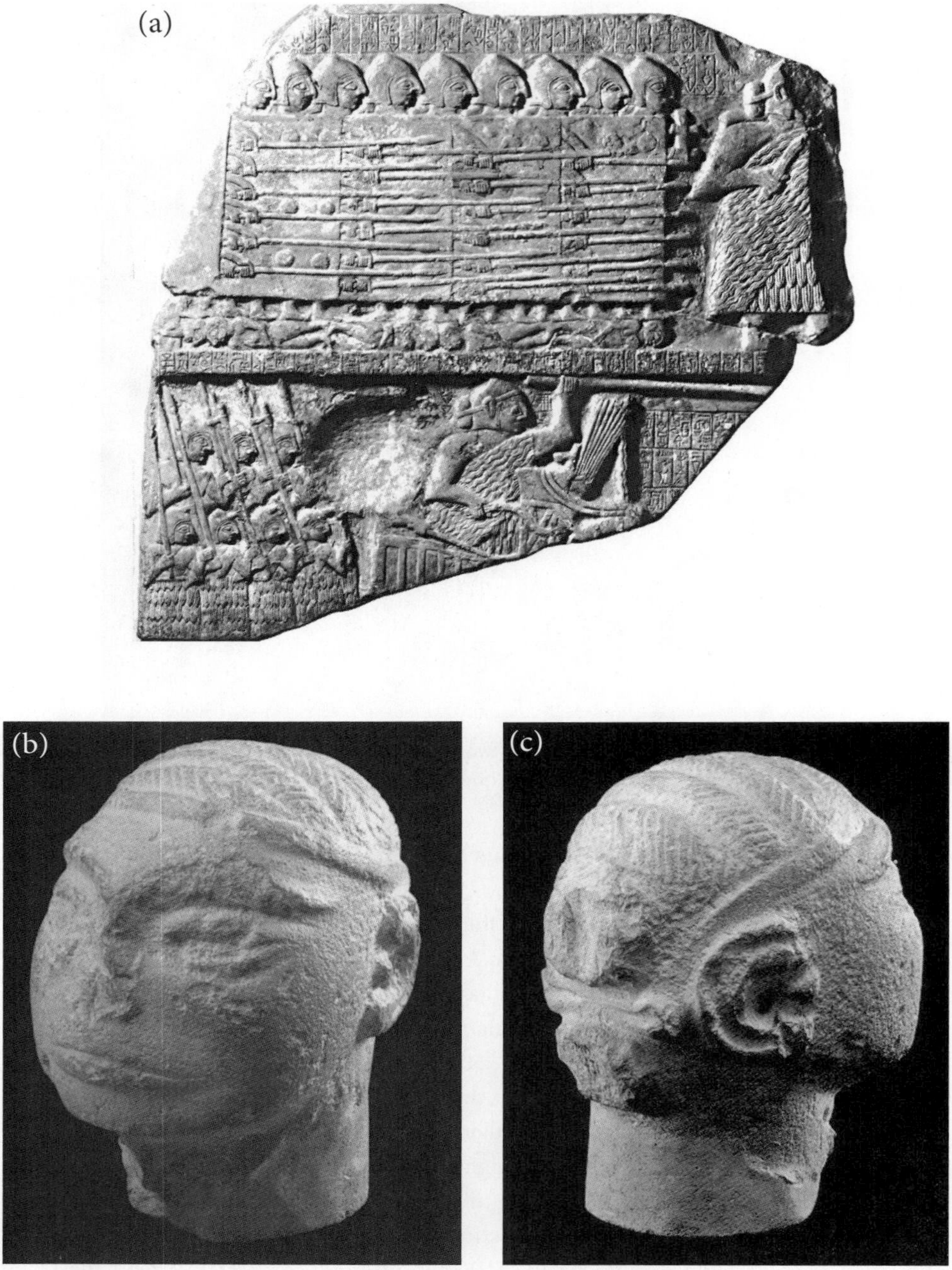

FIGURE 18.7 The "double-bun" headdress. (a) Eannatum, the Sumerian king of Lagash, leading his soldiers on the Stele of the Vultures (EDIIIA, *c.* 2600–2500 BCE) from Telloh in the Musée du Louvre. After Strommenger 1962: pl. 66. Photo Max Hirmer, © Hirmer Fotoarchiv, München, courtesy Musée du Louvre/Béatrice André-Salvini. (b–c) A sandstone sculpture of a male head from Mohenjo-daro in the Mohenjo-daro Museum. After NHK 2000:83, no. 320. Courtesy NHK & NHK Promotions and DAMGP.

was first noted by Elisabeth C. L. During Caspers (1979:133–135), who refers to a number of human portrayals on Indus seals and sculptures: "In each case, the hair is dressed in a bun, which is then secured horizontally, by means of a ribbon or hair-slide of some sort, resulting in the division of hair into two protuberances one above the other." Other examples, additional to those of During Caspers, are as follows. In a cylinder seal from Kalibangan depicting a military context corresponding to the Sumerian helmets, two warriors, both with the divided chignon at the back of the head, fight each other with spears while the goddess of war (who is also shown riding a tiger in this scene) holds them by the hand (Fig. 19.5). In the "fig-deity" seal from Mohenjo-daro, a human head placed on an offering table in front of the deity is probably is a warrior's head since it appears to have the two-parted chignon (Fig. 21.9). Among three sculptures of human heads from Mohenjo-daro, the male head illustrated here has its hair gathered at the nape of the neck into a bun, which is divided into two (now-broken) parts by a horizontal pin connected at both ends with the ribbon encircling the head (Fig. 18.7b–c). There are examples of the Harappan hero of the "contest" scene also wearing the divided chignon.

In the Sumerian language, this hairstyle was called *gú.bar*, whence Akkadian *gubāru* / *gupāru* (*gú* denotes "the nape of the neck"). It is possible that it survived as a warrior's hairstyle to the Vedic Vrātya rites, for the war god Rudra wears a hairstyle known as *kaparda*. This Sanskrit word is likely to be derived from the Proto-Dravidian root **kavar*, "to bifurcate, be divided into two," and the Proto-Dravidian noun **kavaram* / **kavari*, "braided hair," which became a loanword in Sanskrit, *kabara-* / *kabarī-*, "plaited hair" (first attested in Pāṇini's grammar).

In the Old Akkadian royal seals, the bull of the "contest" motif is suddenly replaced by the water buffalo during the last third of the sixty-year-long rule of Sargon the Great (Fig. 18.8a). At the end of the Old Akkadian period, the water buffalo disappears from the Mesopotamian iconography. The water buffalo did not exist in Mesopotamia before this, nor was it reintroduced to Mesopotamia before the Sasanid period some 2500 years later. The water buffalo is so well carved in the Akkadian seals that the craftsmen must have seen the animal alive. In ancient times exotic animals were royal gifts. It has been plausibly suggested that Harappans brought some water buffaloes from the Indus Valley by ship, given that Sargon boasts that ships came from far-off Meluhha to his new capital Akkad. These water buffaloes would have been kept in his royal park, where they apparently soon died (Boehmer 1975). It is noteworthy that the Akkadian artists connect the water-buffalo with the water god Enki/Ea: his servants slake the thirst of the buffalo (Fig. 18.8b).

A notable new iconographic detail is associated with Akkadian seals depicting water buffaloes: the hero places his foot upon the conquered enemy (Fig. 18.8a). From now on, this is the conventional symbol of victory in Mesopotamian art. There are several representations of buffalo spearing in Harappan seals and tablets, and in each case the hero who kills the buffalo raises his foot on the head of the beast (Fig. 18.9). In reality, it would be impossible to put one's foot on a buffalo's head while spearing it. So this pose is simply a conventional symbol of "domination," like the restraining of two lions or tigers with bare hands. In Akkadian glyptics the pose is a natural development, less so in some Harappan examples, which have the appearance of rather clumsy imitations. It is just one addition to the several motifs already

(a)

(b)

FIGURE 18.8 The water buffalo in Old Akkadian seals. (a) A hero grappling with a water buffalo victoriously puts his foot on the head of the beast in a "contest" scene on a seal from Mari in the Damascus Museum. After Parrot 1960: 186 no. 224. Courtesy Musée du Louvre/Béatrice André-Salvini. (b) Enki's servants (nude heroes with hair in six locks) slake the thirst of water buffaloes on an Akkadian cylinder seal in the De Clercq collection of the Musée du Louvre (AO 22303). Inscribed: "Šarkališarri, King of Akkad: Ibnišarrum, the scribe, (is) your servant." After Collon 1987:124 no. 529. Courtesy Dominique Collon and Musée du Louvre/Béatrice André-Salvini.

enumerated that the Harappans adopted from West Asia during the period from Late Early Dynastic to Sargonic times.

In Mesopotamia, the lion and bull had astral counterparts in the zodiacal signs Leo and Taurus. Sumerian sculptures dating from 3100–2900 and 2100–1900 BCE show a reclining bull covered with inlaid trefoils (Fig. 18.10a). These "Bulls of Heaven" may be compared with the cow-shaped Egyptian "Lady of Heaven," since both the bull and the cow are covered in trefoils. The trefoil motif resembles the Sumerian pictogram *mul*, "constellation," consisting

FIGURE 18.9 A hero places his foot on the horns of a water buffalo while spearing it in front of an erect cobra. One side (C) of the molded tablet M-492 (DK 8120, NMI 151) from Mohenjo-daro in the collection of the National Museum of India, New Delhi. After CISI 3.1:396. Photo EL, courtesy NMI.

of three stars placed in a triangle. From Mohenjo-daro comes a fragmentary steatite sculpture of a bull covered with trefoils (Fig. 18.10b).

West Asian gods and divine kings had festive cloths with golden stars, rosettes, and so forth sewn on to them, which were known in Sumerian and Akkadian as "sky garments." What this term meant was apparently stated in the fifth century CE, when the poet Nonnos, writing in Greek, described a Syrian deity as "clad in a patterned robe like the sky" and "called Starclad, since by night starry mantles illuminate the sky." The cloak of the "priest-king" statue from Mohenjo-daro is clearly a form of "sky garment" decorated with trefoils, originally filled with red paste (Fig. 18.11). This Indus garment seems to have been transmitted to the Vedic royal consecration, in which the king is invested with a so-called *tārpya* garment. The Vedic texts ascribe this garment to the divine king Varuṇa, who is associated with the night sky, and state that it had images of sacrificial fireplaces (*dhiṣṇya*) sewn onto it. In the Mahābhārata (3,43), the stars are described as heavenly fireplaces (*dhiṣṇya*) of pious ancient sages. As discussed in chapter 16, this conception can be traced to early Vedic texts.

What does the Harappan borrowing of the "contest" motif—which contained centrally important symbols of kingship in the Late Uruk, Proto-Elamite and Old Akkadian cultures—tell us about kingship in the Indus Valley? When the Harappans adopted this motif, and the royal "double-bun" headdress and "sky garment" of Mesopotamian rulers, did they retain their royal associations? In my view, the answer is yes: the Indus people were ruled by kings.

As discussed in chapters 15 and 16, the Vedic god Varuṇa, the divine king, seems to have succeeded the Harappan water god, symbolized by the fish, crocodile, and water buffalo. Buffalo horns connect this water god with the four-faced Proto-Śiva, who seems to be connected with the sun as the lord of the four directions in the center, and is seated on a throne (Fig. 16.6). This apparently royal divinity is represented on a Harappan-style cylinder seal, where he is balanced by a standing hero who holds back tigers (Fig. 18.12). Beneath the god seated on a throne with bovine legs is a pair of water buffaloes, and he is surrounded by fish and horned snakes. Beneath the standing god is the markhor goat of the Hindu Kush. In later Indian mythology the markhor goat is an animal form of the fire god Agni, who in Vedic texts is equated with Rudra, the divine robber, predecessor of Skanda, the divine warrior in Hinduism.

(a)

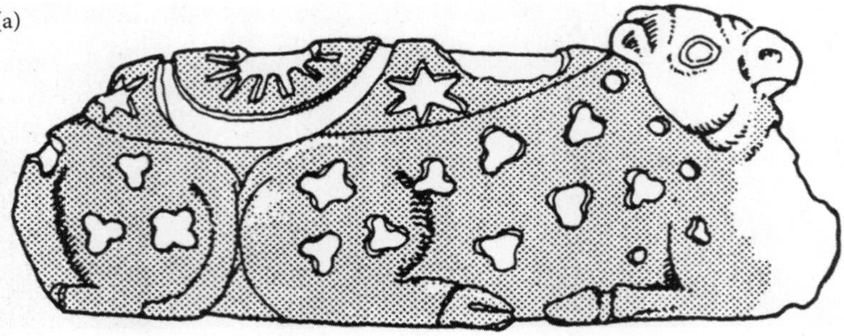

(b)

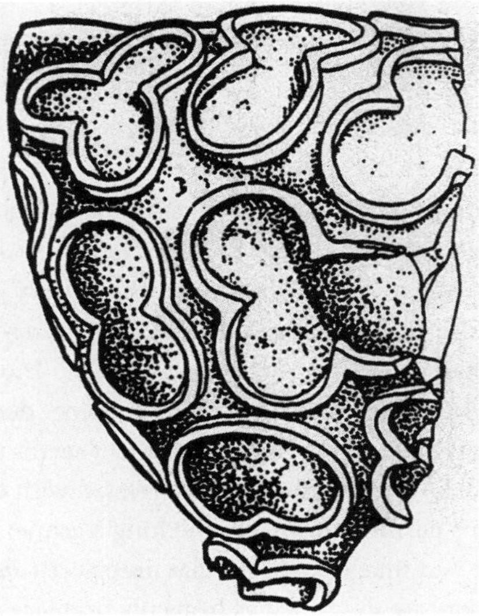

FIGURE 18.10 The Bull of Heaven decorated with trefoils and other astral motifs. (a) A Neo-Sumerian steatite bowl from Ur (U.239), bearing also symbols of the sun and the moon. (b) A fragmentary steatite statuette from Mohenjo-daro. After Ardeleanu-Jansen 1989:205, fig. 19 and 196, fig. 1. Courtesy © Michael Jansen.

Exceptionally in Harappan seal iconography, there is also a bird, probably the vulture, beneath this standing god. In the *agnihotra* ritual of Vedic India, the sacrificer must stand up while pouring the offering libation for the rising sun in the morning, but in the evening, while pouring the offering for the setting sun, he must be seated. If standing and sitting in the cylinder seal discussed refer to the rising and setting sun, or the day sun and the night sun (or the moon), the antithetical pair would represent youth and old age, fire and water, and war/destruction and peace/prosperity. The entire composition reminds one of ideas connected with kingship in later Indian tradition (cf. Heesterman 1957; 1989): the old king resides in the capital in the center of his realm and looks after the welfare of his subjects in all peace, while the crown prince, called *yuvarāja*, "young king," or *kumāra*, "prince," is in charge of war expeditions.

This cylinder seal is to some extent paralleled by an Early Dynastic III chlorite box from Khafajeh in Mesopotamia, where we see the lion-bull antithesis. A divine hero stands on two

FIGURE 18.11 The "priest-king" statuette from Mohenjo-daro, with a robe decorated with trefoils. After Marshall 1931: III, pl. 98.3. Courtesy ASI.

FIGURE 18.12 Impression of an unprovenanced Harappan-style cylinder seal in the Département des Antiquités Orientales, Musée du Louvre (Collection De Clercq 1.26). Photo courtesy Musée du Louvre/ Béatrice André-Salvini.

FIGURE 18.13 Two sides of a chlorite box carved in the "intercultural style" of eastern Iran, Early Dynastic III period (*c.* 2600–2334 BCE), from Khafajeh, Mesopotamia, in the British Museum (Reg. No. 1936,1217.2, BM 12887). (a) A male deity (marked as such with the star or rosette symbol) standing upright on two lionesses and holding a snake in both of his hands. (b) A male deity (marked as such with the star or rosette symbol) seated upon two zebu bulls and holding streams of water in both of his hands. He is surrounded by the sickle of moon and ears of corn. Photos AN 319934001 and AN 6044191001 © The Trustees of the British Museum.

FIGURE 18.13 (Continued)

lionesses and masters two snakes (Fig. 18.13a). On another side of the same box, a deity sits upon two bulls and holds streams of water in his hands (Fig. 18.13b). Both men are marked as divine by a rosette that appears to function like the determinative for divine names in the cuneiform script, the star pictogram. Beside the head of the god sitting on the bulls is also the sickle of the moon. Above the bulls are ears of corn. The sickle of the moon connects the man upon the bulls with night, which is cool and pleasant like the fertilizing waters. The snakes conquered by the man standing upon the lionesses are nightly creatures. The day-night opposition is present also in the standing versus seated posture of the two deities.

Chapter 16 argued that the sun was a symbol of the king and the ruling power in the Early Harappan culture, and that the conceptions associated with the pole star go back to the Indus civilization: the Vedic texts connect the pole star with the king of the country, with the divine king Varuṇa and his banyan tree, yet another symbol of royalty. In the present chapter we have seen that the Indus elite adopted iconographic symbols of royalty from Mesopotamia. The next chapter argues that the most important royal rituals of West Asia had a counterpart in the Indus civilization, and that they were continued with some modification in the Vedic rites of kingship.

19

The Goddess and the Buffalo

In chapter 15 we saw that the principal evidence of the folk religion in the Greater Indus Valley from 7000 BCE onwards consists of statuettes of human females and bulls. It is fairly safe to assume that they represent Mother Earth and Father Sky, an archetypal couple who unite sexually when the roaring sky-bull inseminates the earth with rain. Such ideas appear throughout the texts of West Asia that throw light on the religion of early agricultural communities.

A typical example is the religion of Syria in the fourteenth century BCE. Here Ba'al, the god of thunder and rain, was symbolized by the bull, and Anat, the virgin earth goddess, who personified nature's power of reproduction, was symbolized by the cow, the lioness, the furrow, and the fruit tree. Ba'al—the name means "husband, owner, lord"—was understood to own the cultivated land, just as a husband owned his wife, for whom he had paid the bride-price. The cult culminated in their sacred marriage. Ba'al ruled the season of inseminating rains, fresh vegetation, and growth, whereafter he had to abdicate and descend to the netherworld. After his death, Anat gave birth to a male calf, the young Ba'al, with whom she was to unite the next year. Ba'al was succeeded to the throne by Mot, the god of drying wind and drought, which made everything fade and die, but also ripened the corn. Eventually Anat furiously attacked Mot and cut off his head as if she were harvesting ripe corn. Ba'al's return to the throne coincided with the new-year festival and a further sacred marriage with Anat, whose virginity was renewed each year.

In all these early religions, the earth goddess gave birth to new life, but also took back the life she had given: the dead were buried in the earth, her womb. Indeed, the production of new corn presupposed the sacrifice and burial of seed corn, so birth demanded death. Correspondingly, living beings, especially seed-laying males, whether human or animal, were sacrificed to the earth goddess, but these victims were also supposed to be resurrected. The worship of the earth goddess developed into mystery cults in which not only the goddess but also her devotees partook of the life-containing blood and flesh of the victim.

Around 6000 BCE the earth goddess is represented at Çatal Höyük in Turkey as a fat woman who gives birth while seated on a throne flanked by felines (Fig. 19.1). Bulls are sacrificed in her shrines. Known to the Hittites as Kubaba and to the Greeks and Romans as

FIGURE 19.1 Clay figurine of the Great Goddess seated on a throne flanked by felines. Neolithic Çatal Höyük in Anatolia, *c.* 6000 BCE. The figurine is on permanent display at the Anatolian Civilization Museum in Ankara. Photo courtesy © Çatalhöyük Research Project, Stanford University.

Kybele, this ancient Anatolian goddess was in historical times worshipped with an orgiastic cult that involved the castration of her young lover Attis and also her priests. An important part of Kybele's mystic cult was the *taurobolium*, a sacramental ceremony of cleansing the worshipper of sins with the blood of a sacrificed bull and eating its testicles.

The earth goddess also came to preside over killing and bloodshed that took place in war. From early Neolithic times all over West Asia and the Aegean she was represented by a lion or some other feline, who safeguards her worshippers as a lioness fiercely guards her cubs. Lionesses guard the gates of many ancient cities, such as the Hittite capital Boğazköy in Anatolia, Zincirli and Carchemish in Syria, and Mycenae in Greece. The protective function of the earth goddess manifests itself, too, in the concept of a "mural crown," that is, a crown depicting the (often crenelated) walls of a city. Kybele—who defended Rome against Hannibal—wears such a crown, while the goddess of the city of Mari in Syria was known as "mistress of the city walls."

In chapter 18 we have seen that in Proto-Elamite art (*c.* 3200–2600 BCE) the lion and the bull are represented as each other's adversaries. Thus on one seal from Susa, an enormous bull masters two small lions, and a giant lion dominates two small bulls (Fig. 19.2). They have been interpreted as representatives of opposite and complementary cosmic forces, which appear to have included heaven and earth, male and female. Next to the lion there is a triangular pictogram similar to the Sumerian sign KI, which denotes "earth." The pictogram occurs on other seals, where a lioness is represented, Atlas-like, upholding with her paws tree-clad mountains, apparently as a chthonic deity (Fig. 19.3). According to the Babylonian "Epic of Creation," after the separation of heaven and earth, the sky-god An was the father of the natural deities, the earth-goddess Ki their mother.

The principal Mesopotamian goddess, called in Sumerian Inanna and in Akkadian Ištar, was symbolized by both the lion and the planet Venus. As the evening star she presided

FIGURE 19.2 A Proto-Elamite seal impression from Susa, with lions and wild bulls dominating each other in turn. The script sign KI flanks the lion on either side. After Amiet 1980: no. 585. Courtesy Pierre Amiet.

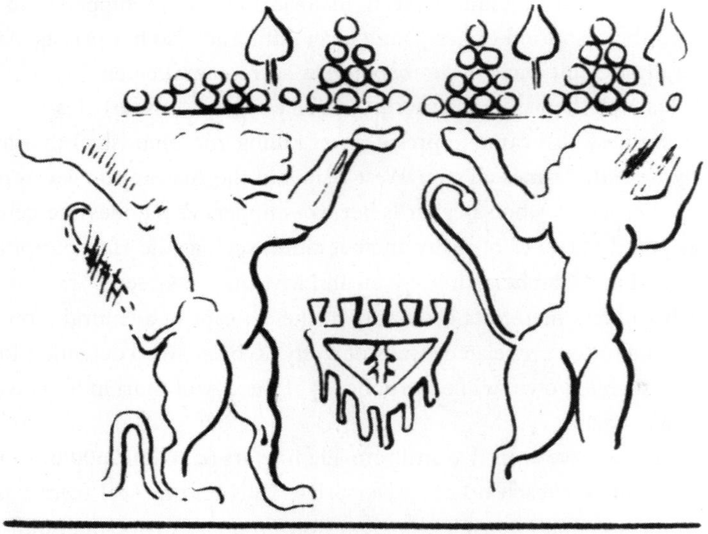

FIGURE 19.3 Impression of a Proto-Elamite seal, showing lionesses upholding mountains and trees, and the script sign KI. After Amiet 1980: no. 577. Courtesy Pierre Amiet.

over sexual love and prostitutes. As the morning star, she was a bloodthirsty warrior about to begin the battle, standing by her princely favorites. The fertility of vegetation, animals, and humans was believed to depend upon the union of Inanna and Dumuzi (Akkadian Tammuz), her young shepherd lover. Dumuzi's death was ritually lamented. (According to one variant of the myth, when Inanna visited the underworld ruled by her sister, she could not return to the earth without a substitute, so demons kidnapped Dumuzi to replace Inanna. However, Dumuzi was allowed to return to the earth for six months every year.) Dumuzi was identified with the king, but the sacred marriage was enacted by priestly personnel. This was the most important festival, celebrated on the new year's day, with processions, dance, music, and feasting.

Turning now to the Indus civilization, we find evidence for the presence of key elements of a West Asian kind of cult of the earth goddess. A seal from Chanhu-daro depicts a "sacred marriage": a bison bull with exposed long penis is about to mount a prostrate human female with an elaborate headdress whose legs are apart and vulva is visible (Fig. 19.4). Importantly, the groom is an animal (bull) and the bride a woman (priestess?), as with the stallion and chief queen in the Vedic horse sacrifice discussed in chapter 12, where the early Indo-Aryans (of the Atharvavedic wave) seem to have substituted their principal sacrificial animal (the horse) for the victim of the Harappan tradition (chiefly the water-buffalo).

FIGURE 19.4 Intercourse of a bison bull and an anthropomorphic priestess. Impression of a lost Indus seal excavated at Chanhu-daro in Sindh (cf. Mackay 1943: pl. 51, no. 13). Exposure 3148 of the old print B7392 in the Museum of Fine Arts, Boston. Courtesy Museum of Fine Arts, Boston.

FIGURE 19.5 A tiger-riding goddess wearing the horns of a mountain goat under an acacia tree. She is also shown, without her mount, as holding by hand two warriors spearing each other. The warriors wear their hair in a two-parted chignon at the nape of the neck. There are two signs of the Indus script, one representing the numeral three. Modern impression of the cylinder seal K-65 (KLB2-9734, ASI 68.1.77) from Kalibangan. After CISI 1:311. Photo EL, courtesy ASI.

The Harappans also had a tiger-riding goddess of war, depicted on a cylinder seal from Kalibangan (Fig. 19.5). Mesopotamian influence is visible in the type of the seal and in the hairstyle of the seal's warriors, which sports a band forming a "double bun," as worn by princes in West Asia around 2400 BCE. But the goddess herself looks native: she has a long skirt and long plaited hair, and holds the hands of two warriors who are spearing each other. Next to this group she is depicted again, now with the body of a tiger and wearing an elaborate crown with the horns of the markhor goat topped by a branch of acacia. In this latter form she also appears on a Harappan-type square seal, found in the same house as the cylinder seal. The inscriptions on these two seals are very similar, but not identical.

The West Asian sacrifice of the bull is also paralleled in the Indus civilization. The sacrifice of a water buffalo bull by spearing is represented on an Indus seal and on several Harappan tablets. We have seen in chapter 18 that the Harappan water buffalo, imported from the Indus Valley, is the counterpart of the West Asian urus bull in the Sargonid "contest" seals, and that the "victor's pose," one foot placed on the head of the buffalo, is replicated in Mesopotamia and in the Indus Valley (Figs. 18.8a, 18.9). The buffalo sacrifice also takes place in front of an erect cobra (Fig. 18.9); according to Vedic texts, "the Queen of the snakes (*sārparājñī*) is the earth" (PB 4,9,6).

In the ancient West Asia and Mediterranean, notably in Minoan Crete, acrobatic bull-baiting has been an integral part of the cult; the sport continues in Spain today. Some Indus seals depict people (in one case clearly women) jumping over a water buffalo (Fig. 19.6). Two bulls facing each other as if in fight are also depicted (H-1997 B). Some tablets from Harappa show men grappling with bison or buffalo bulls, holding them from

(a) (b)
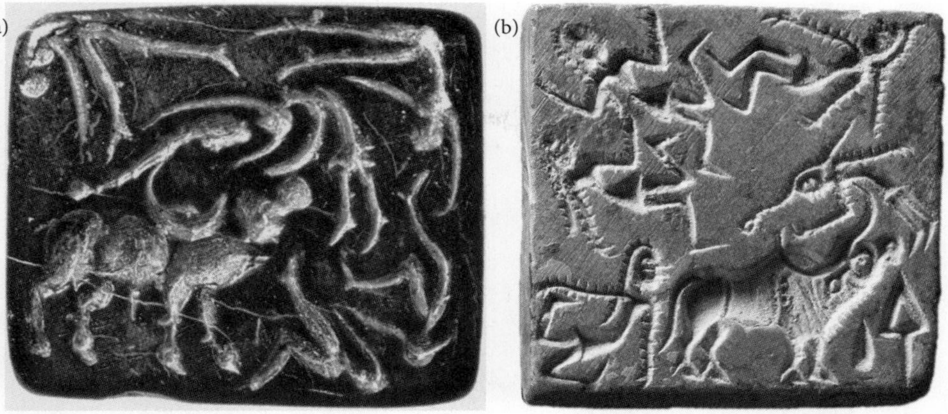

FIGURE 19.6 Jumping over the water buffalo in Indus seals. (a) The seal M-312 (DK 8321, NMI 147) from Mohenjo-daro in the collection of the National Museum of India, New Delhi. After CISI 1:385. Photo EL, courtesy NMI. (b) An Indus seal from Banawali. Photo courtesy ASI.

horns (H-2023 C to H-2030 C). According to seven Old Tamil poems describing life in the pastoral landscape, Kalittokai 101–107, herding communities regularly arranged festive contests of bull grappling (*ēṟu-kōḷ* or *ēṟu-taḻuvu*), where wild bulls with sharpened horns were let loose in the arena, and young men showed their physical prowess in order to win girls in marriage; the poems describe how they could be gored or trampled to death. Bull baiting is still popular in some parts of south India, especially Tamil Nadu, where it is currently known as *erutu-k-kaṭṭu* or *calli-k-kaṭṭu*.

Hindu India reveres a fight between the lion or tiger and the buffalo in the battle between the goddess Durgā and the buffalo demon, Mahiṣa Asura, a ferocious warrior. The beautiful granite panel of the Pallava dynasty (*c.* 700 CE) at Māmallapuram in Tamil Nadu depicts the lion-riding goddess Durgā shooting her opponent with bow and arrows, while the buffalo demon Mahiṣa Asura has the club as his weapon (Fig. 19.7). This composition offers a striking parallel to the Proto-Elamite seal where the lion kills the bull by shooting it with bow and arrows, while the bull clubs the lion with a mace (Fig. 19.8).

But is this comparison really warranted? It is generally thought that the goddess Durgā and her cult did not exist in South Asia until the Iranian-speaking Kuṣāṇas introduced it from Afghanistan in the first century CE. In my view, however, as I shall now discuss, although the name Durgā is indeed not attested in early sources, the Vedic texts do refer to a similar goddess of war and victory, associated with the earth, the lioness, and the buffalo: the goddess Vāc, who figures prominently in the Vrātya rite of *mahāvrata* (chapter 12). Moreover, I argue for a Vrātya origin of the cult of Durgā and therewith of the worship of the Goddess, with bloody sacrifices, even of human victims, and sexual intercourse in which all taboos might be broken: the so-called left-hand Śākta Tantrism. (In "right-hand" worship these practices are replaced with harmless symbols, for example, cutting a water-melon instead of a head, using colored water instead of blood.)

The earliest images of Durgā as Mahiṣāsuramardinī, "crusher of the buffalo demon," date from early Kuṣāṇa times, around 100 CE. The earliest, and most important, full account

FIGURE 19.7 The lion-riding goddess Durgā shoots the buffalo-headed Mahiṣa Asura who wields a club. Rock panel at Māmallapuram, Tamil Nadu, South India, eighth century CE. After Kramrisch 1954: pl. 86. Research inconclusive: copyright Philadelphia Museum of Art may apply.

FIGURE 19.8 A Proto-Elamite seal in which an upright-standing lion shoots a seated bull and an upright-standing bull clubs a seated lion. After Amiet 1980: no. 591. Courtesy Pierre Amiet.

of the Goddess's victory over the demon is that of chapters 2–3 in the Devī-Māhātmya, which appears in the Mārkaṇḍeya-Purāṇa. Here the beautiful virgin goddess is created from the united fiery energy representing the fury of the main gods Brahmā, Viṣṇu, and Śiva, while the other gods provided her with a range of weapons for the annihilation of Mahiṣa; she also drinks wine to increase her fury for the fight. During the battle, the demon changes himself from a buffalo first into a lion, then into a man (a warrior), then an elephant, then back into a buffalo, and a man. In the Devī-Bhāgavata-Purāṇa (5,18,2–70), the demon first has a human form, then successively changes into a lion, an elephant, a śarabha, and a buffalo. In the Śiva-Purāṇa (5,46,48–55), the forms assumed by the demon are those of a buffalo, a lion, an elephant, and a man.

Comparing the available stone iconography with the descriptions in these texts, Heinrich von Stietencron (1983) has proposed that none of the textual accounts can predate the fifth century CE. The earliest icons of the Kuṣāṇa period, where the Goddess embraces the buffalo and breaks its back, have no textual counterpart. The Devī-Māhātmya states that the Goddess jumped onto the back of the buffalo demon, which corresponds to the images at Elephanta, Ellora, and Aihole dated to the sixth and seventh centuries CE; but another detail of the fight mentioned in the Devī-Māhātmya (and the Vāmana-Purāṇa)—the demon's final emergence from the buffalo's mouth in human form—is not known from iconography before the eighth century.

Von Stietencron sees a development of the myth in the texts, conditioned by the growing *bhakti* movement of the first millennium CE. In the Devī-Māhātmya (and in the Śiva- and Vāmana-Purāṇa), the buffalo demon is only a straightforward enemy of the Goddess. In later Purāṇas, though, the demon is driven to battle not by enmity but by passion for the Goddess. The Goddess, however, is unable to accept the lowly demon as her husband. In the latest versions of this textual history Mahiṣa's love is so great that he chooses death at the hand of his beloved rather than life without her. The demon's *bhakti* evokes pity and grace in the Goddess. She offers him friendship if he will return to the netherworld, but this does not satisfy the demon. He is slain by the Goddess, and thereby attains liberation.

In the Devī-Purāṇa, Mahiṣa had been in love with the Goddess in a previous incarnation in the form of the demon called Dundubhi ("Drum"), who had been burnt to ashes by the jealous Śiva. According to an Orissan tradition, at his death Mahiṣa could kiss the female organ of the Goddess, becoming liberated through this intimate contact with her. In the Kālikā-Purāṇa (*c.* 1000 CE), the love is finally legitimized, as Mahiṣa is identified with Śiva. Now the motive for Mahiṣa's death must also change, as he is no longer striving for something forbidden; instead, Śiva is said to have been cursed by an enraged sage.

Von Stietencron's hypothesis explains the evolution of the Goddess and Mahiṣa myths of the Purāṇa texts well, conforming to the history of Indian religions during the corresponding period. Even so, it does not necessarily follow that the theme of love between the Goddess and the buffalo demon is as recent as the sixth century CE; it may have been latent in the earlier tradition. Indeed, David Shulman (1980) has argued for an opposite development in the Tamil texts of South India: that the myth of divine marriage is central to the Tamil religion, and the murder of the male spouse by the virginal bride—for the sake of the god's rebirth—is its most essential element. Brahmanical ideology later imported from North India has tampered with the texts and changed the myths, in particular eliminating the idea of the god's death and projecting it onto the Goddess's fight with demons.

Old Tamil literature speaks of a goddess of war, Kotti or Ko<u>tt</u>avai, who gives victory (*ko<u>tt</u>am*), lives in a great forest, and dances the *tuṇaṅkai* dance. She is generally considered to be a native Dravidian divinity, although the Tamil epic Cilappatikāram (probably composed between 450 and 750 CE), identifies her with the north Indian goddess Durgā Mahiṣāsuramardinī. Her name Koṯṯi is homonymous with South Dravidian *koṯṯi*, "cat"; both words are probably derived from Proto-Dravidian **kol*, "to kill." Koṯṯi's connection with the *tuṇaṅkai* dance appears to me very significant. *Tuṇaṅkai* is danced on the battlefield by men, women, and ghosts, who beat their sides with their arms bent at the elbows. The derivation of *tuṇaṅkai* from the Proto-Dravidian root **tuḷaṅku*, "to shake, sway, be agitated, move violently to and fro or up and down," proposed in the *Tamil lexicon*, seems to suit the situation in the battlefield as an expression of "grief, sorrow" (Tamil *tuḷakku*) for the dead. Several rituals of Vrātya affinity (discussed in chapter 12), including an archaic funeral and the horse sacrifice, include a dance around the deceased, in which the dancers beat their thighs.

The forms of the demon slain by the Goddess consist of the males of various powerful animals. In Old Tamil poems, the tiger, elephant, and wild buffalo are used as similes to portray the anger and courage of heroes; a special theme of Old Tamil poetics is *erumai-maṟam*, comparing the ferocious attack of a hero to the charging of a wild buffalo. The buffalo, lion, *śarabha*, and man, mentioned as metamorphoses of Mahiṣa Asura in his fight with the Goddess, figure high in the list of sacrificial victims in Kālikā-Purāṇa 71,6–18. Here it is specified which particular animal will give pleasure to the Goddess for which length of time—which is also the length of time that she will bless the sacrificer of this particular animal (Table 19.1). The identity of the *śarabha*, which occupies a prominent place in this list, is problematic and will be discussed in chapter 20.

The different sacrificial victims offered to the Goddess represent the metamorphoses of the valiant male, who on the one hand has been killed by the Goddess and at the same time is her late husband or suitor. The victims of the Vedic Vrātya rituals similarly represent the metamorphoses of the creator god Prajāpati, who is the father and husband of Vāc, in my opinion Durgā's predecessor as the goddess of victory and fertility. He is killed on account of his illicit pairing with Vāc. Prajāpati is expressly said to be the "lord/husband of (the goddess)

TABLE 19.1

victim	time
fish, tortoise	1 month
crocodile	2 months
nine species of wild animals	9 months
wild bull, guana	1 year
black antelope, wild boar	12 years
śarabha	25 years
buffalo, rhinoceros, tiger	100 years
lion, śarabha, man	1000 years
three men	100,000 years

speech" (*vācaspati*) (ŚB 5,1,1,16). In Kaṭha-Saṁhitā 12,5 the creation is described in the following manner: "In the beginning Prajāpati (alone) was this (whole universe). His Voice (*vāc-*, fem.) became a second (being). He paired with her. She conceived an embryo. She went away from him. She delivered these creatures." Rigveda 5,42,13 speaks of the creator god Tvaṣṭar, "who, wanton in his own daughter's womb, changing forms made this (form) of ours."

A more extensive version is in Bṛhad-Āraṇyaka-Upaniṣad 1,4:

> 1. In the beginning this world was self (*ātman*) alone in the form of a man (*puruṣa*) . . . 3. . . . He desired a second. He was, indeed, as large as a woman and a man closely embraced. He caused that self to fall (*pat*) into two pieces. Therefrom arose a husband (*pati*) and a wife (*patnī*). . . . He copulated with her. Therefrom human beings were produced. 4. And she then bethought herself: "How now does he copulate with me after he has produced me just from himself? Come, let me hide myself." She became a cow. He became a bull. With her he did indeed copulate. Then cattle were born. She became a mare, he a stallion. She became a female ass, he a male ass; with her he copulated. Thence were born solid-hoofed animals. She became a she-goat, he a he-goat; she a ewe, he a ram. With her he did verily copulate. Therefrom were born goats and sheep. Thus, indeed, he created all, whatever pairs there are, even down to the ants. (Translated Hume 1931:81, slightly modified)

Here the males and females of all the animal species are different manifestations of just one and the same primeval pair, Prajāpati and Vāc. This idea seems to be reflected in the iconography of the Indus civilization, too, for a number of Harappan seals and amulets portray fantastic animals, whose body parts belong to different species. Thus, a composite animal has the horns of a zebu bull, a human face, the trunk and tusks of an elephant, the forequarters of a ram, the hindquarters of a tiger, and a snake for the tail. These mythical creatures may express the idea that all the species represented by the different parts belong to just one and the same being, who can assume different appearances.

In the Vādhula-Anvākhyāna (4,16) the primeval couple is Prajāpati and Vāc, but Prajāpati also has the sacrifice (*yajña-*), that is, the sacrificial victim, as his alter ego. "Prajāpati created (emitted, poured out) the sacrifice (*yajña-*, masc.); after it had been created, it went away from him." (The expression *parāṅ ait*, "went away," usually refers to dying; in ŚB 13,2,5,1, it is used of the pouring out of the sap of life—apparently blood—of the sacrificial horse just slaughtered.)

> He (the sacrifice, the male victim) wished to pair with . . . the (goddess) Speech (*vāc-*, fem.) (in the form of) the *anuṣṭubh* verse . . . he united with her. She became a mare (*aśvā-*), he a stallion (*aśva-*); she became a wild ass mare (*gaurī-*), he a wild ass stallion (*gaura-*); she a bison cow (*gavayī-*), he a bison bull (*gavaya-*); she a female camel (*uṣṭrī-*), he a male camel (*uṣṭra-*); she a she-goat (*ajā-*), he a he-goat (*basta-*); she a female śarabha (*śarabhī-*), he a male śarabha (*śarabha-*); she a she-antelope (*eṇī-*), he a black buck (*kṛṣṇa-*); she a red

female nilgau (*rohit-*), he a male nilgau (*ṛśya-*). Thus they went through becoming all the beings, both of them taking one form after another.

Then Vāc went into the man (*puruṣa*) and "made defence walls (*puraḥ*) (against him), namely the teeth." Then Prajāpati took the form of the porridge (*odana*) sacred to Vāc, which he knew Vāc desired. To enhance her lust, he decorated himself with melted butter. Vāc could not resist him; she removed the defense and swallowed him, thus finally becoming united with him.

In this variant, Vāc possesses defensive walls (*puraḥ*) like Durgā as the goddess of the fortress (*durga*), and the West Asian goddesses like Kybele wearing a mural crown. Moreover, it is stated that Prajāpati and Vāc copulated in the form of all beings (*sarvāni bhūtāni*). Aitareya-Āraṇyaka 5,1,5 speaks of the mating of many animal couples (*bhūtānāṃ ca maithunam*) at the *mahāvrata*. Mating of animal couples takes place in popular festivals in India even today: thus a bull and cow that copulate may represent the marriage of Rāma and Sītā. From the Vādhūla-Śrautasūtra (11,19,25–30) it appears that at the Vedic horse sacrifice there was full sexual license for all the human participants, as in the Śābarotsava of Durgā's "tenth day of victory."

In the variant of the Vādhūla-Anvākhyāna, the enumeration of the animals stops at the pair of the nilgai antelope, *rohit* and *ṛśya*. (The "unicorn" bull, which is so prominent

FIGURE 19.9 Nilgai, "the blue bull" (*ṛśya* in Sanskrit). After Roberts 1977:176, ill. 52. Courtesy F. Roberts and Ruth W. A. Sloan.

in the Harappan iconography, seems to be a cross between the wild urus bull—borrowed as "unicorn" from Mesopotamia, but not present in the Indus Valley fauna—and the native nilgai antelope, which represents the creator god in these Vedic myths: Figs. 19.9, 19.10.) This is the only pair mentioned in a number of other, clearly abbreviated, versions dealing with Prajāpati's incest with his own daughter, among them Aitareya-Brāhmaṇa 3,33, which states that Prajāpati was killed in punishment:

> Prajāpati desired his own daughter. . . . Having become a nilgai bull he approached her who had become a nilgai cow. The gods saw him and said: "Prajāpati is doing a deed that is not done." They sought someone to punish him; they did not find such a person among themselves. They united their most terrible manifestations. Those became This Deity [a euphemism for the dreaded god Rudra]. . . . The gods said to him: "This Prajāpati here has done a deed that is not done; pierce him (with an arrow)." "Be it so," he (Rudra) replied. . . . He aimed and pierced him . . .

Rudra's birth from the most terrible manifestations of the various gods in order to kill Prajāpati is closely paralleled in the Devi-Māhātmya by the birth of Devī from the combined forces of the gods so as to dethrone the buffalo demon on the tenth day. While in the mythology

FIGURE 19.10 An antelope-like "unicorn" on an Indus seal Nd-1 (Exc. Branch 1187) from Nindowari. After CISI 2:419. Photo AV, courtesy DAMGP.

of the Goddess it is the virgin (*kumārī*) goddess herself in her warrior manifestation who kills the demon that has dared to approach her, in the Vedic myth it is her male counterpart, the youthful (*kumāra*) war god Rudra, born at the instance of the incestuous union of the sinful father and his daughter. There is an epic version of the Mahiṣa myth, in which the buffalo demon is killed by the war god Skanda, the Hindu successor of Vedic Rudra. Skanda's birth myth and metronym Kārttikeya connect him with the autumn, when the buffalo is sacrificed in Durgāpūjā.

In the Purāṇas, a lion- or tiger-riding young goddess kills a demon in the shape of a male buffalo. In Kerala, there is a myth of a tiger-riding young male god (Ayyappan) who kills a demoness having the form of a she-buffalo (*mahiṣī*). This Keralan myth underlines the capacity of a divinity to assume either a male or a female appearance. The lion or tiger and the buffalo are both symbols for the fearless and destructive warrior, who personifies war, as does the goddess of victory. Among different Semitic tribes, the war god was either male, Aštar, or female, Aštart. Based on the myth variants discussed in the preceding paragraph, I would like to argue that a similar relationship prevails between the male war god Rudra/Skanda, and the female goddess of war, Durgā, and her doubles, such as Sarasvatī. In Hinduism, these deities share a number of common attributes (such as the peacock and the harp), epithets, and myths. They are youthful and virginal, the male one being called Kumāra, the female Kumārī; these epithets/names imply also sexual chastity (*brahmacaryā*) required in learning wisdom that also characterizes these deities. The Goddess rides a tiger, and in the Veda it is Rudra who is called "the lord of the wild animals" (*araṇyānāṃ pati*, TS 4,5,3e), an epithet otherwise given to the tiger only (cf. AB 8,6 *kṣatraṃ vā etad araṇyānāṃ paśūnāṃ yad vyāghraḥ*).

From the Brāhmaṇa texts it appears not only that Prajāpati assumed the forms of the various animals in creating them but also that he was sacrificed in these forms. Thus the vegetarian offering is explained in Śatapatha-Brāhmaṇa 2,1,3,6–9 to be a substitute for an original bloody sacrifice, starting with the human sacrifice:

> 6. At first . . . the gods offered up a man as the victim. When he was offered up, the sacrificial essence went out of him. It entered into the horse. They offered up the horse. When it was offered up, the sacrificial essence went out of it. It entered into the ox. They offered up the ox. When it was offered up, the sacrificial essence went out of it. It entered into the sheep. They offered up the sheep. When it was offered up, the sacrificial essence went out of it. It entered into the goat. They offered up the goat. When it was offered up, the sacrificial essence went out of it. 7. It entered into this earth. They searched for it, by digging. They found it (in the shape of) those two (substances), the rice and barley. . . . 9. The man (*puruṣa*) whom they had offered up became a bard (*kiṃpuruṣa*). These two, the horse and the ox, which they had sacrificed, became a wild ass and a bison respectively. The sheep which they had sacrificed, became a camel. The goat which they had sacrificed, became a *śarabha*. For this reason one should not eat (the flesh) of these animals, for these animals are deprived of the sacrificial essence (are impure). (Translated Eggeling 1882:I,50–52, modified)

Here two series of animals are correlated, the first being pure animals, which may be sacrificed, and the second impure animals, which are unfit for sacrifice. (For an interpretion of *kiṃpuruṣa*

TABLE 19.2

tame	wild
1. puruṣa	1. kiṃpuruṣa/mayu
2. aśva	2. gaura
3. go/vṛṣabha	3. gavaya
4. avi/vṛṣṇi	4. uṣṭra/meṣa
5. aja/basta	5. śarabha

as a "bard", see chapter 14.) The five pure animals are those whose heads are placed in the lowest layer of the fire altar (*agniciti*). The mantras that are employed in placing these heads also mention the impure animals, here characterized as "belonging to the forest" (*araṇya*), that is, wild, while the pure animals by implication belong to the village, that is, are tame (Table 19.2).

The worship of Durgā (*durgāpūjā*) takes place especially in the autumn, during Dussehra, from Hindi *daśahrā* (< **daśāharaka*), "festival lasting ten days." It consists of the "nine-day festival" (*nava-rātra* or *nava-rātri*) followed by "the tenth day of victory" (*vijaya-daśamī*), which celebrates Durgā's victory over Mahiṣa. Everything culminates in the festival celebrated in the manner of Śabaras (understood to denote "wild tribals," but another explanation is offered in chapter 20) on the tenth day, when the Goddess is "dismissed" and the king lustrates his army before marching to battle. Hindu kings have traditionally started their military operations when the roads have dried up after the rainy season and there is abundant fodder and grain available.

Another festival, the now less-known *vasanta-navarātri*, also connected with the worship of Durgā, is celebrated around the vernal equinox. In Nepal the goddesses of war called "Nine Durgās" are worshipped from the autumnal *dasaīṃ* (< *daśamī*) festival to the end of May, but not during the rainy season. The two Durgā festivals of the year may originally have had the same function as the Vedic *vrātyastoma* rites. One *vrātyastoma* was celebrated when the Vrātyas set out on a raiding expedition, confirming their mutual covenant; another *vrātyastoma* was performed on their return, to purify them of the violent deeds they had committed during the raids. If this was the case, the year was divided into two halves of violence and peace: the inauspicious *dakṣiṇāyana* (the sun's southern course) of raiding, living outside the village, in the wilderness; and the auspicious *uttarāyaṇa* of agriculture (the sun's northern course), living in the village.

This hypothesis would explain the two series of sacrificial animals, tame and wild, used respectively during the two festivals celebrating the two diametrically opposed turning points of the year. When the fire altar is completed (at *mahāvrata*) and the tame animals are sacrificed, the wild ones are released. At the horse sacrifice, however, all possible kinds of wild animals are sacrificed as subsidiary victims. For example, Maitrāyaṇī Saṃhitā 3,14,10 and Vājasaneyi-Saṁhitā 24,28 state:

To the Lord (Īśāna, i.e., Rudra) he sacrifices rhinoceroses (*parasvatāḥ*),
to Mitra wild asses (*gaurān*),

to Varuṇa water buffaloes (*mahiṣān*),
to Bṛhaspati bisons (*gavayān*),
to Tvaṣṭar camels (*uṣṭrān*).

At the autumnal equinox the sacred couple was father (Prajāpati) and daughter (Vāc), who seem to represent the dying "old year" and the virginal "new year": their union coincides with the death of the old and birth of the new year/sun. At the vernal equinox the "sacred marriage" would also be incestuous but with an inversion of the roles: son and mother. The dying groom would be the "young sun" born out of the preceding marriage, that is, the leader of the *vrātya* sodality who had been raiding during the past six months, that is, the Vedic god Rudra personified by a war bard (*kiṃpuruṣa, māgadha*), and the bride would be the chief (seniormost) queen (*mahiṣī*, "buffalo cow," symbolizing Mother Earth). This reconstruction fits the reasonable assumption (presented in chapter 16) that the earliest Indian calendar consisted of the opposing asterisms *rohiṇī* and *jyeṣṭhā*, associated respectively with a young virgin girl just coming of age, and "the eldest lady," representing respectively the goddess of welfare and goddess of misfortune.

I suggest that the two Durgā festivals correspond to the two great festivals of the Vedic sacrificial year, the *mahāvrata* and the *viṣuvat*. *Mahāvrata* is always preceded by a ten-day rite (*daśarātra*)—equal to Dussehra—and in the year-long sacrificial session this combination occurs only once, at the end of the yearly cycle. It may be that originally the *mahāvrata* coincided with the tenth day, for the tenth day is sacred to the creator god Prajāpati; riddles about the creation of the world are followed by an abuse of the evil deeds of Prajāpati, that is, his incest with his daughter resulting in his death. The Vedic texts contain statements indicating that a human victim was once sacrificed on this day and that his flesh was eaten by the participants (Falk 1986:37–42)—as was done on the "tenth day of victory" until the British period in Karnataka—by men leaving for raids (Silva 1955).

I argue that the *mahāvrata* and *viṣuvat* originally had the same function as the Durgā festivals, and that they too were celebrated at the autumnal and vernal equinox, respectively. Most scholars have connected the *mahāvrata* with the winter or summer solstice, and indeed in several Vedic texts the *mahāvrata* and the middle day of the year, *viṣuvat*, clearly denote the solstices. However, some facts suggest that, earlier, the *mahāvrata* celebrated the autumnal equinox. For one thing, the Pleiades constitute the first asterism of the oldest *nakṣatra* lists, and hence their conjunction with the full moon marked the beginning of the year, and several of the individual star names of this asterism relate to rain. Secondly, one characteristic action of the *mahāvrata* day is the sounding of different musical instruments (chapter 12), so that "all (manner of) voices (i.e., music) resound" (*sarvā vāco vadanti*, TS 7,5,9,3; PB 5,5,20). According to Taittirīya-Brāhmaṇa 1,8,4,2 this takes place in the rainy season (*prāvṛṣi sarvā vāco vadanti*), and the rainy season lasts from about the middle of July to the middle of September. The Taittirīya-Brāhmaṇa passage speaks of rites connected with the regular plundering tours of the Vedic Kuru and Pañcāla tribes. While the *mahāvrata* concludes the year-long sacrifice, the mid-point of the year is the *viṣuvat* day, and *viṣuvat* or *viṣu* denotes the "vernal equinox" in many Indian languages and is celebrated today as such in many parts of India. Finally, thus the yearly cycle of the sun comes to correspond with the daily cycle (sunrise–noon–sunset : new year at vernal equinox–summer solstice–autumnal equinox, see chapter 16).

The Kālikā-Purāṇa describes the celebration of the *śābarotsava* in chapters 60–61 (in another version 62–63). I quote the text at length to enable comparison with the celebration of the Vrātya rite *mahāvrata* described in chapter 12, with Goddess Vāc as its central divinity, and with the spring festival of Holī celebrating the death and resurrection of the love god Kāma, which in chapter 15 was found to be related to the south Indian buffalo sacrifices:

> 31–32. Afterwards the Goddess was dismissed with Śabara-festivals, on the tenth day . . . 42–43. A king should hold a lustration of the army . . .; a performance must be made with charming women . . . ; 43–48. One should worship the Supporteress of the worlds with dance, song, play, festivity and benediction; with sweetmeat, cakes, drinks, foods . . . with parched grain . . . and various kinds of meat, spiritous liquors . . . with various sorts of wild animals which belong to the class of offerings . . . with flesh, blood . . . 50–52 . . . . The eight beautiful Yoginis . . . are also to be worshipped, and also the sixty-four Yoginīs, and the ten-million Yoginīs; the beautiful nine Durgās, . . . and Jayantī, etc., . . . because they are the Goddess's shapes. 52–53. One should always worship all weapons of the goddess Mahiṣāsuramardinī and in the same way her ornaments . . . ; and also the lion, her mount, with a view to obtaining success. (Translated van Kooij 1972:109–111)

> 17–23. On the tenth day in Śravaṇa one should dismiss her [the Goddess] with Śābara-festivals. . . . People should be engaged in amorous plays with single women, young girls, courtesans and dancers, amidst the sounds of horns and instruments, and with drums and kettle-drums, with flags and various sorts of cloths, covered with a miscellany of parched grain and flowers; by throwing dust and mud; with auspicious ceremonies for fun; by mentioning the female and male organs, with songs on the male and female organs, and with words for the female and male organs, until they have enough of it. If one is not derided by others, if one does deride others, the Goddess will be angry with him and utter a very dreadful curse. (Translated van Kooij 1972:121)

The *śābarotsava* includes feasting with meat of sacrificial victims and with alcohol, obscene abuses, and sexual intercourse. I am convinced that the notorious "circular worship" (*cakra-pūjā*) of left-hand Śākta Tantrism is derived from a military festival such as the *śābarotsava* (see chapter 20). In the *cakra-pūjā*, the goddess in the center of a ritual circle may be represented by a nude virgin surrounded by couples including "heroes" (*vīra*) and their mates, who may belong to any caste or even be their own mothers or daughters: they indulge in eating meat, fish, and cereals, drinking alcohol, and sexual intercourse: these are the famous "five m's" (*pañca makārāḥ*), denoted with five Sanskrit words beginning with *m-* (*madya*, "intoxicant"; *māṃsa*, "flesh"; *matsya*, "fish"; *mudrā*, "seal-impressed wafer"; and *maithuna*, "sexual intercourse"). The Tantric cult also mentions circles with an ithyphallic male god in the center surrounded by "Mothers," such as the harp-playing god Tumburu (identified with Bhairava, Rudra Tryambaka, Śiva, etc.) surrounded by four goddesses connected with "victory" through their names, Jayā, Vijayā, Ajitā, and Aparājitā; the "mothers" work themselves up to the state of the utmost revelry, dancing, singing, laughing, mocking people, drinking, and devouring quantities of raw flesh.

Even the nude virgin of the Śākta Tantric *cakrapūjā* has a counterpart in the Vedic horse sacrifice. When the four wives of the sacrificing king are led to the victim who is being slain, a "virgin" (*kumārī*) follows them as the fifth (ŚB 13,5,2,1). The chief queen lies with the horse in the center, while the other wives and their companions go around them, beating their thighs. The archaic Vādhūla-Śrautasūtra (10,20) details the role of the virgin:

> Then he (the *adhvaryu* priest) gives her (the chief queen, *mahiṣī*) a blade of grass broken at both ends; she wipes with it that (part of her body) where the male member of the stallion was placed. They lead to the place this virgin (*ānayanty etāṃ kumārīm*). . . . She (the queen) should throw that blade of grass upon this girl, saying: "I pierce you with the burning of the sexual union" (*mithunasya tvā śucā vidhyāmīti*). She is called Sāhā ("mighty, vanquishing") and can from now on leap forth into the (men's) hall (*sāhety āhur īśvarā sabhāṃ praskand[it]or*) which according to the commentary means that she becomes a prostitute (*sabhāṃ praveṣṭuṃ samarthā, puṃścalī syād iti matam*).

The prostitute who accompanies the *vrātyas* on their raids and performs the sexual intercourse with a *māgadha* bard or a student (*brahmacārī*) evidently represents goddess Vāc, whose double is goddess Sarasvatī, also called Vāg-īśvarī, the patron goddess of the courtesans and the fine arts in later Hinduism. In Aitareya-Brāhmaṇa 1,27, the goddess Vāc is "a great naked lady" (*mahānagnī*) with whom the gods purchase Soma from the Gandharvas "desirous of women."

The Vedic texts speak of goddess Vāc as an "invincible" goddess of victory associated with the lion. Vāc is represented by the chief wife (*mahiṣī*) of the sacrificing king, and both are identified with the earth (ŚB 6,5,3,1–4; 7,4,2,32–39). The queen (and earth) is fertilized by the male partner in the "sacred marriage" of the horse sacrifice. Thus the sacrificial victim is the "husband" of the goddess Vāc. This is clear also from Śatapatha-Brāhmaṇa 3,2,1,18–26, where the Brahmanical author confesses that originally the goddess Vāc belonged to the Asuras, that is, "demon" worshippers speaking an Indo-Aryan dialect similar to the Māgadhī Prakrit of eastern India; however, Vāc was taken away from them by the gods, that is, Vedic Aryans worshipping Devas. The last section of this passage runs:

> 25. That Yajña (sacrifice) lusted after Vāc (speech), thinking, "May I pair with her!" He united with her. 26. Indra then thought within himself, "Surely a great monster will spring from this union of Yajña and Vāc: (I must take care) lest it should get the better of me." Indra himself then became an embryo and entered into that union. (Translated Eggeling 1885:II,30–32).

This suggests that Indra, the Vedic war god, was afraid of the birth of the war god of the Asura mythology, that is, Rudra, who according to the Aitareya-Brāhmaṇa (3,33) was born at the moment Prajāpati united with Vāc.

In the Purāṇic ritual, the Goddess is offered the sacrificial victim's blood and head immediately after the decapitation. According to Śatapatha-Brāhmaṇa 3,5,1,22–23 and 3,5,2,9ff., Vāc, as the goddess of victory, went over to the side of the gods on the condition that the offering should reach her before it reached the sacrificial fire: therefore they pour ghee on the high altar (*uttaravedi*), which represents Vāc, with the mantra "Thou art a lioness, Hail!" (VS 5,12). Taittirīya-Saṁhitā 6,2,7,3, in dealing with the construction of the *uttara-vedi*, states: "'Thou art a lioness; thou art a buffalo cow' (*simhīr asi mahiṣīr asi*), he says, for it (i.e., the high altar) taking the form of a lioness went away and remained between the two parties." The two parties referred to are those of the gods (*deva*) and the demons (*asura*), who were contending with each other. In Taittirīya-Saṁhitā 6,2,8,1 this is continued: "The high altar said, 'Through me ye shall obtain all your desires'. The gods desired, 'Let us overcome the Asuras our foes.' They sacrificed (with the words), 'Thou art a lioness, overcoming rivals; hail! (*simhīr asi sapatnasāhī svāhā*)' They overcame the Asuras, their foes" (translated Keith 1914:II,509; the two formulae are also given in the mantra collection in TS 1,2,12,2 as *e* and *k*).

The buffalo sacrifice to the Goddess is the cultic counterpart of the Mahiṣāsuramardinī myth, and really central to the Durgā cult. "The sacrifice of the buffalo in India is offered exclusively to the Goddess, either at the feast of her temple in the beginning of the spring, or during the Navarātri," says Madeleine Biardeau (1981:215, translated). In Nepal, the royal cult of the living virginal goddess Kumārī has until quite recently involved the sacrifice of hundreds of water buffaloes. The water buffalo is native to India and was sacrificed in the Indus civilization, while the horse, first imported to South Asia by the Indo-Aryans, was their most prestigious animal. It is understandable that in Vedic India the horse sacrifice came to be the king of the sacrifices.

According to Rigveda 1,162,10–15, the flesh of the sacrificial horse was cooked and roasted, and eaten with great pleasure. But we are surprised to read in RV 6,17,11 that "(Agni) cooked a hundred buffaloes" to Indra; RV 5,29,7–8 states that Agni cooked 300 buffaloes for his friend Indra upon his wish; "and after Indra had eaten the flesh of 300 buffaloes and drunk 3 oceans full of *soma*, all the gods shouted 'Victory!' to him . . . because he had killed Vrtra." In RV 8,12,8 Indra gains his real strength only after he has eaten a thousand buffaloes. Indra's feasting on buffalo meat increased his warring powers: this sacrificial feast was therefore performed just before leaving for a warring expedition. It seems evident that for a short while after their entrance to South Asia, some Rigvedic Aryans adopted the local way of celebrating the military feast.

However, every trace of those enormous buffalo sacrifices to Indra has been wiped out from the Brāhmaṇa texts, and with the sole exception of the subsidiary buffalo sacrifice to Varuṇa in connection with the horse sacrifice, there is no later Vedic buffalo sacrifice. This suggests a deliberate discrimination against the buffalo by the conservative circles of the Vedic priesthood. There is some concrete evidence that sides were taken for and against the horse and the buffalo as sacrificial victims. The Brahmanical discrimination of the buffalo is matched by the express prohibition of ever offering horses to the Goddess in the Kālikā-Purāṇa (71,46), which prescribes (71,57–58) the following mantra to be addressed to the buffalo when it is decapitated: "As you hate a horse and as you carry Caṇḍikā, so kill my enemies and bring happiness, O buffalo ..." (translated Kane 1955:V.1,167).

In the Rigveda, Indra has adopted even other elements of the earlier local religion, among them the magic ability to assume different shapes, including shapes of different animals (usually this *māyā* of the Asuras belongs to Varuṇa). Most significant among Indra's metamorphoses is that referred to in RV 1,121,2b: "as a water buffalo (*mahiṣa*) he desired the lusty female born from himself." This replicates Prajāpati's incestuous approach to his own daughter (AB 3,33) and reveals that early on Prajāpati was conceived to have the shape of a water buffalo.

The Vedic texts prescribe a human sacrifice (*puruṣamedha*), identical with the *aśvamedha*, save the chief victim. This is thought to be theoretical priestly extension, but Vādhūla-Śrautasūtra 11,21 mentions as the carver of the sacrificed horse a virginal youth (*kumāra*), son of a celebrated bard (*sūta*), who was garlanded and lamented as if he were to die, because in former times he himself was to be cut up. This makes a striking parallel with the lamentation of the dying bridegroom of the Goddess in the West Asian mystery cults. This sacrificed youth seems to have personified the divine Kumāra, whose name Rudra the Brāhmaṇa texts connect with the verb *rud-*, "to cry, lament"; originally the name is likely to have been Rudh(i)ra, "red," referring both to the rising sun and to the planet Mars, as do many names of the Old Tamil war god Murugan "youth," such as Cēy, "the red one." The human victim represented the Primeval Man (*puruṣa*) out of whose severed limbs the world came into being according to RV 10,90,6–16. Sacrifice of a human warrior to the Goddess is implied by the Mahiṣa Asura myth, and indeed south Indian heroes are supposed even to have cut off their own heads in order to secure the Goddess's favor and victory to their king. The severed head of a warrior, recognizable from the "double-bun" hair-braid at the nape of the neck (chapter 18), is placed on an offering-table in front of a deity inside a fig tree, whose worship is depicted on a famous Indus seal; one sign of its inscription can be interpreted as the Dravidian name of the *rohiṇī nakṣatra*, the very earliest new-year star connected with the goddess of victory (chapter 21, Fig. 21.9).

20

Early Iranians and "Left-Hand" Tantrism

The previous chapter argued that the Harappans worshipped the earth goddess using symbols, rituals, and conceptions shared with West Asia: the Goddess presides over fertility, death, and war, is represented by a feline, and undergoes a sacred marriage at the new-year festival, involving the death and rebirth of the bridegroom, represented by a bull or some other male, including a human. I also presented Vedic evidence for the continuity of this Harappan Goddess worship in the Vrātya rituals of the Indo-Aryan speakers of the early Atharvavedic wave, coming from the BMAC culture of southern Central Asia around 2000–1700 BCE. A further suggestion of mine is that the Vrātya rituals largely form the basis of the Śākta Tantric worship of the Goddess that begins to emerge in Hindu and Buddhist sources around the middle of the first millennium CE, at the same time as the earliest Purāṇic accounts of the myth of the warrior goddess Durgā and her victory over the buffalo demon.

These texts were written later than the first images of the goddess Mahiṣāsuramardinī, which date from first centuries CE and come from the Kuṣāṇa-dominated region of Mathurā. The Kuṣāṇas conquered Bactria (northern Afghanistan) around 150 BCE and adopted there the local Middle Iranian language called Bactrian for administrative purposes. Their own, little-known language was different, however. The Kuṣāṇas descended from the nomadic tribe called Yuezhi in Chinese sources, whose original homeland was the eastern end of the Takla Makan desert in the Tarim basin of Xinjiang; tribes called Wusun and Hsiungnu pushed them to the steppes of Central Asia, from where they came to Bactria after a few decades. In the late first century BCE the Kuṣāṇas extended their core area to Gandhāra, which extends from the Kabul Valley to the Swat Valley. From this base they ruled the northern plains of South Asia up to Kashmir and the Ganges-Yamuna doab for the first three centuries CE, at times even as far as Magadha. The Kuṣāṇa kings favored Buddhism but also honored Greek and Iranian deities. Their coins were first in Greek and then in Bactrian; Sanskrit was used in inscriptions, but their own texts are written in Greek, in Bactrian, and in an "unknown" script and language in one case (Vima Takhtu in Dasht-e Nawur) (Harry Falk, personal communication 2014).

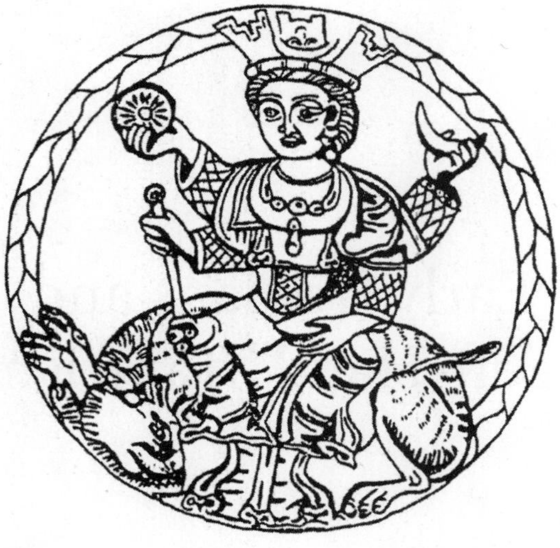

FIGURE 20.1 The goddess Nanaya wearing a mural crown and seated on a feline, holding the sun and the moon in her back pair of hands. A Khwarezmian seventh-century silver bowl in the British Museum, diameter 12.7 cm. After Azarpay 1976:540, fig. 6. Courtesy Guitty Azarpay.

In Afghanistan the Kuṣāṇas adopted, among other local divinities, the goddess called Nana and Nanaya, who is depicted as riding the lion and wearing the mural crown (Fig. 20.1). On the basis of her iconography and name, many scholars have derived Nana from West Asia. A goddess called Na-na-a(-a) is mentioned in cuneiform documents as a goddess whose character is very similar to that of Inanna, being described as follows in cuneiform tablets found in the Temple of Marduk at Babylon: "Lady of ladies, goddess of goddesses, directress of mankind, mistress of the spirits of heaven, possessor of sovereign power; the light of heaven and earth, daughter of the Moon God, ruler of weapons, arbitress of battles; goddess of love; the power over princes and over the sceptre of kings" (translated L. W. King quoted in Rosenfield 1967:85).

Nana first appears in the Mesopotamian lists of gods in the Ur III period (*c.* 2100–2000 BCE), classified in the same section as Inanna. Daniel Potts (2001) plausibly suggests that Nana came to Bactria with the lapis lazuli trade by the end of the third millennium BCE, probably via Susa, where this goddess apparently had a temple around 2300 BCE and where her worship continued until Hellenistic times. Besides, many BMAC objects have been found at Susa. BMAC seals from Afghanistan with a winged goddess escorted by lions very probably depict Nana, nearly two millennia before the Kuṣāṇas (Fig. 20.2).

Almost two millennia after the Kuṣāṇas, local people worship "Bībī Nānī" at Hinglāj, in Las Bela district of Baluchistan. The name comes from Sanskrit *hiṅgulāja*, "vermilion, cinnabar," the red paste applied on the body and on images by Hindus. Hinglāj is the westernmost of the Śākta *pīṭhas*, famous temples of the Hindu Goddess, where she is worshipped as the feline-faced manifestation of Durgā, known as Carcā or Carcikā, a name that might derive from Proto-Dravidian **caṟ-*, "tear, rend, cut with teeth." The Kuṣāṇas seem to have taken the worship of Nana to the Kulu Valley in Himachal Pradesh and to Nainital in the Kumaon foothills of Uttarakhand: both places have a famous temple of Goddess Nainā.

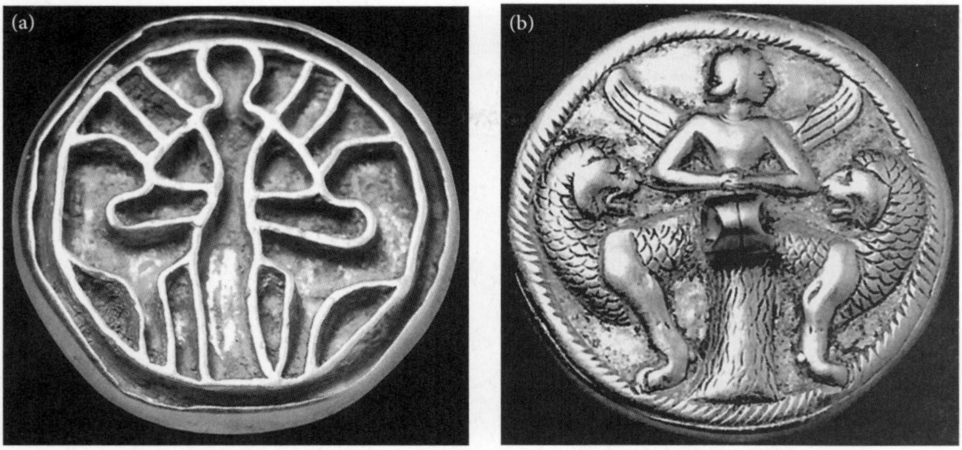

FIGURE 20.2 A lion-escorted and winged goddess with a Mesopotamian-type *kaunakes* skirt on a compartmented BMAC seal made of gold, *c.* 1900 BCE. (a) The compartmented stamp side on the obverse. (b) The reverse. After Ligabue & Salvatori [1989]:202, pl. 58–59. Courtesy Centro Studi Ricerche Ligabue, Venice.

Nana's mural crown connects her with Kybele and Mesopotamian Ištar, known at Mari in Syria as "mistress of the city wall." Durgā's name is supposed to come from the name of a demon slain by her called Durga; the texts call her *durga-ghnā*, "remover of adversity or danger." As an adjective, *dur-ga-* means "difficult to go to, unapproachable," and as a noun "inaccessible place, stronghold, citadel, fortress" (as first attested in Rigveda 5,34,7), as well as "adversity, danger." "Fortress" seems the preferable meaning because Durgā's manifestations have several other names associated with "fortress."

Most notable among Durgā's "fortress" names is Tripurā, "goddess of the triple fort," or Tripura-Sundarī, "the beauty of Tripura." Hindu mythology understands Tripura as "three cities" of the *asuras* (demons) vanquished by Śiva, but the concept seems to go back to the BMAC "temple-forts" such as that of Dashly-3 in northern Afghanistan, from around 1900 BCE, with three concentric circular walls within a square fort surrounded by a moat (Fig. 20.3a). The tradition of building such temple-forts continued in Afghanistan until Achaemenid times (Fig. 20.3b), thus embracing the time when the Rigvedic Aryans had confrontations with the Dāsas. In his study of the Rigvedic passages mentioning Dāsa citadels (*pur-*), Wilhelm Rau concluded that "the evidence does not fit the cities of the Indus civilization. It rather suggests the existence of numerous, frequently concentric, mud or stone ramparts of round or oval ground plan" (Rau 1976:52). This type of fort seems to have come to the BMAC from the Sintashta culture of southern Urals, which had fortified settlements with concentric circular walls (see Fig. 7.4 and chapters 7 and 8).

The Dāsa fortresses are several times described as "autumnal" in the Rigveda (RV 1,131,4b and 1,174,2b = 6,20,10c *puraḥ . . . śāradīḥ*). The exact meaning of this epithet has remained unclear. My own suggestion is that the fortresses were venues for the Goddess's autumn festival. In Kashmir, Durgā is for this very reason called Śāradā ("autumnal"), and

(a)

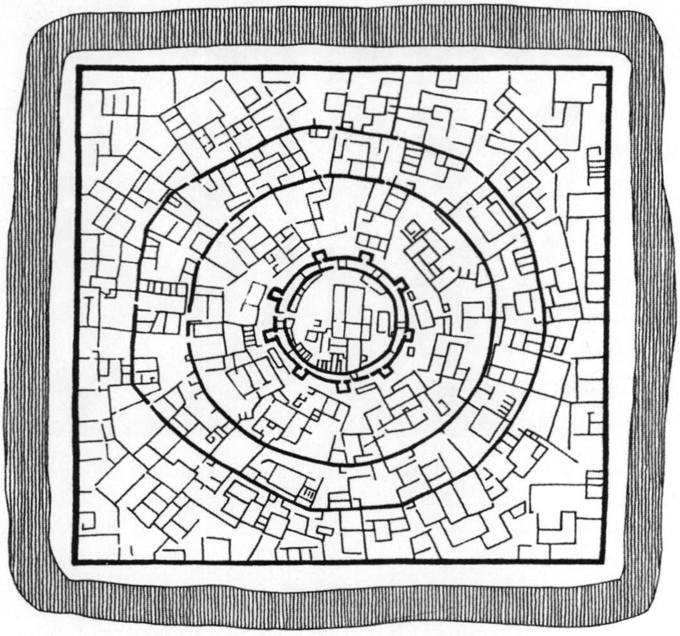

(b)

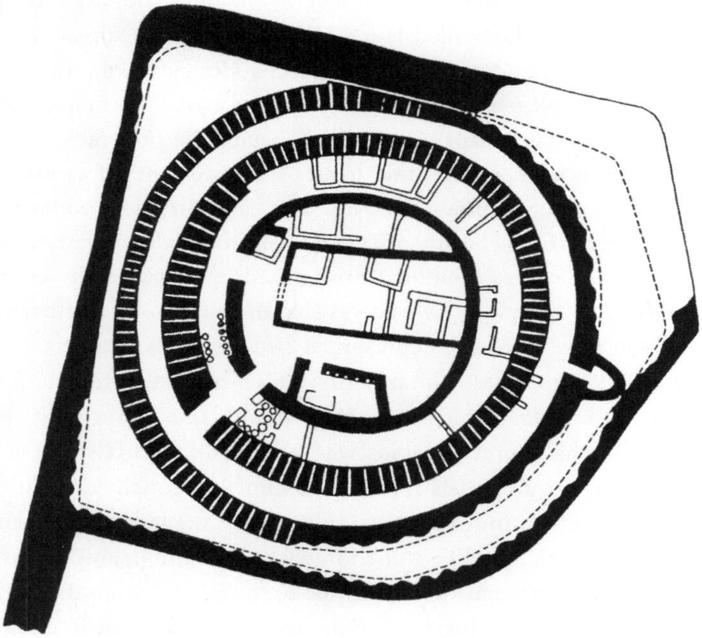

FIGURE 20.3 Fortress with triple concentric walls in Afghanistan. (a) The BMAC "temple-fortress" of Dashly-3 in Bactria, northern Afghanistan, *c.* 1900 BCE. After Sarianidi 1986:59. Courtesy Margiana Archaeological Expedition. (b) The fortress of Kutlug Depe, Achaemenid period (559–330 BCE). After Sarianidi 1986:73. Courtesy Margiana Archaeological Expedition.

one of the principal sites of her worship is a fortified place called Śār(a)dī. In present-day Nepal, where the Goddess is the guardian of the country, the *navarātri* festival is always celebrated in a fortress.

The historical connection of the BMAC *tripura* with later Tantrism is strongly endorsed by the layout of the "palace" of Dashly-3 (Fig. 20.4). This is practically identical with the later Tantric *maṇḍala* in its square form that represents the king's palace or fortified city with a T-shaped gate in the middle of each side. It symbolizes the residence of the supreme ruler of the whole world extending to all four directions. This cosmogram, centered on an image of the divinity, has been widely used as a means of worship and reintegration (Fig. 20.5). It must have been transmitted through the centuries in the form of ephemeral *maṇḍala* paintings made with colored powders for ritual purposes. Ritual powder paintings are found all over South Asia and spread from there to Tibet. In historical times this particular *maṇḍala* cosmogram first reappears in the so-called "TLV-mirrors" of Han-dynasty China (*c.* 200 BCE), which, with their T-, L-, and V-shaped projections, replicate even more closely the Dashly-3 "palace" with its external corridors.

The autumnal worship of the Goddess culminates on the final (tenth) day of the "festival of Śabaras." Since the 1920s, *śabara-* has been connected with Śambara, the proper name of one of the principal Dāsas, whose fortifications were broken by Indra, as mentioned in the Rigveda (chapter 9). Both words have generally been considered to be of non-Aryan, probably Austro-Asiatic, origin, mainly because the ethnic name Sora or Saora of an Austro-Asiatic speaking tribe in Orissa derives from Sanskrit *śabara*. It is true that Śabara, when first attested (in AB 7,18), is the name of one of the Dasyu tribes (along with Andhra, Puṇḍra, Pulinda, and Mūtiba) who live beyond the eastern borders of the Vedic realm. However, determining the ethnic affinity of the people called Śabara in Vedic times from the fact that Austro-Asiatic speakers are called Sora or Saora today, is tantamount to claiming that the Mleccha people, who likewise were met by the Vedic Aryans on their eastern border, were Muslims because the Muslims were later called Mleccha. Yet the Śatapatha-Brāhmaṇa (3,2,1,18–24) makes it plain that those early Mlecchas spoke an Indo-Aryan language sharing characteristics with the later Māgadhī Prakrit of eastern India. It is significant that people called Śabara were labeled Dasyu (which is another appellation of the Dāsas in the Rigveda), and that they were encountered by the Vedic Aryans in eastern India; the Mleccha parallel suggests that they were Aryan speakers.

Śambara as an enemy of Indra is also known from the Mahābhārata, and as the name of a fierce Tantric Buddhist deity, derived from the Indian Śaiva Tantric tradition. In both cases the name Śambara has a variant form Saṃvara, which allows a good Aryan etymology, suggesting a Māgadhī-like sound change *s* > *ś*. The first part is the prefix *sam-*, "together, fully, completely," often appearing in the reduced grade **sṃ-* > *sa-*; the second part, *vara-* means "enclosing, protecting" as well has "obstructing, hindering" (in RV 1,143,5, with reference to an enemy army), from the root *var-*, "to surround, enclose, protect, ward off." In the neuter gender, *śambara-* is used to mean "wall, rampart, fortification." In this sense Sanskrit *śambara-/saṃ-vara-* and *(saṃ-)varaṇa-* correspond to Avestan *vara-*, "fortress," which is the word used to describe the castle built by Yima, the primeval king of the Iranian tradition. That *vara-* also existed in the Iranian Saka language spoken on the Eurasiatic steppes can

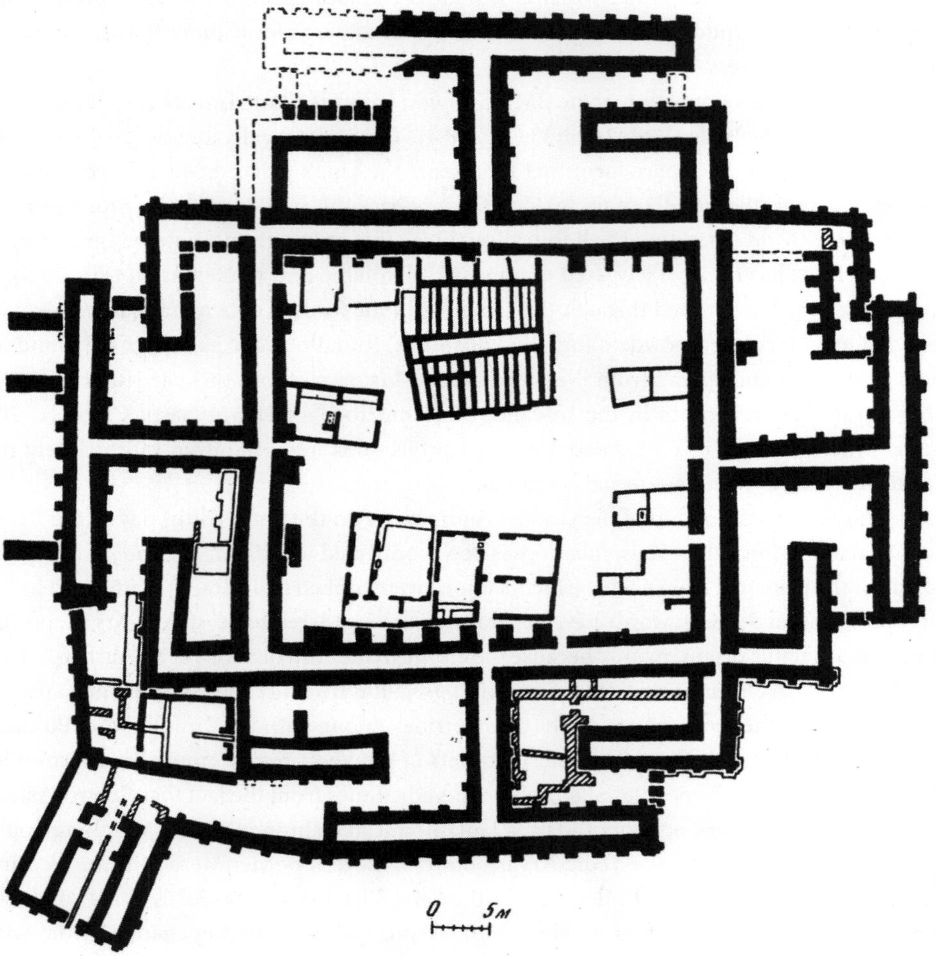

FIGURE 20.4 The ground plan of the BMAC "palace" of Dashly-3 in north Afghanistan, *c.* 1900 BCE. After Sarianidi 1986:53. Courtesy Margiana Archaeological Expedition.

be seen from its borrowing into Hungarian, where *var* means "fort, citadel." Dāsa Śambara seems to have been the Dāsa counterpart of Indra as the god of war, close to the Avestan deity of war *Ham-varti-*, personification of "manly courage."

This conclusion warrants a more general consideration of the Dāsas and their proposed connection with eastern India. It is very likely that when Old Iranian (Saka)-speaking Dāsas entered Afghanistan around 1500 BCE, as suggested in chapter 9, they also entered the northern plains of South Asia, like the Kuṣāṇas and Mughals long after them. This is suggested also by the presence of tribal names cognate with Dasa/Dāsa, known from the Upper Indus Valley (Sanskrit *dāsamīya* and *dāśamīya*, "non-Brahmanical tribe"), the western Indus Valley (Lahnda *ḏahā*, "a tribe of Jaṭs," *ḏāhrā*, "a division of the Kerār tribe"), Sindh (Sindhi *ḏāharī*

FIGURE 20.5 The Hindu Tantric *maṇḍala* of Mahā-Kālī, the triangle in the center symbolizing the female organ. After Preston 1980:65, fig. 2. Courtesy James Preston.

and *ḏāhirī*, "name of a Sindhi tribe"), and Marwar (Sanskrit *daśeraka* and *dāśeraka*, "name of the people of Maru"; cf. *Dāseraka*, "name of a people"). The alternation of the dental and palatal sibilant in the above tribal names is attested in the name Dāsa- itself: besides Rigvedic *dāsa-*, "name of enemy people" and "slave," there is *dāśa-*, "name of a mixed caste" (Manu) and "servant" (VS 30,16). In the meaning "son of a slave girl, bastard," we have in Sanskrit also both *dāsera-* and *dāśera-*, and *dāseya-* and *dāśeya-*.

The sound change *s* > *ś* (which may be due to Dravidian substratum influence) characterized the late Prakrit of northern Sindh called Vrācaḍa (this name is derived from the Sanskrit word *vrātya-*) as well as the Gāndhārī and Māgadhī Prakrits. Gāndhārī (spoken in Gandhāra) and Māgadhī (spoken in Magadha in eastern India) have also some other features in common, notably the change **az* > *e* (instead of **az* > *o* in Sanskrit), which is attested once in the Rigveda. The testimonies of the Dāsa language in the Rigveda are very scarce, and it therefore seems significant that three features connect it with Māgadhī: *s* > *ś*, *v* > *b*, and the presence of the phoneme *l* (which in Proto-Rigvedic and Avestan was replaced by *r*). This suggests considerable Dāsa influence upon the earliest Indo-Aryan-speaking immigrants in eastern India, who may be connected with the Ochre Coloured Pottery (OCP) or Copper Hoards culture of the Upper Ganges Valley in the early second millennium BCE (chapter 8).

Śākta Tantrism has been particularly strong in eastern India, and it may have been taken there by Harappan and early Indo-Aryan immigrants. In the Vedic realm the Vrātya religion was more or less extinguished by orthodox Brahmins. The Brahmins of the "Aryan Midland" were horrified by the "immoral" customs in marginal areas, such as Gandhāra and the western Punjab: their festivals resembling the *śābarotsava* are described with strong disapproval in the eighth book of the Mahābhārata.

The name Śambara/Saṃvara of the Tantric deity thus seems to be an Iranian (Dāsa) contribution to Goddess worship in South Asia. He is often called Cakra-Saṃvara from the fact that his square *maṇḍala* contains three concentric circles (*cakra*) (Fig. 20.6). This replicates the Dashly-3 type *tripura*, "triple fort" (Fig. 20.3a), which, as argued above, also seems to be a Dāsa import, reinforcing Śambara's suggested origin. This terrifying Tantric god has come to Buddhism from the Śaiva circles, in particular from the "skull-bearing" Kāpālika

FIGURE 20.6 The Tantric *maṇḍala* of the four-faced and twelve-armed god Śambara embraced by his consort Vajra-Varāhī and surrounded in the four directions by four other fierce goddesses. After Raghu Vira and Lokesh Chandra 1995: fig. 65. Courtesy Prof. Lokesh Chandra.

sect notorious for its antinomian practices. A Mahiṣa-Saṃvara is worshipped in Nepal, and Śambara is identified with the fierce god Heruka, whose name may come from the Proto-Dravidian word **ēṟu*, "bull, male of any animal remarkable for its physical strength, male buffalo"—in several Sanskrit loanwords from Dravidian the initial *h-* represents the glottal stop that in Central and North Dravidian reinforces a word-initial vowel. (The same phenomenon is found in Hindi: I have heard a Hindi speaker pronouncing English "empty" as *hempty*.) Some Tantric texts speak of *herukas* as demonical beings, who according to Tibetan and Chinese commentaries are "blood drinkers."

The Tantric skull cult, at least the use of the skull as a drinking bowl for wine and blood, may be a contribution of the Iranian Dāsas. The word used for "skull-cup" in Tantric and Purāṇic texts is Sanskrit *kapāla-*, attested in the meaning "skull" in the Atharvaveda, and cognate with Middle and Modern Persian *kabāra, kabārag*, "bowl"; it is suspected to come from the lost original language of the BMAC. The Vedic Hiraṇyakeśi-Gṛhyasūtra (2,3,7) speaks of demons "drinking out of skulls" (*kapāla-pa-*).

According to Herodotus (4,64), the Scythian warrior always cut off the heads of the enemies he had slain and carried them to his king, because the heads alone entitled him to a share of the booty. His esteem also depended upon the number of enemies he had killed, and this he exhibited by hanging their scalps from his bridle-rein, or making himself a cloak by sewing many scalps together. Others covered their quivers with the skin flayed from the right arm of the enemy. Herodotus devotes a full chapter (4,65) to describing how the Scythians made enemy skulls into drinking cups, which were handed around when they had any worthy visitors, the host telling its story. Moreover, once a year the ruler of each district

> mingles a bowl of wine, of which all Scythians have a right to drink by whom foes have been slain; while they who have slain no enemy are not allowed to taste of the bowl, but sit aloof in disgrace. No greater shame than this can happen to them. Such as have slain a very large number of foes, have two cups instead of one, and drink from both. (Herodotus 4,66; translated Rawlinson [1860] 1942:316)

The Nuristani languages of northeastern Afghanistan seem to represent the mixed Iranian and Indo-Aryan language spoken by a group of people who very early departed from the mainstream and migrated into those valleys where they have in relative isolation preserved some very archaic linguistic and cultural features. Thus the depalatalized affricates reconstructed for the Iranian protolanguage are attested in appropriate words only in Nuristani languages (chapter 9), while some other linguistic features connect these languages with early Indo-Aryan. The former "Kāfir" (pagan) religion of the Nuristani speakers is likely to have preserved elements that may go back to around the middle second millennium BCE, as do those aspects of the Dāsa religion that we may understand from the scanty Rigvedic references.

Among the Ashkun Kāfirs (on the upper reaches of the Alingar River), a man was worth nothing until he had killed an enemy. The more people he had killed, the higher his rank, which was exhibited by various symbols. Specific titles were earned after four, eight, and twelve kills, as were garments of honor with embroidered ornamentation and bells hanging from the belt and trousers, and so on. A man with four kills was allowed to erect in the main gathering place of the village a post in which each kill was recorded with a willow twig put through a hole, the top being decorated with a red cloth. This social ranking system led to regular head-hunting expeditions; the trophies, especially severed heads, scalps, or ears, were brought back to the village in a triumphal procession and exhibited during the victory feast.

We have an eyewitness account of how the Kāfirs celebrated immediately before leaving for a war expedition:

> [feasting and dancing is] kept up with great spirit, until about midnight, when on a given signal, the lights are suddenly extinguished; the men rush on the women; and each man seizes the hand of the nearest female, or one whom he may have selected beforehand, if he can manage to approach her in the scuffle which now ensues. He then takes her away to some private place and retains her until the morning. On these occasions it makes very little difference who the fair one is, whether his own wife or that of another—his own daughter or sister or another's. (Raverty 1859:353–354)

Sexual promiscuity ensured that as many women of the tribe as possible became pregnant, so that the tribe produced new men, in case all the elders should perish on the war path. This should be how the Tantric *cakrapūjā* discussed in chapter 19 originated.

The most important Kāfir goddess, Disani, resembles the Hindu Durgā, for she is also "known to excite sexual desire, the prerequisite of procreation. . . . Disani is at the same time a deity of death . . . who takes the deceased home into the house of the Great Mother . . . the women pray to her when they fear for the lives of their men who participate in a war-party. . . . She is armed when in human form, and allegedly carries a bow and quiver. In another story, she kills with a dagger" (Jettmar 1986:69–70).

Georg Morgenstierne (1953:164) has suggested that Disani's name might be etymologically related to that of the obscure Vedic goddess Dhiṣaṇā, but the origin and exact meaning of both words are debated. I propose connecting Dizani—the form of the more archaic Kāmdeshi and Urtsun dialects of Kati—with Old Persian *didā-* from earlier **dizā-*, "wall, palisade, fortress," Bactrian *dizā*, "fortress," and Middle and Modern Persian *diz*, "fortress," with cognates in Sanskrit *dehī-*, "wall" (in RV 6,47,2 used of Śambara's walls), and Greek *teîkhos*, "wall."

This etymology agrees with that proposed above for Durgā's name. In a Kati song Disani is actually said to have made a four-cornered golden fortress (*kuṭ*) with seven doors. According to the Prasun Kāfirs, again, goddess Disani constructed a tower from which seven lanes lead outwards. The seven gates in Disani's fortress can be compared to Indra's seven daughters, including Disani in Ashkun Kāfir mythology. Other Kāfirs worshipped seven daughters of the highest god Imra (whose name comes from Yama-rāja), alias Māra (see chapter 12); Disani was born out of the creator god Imra's breast and was the wife of Gish, the fierce god of war. The seven daughters of Kāfir Māra compare with the daughters of Māra, the god of death, who tempted the Buddha on the verge of his enlightenment. In Hinduism they have a counterpart in the "Seven Mothers" of the Hindu war god Skanda, who follow him on war expeditions; these represent the stars of the Pleiades, mythically the wives of the Seven Sages (chapter 16).

Disani is also said to assume the appearance of a markhor goat. The markhor is prominently depicted on Indus seals, and the Harappan goddess of war with tiger vehicle on the Kalibangan cylinder seal wears the horns of a markhor goat (Fig. 19.5). The important "fig deity" seal from Mohenjo-daro shows a human-faced markhor behind the priest(ess?) who kneels and raises hands in prayer to the deity (probably a predecessor of Durgā) inside a fig tree, while a warrior's severed head has been placed upon an altar table (Fig. 21.9).

On the basis of the cognates in (Nuristani) Kati, in the Dardic languages of the northwest and in Sindhi, I have suggested that *śarabha* originally denoted "markhor" (*Capra falconeri*), the wild goat of the northwestern mountains. In the Vedic texts discussed in chapter 19, *śarabha* is the wild counterpart of the domestic goat. The meaning "markhor" also fits verse 54 of Kālidāsa's Meghadūta, where *śarabha* is a proud animal of the Himalayas, jumping high into the air at the risk of breaking its limbs. Elsewhere in classical Sanskrit literature *śarabha* denotes "a fabulous kind of deer with eight legs, which was supposed to kill elephants and lions." Most Sanskrit speakers presumably never set eyes on a real markhor because they lived in areas outside the animal's geographical range. Cognates of Sanskrit *śarabha* have survived also in the Neo-Indo-Aryan languages of the north (Kashmiri, Panjabi, Pahari, Kumaoni, Nepali, and dialects of Hindi) as well as in the Sinhalese, but in these words the meaning has mutated into another jumping creature, a locust or grasshopper (Turner 1966:714–715). And yet the Kālikā-Purāṇa, written as far east as Assam around 1000 CE, places the *śarabha* on the same level as the water buffalo in its list of sacrificial victims to the Goddess, second only to man, as we saw in chapter 19.

In this chapter I have argued among other things that a goddess related to Hindu Durgā was worshipped in Afghanistan from at least as early as 2000 BCE, then by the Iranian-speaking Dāsas who arrived there around 1500 BCE, and then again by the Iranian-speaking Kuṣāṇas who arrived more than a thousand years later. The Iranians seem to have contributed to the Goddess worship of South Asia by introducing generally abhorrent practices that nevertheless make sense in a military context: sexual promiscuity before a war expedition, head-hunting, and use of skulls as bowls for drinking wine and blood. However, similarly gory and revolting elements characteristic of "left-hand" Tantrism undoubtedly existed in South Asia even before it received this Iranian reinforcement. The West Asian cults of goddesses of war and fertility, such as Inanna-Ištar, are full of cruelty and sexuality, which seems to be replicated in Harappan art. Old Tamil poems, too, describe bloody sacrifices to the goddess of war on the battlefield, and amorous pleasures of warriors returning from their victorious expeditions.

21

Religion in the Indus Script

The iconography of Harappan seals and molded and engraved tablets, motifs of painted pottery, terracotta figurines, stone sculptures, buildings, and city planning are important sources of Harappan religion. The foregoing chapters have endeavored to interpret their imagery with the help of better-documented parallels, especially in South Asia and West Asia, connected with the Indus civilization by cultural continuity and trade relations. Yet to be considered are the signs of the Indus script. Though an undeciphered system of writing, it is uniquely important in having the potential to tell us the actual names used by the Harappans of their gods, and thus to verify assumptions regarding cultural continuity with later times and religions. For, in the other earliest civilizations, writing served religion and administration, and names of gods were often mentioned, whether independently or as components of human proper names.

The decipherment of a logosyllabic script without bilinguals presents a tougher challenge than that of a syllabic or alphabetic script. Syllabaries and alphabets form closed systems that include the entire phonology of a language; in favorable circumstances they can be fully deciphered with the help of just a few external phonetic clues. Logosyllabic scripts have many more signs and variables than syllabaries and alphabets; the phonetic links between their signs are weaker. With minimal marking of grammatical forms, and a presumably more complex syllabic structure, logosyllabic scripts offer no opportunity to build phonetic "grids" of the kind utilized in the decipherment of the Linear B. In that case, sign groups that were likely to be proper nouns with three different case endings were identified from their context in Linear B tablets, and the signs of these hypothesized case endings, probably standing for open syllables, were tabulated according to their shared consonants or vowels in rows and columns (the grid). The proper nouns were then guessed to be the names of Cretan towns, such as Knossos (*ko-no-so*), which provided the initial syllabic values from which other syllabic values and readings could be deduced and applied to wholly unfamiliar sign groups. (One Indus script sign occurs in eleven out of the seventy-four inscriptions excavated at Chanhu-daro, but nowhere else, five times alone forming a second line. It may therefore express the Harappan name of the town. For an interpretation connecting it with the town of Pātāla, which according to Hellenistic sources stood near the Indus estuary, see Parpola 1975b; 2003:558; Parpola & Janhunen 2011:84–90.)

On the assumption that the Indus script is logosyllabic, a complete phonetic decipherment is certainly not possible with the presently available inscriptions. We can hope to decipher only a few Indus signs by assuming that the underlying language is Proto-Dravidian. But to reach even this limited goal we need valid methods.

Most early script signs were originally pictures denoting the objects or ideas they represented. But while this representation works well enough for concepts such as "tree" or "eat," abstract concepts such as "life" are more difficult to express pictorially. These were expressed by extending the meaning ascribed to a pictogram or ideogram from the word for the depicted object to comprise all the word's homophones, that is, words having a similar phonetic shape but a different meaning. Thus the English phrase, "to be or not to be," might be written using the following pictograms: 2 bee oar knot 2 bee. This phonetic functioning of pictograms in early logosyllabic scripts is called a *rebus* (Latin, "by means of things").

Ideally, the homophony in such punning should be exact. However, there are too few exact homophones in any language to yield an effective writing system. So, if we were to write English in rebus form, a picture of a "sun" might conceivably be used to represent the concept "son," a near-homophone of "sun." In the Egyptian and Semitic writing systems, vowel differences are not written, making near-homophony easier to use. But this is not so in Dravidian scripts, which do write vowels. In deciphering the Indus script we should therefore demand near-exact consonant and vowel homophony, generally allowing only those differences that occur commonly within Dravidian etyma, such as a difference in the length of a given consonant or vowel, for example, *kaṇ* and *kaṇṇu*, "eye," and *kāṇ*, "to see."

In the Sumerian script, the problem of representing "life" was solved by drawing a picture of an arrow. This sign denotes not only "arrow" but also "life" and "rib," because the same sound, *ti*, has three different, homophonous, meanings in the Sumerian language. Puns such as this must surely have been employed in oral folklore long before they appeared in Sumerian writing. But because they are language-specific, their point is lost when they are translated into another language. The biblical myth of Eve's creation out of Adam's "rib" makes sense only in the light of its Sumerian origin. In the Sumerian paradise myth, the rib of the sick and dying water god Enki is healed by the goddess Nin-ti, the "Mistress of life." The punning connection in Sumerian between *ti* ("rib") and *ti* ("life") does not exist in Hebrew between *ṣelāᶜ* ("rib") and Eve's name *Ḥawwā* (although the latter word is still connected with the concept of "life," according to Genesis 3,20: "Adam called his wife's name Eve; because she was the mother of all living.").

This means that rebuses may help to identify the language underlying a script and to decipher some signs of it, if we can guess the meaning of a sign from its pictorial form and/or its context. But its pictorial meaning may not always coincide with its contextual meaning. Yet, even if the pictorial and contextual meanings differ, they may still be connected by homophony. If the pictorial and contextual meanings of a particular sign can be independently determined, and turn out to be the same, the coincidence strengthens the assumed shared meaning, though without yielding a phonetic reading.

FIGURE 21.1 The U-shaped sign in an Indus inscription and a kneeling worshipper extending a U-shaped vessel toward a sacred tree. Obverse of a molded tablet M-478 (DK 10237, IM 10387) from Mohenjo-daro. After CISI 3.1:403. Photo EL, courtesy Indian Museum, Kolkata.

As an example, consider an Indus text on a tablet from Mohenjo-daro (Fig. 21.1). It shows the common U- or V-shaped sign, in the middle of the inscription and near the right-hand end. In the first occurrence, the sign's pictorial meaning might include a pot or vessel, though other interpretations are certainly possible. But in the second occurrence, a kneeling human figure holds the very same U- or V-shaped sign in its hands and offers it to a sacred tree—an iconographic motif. From this contextual meaning, it appears that the sign must represent an offering vessel. The contextual meaning of the sign supports its pictorial meaning, without any postulation of an underlying language. Nonetheless, without postulating a language, we have no idea of the word for "offering vessel" in the Indus language, nor of the phonetic value of the sign in the first occurrence.

A phonetic decipherment of a logosyllabic script demands that four conditions are simultaneously fulfilled:

(1) the object depicted in a pictogram can be recognized;
(2) the pictogram has been used as a rebus in a particular context;
(3) the contextual meaning of the rebus can be deduced;
(4) a linguistically satisfactory homophony between these two meanings exists in a historically likely language.

Deduction can begin at any stage; it does not have to follow the order 1, 2, 3, 4.

Unfortunately, the pictorial meaning of most Indus signs is not clear, or at least not unambiguous. Furthermore, it is not always possible to identify every instance of a particular sign, because sometimes it may have been simplified. In most scripts, including the Egyptian hieroglyphic and Mesopotamian cuneiform scripts, the demand for fluency led to a radical simplification of sign shapes. This variation in the graphemic shape of a sign is important, for some variants (known as allographs) may render the pictorial meaning better than others; also, the proposed pictorial interpretation should fit all of the allographs.

Another kind of contextual clue comes from the function of inscribed artifacts. The vast majority of Indus texts are seal stamps and seal impressions in clay. In the warehouse of the Harappan harbor town at Lothal, which burned down, nearly one hundred clay tags

(a)

(b)

FIGURE 21.2 A clay tag from Umma, Mesopotamia, in the Department of the Ancient Near East (1931.120), Ashmolean Museum, Oxford. (a) The obverse with impression of a square Indus seal. (b) The reverse with a textile impression. After Parpola 1994:113, fig. 7.16. Photo courtesy Ashmolean Museum, Oxford.

carrying seal impressions were baked in the fire and have therefore survived. The tags were once attached to bales of goods, for there are traces of cloth, strings, and other packing material on the reverse of the impressions. The Harappans must have used these seals to control commercial transactions, to prevent their merchandise from being tampered with. Some of the clay tags carry seal impressions made with different seals, indicating the need for several witnesses.

A clay tag found in Mesopotamia is stamped with a normal Indus-type square seal bearing the script and the "unicorn" motif on the obverse and a cloth impression on the reverse (Fig. 21.2). This usage ties in with similar usage of seals among the Sumerians and Akkadians. The inscriptions on such Sumerian and Akkadian seals comprise chiefly the proper names of persons, with or without their occupational or official titles and descent (Edzard 1968). The Harappans' long-time presence in West Asia makes it highly probable that the same content may be expected in the Indus seal inscriptions, whether they are found in Mesopotamia or in the Indus Valley.

In Mesopotamian and classical Indian onomastics, the names of gods were used to form personal names. We can therefore expect to have theophoric components in both proper names and priestly titles in some fairly large and uniformly distributed sign groups in the Indus seals. Might this practice apply to the "fish" sign, both in its plain form and when it is modified with various diacritical additions, which occurs so frequently on Indus seals that almost every tenth sign is either a plain "fish" or a modified "fish" (Fig. 21.3)?

That the Indus pictograms looking like fish really do have this pictorial meaning is supported by some Indus iconography, in which the pictogram is placed in the mouth of a fish-eating crocodile (Fig. 15.5). Harappans may have offered fish to sacred crocodiles, as people have done at the Magar Talão or "Crocodile Pool" near Karachi until recently, despite the millennial presence of Islam in the Indus Valley. That fish indeed were offered, either to sacred crocodiles or to sacred trees, as in later Hinduism, and that the "fish" sign in some contexts means "fish," is suggested by some Indus tablets (not seals) that seem to mention offerings of "four pots of fish" or "four fish-pots" (Fig. 21.4). Here the simple "fish" occurs before or after the U- or V-shaped sign, while the three-sign text begins with number 4, represented by four vertical strokes. The addition of the fish sign in these tablets is exceptional. The U- or V-shaped sign occupies the reverse side of most of such tablets either alone or preceded by just one, two, three, or four vertical strokes representing the numbers 1, 2, 3, and 4 (in some rare cases there are no strokes but the U sign is repeated: UUU, "three pots"). Occasionally in such a context, the U sign is placed in the hand or hands of an adjacent sign depicting a man, either standing or kneeling. This connects the U sign with the previously discussed iconographic scene in which the U sign is extended toward to a sacred tree by a kneeling worshipper (Fig. 21.1). The occasional addition of the "worshipper" suggests that on these tablets the U signs stand for pots of offerings.

In contemporary Mesopotamia fish offerings were made in temples. Yet, although Mesopotamian administrative texts in cuneiform tablets often record rations of fish, fish are *never* mentioned in Mesopotamian seal inscriptions. This is not surprising, if the seals contained chiefly proper names. Assuming that the Indus Valley followed Mesopotamian

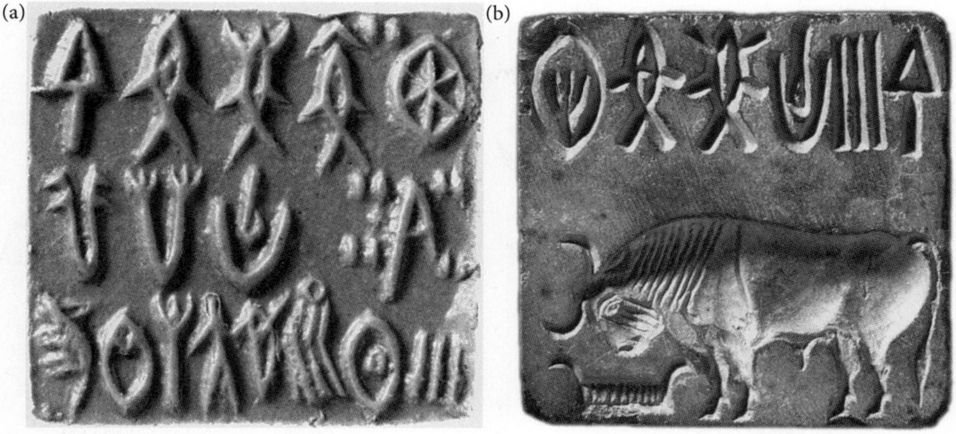

FIGURE 21.3 Two Indus seals with fish signs from Mohenjo-daro. (a) Impression of the seal M-314 (HR 3005, ASI 63.10.366) with the longest Indus text on one side of an object. After CISI 1:78. Photo EL, courtesy ASI. (b) The seal stamp M-236 (DK 10965, NMI 103) in the collection of the National Museum of India, New Delhi. After CISI 3.1:371. Photo EL, courtesy NMI.

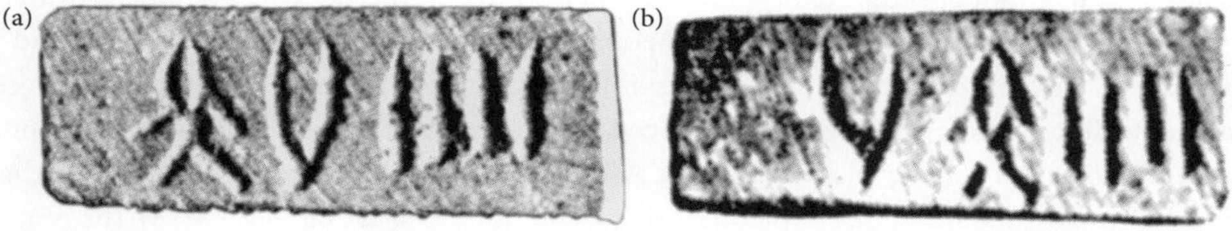

FIGURE 21.4 Reverse sides of two incised tablets from Harappa, probably meaning: (a) "Four pots of fish" (H-1191), and (b) "Four fish-pots" (H-1192). After CISI 3.1:164. Photo Punjab 41:4395, courtesy ASI.

practice, it is likely that in the Indus seal inscriptions the fish sign denotes something other than fish and may be used as a rebus.

The most commonly used word for "fish" in more than one subgroup of the Dravidian languages is **mīn*. A homophonous word means "star." Both meanings, fish and star, are likely to derive from the verb root **min*, "to sparkle, to glitter," which can be reconstructed for Proto-Dravidian. It is known that Old Tamil speakers imagined the stars to be fish swimming in the ocean of the night sky. Might the "fish" sign in the Indus seals denote "star," rather than "fish"? Two pieces of evidence independent of the Dravidian hypothesis support this proposal. An artistic motif showing fishes with stars occurs on Mature Harappan painted pottery (Fig. 21.5). Moreover, the "star" symbol appears alone on Early Harappan pottery. Secondly, there is no "star" pictogram in the signs of the Indus script (although stars do appear as iconographic motifs on Indus seals); this is understandable, following the principle of parsimony, if the "fish" sign could also denote "star." The meaning "star" suits the expected role of the "fish" signs as a component of theophoric proper names in seal inscriptions.

In Mesopotamian inscriptions, by contrast, the pictogram showing a star is easily recognizable. Indeed, whenever a god or goddess is mentioned in cuneiform texts, the

FIGURE 21.5 The "fish" and "star" motifs combined on Indus pottery from Amri. After Casal 1964:II, fig. 92 no. 487 and fig. 78 no. 343. Courtesy Mission Archéologique de l'Indus, CNRS/Musée Guimet, Paris.

"star" pictogram is prefixed to the name as its determinative, so as to indicate that what follows is divine. In the Sumerian script, the "star" pictogram denotes not only "god" but also "sky." It is thought to have originated as an attribute of the sky god An. Since An was the leading divinity of the Sumerian pantheon, his symbol would have come to mean "god" in general. Astronomy, including the use of a star calendar, played an important role in ancient Mesopotamia, and deeply influenced its religion: all the main gods were symbolized by particular stars or planets. In West Asia, one or two "star" symbols placed near the head distinguished divinities in pictorial representations (Fig. 21.6a; Fig. 18.13) The practice seems to have been borrowed by the Indus civilization, for a seal from Mohenjo-daro depicts an Indus deity with a star on either side of his head enclosed by a pair of curved horns (Fig. 21.6b).

The "fish" sign, with the rebus meaning "star," could well have been a building block for Harappan proper names. Certainly, there is a long tradition of Indians having astral names derived from their birth star or constellation; already in early Buddhist texts astral names are common. But this tradition does not seem to have Indo-Aryan roots. In Vedic texts astral names are rare, and they are supposed to be kept secret. Hindu law books recommend that Aryan men should not marry girls "named after a star or constellation (*ṛkṣa*), a tree, or a river, nor one bearing the name of a low caste, or of a mountain, nor one named after a bird, a snake, or a slave, nor one whose name inspires terror" (Manu 3,9). This suggests that names derived from stars are of non-Aryan, possibly Harappan, origin.

Thus, the interpretation of the plain "fish" sign as denoting Dravidian *mīn* in the sense of both "fish" and "star" seems to be a plausible fit with Harappan, Mesopotamian, and post-Vedic Indian religious practice. We must now attempt to check it against other evidence, both internal and external to the script.

Internal checking can be compared to doing a crossword puzzle, in which we guess a word on the basis of the given clue and the number of slots for letters. Whether we are correct is initially uncertain. If we can fill in another word interlocking with the first guess our

(a) (b)

FIGURE 21.6 Star on either side of an anthropomorphic deity. (a) Six-locked nude hero with water streams flowing from his shoulders (as from the Sumerian water god Enki) on a Syrian seal without an archaeological provenance (VA 2928), dated *c.* 1980–1880 BCE (cf. Eder 1996: Dok. 188). © bpk / Staatliche Museen zu Berlin, Vorderasiatisches Museum / Fotoarchiv. (b) The Indus seal M-305 (DK 3884, ASI 60.10.62) from Mohenjo-daro. After CISI 1:383. Photo EL, courtesy ASI.

first guess becomes more probable; the more interlocking words we can fill in, the greater is our confidence in our first guess. In Indus decipherment, we should try to apply similar basic assumptions and methods of interpretation to a new sign closely associated with the first sign we have interpreted—either so that two successive signs make a recurring sequence that probably stands for a compound word, or so that together the signs form a compound sign, where one sign may function as an auxiliary phonetic or semantic indicator to the other sign.

External checking requires us to propose an underlying language and see if this assumption generates credible words in the undeciphered script. If we assume that two successive signs probably form a compound word in a Dravidian language, for example, we must see if this compound word is actually attested in Dravidian languages, notably Old Tamil. A key stage in the phonetic decipherment of the Mayan script shows this process at work. In the later nineteenth century, Léon de Rosny discovered what appeared to be pictorial translations of accompanying glyphs in a Mayan manuscript known as the Madrid Codex.

> He realized that the glyphs for certain animals, such as dog, turkey, parrot and jaguar, could be identified by examining the glyphs above the pictures of these creatures. … He now applied [Bishop de Landa's putative Spanish-Mayan "alphabet" of 1566] to what seemed to be the first sign in the glyph for "turkey." Rosny read the first sign in the glyph as *cu*, by comparing it with Landa's *cu*. He then hazarded a guess that the entire glyph might be read *cutz(u)*, since the Yucatec Mayan word for turkey is *cutz*. (Robinson 2002:121)

In 1952, Rosny's surmise was validated by Yuri Knorozov, who

> noticed that the first sign in the dog glyph was the same as the second sign in the turkey glyph. If the first sign in the dog glyph had the phonetic value *tzu* (as proposed by Rosny), the second could be assigned the value *l(u)*, on the basis of its resemblance to Landa's symbol *l*. Hence the dog glyph might stand for *tzul*. Was there a Yucatec word *tzul* in the dictionary? There was. It meant "dog." (Robinson 2002:123–125).

In deciphering sequences of Indus signs it is obviously essential to read them in the correct direction, as with any writing system. We can be sure that the normal direction is from right to left in the Indus seal impressions. (In the seal stamps, by contrast, the reading direction is from left to right; the stamp texts are mirror images of the seal impressions.) One bit of evidence for the direction of the writing comes from the overlapping of the Indus signs as they were drawn in wet clay. A second bit comes from seals in which part of an edge remains blank, for example, a seal carved on only three of its four sides, with a gap left at what must be the end of the inscription (Fig. 21.7). A third bit comes from lines in which the signs are cramped, or overspill the line, because the writer must have run out of space. Finally, the frequent repetition of certain signs and sign sequences allows them to be identified as being typical of the beginning or end of an inscription. Occasionally, however, the small tablets from Harappa apparently use a reverse order compared to the normal one, as shown by the fact any asymmetrical signs are reversed. Unless otherwise noted, the sign sequences in this book are printed in the order of the impression, not the stamp, and should therefore be read from right to left.

The numerals are among the few Indus signs of which the function and meaning can be deduced with fair certainty, for two reasons. First, the signs consist of groups of vertical strokes, which is how numerals are represented in many ancient scripts. Second, they are mutually interchangeable before specific signs, including the simple "fish" sign. Reading the sequence "six vertical strokes" + "fish" in Dravidian yields the Old Tamil name of the Pleiades, *a<u>r</u>u-mīn*, "six stars." "Seven vertical strokes" + "fish" yields the Old Tamil name of Ursa Major, alias the Big

(a) (b) (c) (d)

FIGURE 21.7 The direction of writing in the Indus script, and dividing longer texts into shorter phrases. (a) Impression of the seal H-103 (2789, ASI 63.11.116) from Harappa, with an inscription carved along three of its sides. The text runs anticlockwise: the uppermost side was written first and is full, running from the right end to the left; the line written next starts beneath the first line and continues to the end of the side; the line written last (upside down in the picture) starts from the side of line 2 and on account of its shortness leaves a gap at the end. Each of the three lines of H-103 forms a phrase that occurs as a complete text among shorter Indus texts from Mohenjo-daro. (b) Impression of the seal M-1680 (DK 8856), parallel to the first line of H-103, except that it lacks the first sign. After CISI 3.1:13. Photo Sind 20:212, courtesy ASI. (c) Impression of the seal M-122 (DK 12523, ASI 63.10.40). After CISI 1:41. Photo courtesy ASI. (d) Impression of the seal M-197 (DK 10924). After CISI 1:53. Photo Sind 22:446, courtesy ASI.

Dipper, *eḻu-mīn*, "seven stars." The latter sequence forms the entire inscription on one big seal from Harappa (which might be compared to the Mesopotamian dedicatory seals sometimes presented to divinities) (Fig. 21.8). In India, since Vedic times, the stars of Ursa Major have been identified with the "Seven Sages," the mythical ancestors of priestly clans. The Pleiades and Ursa Major play a very important role not only in early Indian mythology—including the mythical origin of Śiva's *liṅga* cult—but also in the early history of Indian calendrical astronomy, which is probably of Harappan origin, as discussed in chapter 16.

FIGURE 21.8 The sign sequence "7" + "fish" on the seal H-9 (115, ASI 80.2.4) from Harappa. Depicted here is the seal stamp, where the text is in mirror image and reads from left to right instead of the normal writing direction right to left. After CISI 1:166. Photo EL, courtesy ASI.

Even the modified attributes of the "fish" sign can be interpreted using similar premises, if more tentatively than the numerals or constellations. One diacritical mark over the "fish" sign looks like a "roof" (see the third sign from the right in the top row of Fig. 21.3a). The most widespread lexeme for "roof" in Dravidian languages is **vēy / *mēy*. Using phonological variations reconstructed for Proto-Dravidian, the early form of the word for "roof" was homophonous with **may*, "black." The modified "roof-fish" sign can thus be read as **mēy-mīn*, functioning as a rebus for **may-mīn*, "black star," a compound word actually attested in Old Tamil *mai-m-mīṉ* as the name of Saturn. Saturn is indeed a dim planet, connected with the color black in Sanskrit sources. In Sanskrit, Saturn is called *Śani* or *Śanaiścara*, "slowly moving," on account of the planet's slow pace. In Buddhist and Jaina iconography, the god Saturn rides a proverbially slow tortoise. Conceivably, the Indus "roof-fish" pictogram symbolizes Saturn not only phonetically but even pictorially through his vehicle—for the tortoise, as an aquatic animal, might be regarded as a kind of "fish," while its shell is a kind of roof!

Another diacritic modifying the "fish" sign is a straight line drawn directly or obliquely across the body of the "fish" pictogram, halving the fish (see the second sign from the left in Fig. 21.3b). Dividing a fish into two equal parts for its catchers is a narrative motif in Indian folklore. The Proto-Dravidian root **pacu*, "to halve, divide into two," is homophonous with **pacu*, "green." The resulting compound word *pacu-mīn* is attested in Old Tamil with the meaning "green fish," while *paccai*, literally "greenness," is a Tamil name for the planet Mercury. *Paccai* is also a Tamil name for Viṣṇu as green-hued, and one of Viṣṇu's Sanskrit names is *Hari*, "green." All this agrees with the Indian astrological tradition, according to which Mercury is the lord of green things and Viṣṇu is his presiding deity.

"Fish with a dot in its stomach" is yet another "fish" diacritic (see the second sign from the left in the top row of Fig. 21.3a). What could the dot mean? Here one is reminded of a dot of deep significance for Hindus, namely the red dot put on the forehead, especially by married women whose husband is alive, known in Sanskrit and Hindi as a *bindu*, "dot, drop." Men put the *bindu* on the forehead after worshipping the Goddess; according to the Kālikā-Purāṇa, this should be done with the blood from the sword used in decapitating the sacrificial victim, while pronouncing the mantra: "Whomever I touch with my foot, whomever I see with my eye, he must come into my power." This "fish-with-a-dot" sign occurs prominently on the "fig deity" seal which seems to depict an offering of a warrior's head to the Goddess (see chapter 19) (Fig. 21.9).

FIGURE 21.9 The "fig deity" seal M-1186 (DK 6847, NMP 50.295) from Mohenjo-daro. (This is the seal stamp, not its impression.) After CISI 2:425. Photo JL, courtesy DAMGP.

In north India, the rite of applying red powder to the bride's forehead and the parting of the hair (*sindūra-dāna*) is sometimes the only marriage rite, and often the binding part of the ritual. Archaeological evidence suggests that the custom has age-old Harappan roots, for terracotta female figurines from Nausharo IB (2800–2600 BCE) have traces of red pigment in their hair parting (cf. Kenoyer 1998:44–45,186). However, the Vedic manuals of domestic ritual do not prescribe this custom as part of the marriage ritual, which strongly suggests that it is of non-Aryan origin.

In Dravidian south India, the red dot put on the forehead is called *poṭṭu* (the word also means "drop," like Sanskrit *bindu*). The compound word *poṭṭu-mīn* has been recorded in the Central Dravidian language Pengo with the meaning "a kind of fish," identifiable as a carp species, *Cyprinus/Labeo rohita*. In Sanskrit *rohita* denotes both "red" and "carp." It has been the custom in Karnataka that the bride and groom, at the time of their marriage, catch a carp and use its red scales to mark each other's forehead. Carp scales were also used to mark the forehead in Kashmir. Perhaps the custom was connected with the fish-scale motif popular on Early and Mature Harappan pottery.

Rohiṇī, the feminine form of *rohita*, "red," is the Sanskrit name of the red star Aldebaran, which rose together with the sun at the vernal equinox in 3054 BCE, in Early Harappan times. As discussed in chapter 16, Rohiṇī was probably the original new-year star of the *nakṣatra* calendar. The Gṛhyasūtras and Old Tamil texts mention Rohiṇī as the star most auspicious for marriage, and Rohiṇī as the faithful wife of the moon is among the foremost models for a Hindu wife. The Atharvaveda (AVŚ 13,1,22), however, makes Rohiṇī the mate of the rising sun, Rohita, and a goddess of war. In Sanskrit, *rohiṇī* also denotes a marriageable young virgin who has just attained menstruation. The red Rohiṇī star, therefore, may be imagined to be a drop of menstrual blood, a most suitable symbol for the Goddess. Like the red dot on the forehead, it also resembles the third eye of the virginal warrior Goddess, glaring red from anger. (In the Mesopotamian tradition, Aldebaran represents the "eye" of Taurus, the Bull of Heaven.)

One recurring two-sign sequence, with the simple "fish" sign as its last member, begins with a sign of which the pictorial meaning seems to be "fig tree" (Fig. 21.10). Can this sequence, too, be a Dravidian compound word with an astral meaning?

The pictorial interpretation as "fig" is based on a comparison with a motif on Harappan painted pottery, which depicts a "three-branched fig tree" from the Early through the Mature to the Late phase. In one variant from Nausharo, phase I D, dating from *c.* 2600 BCE (about the time the Indus script was created), four strokes are attached to either side of the middle stem (Fig. 21.11). In the Indus sign, the fig tree is shown as three-branched, just as on the painted pottery, except where the central "branch" is omitted to make a compound sign in which a second sign (the "crab" sign) is inserted in place of the central "branch." In some cases, the branches end in fig leaves as they do on the painted pottery, but in others, the fig leaves are simplified, even into straight lines (Fig. 21.12). The lines or strokes seem to represent the rope-like air roots of the banyan fig, *Ficus bengalensis* or *Ficus indica* (Fig. 16.9).

This mighty tree is native to South Asia and does not grow in the regions from which the Indo-Aryan speakers came. A post-Vedic name for the banyan fig is *vaṭa*. Though a Sanskrit word, *vaṭa* is a loanword from Dravidian, ultimately derived from Proto-Dravidian

FIGURE 21.10 The sequence of Indus signs "fig" + "fish" on two seals from Mohenjo-daro. (a) The seal M-414 (DK 3431, ASI 63.190.208), and (b) its impression. After CISI 3.1:409 (photo EL) and CISI 1:100 (photo Sind 18:587). Courtesy ASI. (c) The seal M-172 (BJ4), and (d) its impression. After CISI 3.1:132 (photo Sind 6:I.67) and CISI 1:50 (photo Marshall 1931: pl. 106:71). Courtesy ASI.

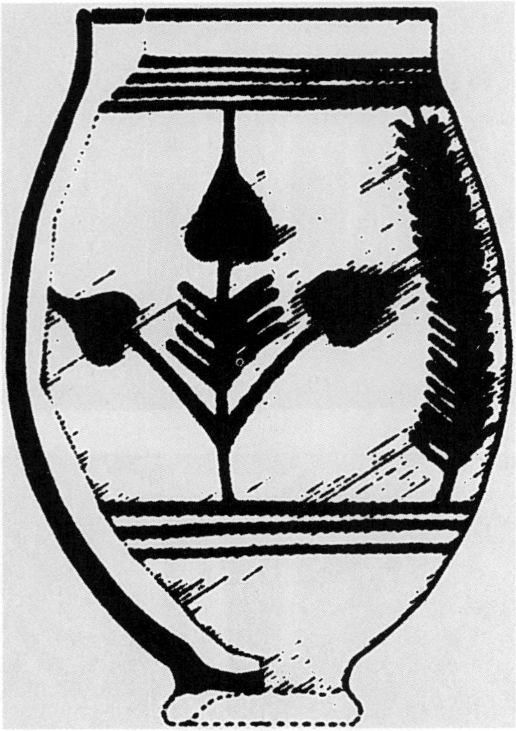

FIGURE 21.11 The "three-branched fig" motif on a Harappan painted goblet from Nausharo, period I D, *c.* 2600–2500 BCE. After Samzun 1992: 250, fig. 29.4 no. 2. Courtesy Mission Archéologique de l'Indus, CNRS/ Musée Guimet, Paris.

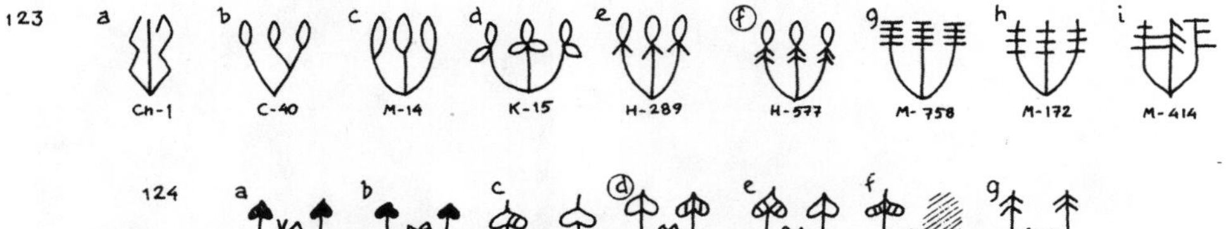

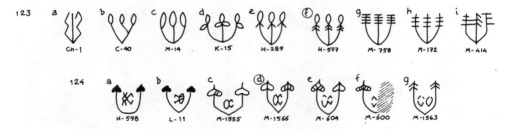

FIGURE 21.12 Variants of the "fig" and "fig" + "crab" signs. After Parpola 1994:235, fig. 13.15.

**vaṭam*, "rope, cord." As a name of the banyan fig, *vaṭam* is short for the compound word *vaṭa-maram*, "rope tree," which is attested in Tamil. *Vaṭam* has a Proto-Dravidian homophone **vaṭa*, "north, northern." This yields the expected astral meaning for the sign sequence "fig" + "fish." *Vaṭa-mīn*, "north star," is attested in Old Tamil; according to the medieval commentaries, it is the name of the star Alcor in Ursa Major. In Old Tamil texts, *vaṭa-mīn* is a symbol of marital fidelity and during the wedding the star is pointed out to the bride as an object for emulation. As discussed in chapter 16, *vaṭa-mīn* probably originally denoted the pole star, which in the third millennium was the nearby star Thuban (Fig. 16.8). The pole star is of course the "immobile" center of the rotating heavens, known in Sanskrit as *dhruva*, "fixed, firm, immovable, constant." It is a fitting symbol of fidelity; indeed in the Vedic marriage ritual the pole star is pointed out to the bride as a model, in addition to Alcor.

This interpretation explains in a new way some peculiar cosmological conceptions of the Purāṇa texts. In the first place, the mythical central mountain of the world, Meru, is surrounded by four great mountains in the four cardinal directions, on the tops of which grows a specific variety of gigantic tree. The tree on the northern mountain is the banyan fig (*vaṭa*). Homophony connects *vaṭa*, "banyan," with *vaṭa*, "north," in Dravidian, but there is no such association in Indo-Aryan languages, where the Sanskrit for "north" is *uttarā* or *udīcī diś-*, literally, the "upper, upward" or "left" direction (north being on the left when one faces east, the "forward" direction). Secondly, in reply to the question why the stars and planets do not fall down from the sky, the Purāṇas say that the heavenly bodies are bound to the pole star with invisible "ropes of wind." In Dravidian *vaṭa-mīn*, besides being the name of the pole star, can also be read as "rope star" and "banyan star." Around 1000 BCE, a late hymn of the Rigveda (1,24,7) speaks of the roots of a cosmic banyan tree being held up in the sky by Varuṇa (see chapter 16). Both Vedic and Hindu texts repeatedly refer to a heavenly fig tree. This conception seems to be reflected on an Indus tablet, which depicts an anthropomorphic deity inside a fig tree. At the bottom the fig tree is flanked on either side by a star, suggesting a heavenly connection for the tree (Fig. 16.10).

The above interpretation of the "fig" sign can be further checked by attempting to understand the compound sign in which the "crab" sign has been substituted for the middle branch of the "fig" sign. The "crab" sign has two variants, with legs and without legs, as demonstrated by the similar context of the two variants in two different seals. On both seals the compound sign is followed by the same two other signs (Fig. 21.13).

Let us first consider the likely meaning of the "crab" sign. It occurs more than 150 times as an uncompounded sign, mostly simplified to a round body with claws (Fig. 21.14). The visual emphasis on the claws suggests that the sign expresses "grasping" or "seizing," which is consistent with the behavior of the crab in Indian folklore. Thus, in the Buddhist Baka-Jātaka, a crab tells a heron who has promised to carry the crab away from a pond that is drying up to some other pond (as a pretext for eating the crab): "You'd never be able to hold me tight enough, friend heron; whereas we crabs have got an astonishingly tight grip." Then "the crab gripped hold of the heron's neck with its claws, as with the pincers of a smith."

Crab's claws are compared with blacksmith's pincers in Old Tamil texts, where the root *koḷ*, "to grab, seize, take," expresses the "seizing." Indo-Aryan texts use the synonymous Sanskrit root *grah- / grabh-*, which is related to English "grab." The "crab" sign often occurs close to "fish" signs and might therefore have an astral meaning. Proto-Dravidian **kōḷ*, "seizure," means "planet" in Tamil. Surprisingly, this double meaning is also true of Sanskrit *graha*—but not true of other Indo-European languages. Sanskrit *graha* is therefore more likely to be a loan translation from Dravidian **kōḷ* than *kōḷ* is to be a loan translation from Sanskrit *graha*. In both the oldest Tamil and the oldest Sanskrit texts *kōḷ* and *graha* refer to the invisible heavenly demon that causes eclipses, by seizing the sun and moon.

FIGURE 21.13 Two variants of the "fig" + "crab" sign (cf. Parpola 1994:232 fig. 13.12). (a) The seal stamp H-598 (13751, HM 200) from Harappa. After CISI 2:297. Photo AV, courtesy DAMGP. (b) Impression of the seal L-11 (4879, LTH.SRG 1261) from Lothal. After CISI 1:241. Photo EL, courtesy ASI.

FIGURE 21.14 [See Fig. 21.12] Variants of the "crab" sign. After Parpola 1994:232.

The planets are firmly believed in both Tamil and Sanskrit texts to "seize" people and afflict them with ills. The Sanskrit author Daṇḍin, writing in about 700 CE, speaks of the "terrifying stars and planets," which the sorcerers control with magical diagrams. From the eighteenth century comes a graphic description of such incantations:

> The term *graha*, by which they are designated, signifies the act of seizing, that is, of laying hold of those whom they are enjoined by the magical enchantments to torment. . . . The magician . . . exclaims as though in a vehement rage, "Grasp it! Grasp it!" . . . No sooner is this done than the *grahas* or planets take possession of the person against whom such incantations are directed, and afflict him with a thousand ills. (Dubois [1825] 1906:387f.)

We can check our interpretation of both the "crab" and "fig" signs by examining the compound sign with the "crab" inside the "fig tree." Luckily, this is among the few Indus signs for which there are "pictorial bilinguals," that is, tablets that mediate the sign's intended meaning visually with an accompanying iconographic motif. The 240 copper tablets from Mohenjo-daro are a rare category of Indus objects, because they show a clear interdependence between the inscription on the obverse and the iconographic animal- or human-shaped motif on the reverse. Numerous duplicates form sets of identical tablets. In some sets, a single sign appears on the reverse instead of an iconographic motif. By comparing tablets having the same inscription on the obverse side but different reverse sides, it is possible to link these single signs with their corresponding iconographic motifs. It appears that the single sign

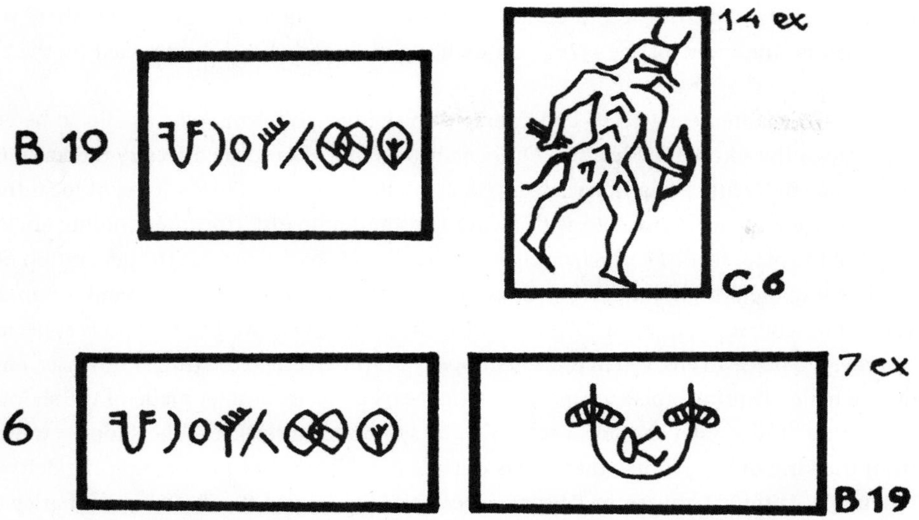

FIGURE 21.15 A "pictorial translation" of an Indus sign: the identical inscriptions on the obverse sides correlate the "horned archer" on the reverse of the type B-19 (there are fourteen identical tablets of this type) and the "fig" + "crab" sign on the reverse of the type C-6 (there are seven identical tablets of this type) among the copper tablets from Mohenjo-daro. After Parpola 1994:234, fig. 13.13.

represented the name of the divinity depicted in the motif. The "crab inside fig" sign can thus be equated with a "horned archer," a male figure armed with a bow and arrows, anthropomorphic apart from its horns and a tail, and with protruding eyes (Fig. 21.15).

In West Asian and Chinese scripts, an inserted sign often functions as a semantic or phonetic determinative. The inserted "crab" sign could be a phonetic determinative indicating that the "fig" sign is not to be read with its usual phonetic value as *vaṭam*, "banyan tree." While the meaning, "fig," is retained, the phonetic shape of the word is similar to that expressed by the "crab" sign, *kōḷ*. Proto-South-Dravidian possesses exactly such a word: **kōḷi*. This word denotes a fig tree, both as a grasping epiphytic plant that strangles its host tree and as a plant that bears fruit without blossoming. In this latter sense *kōḷi* is related to Old Tamil *kōḷ*, "the act of bearing fruit." Both are derived from the root *koḷ*, "to take." Sanskrit *grabh-* has the same additional sense of "bearing fruit." Even the structure of this compound sign seems to express this ambivalent deity, who both "seizes or kills" and "bears fruit or fructifies," for the crab sign is placed inside the fig sign, just as anthropomorphic deities are placed inside fig trees in Indus glyptics.

But how can this word **kōḷi* be connected with the "horned archer" depicted on the copper tablets? In early Vedic texts the grasping fig strangling its host tree and breaking buildings is implored for help in crushing enemies. This suggests that the fig could be a symbol for Rudra, the god who is described in Vedic texts as a cruel hunter and raider who, with his bow, shoots arrows at animals and people. He is also called in Sanskrit *Hara*, "seizer, taker, robber," which could reflect the Dravidian word *kōḷ*, "seizure, plunder, robbery." There is also a homonym *kōḷ*, "hitting, killing," from the root *koḷ*, "hit, shoot with bow, kill." Rudra, whose original name was probably **Rudhra*, "Red," seems to have been represented by the red planet Mars, called in Sanskrit *Rudhira*, "red," "blood," and *Aṅgāra*, "live coal." The latter name has a counterpart in Proto-South-Dravidian **koḷḷi*, "firebrand, glowing ember," which may also be the name of the Harappan archer-god intended to be expressed by the compound sign "fig" + "crab."

Rudra is often equated in Vedic texts with the fire-god Agni, who is said to be either the mate or the son of the Pleiades. Agni's name has Indo-European ancestry (cf. Latin *ignis*, "fire"), but the Vedic fire-god has absorbed attributes and myths likely to be of local Indian origin since they are connected with local plants and animals. Thus the kindling stick was made of the pipal fig or *Ficus religiosa*, which has flame-shaped leaves. The generation of fire by churning the upright kindling stick in the hole of a horizontal wooden plank symbolized sexual intercourse (chapter 11). Agni is called the "embryo of forest trees" and is appealed to by prayer to place an embryo in the worshipper's womb. In the Vedic ritual known as "engendering male offspring" (*puṁsavana*), the wife wears a phallic amulet made of the shoot of a banyan fig. The amulet should have two fruits symbolizing testicles. The shoot is to be cut from the king of banyan figs that grows outside the village after propitiating the deity who inhabits it. Jaimini-Gṛhyasūtra 1,5 prescribes: "Having shaped two beans and a barley corn into shape of a male organ of procreation, he [the worshipper] should give it her [his wife] to eat. ... Then having with two threads . . . fastened a shoot of the banyan fig which has two fruits, she should bear it on her throat. This, they say, is a sure means to get a son."

On a tablet from Harappa we see a ram-headed but otherwise anthropomorphic deity inside a fig tree (Fig. 21.16a). The god's arms are covered in bangles and in their great length the arms resemble the air roots of the banyan. This Harappan ram-headed fig deity has a relatively little-known successor in later Indian tradition. Nejameṣa (*meṣa* means "ram")

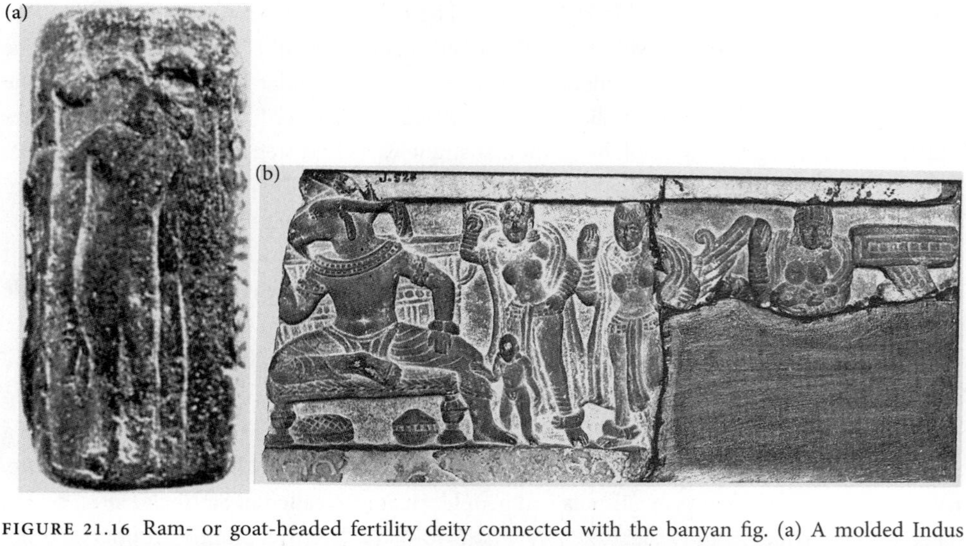

FIGURE 21.16 Ram- or goat-headed fertility deity connected with the banyan fig. (a) A molded Indus tablet H-178 B (7483, ASI 63.11.69) from Harappa. After CISI 1:209. Photo EL, courtesy ASI. (b) The god Naigameṣa flanked by a child and three women. A stūpa railing from Mathurā, *c.* 100 CE. Now in Lucknow Museum (J 626). Photo courtesy American Institute of Indian Studies.

is a fertility god who should be appealed to by a woman who cannot conceive, while she touches her genitals and utters this Vedic verse: "O Nejameṣa! Fly away, and fly hither again bringing back a beautiful son; to me here who is longing for a son grant thou an embryo, and that a male one" (RV Khila 30,1, translated Winternitz 1895:150–151). In later Hindu sources, a related ram-faced deity, Naigameṣa, is said to be a constant companion of Skanda. Another deity, Hari-Naigameṣin, is known from the Jain Kalpasūtra, where this deity transfers the embryo of Mahāvīra Jina to the womb of his mother. According to the Kalpasūtra, Hari-Naigameṣin is the leader of the divine army with a peacock as his mount; he is thus clearly a double of the Hindu war-god Skanda who rides a peacock. On a second-century relief from Mathurā, the goat- or ram-headed fertility god Naigameṣa is flanked on his left side by a baby boy and three women (Fig. 21.16b). The relief is broken, but may originally have shown three women on the god's right side, too. Together, these six women would have represented the Pleiades as mother goddesses.

The unexplained first part of the names of Neja-meṣa and Naiga-meṣa seems to derive from the root *nij-*, "to wash, cleanse." Sanskrit medical texts prescribe bathing the new-born baby under the banyan tree, if its disease is diagnosed as caused by Naigameṣa, along with a bloody offering (*bali*, perhaps originally of a ram or goat) to this deity at a banyan on the sixth day after birth, accompanied by this prayer: "May God Naigameṣa, the child's father, protect the child, (this) greatly famed (Naigameṣa) who is goat-faced, who has moving eyes and eye-brows, and who can take any shape at will." (Suśruta-Saṁhitā, Uttaratantra 36,10–11)

The sections on the illnesses of new-born babies in medical texts speak of a group of nine malignant demons keen to attack and seize infants, if proper respect is not shown to them and the rules of cleanliness and nursing are not followed. The group's name, *nava-graha*, is identical with the classical group of "nine planets," among whom the planet Mars represents the war-god Skanda. The lord of the demons is Skanda-Graha, plus two forms of the goat-headed Naigameṣa and six goddesses. The nine demons were created by the fire-god Agni and Śiva along with the six Pleiades, in order to protect the new-born god Skanda.

The best-known version of the Pleiades myth describes the birth of the ever-youthful war-god Skanda. Kāma, the god of love, shot his arrows of desire at Śiva, whose seed "leapt" (*caskanda*) and fell into the River Ganges. The wives of the Seven Sages were bathing in this heavenly river, and became either the mothers or the wet-nurses of the instantly born boy, who rides a peacock.

Now, Skanda has a counterpart in the principal native deity of south India, the youthful god of war, wisdom, and fertility, Murugan or Murukan, whom Tamils worship today as their "national god." Common people pray to Murukan for sons. His mount is a peacock and his weapon a spear. In Old Tamil literature Murukan is both the hunter-god of the hill forests, much like the Vedic Rudra, and the god of love and fertility. From 300 CE onwards, Murukan is explicitly amalgamated with Skanda.

Given his importance to Dravidian speakers, Murukan's name or names are likely to be present in Indus texts. But how to locate them? Skanda's association with the Pleiades offers a clue. As already suggested, the Pleiades can be identified as the sign sequence "six" + "fish." Two Indus seals share a unique sequence of three signs (the first sign, which is very rare, is

(a)

(b)

FIGURE 21.17 Two Indus texts sharing a unique three-sign sequence. (a) Impression of the seal M-112 (DK 11359, ASI 63.10.81) from Mohenjo-daro. After CISI 1:40. Photo EL, courtesy ASI. (b) The seal M-241 (HR 5787, NMI 106) from Mohenjo-daro in the collection of the National Museum of India, New Delhi; reversed to show the signs as they would appear in an impression. After CISI 1:60. Photo EL, courtesy NMI.

represented by two allographs), suggesting that the two seals may be speaking about the same thing (Fig. 21.17).

In both of the seals the said rare three-sign sequence begins the inscription, and may therefore contain a qualifying phrase—for in Dravidian languages the qualifier precedes the qualified. The following, longer sequence in one of these two seals includes the signs "six" + "fish," and may therefore refer to "Skanda, son of the Pleiades." Thus there is a chance, because the initial phrase connects these two seals, that the corresponding latter part of the other seal might include a name of Murukan. The three-sign sequence occurring here is found very frequently in Indus inscriptions. Read in the normal direction of writing, the three signs are the "two intersecting circles," the "two long vertical strokes" and the "bull's head."

Contextual clues suggest that this sign sequence could indeed refer to a deity. For example, on a tablet from Harappa, the only inscription (exactly repeated on the obverse and the reverse) is the very same sign sequence, "two intersecting circles," the "two long vertical strokes," and the "bull's head," along with various images (Fig. 21.18). On a tablet from Mohenjo-daro, the same sign sequence concludes the inscription on the obverse, while the reverse shows a god sitting on a throne, flanked on either side by a kneeling worshipper and a cobra (Fig. 21.19). In South India, Murukan is associated with a phallic snake cult, and his peacock feeds on snakes.

If the "intersecting circles" sign really does express Murukan's name, or at least the first part of it, I suggest that it might be read in Proto-Dravidian as **muruku*, "young man, baby boy, Murukan." This name is a synonym of Sanskrit *kumāra*, "youth, baby boy," one of the names of Skanda and Rudra. Muruku has an exact and ancient homophone, namely **muruku*, "ring, earring, bangle"—which nicely fits the pictorial meaning of "intersecting circles."

(a)
(b)

FIGURE 21.18 The sign sequence "two intersecting circles" + || occurs on both sides of the Indus tablet H-182 (201, NMI 33) from Harappa in the collection of the National Museum of India, New Delhi: (a) with a drummer and a tiger on the obverse, and (b) with swastikas on the reverse. After CISI 1:209. Photo EL, courtesy NMI.

(a)
(b)

FIGURE 21.19 A molded faience tablet M-453 (DK 7991, ASI 63.190.217) from Mohenjo-daro. (a) The obverse with an inscription. (b) The reverse showing an erect cobra behind a kneeling worshipper (one extending a vessel of offerings, the other with hands raised in prayer) on either side of an anthropomorphic deity seated on a throne. After CISI 1:111 and 386. Photo EL, courtesy ASI.

This proposed reading, **muruku*, for the "intersecting circles" sign is endorsed by its frequent depiction on forty or more inscribed stoneware bangles. Several of these bangles are inscribed with this sign—and no other sign. It is not unusual for ancient inscriptions to mention the name of the inscribed object, especially if the object is a votive offering. These stoneware bangles were manufactured with a difficult process, heated in closed and sealed containers to 1200°C, and must have been very expensive. In this case, the "intersecting circles" sign could denote not only the bangle itself but also—by homophony—the boy child desired by the donor and/or the proper name of the child-granting divinity, himself the divine child par excellence. Even today, many Tamil couples desiring a male child make a pilgrimage to a shrine of Murukan and, following the birth, name their son after the god.

Furthermore, bangles have a strong association with pregnancy in many parts of India. During pregnancy and childbirth mother and baby are both in danger of being attacked by demons, and the bangle symbolizes an enclosed circle of protection. In Tamil Nadu, the expectant mother is ritually adorned with bangles and blessed by older women in the seventh month of the first pregnancy. In the Atharvaveda, bangles are charms to encourage reproduction. Hymn 6,81 of the Atharvaveda (Śaunaka-śākhā) addresses *pari-hasta*, the "bracelet" (literally, "what is around the arm"), as follows: "O bracelet, open up the womb, that the embryo be put (into it)! Do thou . . . furnish a son, bring him here . . . The bracelet that (goddess) Aditi wore, when she desired a son, (god) Tvaṣṭar shall fasten upon this woman, intending that she shall beget a son" (translated Bloomfield 1897:96f.).

In Indian folk religion, Hindus, and even Muslims, offer pregnancy bangles to tree spirits. People anxious to have children hang as many bangles as they can afford on the branches of a sacred tree. If the tree spirit favors their wish, the tree "snatches up the bangles and wears them on its arms" (Crooke 1926:417). This widespread folk custom is likely to go back to Harappan traditions. The deity standing inside the fig tree in the "fig deity" seal from Mohenjo-daro (Fig. 21.9) surely wears bangles on both arms. So do the seven anthropomorphic figures at the bottom of this seal, wearing their hair in the traditional fashion of Indian women, who likely represent the "Seven Mothers," the wives of the Seven Sages, famous as goddesses capable of child-granting and child-killing, like their son Skanda.

My tentative reading of "intersecting circles" as *muruku* might be corroborated by means of the sign that frequently accompanies it, the "two long vertical strokes." This lends itself to various pictorial interpretations, and it is difficult to decide which of them, if any, is correct. However, we may also consider the fact that the "two long vertical strokes" sign often precedes the simple "fish" sign (Fig. 21.20).

Let us collect together any attested Old Tamil compound words that start with *muruku-* and all compound words that end with *-mīn*, that is, X in *muruku-*X and X-*mīn*. If these two different sets of compound words reveal a word, X, that is common to the attested lists, we may test X by asking whether its meaning adequately explains the pictorial shape, "two long vertical strokes."

Among the Old Tamil compound names of Murukan is Muruka-Vēḷ. The word *vēḷ* means "love, desire," and is sometimes used alone as a name of Murukan, that is, Vēḷ. Old

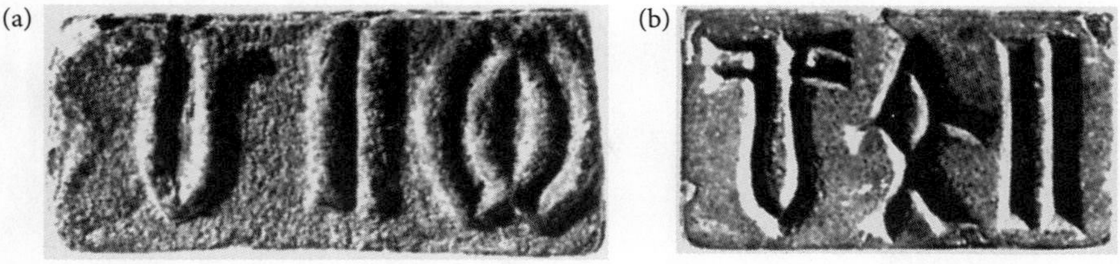

FIGURE 21.20 Cross-checking *Muruku* and *mīn*. (a) The obverse of the molded tablet H-723 (H775, HM 290) from Harappa. After CISI 2:319. Photo AV, courtesy DAMGP. (b) The seal H-669 (P I-44, Lahore Museum P-909) from Harappa, reversed to show the signs as they would appear in an impression. After CISI 2:310. Photo AV, courtesy Lahore Museum.

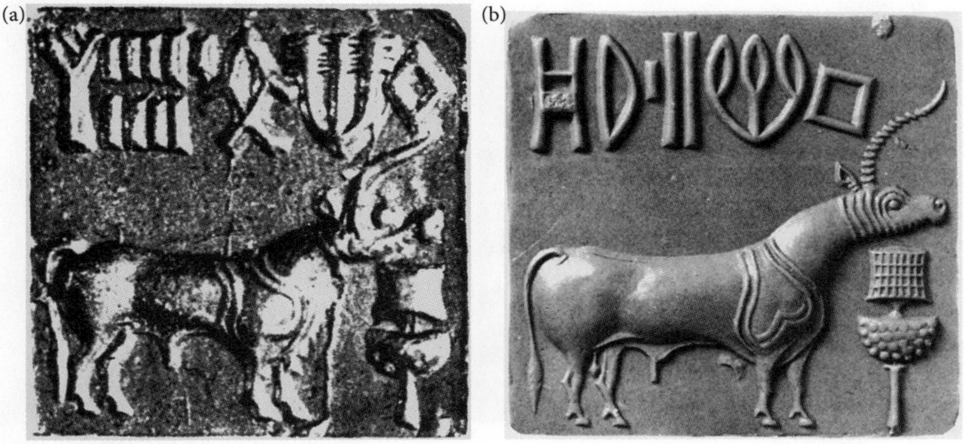

FIGURE 21.21 Impressions of two Indus seals. (a) M-172 (BJ 4) from Mohenjo-daro. After CISI 1:50, photo Marshall 1931: pl. 106.71. Courtesy ASI. (b) H-6 (P I.39, NMI 10) from Harappa in the collection of the National Museum of India, New Delhi. After CISI 1:162. Photo EL, courtesy NMI.

Tamil *veḷ-mīn* denotes the planet Venus, the brightest star of the sky. In this case, *veḷ* means "white, bright." Its derivative *veḷḷi* denotes "Venus" in several Dravidian languages. The shared component of these two compound words, *muruka-vēḷ* and *veḷ-mīn*, thus has the phonetic shape *veḷ* or *vēḷ*. And these words have a further, so far unmentioned, homophone, Proto-Dravidian **veḷ(i)*; its meaning, "space between," such as "space between furrows," matches fairly well the pictorial shape, "two long vertical strokes."

In the Indus compound word read as *veḷ-mīn* or *veḷḷi-mīn*, "bright star, Venus," the "two long vertical strokes" sign is used as an adjectival qualifier ("bright") of the head word ("star"). But in Tamil, *veḷḷi* is used not only as a qualifier of *mīn* but also as a synonym of *mīn; veḷḷi* can mean both "bright" and "star (in general)." Thus, two Tamil dictionary renderings for "star" are *viṇ-mīn* and *vāṉ-veḷḷi*. The words *viṇ* and *vāṉ* both mean "sky"; the prefix is there to avoid confusion of the second part of the compound with other possible meanings such as *mīn*, "fish," and *veḷḷi*, "white metal, silver." Synonymous use of *veḷḷi* and *mīn* is

FIGURE 21.22 The "squirrel" sign of the Indus script. (a) Part of the text engraved on the Indus seal Nd-1 (Exc. Branch 1187) from Nindowari, reversed. After CISI 2:419 no. 5. Photo AV, courtesy DAMGP. (b) The seal M-1202 (DK 2797, Lahore Museum P-1749) from Mohenjo-daro, and (c) its modern impression. After CISI 2:143. Photo AV and S.M. Ilyas, courtesy Lahore Museum. (d) Obverse of the molded tablet H-771 (657, HM 474) from Harappa. After CISI 2:324. Photo AV, courtesy DAMGP. (e) First three signs carved on an Indus seal from Nausharo (excavation no. NS 95.05.17.01), to be published in CISI 3.2. Reversed to show the signs as they would appear in an impression. Photo Catherine Jarrige, courtesy Mission archéologique de l'Indus/Jean-François Jarrige.

further attested in two Tamil compounds, both meaning "the star of the dawn," *viṭi-mīṉ* and *viṭi-veḷḷi*. That *veḷḷi* was used as a synonym of *mīn* in the Indus language, too, can be seen by comparing two inscriptions which otherwise share the same four-sign-long sequence, though three of the signs have variant forms (Fig. 21.21). The "fish" sign is here preceded by the "fig" sign, yielding the already-discussed compound word *vaṭa-mīn*, "north star." We also have "fig" + "two long vertical strokes," yielding *vaṭa-veḷḷi*.

One rare but delightful Indus sign has a very narrow pictorial meaning. From distinctly carved occurrences, such as a seal from Nindowari, the sign can be recognized as depicting the palm squirrel, head down, tail at right angles to its body, with its four paws clinging onto a vertical tree trunk (Fig. 21.22a). In this typical pose, the palm squirrel can sleep for hours, hence its Sanskrit name, "tree-sleeper" (*vṛkṣa-śāyikā*). It still inhabits the entire Indus Valley and is represented in tiny faience figurines from Mohenjo-daro.

The "intersecting circles" sign, which we have interpreted as *muruku*, is followed by the "palm squirrel" sign in three different inscriptions (Fig. 21.22b–e). May this sequence, too, be read in Dravidian, so that the resulting compound is among the attested composite names of Murukan? One of the inscriptions comprises just this sequence followed by the sign read as Vēḷ, one of Murukan's names.

In modern Tamil, the palm squirrel is called *aṇil* or *aṇil-piḷḷai*. The word *piḷḷai* means "child, infant, son, boy," as well as "young of animals and trees." It is tacked on to *aṇil* to form an affectionate diminutive, and even used on its own to refer to a squirrel. (It is used in the same way to form words for "young mongoose" and "young parrot.") Crucially for our argument, it is also added to the various names of Murukan to form pet names that are popular as male proper names in Jaffna Tamil, such as *Muruka-piḷḷai*. This Tamil usage goes back to Proto-Dravidian, for the Central Dravidian languages preserve cognates of *piḷḷai* with the meaning "squirrel." As an honorific plural, Piḷḷaiyār is the Tamil name of the popular god known as Gaṇeśa or Gaṇapati in Sanskrit ("Leader of the Host"). He is an ancient double of Skanda and of Rudra (chapter 12).

The fact that even such uncommon Indus symbols as the palm squirrel, which have a narrow pictorial meaning, find a natural and fitting explanation within a Dravidian linguistic framework is a hopeful sign. As we have seen, a number of Dravidian-based rebus interpretations interlock with each other and with external linguistic and cultural data, making sense within ancient Indian cultural history and the Indus civilization. The interpretations restrict themselves to ancient Indian astronomy and time-reckoning and its associated mythology, the chief deities of Hindu and Old Tamil religion and the fertility cult connected with fig trees. These contexts enable some progress to be made in spite of difficulties, and suggest possible avenues for future progress. Although our knowledge of Proto-Dravidian vocabulary, especially compound words, is deplorably defective, it nevertheless allows some cross-checking.

Conclusion

22

Prehistory of Indo-Aryan Language and Religion

In summarizing the book's most important conclusions, I try to outline my research on the early Aryan and Harappan religions and their survival in the Vedas and Hinduism. At the same time I take the opportunity of making a few more suggestions, particularly in chapter 24, hoping that these will stimulate further research.

The vocabulary common to the different Indo-European languages permits conclusions about the natural and cultural environment of the PIE language. On this basis, the best-informed scholars have long placed the PIE homeland in the Pontic-Caspian steppes, among its pastoralist cultures—known as Khvalynsk, Srednij Stog, and Skelya—of the Neolithic and Copper Age (*c*. 5000–3400 BCE). At present, leading researchers hold the Yamnaya cultures (*c*. 3300–2500 BCE), the immediately succeeding Early Bronze Age cultures of the Pontic-Caspian steppes, as the archaeological correlate of the Late PIE phase. This hypothesis, however, creates certain difficulties. The Corded Ware cultures, which must have played a central role in the dispersal of the IE languages in northwestern Europe, cannot be credibly derived directly from the Yamnaya cultures. Another problem is to explain where the PIE speakers got their wheeled vehicles from. The PIE vocabulary relating to wheeled vehicles has emerged as a particularly important clue to dating the PIE language. I make a suggestion that removes these difficulties: the Early PIE speakers took over the Tripolye culture of Moldavia and Ukraine, and the Late PIE language developed in the Late Tripolye culture (*c*. 4100–3400 BCE).

There is a fair degree of unanimity on the constituents necessary for this solution. It is agreed that the pastoralist Skelya culture invaded the Balkans causing great destruction there around 4300–4100 BCE, and a credible trail of archaeological cultures from the Pontic steppes to Anatolia can be proposed as the archaeological correlate for the prevailing view that the Anatolian languages were the first to separate from the PIE speech community and that they are the only ones to preserve the laryngeal phoneme(s) reconstructed for Early PIE. It is also agreed that the Skelya pastoralists, at the time of their invasion of the Balkans, also attacked sites of the Tripolye culture, with which they had been longer in contact, the

Tripolye culture being the source of their metal and other prestige goods. The volume of the crude handmade ceramics typical of the Skelya culture gradually increases within the Late Tripolye culture until it is eventually the predominant type of Tripolye pottery, from which the Corded Ware can be derived. It is further thought that the stone-headed maces, which are sometimes shaped like a horse-head, have a steppe origin and were probably used as scepters, symbols of power suggesting the importation of a chieftainship type of social structure that made the Tripolye culture expand and flourish, but also led to internal strife.

The long-dominant view that the first wheeled vehicles were invented by the Sumerians in the late fourth millennium BCE has been challenged by numerous new finds in Europe datable to the second half of the fourth millennium. In the fourth millennium, the Tripolye culture alone shows some evidence (in the form of model wheels and wagon-shaped drinking cups) for wheeled vehicles before 3500 BCE. Being the most advanced culture anywhere in agriculture and having the largest settlements of the Copper Age world, it also had the incentive to improve the means of transport. There are many models of ox-pulled sledges, from which the wheeled wagon is thought to have evolved from logs rolling under sledges with heavy loads. Since inventors usually name their inventions, and the PIE vehicle terminology is derived from PIE roots, by this time the language spoken in the Late Tripolye culture must have shifted from non-Indo-European to Late PIE. The terms used for wheeled wagons in Kartvelian and Sumerian make it appear that the invention spread to West Asia over the Caucasus, where the steppe and Mesopotamian Uruk cultures met around 3500 BCE.

The Tripolye culture cultivated the most fertile fields in Europe with plows, and during the fourth millennium its population increased phenomenally. When some kind of climatic crisis around 3400 BCE brought this thriving culture to a sudden end, hundreds of Tripolye sites were abandoned and tens of thousands of Late Tripolye people adopted the mobile pastoralist lifestyle dispersing in wheeled vehicles in every direction. This dispersal of many people from a central source created the two major cultural chains, both dated to *c.* 3300–2500 BCE, which have long been held responsible for the spread of the PIE language to most places where its branches first historically emerge: the Corded Ware or Battle Axe cultures, ranging from the Netherlands to Russia across northwestern Europe, and the Yamnaya cultures, ranging from the Danube to the Urals across southeastern Europe. Both the Corded Ware and the Yamnaya cultures possessed wheeled vehicles, buried as prestige objects in elite graves, and pottery and other artifacts that can be derived from the Late Tripolye culture.

The Yamnaya cultures came into being when the Late Tripolye people, probably speaking Late PIE, spread to the Pontic-Caspian steppes. The archaic substratum is likely to have differentiated the language of the Yamnaya cultures from the other early IE languages. The Yamnaya languages spoken in the western half of the continuum (from the Danube to the Dnieper, which has often functioned as a cultural border) are likely to have been ancestral to Greek and Armenian, and those spoken in the eastern half (from the Dnieper to the Urals) Indo-Iranian. These languages share the augment, the prefix **e* functioning as a past-time marker of verbs, and some other features not present in other IE languages. Unlike Greek, Armenian is a satem language, so its ancestor is likely to have been closer to that of Indo-Iranian and Balto-Slavic, which also share the innovative satemization. Because the ancestor of Balto-Slavic with great probability has as its archaeological correlate the eastern variants of the Corded Ware culture (Middle Dnieper, Fatyanovo, and Balanovo), the original homeland of the Indo-Iranian languages cannot have been in Central Asia, as is often claimed, but has to be in the Pontic-Caspian steppes. Only this location in the European steppes allows for the development of the considerable differences that exist between the "Iranian" and "Indo-Aryan" branches.

Another important, indeed crucial, component for the identification of the Proto-Aryan homeland is the fact that Uralic (Finno-Ugric) languages contain about a hundred early Aryan loanwords. Some of the words had been borrowed before some sound changes characteristic of the Proto-Aryan language (as reconstructed on the bases of the later Indo-Iranian languages) had taken place (Proto-West Uralic **kekrä* vs. Proto-Aryan **cakra-*), while some of the loanwords had clearly come from Proto-Indo-Aryan (**mete-śišta-*, "beeswax," has an exact counterpart in Sanskrit *madhu-śiṣṭa*, literally "what is left over of honey," while even the verb *śiṣ-*, "to leave," lacks a counterpart in Iranian). The latest research suggests, moreover, that Proto-Uralic had Aryan loanwords before its disintegration, which makes it possible to narrow the possibilities for locating the homeland of Proto-Uralic, traditionally sought in the forested eastern part of European Russia.

The above considerations have made it possible to suggest for the first time a more definite network of archaeological correlations that comprises the whole web of Uralic and Indo-Iranian languages (Parpola 2012 [2013]). Carpelan and Parpola (2001) proposed that the Proto-Aryan community split into its two branches around 2300 BCE, when the Late Yamnaya and Poltavka cultures of the forest steppes of the Upper Don and Lower Volga regions expanded to the Mid-Volga and the Lower Kama rivers, forming the Abashevo culture (*c.* 2300–1850 BCE). The primary incentive for this expansion seems to have been the copper resources of this area for which these presumably Proto-Indo-Aryan speakers fought with the Balanovo extension of the Fatyanovo culture. The Abashevo people seem to have lived in symbiosis with the local Garino-Bor people, who probably spoke Proto-Uralic.

Proto-Uralic has native terms both for "copper" (**wäśka*) and for "tin" (**äsa*), which occur together in the compound **äsa-wäśka*, "tin-bronze." Tin-bronze was produced in the great intercultural network of warrior traders that operated around 2100–1600 BCE and mediated high-quality weapons and tools between the Altai Mountains (the source of the tin) and Finland. This network came into being after the Abashevo culture had expanded further east, to the other side of the Ural Mountains, and given rise to the Sintashta culture (*c.* 2100–1700 BCE) of the southern Urals and its eastern offshoot, the Petrovka culture (*c.* 2000–1700 BCE), which reached the Altai Mountains. It seems likely that the European wing of this Sejma-Turbino network was operated by Proto-Uralic speakers and was instrumental in the westward expansion of the Uralic languages.

The Sintashta and Petrovka peoples were not only metallurgists but also pastoralists. They started the Andronovo cultures that dominated the Asiatic steppes of Russia, Kazakhstan, and Turkmenistan around 2000–1450 BCE. The elites of all these cultures possessed the horse-drawn chariot, which was used for racing, hunting, and fighting, and buried together with its owner. It appears that the horse was first yoked to pull the chariot in the Sintashta culture around 2100–2000 BCE, after which it quickly spread in all directions.

From Sintashta both the domesticated horse and the chariot came to the semiurban agriculturally based Bactria and Margiana Archaeological Complex (BMAC) in southern Central Asia and to its extension around Tepe Hissar III in northern Iran. I have argued since 1988 that in the twentieth century BCE, rule in the BMAC was taken over by incoming Proto-Indo-Aryan speakers, who apparently adopted wholesale this impressive culture that preserved its original "Trans-Elamite" shape in its urban phase (*c.* 2300–1700 BCE). While the distribution of the steppe cultures reaches the BMAC, it does not continue further south or west, whereas the BMAC people came to the borders of the Indus Valley as early as around 1900 BCE and simultaneously spread to northern Iran and southwards to the Iranian plateau. Since the twentieth century BCE, the BMAC people were in trade relations with Syria; Assyrian merchants in Cappadocia were importing tin from southern Central Asia.

The easy adoption of a new culture by an incoming powerful minority was also assumed in the case of the Late Tripolye culture, and is actually evidenced in the case of the Mitanni kingdom. That the Mitanni rulers (*c.* 1500–1300 BCE) were Proto-Indo-Aryan speakers can be seen only from texts. An archaeological correlate for the movement of Proto-Indo-Aryan speakers to West Asia is the appearance of the Early West Iranian Grey Ware around 1500 BCE; its origins are seen in Gorgan Grey Ware that was connected with the BMAC extension at Tepe Hissar around 1900 BCE. That the Mitanni Proto-Indo-Aryans initiated chariotry in West Asia on a grand scale is seen above all from the adoption of the Indo-Aryan term *marya-*, "chariot-warrior, nobleman," with these meanings in the Hurrian, Assyrian, West Semitic, and Egyptian languages. A newly found text suggests that the Hurrians had *marya* mercenaries as early as about 1760 BCE (Eidem 2014). Before the westward move of the BMAC-related people of Gorgan in northern Iran, they had probably fused with a new wave of Proto-Indo-Aryan-speaking immigrants from the steppes of Kazakhstan, this time people of the Fëdorovo Andronovo culture, who came to the BMAC in its late, posturban phase, around 1700 BCE. Andronovo campsites surround practically all BMAC settlements, and several hybrid Andronovo-BMAC cultures came into being in southern Central Asia.

In southern Central Asia, the BMAC was replaced by the Yaz I–related cultures (*c.* 1500–1000 BCE). These belong to the "roller pottery" cultures that came from the European steppes. After the departure of the Proto-Indo-Aryan branch (the formation of the Abashevo culture), the Iranian branch remained in the Proto-Aryan homeland, the Pontic-Caspian steppes, where, after the Yamnaya cultures, largely similar pastoralist cultures followed one another, of course with varying distributions. But they did not move to the Asiatic steppes until around 1500 BCE, when the newly formed "roller pottery" cultures suddenly expanded in every direction. This seems to be connected with large-scale adoption of horse riding by Proto-Iranian speakers. While Proto-Iranian has a special verb for "riding," such a verb is not found in PIE or in Proto-Aryan or in Proto-Indo-Aryan.

Having no known graves, the Yaz I people probably practiced "sky" burial (exposure to carrion birds) and created the religion that would become, after its reform, Zoroastrianism, around 1000 BCE. The cenotaphs that occur in increasing numbers in the BMAC suggest that this kind of burial, which has no antecedents in the steppes, was adopted by Proto-Iranian speakers in southern Central Asia. The terracotta figurines of horse riders from Pirak in Baluchistan, datable to around 1500 BCE, are anthropomorphic except for their bird's-beak heads. I compare them with the mounted Saka horsemen from the frozen tombs of the Altai Mountains (*c.* 500–200 BCE), who wear pointed felt caps, often topped by bird's-beak heads.

The people of the Yaz I culture, who probably spoke Proto-East Iranian or Proto-Saka, continued some traditions of the earlier BMAC culture. The Yaz I–related fortress of Tillya Tepe in eastern Afghanistan is similar to the BMAC forts, and the tradition of building such fortresses seems to have survived to the present day in the fortified manors of Pashto-speakers in Waziristan. I suggest that the Yaz I forts are the Dāsa citadels conquered by the Rigvedic Indo-Aryans on their way through the mountains from the Kandahar region (where King Divodāsa was born on the banks of the Sarasvatī River) to Swat and the Punjab. Dāsa or Dasa is an ethnic name of Saka speakers in the Indo-Iranian borderlands (meaning "man, human being, hero" in Khotanese Saka and Wakhi), known as Dā(h)a and Daha in Greek and Old Persian sources. Among the proper names of the Dāsa chiefs mentioned in the Rigveda is the patronym Kānīta, which has been compared to the Scythian proper names Kanītēs and Kanītos; some other names of Dāsa chiefs seem to come from the original non-Indo-European language of the BMAC. This solution to the Dāsa problem provides a new basis for estimating the date of the Rigvedic migration to South Asia; it may have taken place around the fourteenth century BCE, which agrees with the usual estimates.

The Rigvedic Indo-Aryans would thus have arrived in South Asia some 500 years later than the first Proto-Indo-Aryan-speaking immigrants coming from the "urban" phase of the BMAC. I have been ascribing the linguistic and religious differences between the Rigveda and the Atharvaveda to these two separate waves of Indo-Aryan speakers, whose gradual fusion is reflected in the formation of the Vedic literature. This is a controversial issue, as traditionally the evolution of the Vedic texts and religion has been seen as a unilinear development, the differences between the Rigveda and the Atharvaveda being interpreted as due to a dichotomy into a "hieratic" religion of the priests and a "popular" religion of the common people. This view is mainstream opinion, so the question has been dealt with at length in this book. Among the numerous linguistic differences, one is particularly important. In the original Rigvedic dialect every original PIE **l* had merged with **r*; this rhotacism had happened already before the Rigvedic Aryans entered South Asia. Although *l* was later reintroduced into the Rigvedic language, where it occurs mainly in foreign names, the Rigvedic Sanskrit cannot be the source of the Atharvavedic dialect, in which many words have preserved the original PIE **l*. The religious evidence will be discussed shortly.

The Vedic hymns were collected and the Vedic literature created during the rule of the Kuru kings. Temporally, geographically, and culturally (in its use of the horse, iron, only a few and small towns), the Kuru kingdom corresponds closely to the early phase (*c.* 1100–700 BCE) of the culture distinguished by the Painted Grey Ware (PGW). The legendary war between the Kauravas and the Pāṇḍavas, the main story of the Mahābhārata, seems to have taken place during the latter phase (*c.* 700–350 BCE) of the PGW culture (which includes a number of towns, such as Mathurā). None of the Pāṇḍava heroes is known to the Vedic literature before the Gṛhyasūtras, while the grammarian Pāṇini (*c.* 350 BCE) mentions the Mahābhārata and several key names associated with it.

I suggest connecting the Pāṇḍavas with the people who came to South Asia via Sindh, Gujarat, and Rajasthan around 800 BCE and brought with them the so-called Megalithic culture, adopting the earlier local Black-and-Red Ware as their pottery. The father of the five Pāṇḍava brothers is Pāṇḍu, meaning "pale," who was destined to be born pale-skinned; the name (which is Sanskrit with a Dravidian etymology) seems to represent the local Indian appellation for newly arrived foreigners with a slightly paler skin color. The Megalithic graves, the horse equipment found in them, and the associated round, yurt-like houses have parallels in Central Asia, the Caucasus, and western Iran, and suggest that the immigrants originally spoke an Iranian language, a hypothesis supported by the un-Indian polyandric marriage of the Pāṇḍavas, which can be compared with customs of Iranian tribes.

The Rāmāyaṇa seems to reflect the movement of the Megalithic culture to Sri Lanka and southern India, and the takeover of power in these regions by Aryan-speaking adventurers from the Indus Valley, Gujarat, and the Mathurā region. The Buddhist chronicles of Sri Lanka link the Aryan conquest of the island with Prince Vijaya, who came from Gujarat and raided towns on the west coast. The Pāṇḍya kings of Tamil Nadu and their capital Madurai, the southern Madhurā, are connected with the northern Madhurā, that is, Mathurā.

There is general agreement that the "family books" 2–7 represent the oldest part of the Rigveda and most truly reflect the original religion of the Rigvedic Aryans. In these old books, the chief deity is Indra, who is worshipped by offering praise songs and the sacred drink *soma*. The Aśvins or Nāsatyas, the twins who circle around the world in their flying chariot, are divine medicine men, deities of lower rank who were originally excluded from the *soma* cult. Mitra and Varuṇa, another divine dual, vie with Indra but have remarkably few hymns addressed to them. Mitra and Varuṇa, Indra and the Nāsatyas (but no other Aryan god) are all invoked by the Mitanni king Sātivāja to be the divine witnesses of his pact with the Hittite king around 1350 BCE. They seem to have been the most important members of the Proto-Indo-Aryan pantheon at that time, presumably around 1500 BCE, when Mitanni rule started. Here Mitra and Varuṇa hold the first place, while in the Rigveda Indra is clearly the principal deity.

My suggestion is that the religion of the two waves of Proto-Indo-Aryans that came to the BMAC around 2000–1900 BCE and 1700–1600 BCE had already slightly drifted apart. The later wave, that of the Fëdorovo Andronovo people, worshipped Indra. Their cultic drink **sauma* was neither of Proto-Indo-European nor—on the evidence of Herodotus and the Aryan loanwords in Uralic languages—of Proto-Aryan origin, but seems to have been adopted somewhere in Central Asia. (Mummies discovered in Xinjiang and connected with Andronovo people have pouches filled with *Ephedra* twigs in their funeral dress.) Indra, however, may have been the original Proto-Aryan head of the pantheon, the inherited PIE god of the "sky" and the "day," like Zeus (< *Dyeus) in Greece and Ju(piter) (< *Dius) in Rome. Indra is called *deva-*, "god," and has the epithet *dyumat-*, "shining, splendid, heavenly," both from the root *dyav- / div-* (PIE **dyev- / div-*), "to shine." The word for "(highest) god" in Proto-Uralic was **juma* (i.e., *yuma*) from Proto-Indo-Aryan **dyumat-*. The name Indra itself has proved difficult to explain etymologically. I propose deriving it from **Inmar*, the Proto-Central-Uralic name for the god of sky and thundery weather. The West-Uralic cognate *Ilmari* (from *ilma*, "air, weather, atmosphere") occurring in Finnic epic poems is the name of the divine smith who has made the sky and its luminaries; he also created the sky-propping world pillar *sampo / sampas* < Proto-Indo-Aryan **stambha-s*. People belonging to the probably Proto-East-Uralic-speaking Cherkaskul' culture of the Mid-Urals collaborated with the Fëdorovo Andronovo people, and some of them became pastoralists, moving long distances with Andronovo people, even to southern Central Asia.

The first wave of Proto-Indo-Aryan immigrants to the BMAC came from Sintashta in the south Urals, and are supposed to have invented the horse-drawn light chariot around 2100–2000 BCE. The chariot must have enjoyed immense importance in their culture. The layout of their fortified settlements is circular and resembles the chariot wheel. The horse-chariot was a crucial marker of rank, being the most important prestige symbol of elite graves. With the chariot there came into being new deities, who do not have a PIE ancestry as is usually assumed. The new gods associated with the horse-chariot are called "the two sons of the Sky" in the Indo-Aryan, Greek, and Baltic languages: ever since PIE times, the Sky had until this time been the highest god, and his paternity gave prestige to the new gods, who were raised to the top of the divine pantheon. It appears to me that the two-man chariot team was made into a model for a real system of dual kingship, as in Dorian Greece; in India, this dual kingship survives in the collaboration of the king with the priest of the royal house, the *purohita*. The king was the chariot-warrior, his high priest the charioteer—as they were in ancient India in bygone times, according to the Jaiminīya-Brāhmaṇa (3,94).

While the Aśvins clearly are the Indo-Aryan counterparts of the Dorian Greek Dioskouroi, they are not dual kings. Instead, Mitra-and-Varuṇa are dual kings. To explain this, I have suggested that the Aśvins were dual kings when they came to the BMAC. But when the early Proto-Indo-Aryans of the BMAC had trade relations with the Assyrians from the second half of the twentieth century BCE, they probably became acquainted with the Assyrian religion, where social virtues are represented as subsidiary deities, personifications of the qualities of the high god Aššur, surrounding Aššur like a king is surrounded by his closest officials. I assume that the Proto-Indo-Aryans of the BMAC imitated this Assyrian model and provided their own highest gods (i.e., the Aśvins) with similar attributes, namely the Āditya gods. For some reason, the two most important ones among these new attribute gods, Mitra and Varuṇa, came to be associated with the Aśvins' dual kingship, and the Aśvins were reduced to the role of saviors, divine medicine men, and funeral gods. Yet they preserved their inherent connection with the horse-drawn chariot and its two-man team.

In the steppes, chiefs were buried with their chariots. All three divine twins seem to have been funeral gods, too, associated with a funeral chariot race both in Greece and India (if my suggestion about Yama's prize-race in Rigveda 1,116,2 is accepted), and a funeral horse-riding race in the Baltics. The charioteer's chief duty was to "save" his master, the chariot-warrior, and "bring him safely home." This latter sense is the meaning of the PIE root **nes-*, from which derives Greek Nestor, the Homeric hero famed as a charioteer; Greek *nostos*, "home-coming," corresponds with Sanskrit **nasati-*, "homecoming," which is implied by the Aśvins' alternative name, Nāsatya. Like the Aśvins, the Greek Dioskouroi act as *sōtêres*, "saviors," who help people in dire need. In the Rigveda, the Aśvins save decrepit people—sometimes described as lying underground, "like the dead"—by rejuvenating them, which suggests to me that they look after the rebirth of the deceased.

The Aśvins' function as funeral deities seems to be confirmed by the funerary "face urns" of the Gandhāra Grave culture. The connection with the Aśvins is suggested by the urns' lids, which have horse-shaped handles, and above all by the large "nose" that stands out from the "face" of many of these vessels. PIE **nes-*, "to come safely home," has become in Indo-Iranian *nas-*, "to come safely home." The existence of the homophonous word *nas-*, "nose," has given rise among Indo-Aryan-speakers to the myth of the Nāsatyas' "nose-birth" (their conception is said to have taken place when their mother, in the shape of a mare, sniffed the semen inadvertently laid on the ground by the Aśvins' stallion-shaped father). The myth in turn has led to rituals of generation, in which material symbolizing seed is inserted into the wife's nose. The nose thus symbolizes (re)generation.

A "nose" similar to those of the Gandhāra Grave face-urns is prescribed also for the *mahāvīra* or *gharma* pot sacred to the Aśvins; this *gharma* pot is said to be the head of a decapitated hero. At the end of the *gharma* ritual this pot, along with other utensils of the ritual, is to be laid out on ground in the shape of a human being. This ritual act has a parallel in the Vedic funeral, where a deceased sacrificer's ritual implements are laid on the various parts of his corpse. The two officiating priests in charge of the *gharma* ritual are the *adhvaryu* and the *pratiprasthātar*, who personify the two Aśvins among the Vedic sacrificial priests.

In the Rigveda, the worship of Indra with the *soma* cult clearly predominates, although the inclusion of hymns to Mitra, Varuṇa, and the Aśvins in the "family" books suggests that their cult had already been adopted in southern Central Asia, as does the Mitanni pact of around 1350 BCE. On their arrival in South Asia, however, the Rigvedic Aryans appear to have met Indo-Aryan speakers originating from the urban phase of the BMAC whose principal Aryan divinities were the Aśvins and Mitra-Varuṇa, but who had not previously known Indra; on the other hand, they had long been exposed to the substratum influence of the Indus people and their descendants.

The Kāṇva and Āṅgirasa poets, whose traditions favored the tristich structure and the *gāyatrī* and *pragātha* meters, belonged to the early wave of Proto-Indo-Aryan immigrants to South Asia. It appears that the Atri clan of the fifth book of the Rigveda, which is part of the "family" books and therewith belongs to the later, Rigvedic immigrants, adopted the worship of the Aśvins in Gandhāra from the Kāṇvas. The Atri clan adapted the worship of Aśvins as funeral gods to their newly introduced cremation burial by developing the *gharma* or *pravargya* ritual, which seems to be connected with the "face urns" of the second phase of the Gandhāra Grave culture (in 2014 dated to *c.* 1100–800 BCE).

Part of the Kāṇvas and Āṅgirasas appear to have joined the Indra-worshippers of the Rigvedic Aryans more or less immediately after the latter's entrance to South Asia, and created the Sāmaveda. The earliest references to *sāmans* in the Rigveda are connected with the *gharma* ritual, hence the worship of the Aśvins, whose original sacred drink appears to have been honey-beer (*madhu-surā*). From the *sautrāmaṇī* ritual we know that the preparation of *surā* included its purification through a filter of horsehair, while in the *yasna* ritual of the Zoroastrians the *haoma* was filtered through bull's hair. It seems to me that the *sāmans* originally used in the Aśvin-related rites were now adapted to the worship of Indra and his *soma* drink, resulting to the first great addition to the collection of Rigvedic hymns after the "family" books. The principal priests of the Yajurveda are, again, the *adhvaryu* and the *pratiprasthātar*, officiants of the *gharma/pravargya* ritual, said to be the human counterparts of the two Aśvins. This suggests that priests who were once Aśvin-worshippers probably had a major role in the creation of the Yajurveda.

Some Kāṇvas and Āṅgirasas remained faithful to their original traditions, however. Their Atharvavedic hymns were accepted as part of the Vedic culture after they too had at least nominally accepted the Indra cult. This happened in the last additions to the Rigveda, especially in Book 10, where many hymns have an Atharvavedic character. But the core of this earlier, Atharvavedic religion is in many respects rather different from the Rigvedic religion. Particularly noteworthy is sorcery—harming enemies and rivals of the king by magic means—which is among the primary duties of the royal priest, the *purohita*.

Consonant with this violent character of the Atharvaveda are the Vrātya rituals, first described in the Atharvaveda (Book 15 in the Śaunaka recension) and the Brāhmaṇas of the Sāmaveda. The *vrātyastomas* are performed at the beginning and end of raiding expeditions by their participants. The details of the *vrātyastomas* connect them with archaic royal rituals (the horse or human sacrifice, the royal consecration, the *vājapeya*, and the piling of the fire altar, *agnicayana*), as well as the "popular" festival of *mahāvrata* performed at the end of the year, usually coinciding with the completion of the fire altar. Besides the gods of ancient Aryan background, the Aśvins, Varuṇa, and Bṛhaspati (who is a divine *purohita* and charioteer), important divinities in these rites as well as in the Atharvaveda and the Brāhmaṇa literature (which linguistically continues the Atharvavedic rather than Rigvedic tradition) there were the creator god Prajāpati, the goddess Vāc and Rudra. It is these deities, in my opinion, who are most likely to be survivals of the main gods of the Harappan pantheon, though we can also expect that gods who are originally Aryan, such as Varuṇa, may have absorbed some of the functions and attributes of their approximate counterparts in the religion of the Indus civilization.

The Greek ambassador Megasthenes, who lived in Pāṭaliputra around 300 BCE, tells the legend of Princess Pandaíē (i.e., Pāṇḍu's daughter), who was married by his own father, the Indian Heracles. The story resembles the Sāvitrī legend, which connects this myth with the Vedic goddess Sītā-Sāvitrī, and thus with Sītā, the heroine of the Rāmāyaṇa. The Indian Heracles can be identified as Bala-Rāma—according to Cicero, this Heracles was called Belus—while in the Mahābhārata, Bala-Rāma is called simply Rāma, and seems to be originally identical with the hero of the Rāmāyaṇa. In the Rāmāyaṇa, Sītā (whose name means "furrow") was born out of a furrow when King Janaka ("generator, father") was plowing a field, and Bala-Rāma is a deity whose characteristic weapon and attribute is the plow.

Mathurā is connected with the worship of Kṛṣṇa ("black") and his elder brother Bala-Rāma (whose skin-color is white). They belong to the Yādava clan, whose ancestor Yadu is connected with one of the early tribes mentioned in the Rigveda, apparently belonging to the earlier Proto-Indo-Aryan wave of Aśvin worshippers. The Pāṇḍavas united with Kṛṣna of Mathurā, and Kṛṣṇa served as the charioteer of the main Pāṇḍava hero, Arjuna, whose name means "white." In my opinion this chariot team reflects the Aśvins, whose cult had survived among the Yādavas of Mathurā. The same applies to the brothers Bala-Rāma and Kṛṣṇa, who are not on good terms with Indra, for example in the Govardhana episode. The colors white and black suit the Aśvins, who drive around the world in their airborne chariot in a day, apparently personifying, like Mitra and Varuṇa, the day or sun, and the night or moon.

Naturally, this Aśvin heritage is only one side of these divinities. Kṛṣṇa as both a naughty boy and a dark-skinned native cowherd strikingly resembles the low-caste Keralan deity Kuṭṭiccāttan, whose myth and cult suggest how an originally low-caste or aboriginal deity might have been adopted into the Brahmanical pantheon (Parpola 1999c). Bala-Rāma, in his turn, as an addicted toddy-drinker seems to have replaced an earlier local deity worshipped for the same (in)capacity, a demon in the shape of a wild ass (Dhenuka in Harivaṁsa 57). The wild ass (Sanskrit *gaura-*, "wild ass," not "bison" as in dictionaries) is an animal with a phenomenal capacity to drink large amounts of water, mentioned as a model for the *soma*-thirsty Indra in the Rigveda. It lives in the salt desert, and seems to have been worshipped in the Indus civilization as a god of death and fertility (qualities also ascribed to salt) (Parpola & Janhunen 2011). Bala-Rāma also seems to continue as an earlier agricultural divinity connected with the plow, perhaps a predecessor of Hindu Śiva, whose names include Lāṅgaleśvara, "Lord of the Plow."

23

Harappan Religion in Relation to West and South Asia

One of the most crucial problems in the investigation of the Indus civilization and its religion is its linguistic identity. With the Indus population estimated at about one million, the Harappan language could not possibly have disappeared without leaving traces in the Vedic texts, which began to be composed in the Indus Valley toward the end of the second millennium BCE. I think it can now be stated with fair confidence that there was only one written Harappan language, and that it was an early member of the Dravidian language family, by far the largest in South Asia after Indo-Iranian. This conclusion is supported by the many Dravidian loanwords in the Vedic language, including the oldest available source, the Rigveda. Among these early Dravidian loans (which include several new etymologies proposed here) are religious terms that are important in both the Vedic and Hindu religions, such as the sacred syllable *oṁ*. Furthermore, the present-day distribution of Dravidian languages in central and southern India favors Dravidian as the Harappan language, since the Chalcolithic cultures of Gujarat, Rajasthan, Maharashtra, and Karnataka are derived from the Early and Mature Harappan cultures of the Indus Valley. In addition, there is the Dravidian kinship system (radically different from the Aryan system of North India) and Dravidian toponyms, which span from southern India up to Gujarat. None of the minority languages of South Asia, distributed in marginal areas, is a serious competitor with Dravidian.

The Dravidian identification is borne out by the Indus inscriptions. They are written in a language-based logosyllabic and pictographic script, based on the same principles as those of other very early writing systems, such as Archaic Sumerian and the Egyptian hieroglyphic. Using methods proven in successful decipherments, it is possible to interpret two or three dozen Indus signs phonetically, even without bilinguals. The interpretations can be checked because they form compound words that support each other like a crossword puzzle, and also because they agree with external clues on Harappan objects and above all with compound words attested in Dravidian languages.

Another problem concerns the cultural continuity from the Indus civilization to historical times, which has often been questioned. One striking testimony to an unbroken continuity of Harappan cults down to the present day is provided by the unique crocodile worship in fifty tribal villages of southern Gujarat. Horizontal wooden crocodile images erected upon vertical poles by these Gujarati tribals in their sanctuaries have a precise ancient antecedent painted on a Mature Harappan potsherd excavated at Amri in Sindh, depicting a pair of gavials, fish-eating river crocodiles, without back legs but with a projection sticking out of the body at a ninety-degree angle, which anchors the crocodiles to the "ground" of the scene. The swelling protuberance, which is at the tip of their long and narrow snout in the males, is hunted as a powerful aphrodisiac, rendering the animal almost extinct. A tablet from Harappa depicts a male gavial pushing its snout into the vagina of a human female with splayed legs. A tablet from Dholavira seems to depict a sacrifice of little children to crocodiles. Votive offerings of first-born babies to crocodiles were performed by couples wanting offspring in Bengal until around 1810 CE; a similar promise to sacrifice his first-born son was forced upon King Hariścandra when he approached god Varuṇa for an heir in the Vedic Śunaḥśepa legend recited at the royal consecration. Varuṇa is a god of waters and the lord of aquatic animals, who in Hindu iconography rides a crocodile. He is also connected with the night sky, and a heavenly crocodile consisting of stars, the pole star being in its tail, is mentioned in Vedic and Purāṇic texts.

Here we have entered the topic of "village Hinduism," the essential components of which appear to date back at least as early as the Early and Mature Harappan villages of the third millennium BCE. A mother goddess as the guardian deity of the village, her husband or servant symbolized by the bull or buffalo, and their worship in the shape of clay or stone images, are basic elements of this age-old folk religion—likewise the cult of sacred trees and their divine inhabitants. Fig trees, especially the pipal and banyan, the bull, the water buffalo, the fish, and the peacock are some of the important motifs of Early and Mature Harappan painted pottery, which are also among the principal religious symbols of "village Hinduism." Its main concerns are the promotion of human and animal fertility and averting disease, drought, and other misfortunes. John Marshall (1931) suggested an unbroken continuity in Indian folk religion from Harappan times to the present day, and this thesis has enjoyed wide scholarly support.

In my efforts to penetrate deeper into Harappan ideology, I have tried to interpret the manifestations of Early and Mature Harappan religion by relating them to the better- known and better-understood religions of later South Asia, and also those of West Asia, which was in direct contact with the Indus civilization and shared a comparable economic foundation.

During the first quarter of the third millennium BCE, the relatively short-lived Proto-Elamite civilization spread from the region of Susa over most parts of the Iranian plateau, giving rise to the "Trans-Elamite" cultures of Kerman, Seistan, and southern Central Asia, reaching as far east as the Makran in Pakistan. The Proto-Elamites had a language-based pictographic script. The idea of such a script was therefore within reach of the Early Harappans, whose ceramics have been found at Shahr-i Sokhta in Iran. This site in Seistan has yielded a tablet in the Proto-Elamite script. I suspect that the "yoga posture" of the Harappan anthropomorphic deities in the seal iconography is derived from the "sitting bulls" of Proto-Elamite seals. The horns of the Harappan gods may also have prototypes in

Proto-Elamite iconography (where human beings and gods are represented with animals), although gods and kings with horns are also found in Mesopotamia and in many other places.

Indus merchants appear to have first arrived in northern Mesopotamia overland, following caravan routes via which lapis lazuli was imported to West Asia from Bactria—called Aratta in Sumerian sources, which seems to me the original location of the country of Āraṭṭa mentioned in Sanskrit sources. In any case, Harappans would have been present in Mesopotamia towards the end of the Early Dynastic period, since they mediated to the Indus Valley art motifs and modes of dressing—particularly the royal hair-dress—that were current in West Asia in those times.

From the Old Akkadian to Ur III periods (*c.* 2300–2000 BCE), cuneiform documents refer to a sea trade with the Greater Indus Valley, called Meluhha. Sargon himself boasts that these far-off foreigners moored their ships at the dock of his newly built capital city, Akkad. They must have brought the great king living water buffaloes as gifts, as buffaloes suddenly appear in the iconography of royal cylinder seals, replacing the wild urus bull in the favorite Akkadian motif. This "contest" motif had developed from the fight between the lion and the bull in Proto-Elamite seals. In the earlier Late Uruk iconography of Mesopotamia and Egypt, the king is depicted as holding back two lions with his bare hands, or as hunting these mighty beasts. In the Indus Valley, too, a male figure holding back two tigers with his bare hands is likely to have the same symbolism of power.

Some Meluhhans stayed in Mesopotamia and the Gulf for generations, becoming fully integrated in the local society, speaking Sumerian and even giving their children Sumerian names. At the same time, as trade agents, they also spoke their native Meluhhan language, which was not generally understood in Mesopotamia. Translators were needed. Occasionally Harappan agents wrote their foreign names in the Indus script on seals. Sumerians and Akkadians, on the other hand, never seem to have come to the Indus Valley, though some Old Akkadian kings in their war expeditions toward the east conquered the Kerman region in southeastern Iran, the seat of the recently discovered Jiroft culture. One cuneiform text reports that among the participants of a worldwide rebellion against the Old Akkadian ruler Narām-Sīn was a king from Meluhha. Unfortunately the tablet is broken and we know only the last part of this Meluhhan king's name, "[. . .]-ib-ra." This name is the one and only known record of the political history of the Greater Indus Valley, in the form of a peripheral member of the West Asian cultural sphere.

Cultural influences came from West Asia to the Indo-Iranian borderlands much earlier than historical times. A settled way of life with agriculture and animal husbandry is supposed to have started in Anatolia some ten thousand years ago or earlier (the newly discovered, and impressive, temple at Göpekli Tepe in Anatolia is dated to 13,000 BCE!), from which it gradually spread. Around 6000 BCE the village of Çatal Höyük in Anatolia had a temple of a Mother Goddess, seated on a throne guarded by panthers, and worshipped with bull sacrifices. During the following millennia a similar cult (with variations) is found all over West Asia and the Mediterranean. The Goddess, usually associated with the lion and the planet Venus, presides over birth and death, granting fertility and military success. She is the personification of the Earth, which yields grain and other plants including fruit trees, and she receives in her womb both the dead and the seed grains, "sacrificed" but reborn as the new harvest. The bull personifies her husband, the Sky, who roars as thunder and fertilizes the Earth with his rain-seed.

The marriage of this primeval couple was celebrated at the new year, the bull being sacrificed and the people feasted with its meat. The king, who was responsible for the welfare of the country, represented the son-husband of the Goddess, and as her protégé could count on victory in war. He did not, however, personally perform this role in the sacrificial drama enacted on the greatest festival of the year, the "sacred marriage" of the Goddess (represented by her high priestess) at the new year. The drama ended with the death of the bridegroom, which was ritually lamented. This and related rituals elsewhere in West Asia developed into secret mysteries, in which participants killed human victims, ate the flesh, and drank the blood.

In the Proto-Elamite "contest" seals, the lion and the bull are both alternately represented as winners and losers. This has been interpreted to mean that they stand for opposite and complementary cosmic powers, not only female (lion) and male (bull), but also sun/day (lion) and moon/night (bull), fire (lion) and water (bull), and so on. The Sun and Moon are the principal heavenly bodies, whose movements define the time, and are the prime objects of study in astronomy/astrology, which in West Asia was the most important science, used for making predictions, especially about the fate of kings and countries. Very significant, too, were the five planets visible with the naked eye, distinguished by their independent movement and brightness from the fixed stars, which were also important in marking the route through the heavens of the sun, the moon, and the planets, which were all considered divinities in their own right or astral aspects of gods known by other names.

Settled life in the Indo-Iranian borderlands starts around 7000 BCE. The principal religious artifacts are terracotta images of human females and bulls, which presumably have the same meaning as their counterparts in West Asia: Mother Earth and Father Sky. Similar images have been made in South Asian villages ever since, and in most places the principal yearly festival of the villagers has been the marriage of the guardian goddess of the village, involving the sacrifice of the bull or buffalo who represented the goddess's husband. Everywhere in South India the water buffalo was until recently the preferred victim for the goddess, although other male animals could be offered—nowadays they are chiefly goats or chickens. The Daimabad hoard not far from Mumbai with its bronze statue of a water buffalo proves that it was a sacred animal in central Maharashtra in Late Harappan times around 1800 BCE.

In the Old Akkadian seals, the water buffalo imported from the Indus civilization shares the symbolism of the wild bull of the earlier Mesopotamian iconography. Harappans killed the water buffalo by spearing it. The spearman's hair is bound into a "double-bun" at the nape of the neck, which was the hairdo of the royal warrior in West Asian art around 2400 BCE. The Harappan buffalo-spearer also places his foot on the head of the beast, like the naked hero vanquishing the buffalo on Akkadian seals. A seal from Chanhu-daro depicts the sexual intercourse of a bison bull and an anthropomorphic female lying on the ground with open legs. Thus in the Harappan "sacred marriage" the sacrificed bridegroom of the goddess was a water buffalo or bison bull. The sacrificial buffalo may be assumed to personify the important Harappan god called Proto-Śiva, who wears the horns of the water buffalo, and his human counterpart, the king.

The Harappan "sacred marriage" as a royal institution was taken over by the first ("Atharvavedic") wave of Indo-Aryan speaking immigrants, who replaced the water buffalo as the sacrificed bridegroom with the horse, their own most prestigious sacrificial animal. A reminiscence of the Harappan buffalo is the title of the king's chief queen who lies with the horse, *mahiṣī*, "water buffalo cow." The chief queen is said to personify the Earth and the most important goddess of the Vedic Brāhmaṇa texts, Vāc, "Sound." As the goddess of victory, Vāc is called *siṁhī*, "lioness," and is worshipped at the mahāvrata festival with the sound of war-drums and other musical instruments. Vāc is the daughter of the creator god Prajāpati, approached by her father in an incestuous "sacred marriage" that created all beings, but led to Prajāpati's slaughter as punishment for his sin. This marriage is imitated by couples participating in the *mahāvrata*, who do not need to care for social differences.

The *mahāvrata* was originally celebrated at the autumnal equinox, the traditional time of starting war expeditions after the rains. As a vrātya ritual, it had the same function as the *vrātyastoma*, uniting the warriors leaving for war. It survives to the present day in the *navarātri/daśahrā* festival of Goddess Durgā, who, on the "tenth day of victory," vanquishes her ferocious opponent, the Buffalo Demon, who according to some variants of the myth, made amorous passes or even married her on false pretexts, thereby leading to his slaughter. Durgā has been the guardian goddess of many Indian royal houses. On leaving for a war expedition, kings have lustrated their armies at the *navarātri/daśahrā* festival, and sometimes offered hundreds of water buffaloes to the goddess to capture her favor and obtain victory.

The myth of the lion-riding warrior goddess Durgā's fight with the buffalo demon Mahiṣa Asura emerges in Indian literature very late, around 700 CE, but by means of iconographical representations it can be traced back to the first centuries CE, and is supposed to have been introduced to India by the Kuṣāṇas, who a little earlier had in Afghanistan adopted the local worship of the lion-escorted goddess Nanaya. Nanaya's cult was brought to Afghanistan by about 2000 BCE from West Asia, where she was a variant of Inanna/ Ištar, the goddess of love and war. But a tiger-riding goddess of war is attested also in a Harappan cylinder seal from Kalibangan. A few Rigvedic hymns, in which hundreds of water buffaloes are killed for Indra to consume before a battle, prove the existence of such rituals for the sake of victory in the Indus Valley at the end of the second millennium BCE, when the Rigvedic Aryans were reaching South Asia. The water buffalo is a South Asian animal, and the almost complete later silence about the sacrifice of the water buffalo in subsequent Vedic texts shows that it was an alien custom. The water buffalo sacrifice is mentioned in later Vedic literature in one context only: the animal is one of the many subsidiary victims in the horse sacrifice, sacred to Varuṇa, the divine king.

In the BMAC-related religion of the Indo-Aryan speakers, Varuṇa seems to have originally represented the "priest-king," the charioteer of the two-man royal chariot team of the Aśvins, associated with the moon, night, and water (while Mitra was the chariot-warrior associated with the sun, day, and fire). The first Indo-Aryan speakers coming to South Asia substituted Varuṇa for the divine king of the Harappan religion, who was the god of waters, and the god of creation and death, surviving in the Brāhmaṇa texts as the creator god Prajāpati, who was killed in punishment of his incest (thus becoming the first dead person and the king of the deceased, like the god Yama of the originally Iranian tradition also preserved in the Veda).

That Varuṇa inherited the position and attributes of the Harappan "priest-king" is also suggested by Varuṇa's *tārpya* garment, with which the Vedic king is invested in the ritual of royal consecration. The *tārpya* garment is said to be decorated with images of *dhiṣṇyas*, a term that denotes both a "sacrificial hearth" and a "star," and agrees with the Vedic conception that the stars are ancient sages transferred to the sky who stand by their sacrificial hearths. The Priest-King statuette from Mohenjo-daro is draped in a garb decorated with trefoil motifs originally filled with a red paste. The trefoil has an astral significance in West Asia, where it covers statuettes depicting the "Bull of Heaven"; a fragment of a trefoil-decorated bull-figurine has been excavated at Mohenjo-daro, too. Mesopotamian kings and gods were dressed in a garment decorated with the figures of stars, rosettes, and crosses, called a "sky-garment," in imitation of the starry night sky.

In the elite religion of the Indus civilization, as in Mesopotamia and other early urban civilizations, astronomy and time-reckoning played an important role from the Early Harappan period. This is clear from the orientation of the towns according to the cardinal directions, from sun-like art motifs and from what seem to be gnomon stands. Vedic and epic traditions connected with the *nakṣatra* calendar suggest that its origins date to about 3000 BCE when the new-year star was Aldebaran (Sanskrit *rohiṇī*), observed when it rose together with the sun at the vernal equinox. Around 2400 BCE, the calendar was apparently revised by the Indus people, who made it luni-solar and shifted the new year to the sun's conjunction with the Pleiades (Sanskrit *kṛttikāḥ*). This shift seems to be reflected in the principal astral myths of the Veda and epic-purāṇic Hinduism, the abduction of Tārā ("star"), the wife of Bṛhaspati, by Soma the Moon; and the birth of Skanda-Kumāra in the place where the Kṛttikās were bathing in the (heavenly) Ganges. Names of the planets known from Old Tamil texts can be plausibly read in Indus texts, while the Vedic tradition is curiously silent about these luminaries of the sky.

Particularly important is the identification of the Old Tamil name of the pole star in the Indus inscriptions: *vaṭa-mīn*, which literally means "north star," through Dravidian homophony (utilized in the Indus script) also means "rope star" and "banyan star." These meanings make it possible to understand the concepts of a heavenly banyan tree, which the Rigveda (1,24,7) connects with the divine king Varuṇa, and the idea fundamental to the Purāṇic cosmology, according to which all the stars and planets are maintained in the heavens by invisible ropes binding them with the pole star. Mantras addressed to the pole star by the Vedic bridegroom preserve a tradition that probably once was part of the royal consecration, making the pole star a symbol of kingship as it was in China.

The banyan, the mightiest native tree of South Asia, got its name *vaṭa-* (not attested in Sanskrit before the epics) from the Proto-Dravidian word **vaṭam*, "rope," which refers to the hanging air roots characteristic of the banyan. From RV 1,24,7 we know that Vedic people thought the invisible air roots of the heavenly banyan were attached to living beings, supplying them with life-energy. The Sanskrit word *raśmi-*, which is used of them, means not only "rope" but also "ray," a meaning confirmed by the word *ketavaḥ*, "rays," applied to them in this context in RV 1,24,7. Thus they can fully be compared to the rays of the sun, which according to the Vedic and Purāṇic conception feed the heavenly bodies and living beings. This parallelism between the rays of the sun and the air roots of the heavenly banyan tree strongly suggests a Harappan-Dravidian ancestry to some related cosmological conceptions. They also provide new evidence for the hypothesis that beginnings of yoga lie in the Indus civilization.

Thus the Purāṇa texts have specific names, *suṣumṇa-* and others, for the principal rays of the sun, which feed the moon and the five planets. *Suṣumṇa-* is known as the name of a solar ray in the earliest Yajurvedic texts, and the old Upaniṣads know *suṣumṇā-* as the name of the principal vein in the human body, which is said to have 72,000 veins. Moreover, the veins of the human body are linked with the rays of the sun, and they function as paths through which the soul can move from human heart to the sun in deep sleep and at the moment of death, the sacred syllable *oṁ* being connected with this passage. These ideas are clear precedents of concepts central to the later *haṭha-* or *kuṇḍalinī-yoga*, and their Harappan origin is further supported by the fact that the old Upaniṣads ascribe to both veins and solar rays the same five colors that the five planets have in Indian iconography, and from which derive their Dravidian names, attested both in Old Tamil texts and in Indus inscriptions.

The parallelism of the air roots of the heavenly banyan and the rays of the sun also make it likely that the pole star is the nightly counterpart of the midday sun of the zenith. Vedic texts have preserved the conception that the sun does not go beneath the horizon in the evening but simply turns around so that its dark side is toward the earth and then returns invisible through the sky to the east, where it turns its bright side toward the earth. The Brāhmaṇa texts mention as a symbol of the sun the tortoise. The starred tortoise of South Asia has a black shell studded with several bright star-like ornaments.

Several Dravidian names of the tortoise are derived from verbs denoting "contraction," which refers to the tortoise's habit of drawing its limbs beneath its shell. These verbs also mean "to go into hiding" and, when speaking of the sun, "to set," as the setting sun draws in its rays like the tortoise its limbs. Significantly, the Dravidian verbs just mentioned are also used of an ascetic or yogi who is curbing his mind by drawing the senses back from their objects, and also the Bhagavadgītā and other texts compare this act of *pratyāhāra* to the "contraction" of the tortoise.

The Brāhmaṇa texts specifically connect the tortoise with the head and its seven openings, which represent the sense organs and are associated with the Seven Sages. The Seven Sages are identified with the seven stars of Ursa Major, next to the pole star, whose place in the zenith corresponds to the suture at the top of the human skull, the *brahma-randhra* through which the soul is supposed to exit from the body, corresponding to the sun as the door to the world of Brahman. The pole star is also the pivot on which the night sky turns, and all post-Vedic texts, Hindu, Buddhist, and Jaina, assume that the cosmic mountain Meru connects the center of the earth with the pole star. Together these concepts may be behind the myth of the churning of the cosmic ocean (i.e., the ocean of the sky), in which Mount Meru was the churning stick and the tortoise the steady pivot (i.e., the pole star as *dhruva*, "fixed, immobile, constant"). I have proposed tentative Dravidian etymologies for the Sanskrit names of *Meru* and the (cosmic) tortoise, *kūrma*.

The proverbially slow tortoise is also the vehicle of the slow planet Saturn in Buddhist iconography. In chapter 21 it was suggested that while the Harappans wrote Saturn's Proto-Dravidian name, **may-mīn*, "black star," they wanted to refer to the planet not only phonetically but also pictorially, choosing rebuses that mean "roof-fish": the tortoise is an aquatic animal and hence a kind of "fish," which carries a roof over itself. But Saturn is also usually very dim and is assigned the dark blue or black color. Saturn is supposed to be son of the Sun-god, undoubtedly representing the Sun's nightly aspect. This may be the same as Saturn's overlord Yama, the god of death, who is called "the Righteous King" (*dharma-rāja*) as the judge of the deceased. In this respect he is like Varuṇa, the divine king who guards the law (*ṛta-*) and punishes the sinners. Varuṇa is also the god and husband of the waters and the lord of all aquatic animals.

It should by now have become clear that I argue, against the prevailing wisdom, that the Indus civilization had kings or priest-kings, even though their palaces are not as easily recognizable as in other ancient civilizations. (The complex of buildings in Mohenjo-daro, in which both the "Proto-Śiva" seal and the "fig deity" seal were excavated, is a likely candidate for a palace. See Possehl 2002:208–210; Vidale 2010.) From the Early Harappan period, there is evidence of an increasing concentration of power, which enabled wide standardization of culture and preplanned towns. The Kot Diji seals, with their four or five sets of concentric circles, and the Mehrgarh pot painted with the motif "sun in four quadrants," point to the ideology of a solar ruler, governing the four regions and the zenith, an ideology reflected in Vedic royal consecration and in the epics.

I assume that the Harappans had two principal male gods connected with kingship, the "old" divine king (comparable to Vedic Varuṇa and Prajāpati and to Hindu Śiva in his ascetic aspect), ruling in his central palace or capital, and his "young" alter ego, the crown prince (comparable to Vedic Rudra < *Rudh(i)ra, "Red," and also with Prince Rohita, "Red," in the Śunaḥśepa legend), who was in charge of military expeditions, as in the Vedic royal consecration. This is the "young sun," the red, newly born sun of the morning, and the "new year," the sun (re)born at the asterism of the Pleaides, the war-god Skanda nursed by the Kṛttikās, also called Kumāra, "baby, youth," also the name of Skanda's Vedic counterpart. The Old Tamil name of this divinity is Muruku or Murukaṉ, "baby, youth," which I have suggested reading in the Indus inscriptions, called in Tamil also Cēy, "the Red one," yet to be identified in the Indus texts.

In my view these two "royal" deities were connected with the two halves of the year, which ended, respectively, in the *mahāvrata* and *viṣuvat* festivals at the autumnal and vernal equinoxes, and in both of which a "sacred marriage" took place. The old king slept with his young virgin daughter (like Vedic Prajāpati with his own daughter Vāc), while the young prince (Rudra, a harp player and singer, a *kinnara*) slept with his old mother (*mahiṣī*, symbolizing the earth, the mother of the planet Mars, Rudhira). In both cases, the male partner was killed. As in ancient Mesopotamia and in the Vedic horse/human sacrifice, these rituals were enacted not by the king himself but by substitute victims.

The goddess with whom these two male gods fatally united, had two aspects like the Mesopotamian goddess Inanna/Ištar, symbolized by the planet Venus. As the morning star, Ištar was a bloodthirsty warrior goddess; as the evening star, she was a prostitute dedicated to sexual love. The Vedic goddess Vāc as the virginal daughter of Prajāpati is said to represent the Dawn. Vāc, also said to be a lioness and goddess of victory, was thus a predecessor of Durgā, the virginal, lion- or tiger-riding Hindu goddess of victory. The most ancient new-year star, Rohiṇī ("the red female"; the Sanskrit word *rohiṇī* also denotes a young girl just coming of age), was according to the Atharvaveda (13,1,22) a goddess of war. But Vāc is also the Indian counterpart of the Akkadian Ištar as a prostitute. In the Vedic *mahāvrata*, Vāc is worshipped with sexual intercourse, sumptuous feasting, and the sounding of many musical instruments. The Śābara-utsava of the Hindu *navarātri/daśahrā* festival of Durgā is a direct continuation of the Vedic *mahāvrata*. Another Hindu counterpart of Vedic Vāc is goddess Sarasvatī, Vāg-īśvarī, "Mistress of Sound," who plays harp and is the guardian deity of the courtesans and the patroness of fine arts.

I would like to conclude this chapter with some speculations on the Vedic name of the Goddess Vāc, which means "sound, voice," being a cognate of Latin *vox*. It is connected with music making, which clearly played an important part in her "Atharvavedic" cult, while instrumental music seems to have had no place in the Rigvedic tradition. This is particularly true of the Goddess's warrior aspect evidenced in the sounding of the "earth drum" in the *mahāvrata* (see chapter 12), while the war drum is a key object of worship in the Old Tamil religion. But I believe the full meaning of the name Vāc can be understood only if we can find the original Proto-Dravidian word from which Vāc was translated. For this I propose two homophonous Proto-Dravidian roots having the shape **viḷ / *veḷ*. One root spans the meanings "to say, speak, cry (a war-cry), summon, proclaim, reveal, make known; to sound, to sing," while the other root means "to break (as the day), become bright, white, clear," with derived nouns denoting "light, lamp, brightness, dawn, the planet Venus, purity." The interference between these two roots can be seen from terms intimately connected with the worship of the Goddess Bhadra-Kāḷī or Durgā in Kerala. The Goddess is represented by a sword-bearing oracle priest called in Malayalam *veḷiccappāṭu*, through whom the goddess "speaks out" and "reveals her heart." The priest's name is derived from the word *veḷiccam*, "light of lamp or dawn, showing oneself, revelation."

The lamp, *viḷakku*, is one of the most important symbols of the Goddess in South India. A lamp is lighted on the severed head of the buffalo sacrificed to the Goddess (see chapter 15). It represents her as the vanquisher of the dark forces of night and death that the black buffalo symbolizes. In Mesopotamia, Goddess Inanna-Ištar is symbolized by the planet Venus, which as the morning star brings the first light to the darkness of night, being in this sense comparable to the dawn, imagined as the solar lion of the morning who kills the black buffalo of night. It therefore seems possible that the planet Venus was the star of the Goddess also in the ancient Indus Valley (in addition to Rohiṇī). In modern Hinduism, Friday, the day of the planet Venus, is sacred to the Goddess, but the seven-day week came to India only with Hellenistic astronomy and astrology.

24

Retrospect and Prospect

The summaries in chapters 22 and 23 have not reported all of the new research into the religions of the Indus civilization, the Vedas, and Hinduism published in this book. I have concentrated on major topics, with the aim of showing that some key issues can be satisfactorily solved, although further work will undoubtedly refine the proposals offered here. The trail of the Indo-Iranian languages from their East European homeland to their historical speaking areas can be followed in the archaeological record. I further claim that the Harappan language was Proto-Dravidian or close to it, and that Old Tamil literature has preserved important elements of Harappan heritage, such as the names of the planets and some stars, notably the pole star, and such original Harappan names of deities as Muruku and Vēḷ. I also maintain that a decisive beginning has been made in the decipherment of the Indus script, with a number of cross-checked interpretations that are in full agreement with the Harappan context and the wider cultural traditions of West and South Asia. Applying the same methods and working hypotheses, it should be possible to penetrate the script further, although a complete decipherment is clearly impossible with presently available materials. Among the "sects" of later Hinduism, Śaiva-Śākta Tantrism seems to me to be closest to the Harappan and "Atharvavedic" religions, although it, too, has many elements from external sources, including those introduced by the originally Proto-Saka-speaking Dāsas.

There is, however, much more to be discovered. I should like to conclude with some speculations on the social structure of the Indus civilization and the mode of thinking among its priestly administrators. My starting point is the five visible planets. It appears that the planets were connected with five different colors in their original Proto-Dravidian names, for such names are preserved in Tamil texts and seem to occur in the Indus script:

**pon-mīn*, "golden star" = Jupiter
**veḷ(ḷi)-mīn*, "white star" = Venus
**kem-mīn*, "red star" = Mars
**pacu-mīn*, "green star" = Mercury
**may-mīn*, "black star" = Saturn

The Indus signs for Mercury, Saturn, and Venus are identified and briefly explained in chapter 21; some comments on the names of Jupiter and Mars follow. The compound pon̲-mīn̲ is attested in Tamil, but only as the name of a "golden fish," namely *mahsir*, a large carp fish (*Barbus/Cyprinus tor*). However, *pon̲*, "gold," *por̲-kōḷ*, "golden planet," and *ponnan̲* and *ponnavan̲*, "he who is golden," are Tamil names of the planet Jupiter, which is yet to be identified among the "fish" signs of the Indus script.

The expected Proto-Dravidian name of Mars, **kem-mīn*, "red star," survives (with the Tamil-Malayalam affrication *k > c) in Old Tamil *cem-mīn̲*, denoting Mars in Pur̲anāṉūr̲u 60,2. *Cem-mīn̲* ("red fish") is used in Tamil of the sperm whale (*Euphysetes macrocephalus*), and in Malayalam of "prawn, shrimp." But neither of these meanings explains the "fish" pictogram, which I suspect denotes Mars (see the middlemost "fish" sign in Fig. 21.3a), because this particular "fish" sign is found immediately before the sign sequence read as *Muruku-Vēḷ* (as in Fig. 21.19a—here the reading of this "fish" sign is uncertain, but there are other clear parallels). Muruku is the Tamil counterpart of the Hindu war-god Skanda, whom the planet Mars represents according to Jaiminīya-Gṛhyasūtra 2,9 (*vidyād . . . skandam aṅgārakam*); moreover, both Muruku and the planet Mars are called in Old Tamil *cēy*, "redness." Only while writing this chapter did I discover that in Kannada *kem-mīn* is the name of a locally restricted red-colored carp fish (Maclean 1893:410b;763a). Its Sanskrit synonym, *rohita-matsya*, "red fish," denotes *Labeo rohita*, a delicious carp fish common everywhere in the subcontinent except South India; its absence in the south explains why the inherited Dravidian name is applied to several other varieties of fish in South Dravidian languages. The suspected Indus sign can easily be understood as a picture of a carp fish, with characteristic barbels hanging from the sides of the mouth, as suggested by Nikita Gurov (1968:40–42) long ago. Gurov proposed to read it in Proto-Dravidian as **kay/*key*, "carp," (on the basis of Tamil *kayal, cēl*, "carp," and cognates in DEDR no. 1252) to stand for Proto-Dravidian **key/*kēy/*ke-*, "red." About half a dozen times the "carp" sign is followed by the plain "fish" sign, and these sign sequences Gurov interpreted to form the compound **kem-mīn*, "planet Mars." (In my opinion, the word **mīn* is included in the "carp" sign, as seems to be the case with other "fish" signs having diacritics, see chapter 21: the "carp" sign stands for **kem-mīn*, "red fish" as well as "red star.")

The above Dravidian planetary colors agree with those connected with the planets in Sanskrit texts dealing with planetary worship, starting with the late Vedic Gṛhyasūtras.

In the Purāṇic cosmology, as we have seen in chapter 16, the planets are fed by specific rays of the sun having five different colors. These solar rays correspond to veins of five different colors in the human body, according to the Upaniṣads and much later texts of the Yoga tradition.

In ancient Mesopotamia and China, too, the planets are connected with different colors. The Babylonians correlated the planets with different metals, with the quarters of space, and with the times of the sun's daily and yearly circulation (Jeremias 1929). In the third century BCE, the Chinese naturalists had a whole system of correlative thinking involving—in addition to the planets, the colors, the cardinal points, and the seasons—the five elements, tastes, smells, numbers, musical notes, and many other things.

In the Vedic Brāhmaṇa texts, such correlative thinking plays a major role. Different conceptual categories are classified hierarchically, and the correspondences between them are interpreted in terms of equivalences. One of the main purposes of this "classification of the universe," as suggested by Brian K. Smith (1994), is to justify with cosmic parallels the highest social position occupied by the Brahmins. In this classification of the Brāhmaṇa texts, too, the colors play a major role; indeed, each of the traditional four social classes of ancient India is symbolized by a specific color, and the Sanskrit word *varṇa*, "color," also denotes "social class." Much of the Brāhmaṇa classification is ad hoc and unsystematic, with several different systems having different numbers of members. However, the systems with four and five members stand out as most important, and can at least partially be traced back to the latest parts of the Rigveda. Thus in the Puruṣa hymn (RV 10,90), the four social classes are correlated with the different body parts of the "cosmic man": the *brāhmaṇas* with the head, the *kṣatriyas* with the arms, the *vaiśyas* with the loins, and the *śūdras* with the feet. This idea of the cosmos originally consisting of a primeval man who was sacrificed by the gods is unknown in older Rigvedic tradition, but closely connected with religious concepts that seem to have a Harappan origin, such as the creator-god Prajāpati and the human sacrifice, in which the victim was the bridegroom of a "sacred marriage" (chapters 16 and 17).

Table 24.1 shows some basic equivalences. Each column consists of a category: numbers, directions, times of day, seasons, colors, elements, and social classes. Each row comprises equivalent concepts.

Could these most basic correlative classifications of the Brāhmaṇas derive from the Harappans? In that case the planets—connected with the colors—are likely to have been among the ancient categories, too. Colors are associated with the directions of space in that type of Tantric *maṇḍala* (Tucci 1961), which has its prototype in the BMAC "palace" of Dashly-3 (chapter 20). In Tantric iconography, the square *maṇḍala* is the palace or capital of the divinity depicted as the ruler in its center, with palace or city gates in the four cardinal directions. As a cosmogram, the *maṇḍala* also represents the square earth (RV 10,58,2) of the Vedic cosmos, divided according to the cardinal directions (Kirfel 1920:10).

The four cardinal directions form the pattern of cross, providing the basic framework for the fourfold classification. The center of the cross, symbolizing the fifth direction to the zenith, unites and exceeds the four; it is therefore an appropriate symbol for the king who unites the four social classes and is above them. This is reflected in the Vedic royal consecration, where the king takes a step in each of the five directions, thereby ascending to the zenith, the exalted place of the midday sun and the pole star (chapter 16). One is reminded of

TABLE 24.1

5	center/zenith			golden		king
4	east	morning	spring	white	air	brāhmaṇa
3	south	noon	summer	red	fire	kṣatriya
2	west	evening	autumn	green	water	vaiśya
1	north	midnight	winter	black	earth	śūdra

the Early Harappan seals that have four or five sets of concentric circles (Fig. 16.3), which can be assumed to symbolize the sun and its daily and yearly rotation through the four directions and the four seasons defined by the equinoctial and solstitial points.

If the east is in the front, as it is in the traditional orientation of the Vedic texts, the horizontal axle of the cross contains the colors black (in the north) and red (in the south), corresponding to the planets Saturn and Mars, counterparts of the evening/night sun and the morning/day sun. They represent the solar/Śaiva gods Kāla, "Black," and Rud[h]ra, "Red." Śiva is worshipped in the ancient temple of Ujjain (praised by Kālidāsa in Meghadūta) as Mahā-Kāla; Rudra is the youthful Kumāra. These male deities have female counterparts in the black Kālī (often represented as an ugly old hag) and the red Rohiṇī/Durgā (a youthful and beautiful virgin, Kumārī). In this connection it is very significant to note that Sanskrit *kāla* (not attested before the fourth century BCE) and Pali *kāḷa*, "black," almost certainly are derived from Proto-Dravidian **kāẓ*, "black" (DEDR no. 1494).

The vertical axle of the cross contains the colors white (in the east) and greenish-yellow (in the west), corresponding to the planets Venus and Mercury, which probably primarily represent the new moon and the full moon. I suspect that besides the harsh solar gods the Indus people also worshipped milder "lunar" gods. Chapter 13 suggested that the Vaiṣṇava gods Bala-Rāma (white) and Kṛṣṇa (black) are continuations of the Aśvins, divine twins of Aryan origin, connected with the chariot team as well as the sun/day and moon/night. But behind these Vaiṣṇava gods are undoubtedly also earlier local divinities, partly surviving in the texts as "demons" vanquished and replaced by Bala-Rāma and Kṛṣṇa.

The color white characterizes the demons who had the shape of a conch (Pañcajana) and the wild ass (Dhenuka), while the white cosmic snake Śeṣa (used as the rope in the churning of the cosmic milk ocean) is expressly identified with Bala-Rāma. Bala-Rāma's weapon, the plowshare, resembles the sickle of the new moon, while Kṛṣṇa is said to be the "full" incarnation of Viṣṇu, a hint of the full moon. Kṛṣṇa's circular dance with the milkmaids seems to represent the full moon's conjunctions with the various asterisms along its circular path: according to the Śatapatha-Brāhmaṇa (9,4,1,9), the moon is a heavenly playboy, a *gandharva*, and the asterisms are his heavenly mistresses, *apsarases* (chapter 16). Kṛṣṇa's name meaning "black" connects him with the dark-hued aboriginal cowboys of the Vraja tract. But he is actually often depicted as green-hued and called Hari, "greenish-yellow," which is the color of the moon (cf. Hariścandra in chapter 16) and honey: Madhu, "honey," is a demon vanquished by Kṛṣṇa, and symbol for the sweet pleasures of love associated with Kṛṣṇa.

With these hopefully thought-provoking speculations, the book must close.

Bibliographical Notes

Detailed documentary annotation and copious references to further literature can be found in my previous publications, on which this book is mostly based. Unfortunately space forbids giving this apparatus in the present book and thus fully acknowledging here as well my indebtedness to all the scholars involved. Therefore, listed below are references to the principal sources of chapters 6 to 21: first my own publications on the topic (including earlier versions, which may be partially dated, especially with regard to the Dāsas or the first wave(s) of Aryan immigrants to South Asia; the principal ones are in bold), followed by some other works of fundamental importance, in alphabetical order.

CHAPTER 6 *PROTO-INDO-EUROPEAN HOMELANDS*

Parpola ***2008a; 2012 (2013)***; Carpelan & Parpola 2001.

Anthony 1995; 2007. Burmeister 2004. Chernykh 1992. Dergachev 1998; 2007. Gusev 1998. Hänsel & Zimmer 1994. Kohl 2007. Levine, Renfrew, & Boyle 2003. Littauer & Crouwel 1979; 2002. Mallory 1989 through 2002. Mallory & Adams 1997. Maran 2004a; 2004b. Piggott 1983; 1992. Rassamakin 1999; 2004. Videiko 1994; 1995 (1996).

CHAPTER 7 *EARLY INDO-IRANIANS ON EURASIAN STEPPES*

Parpola 1974; 1988a; 1995; 1998a; 1999a; 2002a; ***2012 (2013)***; Carpelan & Parpola 2001.

Anthony & Vinogradov 1995. Bader, Krajnov, & Kosarev 1987. Chernykh 1992; 2007. Chernykh & Kuz'minykh 1987; 1989. Chlenova 1984. Gening, Zdanovich & Gening 1992. Häkkinen 2009. Joki 1973. Koivulehto 2001. Koryakova & Epimakhov 2007. Kovtun 2013. Kuz'mina 2007. Kuz'minykh 2011. Parzinger 2006. Pryakhin & Khalikov 1987. Rédei 1988; 1988–1991. Sinor 1988. Young 1985. Zdanovich & Zdanovich 2002.

CHAPTER 8 *THE BMAC OF CENTRAL ASIA AND THE MITANNI OF SYRIA*

Parpola 1988a; 1995; 1999a; ***2002a, 2002b***; 2004; ***2005d***.

Amiet 1979; 1986. Baghestani 1997. Bobomulloev 1997. Brisch & Bartl 1995. Burrow 1973. Collon 1987. Francfort 2005. Ghirshman 1977. Gubaev, Koshelenko, & Tosi 1998. Hiebert 1994. Jarrige 1991. Lamberg-Karlovsky 1986. Lawergren 2003. Ligabue & Salvatori 1989. Lubotsky 2001. Mayrhofer 1966; 1974. Moran 1992. Raulwing 2005 (2006). Sarianidi 1977 through 2007; Sarianidi et al. 2011 (2012). Schmidt 1933; 1937. Shinde, Possehl, & Ameri 2005. Stein 1994. Thieme 1960. Teufer 2012. von Dassow 2008. Wilhelm 1994. T. C. Young 1985.

CHAPTER 9 *THE RIGVEDIC INDO-ARYANS AND THE DĀSAS*

Parpola 1988a; 2002a; 2002b; 2004; ***2012a***.

Bailey 1959 (1960). Burrow 1976 (1977). Chernykh 1992. Falk 1994. Francfort 2001; 2005. Hillebrandt 1927–1929. Hintze 1998. Jamison & Brereton 2014. Jarrige 1985. Rau 1976. Schmitt 1989; 2000. Szabo & Barfield 1991. Teufer 2013. Wheeler 1947. Witzel 1995b.

CHAPTER 10 *THE AŚVINS AND MITRA-VARUṆA*

Parpola ***2005a***.

Brereton 1981. Falk 1989. Frame 1978; 2010. Gonda 1974; 1975; 1977; 1978. Hillebrandt 1927–1929. Hopkins 1889. Jamison & Brereton 2014. Jamison & Witzel 1992. Lüders 1951–1959. Macdonell 1897. Nyberg 1995. Oberlies 1993; 2012. West 2007. Zeller 1990.

CHAPTER 11 *THE AŚVINS AS FUNERARY GODS*

Parpola ***2005a; 2005c; 2009.***

Caland 1896; 1914. Hopkins 1896. Houben 1991; 2000. Oldenberg 1884. Rönnow 1929. Sparreboom 1985. Stacul 1970; 1971. van Buitenen 1968.

CHAPTER 12 *THE ATHARVAVEDA AND THE VRĀTYAS*

Parpola ***1983; 1988a; in press b,e.***

Bloomfield 1899. Caillat 1989. Caland 1896; 1900; 1908; 1931. Charpentier 1911. Emeneau 1966. Falk 1986. Gonda 1971. Hauer 1927. Heesterman 1957; 1962; 1967. Hillebrandt 1897. Hopkins 1896. Horsch 1966. Insler 1998. Kuiper 1979. Oldenberg 1884. Rolland 1973. von Hinüber 2001. Wackernagel 1896. Wackernagel & Debrunner 1954. Weber 1849. Witzel 1989.

CHAPTER 13 *THE MEGALITHIC CULTURE AND THE GREAT EPICS*

Parpola 1984b; ***1998b; 1999c; 2002c; 2004 (2006).***

Allchin 1995. Brockington 1998. Coningham & Allchin 1995. Ghosh 1989. Goldman 1984. Hopkins 1915. Horsch 1966. Jaiswal 1981. Leshnik 1974. Maloney 1970. van Buitenen 1973–1978. Weber 1850; 1870 (1871). Witzel 1995b; 1997.

CHAPTER 14 *THE LANGUAGE OF THE INDUS CIVILIZATION*

Parpola ***1981; 1994a; 1997a; 1997b; 2003; 2010; 2011a; in press c, d;*** Parpola & Janhunen ***2011.***

Anderson 2008. Burrow & Emeneau 1984. Caldwell 1856; 1875. Hart 1975. Krishnamurti 2003. Osada 2006. Pinnow 1959. Trautmann 1981. Zvelebil 1970 through 1990.

CHAPTER 15 *FERTILITY CULTS IN FOLK RELIGION*

Parpola ***1994a; 2003; 2011a; 2011b.***

Biardeau 2004. Charpentier 1926. Coomaraswamy 1928–1931. Crooke 1906; 1926. Fischer & Shah 1971. Hiltebeitel 1978. Jarrige et al. 1995. Marshall 1931a; 1931b. Ward 1811. Whitehead 1921.

CHAPTER 16 *ASTRONOMY, TIME-RECKONING, AND COSMOLOGY*

Parpola ***1985; 1990; 1994a; 2013; 2014.***

Filliozat 1962. Geldner 1889. Kirfel 1920; 1952; 1954. Liebert 1968 (1969). Mackay 1938. Needham 1959. Pankenier 2004; 2013. Scherer 1953. Uesugi 2011. Vahia & Menon 2011. Wanzke 1987. Weber 1853; 1861 (1862). Winternitz 1892.

CHAPTER 17 *DILMUN, MAGAN, AND MELUHHA*

Parpola ***1994a; 1994b; 2002***; Parpola, S., A. Parpola, & Brunswig ***1977.***

Bibby 1972. Franke-Vogt 1995. Laursen 2010. Maekawa & Mori 2011. Olijdam & Spoor 2008. Potts 2008. Reade 1995; 2008. Steinkeller 1982. Vermaak 2008.

CHAPTER 18 ***ROYAL SYMBOLS FROM WEST ASIA***

Parpola ***1984a; 1985; 1994a; 2011b; 2011c; in press c.***

Amiet 1956; 1980. Black & Green 1992. Boehmer 1974; 1975. Collon 1987. Franke-Vogt 1991 (1992). Heesterman 1957; 1989. Leick 1991. Mode 1944. Petrie 1939. Porada 1950. Rothman 2001. Sievertsen 1992; 1999.

CHAPTER 19 ***THE GODDESS AND THE BUFFALO***

Parpola 1983; 1984a; 1985; 1988a; 1989; ***1992a; 1994a; 1998b; 1999b; 2002b&c; 2011c; 2012b; in press e.***

Beck 1981. Biardeau 1981; 2004. C. J. Fuller 1992. Hiltebeitel 1978. Kane 1941–1958. Kinsley 1986. Shulman 1980. Silva 1955. van Kooij 1972. Vermaseren 1977. von Stietencron 1983. Whitehead 1921.

CHAPTER 20 ***EARLY IRANIANS AND "LEFT-HAND" TANTRISM***

Parpola 1988a; ***2002b.***

Azarpay 1976. Brentjes 1983. Degener 2002. Jettmar 1986. Potts 2001.

CHAPTER 21 ***RELIGION IN THE INDUS SCRIPT***

Parpola 1975a; 1975b; 1986a; 1986b; 1988b; 1990a; 1990b; 1992b; ***1994a***; 1998b; 2003; 2005b; 2008b; ***2011a; 2011c***; Parpola & Janhunen ***2011***; CISI.

Baines 1999. Chadwick 1958. Daniels 1996. Geldner 1889. Hart 1975. Robinson 2002. Van Buren 1948. Winternitz 1895.

CHAPTER 24 ***RETROSPECT AND PROSPECT***

Parpola 1999d. Parpola & Janhunen 2011.

Maclean 1893. Smith 1994.

References

Allchin, Bridget, & Raymond Allchin. 1968. *The birth of Indian civilization: India and Pakistan before 500 B.C.* Harmondsworth: Penguin.

———. 1982. *The rise of civilization in India and Pakistan.* Cambridge: Cambridge University Press.

Allchin, F. R. 1995. *The archaeology of early historic South Asia: The emergence of cities and states.* With contributions from George Erdosy, R. A. E. Coningham, D. K. Chakrabarti, and Bridget Allchin. Cambridge: Cambridge University Press.

Amiet, Pierre. 1956. Le symbolisme cosmique du répertoire animalier en Mésopotamie. *Revue d'Assyriologie et d'Archéologie Orientale* 50:113–126.

———. 1979. Archaeological discontinuity and ethnic duality in Elam. *Antiquity* 53:195–204.

———. 1980. *La glyptique mésopotamienne archaïque.* Deuxième édition revue et corrigée avec un supplément. Paris: Éditions du Centre National de la Recherche Scientifique.

———. 1986. *L'âge des échanges inter-iraniens 3500–1700 avant J.-C.* Paris: Éditions de la Réunion des musées nationaux.

Anderson, Gregory D. S. 2008. Introduction to the Munda languages. Pp. 1–10 in: Gregory D. S. Anderson (ed.), *The Munda languages.* (Routledge Language family series.) London and New York: Routledge.

Anthony, David W. 1995. Horse, wagon and chariot: Indo-European languages and archaeology. *Antiquity* 69:554–565.

———. 2007. *The horse, the wheel, and language: How Bronze-Age riders from the Eurasian steppes shaped the modern world.* Princeton, NJ: Princeton University Press.

Anthony, David W., & N. B. Vinogradov. 1995. Birth of the chariot. *Archaeology* 48(2):36–41.

Ardeleanu-Jansen, Alexandra. 1989. A short note on a steatite sculpture from Mohenjo-Daro. Pp. 196–210 in: Karen Frifelt & Per Sørensen (eds.), *South Asian Archaeology 1985.* (Scandinavian Institute of Asian Studies, Occasional Papers 4.) London: Curzon.

Aruz, Joan (ed.). 2003. *Art of the first cities: The third millennium B.C. from the Mediterranean to the Indus.* New York: Metropolitan Museum of Art; New Haven, CT: Yale University Press.

Avanesova, N. A. 2010. Zarafshanskaya kul'turnaya provintsiya Baktrijsko-Margianskoj tsivilizatsii. Pp. 334–364 in: P. M. Kozhin, M. F. Kosarev, & N. A. Dubova (eds.), *Na puti otkrytiya tsivilizatsii: Sbornik statej k 80-letiyu V. I. Sarianidi.* (Trudy Margianskoj arkheologicheskoj èkspeditsii [3].) St. Petersburg: Aletejya.

Azarpay, G. 1976. Nanā, the Sumero-Akkadian goddess of Transoxiana. *Journal of the American Oriental Society* 96(4):536–542.

Bader, O. N., D. A. Krajnov, & M. F. Kosarev (eds.). 1987. *Arkeologiya SSSR: Èpokha bronzy lesnoj polosy SSSR.* Moscow: Nauka.

Baghestani, Susanne. 1997. *Metallene Compartimentsiegel aus Ost-Iran, Zentralasien und Nord-China.* (Archäologie in Iran und Turan 1.) Rahden, Westfahlen: Marie Leidorf.

Bailey, Harold Walter. 1959 (1960). Iranian *Arya-* and *Daha-*. *Transactions of the Philological Society* 1959:71–115.

Baines, John. 1999. Writing, invention and early development. Pp. 882–885 in: Kathryn A. Bard (ed.), *Encyclopedia of the archaeology of ancient Egypt*. London and New York: Routledge.

Barnett, Lionel D. (trans.). 1907. *The Antagaḍa-dasāo and Aṇuttarovavāiya-dasāo*. Translated from the Prakrit. (Oriental Translation Fund NS 17.) London: Royal Asiatic Society.

Bartl, Karin, Reinhard Bernbeck, & Marlies Heinz (eds.). 1995. *Zwischen Euphrat und Indus: Aktuelle Forschungsprobleme in der Vorderasiatischen Archäologie*. Hildesheim: Georg Olms.

Beck, Brenda E. F. 1981. The goddess and the demon: A local South Indian festival and its wider context. Pp. 83–136 in: Biardeau 1981.

Benfey, Theodor. 1869. *Geschichte der Sprachwissenschaft und orientalischen Philologie in Deutschland seit dem Anfange des 19. Jahrhunderts, mit einem Rückblick auf die früheren Zeiten*. (Geschichte der Wissenschaften in Deutschland 8.) Munich: J. G. Cotta.

Besenval, Roland. 2011. Between East and West: Kech-Makran (Pakistan) during Protohistory. Pp. 41–164 in: Osada & Witzel 2011.

Biardeau, Madeleine (ed.). 1981. *Autour de la déesse hindoue*. (Puruṣārtha 5.) Paris: Éditions de l'École des Hautes Études en Sciences Sociales.

———. 2004. *Stories about posts: Vedic variations around the Hindu Goddess*. Translated by Alf Hiltebeitel, Marie-Louise Reiniche, & James Walker, edited by Alf Hiltebeitel & Marie-Louise Reiniche. Chicago: University of Chicago Press.

Bibby, Geoffrey. 1972. *Looking for Dilmun*. Harmondsworth: Penguin.

Black, Jeremy, & Anthony Green. 1992. *Gods, demons and symbols of ancient Mesopotamia: An illustrated dictionary*. Illustrations by Tessa Rickards. London: British Museum Press.

Bloomfield, Leonard. 1933. *Language*. New York: Henry Holt.

Bloomfield, Maurice (trans.). 1897. *Hymns of the Atharva-Veda*. (Sacred Books of the East 42.) Oxford: Clarendon Press.

———. 1899. *The Atharva-Veda and the Gopatha-Brāhmaṇa*. (Grundriss der indo-arischen Philologie und Altertumskunde 2:1:B.) Strasbourg: Karl J. Trübner.

Bobomulloev, Saïdmurâd. 1997. Ein bronzezeitliches Grab aus Zardča Chalifa bei Pendžikent (Zeravšan-Tal). *Archäologische Mitteilungen aus Iran und Turan* 29:121–134.

Boehmer, Rainer Michael. 1974. Das Rollsiegel im prädynastischen Ägypten. *Archäologischer Anzeiger* 1974:495–514.

———. 1975. Das Auftreten des Wasserbüffels in Mesopotamien in historischer Zeit und seine sumerische Bezeichnung. *Zeitschrift für Assyriologie* 64:1–19.

Bopp, Franz. 1816. *Über das Conjugationssystem der Sanskritsprache in Vergleichung mit jenem der griechischen, lateinischen, persischen und germanischen Sprache*. Herausgegeben und mit Vorerinnerungen begleitet von K. J. Windischmann. Frankfurt am Main: Andreäische Buchhandlung.

Boyle, Katie, Colin Renfrew, & Marsha Levine (eds.). 2002. *Ancient interactions: East and west in Eurasia*. Cambridge, UK: McDonald Institute for Archaeological Research.

Brentjes, Burchard. 1983. Das "Ur-Mandala" (?) von Daschly-3. *Iranica Antiqua* 18:25–49 and Table I.

Brereton, Joel Peter. 1981. *The Ṛgvedic Ādityas*. (American Oriental Series 63.) New Haven, CT: American Oriental Society.

Brisch, Nicole, & Karin Bartl. 1995. Die altassyrischen Handelskolonien in Anatolien. Pp. 134–147 in: Bartl, Bernbeck, & Heinz 1995.

Brockington, John. 1998. *The Sanskrit epics*. (Handbuch der Orientalistik, Abt. 2: Indien 12.) Leiden: Brill.

Brunt, P. A. 1976–1983. *Arrian with an English translation* I–II. (Loeb classical library 236, 269.) Cambridge, MA: Harvard University Press; London: William Heinemann.

Bryant, Edwin. 2001. *The quest for the origins of Vedic culture: The Indo-Aryan migration debate*. New York: Oxford University Press.

Burlingame, Eugene Watson (trans.). 1921. *Buddhist legends* I–III. Translated from the original Pali text of the Dhammapada commentary. (Harvard Oriental Series 28–30.) Cambridge, MA: Harvard University Press.

Burmeister, Stefan. 2004. Der Wagen im Neolithikum und in der Bronzezeit: Erfindung, Ausbreitung und Funktion der ersten Fahrzeuge. Pp. 13–40 in: Fansa & Burmeister 2004.

Burrow, Thomas. 1973. The Proto-Indoaryans. *Journal of the Royal Asiatic Society of Great Britain and Ireland* 1973(2):123–140.

———. 1976 (1977). Review of Rau 1976. *Kratylos* 21:72–76.

Burrow, Thomas, & M. B. Emeneau. 1984. *A Dravidian etymological dictionary*. 2nd ed. Oxford: Clarendon Press. (= DEDR)

Caillat, Colette (ed.). 1989. *Dialectes dans les littératures indo-aryennes*. (Publications de l'Institut de civilisation indienne, Série in-8° 55.) Paris: Collège de France, Institut de civilisation indienne.

Caland, Willem. 1896. *Die altindischen Todten- und Bestattungsgebräuche*. (Verhandelingen der Koninklijke Akademie van Wetenschappen te Amsterdam, Afdeeling Letterkunde, I:6.) Amsterdam: Johannes Müller.

______. 1900. *Altindisches Zauberritual: Probe einer Uebersetzung der wichtigsten Theile des Kauśika Sūtra*. (Verhandelingen der Koninklijke Akademie van Wetenschappen te Amsterdam, Afdeeling Letterkunde, Nieuwe Reeks, III:2.) Amsterdam: Johannes Müller.

———. 1908. *Altindische Zauberei: Darstellung der altindischen "Wunschopfer."* (Verhandelingen der Koninklijke Akademie van Wetenschappen te Amsterdam, Afdeeling Letterkunde, N.R. 10:1.) Amsterdam: Johannes Müller.

———. 1914. Die vorchristlichen baltischen Totengebräuche. *Archiv für Religionswissenschaft* 17:476–512.

——— (trans.). 1931. *Pañcaviṃśa-Brāhmaṇa: The Brāhmaṇa of twenty five chapters*. (Bibliotheca Indica, Work 255.) Calcutta: Asiatic Society of Bengal.

Caldwell, Robert. 1856. *A comparative grammar of the Dravidian or South-Indian family of languages*. London: Harrison.

———. 1875. *A comparative grammar of the Dravidian or South-Indian family of languages*. 2nd ed. Madras: University of Madras.

Campbell, Lyle. 2004. *Historical linguistics: An introduction*. 2nd ed. Edinburgh: Edinburgh University Press; Cambridge, MA: MIT Press.

Cardona, George. 1976. *Pāṇini: A survey of research*. (Trends in Linguistics, State-of-the-art Reports 6.) The Hague: Mouton.

Carpelan, Christian, & Asko Parpola. 2001. Emergence, contacts and dispersal of Proto-Indo-European, Proto-Uralic and Proto-Aryan in archaeological perspective. Pp. 55–150 in: Carpelan, Parpola, & Koskikallio 2001.

Carpelan, Christian, Asko Parpola, & Petteri Koskikallio (eds.). 2001. *Early contacts between Uralic and Indo-European: Linguistic and archaeological considerations*. (Mémoires de la Société Finno-Ougrienne 242.) Helsinki: Suomalais-Ugrilainen Seura.

Casal, Jean-Marie. 1964. *Fouilles d'Amri* I–II. (Publications de la Commission des Fouilles Archéologiques: Fouilles du Pakistan.) Paris: C. Klincksieck.

Chadwick, John. 1958. *The decipherment of Linear B*. Cambridge: Cambridge University Press.

Charpentier, Jarl. 1911. Bemerkungen über die vrātya's. *Wiener Zeitschrift für die Kunde des Morgenlandes* 25:355–388.

———. 1926. Über den Begriff und die Etymologie von *pūjā*. Pp. 276–297 in: Willibald Kirfel (ed.), *Beiträge zur Literaturwissenschaft und Geistesgeschichte Indiens: Festgabe Hermann Jacobi zum 75. Geburtstag dargebracht von Freunden, Kollegen und Schülern*. Bonn: Fritz Klopp.

Chernykh, E. N. 1970. *Drevnejshaya metallurgiya Urala i Povolzh'ya*. Moscow: Nauka.

———. 1992. *Ancient metallurgy in the USSR: The early metal age*. Translated by Sarah Wright. (New Studies in Archaeology.) Cambridge: Cambridge University Press.

———. 2007. *Kargaly: Fenomen i paradoksy razvitiya. Kargaly v sisteme metallurgicheskikh provintsij. Potaennaya (sakral'naya) zhizn' arkhaichnykh gornyakov i metallurgov*. (Kargaly 5.) Moscow: Yazyki slavyanskoj kul'tury.

Chernykh, E. N., & S. V. Kuz'minykh. 1987. Pamyatniki sejminsko-turbinskogo tipa v Evrazii. Pp. 84–105 in: Bader, Krajnov, & Kosarev 1987.

———. 1989. *Drevnyaya metallurgiya severnoj Evrasii (Sejminsko-Turbinskij fenomen)*. Moscow: Nauka.

Childe, V. Gordon. 1926. *The Aryans: A study of Indo-European origins*. London: Kegan Paul.

Chlenova, N. L. 1984. Arkheologicheskie materialy k voprosu ob irantsakh doskifskoj èpokhi i indo-irantsakh. *Sovetskaya Arkheologiya* 1984(1):88–103.

Cierny, Jan, Thomas Stöllner, & Gerd Weisgerber. 2005. Zinn in und aus Mittelasien. Pp. 431–448 in: *Bergbau, Metallurgie, Industriezentren und Werkstätten von Handelsgütern*. Bochum: Deutsches Bergbau-Museum.

CISI = *Corpus of Indus Seals and Inscriptions*. 1 = Joshi & Parpola 1987. 2 = Shah & Parpola 1991. 3.1 = Parpola, Pande, & Koskikallio 2010.

Clauson, Gerard, & John Chadwick. 1969. The Indus script deciphered? *Antiquity* 43(71):200–207.

Coningham, R. A. E., & F. R. Allchin. 1995. The rise of cities in South Asia. Pp. 152–184 in: Allchin 1995.

Coeurdoux, Gaston-Laurent. 1777. *Moeurs et coutumes des Indiens*. See Murr 1987.

Collon, Dominique. 1987. *First impressions: Cylinder seals in the ancient Near East*. London: British Museum Publications.

Coomaraswamy, Anand K. 1928–1931. *Yakṣas* I–II. (Smithsonian Institution Publications 2926, 3059.) Washington, DC: Smithsonian Institution.

Crooke, William. 1906. *Things Indian, being discursive notes on various subjects connected with India*. London: John Murray.

———. 1926. *Religion and folklore of Northern India*. Prepared for the press by R. E. Enthoven. London: Oxford University Press.

Cunningham, Alexander. 1875. Harapâ. Pp. 105–108 and pl. XXXII–XXXIII in: *Archaeological Survey of India, Report for the year 1872–73*. ([Reports, Old series] vol. V.) Calcutta: Office of the Superintendent of Government Printing, India.

Daniel, J. C. 1983. *The book of Indian reptiles*. Bombay: Bombay Natural History Society and Oxford University Press.

Daniels, Peter T. 1996. Methods of decipherment. Pp. 141–159 in: Daniels & Bright 1996.

Daniels, Peter T., & William Bright (eds.). 1996. *The world's writing systems*. New York: Oxford University Press.

DEDR = Burrow & Emeneau 1984.

Degener, Almuth. 2002. The Nuristani languages. Pp. 103–117 in: Sims-Williams 2002.

Dergachev, Valentin A. 1998. Kulturelle und historische Entwicklungen im Raum zwischen Karpaten und Dnepr: Zu den Beziehungen zwischen frühen Gesellschaften im nördlichen Südost- und Osteuropa. Pp. 27–64 in: Bernhard Hänsel & Jan Machnik (eds.), *Das Karpatenbecken und die osteuropäische Steppe*. (Südosteuropa-Schriften 20; Prähistorische Archäologie in Südosteuropa 12.) Munich: Südosteuropa-Gesellschaft; Rahden, Westfalen: Marie Leidorf.

———. 2007. *O skipetrakh, o loshadyakh, o vojne: ètyudy v zashchitu migratsionnoj kontseptsii M. Gimbutas*. St. Petersburg: Nestor.

Didier, Aurore. 2013. *La production céramique du Makran (Pakistan) à l'âge du bronze ancien: Contribution à l'étude des peuplements des régions indo-iraniennes*. (Mémoires des Missions archéologiques françaises en Asie centrale et en Asie moyenne 14. Série Indus-Balochistan.) Paris: De Boccard.

Dixit, Yama, David A. Hodell, & Cameron A. Petrie. 2014. Abrupt weakening of the summer monsoon in northwest India ~4100 yr ago. *Geology* 42(4), 24 Feb 2014. http://www.cam.ac.uk/research/news/decline-of-bronze-age-megacities-linked-to-climate-change.

Doniger, Wendy. 2009. *The Hindus: An alternative history*. New York: Penguin.

Dubois, Jean Antoine. [1825] 1906. *Hindu manners, customs and ceremonies*. Translated from the author's later French MS. and edited with notes, corrections, and biography by Henry K. Beauchamp. 3rd ed. Oxford: Clarendon Press.

[Dubois pirated the unpublished work of Coeurdoux 1777, see Murr 1987.]

During Caspers, E. C. L. 1979. Sumer, coastal Arabia and the Indus Valley in Protoliterate and Early Dynastic eras: Supporting evidence for a cultural linkage. *Journal of the Economic and Social History of the Orient* 22(2):121–135.

Durrani, F. A. 1988. *Excavations in the Gomal Valley: Rahman Dheri excavation report no. 1*. (Ancient Pakistan 6.) Peshawar: Department of Archaeology, University of Peshawar.

Durrani, F. A., I. Ali, & G. Erdosy. 1994–1995. Seals and inscribed sherds. Pp. 198–223 in: Taj Ali (ed.), *Excavations in the Gomal Valley: Rehman Dheri report no. 2*. (Ancient Pakistan 10.) Peshawar: Department of Archaeology, University of Peshawar.

Eder, Christian. 1996. *Die ägyptischen Motive in der Glyptik des östlichen Mittelmeerraumes zu Anfang des 2. Jts. v.Chr.* (Orientalia Lovanensia analecta 71.) Leuven: Peeters.

Edzard, Dietz Otto. 1968. Die Inschriften der altakkadischen Rollsiegel. *Archiv für Orientforschung* 22:12–20.

Eggeling, Julius (trans.). 1882–1900. *The Śatapatha-Brāhmaṇa according to the text of the Mādhyandina school* I–V. (Sacred Books of the East 12, 26, 41, 43, 44.) Oxford: Clarendon Press.

Ehlers, Gerhard. 2007. Sieben Seher, sieben Wasser. Pp. 145–150 in: Konrad Klaus & Jens-Uwe Hartmann (eds.), *Indica et Tibetica: Festschrift für Michael Hahn zum 65. Geburtstag von Freunden und Schülern überreicht.* (Wiener Studien zur Tibetologie und Buddhismuskunde 66.) Vienna: Arbeitskreis für tibetische und buddhistische Studien, Universität Wien.

Eichmann, Ricardo, & Hermann Parzinger (eds.). 2001. *Migration und Kulturtransfer: Der Wandel vorder- und zentralasiatischer Kulturen im Umbruch vom 2. zum 1. vorchristlichen Jahrtausend.* Bonn: Dr Rudolf Habelt.

Eidem, Jesper. 2014. The kingdom of Šamšī-Adad and its legacies. Pp. 137–146 in: Eva Cancik-Kirschbaum, Nicole Brisch & Jesper Eidem (eds.), *Constituent, confederate and conquered space: The emergence of the Mittani state.* (Topoi 17.) Berlin: Walter de Gruyter.

Ellis, Francis Whyte. 1816. Dissertation on the Telugu language [= "Note to the introduction."]. Pp. 1–31 in: A. D. Campbell, *A grammar of the Teloogoo language.* Madras: College Press.

Eltsov, Piotr Andreevich. 2008. *From Harappa to Hastinapura: A study of the earliest South Asian city and civilization.* (American School of Prehistoric Research Monograph series.) Leiden: Brill.

Emeneau, M. B. 1966. The dialects of Old Indo-Aryan. Pp. 123–138 in: Henrik Birnbaum & Jaan Puhvel (eds.), *Ancient Indo-European dialects.* Berkeley: University of California Press.

Erdosy, George (ed.). 1995. *The Indo-Aryans of ancient South Asia: Language, material culture and ethnicity.* (Indian Philology and South Asian Studies 1.) Berlin: Walter de Gruyter.

Falk, Harry. 1986. *Bruderschaft und Würfelspiel. Untersuchungen zur Entwicklungsgeschichte des vedischen Opfers.* Freiburg: Hedvig Falk.

———. 1989. Soma I and II. *Bulletin of the School of Oriental and African Studies, University of London* 52(1):77–90.

———. 1993. *Schrift im alten Indien: Ein Forschungsbericht mit Anmerkungen.* (ScriptOralia 56.) Tübingen: Gunter Narr.

———. 1994. Das Reitpferd im vedischen Indien. Pp. 91–101 in: Hänsel & Zimmer 1994.

Fansa, Mamoun, & Stefan Burmeister (eds.). 2004 *Rad und Wagen: Der Ursprung einer Innovation. Wagen im Vorderen Orient und Europa.* (Beiheft der Archäologischen Mitteilungen aus Nordwestdeutschland 40.) Mainz: Philipp von Zabern.

Farmer, Steve, Richard Sproat, & Michael Witzel. 2004. The collapse of the Indus script thesis: The myth of a literate Harappan Civilization. *Electronic Journal of Vedic Studies* 11(2):19–57.

Farnell, Lewis Richard. 1921. *Greek hero cults and ideas of immortality.* Oxford: Clarendon Press.

Filliozat, Jean. 1962. Notes d'astronomie ancienne de l'Iran et de l'Inde (I, II et III). *Journal Asiatique* 250:325–350.

Fiordalis, David V. 2013. The smile of the Buddha: Enigma, illumination, and majesty. Paper read at the 223rd annual meeting of the American Oriental Society in Portland, Oregon, March 15, 2013.

Fischer, Eberhard, & Haku Shah. 1971. *Mogra Dev, tribal crocodile gods: Wooden crocodile images of Chodhri, Gamit and Vasava tribes, South Gujarat (India).* (Art for tribal rituals in South Gujarat 1.) Ahmedabad: Gujarat Vidyapith.

Flattery, David Stophlet, & Martin Schwartz. 1989. *Haoma and harmaline: The botanical identity of the Indo-Iranian sacred hallucinogen "Soma" and its legacy in religion, language, and Middle Eastern folklore.* (University of California publications, Near Eastern studies 21.) Berkeley: University of California Press.

Fortson, Benjamin W., IV. 2010. *Indo-European language and culture: An introduction.* 2nd ed. Oxford: Blackwell.

Frame, Douglas. 1978. *The myth of return in early Greek epic.* New Haven, CT: Yale University Press.

———. 2010. *Hippota Nestor.* (Hellenic Studies 37.) Washington, DC: Center for Hellenic Studies.

Francfort, Henri-Paul. 1989. *Fouilles de Shortughaï: Recherches sur l'Asie Centrale Protohistorique* I–II. (Mémoires de la Mission Archéologique Française en Asie Centrale 2.) Paris: Diffusion De Boccard.

Francfort, Henri-Paul. 2001. The cultures with painted ceramics of south Central Asia and their relations with the northeastern steppe zone (late 2nd/early 1st millennium BC). Pp. 221–235 in: Eichmann & Parzinger 2001.

———. 2005. La civilisation de l'Oxus et les Indo-Iraniens et Indo-Aryens. Pp. 253–328 in: Fussman et al. 2005.

Franke, Ute. 2010. From the Oxus to the Indus: Two compartmented seals from Mohenjo-daro (Pakistan). Pp. xvii–xliii in: CISI 3.1.

Franke-Vogt, Ute. 1991 (1992). *Die Glyptik aus Mohenjo-Daro. Uniformität und Variabilität in der Induskultur: Untersuchungen zur Typologie, Ikonographie und räumlichen Verteilung* I–II. (Baghdader Forschungen 13.) Mainz: Philipp von Zabern.

———. Der Golfhandel im späten 3. und frühen 2. Jt. v. Chr. Pp. 114–133 in: Bartl, Bernbeck, & Heinz 1995.

Frankfort, Henri. 1955. *Stratified cylinder seals from the Diyala region.* (University of Chicago Oriental Institute Publications 72.) Chicago: University of Chicago Press.

Fujii, Masato. 2012. The Jaiminīya Sāmaveda traditions and manuscripts in South India. Pp. 99–118 in: Saraju Rath (ed.), *Aspects of manuscript culture in South India.* (Brill's Indological library 40.) Leiden: Brill.

Fuller, C. J. 1992. *The camphor flame: Popular Hinduism and society in India.* Princeton, NJ: Princeton University Press.

Fuller, Dorian Q. 2006. Agricultural origins and frontiers in South Asia: A working synthesis. *Journal of World Prehistory* 20(1):1–86.

Fussman, Gérard, Jean Kellens, Henri-Paul Francfort, & Xavier Tremblay. 2005. *Âryas, Aryens et iraniens en Asie centrale.* (Collège de France, Publications de l'Institut de Civilisation Indienne 72.) Paris: Diffusion De Boccard.

Gadd, C. J., & Sidney Smith. 1924. The new links between Indian and Babylonian civilizations. *Illustrated London News*, October 4, 1924:614–616.

Gamkrelidze, T. V., & V. V. Ivanov. 1995. *Indo-European and the Indo-Europeans* I–II. Translated by Johanna Nichols. (Trends in Linguistics, Studies and Monographs 80.) Berlin: Mouton de Gruyter.

Geldner, Karl F. 1889. Ficus Indica in RV. 1,24,7. Pp. 113–115 in: Richard Pischel & Karl F. Geldner, *Vedische Studien* I. Stuttgart: W. Kohlhammer.

Gening, V. F., G. B. Zdanovich, & V. V. Gening. 1992. *Sintashta: Arkheologicheskie pamyatniki arijskikh plemen Uralo-Kazakhstanskikh stepej* I. Chelyabinsk: Yuzhno-Ural'skoe knizhnoe izdatel'stvo.

Ghirshman, Roman. 1977. *L'Iran et la migration des Indo-Aryens et des Iraniens.* Leiden: Brill.

Ghosh, A. (ed.). 1989. *An encyclopaedia of Indian archaeology* I–II. New Delhi: Munshiram Manoharlal.

Gimbutas, Marija. 1997. *The Kurgan Culture and the Indo-Europeanization of Europe: Selected articles from 1952 to 1993.* Edited by Miriam Robbins Dexter and Karlene Jones-Bley. (Journal of Indo-European Studies Monograph 18.) Washington, DC: Institute for the Study of Man.

Goldman, Robert P. 1984. *The Rāmāyaṇa of Vālmīki: An epic of ancient India* I: *Bālakāṇḍa.* Introduction and translation by Robert P. Goldman. Annotation by Robert P. Goldman and Sally J. Sutherland. Princeton, NJ: Princeton University Press.

Gonda, Jan. 1971. *Old Indian.* (Handbuch der Orientalistik II.1.1.) Leiden: Brill.

———. 1974. *The dual deities in the religion of the Veda.* (Verlandelingen der Koninklijke Nederlandse Akademie van Wetenschappen, Afdeeling Letterkunde, Nieuwe Reeks 81.) Amsterdam: North-Holland.

———. 1975. *Vedic literature (Saṃhitās and Brāhmaṇas).* (A history of Indian literature I:1.) Wiesbaden: Otto Harrassowitz.

———. 1977. *The ritual Sūtras.* (A history of Indian literature I:2.) Wiesbaden: Otto Harrassowitz.

———. 1978. *Die Religionen Indiens* I: *Veda und älterer Hinduismus.* 2nd ed. (Die Religionen der Menschheit 11.) Stuttgart: W. Kohlhammer.

Gordon, D. H. 1960. *The Prehistoric background of Indian culture.* 2nd ed. Bombay: Bhulabhai Memorial Institute.

Grimm, Jakob. 1822. *Deutsche Grammatik* I. Zweite Ausgabe. Göttingen: Dieterichische Buchhandlung.

Gubaev, A., G. Koshelenko, & M. Tosi (eds.). 1998. *The archaeological map of the Murghab Delta: Preliminary reports 1990–95.* (Istituto Italiano per l'Africa e l'Oriente, Centro Scavi e ricerche archaeologiche, Reports and Memoirs, Series Minor 3.) Rome: IsIAO.

Gundert, Hermann. 1869. Die dravidischen Elemente in Sanskrit. *Zeitschrift der Deutschen Morgenländischen Gesellschaft* 23:517–530.

Gurov, Nikita V. 1968. Prospects for the linguistic interpretation of the Proto-Indian texts (on the basis of Dravidian languages). Pp. 28–54 in: *Proto-Indica: 1968. Brief report on the investigation of the Proto-Indian texts.* (VIII International Congress of Anthropological and Ethnographical Sciences, Tokio, September, 1968.) Moscow: Institute of Ethnography, Academy of Sciences of USSR.

———. 2000. On the substratum heritage in the vocabulary of the Ṛgveda (in connection with recent works by F. B. J. Kuiper and M. Witzel). Paper read at the 21st Zograph conference "Traditional Indian texts: Problems of interpretation", St. Petersburg, April 24–26, 2000.

Gusev, S. A. 1998. K voprosu o transportnykh sredstvakh tripol'skoj kul'tury. *Rossijskaya Arkheologiya* 1998(1):15–28.

Häkkinen, Jaakko. 2009. Kantauralin ajoitus ja paikannus: perustelut puntarissa. *Journal de la Société Finno-Ougrienne* 92:9–56.

Hänsel, Bernhard, & Stefan Zimmer (eds.). 1994. *Die Indogermanen und das Pferd.* (Archaeolingua 4.) Budapest: Archaeolingua.

Hansen, Donald P. 2003a. Art of the early city-states. Pp. 21–42 in: Aruz 2003.

———. 2003b. Art of the Akkadian Dynasty. Pp. 189–233 in: Aruz 2003.

Hart, George L. 1975. *The poems of ancient Tamil: Their milieu and their Sanskrit counterparts.* Berkeley: University of California Press.

Hauer, J. W. 1927. *Der Vrātya: Untersuchungen über die nichtbrahmanische Religion Altindiens* I. Stuttgart: W. Kohlhammer.

Heesterman, J. C. 1957. *The ancient Indian royal consecration: The rājasūya described according to the Yajus texts and annotated.* (Disputationes Rheno-Trajectinae 2.) 's-Gravenhage: Mouton.

———. 1962. Vrātya and sacrifice. *Indo-Iranian Journal* 6(1):1–37.

———. 1967. The case of the severed head. *Wiener Zeitschrit für die Kunde Süd- und Ostasiens* 11:22–43.

———. 1989. King and warrior. Pp. 97–122 in: J. C. Galey (ed.), *Kingship and the kings.* (History and anthropology 4.) London: Harwood Academic.

Heras, Henry. 1953. *Studies in Proto-Indo-Mediterranean Culture* I. (Studies in Indian History 19.) Bombay: Indian Historical Research Institute.

Hévesy, Guillaume de [Vilmos Hevesy]. 1933. Océanie et Inde préaryenne: Mohenjo-daro et l'Ile de Pâques. *Bulletin de l'Association française des amis de l'orient* 14–15:29–50.

Hickmann, Hans 1946. *La trompette dans l'Egypte ancienne.* (Supplément aux Annales du Service des Antiquités de l'Egypte, Cahier 1.) Cairo: [n.p.].

Hiebert, Fredrik Talmage. 1994. *Origins of the Bronze Age oasis civilizations of Central Asia.* (Bulletin of the American School of Prehistoric Research 42.) Cambridge, MA: Peabody Museum.

———. 1995. South Asia from a Central Asian perspective. Pp. 192–205 in: Erdosy (ed.) 1995.

Hillebrandt, Alfred. 1897. *Ritual-Litteratur, vedische Opfer und Zauber.* (Grundriss der Indo-Arischen Philologie und Altertumskunde III:2.) Strasbourg: Karl J. Trübner.

———. 1927–1929. *Vedische Mythologie* I–II. Zweite veränderte Auflage. Breslau: M. & H. Marcus.

Hiltebeitel, Alf. 1978. The Indus Valley "Proto-Śiva", reexamined through reflections on the goddess, the buffalo, and the symbolism of vāhanas. *Anthropos* 73:767–797.

Hintze, Almut. 1998. The migrations of the Indo-Iranians and the Iranian sound change *s* > *h*. Pp. 139–153 in: Wolfgang Meid (ed.), *Sprache und Kultur der Indogermanen.* (Innsbrucker Beiträge zur Sprachwissenschaft 93.) Innsbruck: Institut für Sprachwissenschaft der Universität Innsbruck.

Hoffmann, Karl. 1940. Vedische Namen. *Wörter und Sachen* 21:139–161.

Honoré, Emmanuelle. 2007. Earliest cylinder-seal glyptic in Egypt: From Greater Mesopotamia to Naqada. Pp. 31–45 in: Hany Hanna (ed.), *The International conference on heritage of Naqada and Qus region, January 22–28, 2007, Naqada, Egypt* I. Alexandria: International Council of Museums (ICOM).

Hopkins, E. Washburn. 1889. The social and military position of the ruling caste in ancient India, as represented by the Sanskrit epic; with an appendix on the status of woman. *Journal of the American Oriental Society* 13:57–376.

———. 1896. Prāgāthikāni I. *Journal of the American Oriental Society* 17:23–92.

———. 1915. *Epic mythology.* (Grundriss der indo-arischen Philologie und Altertumskunde III:1:B.) Strasbourg: Karl J. Trübner.

Horsch, Paul. 1966. *Die vedische Gāthā- und Śloka-Literatur.* Bern: Francke.

Houben, Jan E. M. (ed. and trans.). 1991. *The Pravargya Brāhmaṇa of the Taittirīya Āraṇyaka: An ancient commentary on the Pravargya ritual.* Introduction, translation, and notes. Delhi: Motilal Banarsidass.

———. 2000. On the earliest attestable forms of the Pravargya ritual: Ṛg-Vedic references to the Gharma-Pravargya, especially in the Atri-family book (book 5). *Indo-Iranian Journal* 43:1–25.

Hume, Robert Ernest (trans.). 1931. *The thirteen principal Upanishads.* London: Oxford University Press.

Hunter, G. R. 1934. *The script of Harappa and Mohenjo-daro and its connection with other scripts.* (Studies in the History of Culture 1.) London: Kegan Paul, Trench, Trubner.

Indus Civilization Exhibition, Tokyo Metropolitan Art Museum, 5th August – 3rd December, 2000. Tokyo: NHK, NHK Promotions, 2000.

Insler, Stanley. 1996. Avestan *vāz* and Vedic *vāh*. *Studien zur Indologie und Iranistik* 20:169–186.

———. 1998. On the recensions of the Atharva Veda and Atharvan hymn composition. *Wiener Zeitschrift für die Kunde Südasiens* 42:5–21.

Jacobsen, Knut A. (ed.). 2009–2013. *Brill's Encyclopedia of Hinduism* I–V. (Handbook of Oriental Studies, Section 2: South Asia 22.) Leiden: Brill.

Jaiswal, Suvira. 1981. *Origin and development of Vaiṣṇavism: Vaiṣṇavism from 200 BC to AD 500.* Second revised and enlarged edition. New Delhi: Munshiram Manoharlal.

Jamison, Stephanie W., & Joel P. Brereton (ed. and trans.). 2014. *The Rigveda* I–III. New York: Oxford University Press.

Jamison, S. W., & M. Witzel 1992. Vedic Hinduism. http://www.people.fas.harvard.edu/~witzel/vedica.pdf.

Jansen, Michael. 1993. *Mohenjo-Daro: Stadt der Brunnen und Kanäle: Wasserluxus vor 4500 Jahren.* (Schriftenreihe der Frontinus-Gesellschaft, Supplementband 2.) Bergisch Gladbach: Frontinus-Gesellschaft.

Jansen, Michael, Máire Mulloy, & Günter Urban (eds.). 1991. *Forgotten cities on the Indus: Early civilization in Pakistan from the 8th to the 2nd millennium B.C.* Mainz: Philipp von Zabern.

Jarrige, Catherine, Jean-François Jarrige, Richard H. Meadow, & Gonzague Quivron. 1995. *Mehrgarh field reports, 1974–1985: From Neolithic times to the Indus Civilization.* Karachi: Sind Culture Department.

Jarrige, Jean-François. 1985. The Indian world: The archaeological background. Pp. 238–247 in: *The world atlas of archaeology.* London: Mitchell Beazley.

———. 1991. The cultural complex of Mehrgarh (Period VIII) and Sibri. The "Quetta hoard." Pp. 94–103 in: Jansen, Mulloy, & Urban 1991.

Jeremias, Alfred. 1929. *Handbuch der altorientalischen Geisteskultur.* Zweite Aufl. Berlin: Walter de Gruyter.

Jettmar, Karl. 1986. *The religions of the Hindukush* I: *The religion of the Kafirs. The pre-Islamic heritage of Afghan Nuristan.* Translated by Adam Nayyar. With contributions from Schuyler Jones and Max Klimburg and a glossary by Peter S. C. Parkes. Warminster: Aris & Phillips.

Joki, Aulis J. 1973. *Uralier und Indogermanen: Die älteren Berührungen zwischen den uralischen und indogermanischen Sprachen.* (Mémoires de la Société Finno-Ougrienne 151.) Helsinki: Suomalais-Ugrilainen Seura.

Jones, William. 1788. On the Hindús. The third anniversary discourse [delivered at the Asiatic Society, Calcutta, on February 2, 1786]. *Asiatick Researches* 1:415–431.

Joshi, Jagat Pati, & Asko Parpola. 1987. *Corpus of Indus seals and inscriptions* I: *Collections in India.* (Annales Academiae Scientiarum Fennicae B239.) Helsinki: Suomalainen Tiedeakatemia. (= CISI 1)

Kane, P. V. 1941–1958. *History of Dharmaśāstra* I–V. Partly 2nd ed. (Government Oriental Series B6.) Poona: Bhandarkar Oriental Research Institute.

Karttunen, Klaus, & Petteri Koskikallio (eds.). 2001. *Vidyārṇavavandanam: Essays in honour of Asko Parpola.* (Studia Orientalia 94.) Helsinki: Finnish Oriental Society.

Kaw, R. N. 1989. Burzahom. Pp. 86–89 in: Ghosh 1989 II.

Keith, Arthur Berriedale (trans.). 1914. *The Veda of the Black Yajus school entitled Taittirīya Sanhitā* I–II. (Harvard Oriental Series 18–19.) Cambridge, MA: Harvard University Press.

——— (trans.). 1920. *Rigveda Brahmanas: The Aitareya and Kauṣītaki Brāhmaṇas of the Rigveda.* (Harvard Oriental Series 25.) Cambridge, MA: Harvard University Press.

Kenoyer, Jonathan Mark. 1998. *Ancient cities of the Indus Valley civilization.* Karachi: Oxford University Press.

Khan, F. A. 1965. Excavations at Kot Diji. *Pakistan Archaeology* 2:11–85.

Kharakwal, J. S., Y. S. Rawat, & Toshiki Osada (eds.). 2012. *Excavation at Kanmer 2005–06 - 2008–09. Kanmer Archaeological Research Project: An Indo-Japanese collaboration*. Kyoto: Indus Project, Research Institute for Humanity and Nature.

Kinsley, David. 1986. *Hindu goddesses: Visions of the divine feminine in the Hindu religious tradition*. Berkeley: University of California Press.

Kirfel, Willibald. 1920. *Die Kosmographie der Inder, nach den Quellen dargestellt*. Bonn and Leipzig: Kurt Schroeder.

———. 1952. Der Mythos von der Tārā und der Geburt des Budha. *Zeitschrift der Deutschen Morgenländischen Gesellschaft* 102:66–90.

———. 1954. *Das Purāṇa vom Weltgebäude (Bhuvanavinyāsa): Die kosmographischen Traktate der Purāṇa's, Versuch einer Textgeschichte*. (Bonner Orientalistische Studien N.S.1.) Bonn: Selbstverlag des Orientalischen Seminars der Universität.

Knorozov, Yurij V. 1952. Drevnyaya pis'mennost' tsentral'noj Ameriki. *Sovetskaya ètnografiya* 1952(3):100–118.

Knorozov, Yuri V., M. F. Albedil, & B. Ya. Volchok. 1981. *Proto-Indica: 1979. Report on the investigation of the Proto-Indian texts*. Moscow: Nauka.

[Knorozov, Yuri V., et al.] *Proto-Indica: 1968. Brief report on the investigation of the Proto-Indian texts*. Moscow 1968. [Presented at the VIII International Congress of Anthropological and Ethnographical Sciences, Tokyo, September 1968.]

Kohl, Philip L. 2007. *The making of Bronze Age Eurasia*. Cambridge: Cambridge University Press.

Koivulehto, Jorma. 2001. The earliest contacts between Indo-European and Uralic speakers in the light of lexical loans. Pp. 235–263 in: Carpelan, Parpola, & Koskikallio 2001.

Koryakova, Ludmila, & Andrej Epimakhov. 2007. *The Urals and Western Siberia in the Bronze and Iron Ages*. (Cambridge World archaeology.) Cambridge: Cambridge University Press.

Koskenniemi, Kimmo. 1981. Syntactic methods in the study of the Indus script. *Studia Orientalia* 50:125–136.

Koskenniemi, Kimmo, & Asko Parpola. 1979. *Corpus of texts in the Indus script*. (Department of Asian and African Studies, University of Helsinki, Research Reports 1.) Helsinki.

———. 1980. *Documentation and duplicates of the texts in the Indus script*. (Department of Asian and African Studies, University of Helsinki, Research Reports 2.) Helsinki.

———. 1982. *A concordance to the texts in the Indus script*. (Department of Asian and African Studies, University of Helsinki, Research Reports 3.) Helsinki.

Koskenniemi, Seppo, Asko Parpola, & Simo Parpola. 1970. A method to classify characters of unknown ancient scripts. *Linguistics* 61:65–91.

———. 1973. *Materials for the study of the Indus script* I: *A concordance to the Indus inscriptions*. (Annales Academiae Scientiarum Fennicae B185.) Helsinki: Suomalainen Tiedeakatemia.

Kovtun, I. V. 2013. *Predystoriya indoarijskoj mifologii*. Kemerovo: Rossijskaya Akademiya Nauk, Sibirskoe otdelenie, Institut èkologii cheloveka.

Kramrisch, Stella. 1954. *The art of India: Traditions of Indian sculpture, painting and architecture*. London: Phaidon.

Krishnamurti, Bhadriraju. 2003. *The Dravidian languages*. (Cambridge Language Surveys.) Cambridge: Cambridge University Press.

Kriyā. 2008. *Kriyāvin̲ tar̲kālat tamil̲ akarāti: Tamil̲-tamil̲-āṅkilam*. 2nd ed. Chennai: Kriyā (Cre-A).

Kuiper, F. B. J. 1979. *Varuṇa and Vidūṣaka: On the origin of the Sanskrit drama*. (Verhandelingen der Koninklijke Nederlandse Akademie van Wetenschappen, Afd. Letterkunde, Nieuwe Reeks 100.) Amsterdam: North Holland.

———. 1991. *Aryans in the Rigveda*. (Leiden Studies in Indo-European 1.) Amsterdam: Rodopi.

Kuz'mina, Elena E. 2007. *The origin of the Indo-Iranians*. Translated by S. Pitina and P. Prudovsky. Edited by James P. Mallory. (Leiden Indo-European Etymological Dictionary Series 3.) Leiden: Brill.

Kuz'minykh, S. V. 2011. Sejminsko-turbinskaya problema: Novye materialy. *Kratkie soobshcheniya Instituta Arkheologii RAN* 225:240–263.

Lamberg-Karlovsky, C. C. 1986. Third millennium structure and process: From the Euphrates to the Indus and the Oxus to the Indian Ocean. *Oriens Antiquus* 25(3–4):189–219.

———. 2002. Archaeology and language: The Indo-Iranians. *Current Anthropology* 43(1):63–88.

Lambrick, H. T. 1964. *Sind: A general introduction*. Hyderabad (Sind): Sindhi Adabi Board.

Lassen, Christian. 1847–1852. *Indische Alterthumskunde* I–II. Bonn: H. B. Koenig.

Laursen, Steffen Terp. 2010. The westward transmission of Indus Valley sealing technology: Origin and development of the "Gulf Type" seal and other administrative technologies in Early Dilmun, *c*. 2100–2000 BC. *Arabian Archaeology and Epigraphy* 21:96–134.

Law, Randall William. 2011. *Inter-regional interaction and urbanism in the ancient Indus Valley: A geologic provenience study of Harappa's rock and mineral assemblage*. (Linguistics, archaeology and the human past, Occasional Paper 11.) Kyoto: Indus Project, Research Institute for Humanity and Nature.

Lawergren, Bo. 2003. Oxus trumpets, ca. 2200–1800 BCE: Material overview, usage, societal role and catalogue. *Iranica Antiqua* 38:41–118.

Lawler, Andrew. 2004. The Indus script: Write or wrong? *Science* 306 (December 17, 2004):2026–2029.

Legrain, L. 1921. *Empreintes de cachets élamites*. (Mémoires de la Mission Archéologique de Perse 16.) Paris: Ernest Leroux.

Leick, Gwendolyn. 1991. *A dictionary of ancient Near Eastern mythology*. London and New York: Routledge.

Leshnik, Lawrence S. 1974. *South Indian "Megalithic" burials: The Pandukal complex*. Wiesbaden: Franz Steiner.

Liebert, Gösta. 1968 (1969). Beitrag zur Frage des Polarsterns in der altindischen Literatur. *Orientalia Suecana* 17:155–170.

Levine, Marsha, Colin Renfrew, & Katie Boyle (eds.). 2003. *Prehistoric steppe adaptation and the horse*. (McDonald Institute Monographs.) Cambridge: McDonald Institute for Archaeological Research.

Ligabue, Giancarlo, & Sandro Salvatori (eds.). [1989]. *Bactria: An ancient oasis civilization from the sands of Afghanistan*. (Studies and documents 3.) Venice: Erizzo.

Littauer, M. A., & J. H. Crouwel. 1979. *Wheeled vehicles and ridden animals in the ancient Near East*. Drawings by J. Morel. (Handbuch der Orientalistik 7:1:2:B:1.) Leiden: Brill.

———. 2002. *Selected writings on chariots and other early vehicles, riding and harness*. Edited by Peter Raulwing. (Culture and history of the ancient Near East 6.) Leiden: Brill.

Lubotsky, Alexander. 2001. The Indo-Iranian substratum. Pp. 301–317 in: Carpelan, Parpola, & Koskikallio 2001.

Lüders, Heinrich. 1951–1959. *Varuṇa* I–II. Aus dem Nachlass herausgegeben von Ludwig Alsdorf. Göttingen: Vandenhoeck & Ruprecht.

Macdonell, A. A. 1897. *Vedic mythology*. (Grundriss der indo-arischen Philologie und Altertumskunde III:1:A.) Strasbourg: Karl J. Trübner.

Mackay, Ernest J. H. 1938. *Further excavations at Mohenjo-daro* I–II. Delhi: Manager of Publications, Government of India.

———. 1943. *Chanhu-daro excavations, 1935–36*. (American Oriental Series 20.) New Haven, CT: American Oriental Society.

Maclean, C. D. 1893. *Glossary of the Madras Presidency*. (Manual of the administration of the Madras Presidency 3.) Madras: Government Press.

Maekawa, Kazuya, & Wakaha Mori. 2011. Dilmun, Magan, and Meluhha in early Mesopotamian history: 2500–1600 BC. Pp. 245–269 in: Osada & Witzel 2011.

Mahadevan, Iravatham. 1977. *The Indus script: Texts, concordance and tables*. (Memoirs of the Archaeological Survey of India 77.) New Delhi: Archaeological Survey of India.

———. 2003. *Early Tamil epigraphy: From the earliest times to the sixth century A.D.* (Harvard Oriental Series 62.) Chennai: Cre-A; Cambridge, MA: Department of Sanskrit and Indian Studies, Harvard University.

Mahapatra, Piyushkanti. 1972. *The folk cults of Bengal*. Calcutta: Indian Publications.

Mair, Victor H. (ed.). 1998. *The Bronze and Iron Age peoples of eastern Central Asia* I–II. (Journal of Indo-European Studies Monograph 26.) Washington, DC: Institute for the Study of Man.

Mallory, J. P. 1989. *In search of the Indo-Europeans: Language, archaeology and myth*. London: Thames and Hudson.

———. 1994–1995. The Indo-European homeland: An Asian perspective. *Bulletin of the Deccan College Post-Graduate and Research Institute* 54–55:237–254.

———. 1996. The Indo-European homeland: A matter of time. Pp. 1–22 in: Karlene Jones-Bley & Martin E. Huld (eds.), *The Indo-Europeanization of northern Europe*. (Journal of Indo-European Studies Monograph 17.) Washington, DC: Institute for the Study of Man.

———. 1997. The homelands of the Indo-Europeans. Pp. 93–121 in: Roger Blench & Matthew Spriggs (eds.), *Archaeology and language* I. London: Routledge.

———. 1998. A European perspective on Indo-Europeans in Asia. Pp. 175–201 in: Mair 1998:I.

———. 2001. Uralics and Indo-Europeans: Problems of time and space. Pp. 345–366 in: Carpelan, Parpola, & Koskikallio 2001.

———. 2002a. Archaeological models and Asian Indo-Europeans. Pp. 19–42 in: Sims-Williams 2002.

———. 2002b. Comment. Pp. 79–80 in: Lamberg-Karlovsky 2002.

Mallory, J. P., & D. Q. Adams (eds.). 1997. *Encyclopedia of Indo-European culture*. London and Chicago: Fitzroy Dearborn.

Mallory, J. P., & Victor H. Mair. 2000. *The Tarim mummies: Ancient China and the mystery of the earliest peoples from the west*. London: Thames and Hudson.

Mallowan, M. E. L. 1965. *Early Mesopotamia and Iran*. (Library of the early civilizations.) London: Thames and Hudson.

Maloney, Clarence. 1970. The beginnings of civilization in South India. *Journal of Asian Studies* 29(3):603–616.

Maran, Joseph. 2004a. Die Badener Kultur und ihre Räderfahrzeuge. Pp. 265–282 in: Fansa & Burmeister 2004.

———. 2004b. Kulturkontakte und Wege der Ausbreitung der Wagentechnologie im 4. Jahrtausend v.Chr. Pp. 429–442 in: Fansa & Burmeister 2004.

Marshall, John. 1924. First light on a long-forgotten civilization. *Illustrated London News* September 20, 1924:528–532.

———. 1931a. Religion. Pp. 48–78 in: Marshall 1931b:I.

———, (ed.). 1931b. *Mohenjo-Daro and the Indus Civilization* I–III. London: Arthur Probsthain.

Mayrhofer, Manfred. 1966. *Die Indo-Arier im Alten Vorderasien. Mit einer analytischen Bibliographie*. Wiesbaden: Otto Harrassowitz.

———. 1974. *Die Arier im Vorderen Orient—ein Mythos? Mit einem bibliographischen Supplement*. (Österreichische Akademie der Wissenschaften, Philos.-hist. Klasse, Sitzungsberichte 294:3.) Vienna: Verlag der Österreichischen Akademie der Wissenschaften.

———. 1992–2001. *Etymologisches Wörterbuch des Altindoarischen* I–III. Heidelberg: Universitätsverlag Carl Winter.

———. 2002 (2004). Zur Vertretung der indogermanischen Liquiden in den indo-iranischen Sprachen. *Indologica Taurinensia* 28:149–161.

McIntosh, Jane R. 2008. *The ancient Indus Valley: New perspectives*. (Understanding ancient civilizations.) Santa Barbara, CA: ABC-CLIO.

Meadow, Richard H. 1991. The domestication and exploitation of plants and animals in the Greater Indus Valley, 7th–2nd millennium B.C. Pp. 51–58 in: Jansen, Mulloy, & Urban 1991.

Meadow, Richard H., & Ajita K. Patel. 1997. A comment on "Horse remains from Surkotada" by Sandor Bökönyi. *South Asian Studies* 13:308–315.

Meriggi, Piero. 1934. Zur Indus-Schrift. *Zeitschrift der Deutschen Morgenländischen Gesellschaft* 87(N.F.12):198–241.

Mode, Heinz. 1944. *Indische Frühkulturen und ihre Beziehungen zum Westen*. Basel: Benno Schwabe.

Monier-Williams, Monier. 1885. *Religious thought and life in India: An account of the religions of the Indian peoples, based on a life's study of their literature and on personal investigations in their own country* I: *Vedism, Brāhmanism and Hindūism*. 2nd ed. London: John Murray.

Moran, William L. (ed. and trans.). 1992. *The Amarna letters*. Baltimore, MD: Johns Hopkins University Press.

Morgenstierne, Georg. 1953. Some Kati myths and hymns. *Acta Orientalia* 21: 161–189.

Mughal, Mohammad Rafique. 1970. *The Early Harappan period in the Greater Indus Valley and Northern Baluchistan (c. 3000–2400 B.C.)*. (PhD dissertation in anthropology, University of Pennsylvania, Philadelphia.) Ann Arbor: University Microfilms.

Müller, Max. 1859. *A history of ancient Sanskrit literature, so far as it illustrates the primitive religion of the Brahmans*. London: Williams and Norgate.

Murr, Sylvia. 1987. *L'Inde philosophique entre Bossuet et Voltaire*. I: *Moeurs et Coutumes des Indiens (1777)*. Un inédit du Père G.-L. Coeurdoux s.j. dans la version de N.-J. Desvaulx, texte établi et annoté par Sylvia Murr. II: *L'Indologie du Père Coeurdoux: Stratégies, apologétique et scientificité*. (Publications de l'École Française d'Extrême-Orient 146.) Paris: École Française d'Extrême-Orient. [I = Coeurdoux 1777]

Needham, Joseph. 1959. *Science and civilisation in China* III: *Mathematics and the sciences of the heavens and the earth*. Cambridge: Cambridge University Press.

Nelson, Harold Hayden, et al. 1932. *Medinet Habu* II: *Later historical records of Ramses III*. (Oriental Institute Publications 9.) Chicago: University of Chicago Press.

NHK 2000. See *Indus Civilization Exhibition*.

Nichols, Johanna. 1997. Modeling ancient population structures and movement in linguistics. *Annual Review of Anthropology* 26:359–384.

Nyberg, Harri. 1995. The problem of the Aryans and the Soma: The botanical evidence. Pp. 382–406 in: Erdosy 1995.

Oates, Joan. 2003. A note on the early evidence for horse and the riding of equids in Western Asia. Pp. 115–125 in: Levine, Renfrew, & Boyle 2003.

Oberlies, Thomas. 1993. Die Aśvin: Götter der Zwischenbereiche. *Studien zur Indologie und Iranistik* 18:169–189.

———. 2012. *Der Rigveda und seine Religion*. Berlin: Verlag der Weltreligionen im Insel Verlag.

Oldenberg, Hermann. 1884. Ṛigveda-Saṃhitā and Sāmavedārcika. Nebst Bemerkungen über die Zerlegung der Ṛigveda-Hymnen in Theilhymnen und Strophen sowie über einige verwandte Fragen. *Zeitschrift der Deutschen Morgenländischen Gesellschaft* 38:439–480.

Olijdam, Eric, & Richard H. Spoor (eds.). 2008. *Intercultural relations between South and Southwest Asia: Studies in commemoration of E.C.L. During Caspers (1934–1996)*. (BAR International Series 1826). Oxford: Archaeopress.

Olivelle, Patrick. 1998. *The early Upaniṣads: Annotated text and translation*. New York: Oxford University Press.

Osada, Toshiki. 2006. How many Proto-Munda words in Sanskrit? With special reference to agricultural vocabulary. Pp. 151–174 in: Toshiki Osada (ed.), *Proceedings of the Pre-symposium of RIHN and the 7th ESCA Harvard-Kyoto Roundtable*. Kyoto: Research Institute for Humanity and Nature.

Osada, Toshiki & Hitoshi Endo (eds.) 2011. *Linguistics, Archaeology and the Human Past: Occasional Paper 12*. Kyoto: Indus Project, Research Institute for Humanity and Nature. Reprinted 2012 with the title: *Current Studies on the Indus Civilization*, IX. New Delhi: Manohar.

Osada, Toshiki, & Michael Witzel (eds.). 2011. *Cultural relations between the Indus and the Iranian Plateau during the third millennium BCE. Indus Project, Research Institute for Humanities and Nature, June 7–8, 2008*. (Harvard Oriental Series, Opera Minora 7.) Cambridge, MA: Department of Sanskrit and Indian Studies, Harvard University.

Pankenier, David W. 2004. A brief history of *Beiji* (Northern Culmen). *Culture and Cosmos* 8(1–2):287–308.

———. 2013. *Astrology and cosmology in early China: Conforming Earth to Heaven*. Cambridge: Cambridge University Press.

Parpola, Asko. 1967 (1968). On the Jaiminīyaśrautasūtra and its annexes. *Orientalia Suecana* 16:181–214.

———. 1968–1969. *The Śrautasūtras of Lāṭyāyana and Drāhyāyaṇa and their commentaries: An English translation and study* I. 1: *General introduction and appendices to vol. 1*. 2: *The agniṣṭoma (LŚS I-II, DŚS I-VI)*. (Commentationes Humanarum Litterarum 42:2 and 43:2.) Helsinki: Societas Scientiarum Fennica.

———.1973. *The literature and study of the Jaiminīya Sāmaveda in retrospect and prospect*. (Studia Orientalia 43:6.) Helsinki: Finnish Oriental Society.

———. 1974. On the protohistory of the Indian languages in the light of archaeological, linguistic and religious evidence: An attempt at integration. Pp. 90–100 in: J. E. van Lohuizen-de Leeuw & J. M. M. Ubaghs (eds.), *South Asian Archaeology 1973*. Leiden: Brill.

———. 1975a. Tasks, methods and results in the study of the Indus script. *Journal of the Royal Asiatic Society of Great Britain and Ireland* 1975(2):178–209.

———. 1975b. Isolation and tentative interpretation of a toponym in the Harappan inscriptions. Pp. 121–143 in: Jean Leclant (ed.), *Le déchiffrement des écritures et des langues: Colloque du XXIXe Congrès International des Orientalistes*. Paris: L'Asiathèque.

———. 1981. On the primary meaning and etymology of the sacred syllable Ōm. *Studia Orientalia* 50:195–213.

———. 1983. The pre-Vedic Indian background of the Śrauta rituals. Pp. 41–75 in: F. Staal 1983:II.

———. 1984a. New correspondences between Harappan and Near Eastern glyptic art. Pp. 176–195 in: Bridget Allchin (ed.), *South Asian Archaeology 1981*. (University of Cambridge Oriental Publications 35.) Cambridge: Cambridge University Press.

———. 1984b. On the Jaiminīya and Vādhūla traditions of South India and the Paṇḍu / Pāṇḍava problem. *Studia Orientalia* 55:429–468.

———. 1985. *The Sky-Garment: A study of the Harappan religion and its relation to the Mesopotamian and later Indian religions*. (Studia Orientalia 57.) Helsinki: Finnish Oriental Society.

———. 1986a. The size and quality of the Indus seals and other clues to the royal titles of the Harappans. *Tamil Civilization* 4(3–4):144–156.

———. 1986b. The Indus script: A challenging puzzle. *World Archaeology* 17(3):399–419.

———. 1988a. The coming of the Aryans to Iran and India and the cultural and ethnic identity of the Dāsas. *Studia Orientalia* 64:195–302.

———. 1988b. Religion reflected in the iconic signs of the Indus script: Penetrating into long-forgotten picto+graphic messages. Pp. 114–135 in: *Visible Religion (Annual for Religious Iconography)* VI: *The Image in Writing*. Leiden: Brill.

———. 1989. Witnessing a hog sacrifice to the Goddess in South Kanara. *NIF Newsletter* 1989(4):20–24. Turku: Nordic Institute of Folklore.

———. 1990a. Astral proper names in India: An analysis of the oldest sources, with argumentation of an ultimately Harappan origin. *Adyar Library Bulletin* 53:1–53.

———. 1990b. Bangles, sacred trees and fertility: Interpretations of the Indus script related to the cult of Skanda-Kumāra. Pp. 263–284 in: Maurizio Taddei (ed.) *South Asian Archaeology 1987* I. (Serie Orientale Roma 66:1.) Rome: Istituto Italiano per il Medio ed Estremo Oriente.

———. 1992a. The metamorphoses of Mahiṣa Asura and Prajāpati. Pp. 275–308 in: A.W. van den Hoek, D.H.A. Kolff, & M.S. Oort (eds.), *Ritual, state and history in South Asia: Essays in honour of J. C. Heesterman*. (Memoirs of the Kern Institute 5.) Leiden: Brill.

———. 1992b. The "fig deity seal" from Mohenjo-daro: Its iconography and inscription. Pp. 277–236 in: Catherine Jarrige (ed.), *South Asian Archaeology 1989* I. (Monographs in World Archaeology 14.) Madison, WI: Prehistory.

———. 1994a. *Deciphering the Indus script*. Cambridge: Cambridge University Press.

———. 1994b. Harappan inscriptions: An analytical catalogue of the Indus inscriptions from the ancient Near East. Pp. 304–315 and (bibliography) 483–492 in: Flemming Højlund & H. Hellmuth Andersen, *Qala'at al-Bahrain* I: *The northern city wall and the Islamic fortress*. (Jutland Archaeological Society Publications 30:1.) Aarhus: Jutland Archaeological Society.

———. 1995. The problem of the Aryans and the Soma: Textual-linguistic and archaeological evidence. Pp. 353–381 in: Erdosy 1995.

———. 1997a. Dravidian and the Indus script: On the interpretation of some pivotal signs. *Studia Orientalia* 82:167–191.

———. 1997b. *Deciphering the Indus script: Methods and select interpretations*. Keynote address delivered at the 25th Annual South Asia Conference, University of Wisconsin, Madison, Wisconsin, October 18–20, 1996. (Occasional Papers Series 2.) Madison: Center for South Asia, University of Wisconsin-Madison.

———. 1997c. The Aryan languages and archaeology, with an excursus on Botaj. Pp. 291–308 in: Raymond Allchin & Bridget Allchin (eds.), *South Asian Archaeology 1995* I. New Delhi: Oxford & IBH.

———. 1998a. Aryan languages, archaeological cultures, and Sinkiang: Where did Proto-Iranian come into being, and how did it spread? Pp. 114–147 in: Mair 1998 I.

———. 1998b. Sāvitrī and resurrection. Pp. 167–312 in: Asko Parpola & Sirpa Tenhunen (eds.), *Changing patterns of family and kinship in South Asia*. (Studia Orientalia 84.) Helsinki: Finnish Oriental Society.

Parpola, Asko. 1999a. The formation of the Aryan branch of Indo-European. Pp. 180–207 in: Roger Blench and Matthew Spriggs (eds.), *Combining archaeological and linguistic aspects of the past.* (World Archaeology: Archaeology and Language series 3.) London: Routledge.

———. 1999b. Vāc as a goddess of victory in the Veda and her relation to Durgā. *Zinbun* 34(2):101–143.

———. 1999c. The iconography and cult of Kuṭṭiccāttan: Field research on the sanskritization of local folk deities in Kerala. Pp. 175–205 in: Johannes Bronkhorst & Madhav M. Deshpande (eds.), *Aryan and Non-Aryan in South Asia: Evidence, interpretation and ideology.* (Harvard Oriental Series, Opera Minora 3.) Cambridge, MA: Department of Sanskrit and Indian Studies, Harvard University.

———. 1999d. Conceptual categories and their classification in Middle Vedic texts: A review of Brian K. Smith's two recent books. Pp. 5–22 in: Folke Josephson (ed.), *Categorisation and interpretation: Indological and comparative studies. A volume dedicated to the memory of Gösta Liebert.* (Meijerbergs arkiv för svensk ordforskning 24.) Göteborg: Styrelsen för Meijerbergs institut vid Göteborgs universitet.

———. 2002a. From the dialects of Old Indo-Aryan to Proto-Indo-Aryan and Proto-Iranian. Pp. 43–102 in: Sims-Williams 2002.

———. 2002b. Pre-Proto-Iranians of Afghanistan as initiators of Śākta Tantrism: On the Scythian/Saka affiliation of the Dāsas, Nuristanis and Magadhans. *Iranica Antiqua* 37:233–324.

———. 2002c. Pandaíē and Sītā: On the historical background of the Sanskrit epics. *Journal of the American Oriental Society* 122(2):361–373.

———. 2003. Sacred bathing place and transcendence: Dravidian *kaṭa(vuḷ)* as the source of Indo-Aryan *ghāṭ, tīrtha, tīrthankara* and *(tri)vikrama.* Pp. 523–574 in: Olle Qvarnström (ed.), *Jainism and early Buddhism: Essays in honor of Padmanabh S. Jaini.* Fremont, CA: Asian Humanities Press.

———. 2004. From archaeology to a stratigraphy of Vedic syncretism: The banyan tree and the water buffalo as Harappan-Dravidian symbols of royalty, inherited in succession by Yama, Varuṇa and Indra, divine kings of the first three layers of Aryan speakers in South Asia. Pp. 479–515 in: Arlo Griffiths & Jan E. M. Houben (eds.), *The Vedas: Texts, language & ritual.* (Groningen Oriental Studies 20.) Groningen: Egbert Forsten.

———. 2004 (2006). Bala-Rāma and Sītā: On the origins of the Rāmāyaṇa. Proceedings of the XIth World Sanskrit Conference (Turin, April 3rd–8th, 2000) II. *Indologica Taurinensia* 30:185–200.

———. 2005a. The Nāsatyas, the chariot and Proto-Aryan religion. *Journal of Indological Studies* 16–17(2004–2005):1–63.

———. 2005b. Study of the Indus script. *Transactions of the International Conference of Eastern Studies* 50:28–66.

———. 2005c. Gandhara Graves and the Gharma pot, the Nasatyas and the Nose: In pursuit of the Chariot Twins. *Ancient Pakistan* 16:73–107.

———. 2005d. Administrative contact and acculturation between Harappans and Bactrians: Evidence of sealings and seals. Pp. 267–274 in: Catherine Jarrige & Vincent Lefèvre (eds.), *South Asian Archaeology 2001* I: *Prehistory.* Paris: Éditions Recherche sur les Civilisations.

———. 2008a. Proto-Indo-European speakers of the Late Tripolye culture as the inventors of wheeled vehicles: Linguistic and archaeological considerations of the PIE homeland problem. Pp. 1–59 in: Karlene Jones-Bley, Martin E. Huld, Angela Della Volpe, & Miriam Robbins Dexter (eds.), *Proceedings of the Nineteenth Annual UCLA Indo-European Conference, November 2–3, 2007.* (Journal of Indo-European Studies Monograph 54.) Washington, DC: Institute for the Study of Man.

———. 2008b. Copper tablets from Mohenjo-daro and the study of the Indus script. Pp. 132–139 in: Olijdam & Spoor 2008.

———. 2008c. Is the Indus script indeed not a writing system? Pp. 111–131 in: *Airavati: Felicitation volume in honour of Iravatham Mahadevan.* Chennai: Varalaaru.com. http://www.harappa.com/script/indus-writing.pdf.

———. 2009. The face urns of Gandhāra and the Nāsatya cult. Pp. 149–162 in: Michael Willis (gen. ed.), *Migration, trade, and peoples* (European Association of South Asian Archaeologists, Proceedings of the Eighteenth Congress, London, 2005), Part 3: *Aryans and nomads,* edited by Asko Parpola. London: British Association for South Asian Studies, British Academy.

———. 2010. *A Dravidian solution to the Indus script problem.* (Kalaignar M. Karunanidhi Classical Tamil Research Endowment Lecture, World Classical Tamil Conference 25-6-2010 Coimbatore.) Chennai: Central Institute of Classical Tamil.

———. 2011a. Crocodile in the Indus civilization and later South Asian traditions. Pp. 1–57 in: Osada & Endo 2011.

———. 2011b. The Harappan unicorn in Eurasian and South Asian perspectives. Pp. 125–188 in: Osada & Endo 2011.

———. 2011c. Motifs of early Iranian, Mesopotamian and Harappan art (and script), reflecting contacts and ideology. Pp. 271–357 in: Osada & Witzel 2011.

———. 2011d. Three ways of chanting in a sacrificial laud: Chapter two of Jaimini-Paryadhyāya (Jaiminīya-Śrautasūtra III) with Bhavatrāta's commentary: Sanskrit text with an annotated English translation. Pp. 141–163 in: Bertil Tikkanen & Albion M. Butters (eds.), *Pūrvāparaprajñābhinandanam: East and West, past and present. Indological and other essays in honour of Klaus Karttunen.* (Studia Orientalia 110.) Helsinki: Finnish Oriental Society.

———. 2011e. Codification of Vedic domestic ritual in Kerala: Pārvaṇa-sthālīpāka— the model of rites with fire offerings—in Jaiminīya-Gṛhyasūtra 1,1-4 and in the Malayāḷam manual of the Sāmaveda Nampūtiri Brahmins of Kerala, the Sāma-Smārtta-Caṭaṅṅu. Pp. 261–354 in: Jan E. M. Houben & Julieta Rotaru (eds.), *Veda-Vedāṅga and Avesta between orality and writing.* (Travaux de symposium international Le Livre, La Roumanie, L'Europe, Troisième édition—20 à 24 Septembre 2011, Tome III: La troisième section—Études euro- et afro-asiatiques, Section IIIA.) Bucarest: Éditeur Bibliothèque de Bacarest. http://www.bibliotecametropolitana.ro/Uploads/Simpozionul%20International_Cartea_Romania_Europa_III_V3_mic.pdf.

———. 2012a. The Dāsas of the Ṛgveda as Proto-Sakas of the Yaz I -related cultures. With a revised model for the protohistory of Indo-Iranian speakers. Pp. 221–264 in: Martin E. Huld, Karlene Jones-Bley, & Dean Miller (eds.), *Archaeology and Language: Indo-European Studies presented to James P. Mallory.* (Journal of Indo-European Studies Monograph 60.) Washington, DC: Institute for the Study of Man.

———. 2012b. Indus civilization (–1750 BCE). Pp. 3–18 in: Jacobsen 2012 IV.

———. 2012c. Chapter headings of the Jaimini-Paryadhyāya (Jaiminīya-Śrautasūtra III). Pp. 423–430 in: L. I. Kulikov & M. A. Rusanov (eds.), *T. Ya. Elizarenkova memorial volume*, Book 2. (Orientalia et Classica 40.) Moscow: Russian State University for the Humanities.

———. 2012 (2013). Formation of the Indo-European and Uralic (Finno-Ugric) language families in the light of archaeology: Revised and integrated "total" correlations. Pp. 119–184 in: Riho Grünthal & Petri Kallio (eds.), *Linguistic Map of Prehistoric Northern Europe.* (Mémoires de la Société Finno-Ougrienne 266.) Helsinki: Suomalais-Ugrilainen Seura.

———. 2013. Beginnings of Indian astronomy, with reference to a parallel development in China. *History of Science in South Asia* 1:21–78. http://hssa.sayahna.org/.

———. 2014. Beginnings of the Indian and Chinese calendrical astronomy. *Journal of the American Oriental Society* 134(1):107–112.

———. in press a. Indus seals and glyptic: An overview. In: Marta Ameri, Sarah Kielt Costello, Gregg M. Jamison, & Sarah Jarmer Scott (eds.), *Small Windows: New Approaches to the Study of Seals and Sealing as Tools of Identity, Political Organization and Administration in the Ancient World.* Cambridge: Cambridge University Press.

———. in press b. Sāmaveda and sorcery. In: V. Sadovsky & J. Rotaru (eds.), *Language and ritual in Indo-Iranian traditions.* Vienna: Österreichische Akademie der Wissenschaften.

———. in press c. Sanskrit *kaparda-* "braided hair": Yet another Harappan symbol of royalty surviving in Vedic "Vrātya rituals". In: Tiziana Pontillo et al. (eds.), *The volatile world of sovereignty: The Vrātya problem and kingship in South Asia.* New Delhi: D. K. Printworld.

———. in press d. Sanskrit *śakaṭī- / śakaṭa-* "ox-cart". In: Gerd J. R. Mevissen & Vijay Kumar Gupta (eds.), *Indology's pulse: Arts in context. Essays presented to Doris Meth Srinivasan in admiration of her scholarly research.* New Delhi: Aryan Publications International.

———. in press e. *Rudra*: "Red" and "cry" in the name of the destroyer god. In a forthcoming Festschrift.

Parpola, Asko. in press f. References to ritual authorities and Vedic schools in the Jaiminīya-Śrautasūtra, collected and evaluated. Pp. 32 in: Jan. E. M. Houben, Julieta Rotaru, & Michael Witzel (eds.), *Vedic śākhās, past, present, future. Proceedings of the Fifth international Vedic workshop, Bucharest 2011.*

Parpola, Asko, & Juha Janhunen. 2011. On the Asiatic wild asses and their vernacular names. Pp. 59–124 in: Osada & Endo 2011.

Parpola, Asko, Seppo Koskenniemi, Simo Parpola, & Pentti Aalto. 1969a. *Decipherment of the Proto-Dravidian inscriptions of the Indus civilization: A first announcement.* (Scandinavian Institute of Asian Studies, Special Publications 1.) Copenhagen.

———. 1969b. *Progress in the decipherment of the Proto-Dravidian Indus script.* (Scandinavian Institute of Asian Studies, Special Publications 2.) Copenhagen.

———. 1970. *Further progress in the Indus script decipherment.* (Scandinavian Institute of Asian Studies, Special Publications 3.) Copenhagen.

Parpola, Asko, & Petteri Koskikallio (eds.). 1994. *South Asian Archaeology 1993: Proceedings of the Twelfth international conference of the European association of South Asian archaeologists held in Helsinki University, 5–9 July 1993.* I–II. (Annales Academiae Scientiarum Fennicae, Series B 271.) Helsinki: Suomalainen Tiedeakatemia.

Parpola, Asko, B. M. Pande, & Petteri Koskikallio. 2010. *Corpus of Indus seals and inscriptions* 3: *New material, untraced objects, and collections outside India and Pakistan* 1: Mohenjo-daro and Harappa, in collaboration with Richard H. Meadow & J. Mark Kenoyer. (Annales Academiae Scientiarum Fennicae, Humaniora 359.) Helsinki: Suomalainen Tiedeakatemia. (= CISI 3.1)

Parpola, Asko, Simo Parpola, & Seppo Koskenniemi. 1966. Computing approach to Proto-Indian, 1965: An interim report. [Helsinki: The authors.]

Parpola, Marjatta. 2000. *Kerala Brahmins in Transition: A Study of a Nampūtiri Family.* (Studia Orientalia 91.) Helsinki: The Finnish Oriental Society.

Parpola, Päivikki. 1987. Väline merkkijoukkojonoa kuvaavan kieliopin löytämiseksi askelittain. Unpublished M.Sc. thesis, Department of computer science, University of Helsinki.

———. 1988. On the synthesis of context-free grammars. Pp. 133–141 in: Matti Mäkelä, Seppo Linnainmaa & Esko Ukkonen (eds.), *STeP-88 (Finnish artificial intelligence symposium, University of Helsinki, August 15–18, 1988)* I. Helsinki: Suomen tekoälyseura.

Parpola, Simo, Asko Parpola, & Robert H. Brunswig, Jr. 1977. The Meluḫḫa village: Evidence of acculturation of Harappan traders in late third millennium Mesopotamia? *Journal of the Economic and Social History of the Orient* 20(2):129–65.

Parrot, André. 1960. *Sumer.* Translated by Stuart Gilbert and James Emmons. (The arts of mankind 1.) London: Thames and Hudson.

Parzinger, Hermann. 2006. *Die frühen Völker Eurasiens: Vom Neolithikum bis zum Mittelalter.* Munich: C. H. Beck.

Pennington, Brian K. 2005. *Was Hinduism invented? Britons, Indians, and the colonial construction of religion.* New York: Oxford University Press.

Petrie, Flinders. 1939. *The making of Egypt.* London: Sheldon.

Piggott, Stuart. 1950. *Prehistoric India to 1000 B.C.* Harmondsworth: Penguin.

———. 1983. *The earliest wheeled transport: From the Atlantic Coast to the Caspian Sea.* London: Thames and Hudson.

———. 1992. *Wagon, chariot and carriage: Symbol and status in the history of transport.* London: Thames and Hudson.

Pinault, Georges-Jean. 1989. Reflets dialectaux en védique ancien. Pp. 35–96 in: Caillat 1989.

Pinnow, Heinz-Jürgen. 1959. *Versuch einer historischen Lautlehre der Kharia-Sprache.* Wiesbaden: Otto Harrassowitz.

Pirart, Éric. 1995. *Les Nāsatya* I: *Les noms des Aśvin. Traduction commentée des strophes consacrées aux Aśvin dans le premier maṇḍala de la Ṛgvedasamhitā.* (Bibliothèque de la Faculté de Philosophie et Lettres de l'Université de Liège 261.) Geneva: Diffusion Librairie Droz.

Pittman, Holly. 1984. *Art of the Bronze Age southeastern Iran, western Central Asia, and the Indus Valley.* With comments on style and iconography by Edith Porada. New York: Metropolitan Museum of Art.

Polos'mak, Nataliya V. 2001. Zur Kleidung der Pazyryk-Bevölkerung aus Ukok, Südaltaj. Pp. 101–126 in: Eichmann & Parzinger 2001.

Porada, Edith. 1950. A leonine figure of the Protoliterate period of Mesopotamia. *Journal of the American Oriental Society* 70:223–226.

Possehl, Gregory L. 1999. *Indus Age: The beginnings*. New Delhi: Oxford & IBH Publishing.

———. 2002. *The Indus Civilization: A contemporary perspective*. Walnut Creek, CA: Alta Mira.

Potts, Daniel T. 2001. Nana in Bactria. *Silk Road Art and Archaeology* 7:23–35.

———. 2008 (2009). Puzur-Inšušinak and the Oxus Civilization (BMAC): Reflections on Šimaški and the geo-political landscape of Iran and Central Asia in the Ur III period. *Zeitschrift für Assyriologie und Vorderasiatische Archäologie* 95:165–194.

Preston, James J. 1980. *Cult of the goddess: Social and religious change in a Hindu temple*. New Delhi: Vikas.

Pritchard, James B. 1969. *The ancient Near East in pictures relating to the Old Testament*. 2nd ed. with supplement. Princeton, NJ: Princeton University Press.

Proferes, Theodore N. 2007. *Vedic ideals of sovereignty and the poetics of power*. (American Oriental Series 90.) New Haven, CT: American Oriental Society.

Pryakhin, A. D., & A. Kh. Khalikov 1987. Abashevskaya kul'tura. Pp. 124–131 in: Bader, Krajnov, & Kosarev 1987.

Quivron, Gonzague. 1980. Les marques incisées sur les poteries de Mehrgarh au Baluchistan, du milieu du IVe millénaire à la première moitie du IIIe millénaire. *Paléorient* 6:269–280.

Raghu Vira & Lokesh Chandra (eds.) 1995. *Tibetan maṇḍalas (Vajrāvalī and Tantra-samuccaya)*. (Śata-Piṭaka Series 383.) New Delhi: International Academy of Indian Culture.

Rao, S R. 1982. *The decipherment of the Indus script*. Bombay: Asia Publishing House.

———. 1991. *Dawn and devolution of the Indus Civilization*. New Delhi: Aditya Prakashan.

Rask, Rasmus. 1818. *Undersøgelse om den gamle Nordiske eller Islandske Sprogs Oprindelse*. Copenhagen: Gyldendal.

Rassamakin, Yuri. 1999. The Eneolithic of the Black Sea Steppe: Dynamics of cultural and economic development, 4500–2300 BC. Pp. 59–182 in: Marsha Levine, Yuri Rassamakin, Aleksandr Kislenko & Nataliya Tatarintseva (eds.), *Late Prehistoric exploitation of the Eurasian steppe*. Cambridge: McDonald Institute for Archaeological Research.

———. 2004. *Die nordpontische Steppe in der Kupferzeit: Gräber aus der Mitte des 5. Jts. bis Ende des 4. Jts. v.Chr.* I–II. (Archäologie in Eurasien 17.) Mainz: Philipp von Zabern.

Ratnagar, Shereen. 1991. *Enquiries into the political organization of Harappan society*. Pune: Ravish.

Rau, Wilhelm. 1976. *The meaning of* pur *in Vedic literature*. (Abhandlungen der Marburger Gelehrten Gesellschaft, Jahrgang 1973:1.) Munich: Wilhelm Fink.

Raulwing, Peter. 2005 (2006). The Kikkuli Text (CTH 284): Some interdisciplinary remarks on Hittite training texts for chariot horses in the second half of the 2nd millennium B.C. Pp. 61–75 in: Armelle Gardeisen (ed.), *Les équides dans le monde méditerranéen antique*. (Monographies d'archéologie méditerranéen 1.) Lattes: èditions de l'Association pour le développement de l'archéologie en Languedoc-Rousillon.

Raverty, H. G. 1859. Notes on Kafiristan. *Journal of the Asiatic Society of Bengal* 28:317–368.

Rawlinson, George (trans.). [1860] 1942. Herodotus, *The Persian Wars*. (Modern Library 255.) New York: Random House.

Reade, Julian. 1995. Magan and Meluhha merchants at Ur? Pp. 597–599 in: U. Finkbeiner, R. Dittmann & H. Hauptmann (eds.), *Beiträge zur Kulturgeschichte Vorderasiens: Festschrift für Rainer Michael Boehmer*. Mainz: Philipp von Zabern.

———. 2008. The Indus-Mesopotamia relationship reconsidered. Pp. 12–18 in: Olijdam & Spoor 2008.

Rédei, Károly. 1988. Die ältesten indogermanischen Lehnwörter der uralischen Sprachen. Pp. 638–664 in: Sinor 1988.

———. 1988–1991. *Uralisches etymologisches Wörterbuch* I–III. Wiesbaden: Otto Harrassowitz.

Renger, Johannes. 2004. Die naturräumlichen Bedingungen im Alten Orient im 4. und frühen 3. Jt. v. Chr. Pp. 41–48 in: Fansa & Burmeister 2004.

Renou, Louis. 1953. *Religions of ancient India*. London: Athlone.

Roberts, T. J. 1977. *The mammals of Pakistan*. London: Ernest Benn.

Robinson, Andrew. 2002. *Lost languages: The enigma of the world's undeciphered scripts.* New York: McGraw Hill.

Rolland, Pierre. 1973. Le Mahāvrata. *Nachrichten der Akademie der Wissenschaften in Göttingen, Philologisch-historische Klasse*, Jahrgang 1973:51–79.

Rönnow, Kasten. 1929. Zur Erklärung des Pravargya, des Agnicayana und der Sautrāmaṇī. *Le Monde Oriental* 23:69–173.

Rosenfield, John M. 1967. *The dynastic arts of the Kushans.* Berkeley: University of California Press.

Rothman, Mitchell S. (ed.). 2001. *Uruk Mesopotamia & its neighbors: Cross-cultural interactions in the era of state formation.* Santa Fe: School of American Research Press.

Ryzhov, S. M. 2003. Glynyani modeli sanej Kukuten'-Trypil's'koï spil'nosti. *Arkheologichnyj litopys livoberezhnoï Ukraïny* 2002:3 & 2003:1:56–57.

Sajnovics, Joannes [János]. 1770. *Demonstratio idioma Ungarorum et Lapponum idem esse.* Turnaviae: Typis Collegii Academici Societatis Jesu.

Salomon, Richard G. 1996. Brahmi and Kharoshthi. Pp. 373–383 in: Daniels & Bright 1996.

Samzun, Anaick 1992. Observations on the characteristics of the Pre-Harappan remains, pottery, and artifacts at Nausharo, Pakistan (2700–2500 BC). Pp. 245–252 in: Catherine Jarrige (ed.), *South Asian Archaeology 1989.* (Monographs in World Archaeology.) Madison, WI: Prehistory.

Sarianidi, Viktor I. 1977. *Drevnie zemledel'tsy Afganistana: Materialy Sovetsko-Afganskoj èkspeditsii 1969–1974 gg.* Moscow: Nauka

———. 1986. *Die Kunst des alten Afghanistan: Architektur, Keramik, Siegel, Kunstwerke aus Stein und Metall.* Übersetzt aus dem Russischen von Sabine Grebe. Weinheim: VCH Verlagsgesellschaft.

———. 1987. South-west Asia: Migrations, the Aryans and Zoroastrians. *Information Bulletin of the International Association for the Study of the Cultures of Central Asia* 13:44–56.

———. 1989. *Khram i nekropol' Tillyatepe.* Moscow: Nauka.

———. 1998a. *Margiana and Protozoroastrism.* Translated from Russian by Inna Sarianidi. Athens: Kapon.

———. 1998b. *Myths of ancient Bactria and Margiana on its seals and amulets.* Moscow: Pentagraphic.

———. 2001. The Indo-Iranian problem in the light of the latest excavations in Margiana. Pp. 417–441 in: Karttunen & Koskikallio 2001.

———. 2002. *Marguş: Murgap derýasynyn köne hanasynyn aýagyndaky gadymy gündogar şalygy / Drevnevostochnoe tsarstvo s staroj del'te reki Murgab / Ancient Oriental kingdom in the old delta of Murghab river.* Aşgabat: Türkmendöwlethabarlary.

———. 2007. *Necropolis of Gonur.* English translation by Inna Sarianidi. Athens: Kapon.

Sarianidi, V. I., P. M. Kozhin, M. F. Kosarev, & N. A. Dubova (eds.). 2011 (2012). *Trudy Margianskoj arkheologicheskoj èkspeditsii* 4. Moscow: Institut ètnologii i antropologii im. N. N. Miklukho-Maklaya, RAN.

Savarkar, V. D. 1938. *Hindutva: Who is a Hindu?* New Delhi: Central Hindu Yuvak Sabha.

Sayce, A. H. 1924. Remarkable discoveries in India. *Illustrated London News*, September 27, 1924:526.

Scherer, Anton. 1953. *Gestirnnamen bei den indogermanischen Völkern.* (Indogermanische Bibliothek 3.1.) Heidelberg: Carl Winter–Universitätsverlag.

Schlerath, Bernfried. 1960. *Das Königtum im Rig- und Atharvaveda. Ein Beitrag zur indogermanischen Kulturgeschichte.* (Abhandlungen für die Kunde des Morgenlandes 33:3.) Wiesbaden: Kommissionsverlag Franz Steiner.

Schmidt, Erich F. 1933. Tepe Hissar excavations, 1931. *Museum Journal* 23(4):323–487.

———. 1937. *Excavations at Tepe Hissar, Damghan.* Philadelphia, PA: University Museum.

Schmitt, Rüdiger. 1967. *Dichtung und Dichtersprache in indogermanischer Zeit.* Wiesbaden: Otto Harrassowitz.

———, (ed.). 1989. *Compendium Linguarum Iranicarum.* Wiesbaden: Dr Ludwig Reichert.

———. 2000. *Die iranischen Sprachen in Geschichte und Gegenwart.* Wiesbaden: Dr Ludwig Reichert.

Schrader, Otto. 1907–1906. *Sprachvergleichung und Urgeschichte: Linguistisch-historische Beiträge zur Erforschung des indogermanischen Altertums* I–II. Dritte neubearbeitete Auflage. Jena: Hermann Costenoble.

Schrader, O. [& A. Nehring]. 1917–1929. *Reallexikon der indogermanischen Altertumskunde.* Zweite, vermehrte und umgearbeitete Auflage herausgegeben von A. Nehring. I–II. Berlin: Walter de Gruyter.

Shah, Sayid Ghulam Mustafa, & Asko Parpola. 1991. *Corpus of Indus seals and inscriptions 2: Collections in Pakistan.* (Annales Academiae Scientiarum Fennicae B240.) Helsinki: Suomalainen Tiedeakatemia. (= CISI 2)

Shinde, V., G. L. Possehl, & M. Ameri. 2005. Excavations at Gilund 2001–2003: The seal impressions and other finds. Pp. 159–169 in: Ute Franke-Vogt & Hans-Joachim Weisshaar (eds.), *South Asian Archaeology 2003.* (Forschungen zur Archäologie aussereuropäischer Kulturen 1.) Aachen: Linden Soft.

Shulman, David Dean. 1980. *Tamil temple myths: Sacrifice and divine marriage in the South Indian Śaiva tradition.* Princeton, NJ: Princeton University Press.

Sievertsen, Uwe. 1992. Das Messer vom Gebel el-Arak. *Baghdader Mitteilungen* 23:1–75.

———. 1999. Early buttress-recess architecture in Mesopotamia and Syria. *Baghdader Mitteilungen* 30:7–20.

Silva, Severine. 1955. Traces of human sacrifice in Kanara. *Anthropos* 50:577–592.

Sims-Williams, Nicholas (ed.). 2002. *Indo-Iranian languages and peoples.* (Proceedings of the British Academy 116.) Oxford: Oxford University Press.

Sinor, Denis (ed.). 1988. *The Uralic languages: Description, history, and foreign influences.* (Handbuch der Orientalistik 8:1.) Leiden: Brill.

Smith, Brian K. 1994. *Classifying the universe: The ancient Indian varṇa system and the origins of caste.* New York: Oxford University Press.

Sontheimer, Günther-Dietz. 1989. *Pastoral deities in western India.* Translated by Anne Feldhaus. New York: Oxford University Press.

Southworth, Franklin C. 2005. *Linguistic archaeology of South Asia.* London: RoutledgeCurzon.

Sparreboom, Marcus. 1985. *Chariots in the Veda.* (Memoirs of the Kern Institute 3.) Leiden: Brill.

Speyer, J. S. (ed.). 1906–1909. *Avadānaçataka: A century of edifying tales belonging to the Hīnayāna* I–II. (Bibliotheca Buddhica 3.) St. Pétersbourg: Académie Impériale des Sciences.

Staal, J. F. 1961. *Nambudiri Veda recitation.* (Disputationes Rheno-Traiectinae 5.) 's-Gravenhage: Mouton.

——— (ed.) 1983. *Agni: The Vedic ritual of the Fire Altar* I–II. Berkeley: Asian Humanities Press.

Stacul, Giorgio. 1970. The Grey Pottery in the Swat Valley and the Indo-Iranian connections (*c.* 1500–300 B.C.). *East and West* NS 20(1–2):92–102.

———. 1971. Cremation graves in northwest Pakistan and their Eurasian connections: Remarks and hypotheses. *East and West* NS 21(1–2):9–19.

Stein, Diana L. 1994. Mittan(n)i. B. Bildkunst und Architektur. Pp. 296–299 in: *Reallexikon der Assyriologie und Vorderasiatischen Archäologie* 8(3–4). Berlin: Walter de Gruyter.

Steinkeller, Piotr. 1982. The question of Marḫaši: A contribution to the historical geography of Iran in the third millennium B.C. *Zeitschrift für Assyriologie und vorderasiatische Archäologie* 72:237–265.

Strommenger, Eva. 1962. *Fünf Jahrtausende Mesopotamien: Die Kunst von den Anfangen um 5000 v.Chr. bis zu Alexander dem Grossen.* Aufnahmen von Max Hirmer. Munich: Hirmer.

Szabo, Albert, & Thomas J. Barfield. 1991. *Afghanistan: An atlas of indigenous domestic architecture.* Austin: University of Texas Press.

Tallgren, A. M. 1928. [Review of articles from 1927 by S. Teploukhov, M. P. Gryaznov, P. Rykov, and S. Dubrilin.] *Eurasia Septentrionalis Antiqua* 3:186–188.

Tamil lexicon. 1924–1939. I–VI and Supplement. Madras: University of Madras.

Teufer, Mike. 2012. Der Streitwagen: Eine "indo-iranische" Erfindung? Zum Problem der Verbindung von Sprachwissenschaft und Archäologie. *Archäologische Mitteilungen aus Iran und Turan* 44:270–313.

———. 2013. Vom Grab als Totenhaus zum "Haus des Lobliedes" im Jenseits. Überlegungen zum Aufkommen des Zoroastrismus aus archäologischer Sicht. Pp. 1–44 in: Gunvor Lindström, Svend Hansen, Alfried Wieczorek & Michael Tellenbach (eds.), *Zwischen Ost und West: Neue Forschungen zum antiken Zentralasien.* Darmstadt: Philipp von Zabern.

Thapar, B. K. 1985. *Recent archaeological discoveries in India.* Paris: UNESCO.

Thieme, Paul. 1957. Mitra and Aryaman. *Transactions of the Connecticut Academy of Arts and Sciences* 41:1–96.

———. 1960. The "Aryan" gods of the Mitanni treaties. *Journal of the American Oriental Society* 80:301–317.

Tod, James. 1835. Comparison of the Hindu and Theban Hercules, illustrated by an ancient Hindu Intaglio. *Transactions of the Royal Asiatic Society of Great Britain and Ireland* 3:139–159.

Tokunaga, Muneo (ed.) 1997. *The Bṛhaddevatā: Text reconstructed from the manuscripts of the shorter recension, with introduction, explanatory notes, and indices.* Kyoto: Rinsen.

Trautmann, Thomas R. 1981. *Dravidian kinship.* (Cambridge Studies in Social Anthropology 36.) Cambridge: Cambridge University Press.

——— (ed.) 2005. *The Aryan debate.* New Delhi: Oxford University Press.

Tucci, Giuseppe. 1961. *The theory and practice of the maṇḍala.* Translated by Alan Houghton Brodrick. London: Rider.

Tull, Herman. 1989. *The Vedic origins of karma: Cosmos as man in ancient Indian myth and ritual.* (SUNY series in Hindu studies.) Albany: State University of New York Press.

Turner, Ralph L. 1966. *A comparative dictionary of the Indo-Aryan languages.* London: Oxford University Press.

Uesugi, Akinori. 2011. Development of the inter-regional interaction system in the Indus Valley and beyond: A hypothetical view towards the formation of the urban society. Pp. 359–380 in: Osada & Witzel 2011.

Usachuk, A. N. (ed.) 2004. *Psalii: Èlementy upryazhi i konskogo snaryazheniya v drevnosti.* (Arkheologicheskij al'manakh 15.) Donetsk: Institut arkheologii NAN Ukrainy.

———. 2013. *Drevnejshie psalii (izgotovlenie i ispol'zovanie).* Kiev and Donetsk: Institut arkheologii, Natsional'naya Akademiya Nauk Ukrainy.

Vahia, Mayank N., & Srikumar M. Menon. 2011. A possible astronomical observatory at Dholavira. http://www.tifr.res.in/~archaeo/papers/Harappan%20Civilisation/Observatory%20at%20Dholavira.pdf.

van Buitenen, J. A. B. 1968. *The Pravargya: An ancient Indian iconic ritual described and annotated.* (Deccan College Building Centenary and Silver Jubilee Series 58.) Poona: Deccan College.

——— (trans. and ed.). 1973–1978. *The Mahābhārata* I–III. Chicago: University of Chicago Press.

Van Buren, Elizabeth Douglas. 1948. Fish-offerings in ancient Mesopotamia. *Iraq* 10: 101–121.

van Kooij, K. R. 1972. *Worship of the Goddess according to the Kālikāpurāṇa* I. (Orientalia Rheno-Traiectina 14.) Leiden: Brill.

Vasil'ev, I. B., P. F. Kuznetsov, & A. P. Semenova. 1994. *Potapovskij kurgannyj mogil'nik indoranskikh plemen na Volge.* Samara: Samarskij universitet.

Vermaak, P. S. 2008. Guabba, the Meluhhan village in Mesopotamia. *Journal for Semitics* 17(2):454–471.

Vermaseren, Maarten J. 1977. *Cybele and Attis: The myth and the cult.* London: Thames and Hudson.

Vidale, Massimo. 2007. The collapse melts down: A reply to Farmer, Sproat & Witzel [2004]. *East and West* 57(1–4):333–366.

———. 2010. Aspects of palace life at Mohenjo-Daro. *South Asian Studies* 26(1):59–76.

Vidale, Massimo, Roberto Micheli, Luca Maria Olivieri, & Muhammad Zahir. 2014. New radiocarbon dates and the chronology of protohistorical graves of Swat Valley: The latest evidence from Godgara IV and Udegram (Khyber Pakhtunkhwa, Pakistan). Paper read at the 22nd conference of the European Association for South Asian Archaeology and Art in Stockholm, Sweden, June 30 to July 4, 2014.

Videiko, Mihailo Y. 1994. Tripolye—"pastoral" contacts. Facts and character of the interactions: 4800–3200 BC. *Baltic-Pontic Studies* 2:5–28.

———. 1995 (1996). Grossiedlungen der Tripol'e-Kultur in der Ukraine. *Eurasia Antiqua* 1:45–80.

Vinogradov, N. B. 2003. *Mogil'nik bronzovogo veka Krivoe Ozera v yuzhnom Zaural'e.* Chelyabinsk: Yuzhno-Ural'skoe knizhnoe izdatel'stvo.

von Dassow, Eva. 2008. *State and society in the Late Bronze Age Alalah under the Mittani empire.* (SCCNH = Studies on the civilization and culture of Nuzi and the Hurrians 17.) Bethesda, MD: CDL Press.

von Hinüber, Oskar. 2001. *Das ältere Mittelindisch im Überblick.* Zweite Auflage. (Österreichische Akademie der Wissenschaften, Philosophisch-historische Klasse, Sitzungsberiche 467; Veröffentlichungen der Kommission für Sprachen und Kulturen Südasiens, 20.) Vienna: Österreichische Akademie der Wissenschaften.

von Stietencron, Heinrich. 1983. Die Göttin Durgā Mahiṣāsuramardinī: Mythos, Darstellung und geschichtliche Rolle bei der Hinduisierung Indiens. *Visible Religion* 2:118–66.

———. 1989. Hinduism: On the proper use of a deceptive term. Pp. 11–27 in: Günther D. Sontheimer & Hermann Kulke (eds.), *Hinduism reconsidered.* (South Asian Studies 24.) New Delhi: Manohar.

Wace, Alan J. B., & Frank H. Stubbings (eds.). 1962. *A companion to Homer*. London: Macmillan.

Wackernagel, Jakob. 1896. *Altindische Grammatik* I. Göttingen: Vandenhoeck & Ruprecht.

Wackernagel, Jacob [& Albert Debrunner]. 1954. *Altindische Grammatik*, II,2: *Die Nominalsuffixe*, von Albert Debrunner. Göttingen: Vandenhoeck & Ruprecht.

Waddell, L. A. 1925. *The Indo-Sumerian seals deciphered: Discovering Sumerians of the Indus Valley as Phoenicians, Barats, Goths, and famous Vedic Aryans, 3100 to 2300 B.C.* London: Luzac.

Wanzke, Holger. 1987. Axis systems and orientation at Mohenjo-Daro. Pp. 33–44 in: Michael Jansen & Günter Urban (eds.), *Interim reports 2: Reports on field work carried out at Mohenjo-Daro, Pakistan, 1983–84 by the IsMEO—Aachen-University Mission*. Aachen: RWTH, and Rome: IsMEO.

Ward, William (trans.). 1811. *Account of the writings, religion, and manners, of the Hindoos, including translations from their principal works* I–IV. Serampore: Mission.

Watkins, Calvert. 1995. *How to kill a dragon: Aspects of Indo-European poetics*. New York: Oxford University Press.

Weber, Albrecht. 1849. Ueber die Literatur des Sāmaveda. *Indische Studien* 1(1):25–67.

———. 1850. Zwei Sagen aus dem Çatapatha-Brāhmaṇa über Einwanderung und Verbreitung der Ārier in Indien, nebst einer geographisch-geschichtlichen Skizze aus dem weissen Yajus. *Indische Studien* 1(2):161–232.

———. 1853. Zur Geschichte der indischen Astrologie. *Indische Studien* 2:236–287.

———. 1861 (1862). *Die vedischen Nachrichten von den naxatra (Mondstationen)* II. (Abhandlungen der Königlichen Akademie der Wissenschaften zu Berlin, aus dem Jahre 1861:267–400.) Berlin: Druckerei der Königlichen Akademie der Wissenschaften.

———. 1870 (1871). Über das Rāmāyaṇa. *Abhandlungen der Königlichen Akademie der Wissenschaften zu Berlin, Aus dem Jahre 1870, Philosophisch-historische Klasse*: 1–88.

Wessels-Mevissen, Corinna. 2001. *The gods of the directions in ancient India: Origin and early development in art and literature (until c. 1000 A.D.)*. (Monographien zur indischen Archäologie, Kunst und Philologie, Band 14.) Berlin: Dietrich Reimer.

West, M. L. 2007. *Indo-European poetry and myth*. Oxford: Oxford University Press.

Wheeler, Mortimer. 1947. Harappa 1946: The defences and cemetery R37. *Ancient India* 3:58–130, and pl. XV–LX.

———. 1968. *The Indus civilization*. 3rd ed. Cambridge: Cambridge University Press.

Whitehead, Henry. 1921. *The village gods of South India*. 2nd ed., revised and enlarged. (The religious life of India.) Calcutta: Association Press (YMCA); London: Oxford University Press.

Wilhelm, Gernot. 1994. Mittan(n)i, Mitanni, Maitani. A. Historisch. Pp. 286–296 in: *Reallexikon der Assyriologie und Vorderasiatischen Archäologie* 8(3–4). Berlin: Walter de Gruyter.

Winkelmann, Sylvia. 2004. *Seals of the oasis from the Ligabue collection*. With an introduction by Pierre Amiet and a postscriptum by Gabriele Rossi-Osmida. Padova: Il Punto Edizioni.

Winternitz, Moriz. 1892. *Das altindische Hochzeitsrituell nach dem Āpastamba-Gṛhyasūtra und einigen anderen verwandten Werken*. (Denkschriften der Kaiserlichen Akademie der Wissenschaften in Wien, Philos.-hist. Classe 40:1.) Vienna: In Commission bei F. Tempsky.

———. 1895. Nejamesha, Naigamesha, Nemeso. *Journal of the Royal Asiatic Society of Great Britain and Ireland* 1895:149–155.

———. 1927. *A history of Indian literature* I. Translated by S. Ketkar and revised by the author. Calcutta: University of Calcutta.

Witzel, Michael. 1989. Tracing the Vedic dialects. Pp. 97–265 in: Caillat 1989.

———. 1995a. Early Indian history: Linguistic and textual parameters. Pp. 85–125 in: Erdosy 1995.

———. 1995b. Rgvedic history: Poets, chieftains and polities. Pp. 307–352 in: Erdosy 1995.

———. 1997. The development of the Vedic canon and its schools: The social and political milieu. (Materials on Vedic Śākhās 8.) Pp. 257–345 in: Michael Witzel (ed.), *Inside the texts, beyond the texts: New approaches to the study of the Vedas*. (Harvard Oriental Series, Opera Minora 2.) Cambridge, MA: Department of Sanskrit and Indian Studies, Harvard University.

———. 2000. The home of the Aryans. Pp. 283–338 in: Almut Hintze & Eva Tichy (eds.), *Anusantatyai: Festschrift für Johanna Narten zum 70. Geburtstag*. (Münchener Studien zur Sprachwissenschaft, Beihefte NF 19.) Dettelbach: J. H. Röll.

Witzel, Michael. 2005. Central Asian roots and acculturation in South Asia: Linguistic and archaeological evidence from western Central Asia, the Hindukush and northwestern South Asia for early Indo-Aryan language and religion. Pp. 87–211 in: Toshiki Osada (ed.), *Linguistics, Archaeology and the Human Past: Occasional Paper 1*. Kyoto: Indus Project, Research Institute for Humanity and Nature.

Young, T. C., Jr. 1985. Early Iron Age Iran revisited: Preliminary suggestions for the reanalysis of old constructs. Pp. 361–377 in: J.-L. Huot, M. Yon & Y. Calvet (eds.), *De l'Indus aux Balkans: Recueil à la mémoire de Jean Deshayes*. Paris: Éditions Recherche sur les Civilisations.

Young, Thomas. 1813. Adelung's General History of Languages. *Quarterly Review* (London) 10(19):250–292.

Zdanovich, Gennady B., & Dmitry G. Zdanovich. 2002. The "Country of Towns" of southern Trans-Urals and some aspects of steppe assimilation in the Bronze Age. Pp. 249–263 in: Boyle, Renfrew, & Levine 2002.

Zeller, Gabriele. 1990. *Die vedischen Zwillingsgötter: Untersuchungen zur Genese ihres Kultes*. (Freiburger Beiträge zur Indologie 24.) Wiesbaden: Otto Harrassowitz.

Zide, Norman H. 1969. Munda and non-Munda Austroasiatic languages. Pp. 411–430 in: Thomas A. Sebeok (ed.), *Linguistics in South Asia*. (Current trends in linguistics 5.) The Hague and Paris: Mouton.

Zvelebil, Kamil V. 1970. *Comparative Dravidian phonology*. (Janua Linguarum, Series practica 80.) The Hague: Mouton.

———. 1973. *The smile of Murugan: On Tamil literature of South India*. Leiden: Brill.

———. 1974. *Tamil literature*. (A History of Indian Literature 10:1.) Wiesbaden: Otto Harrassowitz.

———. 1990. *Dravidian linguistics: An introduction*. (Pondicherry Institute of Linguistics and Culture publication 3.) Pondicherry: Pondicherry Institute of Linguistics and Culture.

Index

For reasons of space modern authors and Vedic texts (listed in References and on pages xv–xvi) have been excluded from this index. Attributes defining phases (Proto-, Old, Modern) or dialectal groups (e.g., East, North) of languages and language families, if included in the index, do not constitute separate lemmas but appear under the respective language and language group (e.g., Indo-European).